CONNECT WITH SMARTBOOK® WORKS

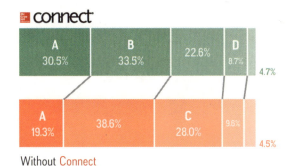

More C students
earn B's

*Study: 690 students / 6 institutions

Over 20%
more students
pass the class
with Connect

*A&P Research Study

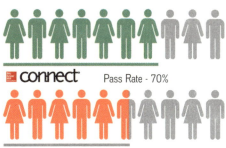

More than 60%
of all students agreed
Connect was a
very or extremely
helpful learning tool

*Based on 750,000 student survey responses

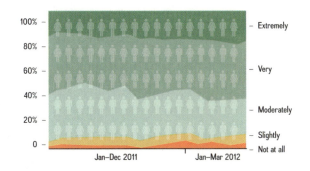

> **AVAILABLE** *ON-THE-GO*

http://bitly.com/TryConnect

> Shop and Sign In

Let's see how confident you are on the question.

Connect Insight helps you track your performance on assignments.

What you know (green) and what you still need to review (yellow), based on your answers

COMPARE AND CHOOSE WHAT'S RIGHT FOR YOU

	PRINT BOOK	SMARTBOOK	ASSIGNMENTS	
connect		✓	✓	SmartBook—all in one digital product for maximum savings!
connect Looseleaf	✓	✓	✓	Pop the pages into your own binder or carry just the pages you need.
connect Bound Book	✓	✓	✓	The #1 Student Choice!
SMARTBOOK® Access Code	✓	✓		The first and only book that adapts to you!
create™	✓	✓	✓	The smartest way to get from a B to an A.

> Buy directly from the source at http://shop.mheducation.com.

Operations and Supply Chain Management: The Core

The McGraw-Hill Education Series Operations and Decision Sciences

OPERATIONS MANAGEMENT

Beckman and Rosenfield
Operations Strategy: Competing in the
21st Century
First Edition

Benton
Purchasing and Supply Chain Management
Third Edition

Bowersox, Closs, and Cooper
Supply Chain Logistics Management
Fifth Edition

Brown and Hyer
Managing Projects: A Team-Based
Approach
Second Edition

Burt, Petcavage, and Pinkerton
Supply Management
Ninth Edition

Cachon and Terwiesch
Operations Management
First Edition

Cachon and Terwiesch
Matching Supply with Demand: An
Introduction to Operations Management
Fourth Edition

Finch
Interactive Models for Operations and
Supply Chain Management
First Edition

Fitzsimmons and Fitzsimmons
Service Management: Operations, Strategy,
Information Technology
Eighth Edition

Gehrlein
Operations Management Cases
First Edition

Harrison and Samson
Technology Management
First Edition

Hayen
SAP R/3 Enterprise Software: An Introduction
First Edition

Hill
Manufacturing Strategy: Text & Cases
Third Edition

Hopp
Supply Chain Science
First Edition

Hopp and Spearman
Factory Physics
Third Edition

Jacobs, Berry, Whybark, and Vollmann
Manufacturing Planning & Control
for Supply Chain Management
Sixth Edition

Jacobs and Chase
Operations and Supply Chain Management
Fourteenth Edition

Jacobs and Chase
Operations and Supply Chain Management:
The Core
Fourth Edition

Jacobs and Whybark
Why ERP?
First Edition

Johnson, Leenders, and Flynn
Purchasing and Supply Management
Fifteenth Edition

Larson and Gray
Project Management: The Managerial Process
Sixth Edition

Schroeder, Goldstein, and Rungtusanatham
Operations Management: Contemporary
Concepts and Cases
Sixth Edition

**Simchi-Levi, Kaminsky, and
Simchi-Levi**
Designing and Managing the Supply Chain:
Concepts, Strategies, Case Studies
Third Edition

Sterman
Business Dynamics: Systems Thinking and
Modeling for a Complex World
First Edition

Stevenson
Operations Management
Twelfth Edition

Swink, Melnyk, Cooper, and Hartley
Managing Operations Across the Supply Chain
Third Edition

Thomke
Managing Product and Service
Development: Text and Cases
First Edition

Ulrich and Eppinger
Product Design and Development
Sixth Edition

Zipkin
Foundations of Inventory Management
First Edition

QUANTITATIVE METHODS AND MANAGEMENT SCIENCE

Hillier and Hillier
Introduction to Management Science: A
Modeling and Case Studies Approach with
Spreadsheets
Fifth Edition

Stevenson and Ozgur
Introduction to Management Science with
Spreadsheets
First Edition

Operations and Supply Chain Management: The Core

Fourth Edition

F. ROBERT JACOBS
Indiana University

RICHARD B. CHASE
University of Southern California

Mc
Graw
Hill
Education

OPERATIONS AND SUPPLY CHAIN MANAGEMENT: THE CORE, FOURTH EDITION

Published by McGraw-Hill Education, 2 Penn Plaza, New York, NY 10121. Copyright © 2017 by McGraw-Hill Education. All rights reserved. Printed in the United States of America. Previous editions © 2013, 2010, and 2008. No part of this publication may be reproduced or distributed in any form or by any means, or stored in a database or retrieval system, without the prior written consent of McGraw-Hill Education, including, but not limited to, in any network or other electronic storage or transmission, or broadcast for distance learning.

Some ancillaries, including electronic and print components, may not be available to customers outside the United States.

This book is printed on acid-free paper.

1 2 3 4 5 6 7 8 9 0 DOW/DOW 1 0 9 8 7 6

ISBN 978-1-259-54972-4
MHID 1-259-54972-0

Senior Vice President, Products & Markets: *Kurt L. Strand*
Vice President, General Manager, Products & Markets: *Marty Lange*
Vice President, Content Design & Delivery: *Kimberly Meriwether David*
Managing Director: *James Heine*
Brand Manager: *Dolly Womack*
Director, Product Development: *Rose Koos*
Lead Product Developer: *Michele Janicek*
Product Developer: *Camille Corum*
Marketing Manager: *Britney Hermsen*
Director of Digital Content Development: *Douglas Ruby*
Digital Product Analyst: *Kevin Shanahan*
Director, Content Design & Delivery: *Linda Avenarius*
Program Manager: *Mark Christianson*
Content Project Managers: *Kathryn D. Wright, Kristin Bradley, and Karen Jozefowicz*
Buyer: *Sandy Ludovissy*
Design: *Debra Kubiak*
Content Licensing Specialists: *Beth Thole and Shawntel Schmitt*
Cover Image: *Earth core structure illustrated with geological layers according to scale—isolated on black (Texture maps from NASA); © Johan Swanepoel/Alamy*
Compositor: *Aptara®, Inc.*
Printer: *R. R. Donnelley*

All credits appearing on page or at the end of the book are considered to be an extension of the copyright page.

Library of Congress Cataloging-in-Publication Data

Names: Jacobs, F. Robert. | Chase, Richard B.
  Title: Operations and supply chain management. The core / F. Robert Jacobs
    Indiana University, Richard B. Chase, University of Southern California.
  Other titles: Operations and supply management. The core
  Description: Fourth edition. | New York, NY : McGraw-Hill/Irwin, [2016] |
    Originally published as: Operations and supply management. The core. |
    Includes bibliographical references and indexes.
  Identifiers: LCCN 2015046932| ISBN 9781259549724 (alk. paper) |
    ISBN 1259549720 (alk. paper)
  Subjects: LCSH: Production management.
  Classification: LCC TS155 .J273 2016 | DDC 658.5—dc23 LC record available at
  http://lccn.loc.gov/2015046932

The Internet addresses listed in the text were accurate at the time of publication. The inclusion of a website does not indicate an endorsement by the authors or McGraw-Hill Education, and McGraw-Hill Education does not guarantee the accuracy of the information presented at these sites.

mheducation.com/highered

To Rhonda, Jennifer, Suzy,
and Jessica.

ABOUT THE AUTHORS

F. Robert Jacobs is Professor Emeritus of Operations and Decision Technologies at Indiana University. He received a B.S. in Industrial Engineering as well as Computer and Information Science, an MBA, and a Ph.D. in Operations Management all from The Ohio State University. He has also taught at the University of Houston and The Ohio State University. He has published 7 books and over 50 research articles on topics that include enterprise resource planning, inventory control, the design of manufacturing facilities, cellular manufacturing, and the scheduling of manufacturing operations. He is a Fellow of the Decision Sciences Institute and Past President and has received teaching honors such as MBA Teaching Award, Students Award for Teaching Excellence in International Business Issues, and Teaching Excellence in Operations Management.

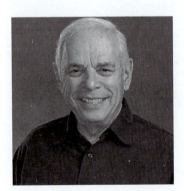

Richard B. Chase is Justin B. Dart Professor Emeritus of Operations Management at the Marshall School of Business, University of Southern California. He received his Ph.D. in Operations Management, as well as an MBA and B.S. from UCLA. He has taught at the Harvard Business School, IMD (Switzerland), and the University of Arizona. His research examines service process design and service strategy. In 2006 he received a POMS Lifetime Achievement Award for his research in service operations and in 2004 received a Scholar of the Year Award by the Academy of Management. In 2009, he was honored in the *Production & Operations Management Journal* for his contributions to Operations Management. He is a Fellow of the Academy of Management, Production Operations Management Society, and the Decision Sciences Institute. He was also an Examiner for the Malcolm Baldrige National Quality Award. Dr. Chase has lectured/consulted recently on service and excellence to such organizations as Cisco Systems, Four Seasons Resorts, General Electric, and the Gartner Group.

PREFACE

The goal of this book is to provide you with the essential information that every manager needs to know about operations and supply chain–related activities in a firm. Things have changed dramatically over the last few years. Organization structures are now much flatter, and rather than being functionally organized, companies often are organized by customer and product groups. Today's manager cannot ignore how the real work of the organization is done. This book is all about how to get the real work done effectively. It makes little difference if you are officially in finance, marketing, accounting, or operations: The value-added work, the process of creating and delivering products, needs to be completed in a manner that is both high quality and maximally efficient. Many of the things you do, or will do, in your job are repetitive, even some of the most creative and high-profile activities. You should think of this course as preparing you to be your most productive and helping you help your organization be its most productive.

We can consider the importance of the material in this book on many levels, but let's focus on three. First, consider your role as a business unit manager with people working under your supervision. Next, in the longer term, you probably have aspirations to become a senior executive with responsibility for multiple businesses or products. Finally, you may decide to specialize in operations and supply chain management as a long-term career.

In your role as a manager with people working under your supervision, one of your major duties will be to organize the way work is done. There needs to be some structure to the work process, including how information is captured and analyzed, as well as how decisions and changes and improvements are made. Without a logical or structured approach, even a small group may be subject to errors, inefficiencies, and even chaos.

Designing efficient process flows is an important element of getting a group to work together. If your group is involved in creative activities such as designing cars, buildings, or even stock portfolios, there still needs to be structure to how the work is done, who is responsible for what, and how progress is reported. The concepts of project management, manufacturing and service process design, capacity analysis, and quality in this text are all directly related to the knowledge you will need to be a great supervisor in your organization, and getting your group to work productively and efficiently will lead to success and more responsibility for you.

Next, think about becoming a senior executive. Making acquisitions, planning mergers, and buying and selling divisions will get your name and picture in business magazines. Deals are easily explained to boards, shareholders, and the media. They are newsworthy and offer the prospect of nearly immediate gratification, and being a deal maker is consistent with the image of the modern executive as someone who focuses on grand strategy and leaves operations details to others. Unfortunately, the majority of deals are unsuccessful. The critical element of success, even with the grandest deals, can still be found most often in the operational details.

Real success happens when operational processes can be improved. Productivity improvements from things such as sharing customer service processes, purchasing systems, distribution and manufacturing systems, and other processes can lead to great synergies and success. Operations accounts for 60 to 80 percent of the direct expenses that limit the profit of most firms. Without these operations synergies, designed and implemented by executives with a keen understanding of the concepts in this book, companies are often left with expensive debt, disappointed customers and shareholders, and pressure on the bottom line—on earnings.

Finally, you may be interested in a career in operations and supply chain management. Well, you are not alone. Professional organizations such as APICS, the Institute for Supply Management, and the Council of Supply Chain Management Professionals have well over 200,000 members participating in regular monthly meetings, annual conferences, and certification programs. Entry-level jobs might be as a forecast strategist, project manager, inventory control manager, production supervisor, purchasing manager, logistics manager, or warehouse specialist. In addition, top operations students may obtain their initial jobs with consulting firms, working as business process analysts and system design specialists.

We encourage you to talk to your instructor about what you want to get out of the course. What are your career aspirations, and how do they relate to the material in this course? Write your instructor a short e-mail describing what you want to do in the future—this is invaluable information for tailoring the material in the course to your needs. As you work through the text, share your experiences and insights with the class. Being an active student is guaranteed to make your experience more valuable and interesting.

ACKNOWLEDGMENTS

Special thanks to Paul Schikora, Indiana State University, for his insight and work on the instructor's material for this edition of the book.

Also, special thanks to William Berry, Professor Emeritus, Queens College, for preparing the Test Bank and accuracy checking Connect material; Ronny Richardson, Kennesaw State University, for preparing narrated learning resources; Gregory DeYong, University of Michigan, Flint, for revising the PowerPoint slides and revising Learnsmart; and Larry White, Eastern Illinois University, for accuracy checking Connect material.

Thanks to the McGraw-Hill development and production team who made this possible—Camille Corum, Product Developer; Dolly Womack, Executive Brand Manager; Kathryn Wright, Core Project Manager; Kristin Bradley, Assessment Project Manager; Britney Hermsen, Marketing Manager; and Debra Kubiak, Senior Designer.

We appreciate our former executive editor, Dick Hercher. His brilliant guidance and unwavering dedication to working with us on early edition of the book, has been a constant motivator.

Last, but certainly not least, we thank our families. We have stolen countless hours away for this project; time that would otherwise be spent with them. We sincerely appreciate their support.

F. Robert Jacobs
Richard B. Chase

A Note to Instructors

Operations and Supply Chain Management: The Core derives its title from a combination of ideas and trends. The book is designed to be lean and focused, much in the tradition of the concepts taught in the book. The topics selected are the result of the study of the syllabi of dozens of representative U.S. universities. There are a wide variety of topics covered, many more than could be covered in a single course. Our "big book," *Operations and Supply Chain Management*, is comprehensive and is intended for those who want to pick and choose topics that best fit the objectives of their course. The "*Core*" book covers the topics most commonly included in these courses and has material sufficient for a 12- to 15-week course.

As is well known in the field, success for companies today requires successfully managing the entire supply flow, from the sources of the firm, through the value-added processes of the firm, and on to the customers of the firm.

In *Operations and Supply Chain Management: The Core 4e*, we take students to the center of the business and focus on the core concepts and tools needed to ensure that these processes run smoothly.

Discussion of Fourth Edition Revisions

Many of the revisions to the fourth edition have been driven by our focus on supply chain analytics. Supply chain analytics involves the analysis of data to better solve business problems. We recognize that this is not really new since data have always been used to solve business problems. But what *is* new is the reality that there are a great deal more data now available for decision making.

In the past, most analysis involved the generation of standard and ad hoc reports that summarized the current state of the firm. Software allowed query and "drill down" analysis to the level of the individual transaction, useful features for understanding what happened in the past. Decision making was typically left to the decision maker based on judgment or simple alerting rules. The new "analytics" movement takes this to a new level using statistical analysis, forecasting to extrapolate what to expect in the future, and even optimization, possibly in real time, to support decisions.

In this new edition we have refined the 11 Analytic Exercises that have proven to be so popular in our books. These Analytic Exercises use settings that are modern and familiar to students taking the course. They include Starbucks, cellphones, notebook computers, Taco Bell Restaurant, Toyota, a retail Website–based company, and industrial products that are sourced from China/Taiwan and sold globally.

In this book, all the of the chapters have been designed to be independent. We have put much effort into the organization of the book, but recognize that our organization might not align with the way you are using the material in your course. In addition, many of you may custom publish a version of the book to exactly meet your needs. The chapters have been design to allow this type of customization.

The chapters are all now tightly organized by special learning objectives. The learning objectives for the chapter are defined at the start. Special contiguous sections are designed to cover each objective. The chapter summary, discussion and objective questions are also organized by learning objective. This new organization allows material to be assigned at the level of learning objective. If the desire might be to skip some advanced techniques, for example, this can be easily done by not assigning the specific learning objective. This allows considerable flexibility in how the material is used in a class.

The material has also been adapted to work well with electronic media, since this is now becoming the media of choice at many universities.

TECHNOLOGY

McGraw-Hill Connect®

Less Managing. More Teaching. Greater Learning.
McGraw-Hill Connect is an online assignment and assessment solution that connects students with the tools and resources they'll need to achieve success. McGraw-Hill Connect helps prepare students for their future by enabling faster learning, more efficient studying, and higher retention of knowledge.

McGraw-Hill Connect Features
Connect offers a number of powerful tools and features to make managing assignments easier so faculty can spend more time teaching. With Connect, students can engage with their coursework anytime and anywhere making the learning process more accessible and efficient. Connect offers you the features described below.

Simple Assignment Management
With Connect, creating assignments is easier than ever, so you can spend more time teaching and less time managing. The assignment management function enables you to:

- Create and deliver assignments easily with selectable end-of-chapter questions and test bank items.
- Streamline lesson planning, student progress reporting, and assignment grading to make classroom management more efficient than ever.
- Go paperless with the eBook and online submission and grading of student assignments.

Smart Grading
When it comes to studying, time is precious. Connect helps students learn more efficiently by providing feedback and practice material when they need it, where they need it. When it comes to teaching, your time also is precious. The grading function enables you to:

- Have assignments scored automatically, giving students immediate feedback on their work and side-by-side comparisons with correct answers.
- Access and review each response; manually change grades or leave comments for students to review.
- Reinforce classroom concepts with practice tests and instant quizzes.

Instructor Library
The Connect Instructor Library is your repository for additional resources to improve student engagement in and out of class. You can select and use any asset that enhances your lecture. The Connect Instructor Library includes:

- PowerPoint Slides
- Text Figures
- Instructor's Solutions Manual
- Test Banks
- Excel Templates

Student Study Center

The Connect Student Study Center is the place for students to access additional resources. The Student Study Center offers students quick access to study and review material.

Student Progress Tracking

Connect keeps instructors informed about how each student, section, and class is performing, allowing for more productive use of lecture and office hours. The progress-tracking function enables you to:

- View scored work immediately and track individual or group performance with assignment and grade reports.
- Access an instant view of student or class performance relative to chapter headings.

Tegrity Campus: Lectures 24/7

Tegrity Campus is a service that makes class time available 24/7 by automatically capturing every lecture in a searchable format for students to review when they study and complete assignments. With a simple one-click start-and-stop process, you capture all computer screens and corresponding audio. Students can replay any part of any class with easy-to-use browser-based viewing on a PC or Mac. Educators know that the more students can see, hear, and experience class resources, the better they learn. In fact, studies prove it. With Tegrity Campus, students quickly recall key moments by using Tegrity Campus's unique search feature. This search helps students efficiently find what they need, when they need it, across an entire semester of class recordings. Help turn all your students' study time into learning moments that are immediately supported by your lecture. To learn more about Tegrity, watch a two-minute Flash demo at www.tegrity.com.

OPERATIONS MANAGEMENT AND THE AACSB

Assurance of Learning Ready

Many educational institutions today are focused on the notion of *assurance of learning*, an important element of some accreditation standards. *Operations and Supply Chain Management* is designed specifically to support your assurance of learning initiatives with a simple yet powerful solution.

Each test bank question for *Operations and Supply Chain Management* maps to a specific chapter learning outcome/objective listed in the text. You can use our test bank software, EZ Test and EZ Test Online, or in *Connect Operations Management* to easily query for learning outcomes/objectives that directly relate to the learning objectives for your course. You can then use the reporting features of EZ Test to aggregate student results in similar fashion, making the collection, presentation, and assurance of learning data simple and easy.

AACSB Statement

McGraw-Hill Education is a proud corporate member of AACSB International. Understanding the importance and value of AACSB accreditation, *Operations and Supply Chain Management* recognizes the curricula guidelines detailed in the AACSB standards for business accreditation by connecting selected questions in the test bank to the six general knowledge and skill areas in the AACSB standards Assessment of Learning Standards.

The statements contained in *Operations and Supply Chain Management* are provided only as a guide for the users of this textbook. The AACSB leaves content coverage and assessment within the purview of individual schools, the mission of the school, and the faculty. While *Operations and Supply Chain Management* and the teaching package make no claim of any specific AACSB qualification or evaluation, we have within the Test Bank labeled questions according to the six general knowledge and skill areas.

McGraw-Hill Customer Experience Contact Information

At McGraw-Hill, we understand that getting the most from new technology can be challenging. That's why our services don't stop after you purchase our products. You can e-mail our Product Specialists 24 hours a day to get product-training online. Or you can search our knowledge bank of Frequently Asked Questions on our support Website. For Customer Support, call **800-331-5094** or visit mpss.mhhe.com. One of our Technical Support Analysts will be able to assist you in a timely fashion.

Walkthrough

Major Study and Learning Features

The following section highlights the key features developed to provide you with the best overall text available. We hope these features give you maximum support to learn, understand, and apply operations concepts.

Chapter Opener

CHAPTER 2

STRATEGY AND SUSTAINABILITY

Learning Objectives

LO2–1 Know what a sustainable business strategy is and how it relates to operations and supply chain management.

LO2–2 Define operations and supply chain strategy.

LO2–3 Explain how operations and supply chain strategies are implemented.

LO2–4 Understand why strategies have implications relative to business risk.

LO2–5 Evaluate productivity in operations and supply chain management.

MISSION STATEMENTS WITH ASPIRATIONS BEYOND MAKING A PROFIT

Companies such as Clif Bar and Whole Foods Market have bold mission statements that depict a focus that goes well beyond profit and shareholder wealth. Consider Clif Bar's 5 Aspirations and Whole Foods Market's Declaration of Interdependence, company mission statements that describe their aspirations related to the environment, the community, their employees, and making a profit. Companies need operations and supply chain strategies that align with the goals of the firm as a whole.

Opening Vignettes

Each chapter opens with a short vignette to set the stage and help pique students' interest in the material about to be studied. A few examples include:

- Mission Statements with Aspirations Beyond Making a Profit, Chapter 2
- From Bean to Cup: Starbucks Global Supply Chain Challenge, Chapter 3
- Inside the iPad, Chapter 9
- The Factoryless Goods Producers, Chapter 13

In the context of major business functions, operations and supply chain management involves specialists in product design, purchasing, manufacturing, service operations, logistics, and distribution. These specialists are mixed and matched in many different ways depending on the product or service. For a firm that sells televisions, like Toshiba, these are the functions responsible for designing televisions, acquiring materials, coordinating equipment resources to convert material to products, moving the product, and exchanging the final product with the

© Robyn Beck/AFP/Getty Images

customer. Some firms are focused on services, such as a hospital. Here, the context involves managing resources, including the operating rooms, labs, and hospital beds used to nurse patients back to health. In this context, acquiring materials, moving patients, and coordinating resource use are keys to success. Other firms are more specialized, such as Amazon. Here, purchasing, Web site services, logistics, and distribution need to be carefully coordinated for success.

In our increasingly interconnected and interdependent global economy, the process of delivering finished goods, services, and supplies from one place to another is accomplished by means of mind-boggling technological innovation, clever new applications of old ideas, seemingly magical mathematics, powerful software, and old-fashioned concrete, steel, and muscle. This book is about doing this at low cost while meeting the requirements of demanding customers. Success involves the clever integration of a great operations-related strategy, processes that can deliver the products and services, and analytics that support the ongoing decisions needed to manage the firm. Our goal in this book is to introduce students to basic operations and supply chain concepts so they understand how things should be done and the importance of these functions to the success of the firm.

No matter what your major is in business, understanding operations and supply chain management is critical to your success. If you are interested in the study of finance, you will find that all of the concepts are directly applicable. Just convert all of those widgets to their value in the currency of your choice and you will

Photos and Exhibits

Photos and exhibits in the text enhance the visual appeal and clarify text discussions. Many of the photos illustrate additional examples of companies that utilize the operations and supply chain concepts in their business.

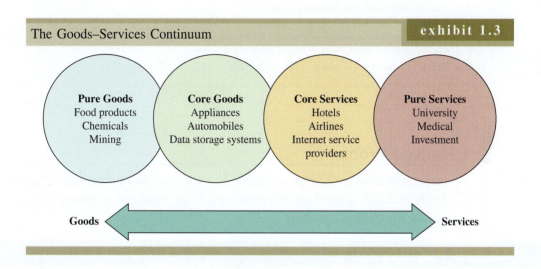

The Goods–Services Continuum   exhibit 1.3

Pure Goods
Food products
Chemicals
Mining

Core Goods
Appliances
Automobiles
Data storage systems

Core Services
Hotels
Airlines
Internet service
providers

Pure Services
University
Medical
Investment

Goods ←————————————————————————→ Services

MARSHMALLOW CANDY PEEPS CHICKS GET A QUALITY CONTROL CHECK AS THEY MOVE DOWN A CONVEYOR BELT INSIDE THE JUST BORN INC. MANUFACTURING FACILITY IN BETHLEHEM, PENNSYLVANIA.

© Mike Mergen/Bloomberg/Getty Images

Concept Connections

Concept Connections draws together various end of chapter sections including Key Terms, Solved Problems, Discussion Questions, Objective Questions, Cases, Analytics Exercises, and Practice Exams.

CONCEPT CONNECTIONS

LO1–1 Identify the elements of operations and supply chain management (OSCM).

- Processes are used to implement the strategy of the firm.
- Analytics are used to support the ongoing decisions needed to manage the firm.

Operations and supply chain management (OSCM) Design, operation, and improvement of the systems that create and deliver the firm's primary products and services.

Process One or more activities that transform inputs into outputs.

Product-service bundling Building service activities into a firm's product offerings to create more value for the customer.

Solved Problems

Representative problems are placed at the end of appropriate chapters. Each includes a worked-out solution giving students a review before solving problems on their own.

SOLVED PROBLEMS

SOLVED PROBLEM 1

Quick Lube Inc. operates a fast lube and oil change garage. On a typical day, customers arrive at the rate of three per hour, and lube jobs are performed at an average rate of one every 15 minutes. The mechanics operate as a team on one car at a time.

Assuming Poisson arrivals and exponential service, find:

a. The utilization of the lube team.
b. The average number of cars in line.
c. The average time a car waits before it is lubed.
d. The total time it takes to go through the system (that is, waiting in line plus lube time).

Solution

$\lambda = 3, \mu = 4$

a. Utilization $\rho = \dfrac{\lambda}{\mu} = \dfrac{3}{4} = 75$ percent.

b. $L_q = \dfrac{\lambda^2}{\mu(\mu - \lambda)} = \dfrac{3^2}{4(4-3)} = \dfrac{9}{4} = 2.25$ cars in line.

c. $W_q = \dfrac{L_q}{\lambda} = \dfrac{2.25}{3} = .75$ hour, or 45 minutes.

d. $W_s = \dfrac{L_s}{\lambda} = \dfrac{\lambda}{\mu - \lambda}/\lambda = \dfrac{3}{4-3}/3 = 1$ hour (waiting + lube).

Practice Exam

The practice exam includes many straightforward review questions, but also has a selection that tests for mastery and integration/application level understanding, that is, the kind of questions that make an exam challenging.

PRACTICE EXAM

1. A strategy that is designed to meet current needs without compromising the ability of future generations to meet their needs.
2. The three criteria included in a triple bottom line.
3. The seven operations and supply chain competitive dimensions.
4. It is probably most difficult to compete on this major competitive dimension.
5. This occurs when a company seeks to match what a competitor is doing while maintaining its existing competitive position.
6. A criterion that differentiates the products or services of one firm from those of another.
7. A screening criterion that permits a firm's products to be considered as possible candidates for purchase.
8. A diagram showing the activities that support a company's strategy.
9. A measure calculated by taking the ratio of output to input.

Answers to Practice Exam 1. Sustainable 2. Social, economic, environmental 3. Cost, quality, delivery speed, delivery reliability, coping with changes in demand, flexibility and speed of new product introduction, other product-specific criteria 4. Cost 5. Straddling 6. Order winner 7. Order qualifier 8. Activity-system map 9. Productivity

Cases

Cases allow students to think critically about issues discussed in the chapter. Cases include:

The Tao of Timbuk2, Chapter 2
Shouldice Hospital: A Cut Above, Chapter 4
Pro Fishing Boats: A Value Stream Mapping Exercise, Chapter 12

CASE: THE TAO OF TIMBUK2*

"Timbuk2 is more than a bag. It's more than a brand. Timbuk2 is a bond. To its owner, a Timbuk2 bag is a dependable, everyday companion. We see fierce, emotional attachments form between Timbuk2 customers and their bags all the time. A well-worn Timbuk2 bag has a certain patina—the stains and scars of everyday urban adventures. Many Timbuk2 bags are worn daily for a decade or more, accompanying the owner through all sorts of defining life events. True to our legend of 'indestructibility,' it's not uncommon for a Timbuk2 bag to outlive jobs, personal relationships, even pets. This is the Tao of Timbuk2."

What makes Timbuk2 so unique? Visit the Web site at www.timbuk2.com and see for yourself. Each bag is custom designed by the customer on the Web site. After the customer selects the basic bag configuration and size, colors for each of the various panels are presented; various lines, logos, pockets, and straps are selected so that the bag is tailored to the

pocket, and strap options. The bag is tailored to the exact specifications of the customer on the Timbuk2 assembly line in San Francisco and sent via overnight delivery directly to the customer.

Recently, Timbuk2 has begun making some of its new products in China, which is a concern to some of its long-standing customers. The company argues that it has designed its new products to provide the best possible features, quality, and value at reasonable prices and stresses that these new products are designed in San Francisco. Timbuk2 argues that the new bags are much more complex to build and require substantially more labor and a variety of very expensive machines to produce. It argues that the San Francisco factory labor cost alone would make the retail price absurdly high. After researching a dozen factories in China, Timbuk2 found one that it thinks is up to the task of producing these new bags. Much as

Analytics Exercises

There are so much more data now available for decision making. The analytics movement takes this to a new level using statistical analysis to extrapolate what to expect in the future to support operations and supply chain decisions. A series of 11 analytics exercises are spread through the chapters. These include

ANALYTICS EXERCISE: DESIGNING A MANUFACTURING PROCESS

Toshiba's Notebook Computer Assembly Line

Toshihiro Nakamura, manufacturing engineering section manager, is examining the prototype assembly process sheet (shown in Exhibit 6.8) for the newest subnotebook computer model. With every new model introduced, management felt that the assembly line had to increase productivity and lower costs, usually resulting in changes to the assembly process. When a new model is designed, considerable attention is directed toward reducing the number of components and simplifying parts production and assembly requirements. This new computer was a marvel of high-tech, low-cost innovation and should give Toshiba an advantage during the upcoming fall/winter selling season.

Production of the subnotebook is scheduled to begin in 10 days. Initial production for the new model is to be 150 units per day, increasing to 250 units per day the following week (management thought that eventually production would reach 300 units per day). Assembly lines at the plant normally are staffed by 10 operators who work at a 14.4-meter-long assembly line. The line is organized in a straight line with workers shoulder to shoulder on one side. The line can accommodate up to 12 operators if there is a need. The line normally operates for 7.5 hours a day (employees work from 8:15 A.M. to 5:00 P.M. and regular hours include one hour of unpaid lunch and 15 minutes of scheduled breaks). It is possible to run one, two, or three hours of overtime, but employees need at least three days' notice for planning purposes.

The Assembly Line

At the head of the assembly line, a computer displays the daily production schedule, consisting of a list of model types and corresponding lot sizes scheduled to be assembled on the line. The models are simple variations of hard disk size, memory, and battery power. A typical production schedule includes seven or eight model types in lot sizes varying from 10 to 100 units. The models are assembled sequentially: All the units of the first model are assembled, followed by all the units of the second, and so on. This computer screen also indicates how far along the assembly line is in completing its

CONTENTS IN BRIEF

CONTENTS

Operations and Supply Chain Management: The Core

CHAPTER 1

OPERATIONS AND SUPPLY CHAIN MANAGEMENT

Learning Objectives

LO1–1 Identify the elements of operations and supply chain management (OSCM).

LO1–2 Evaluate the efficiency of the firm.

LO1–3 Know the potential career opportunities in operations and supply chain management.

LO1–4 Recognize the major concepts that define the operations and supply chain management field.

STRATEGY, PROCESSES, AND ANALYTICS

This book is about designing and operating processes that deliver a firm's goods and services in a manner that matches customers' expectations. Really successful firms have a clear and focused idea of how they intend to make money. Be it high-end products or services that are custom-tailored to the needs of a single customer or generic, inexpensive commodities that are bought largely on the basis of cost, competitively producing and distributing these products is a great challenge.

In the context of major business functions, operations and supply chain management involves specialists in product design, purchasing, manufacturing, service operations, logistics, and distribution. These specialists are mixed and matched in many different ways depending on the product or service. For a firm that sells televisions, like Toshiba, these are the functions responsible for designing televisions, acquiring materials, coordinating equipment resources to convert material to products, moving the product, and exchanging the final product with the

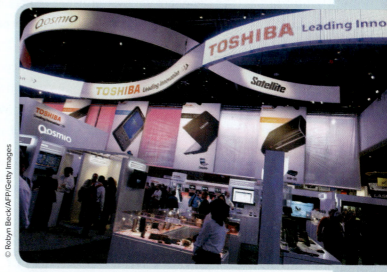

© Robyn Beck/AFP/Getty Images

customer. Some firms are focused on services, such as a hospital. Here, the context involves managing resources, including the operating rooms, labs, and hospital beds used to nurse patients back to health. In this context, acquiring materials, moving patients, and coordinating resource use are keys to success. Other firms are more specialized, such as Amazon. Here, purchasing, Web site services, logistics, and distribution need to be carefully coordinated for success.

In our increasingly interconnected and interdependent global economy, the process of delivering finished goods, services, and supplies from one place to another is accomplished by means of mind-boggling technological innovation, clever new applications of old ideas, seemingly magical mathematics, powerful software, and old-fashioned concrete, steel, and muscle. This book is about doing this at low cost while meeting the requirements of demanding customers. Success involves the clever integration of a great operations-related strategy, processes that can deliver the products and services, and analytics that support the ongoing decisions needed to manage the firm. Our goal in this book is to introduce students to basic operations and supply chain concepts so they understand how things should be done and the importance of these functions to the success of the firm.

Strategy

Processes

Analytics

No matter what your major is in business, understanding operations and supply chain management is critical to your success. If you are interested in the study of finance, you will find that all of the concepts are directly applicable. Just convert all of those widgets to their value in the currency of your choice and you will realize that this is all about dollars and cents moving, being stored, and appreciating in value due to exchanges. What you study in finance class is exactly the same, but we look at things in very different ways due to the physical nature of goods and the intangible features of services. If you are interested in studying marketing, you will realize that the topics presented here are critical to your success. If the product or service cannot be delivered to the customer at an acceptable cost, then no matter how good your marketing program is, no one may buy it. And finally, for the accountants who keep score, the operations and supply chain processes generate most of the transactions used to track the financial health of the firm. Understanding why these processes operate the way they do is important to understanding the financial statements of the firm.

LO1–1 Identify the elements of operations and supply chain management (OSCM).

Operations and supply chain management (OSCM)
The design, operation, and improvement of the systems that create and deliver the firm's primary products and services.

WHAT IS OPERATIONS AND SUPPLY CHAIN MANAGEMENT?

Operations and supply chain management (OSCM) is defined as the design, operation, and improvement of the systems that create and deliver the firm's primary products and services. Like marketing and finance, OSCM is a functional field of business with clear line management responsibilities. OSCM is concerned with the management of the entire system that produces a product or delivers a service. Producing a product such as the Men's Nylon Supplex Parka or providing a service, such as a cellular phone account, involves a complex series of transformation processes.

Exhibit 1.1 shows a supply network for a Men's Nylon Supplex Parka sold on Web sites such as L.L. Bean or Land's End. We can understand the network by looking at the four color-coded paths. The blue path traces the activities needed to produce the Polartec insulation material used in the parkas. Polartec insulation is purchased in bulk, processed to get the proper finish, and then dyed prior to being checked for consistency—or grading—and color. It is then stored in a warehouse. The red path traces the production of the nylon, Supplex, used in the parkas. Using a petroleum-based polymer, the nylon is extruded and drawn into a yarnlike material. From here the green path traces the many steps required to fabricate the clothlike Supplex used to make the parkas. The yellow path shows the Supplex and Polartec material coming together and used to assemble the lightweight and warm parkas. The completed parkas are sent to a warehouse and on to the retailer's distribution center. The parkas are then picked and packed for shipment to individual customers.

Think of the supply network as a pipeline through which material and information flow. There are key locations in the pipeline where material and information are stored for future use: Polartec is stored near the end of the blue pipeline; Supplex is stored near the end of the red pipeline. In both cases, fabric is cut prior to merging with the yellow pipeline. At the beginning of the yellow path, bundles of Supplex and Polartec are stored prior to their use in the fabrication of the parkas. At the end of the yellow path are

exhibit 1.1   Process Steps for Men's Nylon Supplex Parkas

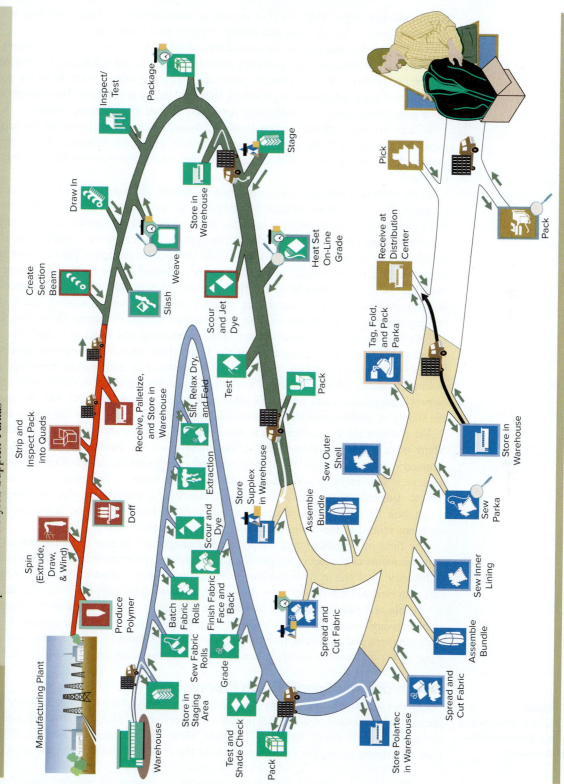

the distribution steps, which involve storing to await orders, picking according to the actual customer order, packing, and finally shipping to the customer.

Networks such as this can be constructed for any product or service. Typically, each part of the network is controlled by different companies, including the nylon Supplex producer, the Polartec producer, the parka manufacturer, and the catalog sales retailer. All of the material is moved using transportation providers, ships and trucks in this case. The network also has a global dimension, with each entity potentially located in a different country.

Success in today's global markets requires a business strategy that matches the preferences of customers with the realities imposed by complex supply networks. A sustainable strategy that meets the needs of shareholders and employees and preserves the environment is critical.

In the context of our discussion, the terms *operations* and *supply chain* take on special meaning. *Operations* refers to manufacturing and service processes that are used to transform the resources employed by a firm into products desired by customers. For example, a manufacturing process would produce some type of physical product, such as an automobile or a computer. A service process would produce an intangible product, such as a call center that provides information to customers stranded on the highway or a hospital that treats accident victims in an emergency room. Planning the use of these processes involves analyzing capacity, labor, and material needs over time. Ensuring quality and making ongoing improvements to these processes are needed to manage these processes.

Supply chain refers to processes that move information and material to and from the manufacturing and service processes of the firm. These include the logistics processes that physically move product, as well as the warehousing and storage processes that position products for quick delivery to the customer. Supply chain in this context refers to providing products and service to plants and warehouses at the input end and also to the supply of products and service to the customer on the output end of the supply chain.

We consider the topics included in this book to be the foundation or "core" material. Many other topics could be included, but these cover the fundamental concepts. All managers should understand these basic principles that guide the design of transformation processes. This includes understanding how different types of processes are organized, how to determine the capacity of a process, how long it should take a process to make a unit, how the quality of a process is monitored, and how information is used to make decisions related to the design and operation of these processes.

The field of operations and supply chain management is ever changing due to the dynamic nature of competing in global business and the constant evolution of information technology. So while many of the basic concepts have been around for years, their application in new and innovative ways is exciting. Internet technology has made the sharing of reliable real-time information inexpensive. Capturing information directly from the source through such systems as point-of-sale, radio-frequency identification tags, barcode scanners, and automatic recognition has shifted the focus to understanding not only what all the information is saying but how good the decisions are that will use it.

Operations and Supply Chain Processes

Process
One or more activities that transform inputs into outputs.

Operations and supply chain **processes** can be conveniently categorized, particularly from the view of a producer of consumer products and services, as planning, sourcing, making, delivering, and returning. Exhibit 1.2 depicts where the processes are used in different parts of a supply chain. The following describes the work involved in each type of process.

1. **Planning** consists of the processes needed to operate an existing supply chain strategically. Here, a firm must determine how anticipated demand will be met with available resources. A major aspect of planning is developing a set of metrics to

Supply Chain Processes   **exhibit 1.2**

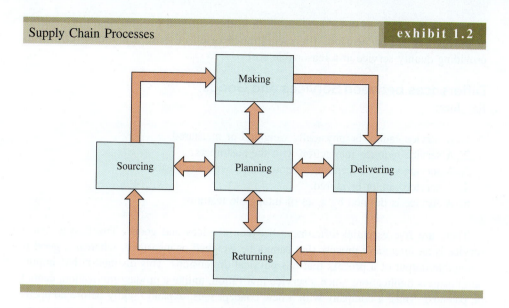

monitor the supply chain so that it is efficient and delivers high quality and value to customers.

2. **Sourcing** involves the selection of suppliers that will deliver the goods and services needed to create the firm's product. A set of pricing, delivery, and payment processes are needed together with metrics for monitoring and improving the relationships between partners of the firm. These processes include receiving shipments, verifying them, transferring them to manufacturing facilities, and authorizing supplier payments.

3. **Making** is where the major product is produced or the service is provided. The step requires scheduling processes for workers and coordinating material and other critical resources such as the equipment to support producing or providing the service. Metrics that measure speed, quality, and worker productivity are used to monitor these processes.

4. **Delivering** is also referred to as a logistics process. Carriers are picked to move products to warehouses and customers, coordinate and schedule the movement of goods and information through the supply network, develop and operate a network of warehouses, and run the information systems that manage the receipt of orders from customers and the invoicing systems that collect payments from customers.

5. **Returning** involves processes for receiving worn-out, defective, and excess products back from customers and support for customers who have problems with delivered products. In the case of services, this may involve all types of follow-up activities that are required for after-sales support.

To understand the topic, it is important to consider the many different players that need to coordinate work in a typical supply chain. The steps of planning, sourcing, making, delivering, and returning are fine for manufacturing and can also be used for the many processes that do not involve the discrete movement and production of parts. In the case of a service firm such as a hospital, for example, supplies are typically delivered on a daily basis from drug and health care suppliers and require coordination among drug companies, local warehouse operations, local delivery services, and hospital receiving. Patients need to be scheduled into the services provided by the hospital, such as operations and blood tests. Other areas, such as the emergency room, need to be staffed to provide service on demand. The orchestration of all of these activities is critical to providing quality service at a reasonable cost.

Differences between Services and Goods

Key Idea:

1. A service cannot be physically weighted or measured.
2. A service requires interaction with the customers.
3. A service varies depending on interaction with the customers.
4. A service cannot be stored.
5. A service is defined by a set of intangible features.

There are five essential differences between services and goods. The first is that a service is an *intangible* process that cannot be weighed or measured, whereas a good is a tangible output of a process that has physical dimensions. This distinction has important business implications since a service innovation, unlike a product innovation, cannot be patented. Thus, a company with a new concept must expand rapidly before competitors copy its procedures. Service intangibility also presents a problem for customers since, unlike with a physical product, customers cannot try it out and test it before purchase.

The second is that a service requires some degree of *interaction with the customer* for it to be a service. The interaction may be brief, but it must exist for the service to be complete. Where face-to-face service is required, the service facility must be designed to handle the customer's presence. Goods, on the other hand, are generally produced in a facility separate from the customer. They can be made according to a production schedule that is efficient for the company.

The third is that services, with the big exception of hard technologies such as automated teller machines (ATMs) and information technologies such as answering machines and automated Internet exchanges, are inherently *heterogeneous*—they vary from day to day and even hour by hour as a function of the attitudes of the customer and the servers. Thus, even highly scripted work, such as found in call centers, can produce unpredictable outcomes. Goods, in contrast, can be produced to meet very tight specifications day-in and day-out with essentially zero variability. In those cases where a defective good is produced, it can be reworked or scrapped.

The fourth is that services as a process are *perishable and time dependent*, and unlike goods, they can't be stored. You cannot "come back last week" for an air flight or a day on campus.

And fifth, the specifications of a service are defined and evaluated as a *package of features* that affect the five senses. These features are:

- Supporting facility (location, decoration, layout, architectural appropriateness, supporting equipment)
- Facilitating goods (variety, consistency, quantity of the physical goods that go with the service; for example, the food items that accompany a meal service)
- Explicit services (training of service personnel, consistency of service performance, availability and access to the service, and comprehensiveness of the service)
- Implicit services (attitude of the servers, atmosphere, waiting time, status, privacy and security, and convenience)

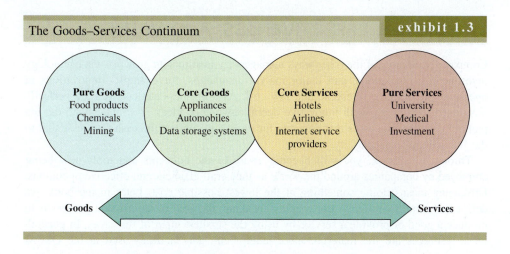

The Goods–Services Continuum   exhibit 1.3

Pure Goods	Core Goods	Core Services	Pure Services
Food products	Appliances	Hotels	University
Chemicals	Automobiles	Airlines	Medical
Mining	Data storage systems	Internet service providers	Investment

Goods ⟷ Services

The Goods–Services Continuum

Almost any product offering is a combination of goods and services. In Exhibit 1.3, we show this arrayed along a continuum of "pure goods" to "pure services." The continuum captures the main focus of the business and spans from firms that just produce products to those that only provide services. Pure goods industries have become low-margin commodity businesses, and in order to differentiate, they are often adding some services. Some examples are providing help with logistical aspects of stocking items, maintaining extensive information databases, and providing consulting advice.

Core goods providers already provide a significant service component as part of their businesses. For example, automobile manufacturers provide extensive spare parts distribution services to support repair centers at dealers.

Core service providers must integrate tangible goods. For example, your cable television company must provide cable hookup and repair services and also high-definition cable boxes. Pure services, such as may be offered by a financial consulting firm, may need little in the way of facilitating goods, but what they do use—such as textbooks, professional references, and spreadsheets—are critical to their performance.

Product-Service Bundling

Product-service bundling refers to a company building service activities into its product offerings for its customers. Such services include maintenance, spare part provisioning, training, and in some cases, total systems design and R&D. A well-known pioneer in this area is IBM, which treats its business as a service business and views physical goods as a small part of the "business solutions" it provides its customers. Companies that are most successful in implementing this strategy start by drawing together the service aspects of the business under one roof in order to create a consolidated service organization. The service evolves from a focus on enhancing the product's performance to developing systems and product modifications that support the company's move up the "value stream" into new markets. This type of strategy might not be the best approach for all product companies, however. A recent study found that while firms that offer product-service bundles generate higher revenues, they tend to generate lower profits as a percent of revenues when compared to focused firms. This is because they are often unable to generate revenues or margins high enough to cover the additional investment required to cover service-related costs.

Product-service bundling
When a firm builds service activities into its product offerings to create additional value for the customer.

EFFICIENCY, EFFECTIVENESS, AND VALUE

LO1–2 Evaluate the efficiency of the firm.

Compared with most of the other ways managers try to stimulate growth—via technology investments, acquisitions, and major market campaigns, for example—innovations in operations are relatively reliable and low cost. As a business student, you are perfectly positioned to come up with innovative operations-related ideas. You understand the big picture of all the processes that generate the costs and support the cash flow essential to the firm's long-term viability.

Through this book, you will become aware of the concepts and tools now being employed by companies around the world as they craft efficient and effective operations. **Efficiency** means doing something at the lowest possible cost. Later in the book, we define this more thoroughly. But roughly speaking, the goal of an efficient process is to produce a good or provide a service by using the smallest input of resources. In general, these resources are the material, labor, equipment, and facilities used in the OSCM processes.

Effectiveness means doing the right things to create the most value for the customer. For example, to be effective at a grocery store it is important to have plenty of operating checkout lines even though they may often stand idle. This is a recognition that the customer's time is valuable and that they do not like waiting to be served in the checkout line. Often maximizing effectiveness and efficiency at the same time creates conflict between the two goals. We see this trade-off every day in our lives. At the checkout lines, being efficient means using the fewest people possible to ring up customers. Being effective, though, means minimizing the amount of time customers need to wait in line.

Related to efficiency and effectiveness is the concept of **value**, which can be abstractly defined as quality divided by price. Here quality is the attractiveness of the product, considering its features and durability. If you can provide the customer with a better car without changing price, value has gone up. If you can give the customer a better car at a *lower* price, value goes way up. A major objective of this book is to show how smart management can achieve high levels of value.

Efficiency
Doing something at the lowest possible cost.

Effectiveness
Doing the right things to create the most value for the customer.

Value
The attractiveness of a product relative to its price.

Efficiency at Southwest Airlines

Getting passengers on a plane quickly can greatly affect an airline's cost. Southwest, considered the fastest at turning a plane around, does not assign seats. For Southwest, the goal is to have its airplanes in the air as much as possible. This is difficult, given the multiple short flights that a Southwest jet flies each day.

On average, Southwest's 550 jets fly about 3,400 flights a day. Without adjusting for jets that are not flying for maintenance, this averages out to over 6 flights a day per jet. Turning a jet around—from landing to takeoff—is critical to this type of airline, and it has been estimated that Southwest can do this in between 30 and 55 minutes, depending on the airport and plane. Think about this: even at 45 minutes per turn, a Southwest jet still spends about 4.5 hours on the ground each day. The precious minutes that Southwest can save in loading passengers results in more flights the airline can fly.

Courtesy of F. Robert Jacobs

How Does Wall Street Evaluate Efficiency?

Comparing firms from an operations and supply chain view is important to investors since the relative cost of providing a good or service is essential to high earnings growth. When you think about it, earnings growth is largely a function of the firm's profitability, and profit can be increased through higher sales and/or reduced cost. Highly efficient firms usually shine when demand drops during recession periods since they often can continue to make a profit due to their low-cost structure. These operations-savvy firms may even see a recession as an opportunity to gain market share as their less-efficient competitors struggle to remain in business.

An interesting relationship between the costs related to OSCM functions and profit is the direct impact of a reduction of cost in one of these functions on the profit margin of the firm. In Exhibit 1.4, we show data from a company's balance sheet. The balance sheet on the left shows the return on investment (ROI) for the company prior to a reduction in raw material cost. The balance sheet on the right shows the same data, but with a reduction of 5% in the cost of raw materials. The cost of raw materials affects the values throughout the supply chain, including the cost of goods sold, inventory value, and total value of assets; therefore, reducing raw material costs by 5% leads to nearly a 29% increase in profit margins and a 30% increase in the company's ROI. Thus, there is an almost 6:1 leverage on every dollar saved by reducing raw materials costs.

A common set of financial indicators that Wall Street tracks to *benchmark* companies are called management efficiency ratios. **Benchmarking** is a process in which one company studies the processes of another company (or industry) to identify best practices. You probably discussed these in one of your accounting classes. It is not our purpose to do an in-depth review of this material, but it is important to recognize the significant impact the operations and supply chain processes have on these ratios. A comparison of a few automobile companies using the ratios is shown in Exhibit 1.5.

Benchmarking
When one company studies the processes of another company to identify best practices.

The Impact of Reducing Raw Material Cost   **exhibit 1.4**

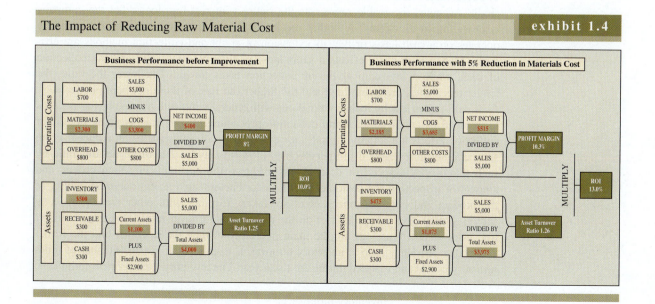

exhibit 1.5	Management Efficiency Measures Used by Wall Street			
A COMPARISON OF AUTOMOBILE COMPANIES				
EFFICIENCY MEASURE	TOYOTA (TM)	GENERAL MOTORS (GM)	FORD (F)	INDUSTRY
Income per employee	$60,266	$50,255	$17,037	$39,170
Revenue (or sales) per employee	$738,754	$1,949,113	$770,465	$799,932
Receivables turnover	3.3	6.4	1.6	3.2
Inventory turnover	10.50	9.7	15.3	9.5
Asset turnover	0.6	0.9	0.7	0.7

The following is a brief review of these ratios. Starting from basic financial data for the firm, the simplest efficiency-related measures relate to the productivity of labor employed by the firm. There are two of these ratios:

- Net income per employee
- Revenue (or sales) per employee

These labor productivity measures are fairly crude since many employees are not directly employed in operations and supply chain–related functions. Also, it is important to recognize that the concepts described in this book are certainly applicable to the other functions in the firm.

A third efficiency ratio measures the number of times receivables are collected, on average, during the fiscal year. This ratio is called the receivables turnover ratio, and it is calculated as follows:

$$\text{Receivables turnover} = \frac{\text{Annual credit sales}}{\text{Average accounts receivable}} \qquad [1.1]$$

The receivables turnover ratio measures a company's efficiency in collecting its sales on credit. Accounts receivable represents the indirect interest-free loans that the company is providing to its clients. A higher receivables ratio implies either that the company operates on a cash basis or that its extension of credit and collection methods are efficient. Also, a high ratio reflects a short lapse of time between sales and the collection of cash, while a low number means collection takes longer. The lower the ratio, the longer receivables are being held and the higher the risk of them not being collected.

A ratio that is low by industry standards will generally indicate that the business needs to improve its credit policies and collection procedures. If the ratio is going up, either collection efforts are improving, sales are rising, or receivables are being reduced. From an operations and supply chain perspective, the firm may be able to impact this ratio by such things as the speed of delivery of products, the accuracy in filling orders, and amount of inspection the customer needs to do. Factors such as the outgoing quality of the product and how customer orders are taken, together with other order-processing activities, may have a huge impact on the receivables turnover ratio. This is particularly true when Internet catalogs are the main interface between the customer and the firm.

Another efficiency ratio is inventory turnover. It measures the average number of times inventory is sold and replaced during the fiscal year. The inventory turnover ratio formula is:

$$\text{Inventory turnover} = \frac{\text{Cost of goods sold}}{\text{Average inventory value}} \qquad [1.2]$$

This ratio measures the company's efficiency in turning its inventory into sales. Its purpose is to measure the liquidity or speed of inventory usage. This ratio is generally compared against industry averages. A low inventory turnover ratio is a signal of inefficiency, since inventory ties up capital that could be used for other purposes. It might imply either poor sales or excess inventory relative to sales. A low turnover ratio can indicate poor liquidity, possible overstocking, and obsolescence, but it may also reflect a planned inventory buildup in the case of material shortages or in anticipation of rapidly rising prices. A high inventory turnover ratio implies either strong sales or ineffective buying (the firm may be buying too often and in small quantities, driving up the buying price). A high inventory turnover ratio can indicate better liquidity, but it can also indicate shortage or inadequate inventory levels, which may lead to a loss in business. Generally, a high inventory turnover ratio when compared to competitors' is good. This ratio is controlled to a great extent by operations and supply chain processes. Factors such as order lead times, purchasing practices, the number of items being stocked, and production and order quantities have a direct impact on the ratio.

The final efficiency ratio considered here is asset turnover. This is the amount of sales generated for every dollar's worth of assets. The formula for the ratio is:

$$\text{Asset turnover} = \frac{\text{Revenue (or sales)}}{\text{Total assets}} \qquad [1.3]$$

Asset turnover measures a firm's efficiency at using its assets in generating sales revenue—the higher the number, the better. It also indicates pricing strategy: companies with low profit margins tend to have high asset turnover, while those with high profit margins have low asset turnover. This ratio varies significantly by industry, so comparisons between unrelated businesses are not useful. To a great extent, the asset turnover ratio is similar to the receivables turnover and the inventory turnover ratio since all three involve the investment in assets. Asset turnover is more general and includes the plants, warehouses, equipment, and other assets owned by the firm. Because many of these facilities are needed to support the operations and supply chain activities, the ratio can be significantly impacted by investments in technology and outsourcing, for example.

These ratios can be calculated from data in a firm's annual financial statements and are readily available on the Internet from Web sites such as **www.dailyfinance.com**.

FORD FIESTAS ON THE ASSEMBLY LINE AT THE FORD FACTORY IN COLOGNE, GERMANY.
© Oliver Berg/Corbis Wire/Corbis

Example 1.1: Comparing the Management Efficiency of Companies in the Same Industry Using Wall Street Measures

Building on the data in Exhibit 1.5, compare the Japanese automobile manufacturer Honda to Toyota, General Motors, and Ford. Specifically address the following questions:

1. How does Honda (stock symbol HMC) differ relative to income per employee, revenue per employee, receivables turnover, inventory turnover, and asset turnover?
2. Speculate on why Honda's Wall Street efficiency measures are different from the other automobile companies'. Be sure to consider the fact that Honda is a smaller company compared to the others.

SOLUTION

The first step is to get comparable data on Honda. One Web site that has these data is, again, www.dailyfinance.com. Hyperlink to this site using your browser and then enter HMC in the "Get Quote" block on the top of the page. Then, from the menu on the left under Rate and Ratios, select Financial Ratios. Check to see that you have the correct data.

Comparable data for Honda are as follows:

Income per employee	30,203
Revenue per employee	585,647
Receivables turnover	4.9
Inventory turnover	6.3
Asset turnover	0.8

Next, we need to try to understand the data. It is probably good to start with asset turnover, since this is the most comprehensive measure. Notice that GM is the highest in the group. Recall that GM recently went bankrupt and was recapitalized, which could explain the higher asset turnover. Honda, though, is fine compared to the industry average on this measure.

On net income per employee, revenue per employee and inventory turn, we see that Honda appears, for the most part, to be stronger than Ford, but weaker than Toyota and General Motors. Ford is strongest in inventory turn. This is surprising since we might expect Toyota to be strong here, given its reputation in managing inventory. It is interesting to see how Ford is weakest in receivables turnover, which may relate to the amount of credit it is giving customers in order to sell vehicles. •

CAREERS IN OPERATIONS AND SUPPLY CHAIN MANAGEMENT

LO1–3 Know the potential career opportunities in operations and supply chain management.

So what do people who pursue careers in OSCM do? Quite simply, they specialize in managing the production and distribution of goods and services. Jobs abound for people who can do this well since every organization is dependent on effective performance of this fundamental activity for its long-term success.

It is interesting to contrast entry-level jobs in OSCM to marketing and finance jobs. Many marketing entry-level jobs focus on actually selling products or managing the sales of products. These individuals are out on the front line trying to push product to potential customers. Frequently, a significant part of their income will depend on commissions from these sales. Entry-level finance (and accounting) jobs are often in large public accounting firms. These jobs involve working at a desk auditing transactions to ensure the accuracy of financial statements. Other assignments involve the analysis of transactions to better understand the costs associated with the business.

Contrast the marketing and finance jobs to OSCM jobs. The operations and supply chain manager is out working with people to figure out the best way to deliver the goods and services of the firm. Sure, OSCM people work with the marketing folks, but rather than being on the selling side, they are on the buying side: trying to select the best materials and hiring the greatest talent. They will use the data generated by the finance people and analyze processes to figure out those goods and services.

OSCM jobs are hands-on, working with people and figuring out the best way to do things.

The following are some typical entry-level and staff jobs in OSCM:

- Plant manager—Oversees the workforce and physical resources (inventory, equipment, and information technology) required to produce the organization's product.
- Hospital administrator—Oversees human resource management, staffing, and finances at a health care facility.
- Branch manager (bank)—Oversees all aspects of financial transactions at a branch.
- Department store manager—Oversees all aspects of staffing and customer service at a store.
- Call center manager—Oversees staffing and customer service activities at a call center.
- Supply chain manager—Negotiates contracts with vendors and coordinates the flow of material inputs to the production process and the shipping of finished products to customers.
- Purchasing manager—Manages the day-to-day aspects of purchasing, such as invoicing and follow-up.
- Logistics manager—Oversees the movement of goods throughout the supply chain.
- Warehouse/Distribution manager—Oversees all aspects of running a warehouse, including replenishment, customer order fulfillment, and staffing.
- Business process improvement analyst—Applies the tools of lean production to reduce cycle time and eliminate waste in a process.
- Quality control manager—Applies techniques of statistical quality control, such as acceptance sampling and control charts, to the firm's products.
- Lean improvement manager—Trains organizational members in lean production and continuous improvement methods.
- Project manager—Plans and coordinates staff activities, such as new-product development, new-technology deployment, and new-facility location.
- Production control analyst—Plans and schedules day-to-day production.
- Facilities manager—Ensures that the building facility design, layout, furniture, and other equipment are operating at peak efficiency.

The OSCM Profession

Operations and Supply Chain Management Professional Societies

If you are interested in career opportunities in operations and supply chain management, you can learn more about the field through the following professional societies. These groups provide industry-recognized certification programs and ongoing training for those seeking to work in the field.

APICS, the Association for Operations Management: **www.apics.org**

Council of Supply Chain Management Professionals (CSCMP): **www.cscmp.org**

Institute for Supply Management (ISM): **www.ism.ws**

The Project Management Institute (PMI): **www.pmi.org**

Chief Operating Officer

So how far can you go in a career in OSCM? One goal would be to become the chief operating officer (COO) of a company. The COO works with the CEO and company president to determine the company's competitive strategy. The COO's ideas are filtered down through the rest of the company. COOs determine an organization's location, its facilities, which vendors to use, and how the hiring policy will be implemented. Once the key decisions are made, lower-level operations personnel carry them out. Operations personnel work to find solutions and then set about fixing the problems.

Managing the supply chain, service, and support are particularly challenging aspects of a chief operating officer's job. Career opportunities in OSCM are plentiful today as companies strive to improve profitability by improving quality and productivity and reducing costs. The hands-on work of managing people is combined with great opportunities to leverage the latest technologies in getting the job done at companies around the world. No matter what you might do for a final career, your knowledge of OSCM will prove to be a great asset.

LO1–4 Recognize the major concepts that define the operations and supply chain management field.

Manufacturing strategy Emphasizes how a factory's capabilities could be used strategically to gain advantage over a competing company.

HISTORICAL DEVELOPMENT OF OPERATIONS AND SUPPLY CHAIN MANAGEMENT

Our purpose in this section is not to go through all the details of OSCM; that would require us to recount the entire Industrial Revolution. Rather, the focus is on major operations-related concepts that have been popular since the 1980s. Exhibit 1.6 will help clarify the dates as you read about the concepts. Where appropriate, how a supposedly new idea relates to an older idea is discussed. (We seem to keep rediscovering the past.)

Manufacturing Strategy Paradigm The late 1970s and early 1980s saw the development of the **manufacturing strategy** paradigm, which emphasized how manufacturing executives could use their factories' capabilities as strategic competitive weapons. Central

exhibit 1.6 Time Line Depicting When Major OSCM Concepts Became Popular

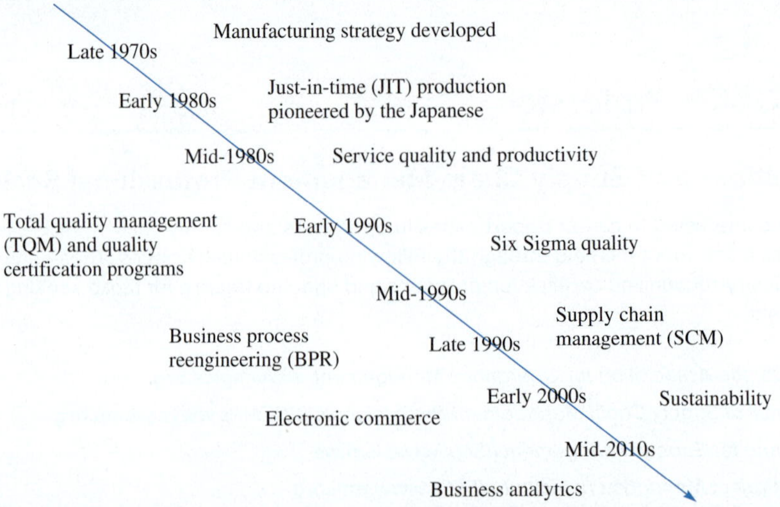

Manufacturing strategy developed — Late 1970s
Just-in-time (JIT) production pioneered by the Japanese — Early 1980s
Service quality and productivity — Mid-1980s
Total quality management (TQM) and quality certification programs — Early 1990s
Six Sigma quality
Supply chain management (SCM) — Mid-1990s
Business process reengineering (BPR) — Late 1990s
Electronic commerce — Early 2000s
Sustainability
Business analytics — Mid-2010s

to this thinking was the notion of manufacturing trade-offs among such performance measures as low cost, high quality, and high flexibility.

Lean Manufacturing, JIT, and TQC The 1980s saw a revolution in the management philosophies and technologies by which production is carried out. **Just-in-time (JIT)** production was the major breakthrough in manufacturing philosophy. Pioneered by the Japanese, JIT is an integrated set of activities designed to achieve high-volume production using minimal inventories of parts that arrive at the workstation exactly when they are needed. The philosophy—coupled with **total quality control (TQC)**, which aggressively seeks to eliminate causes of production defects—is now a cornerstone in many manufacturers' production practices, and the term **lean manufacturing** is used to refer to the set of concepts.

Service Quality and Productivity The unique approach to quality and productivity by McDonald's has been so successful that it stands as a reference point in thinking about how to deliver high-volume standardized services.

Total Quality Management and Quality Certification Another major development was the focus on **total quality management (TQM)** in the late 1980s and 1990s. Helping the quality movement along was the Baldrige National Quality Award, started in 1987 under the direction of the National Institute of Standards and Technology. The Baldrige Award recognizes companies each year for outstanding quality management systems.

The ISO 9000 certification standards, created by the International Organization for Standardization, now play a major role in setting quality standards for global manufacturers.

Business Process Reengineering The need to become lean to remain competitive in the global economic recession in the 1990s pushed companies to seek innovations in the processes by which they run their operations. The **business process reengineering (BPR)** approach seeks to make revolutionary changes as opposed to evolutionary changes (which are commonly advocated in TQM). It does this by taking a fresh look at what the organization is trying to do in all its business processes, and then eliminating non-value-added steps and computerizing the remaining ones to achieve the desired outcome.

Six Sigma Quality Originally developed in the 1980s as part of total quality management, **Six Sigma** in the 1990s saw a dramatic expansion as an extensive set of diagnostic tools was developed. These tools have been taught to managers as part of "Green and Black Belt Programs" at many corporations. The tools are now applied not only to the well-known manufacturing applications, but also to nonmanufacturing processes such as accounts receivable, sales, and research and development. Six Sigma has been applied to environmental, health, and safety services at companies and is now being applied to research and development, finance, information systems, legal, marketing, public affairs, and human resource processes.

Supply Chain Management The central idea of supply chain management is to apply a total system approach to managing the flow of information, materials, and services from raw material suppliers through factories and warehouses to the end customer. Trends such as outsourcing and **mass customization** are forcing companies to find flexible ways to meet customer demand. The focus is on optimizing core activities to maximize the speed of response to changes in customer expectations.

Just-in-time (JIT)
An integrated set of activities designed to achieve high-volume production using minimal inventories of parts that arrive exactly when they are needed.

Total quality control (TQC)
Aggressively seeks to eliminate causes of production defects.

Lean manufacturing
Term used to refer to the set of concepts relating to JIT and TQC.

Total quality management (TQM)
Managing the entire organization so that it excels on all dimensions of products and services that are important to the customer.

Business process reengineering (BPR)
An approach to improving business processes that seeks to make revolutionary changes as opposed to evolutionary (small) changes.

Six Sigma
A statistical term to describe the quality goal of no more than 3.4 defects out of every million units. Also refers to a quality improvement philosophy and program.

Mass customization
The ability to produce a unique product exactly to a particular customer's requirements.

Electronic Commerce The quick adoption of the Internet and the World Wide Web during the late 1990s was remarkable. The term *electronic commerce* refers to the use of the Internet as an essential element of business activity. The use of Web pages, forms, and interactive search engines has changed the way people collect information, shop, and communicate. It has changed the way operations managers coordinate and execute production and distribution functions.

Sustainability

The ability to meet current resource needs without compromising the ability of future generations to meet their needs.

Sustainability and the Triple Bottom Line Sustainability is the ability to maintain balance in a system. Management must now consider the mandates related to the ongoing economic, employee, and environmental viability of the firm (the **triple bottom line**). Economically, the firm must be profitable. Employee job security, positive working conditions, and development opportunities are essential. The need for nonpolluting and non-resource-depleting products and processes presents new challenges to operations and supply managers.

Triple bottom line

A business strategy that includes social, economic, and environmental criteria.

Business Analytics Business analytics involves the analysis of data to better solve business problems. Not that this is something new. Data have always been used to solve business problems. What is new is the reality that so much more data are now captured and available for decision-making analysis than were available in the past. In addition, mathematical tools are now readily available that can be used to support the decision-making process.

Business analytics

The use of current business data to solve business problems using mathematical analysis.

In the past, most analysis involved the generation of standard and ad hoc reports that summarized the current state of the firm. Software allowed querying and "drill down" analysis to the level of the individual transaction, useful features for understanding what happened in the past. Decision making was typically left to the decision maker based on judgment or simple alerting rules. The new "analytics" movement takes this to a new level, using statistical analysis, forecasting to extrapolate what to expect in the future, and even optimization, possibly in real time, to support decisions. These mathematical results can be used either to support the decision maker or to automate decision making.

Take, for example, an airline manager presented with the task of setting price points for tickets on a flight. Real-time demand data, historic demand patterns, and powerful mathematical models can now be applied to setting price points for different classes of tickets. As it is closer to the time of departure for a particular flight, these price points can be adjusted based on how sales are going. These decisions have a major impact on the utilization of aircraft capacity, which impacts both revenue and costs for the airlines. These decisions can even be made using criteria related to weather conditions, fuel prices, crew schedules, and other flights to maximize the profit of the firm.

SOUTHWEST AIRLINES MANAGER MONITORING FLIGHTS AND PASSENGERS TO DECIDE PRICING.

© ERIK S LESSER/Corbis Wire/Corbis

Current Issues in Operations and Supply Chain Management

OSCM is a dynamic field, and issues arising in global enterprise present exciting new challenges for operations managers. Looking forward to the future, we believe the major challenges in the field will be as follows:

1. **Coordinating the relationships between mutually supportive but separate organizations.** Recently, there has been a dramatic surge in the outsourcing of parts, and outsourcing parts and services is common as companies seek to minimize costs. Many companies now even outsource major corporate functions, such as information systems, product development and design, engineering services, and distribution. The ability to coordinate these activities is a significant challenge for today's operations and supply chain manager.

2. **Optimizing global supplier, production, and distribution networks.** The implementation of global enterprise resource planning systems, now common in large companies, has challenged managers to use all of this information. Operations and supply chain *analytics* involves leveraging this information for making decisions related to resources such as inventory, transportation, and production.

3. **Managing customer touch points.** As companies strive to become superefficient, they often scrimp on customer support personnel (and training) required to effectively staff service departments, help lines, and checkout counters. This leads to the frustrations we have all experienced, such as being placed in call-center limbo seemingly for hours, getting bad advice when finally interacting with a company rep, and so on. The issue here is to recognize that making resource utilization decisions must capture the implicit costs of lost customers as well as the direct costs of staffing.

4. **Raising senior management awareness of OSCM as a significant competitive weapon.** Many senior executives entered the organization through finance, strategy, or marketing; built their reputations on work in these areas; and as a result often take OSCM for granted. As we will demonstrate in this book, this can be a critical mistake when we realize how profitable companies such as Amazon, Apple, Taco Bell, and Southwest Airlines are. These are companies where executives have creatively used OSCM for competitive advantage.

CONCEPT CONNECTIONS

LO1–1 Identify the elements of operations and supply chain management (OSCM).

- Processes are used to implement the strategy of the firm.
- Analytics are used to support the ongoing decisions needed to manage the firm.

Operations and supply chain management (OSCM) Design, operation, and improvement of the systems that create and deliver the firm's primary products and services.

Process One or more activities that transform inputs into outputs.

Product-service bundling Building service activities into a firm's product offerings to create more value for the customer.

LO1–2 Evaluate the efficiency of the firm.

Criteria that relate to how well the firm is doing include:

- Efficiency
- Effectiveness
- Value created in its products and services

Efficiency   Doing something at the lowest possible cost.

Effectiveness   Doing the right things to create the most value for the customer.

Value   Ratio of quality to price paid. Competitive "happiness" is being able to increase quality and reduce price while maintaining or improving profit margins. (This is a way that operations can directly increase customer retention and gain market share.)

Benchmarking   When one company studies the processes of another company to identify best practices.

Efficiency Measures:

Income per employee

Revenue (or sales) per employee

$$\text{Receivables turnover} = \frac{\text{Annual credit sales}}{\text{Average accounts receivable}}$$

$$\text{Inventory turnover} = \frac{\text{Cost of goods sold}}{\text{Average inventory value}}$$

$$\text{Asset turnover} = \frac{\text{Revenue (or sales)}}{\text{Total assets}}$$

LO1–3 **Know the potential career opportunities in operations and supply chain management.**

- OSCM people specialize in managing the production of goods and services.
- OSCM jobs are hands-on and require working with others and figuring out the best way to do things.
- The chief operating officer (COO) works with the CEO and company president to determine the company's competitive strategy.
- COOs determine an organization's location, its facilities, which vendors to use, and how the hiring policy will be implemented.

LO1–4 **Recognize the major concepts that define the operations and supply chain management field.**

Many of the concepts that form the OSCM field have their origins in the Industrial Revolution in the 1800s. The focus of this book is on popular concepts developed since the 1980s.

These concepts include:

Manufacturing strategy   Emphasizes how a factory's capabilities could be used strategically to gain advantage over a competing company.

Just-in-time (JIT)   An integrated set of activities designed to achieve high-volume production using minimal inventories of parts that arrive exactly when they are needed.

Total quality control (TQC)   Aggressively seeks to eliminate causes of production defects.

Lean manufacturing   Term used to refer to the set of concepts relating to JIT and TQC.

Total quality management (TQM)   Managing the entire organization so that it excels on all dimensions of products and services that are important to the customer.

Business process reengineering (BPR)   An approach to improving business processes that seeks to make revolutionary changes as opposed to evolutionary (small) changes.

Six Sigma   A statistical term to describe the quality goal of no more than 3.4 defects out of every million units. Also refers to a quality improvement philosophy and program.

Mass customization   Producing products exactly to a particular customer's requirements.

Sustainability   The ability to meet current resource needs without compromising the ability of future generations to meet their needs.

Triple bottom line   A business strategy that includes social, economic, and environmental criteria.

Business analytics   The use of current business data to solve business problems using mathematical analysis.

DISCUSSION QUESTIONS

LO1–1

1. Using Exhibit 1.2 as a model, describe the source-make-deliver-return relationships in the following systems:
   a. An airline
   b. An automobile manufacturer
   c. A hospital
   d. An insurance company
2. Define the service package of your college or university. What is its strongest element? Its weakest one?
3. What service industry has impressed you the most with its innovativeness?
4. What is product-service bundling, and what are the benefits to customers?
5. What is the difference between a service and a good?

LO1–2

6. Some people tend to use the terms *effectiveness* and *efficiency* interchangeably, though we've seen they are different concepts. But is there any relationship at all between them? Can a firm be effective but inefficient? Very efficient but essentially ineffective? Both? Neither?
7. Two of the efficiency ratios mentioned in the chapter are the *receivables turnover ratio* and the *inventory turnover ratio*. While they are two completely separate measures, they are very similar in one way. What is the common thread between these two?

LO1–3

8. Look at the job postings at **www.apics.org** and evaluate the opportunities for an OSCM major with several years of experience.

LO1–4

9. Recent outsourcing of parts and services that had previously been produced internally is addressed by which current issue facing operation management today?
10. What factors account for the resurgence of interest in OSCM today?
11. As the field of OSCM has advanced, new concepts have been applied to help companies compete in a number of ways, including the advertisement of the firm's products or services. One recent concept to gain the attention of companies is promoting *sustainability*. Discuss how you have seen the idea of sustainability used by companies to advertise their goods or services.

OBJECTIVE QUESTIONS

LO1–1

1. What are the three elements that require integration to be successful in operations and supply chain management?
2. Operations and supply chain management is concerned with the design and management of the entire system that has what function?

LO1–2

3. Consider the following financial data from the past year for Midwest Outdoor Equipment Corporation.

Gross income	$25,240,000
Total sales	24,324,000
Total credit sales	18,785,000
Net income	2,975,000
Cost of goods sold	12,600,000
Total assets	10,550,000
Average inventory	2,875,000
Average receivables	3,445,000

  a. Compute the *receivables turnover ratio*.
  b. Compute the *inventory turnover ratio*.
  c. Compute the *asset turnover ratio*.

4. A manufacturing company has entered into a new contract with a major supplier of raw materials used in the manufacturing process. Under the new arrangement, called *vendor managed inventory*, the supplier manages its raw material inventory inside the manufacturer's plant, and bills only the manufacturer when the manufacturer consumes the raw material. How is this likely to affect the manufacturer's inventory turnover ratio?

5. What is the name of the process in which one company studies the processes of another firm in order to identify best practices?

6. A company has recently implemented an automated online billing and payment processing system for orders it ships to customers. As a result, it has reduced the average number of days between billing a customer and receiving payment by 10 days. How will this affect the receivables turnover ratio?

LO1–3

7. Match the following OSCM job titles with the appropriate duties and responsibilities.

_____ Plant manager
_____ Supply chain manager
_____ Project manager
_____ Business process improvement analyst
_____ Logistics manager

A. Plans and coordinates staff activities such as new product development and new facility location.
B. Oversees the movement of goods throughout the supply chain.
C. Oversees the workforce and resources required to produce the firm's products.
D. Negotiates contracts with vendors and coordinates the flow of material inputs to the production process.
E. Applies the tools of lean production to reduce cycle time and eliminate waste in a process.

8. What high-level OSCM manager is responsible for working with the CEO and company president to determine the company's competitive strategy?

LO1–4

9. Order the following major concepts that have helped define the OSCM field on a time line. Use 1 for the earliest concept to be introduced, and 5 for the most recent.

_____ Supply chain management
_____ Manufacturing strategy
_____ Business analytics
_____ Total quality management
_____ Electronic commerce

10. Which major OSCM concept can be described as an integrated set of activities designed to achieve high-volume production using minimal inventories of parts that arrive at workstations exactly when they are needed?

11. _____ leverage the vast amount of data in enterprise resource planning systems to make decisions related to managing resources.

12. Which current issue in OSCM relates to the ability of a firm to maintain balance in a system, considering the ongoing economic, employee, and environmental viability of the firm?

ANALYTICS EXERCISE: COMPARING COMPANIES USING WALL STREET EFFICIENCY MEASURES

The idea behind this exercise is for the class to generate data comparing companies in many different industries. These data will be used to compare these industries from an operations and supply chain view to better understand differences. Be prepared for a lively class discussion for this session.

Step 1: Pick an industry that you find interesting. This may be driven by a company by which you would like to be employed or by some other factor. Within the industry, identify three companies that compete with one another. To ensure comparability, go to www.dailyfinance.com, and then find and enter the company stock symbol. The industry is in the right column. Find three companies that are in the same industry.

Step 2: Collect data related to each company. At a minimum, find the income per employee, revenue per employee, receivables turnover, inventory turnover, and asset turnover for each company. These data are available under Rates and Ratios. Then, select Financial Ratios on the Web site.

Step 3: Compare the companies based on what you have found. Which company appears to have the most productive employees? Which company has the best operations and supply chain processes? Which company is most efficient in its use of credit? Which company makes the best use of its facility and equipment assets?

Step 4: What insights can you draw from your analysis? What could your companies learn from benchmarking each other?

PRACTICE EXAM

1. The pipelinelike movement of the materials and information needed to produce a good or service.
2. A strategy that meets the needs of shareholders, and employees, and that preserves the environment.
3. The processes needed to determine the set of future actions required to operate an existing supply chain.
4. The selection of suppliers.
5. A type of process where a major product is produced or a service is provided.
6. A type of process that moves products to warehouses or customers.
7. Processes that involve the receiving of worn-out, defective, and excess products returned by customers and support for customers who have product problems.
8. A business where the major product is intangible, meaning it cannot be weighed or measured.
9. When a company builds service activities into its product offerings.
10. Doing something at the lowest possible cost.
11. Doing the right things to create the most value for the company.
12. Metaphorically defined as quality divided by price.
13. A philosophy that aggressively seeks to eliminate the causes of production defects.
14. An approach that seeks to make revolutionary changes, as opposed to evolutionary changes (which is advocated by total quality management).
15. An approach that combines TQM and JIT.
16. Tools that are taught to managers in "Green and Black Belt Programs."
17. A program to apply the latest concepts in information technology to improve service productivity.

Answers to Practice Exam 1. Supply (chain) network 2. Triple bottom line strategy 3. Planning 4. Sourcing 5. Making 6. Delivery 7. Returning 8. Service 9. Product–service bundling 10. Efficiency 11. Effectiveness 12. Value 13. Total quality control 14. Business process reengineering 15. Lean manufacturing 16. Six Sigma quality 17. Service science management and engineering

CHAPTER 2

STRATEGY AND SUSTAINABILITY

Learning Objectives

LO2–1 Know what a sustainable business strategy is and how it relates to operations and supply chain management.

LO2–2 Define operations and supply chain strategy.

LO2–3 Explain how operations and supply chain strategies are implemented.

LO2–4 Understand why strategies have implications relative to business risk.

LO2–5 Evaluate productivity in operations and supply chain management.

MISSION STATEMENTS WITH ASPIRATIONS BEYOND MAKING A PROFIT

Companies such as Clif Bar and Whole Foods Market have bold mission statements that depict a focus that goes well beyond profit and shareholder wealth. Consider Clif Bar's 5 Aspirations and Whole Foods Market's Declaration of Interdependence, company mission statements that describe their aspirations related to the environment, the community, their employees, and making a profit. Companies need operations and supply chain strategies that align with the goals of the firm as a whole.

Clif Bar's 5 Aspirations

1. Sustaining our Planet—Keep our impact on the planet small, even as we grow.
2. Sustaining our Community—Be good neighbors. Give back to the community.
3. Sustaining our People—Create an environment where people can live life to the fullest, even from 9 to 5.
4. Sustaining our Business—Grow slower, grow better and stick around longer.
5. Sustaining our Brands—Make what people actually need. Never compromise quality.

© Jorgen Gulliksen/ZUMA Press/Corbis Wire/Corbis

Whole Foods Market's Declaration of Interdependence

Whole Foods Market is a dynamic leader in the quality food business. We are a mission-driven company that aims to set the standards of excellence for food retailers. We are building a business in which high standards permeate all aspects of our company. Quality is a state of mind at Whole Foods Market.

© UPPA/ZUMAPRESS/Newscom

Our motto—Whole Foods, Whole People, Whole Planet—emphasizes that our vision reaches far beyond just being a food retailer. Our success in fulfilling our vision is measured by customer satisfaction, Team Member excellence and happiness, return on capital investment, improvement in the state of the environment, and local and larger community support.

Our ability to instill a clear sense of interdependence among our various stakeholders (the people who are interested and benefit from the success of our company) is contingent upon our efforts to communicate more often, more openly, and more compassionately. Better communication equals better understanding and more trust.

A SUSTAINABLE OPERATIONS AND SUPPLY CHAIN STRATEGY

LO2–1 Know what a sustainable business strategy is and how it relates to operations and supply chain management.

Sustainability
The ability to meet current resource needs without compromising the ability of future generations to meet their needs.

Triple bottom line
Evaluating the firm against social, economic, and environmental criteria.

Strategy should describe how a firm intends to create and sustain value for its current shareholders. By adding **sustainability** to the concept, we add the requirement to meet these current needs without compromising the ability of future generations to meet their own needs. *Shareholders* are those individuals or companies that legally own one or more shares of stock in the company. Many companies today have expanded the scope of their strategy to include stakeholders. *Stakeholders* are those individuals or organizations that are influenced, either directly or indirectly, by the actions of the firm. This expanded view means that the scope of the firm's strategy must not only focus on the economic viability of its shareholders, but should also consider the environmental and social impact on key stakeholders.

To capture this expanded view, the phrase **triple bottom line** has been coined. The triple bottom line, Exhibit 2.1, considers evaluating the firm against social, economic, and environmental criteria. Many companies have developed this expanded view through goals that relate to sustainability along each of these dimensions. Some alternative phrases for the same concept are "People, Planet, and Profit" used by Shell Oil Company, and "Folk, Work, and Place" which originated with the twentieth-century writer Patrick Geddes. The following expands on the meaning of each dimension of the triple bottom line framework.

- **Social** pertains to fair and beneficial business practices toward labor, the community, and the region in which a firm conducts its business. A triple bottom line company seeks to benefit its employees, the community, and other social entities that are impacted by the firm's existence. A company should not use child labor, and should pay fair salaries to its workers, maintain a safe work environment with tolerable working hours, and not otherwise exploit a community or its labor force. A business can also give back by contributing to the strength and growth of its community through health care, education, and other special programs.
- **Economic** means the firm is obligated to compensate shareholders who provide capital through stock purchases and other financial instruments via a competitive return on

exhibit 2.1 The Triple Bottom Line

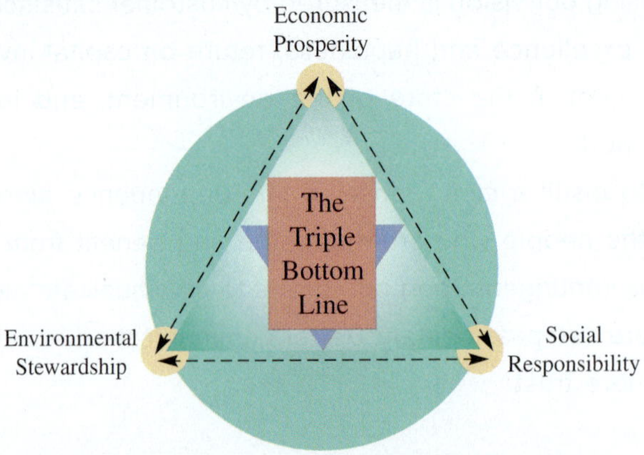

investment. Company strategies should promote growth and grow long-term value to this group in the form of profit. Within a sustainability framework, this dimension goes beyond just profit for the firm; it also provides lasting economic benefit to society.

- **Environmental** refers to the firm's impact on the environment. The company should protect the environment as much as possible—or at least cause no harm. Managers should move to reduce a company's ecological footprint by carefully managing its consumption of natural resources and by reducing waste. Many businesses now conduct "cradle-to-grave" assessments of products to determine what the true environmental costs are—from processing the raw material to manufacture to distribution to eventual disposal by the final customer.

THE GAP CORPORATE HEADQUARTERS BUILDING UTILIZES A GREEN ROOF WITH SOLAR PANELS.

© Steve Proehl/Terra/Corbis

Conventional strategy focuses on the economic part of this framework. Because many of the processes that fall under the domain of operations and supply chain management have a social and environment impact, it is important these criteria be considered as well. Some proponents argue that in many ways European Union countries are more advanced due to the standardized reporting of ecological and social losses that came with the adoption of the euro.

Although many company planners agree with the goals of improving society and preserving the environment, many others disagree. Dissenting arguments relate to the potential loss of efficiency due to the focus on conflicting criteria. Others argue that these goals may be appropriate only for rich societies that can afford to contribute to society and the environment. A company in a poor or developing society/nation must focus on survival. The economic benefit derived from the use of abundant local resources may be viewed as worth their destruction.

In this chapter, we take a customer-centered approach; issues associated with people and the environment are left to an individual case approach. Depending on the country, industry, and scope of the firm, these other issues vary widely, and it would be difficult to provide a general approach for analysis. The issues and their relationship to operations and supply chain management are very real, however, and we anticipate they will become even more relevant in the future.

WHAT IS OPERATIONS AND SUPPLY CHAIN STRATEGY?

Operations and supply chain strategy is concerned with setting broad policies and plans for using the resources of a firm and must be integrated with corporate strategy. So, for example, if the high-level corporate strategy includes goals related to the environment and social responsibility, then the operations and supply chain strategy must consider these goals. A major focus to the operations and supply chain strategy is

Operations and supply chain strategy The setting of broad policies and plans that will guide the use of the resources needed by the firm to implement its corporate strategy.

LO2–2 Define operations and supply chain strategy.

Operations effectiveness
Performing activities in a manner that best implements strategic priorities at minimum cost.

operations effectiveness. **Operations effectiveness** relates to the core business processes needed to run the business. The processes span all the business functions, from taking customer orders, handling returns, manufacturing, and managing the updating of the Web site, to shipping products. Operational effectiveness is reflected directly in the costs associated with doing business. Strategies associated with operational effectiveness, such as quality assurance and control initiatives, process redesign, planning and control systems, and technology investments, can show quick near-term (12 to 24 months) results.

Operations and supply chain strategy can be viewed as part of a planning process that coordinates operational goals with those of the larger organization. Since the goals of the larger organization change over time, the operations strategy must be designed to anticipate future needs. A firm's operations and supply chain capabilities can be viewed as a portfolio best suited to adapting to the changing product and/or service needs of the firm's customers.

Next, we focus on integrating operations and supply chain strategy with a firm's operations capabilities. This involves decisions that relate to the design of the processes and infrastructure needed to support these processes. Process design includes selecting the appropriate technology, sizing the process over time, determining the role of inventory in the process, and locating the process. The infrastructure decisions involve the logic associated with the planning and control systems, quality assurance and control approaches, work payment structure, and organization of the operations and supply functions. A firm's operations capabilities can be viewed as a portfolio best suited to adapting to the changing product and/or service needs of a firm's customers.

Competitive Dimensions

Given the choices customers face today, how do they decide which product or service to buy? Different customers are attracted by different attributes. Some customers are interested primarily in the cost of a product or service and, correspondingly, some companies attempt to position themselves to offer the lowest prices. The major competitive dimensions that form the competitive position of a firm are discussed next.

Cost or Price: "Make the Product or Deliver the Service Cheap" Within every industry, there is usually a segment of the market that buys solely on the basis of low cost. To successfully compete in this niche, a firm must be the low-cost producer, but even this does not always guarantee profitability and success. Products and services sold strictly on the basis of cost are typically commodity-like; in other words, customers cannot distinguish the product or service of one firm from that of another. This segment of the market is frequently very large, and many companies are lured by the potential for significant profits, which they associate with the large unit volumes. As a consequence, however, competition in this segment is fierce—and the failure rate high. After all, there can be only one low-cost producer, who usually establishes the selling price in the market.

Price, however, is not the only basis on which a firm can compete (although many economists appear to assume it is!). Other companies, such as BMW, seek to attract people who want *higher quality*—in terms of performance, appearance, or features—than what is available in competing products and services, even though it means a higher price.

Quality: "Make a Great Product or Deliver a Great Service" There are two characteristics of a product or service that define quality: design quality and process quality. Design quality relates to the set of features the product or service contains. Obviously, a child's first two-wheel bicycle is of significantly different quality than the bicycle of a world-class cyclist. The use of special aluminum alloys and special lightweight sprockets and chains is important to the performance needs of the advanced cyclist. These two types of bicycles are designed for different customers' needs. The higher-quality cyclist product commands a higher price in the marketplace due to its special features. The goal in establishing the proper level of design quality is to focus on the requirements of the customer. Overdesigned products and services with too many or inappropriate features will be viewed as prohibitively expensive. In comparison, underdesigned products and services will lose customers to products that cost a little more but are perceived by customers as offering greater value.

AN AERODYNAMICS EXPERT LOGS RESULTS FROM A WIND TUNNEL TEST FOR CYCLING CLOTHING AND RACING BICYCLE DESIGN.

© Adrian Sherratt/Alamy

Process quality, the second characteristic of quality, is critical because it relates directly to the reliability of the product or service. Regardless of whether the product is a child's first two-wheeler or a bicycle for an international cyclist, customers want products without defects. Thus, the goal of process quality is to produce defect-free products and services. Product and service specifications, given in dimensional tolerances and/or service error rates, define how the product or service is to be made. Adherence to these specifications is critical to ensure the reliability of the product or service as defined by its intended use.

Delivery Speed: "Make the Product or Deliver the Service Quickly" In some markets, a firm's ability to deliver more quickly than its competitors is critical. A company that can offer an onsite repair service in only 1 or 2 hours has a significant advantage over a competing firm that guarantees service only within 24 hours.

Delivery Reliability: "Deliver It When Promised" This dimension relates to the firm's ability to supply the product or service on or before a promised delivery due date. For an automobile manufacturer, it is very important that its supplier of tires provide the needed quantity and types for each day's car production. If the tires needed for a particular car are not available when the car reaches the point on the assembly line where the tires are installed, the whole assembly line may have to be shut down until they arrive. For a service firm such as Federal Express, delivery reliability is the cornerstone of its strategy.

Coping with Changes in Demand: "Change Its Volume" In many markets, a company's ability to respond to increases and decreases in demand is important to its ability to compete. It is well known that a company with increasing demand can do little wrong. When demand is strong and increasing, costs are continuously reduced due to economies of scale, and investments in new technologies can be easily justified. But scaling back when demand decreases may require many difficult decisions about laying off employees and determining reductions in assets. The ability to effectively deal with dynamic market demand over the long term is an essential element of operations strategy.

Flexibility and New-Product Introduction Speed: "Change It" Flexibility, from a strategic perspective, refers to the ability of a company to offer a wide variety of products to its customers. An important element of this ability to offer different products is the time required for a company to develop a new product and to convert its processes to offer the new product.

Other Product-Specific Criteria: "Support It" The competitive dimensions just described are certainly the most common. However, other dimensions often relate to specific products or situations. Notice that most of the dimensions listed next are primarily services in nature. Often, special services are provided to augment the sales of manufactured products.

1. **Technical liaison and support.** A supplier may be expected to provide technical assistance for product development, particularly during the early stages of design and manufacturing.
2. **Meeting a launch date.** A firm may be required to coordinate with other firms on a complex project. In such cases, manufacturing may take place while development work is still being completed. Coordinating work between firms and having them work simultaneously on a project will reduce the total time required to complete the project.
3. **Supplier after-sale support.** An important competitive dimension may be the ability of a firm to support its product after the sale. This involves the availability of replacement parts and, possibly, the modification of older, existing products, bringing them up to new performance levels. The speed of response to these after-sale needs is often important as well.
4. **Environmental impact.** A dimension related to criteria such as carbon dioxide emissions, the use of nonrenewable resources, and other factors that relate to sustainability.
5. **Other dimensions.** These typically include such factors as the colors available, size, weight, location of the fabrication site, the customization available, and product mix options.

The Notion of Trade-Offs

Central to the concept of operations and supply chain strategy is the notion of operations focus and trade-offs. The underlying logic is that an operation cannot excel simultaneously on all competitive dimensions. Consequently, management has to decide which parameters of performance are critical to the firm's success and then concentrate the resources of the firm on these particular characteristics.

For example, if a company wants to focus on the speed of delivery, it cannot be very flexible in its ability to offer a wide range of products. Similarly, a low-cost strategy is not compatible with either speed of delivery or flexibility. High quality also is viewed as a trade-off to low cost.

A strategic position is not sustainable unless there are compromises with other positions. Trade-offs occur when activities are incompatible so that more of one thing necessitates less of another. An airline can choose to serve meals—adding cost and slowing turnaround time at the gate—or it can choose not to, but it cannot do both without bearing major inefficiencies.

Straddling occurs when a company seeks to match the benefits of a successful position while maintaining its existing position. It adds new features, services, or technologies onto the activities it already performs. The risky nature of this strategy is shown by Continental Airlines' ill-fated attempt to compete with Southwest Airlines. While maintaining its position as a full-service airline, Continental set out to match Southwest on a number of point-to-point routes. The airline dubbed the new service Continental Lite. It eliminated meals and first-class service, increased departure frequency, lowered fares, and shortened gate turnaround time. Because Continental remained a full-service airline on other routes, it continued to use travel agents and its mixed fleet of planes and to provide baggage checking and seat assignments.

Trade-offs ultimately grounded Continental Lite. The airline lost hundreds of millions of dollars, and the chief executive officer lost his job. Its planes were delayed, leaving hub cities congested, slowed at the gate by baggage transfers. Late flights and cancellations generated a thousand complaints a day. Continental Lite could not afford to compete on price and still pay standard travel agent commissions, but neither could it do without agents for its full-service business. The airline compromised by cutting commissions for all Continental flights. Similarly, it could not afford to offer the same frequent-flier benefits to travelers paying the much lower ticket prices for Lite service. It compromised again by lowering the rewards of Continental's entire frequent-flier program. The results: angry travel agents and full-service customers. Continental tried to compete in two ways at once and paid an enormous straddling penalty.

Straddling
When a firm seeks to match what a competitor is doing by adding new features, services, or technologies to existing activities. This often creates problems if certain trade-offs need to be made.

Order Winners and Order Qualifiers:
The Marketing–Operations Link

A well-designed interface between marketing and operations is necessary to provide a business with an understanding of its markets from both perspectives. The terms *order winner* and *order qualifier* describe marketing-oriented dimensions that are key to competitive success. An **order winner** is a criterion that differentiates the products or services of one firm from those of another. Depending on the situation, the order-winning criterion may be the cost of the product (price), product quality and reliability, or any of the other dimensions developed earlier. An **order qualifier** is a screening criterion that permits a firm's products to even be considered as possible candidates for purchase. Oxford professor Terry Hill states that a firm must "requalify the order qualifiers" every day it is in business.

For example, consider your purchase of a notebook computer. You might think that such features as screen size, weight, operating system version, and cost are important *qualifying* dimensions. But the order-winning feature that actually *differentiates* one notebook computer candidate from another for you is battery life. In doing your search, you develop a list of computers that all have 14-inch screens, weigh less than three pounds, run the latest Microsoft Windows operating system, and cost less than $1,000. From this list of acceptable computers, you select the one that has the longest battery life.

Order winners
One or more specific marketing-oriented dimensions that clearly differentiate a product from competing products.

Order qualifiers
Dimensions used to screen a product or service as a candidate for purchase.

In an industrial setting where a firm is deciding on a supplier, the decision can be quite different. Here, consider a firm that is deciding on a supplier for its office supplies. Companies such as Office Depot, Quill, or Staples might be candidates. Here, the qualifying dimensions are the following: Can the company supply the items needed? Can the supplier deliver orders within 24 hours? Are the items guaranteed? And is a private Web-based catalog available? Companies that have these capabilities would *qualify* for consideration as possible suppliers. The order winner might be the discount schedule that the company offers on the price of the items purchased.

STRATEGIES ARE IMPLEMENTED USING OPERATIONS AND SUPPLY CHAIN ACTIVITIES—IKEA'S STRATEGY

LO2–3 Explain how operations and supply chain strategies are implemented.

All the activities that make up a firm's operation relate to one another. To make these activities efficient, the firm must minimize its total cost without compromising customers' needs.

To demonstrate how this works, consider how IKEA, the Swedish retailer of home products, implements its strategy using a set of unique activities. IKEA targets young furniture buyers who want style at a low cost. IKEA has chosen to perform activities differently than its rivals.

Consider the typical furniture store, where showrooms display samples of the merchandise. One area may contain many sofas, another area displays dining tables, and there are many other areas focused on particular types of furniture. Dozens of books displaying fabric swatches or wood samples or alternative styles offer customers thousands of product varieties from which to choose. Salespeople escort customers through the store, answering questions and helping them navigate the maze of choices. Once a customer decides what he or she wants, the order is relayed to a third-party manufacturer. With a lot of luck, the furniture will be delivered to the customer's home within six to eight weeks. This is a supply chain that maximizes customization and service, but does so at a high cost.

© Ron Buskirk/Alamy

In contrast, IKEA serves customers who are happy to trade service for cost. Instead of using sales associates, IKEA uses a self-service model with roomlike displays where furniture is shown in familiar settings. Rather than relying on third-party manufacturers, IKEA designs its own low-cost, modular, ready-to-assemble furniture. In the store, there is a warehouse section with the products in boxes ready for delivery. Customers do their own picking from inventory and delivery. Much of its low-cost operation comes from having customers service themselves, yet IKEA offers extra services, such as in-store child care and extended hours. Those services align well with the needs of its customers, who are young, not wealthy, and likely to have children, and who need to shop at odd hours.

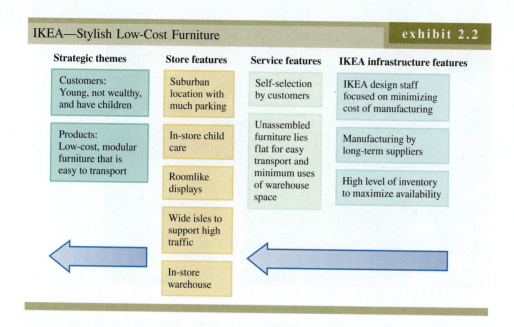

IKEA—Stylish Low-Cost Furniture   exhibit 2.2

Exhibit 2.2 shows how IKEA's strategy is implemented through a set of activities designed to deliver it. **Activity-system maps** such as the one for IKEA show how a company's strategy is delivered through a set of tailored activities. In companies with a clear strategy, a number of higher-order strategic themes (in darker blue) can be identified and implemented through clusters of tightly linked activities. This type of map can be useful in understanding how good the fit is between the system of activities and the company's strategy. Competitive advantage comes from the way a firm's activities fit with and reinforce one another.

Activity-system maps
Diagrams that show how a company's strategy is delivered through a set of supporting activities.

ASSESSING THE RISK ASSOCIATED WITH OPERATIONS AND SUPPLY CHAIN STRATEGIES

The devastating earthquake and tsunami that hit Japan in March 2011 are a grim reminder that managing risk is a critical part of developing an effective operations and supply chain strategy.

The uncertainty in the global environment where most supply chains operate requires strategic planners to evaluate the relative riskiness of their operations and supply chain strategies. **Supply chain risk** is defined as the likelihood of a disruption that would impact the ability of the company to continuously supply products or services. Supply chain disruptions are unplanned and unanticipated events that disrupt the normal flow of goods and materials within a supply chain, and that expose firms within the supply chain to operational and financial risks. Operations and supply chain strategies must consider the risk in their supply chains and develop initiatives to cope with these disruptions and mitigate their impact on the business.

LO2–4 Understand why strategies have implications relative to business risk.

Supply chain risk
The likelihood of a disruption that would impact the ability of a company to continuously supply products or services.

THE PORT OF TOKYO IS EMPTY OF SHIPPING VESSELS TWO WEEKS AFTER THE DEVASTATING EARTHQUAKE AND TSUNAMI IN 2011 THAT TRIGGERED A NUCLEAR CRISIS. SHIPPING COMPANIES AVOIDED DOCKING THEIR SHIPS DUE TO RADIATION FEARS, CAUSING MAJOR DELAYS IN JAPAN'S SUPPLY CHAIN.

© Kyodo/Newscom

We can categorize risk by viewing the inherent uncertainties related to operations and supply chain management along two dimensions: (1) supply chain coordination risks that are associated with the day-to-day management of the supply chain, which are normally dealt with using safety stock, safety lead time, overtime, and so on; and (2) disruption risks, which are caused by natural or human-made disasters, such as earthquakes, hurricanes, and terrorism.

In this section, our focus is on the concepts and tools that are useful for managing the problems related to disruption risks. The events related to these risks are highly random and virtually impossible to predict with any precision.

Other than the Japan earthquake and tsunami mentioned above, the following are examples of the types of events this section relates to:

- In 1996, General Motors experienced an 18-day labor strike at a brake supplier factory. This strike idled workers at 26 assembly plants and led to an estimated $900 million reduction in earnings.
- In 1997, a Boeing supplier's failure to deliver two critical parts led to a loss of $2.6 billion.
- In 2000, a 10-minute fire at a Phillips plant that supplied integrated circuits led to a $400 million loss to the firm.
- There are many other examples, including the 2010 Toyota recalls and the BP oil rig fire in the Gulf of Mexico.

Risk Management Framework

The nature of these types of risks lends them to a three-step risk management process that can be applied to situations where disruptions are possible. The three steps are as follows:

1. Identify the sources of potential disruptions. Assessing a type of vulnerability is the first step in the risk management framework. These are highly situation-dependent, but the focus should be on highly unlikely events that would cause a significant disruption to normal operations. Such types of events include: natural disasters, capacity failures, infrastructure failures (e.g., air traffic system), terrorists, supplier failures, labor actions, equipment failures, commodity price volatility, and military/civil conflict.

2. Assess the potential impact of the risk. Here the goal is to quantify the probability and the potential impact of the risk. Depending on the specific incident, this assessment could be based on financial impact, environmental impact, ongoing business viability, brand image/reputation, potential human lives, and so on.

3. Develop plans to mitigate the risk. A detailed strategy for minimizing the impact of the risk could take many different forms, depending on the nature of the problem.

Risk mapping involves assessment of the probability or relative frequency of an event against the aggregate severity of the loss. Depending on the evaluation, some risks might be deemed acceptable and the related costs considered a normal cost of doing business. In some cases, the firm may find it is possible to insure against the loss. There may be other cases where the potential loss is so great that the risk would need to be avoided altogether.

A matrix (see Exhibit 2.3) that maps risks against specific operations and supply chain strategies is commonly used. The matrix helps us understand the impact of different types of supply chain disruptions when using specific operations and supply chain strategies.

Risk Mitigation Strategies

exhibit 2.3

RISKS	RISK MITIGATION STRATEGY
Natural disaster (e.g., climate change, weather)	Contingency planning (alternate sites, etc.), insurance
Country risks	Hedge currency, produce/source locally
Supplier failures	Use multiple suppliers
Network provider failure	Support redundant digital networks
Regulatory risk (e.g., licensing and regulation issues)	Up-front and continuing research; good legal advice, compliance
Commodity price risks	Multisource, commodity hedging
Logistics failure	Safety stock, detailed tracking and alternate suppliers
Inventory risks	Pool inventory, safety stock
Major quality failure	Carefully select and monitor suppliers
Loss of customers	Service/product innovation
Theft and vandalism	Insurance, security precautions, knowledge of likely risks, patent protection, etc.

	Natural/human-made disasters	Country risks	Supplier failure	Network provider failure	Regulatory risk	Commodity price risks	Logistics failure	Inventory risks	Quality risks
Outsourcing	Moderate	High	No	High	High	High	Moderate	No	High
Sole sourcing	High	Moderate	High	High	No	Moderate	No	No	High
Lean practices	High	No	Moderate	No	No	Moderate	High	High	Moderate
Distribution hubs	High	No	No	Moderate	No	No	High	No	No

High impact	Moderate impact	No impact

For example, the first column evaluates the impact of natural hazards. Here, we see that sole sourcing, lean practices, and the use of distribution hubs can have a major impact on the firm.

Unfortunately, some of the most cost-effective strategies are also the riskiest. It is important to keep this in mind as you consider each concept. Thus far in the book, we have not discussed specific operations and supply chain strategies, such as outsourcing and sole sourcing. You will learn about these as we progress through the book.

PRODUCTIVITY MEASUREMENT

LO2–5 Evaluate productivity in operations and supply chain management.

Productivity
A measure of how well resources are used.

Productivity is a common measure of how well a country, industry, or business unit is using its resources (or factors of production). Since operations and supply chain management focuses on making the best use of the resources available to a firm, productivity measurement is fundamental to understanding operations-related performance. In this section, we define various measures of productivity. Throughout the rest of the book, many other performance measures will be defined as they relate to the material.

In its broadest sense, productivity is defined as

$$\text{Productivity} = \frac{\text{Outputs}}{\text{Inputs}} \qquad [2.1]$$

To increase productivity, we want to make this ratio of outputs to inputs as large as practical.

Productivity is what we call a *relative measure*. In other words, to be meaningful, it needs to be compared with something else. For example, what can we learn from the fact that we operate a restaurant and that its productivity last week was 8.4 customers per labor hour? Nothing!

Productivity comparisons can be made in two ways. First, a company can compare itself with similar operations within its industry, or it can use industry data when such data are available (e.g., comparing productivity among the different stores in a franchise). Another approach is to measure productivity over time within the same operation. Here we would compare our productivity in one time period with that in the next.

As Exhibit 2.4 shows, productivity may be expressed as partial measures, multifactor measures, or total measures. If we are concerned with the ratio of some output to a single input, we have a *partial productivity measure*. If we want to look at the ratio of some output to a group of inputs (but not all inputs), we have a *multifactor productivity measure*. If we want to express the ratio of all outputs to all inputs, we can use a *total factor measure of productivity* to describe the productivity of an entire organization or even a nation.

A numerical example of productivity appears in Exhibit 2.4. The data reflect quantitative measures of input and output associated with the production of a certain product. Notice that for the multifactor and partial measures, it is not necessary to use total output as the numerator. Often, it is desirable to create measures that represent productivity as it relates to some particular output of interest. Using Exhibit 2.4 as an example, total units might be the output of interest to a production control manager, whereas total output may be of key interest to the plant manager. This process of aggregation and disaggregation of productivity measures provides a means of shifting the level of the analysis to suit a variety of productivity measurement and improvement needs.

Examples of Productivity Measures

exhibit 2.4

Partial measure	$\dfrac{\text{Output}}{\text{Labor}}$ or $\dfrac{\text{Output}}{\text{Capital}}$ or $\dfrac{\text{Output}}{\text{Materials}}$ or $\dfrac{\text{Output}}{\text{Energy}}$
Multifactor measure	$\dfrac{\text{Output}}{\text{Labor + Capital + Energy}}$ or $\dfrac{\text{Output}}{\text{Labor + Capital + Materials}}$
Total measure	$\dfrac{\text{Output}}{\text{Inputs}}$ or $\dfrac{\text{Goods and services produced}}{\text{All resources used}}$

INPUT AND OUTPUT PRODUCTION DATA ($1,000)

OUTPUT

1. Finished units	$10,000
2. Work in process	2,500
3. Dividends	1,000
Total output	$13,500

INPUT

1. Labor	$ 3,000
2. Material	153
3. Capital	10,000
4. Energy	540
5. Other expenses	1,500
Total input	$15,193

PRODUCTIVITY MEASURE EXAMPLES

Total measure

$$\frac{\text{Total output}}{\text{Total input}} = \frac{13,500}{15,193} = 0.89$$

Multifactor measures:

$$\frac{\text{Total output}}{\text{Labor + Material}} = \frac{13,500}{3,153} = 4.28$$

$$\frac{\text{Finished units}}{\text{Labor + Material}} = \frac{10,000}{3,153} = 3.17$$

Partial measures:

$$\frac{\text{Total output}}{\text{Energy}} = \frac{13,500}{540} = 25$$

$$\frac{\text{Finished units}}{\text{Energy}} = \frac{10,000}{540} = 18.52$$

Excel:
Productivity Measures

Partial Measures of Productivity

BUSINESS	PRODUCTIVITY MEASURE
Restaurant	Customers (meals) per labor hour
Retail store	Sales per square foot
Chicken farm	Lb. of meat per lb. of feed
Utility plant	Kilowatt-hours per ton of coal
Paper mill	Tons of paper per cord of wood

Exhibit 2.4 shows all units in dollars. Often, however, management can better understand how the company is performing when units other than dollars are used. In these cases, only partial measures of productivity can be used, because we cannot combine dissimilar units such as labor hours and pounds of material. Examples of some commonly used partial measures of productivity are presented in Exhibit 2.4. Such partial measures of productivity give managers information in familiar units, allowing them to easily relate these measures to the actual operations.

Each summer, *USA Today* publishes annual reports of productivity gains by the largest U.S. firms. Productivity has been on the rise for many years now, which is very good for the economy. Productivity often increases in times of recession; as workers are fired, those remaining are expected to do more. Increases also come from technological advances. Think of what the tractor did for farm productivity.

CONCEPT CONNECTIONS

LO2–1 **Know what a sustainable business strategy is and how it relates to operations and supply chain management.**

- A strategy that is sustainable needs to create value for the firm's shareholders and stakeholders.
- The shareholders are equity owners in the company.
- The stakeholders are those individuals and organizations that are influenced by the actions of the firm.
- This view means that a firm's strategy must focus not only on economic viability, but also on the environmental and social impact of its actions.

Sustainability   The ability to meet current resource needs without compromising the ability of future generations to meet their needs.

Triple bottom line   Evaluating the firm against social, economic, and environmental criteria.

LO2–2 **Define operations and supply chain strategy.**

- This involves setting the broad policies of a firm and creating a plan for using that firm's resources.
- The operations and supply chain strategy coordinates operational goals with those of the larger organization.
- A firm's operational capabilities should match the changing product or service needs of the firm's customers.

Major competitive dimensions that form the competitive position of a firm include:

- Cost
- Quality
- Delivery speed and reliability
- Changes in volume
- Flexibility and new-product introduction speed
- Other product-specific criteria

Usually there are trade-offs that occur relative to these competitive dimensions.

Operations and supply chain strategy   The setting of broad policies and plans that will guide the use of the resources needed by the firm to implement its corporate strategy.

Operations effectiveness   Performing activities in a manner that best implements strategic priorities at minimum cost.

Straddling   When a firm seeks to match what a competitor is doing by adding new features, services, or technologies to existing activities. This often creates problems if trade-offs need to be made.

Order winners   One or more specific marketing-oriented dimensions that clearly differentiate a product from competing products.

Order qualifiers   Dimensions used to screen a product or service as a candidate for purchase.

LO2–3 **Explain how operations and supply chain strategies are implemented.**

- Strategies are implemented through a set of activities designed to deliver products and services in a manner consistent with the firm's overall business strategy.

Activity-system maps   Diagrams that show how a company's strategy is delivered through a set of supporting activities.

LO2–4 **Understand why strategies have implications relative to business risk.**

- Operations and supply chain strategies need to be evaluated relative to their riskiness.
- Supply chain disruptions are unplanned and unanticipated events that disrupt the normal flow of goods and materials.

- Risks can be categorized along two dimensions: supply chain coordination risks and disruption risks.
- A three-step risk management framework involves identifying the potential disruptions, assessing the potential impact of the risk, and developing plans to mitigate the risk.

Supply chain risk   The likelihood of a disruption that would impact the ability of a company to continuously supply products or services.

LO2–5 **Evaluate productivity in operations and supply chain management.**

- Productivity measures are used to ensure that the firm makes the best use of its resources.
- Since these are relative measures, they are meaningful only if they are compared to something else. Often, the comparison is to another company.

Productivity   A measure of how well resources are used.

$$\text{Productivity} = \frac{\text{Outputs}}{\text{Inputs}} \qquad [2.1]$$

SOLVED PROBLEM

A furniture manufacturing company has provided the following data (units are $1,000). Compare the labor, raw materials and supplies, and total productivity for the past two years.

		LAST YEAR	THIS YEAR
Output:	Sales value of production	$22,000	$35,000
Input:	Labor	10,000	15,000
	Raw materials and supplies	8,000	12,500
	Capital equipment depreciation	700	1,200
	Other	2,200	4,800

Solution

	LAST YEAR	THIS YEAR
Partial productivities		
Labor	2.20	2.33
Raw materials and supplies	2.75	2.80
Total productivity	1.05	1.04

DISCUSSION QUESTIONS

LO2–1
1. What is meant by a triple bottom line strategy? Give an example of a company that has adopted this type of strategy.
2. Find examples where companies have used features related to environmental sustainability to win new customers.

LO2–2
3. What are the major priorities associated with operations and supply chain strategy? For each major priority, describe the unique characteristics of the market niche with which it is most compatible.
4. Why does the proper operations and supply chain strategy keep changing for companies that are world-class competitors?
5. What do the expressions order winner and order qualifier mean? What was the order winner for your last major purchase of a product or service?

LO2–3
6. Pick a company that you are familiar with and describe its operations strategy and how it relates to winning customers. Describe specific activities used by the company that support the strategy (see Exhibit 2.2 for an example).

LO2–4

7. At times, the dollar shows relative weakness with respect to foreign currencies such as the yen, euro, and pound. This stimulates exports. Why would long-term reliance on a lower-valued dollar be at best a short-term solution to the competitiveness problem?

8. Identify an operations and supply chain–related disruption that recently impacted a company. What could the company have done to minimize the impact of this type of disruption prior to it occurring?

LO2–5

9. What do we mean when we say productivity is a relative measure?

OBJECTIVE QUESTIONS

LO2–1

1. Shell Oil Company's motto "People, Planet, and Profit" is a real-world implementation of what OSCM concept?

2. A firm's strategy should describe how it intends to create and sustain value for what entities?

3. What is the term used to describe individuals or organizations that are influenced by the actions of a firm?

LO2–2

4. How often should a company develop and refine the operations and supply chain strategy?

5. What is the term used to describe product attributes that attract certain customers and can be used to form the competitive position of a firm?

6. What are the two main competitive dimensions related to product delivery?

7. What are the two characteristics of a product or service that define quality?

LO2–3

8. What is the diagram that shows how a company's strategy is delivered by a set of supporting activities called?

9. In implementing supply chain strategy, a firm must minimize its total cost without compromising the needs of what group of people?

LO2–4

10. What is defined as the likelihood of disruption that would impact the ability of a company to continuously supply products or services?

11. What are risks caused by natural and human-made disasters, which are impossible to reliably predict, called?

12. Match the following common risks with the appropriate mitigation strategy:

_____ Country risks	A. Detailed tracking, alternate suppliers
_____ Regulatory risk	B. Careful selection and monitoring of
_____ Logistics failure	suppliers
_____ Natural disaster	C. Contingency planning, insurance
_____ Major quality failure	D. Good legal advice, compliance
	E. Currency hedging, local sourcing

13. What is the term used to describe the assessment of the probability of a negative event against the aggregate severity of the related loss?

LO2–5

14. As operations manager, you are concerned about being able to meet sales requirements in the coming months. You have just been given the following production report:

	JAN	FEB	MAR	APR
Units produced	2,300	1,800	2,800	3,000
Hours per machine	325	200	400	320
Number of machines	3	5	4	4

Find the average of the monthly productivity figures (units per machine hour).

15. Sailmaster makes high-performance sails for competitive windsurfers. Below is information about the inputs and outputs for one model, the Windy 2000. Calculate the productivity in sales revenue/labor expense.

Units sold	1,217
Sale price each	$1,700
Total labor hours	46,672
Wage rate	$12/hour
Total materials	$60,000
Total energy	$4,000

16. Live Trap Corporation received the data below for its rodent cage production unit. Find the total productivity.

OUTPUT	INPUT	
50,000 cages	Production time	620 labor hours
Sales price: $3.50 per unit	Wages	$7.50 per hour
	Raw materials (total cost)	$30,000
	Component parts (total cost)	$15,350

17. Two types of cars (Deluxe and Limited) were produced by a car manufacturer last year. Quantities sold, price per unit, and labor hours are given below. What is the labor productivity for each car? Explain the problem(s) associated with the labor productivity.

	QUANTITY	$/UNIT
Deluxe car	4,000 units sold	$8,000/car
Limited car	6,000 units sold	$9,500/car
Labor, Deluxe	20,000 hours	$12/hour
Labor, Limited	30,000 hours	$14/hour

18. A U.S. manufacturing company operating a subsidiary in an LDC (less-developed country) shows the following results:

	U.S.	LDC
Sales (units)	100,000	20,000
Labor (hours)	20,000	15,000
Raw materials (currency)	$20,000 (US)	20,000 (FC)
Capital equipment (hours)	60,000	5,000

a. Calculate partial labor and capital productivity figures for the parent and subsidiary. Do the results seem confusing?
b. Compute the multifactor productivity figures for labor and capital together. Do the results make more sense?
c. Calculate raw material productivity figures [units/$ where $1 = 10 (FC)]. Explain why these figures might be greater in the subsidiary.

19. Various financial data for the past two years follow. Calculate the total productivity measure and the partial measures for labor, capital, and raw materials for this company for both years. What do these measures tell you about this company?

	LAST YEAR	THIS YEAR
Output: Sales	$200,000	$220,000
Input: Labor	30,000	40,000
Raw materials	35,000	45,000
Energy	5,000	6,000
Capital	50,000	50,000
Other	2,000	3,000

20. An electronics company makes communications devices for military contracts. The company just completed two contracts. The navy contract was for 2,300 devices and took 25 workers two weeks (40 hours per week) to complete. The army contract was for 5,500 devices that were produced by 35 workers in three weeks. On which contract were the workers more productive?

21. A retail store had sales of $45,000 in April and $56,000 in May. The store employs eight full-time workers who work a 40-hour week. In April, the store also had seven part-time workers at 10 hours per week, and in May the store had nine part-timers at 15 hours per week (assume four weeks in each month). Using sales dollars as the measure of output, what is the percentage change in productivity from April to May?

22. A parcel delivery company delivered 103,000 packages last year, when its average employment was 84 drivers. This year, the firm handled 112,000 deliveries with 96 drivers. What was the percentage change in productivity over the past year?

23. A fast-food restaurant serves hamburgers, cheeseburgers, and chicken sandwiches. The restaurant counts a cheeseburger as equivalent to 1.25 hamburgers and chicken sandwiches as 0.8 hamburger. Current employment is five full-time employees who each work a 40-hour week. If the restaurant sold 700 hamburgers, 900 cheeseburgers, and 500 chicken sandwiches in one week, what is its productivity? What would its productivity have been if it had sold the same number of sandwiches (2,100), but the mix was 700 of each type?

CASE: THE TAO OF TIMBUK2*

"Timbuk2 is more than a bag. It's more than a brand. Timbuk2 is a bond. To its owner, a Timbuk2 bag is a dependable, everyday companion. We see fierce, emotional attachments form between Timbuk2 customers and their bags all the time. A well-worn Timbuk2 bag has a certain patina—the stains and scars of everyday urban adventures. Many Timbuk2 bags are worn daily for a decade or more, accompanying the owner through all sorts of defining life events. True to our legend of 'indestructibility,' it's not uncommon for a Timbuk2 bag to outlive jobs, personal relationships, even pets. This is the Tao of Timbuk2."

What makes Timbuk2 so unique? Visit the Web site at www.timbuk2.com and see for yourself. Each bag is custom designed by the customer on the Web site. After the customer selects the basic bag configuration and size, colors for each of the various panels are presented; various lines, logos, pockets, and straps are selected so that the bag is tailored to the exact specifications of the customer. A quick click of the mouse and the bag is delivered directly to the customer in only two days. How does Timbuk2 do this?

This San Francisco–based company is known for producing high-quality custom and classic messenger bags. It has a team of approximately 25 hardworking cutters and sewers in its San Francisco plant. Over the years, it has fine-tuned its production line to make it as efficient as possible while producing the highest-quality messenger bags available.

The local manufacturing is focused on the custom messenger bag. For these bags, orders are taken over the Internet. Customers are offered many configuration, size, color, pocket, and strap options. The bag is tailored to the exact specifications of the customer on the Timbuk2 assembly line in San Francisco and sent via overnight delivery directly to the customer.

Recently, Timbuk2 has begun making some of its new products in China, which is a concern to some of its long-standing customers. The company argues that it has designed its new products to provide the best possible features, quality, and value at reasonable prices and stresses that these new products are designed in San Francisco. Timbuk2 argues that the new bags are much more complex to build and require substantially more labor and a variety of very expensive machines to produce. It argues that the San Francisco factory labor cost alone would make the retail price absurdly high. After researching a dozen factories in China, Timbuk2 found one that it thinks is up to the task of producing these new bags. Much as in San Francisco, the China factory employs a team of hardworking craftspeople who earn good wages and an honest living. Timbuk2 visits the China factory every four to eight weeks to ensure superior quality standards and working conditions.

On the Timbuk2 Web site, the company argues that its team members are the same hardworking group of bag fanatics as before, designing and making great bags and supporting the local community and increasingly competitive global market. The company reports that demand is still strong for the custom messenger bags made in San Francisco and that the new laptop bags sourced from China are receiving rave reviews. The additional business is allowing the company to hire more people in all departments at its San Francisco headquarters—creating even more jobs locally.

*Special thanks to Kyle Cattani of Indiana University for this case.

© Bloomberg/Getty Images

Questions

1. Consider the two categories of products that Timbuk2 makes and sells. For the custom messenger bag, what key competitive dimensions are driving sales? Are the company's competitive priorities different for the new laptop bags sourced in China?

2. Compare the assembly line in China to that in San Francisco along the following dimensions: (1) volume or rate of production, (2) required skill of the workers, (3) level of automation, and (4) amount of raw materials and finished goods inventory.

3. Draw two diagrams, one depicting the supply chain for those products sourced in China and the other depicting the bags produced in San Francisco. Show all the major steps, including raw material, manufacturing, finished goods, distribution inventory, and transportation. Other than manufacturing cost, what other costs should Timbuk2 consider when making the sourcing decision?

PRACTICE EXAM

1. A strategy that is designed to meet current needs without compromising the ability of future generations to meet their needs.

2. The three criteria included in a triple bottom line.

3. The seven operations and supply chain competitive dimensions.

4. It is probably most difficult to compete on this major competitive dimension.

5. This occurs when a company seeks to match what a competitor is doing while maintaining its existing competitive position.

6. A criterion that differentiates the products or services of one firm from those of another.

7. A screening criterion that permits a firm's products to be considered as possible candidates for purchase.

8. A diagram showing the activities that support a company's strategy.

9. A measure calculated by taking the ratio of output to input.

Answers to Practice Exam 1. Sustainable 2. Social, economic, environmental 3. Cost, quality, delivery speed, delivery reliability, coping with changes in demand, flexibility and speed of new product introduction, other product-specific criteria 4. Cost 5. Straddling 6. Order winner 7. Order qualifier 8. Activity-system map 9. Productivity

CHAPTER 3

FORECASTING

Learning Objectives

LO3–1 Understand how forecasting is essential to supply chain planning.

LO3–2 Evaluate demand using quantitative forecasting models.

LO3–3 Apply qualitative techniques to forecast demand.

LO3–4 Apply collaborative techniques to forecast demand.

FROM BEAN TO CUP: STARBUCKS GLOBAL SUPPLY CHAIN CHALLENGE

Starbucks Corporation is the largest coffeehouse company in the world with over 17,000 stores in more than 50 countries. The company serves some 50 million customers each week.

Forecasting demand for a Starbucks is an amazing challenge. The product line goes well beyond drip-brewed coffee sold on demand in the stores. It includes espresso-based hot drinks, other hot and cold drinks, coffee beans, salads, hot and cold sandwiches and panini, pastries, snacks, and items such as mugs and tumblers. Many of the company's products are seasonal or specific to the locality of the store. Starbucks-branded ice cream and coffee are also offered at grocery stores around the world.

The creation of a single, global logistics system was important for Starbucks because of its far-flung supply chain. The company generally brings coffee beans from Latin America, Africa, and Asia to the United States and Europe in ocean containers. From the port of entry, the "green" (unroasted) beans are trucked to six storage sites, either at a roasting plant or nearby. After the beans are roasted and packaged, the finished product is trucked to regional distribution centers, which range from 200,000 to 300,000 square feet in size. Starbucks runs five regional distribution centers

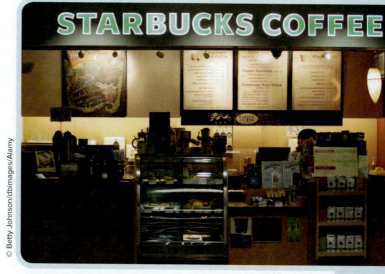

STARBUCKS CAFE IN BUR JUMAN CENTER SHOPPING MALL, DUBAI, UNITED ARAB EMIRATES.

(DCs) in the United States. It has two DCs in Europe and two more in Asia. Coffee, however, is only one of the many products held at these warehouses. They also handle other items required by Starbucks' retail outlets, everything from furniture to cappuccino mixes.

In the Analytics Exercise at the end of the chapter, we consider the challenging demand forecasting problem that Starbucks must solve to be able to successfully run this complex supply chain.

FORECASTING IN OPERATIONS AND SUPPLY CHAIN MANAGEMENT

LO3–1 Understand how forecasting is essential to supply chain planning.

Forecasts are vital to every business organization and for every significant management decision. Forecasting is the basis of corporate planning and control. In the functional areas of finance and accounting, forecasts provide the basis for budgetary planning and cost control. Marketing relies on sales forecasting to plan new products, compensate sales personnel, and make other key decisions. Production and operations personnel use forecasts to make periodic decisions involving supplier selection, process selection, capacity planning, and facility layout, as well as for continual decisions about purchasing, production planning, scheduling, and inventory.

In considering what forecasting approach to use, it is important to consider the purpose of the forecast. Some forecasts are for very high-level demand analysis. What do we expect the demand to be for a group of products over the next year, for example? Some forecasts are used to help set the strategy of how, in an aggregate sense, we will meet demand. We will call these **strategic forecasts**. Relative to the material in the book, strategic forecasts are most appropriate when making decisions related to overall strategy (Chapter 2), capacity (Chapter 4), manufacturing process design (Chapter 6), service process design (Chapter 7), sourcing (Chapter 13), location and distribution design (Chapter 14), and in aggregate operations planning (Chapter 8). These all involve medium- and long-term decisions that relate to how demand will be met strategically.

Strategic forecasts Medium- and long-term forecasts that are used for decisions related to strategy and estimating aggregate demand.

Tactical forecasts Short-term forecasts used as input for making day-to-day decisions related to meeting demand.

Forecasts are also needed to determine how a firm operates processes on a day-to-day basis. For example, when should the inventory for an item be replenished, or how much production should we schedule for an item next week? These are **tactical forecasts** where the goal is to estimate demand in the short term—a few weeks or months. These forecasts are important to ensure that in the short term we are able to meet customer lead-time expectations and other criteria related to the availability of our products and services.

FORECASTING IS CRITICAL IN DETERMINING HOW MUCH INVENTORY TO KEEP TO MEET CUSTOMER NEEDS.

© Sanjit Das/Bloomberg/Getty Images

In Chapter 6, the concept of decoupling points is discussed. These are points within the supply chain where inventory is positioned to allow processes or entities in the supply chain to operate independently. For example, if a product is stocked at a retailer, the customer pulls the item from the shelf and the manufacturer never sees a customer order. Inventory acts as a buffer to separate the customer from the manufacturing process. Selection of decoupling points is a strategic decision that determines customer lead times and can greatly impact inventory investment. The closer this point is to the customer, the quicker the customer can be served. Typically, a trade-off is involved where quicker response to customer demand comes at the expense of greater inventory investment because finished goods inventory is more expensive than raw material inventory.

Forecasting is needed at these decoupling points to set appropriate inventory levels for these buffers. The actual setting of these levels is the topic of Chapter 11, Inventory Management, but an essential input into those decisions is a forecast of expected demand and the expected error associated with that demand. If, for example, we are able to forecast demand very accurately, then inventory levels can be set precisely to expected customer demand. On the other hand, if predicting short-term demand is difficult, then extra inventory to cover this uncertainty will be needed.

The same is true relative to service settings where inventory is not used to buffer demand. Here capacity availability relative to expected demand is the issue. If we can predict demand in a service setting very accurately, then tactically all we need to do is ensure that we have the appropriate capacity in the short term. When demand is not predictable, then excess capacity may be needed if servicing customers quickly is important.

Bear in mind that a perfect forecast is virtually impossible. Too many factors in the business environment cannot be predicted with certainty. Therefore, rather than search for the perfect forecast, it is far more important to establish the practice of continual review of forecasts and to learn to live with inaccurate forecasts. This is not to say that we should not try to improve the forecasting model or methodology or even to try to influence demand in a way that reduces demand uncertainty. When forecasting, a good strategy is to use two or three methods and look at them for the common sense view. Will expected changes in the general economy affect the forecast? Are there changes in our customers' behaviors that will impact demand that are not being captured by our current approaches? In this chapter, we look at both *qualitative* techniques that use managerial judgment and also *quantitative* techniques that rely on mathematical models. It is our view that combining these techniques is essential to finding the best forecasting process for the decisions being made.

QUANTITATIVE FORECASTING MODELS

Forecasting can be classified into four basic types: *qualitative, time series analysis, causal relationships*, and *simulation*.

Qualitative techniques are subjective or judgmental and are based on estimates and opinions. **Time series analysis**, the primary focus of this chapter, is based on the idea that data relating to past demand can be used to predict future demand. Past data may include several components, such as trend, seasonal, or cyclical influences, and are described in the following section. Causal forecasting, which we discuss using the linear regression technique, assumes that demand is related to some underlying factor or factors in the environment. Simulation models allow the forecaster to run through a range of assumptions about the condition of the forecast. In this chapter, we focus on qualitative and time series techniques because these are most often used in supply chain planning and control.

LO3–2 Evaluate demand using quantitative forecasting models.

Time series analysis A type of forecast in which data relating to past demand are used to predict future demand.

Excel:
Components of
Demand

| exhibit 3.1 | Historical Product Demand Consisting of a Growth Trend and Seasonal Demand |

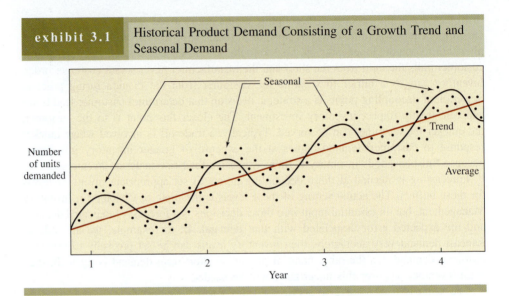

Components of Demand

In most cases, the demand for products or services can be broken down into six components: average demand for the period, a trend, seasonal element, cyclical elements, random variation, and autocorrelation. Exhibit 3.1 illustrates a demand over a four-year period, showing the average, trend, and seasonal components and randomness around the smoothed demand curve.

Cyclical factors are more difficult to determine because the time span may be unknown or the cause of the cycle may not be considered. Cyclical influence on demand may come from such occurrences as political elections, war, economic conditions, or sociological pressures.

Random variations are caused by chance events. Statistically, when all the known causes for demand (average, trend, seasonal, cyclical, and autocorrelative) are subtracted from total demand, what remains is the unexplained portion of demand. If we cannot identify the cause of this remainder, it is assumed to be purely random chance.

Autocorrelation denotes the persistence of occurrence. More specifically, the value expected at any point is highly correlated with its own past values. In waiting line theory, the length of a waiting line is highly autocorrelated. That is, if a line is relatively long at one time, then shortly after that time, we would expect the line still to be long.

When demand is random, it may vary widely from one week to another. Where high autocorrelation exists, the rate of change in demand is not expected to change very much from one week to the next.

Trend lines are the usual starting point in developing a forecast. These trend lines are then adjusted for seasonal effects, cyclical elements, and any other expected events that may influence the final forecast. Exhibit 3.2 shows four of the most common types of trends. A linear trend is obviously a straight continuous relationship. An S-curve is typical of a product growth and maturity cycle. The most important point in the S-curve is where the trend changes from slow growth to fast growth or from fast to slow. An asymptotic trend starts with the highest demand growth at the beginning but then tapers off. Such a curve could happen when a firm enters an existing market with the objective of saturating and capturing a large share of the market. An exponential curve is common in products with explosive growth. The exponential trend suggests that sales will continue at an ever-increasing rate—an assumption that may not be safe to make.

Common Types of Trends

exhibit 3.2

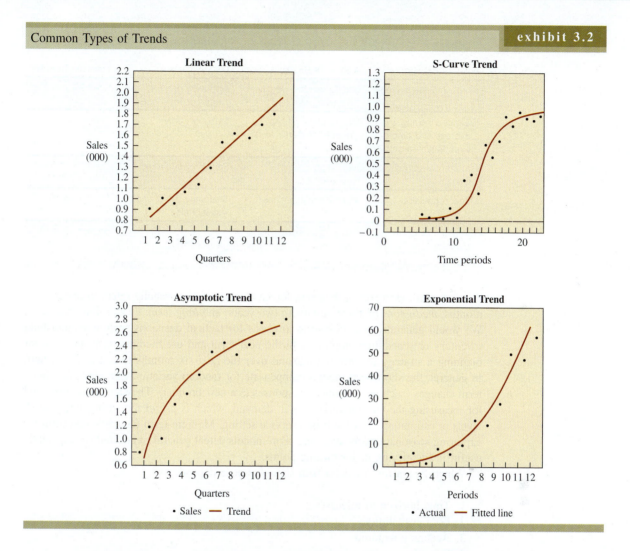

A widely used forecasting method plots data and then searches for the curve pattern (such as linear, S-curve, asymptotic, or exponential) that fits best. The attractiveness of this method is that because the mathematics for the curve are known, solving for values for future time periods is easy.

Sometimes our data do not seem to fit any standard curve. This may be due to several causes essentially beating the data from several directions at the same time. For these cases, a simplistic but often effective forecast can be obtained by simply plotting data.

Time Series Analysis

Time series forecasting models try to predict the future based on past data. For example, sales figures collected for the past six weeks can be used to forecast sales for the seventh week. Quarterly sales figures collected for the past several years can be used to forecast future quarters. Even though both examples contain sales, different forecasting time series models would likely be used.

Exhibit 3.3 shows the time series models discussed in the chapter and some of their characteristics. Terms such as *short, medium,* and *long* are relative to the context in which

exhibit 3.3	A Guide to Selecting an Appropriate Forecasting Method		
FORECASTING METHOD	AMOUNT OF HISTORICAL DATA	DATA PATTERN	FORECAST HORIZON
Simple moving average	6 to 12 months; weekly data are often used	Stationary only (i.e., no trend or seasonality)	Short
Weighted moving average and simple exponential smoothing	5 to 10 observations needed to start	Stationary only	Short
Exponential smoothing with trend	5 to 10 observations needed to start	Stationary and trend	Short
Linear regression	10 to 20 observations	Stationary, trend, and seasonality	Short to medium
Trend and seasonal models	2 to 3 observations per season	Stationary, trend, seasonality	Short to medium

they are used. However, in business forecasting *short term* usually refers to under three months; *medium term*, three months to two years; and *long term*, greater than two years. We would generally use short-term forecasts for tactical decisions such as replenishing inventory or scheduling employees in the near term and use medium-term forecasts for planning a strategy for meeting demand over the next six months to a year and a half. In general, the short-term models compensate for random variation and adjust for short-term changes (such as consumers' responses to a new product). They are especially good for measuring the current variability in demand, which is useful for setting safety stock levels or estimating peak loads in a service setting. Medium-term forecasts are useful for capturing seasonal effects, and long-term models detect general trends and are especially useful in identifying major turning points.

Which forecasting model a firm should choose depends on:

1. Time horizon to forecast
2. Data availability
3. Accuracy required
4. Size of forecasting budget
5. Availability of qualified personnel

In selecting a forecasting model, there are other issues such as the firm's degree of flexibility. (The greater the ability to react quickly to changes, the less accurate the forecast needs to be.) Another item is the consequence of a bad forecast. If a large capital investment decision is to be based on a forecast, it should be a good forecast.

Simple Moving Average

Moving average
A forecast based on average past demand.

When demand for a product is neither growing nor declining rapidly, and if it does not have seasonal characteristics, a **moving average** can be useful in removing the random fluctuations for forecasting. The idea here is to simply calculate the average demand over the most recent periods. Each time a new forecast is made, the oldest period is discarded in the average and the newest period included. Thus, if we want to forecast June with a five-month moving average, we can take the average of January, February, March, April, and May. When June passes, the forecast for July would be the average of February, March, April, May, and June. An example using weekly demand is shown in Exhibit 3.4.

WEEK	DEMAND	3-WEEK	9-WEEK		WEEK	DEMAND	3-WEEK	9-WEEK
1	800				16	1,700	2,200	1,811
2	1,400				17	1,800	2,000	1,800
3	1,000				18	2,200	1,833	1,811
4	1,500	1,067			19	1,900	1,900	1,911
5	1,500	1,300			20	2,400	1,967	1,933
6	1,300	1,333			21	2,400	2,167	2,011
7	1,800	1,433			22	2,600	2,233	2,111
8	1,700	1,533			23	2,000	2,467	2,144
9	1,300	1,600			24	2,500	2,333	2,111
10	1,700	1,600	1,367		25	2,600	2,367	2,167
11	1,700	1,567	1,467		26	2,200	2,367	2,267
12	1,500	1,567	1,500		27	2,200	2,433	2,311
13	2,300	1,633	1,556		28	2,500	2,333	2,311
14	2,300	1,833	1,644		29	2,400	2,300	2,378
15	2,000	2,033	1,733		30	2,100	2,367	2,378

exhibit 3.4 Forecast Demand Based on a Three- and a Nine-Week Simple Moving Average

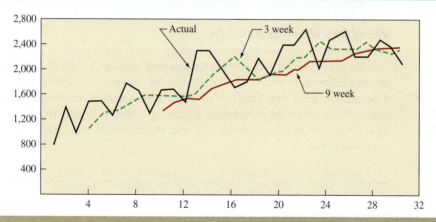

Excel: Forecasting

Here, 3-week and 9-week moving average forecasts are calculated. Notice how the forecast is shown in the period following the data used. The 3-week moving average for week 4 uses actual demand from weeks 1, 2, and 3.

Selecting the period length should be dependent on how the forecast is going to be used. For example, in the case of a medium-term forecast of demand for planning a budget, monthly time periods might be more appropriate, whereas if the forecast were being used for a short-term decision related to replenishing inventory, a weekly forecast might be more fitting. Although it is important to select the best period length for the moving average, the number of periods to use in the forecast can also have a major impact on the accuracy of the forecast. As the moving average period length becomes shorter, and when fewer historic periods are used, there is a closer following of the trend. Conversely, a longer time span with more historic periods gives a smoother response, but lags the trend.

The formula for a simple moving average is

$$F_t = \frac{A_{t-1} + A_{t-2} + A_{t-3} + \cdots + A_{t-n}}{n}$$ [3.1]

where

F_t = Forecast for the coming period
n = Number of periods to be averaged
A_{t-1} = Actual occurrence in the past period
A_{t-2}, A_{t-3}, and A_{t-n} = Actual occurrences two periods ago, three periods ago, and so on, up to n periods ago

A plot of the data in Exhibit 3.4 shows the effects of using different numbers of periods in the moving average. We see that the growth trend levels off at about the 23rd week. The three-week moving average responds better in following this change than the nine-week average; however, overall, the nine-week average is smoother.

The main disadvantage in calculating a moving average is that all individual elements must be carried as data because a new forecast period involves adding new data and dropping the earliest data. For a three- or six-period moving average, this is not too severe. But plotting a 60-day moving average for the usage of each of 100,000 items in inventory would involve a significant amount of data.

Weighted Moving Average

Weighted moving average

A forecast made with past data where more recent data are given more significance than older data.

Whereas the simple moving average assigns equal importance to each component of the moving average database, a **weighted moving average** allows any weights to be placed on each element, provided, of course, that the sum of all weights equals 1. For example, a department store may find that in a four-month period, the best forecast is derived by using 40 percent of the actual sales for the most recent month, 30 percent of two months ago, 20 percent of three months ago, and 10 percent of four months ago. If actual sales experience was

MONTH 1	MONTH 2	MONTH 3	MONTH 4	MONTH 5
100	90	105	95	?

the forecast for month 5 would be

$$F_5 = 0.40(95) + 0.30(105) + 0.20(90) + 0.10(100)$$
$$= 38 + 31.5 + 18 + 10$$
$$= 97.5$$

The formula for a weighted moving average is

$$F_t = w_1 A_{t-1} + w_2 A_{t-2} + \cdots + w_n A_{t-n}$$ [3.2]

where

w_1 = Weight to be given to the actual occurrence for the period $t - 1$
w_2 = Weight to be given to the actual occurrence for the period $t - 2$
w_n = Weight to be given to the actual occurrence for the period $t - n$
n = Total number of prior periods in the forecast

Although many periods may be ignored (that is, their weights are zero) and the weighting scheme may be in any order (for example, more distant data may have greater weights than more recent data), the sum of all the weights must equal 1.

$$\sum_{i=1}^{n} w_i = 1$$

Suppose sales for month 5 actually turned out to be 110. Then the forecast for month 6 would be

$$F_6 = 0.40(110) + 0.30(95) + 0.20(105) + 0.10(90)$$
$$= 44 + 28.5 + 21 + 9$$
$$= 102.5$$

Choosing Weights Experience and trial and error are the simplest ways to choose weights. As a general rule, the most recent past is the most important indicator of what to expect in the future, and, therefore, it should get higher weighting. The past month's revenue or plant capacity, for example, would be a better estimate for the coming month than the revenue or plant capacity of several months ago.

However, if the data are seasonal, for example, weights should be established accordingly. Bathing suit sales in July of last year should be weighted more heavily than bathing suit sales in December (in the Northern Hemisphere).

The weighted moving average has a definite advantage over the simple moving average in being able to vary the effects of past data. However, it is more inconvenient and costly to use than the exponential smoothing method, which we examine next.

Exponential Smoothing

In the previous methods of forecasting (simple and weighted moving averages), the major drawback is the need to continually carry a large amount of historical data. (This is also true for regression analysis techniques, which we soon will cover.) As each new piece of data is added in these methods, the oldest observation is dropped and the new forecast is calculated. In many applications (perhaps in most), the most recent occurrences are more indicative of the future than those in the more distant past. If this premise is valid—that the importance of data diminishes as the past becomes more distant—then **exponential smoothing** may be the most logical and easiest method to use.

Exponential smoothing is the most used of all forecasting techniques. It is an integral part of virtually all computerized forecasting programs, and it is widely used in ordering inventory in retail firms, wholesale companies, and service agencies.

Exponential smoothing techniques have become well accepted for six major reasons:

1. Exponential models are surprisingly accurate.
2. Formulating an exponential model is relatively easy.
3. The user can understand how the model works.
4. Little computation is required to use the model.
5. Computer storage requirements are small because of the limited use of historical data.
6. Tests for accuracy as to how well the model is performing are easy to compute.

In the exponential smoothing method, only three pieces of data are needed to forecast the future: the most recent forecast, the actual demand that occurred for that forecast

Exponential smoothing
A time series forecasting technique in which each increment of past demand data is decreased by $(1 - \alpha)$.

period, and a **smoothing constant alpha (α)**. This smoothing constant determines the level of smoothing and the speed of reaction to differences between forecasts and actual occurrences. The value for the constant is determined both by the nature of the product and by the manager's sense of what constitutes a good response rate. For example, if a firm produced a standard item with relatively stable demand, the reaction rate to differences between actual and forecast demand would tend to be small, perhaps just 5 or 10 percentage points. However, if the firm were experiencing growth, it would be desirable to have a higher reaction rate, perhaps 15 to 30 percentage points, to give greater importance to recent growth experience. The more rapid the growth, the higher the reaction rate should be. Sometimes users of the simple moving average switch to exponential smoothing but like to keep the forecasts about the same as the simple moving average. In this case, α is approximated by $2 \div (n + 1)$, where n is the number of time periods in the corresponding simple moving average.

The equation for a single exponential smoothing forecast is simply

$$F_t = F_{t-1} + \alpha(A_{t-1} - F_{t-1}) \qquad [3.3]$$

where

F_t = The exponentially smoothed forecast for period t
F_{t-1} = The exponentially smoothed forecast made for the prior period
A_{t-1} = The actual demand in the prior period
α = The desired response rate, or smoothing constant

This equation states that the new forecast is equal to the old forecast plus a portion of the error (the difference between the previous forecast and what actually occurred).

To demonstrate the method, assume that the long-run demand for the product under study is relatively stable and a smoothing constant (α) of 0.05 is considered appropriate. If the exponential smoothing method were used as a continuing policy, a forecast would have been made for last month. Assume that last month's forecast (F_{t-1}) was 1,050 units. If 1,000 actually were demanded, rather than 1,050, the forecast for this month would be

$$F_t = F_{t-1} + \alpha(A_{t-1} - F_{t-1})$$
$$= 1,050 + 0.05(1,000 - 1,050)$$
$$= 1,050 + 0.05(-50)$$
$$= 1,047.5 \text{ units}$$

Because the smoothing coefficient is small, the reaction of the new forecast to an error of 50 units is to decrease the next month's forecast by only 2½ units.

When exponential smoothing is first used for an item, an initial forecast may be obtained by using a simple estimate, like the first period's demand, or by using an average of preceding periods, such as the average of the first two or three periods.

Single exponential smoothing has the shortcoming of lagging changes in demand. Exhibit 3.5 presents actual data plotted as a smooth curve to show the lagging effects of the exponential forecasts. The forecast lags during an increase or decrease, but overshoots when a change in direction occurs. Note that the higher the value of alpha, the more closely the forecast follows the actual. To more closely track actual demand, a

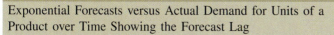

| Exponential Forecasts versus Actual Demand for Units of a Product over Time Showing the Forecast Lag | exhibit 3.5 |

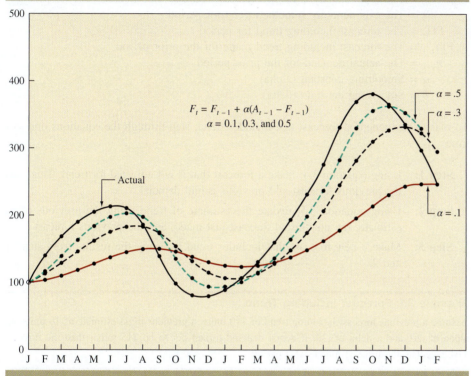

$$F_t = F_{t-1} + \alpha(A_{t-1} - F_{t-1})$$
$$\alpha = 0.1, 0.3, \text{ and } 0.5$$

trend factor may be added. Adjusting the value of alpha also helps. This is termed *adaptive forecasting*. Both trend effects and adaptive forecasting are briefly explained in the following sections.

Exponential Smoothing with Trend

Remember that an upward or downward trend in data collected over a sequence of time periods causes the exponential forecast to always lag behind (be above or below) the actual occurrence. Exponentially smoothed forecasts can be corrected somewhat by adding in a trend adjustment. To correct the trend, we need two smoothing constants. Besides the smoothing constant α, the trend equation also uses a **smoothing constant delta (δ)**. Both alpha and delta reduce the impact of the error that occurs between the actual and the forecast. If both alpha and delta are not included, the trend overreacts to errors.

To get the trend equation going, the first time it is used the trend value must be entered manually. This initial trend value can be an educated guess or a computation based on observed past data.

The equations to compute the forecast including trend (FIT) are

$$F_t = FIT_{t-1} + \alpha(A_{t-1} - FIT_{t-1}) \qquad [3.4]$$
$$T_t = T_{t-1} + \delta(F_t - FIT_{t-1}) \qquad [3.5]$$
$$FIT_t = F_t + T_t \qquad [3.6]$$

Smoothing constant delta (δ)
An additional parameter used in an exponential smoothing equation that includes an adjustment for trend.

where

$$F_t = \text{The exponentially smoothed forecast that does not include trend for period } t$$
$$T_t = \text{The exponentially smoothed trend for period } t$$
$$\text{FIT}_t = \text{The forecast including trend for period } t$$
$$\text{FIT}_{t-1} = \text{The forecast including trend made for the prior period}$$
$$A_{t-1} = \text{The actual demand for the prior period}$$
$$\alpha = \text{Smoothing constant (alpha)}$$
$$\delta = \text{Smoothing constant (delta)}$$

To make an exponential forecast that includes trend, step through the equations one at a time.

Step 1: Using equation 3.4, make a forecast that is not adjusted for trend. This uses the previous forecast and previous actual demand.

Step 2: Using equation 3.5, update the estimate of trend using the previous trend estimate, the unadjusted forecast just made, and the previous forecast.

Step 3: Make a new forecast that includes trend by using the results from steps 1 and 2.

Example 3.1: Forecast Including Trend

Assume a previous forecast including trend of 110 units, a previous trend estimate of 10 units, an alpha of .20, and a delta of .30. If actual demand turned out to be 115 rather than the forecast 110, calculate the forecast for the next period.

SOLUTION

The actual A_{t-1} is given as 115. Therefore,

$$F_t = \text{FIT}_{t-1} + \alpha(A_{t-1} - \text{FIT}_{t-1})$$
$$= 110 + .2(115 - 110) = 111.0$$
$$T_t = T_{t-1} + \delta(F_t - \text{FIT}_{t-1})$$
$$= 10 + .3(111 - 110) = 10.3$$
$$\text{FIT}_t = F_t + T_t = 111.0 + 10.3 = 121.3$$

If, instead of 121.3, the actual turned out to be 120, the sequence would be repeated and the forecast for the next period would be

$$F_{t+1} = 121.3 + .2(120 - 121.3) = 121.04$$
$$T_{t+1} = 10.3 + .3(121.04 - 121.3) = 10.22$$
$$\text{FIT}_{t+1} = 121.04 + 10.22 = 131.26 \bullet$$

Choosing the Appropriate Value for Alpha and Delta Exponential smoothing requires that the smoothing constants be given a value between 0 and 1. Typically, fairly small values are used for alpha and delta in the range of .1 to .3. The values depend on how much random variation there is in demand and how steady the trend factor is. Later in the chapter, error measures are discussed that can be helpful in picking appropriate values for these parameters.

Linear Regression Analysis

Regression can be defined as a functional relationship between two or more correlated variables. It is used to predict one variable given the other. The relationship is usually developed from observed data. The data should be plotted first to see if they appear linear or if at least parts of the data are linear. *Linear regression* refers to the special class of regression where the relationship between variables forms a straight line.

The linear regression line is of the form $Y_t = a + bt$, where Y_t is the value of the dependent variable that we are solving for, a is the Y_t intercept, b is the slope, and t is an index for the time period.

Linear regression is useful for long-term forecasting of major occurrences and aggregate planning. For example, linear regression would be very useful to forecast demand for product families. Even though demand for individual products within a family may vary widely during a time period, demand for the total product family is surprisingly smooth.

The major restriction in using **linear regression forecasting** is, as the name implies, that past data and future projections are assumed to fall in about a straight line. Although this does limit its application sometimes, if we use a shorter period of time, linear regression analysis can still be used. For example, there may be short segments of the longer period that are approximately linear.

Linear regression is used both for time series forecasting and for causal relationship forecasting. When the dependent variable (usually the vertical axis on a graph) changes as a result of time (plotted as the horizontal axis), it is time series analysis. If one variable changes because of the change in another variable, this is a causal relationship (such as the number of deaths from lung cancer increasing with the number of people who smoke).

Linear regression forecasting
A forecasting technique that assumes that past data and future projections fall around a straight line.

We use the following example to demonstrate linear least squares regression analysis:

Example 3.2: Least Squares Method

A firm's sales for a product line during the 12 quarters of the past three years were as follows:

Quarter	Sales	Quarter	Sales
1	600	7	2,600
2	1,550	8	2,900
3	1,500	9	3,800
4	1,500	10	4,500
5	2,400	11	4,000
6	3,100	12	4,900

The firm wants to forecast each quarter of the fourth year—that is, quarters 13, 14, 15, and 16.

SOLUTION

The least squares equation for linear regression is

$$Y_t = a + bt \qquad [3.7]$$

where

Y_t = Dependent variable computed by the equation
y = The actual dependent variable data point (used below)
a = Y_t intercept
b = Slope of the line
t = Time period

The least squares method tries to fit the line to the data *that minimizes the sum of the squares of the vertical distance* between each data point and its corresponding point on the line. If a straight line is drawn through the general area of the points, the difference between the point and the line is $y - Y$. Exhibit 3.6 shows these differences. The sum of the squares of the differences between the plotted data points and the line points is

$$(y_1 - Y_1)^2 + (y_2 - Y_2)^2 + \cdots + (y_{12} - Y_{12})^2$$

The best line to use is the one that minimizes this total.

As before, the straight line equation is

$$Y_t = a + bt$$

In the least squares method, the equations for a and b are

$$b = \frac{\Sigma ty - n\bar{t} \cdot \bar{y}}{\Sigma t^2 - n\bar{t}^2} \qquad [3.8]$$

$$a = \bar{y} - b\bar{t} \qquad [3.9]$$

Excel:
Forecasting

exhibit 3.6   Least Squares Regression Line

where

    a = Y intercept
    b = Slope of the line
    $\bar{y}$ = Average of all ys
    $\bar{t}$ = Average of all ts
    t = t value at each data point
    y = y value at each data point
    n = Number of data points
    Y_t = Value of the dependent variable computed
        with the regression equation

Exhibit 3.7 shows these computations carried out for the 12 data points in the problem. Note that the final equation for Y_t shows an intercept of 441.67 and a slope of 359.6. The slope shows that for every unit change in t, Y_t changes by 359.6. Also note that these calculations can be done with the INTERCEPT and SLOPE functions in Microsoft Excel.

Strictly based on the equation, forecasts for periods 13 through 16 would be

$$Y_{13} = 441.67 + 359.6(13) = 5{,}116.5$$
$$Y_{14} = 441.67 + 359.6(14) = 5{,}476.1$$
$$Y_{15} = 441.67 + 359.6(15) = 5{,}835.7$$
$$Y_{16} = 441.67 + 359.6(16) = 6{,}195.3$$

The standard error of estimate, or how well the line fits the data, is

$$S_{yt} = \sqrt{\frac{\sum_{i=1}^{n}(y_i - Y_i)^2}{n-2}}$$

[3.10]

Least Squares Regression Analysis　　　　**exhibit 3.7**

(1) t	(2) y	(3) $t \times y$	(4) t^2	(5) y^2	(6) Y
1	600	600	1	360,000	801.3
2	1,550	3,100	4	2,402,500	1,160.9
3	1,500	4,500	9	2,250,000	1,520.5
4	1,500	6,000	16	2,250,000	1,880.1
5	2,400	12,000	25	5,760,000	2,239.7
6	3,100	18,600	36	9,610,000	2,599.4
7	2,600	18,200	49	6,760,000	2,959.0
8	2,900	23,200	64	8,410,000	3,318.6
9	3,800	34,200	81	14,440,000	3,678.2
10	4,500	45,000	100	20,250,000	4,037.8
11	4,000	44,000	121	16,000,000	4,397.4
12	4,900	58,800	144	24,010,000	4,757.1
78	33,350	268,200	650	112,502,500	

$\bar{t} = 6.5$　$b = 359.6154$
$\bar{y} = 2{,}779.17$　$a = 441.6667$
Therefore, $Y_t = 441.67 + 359.6t$　$S_{yt} = 363.9$

Excel:
Forecasting

**Excel:
Forecasting**

exhibit 3.8   Excel Regression Tool

	A	B
1	Qtr	Demand
2	1	600
3	2	1550
4	3	1500
5	4	1500
6	5	2400
7	6	3100
8	7	2600
9	8	2900
10	9	3800
11	10	4500
12	11	4000
13	12	4900

Regression

Input
Input Y Range: $B$2:$B$13
Input X Range: $A$2:$A$13
☐ Labels   ☐ Constant is Zero
☐ Confidence Level: 95 %

Output options
◉ Output Range: $A$16
○ New Worksheet Ply:
○ New Workbook

Residuals
☐ Residuals   ☐ Residual Plots
☐ Standardized Residuals ☐ Line Fit Plots

Normal Probability
☐ Normal Probability Plots

[OK] [Cancel] [Help]

SUMMARY OUTPUT

Regression Statistics	
Multiple R	0.96601558
R Square	0.933186102
Adjusted R Square	0.926504712
Standard Error	363.8777972
Observations	12

ANOVA

	df	SS	MS	F	Significance F
Regression	1	18493221.15	18493221	139.6695	3.37202E-07
Residual	10	1324070.513	132407.1		
Total	11	19817291.67			

	Coefficients	Standard Error	t Stat	P-value	Lower 95%	Upper 95%	Lower 95.0%	Upper 95.0%
Intercept	441.6666667	223.9513029	1.972155	0.076869	-57.3279302	940.661264	-57.3279302	940.6612636
X Variable 1	359.6153846	30.42899005	11.81818	3.37E-07	291.8153699	427.415399	291.81537	427.4153993

The standard error of estimate is computed from the second and last columns of Exhibit 3.7:

$$S_{yt} = \sqrt{\frac{(600 - 801.3)^2 + (1{,}550 - 1{,}160.9)^2 + (1{,}500 - 1{,}520.5)^2 + \cdots + (4{,}900 - 4{,}757.1)^2}{10}}$$

$$= 363.9$$

In addition to the INTERCEPT and SLOPE functions, Microsoft Excel has a very powerful regression tool designed to perform these calculations. (Note that it can also be used for moving average and exponential smoothing calculations.) To use the tool, a table is needed that contains data relevant to the problem (see Exhibit 3.8). The tool is part of the Data Analysis ToolPak that is accessed from the Data menu (you may need to add this to your Data options by using the Add-In option under File → Options → Add-Ins).

To use the tool, first input the data in two columns in your spreadsheet; then access the Regression option from the → Data menu. Next, specify the Y Range, which is B2:B13, and the time periods in the X Range, which is A2:A13 in our example. Finally, an Output Range is specified. This is where you would like the results of the regression analysis placed in your spreadsheet. In the example, A16 is entered. There is some information provided that goes beyond what we have covered, but what you are looking for is the Intercept and X Variable coefficients that correspond to the intercept and slope values in the linear equation. These are in cells B32 and B33 in Exhibit 3.8. •

Decomposition of a Time Series

A *time series* can be defined as chronologically ordered data that may contain one or more components of demand: trend, seasonal, cyclical, autocorrelation, and random. **Decomposition** of a time series means identifying and separating the time series data into these components. In practice, it is relatively easy to identify the trend (even without mathematical analysis, it is usually easy to plot and see the direction of movement) and the seasonal component (by comparing the same period year to year). It is considerably more difficult to identify the cycles (these may be many months or years long), the autocorrelation, and the random components. (The forecaster usually calls random anything left over that cannot be identified as another component.)

Decomposition The process of identifying and separating time series data into fundamental components such as trend and seasonality.

When demand contains both seasonal and trend effects at the same time, the question is how they relate to each other. In this description, we examine two types of seasonal variation: *additive* and *multiplicative*.

Additive Seasonal Variation Additive seasonal variation simply assumes that the seasonal amount is a constant no matter what the trend or average amount is.

$$\text{Forecast including trend and seasonal} = \text{Trend} + \text{Seasonal}$$

Exhibit 3.9A shows an example of increasing trend with constant seasonal amounts.

Multiplicative Seasonal Variation In multiplicative seasonal variation, the trend is multiplied by the seasonal factors.

$$\text{Forecast including trend and seasonal} = \text{Trend} \times \text{Seasonal factor}$$

Exhibit 3.9B shows the seasonal variation increasing as the trend increases because its size depends on the trend.

The multiplicative seasonal variation is the usual experience. Essentially, this says that the larger the basic amount projected, the larger the variation around this that we can expect.

Excel:
Forecasting

Additive and Multiplicative Seasonal Variation Superimposed on Changing Trend	exhibit 3.9

A. Additive Seasonal

Amount

January   January   January   January   January
   July   July   July   July

B. Multiplicative Seasonal

Amount

January   January   January   January   January
   July   July   July   July

© Oleksiy Maksymenko/Alamy

© CNP Collection/Alamy

Companies such as Honda manufacture lawnmowers and snow blowers to match seasonal demand. Using the same equipment and assembly lines provides better capacity utilization, workforce stability, productivity, and revenue.

Seasonal Factor (or Index)   A seasonal factor is the amount of correction needed in a time series to adjust for the season of the year.

We usually associate *seasonal* with a period of the year characterized by some particular activity. We use the word *cyclical* to indicate other than annual recurrent periods of repetitive activity.

The following examples show how seasonal indexes are determined and used to forecast (1) a simple calculation based on past seasonal data and (2) the trend and seasonal index from a hand-fit regression line. We follow this with a more formal procedure for the decomposition of data and forecasting using least squares regression.

Example 3.3: Simple Proportion

Assume that in past years a firm sold an average of 1,000 units of a particular product line each year. On average, 200 units were sold in the spring, 350 in the summer, 300 in the fall, and 150 in the winter. The seasonal factor (or index) is the ratio of the amount sold during each season divided by the average for all seasons.

SOLUTION

In this example, the yearly amount divided equally over all seasons is $1,000 \div 4 = 250$. The seasonal factors therefore are

	Past Sales	Average Sales for Each Season (1,000/4)	Seasonal Factor
Spring	200	250	200/250 = 0.8
Summer	350	250	350/250 = 1.4
Fall	300	250	300/250 = 1.2
Winter	150	250	150/250 = 0.6
Total	1,000		

Using these factors, if we expected demand for next year to be 1,100 units, we would forecast the demand to occur as

	EXPECTED DEMAND FOR NEXT YEAR	AVERAGE SALES FOR EACH SEASON (1,100/4)		SEASONAL FACTOR		NEXT YEAR'S SEASONAL FORECAST
Spring		275	×	0.8	=	220
Summer		275	×	1.4	=	385
Fall		275	×	1.2	=	330
Winter		275	×	0.6	=	165
Total	1,100					

The seasonal factor may be periodically updated as new data are available. The following example shows the seasonal factor and multiplicative seasonal variation. •

Example 3.4: Computing Trend and Seasonal Factor from a Linear Regression Line Obtained with Excel

Forecast the demand for each quarter of the next year using trend and seasonal factors. Demand for the past two years is in the following table:

QUARTER	AMOUNT	QUARTER	AMOUNT
1	300	5	520
2	200	6	420
3	220	7	400
4	530	8	700

SOLUTION

First, we plot as in Exhibit 3.10 and then calculate the slope and intercept using Excel. For Excel, the quarters are numbered 1 through 8. The "known y's" are the amounts (300, 200, 220, etc.), and the "known x's" are the quarter numbers (1, 2, 3, etc.). We obtain a slope = 52.3 (rounded) and an intercept = 176.1 (rounded). The equation for the line is

$$\text{Forecast including trend (FIT)} = 176.1 + 52.3t$$

Next, we can derive a seasonal index by comparing the actual data with the trend line, as in Exhibit 3.10. The seasonal factor was developed by averaging the same quarters in each year.

We can compute the forecast for next year, including trend and seasonal factors (FITS), as follows:

$$\text{FITS}_t = \text{FIT} \times \text{Seasonal}$$

$$\text{I} - \text{FITS}_9 = [176.1 + 52.3(9)]1.25 = 808$$

$$\text{II} - \text{FITS}_{10} = [176.1 + 52.3(10)]0.79 = 552$$

$$\text{III} - \text{FITS}_{11} = [176.1 + 52.3(11)]0.70 = 526$$

$$\text{IV} - \text{FITS}_{12} = [176.1 + 52.3(12)]1.28 = 1029$$

Note, these numbers were calculated using Excel, so your numbers may differ slightly due to rounding. •

Excel:
Forecasting

exhibit 3.10 Computing a Seasonal Factor from the Actual Data and Trend Line

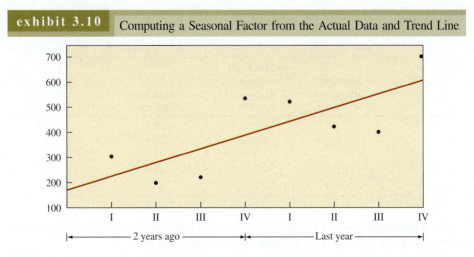

QUARTER	ACTUAL AMOUNT	FROM TREND EQUATION FIT$_t$ = 176.1 + 52.3t	RATIO OF ACTUAL ÷ TREND	SEASONAL FACTOR (AVERAGE OF SAME QUARTERS IN BOTH YEARS)
2 years ago				
I	300	228.3	1.31	
II	200	280.6	0.71	
III	220	332.9	0.66	I 1.25
IV	530	385.1	1.38	II 0.79
Last year		—	—	III 0.70
I	520	437.4	1.19	IV 1.28
II	420	489.6	0.86	
III	400	541.9	0.74	
IV	700	594.2	1.18	

Decomposition Using Least Squares Regression This procedure is different from the previous one and in some cases may give better results. The approach described in Example 3.3 started by fitting a regression line, and given the line, the seasonal indexes are calculated. With this approach we start by calculating seasonal indexes; then, using data that have been "deseasonalized," we estimate a trend line using linear regression. More formally, the process is:

1. Decompose the time series into its components.
   a. Find the seasonal component.
   b. Deseasonalize the demand.
   c. Find the trend component.
2. Forecast the future values of each component.
   a. Project the trend component into the future.
   b. Multiply the trend component by the seasonal component.

Exhibit 3.11 shows the decomposition of a time series using least squares regression and the same basic data we used in our first regression example. Each data point corresponds to using a single three-month quarter of the three-year (12-quarter) period. Our objective is to forecast demand for the four quarters of the fourth year.

| | | | Deseasonalized Demand | | | | | exhibit 3.11 |

| (1) | (2) | (3) ACTUAL DEMAND (y) | (4) AVERAGE OF THE SAME QUARTERS OF EACH YEAR | (5) SEASONAL FACTOR | (6) DESEASONALIZED DEMAND (y_d) COL. (3) ÷ COL. (5) | (7) t^2 (COL. 1)^2 | (8) $t \times y_d$ COL. (1) × COL. (6) |
PERIOD (t)	QUARTER						
1	I	600	(600 + 2,400 + 3,800)/3 = 2,266.7	0.82	735.7	1	735.7
2	II	1,550	(1,550 + 3,100 + 4,500)/3 = 3,050	1.10	1,412.4	4	2,824.7
3	III	1,500	(1,500 + 2,600 + 4,000)/3 = 2,700	0.97	1,544.0	9	4,631.9
4	IV	1,500	(1,500 + 2,900 + 4,900)/3 = 3,100	1.12	1,344.8	16	5,379.0
5	I	2,400		0.82	2,942.6	25	14,713.2
6	II	3,100		1.10	2,824.7	36	16,948.4
7	III	2,600		0.97	2,676.2	49	18,733.6
8	IV	2,900		1.12	2,599.9	64	20,798.9
9	I	3,800		0.82	4,659.2	81	41,932.7
10	II	4,500		1.10	4,100.4	100	41,004.1
11	III	4,000		0.97	4,117.3	121	45,290.1
12	IV	4,900		1.12	4,392.9	144	52,714.5
78		33,350*		12.03	33,350.1*	650	265,706.9

$$\bar{t} = \frac{78}{12} = 6.5 \qquad b = \frac{\Sigma ty_d - n\bar{t}\bar{y}_d}{\Sigma t^2 - n\bar{t}^2} = \frac{265,706.9 - 12(6.5)2,779.2}{650 - 12(6.5)^2} = 342.2$$

$$\bar{y}_d = 33,350/12 = 2,779.2 \qquad a = \bar{y}_d - b\bar{t} = 2,779.2 - 342.2(6.5) = 554.9$$

Therefore, $Y = a + bt = 554.9 + 342.2t$

*The column 3 and column 6 totals should be equal at 33,350. Differences are due to rounding. Column 5 was rounded to two decimal places.

Step 1. Determine the seasonal factor (or index). Exhibit 3.11 summarizes the calculations needed. Column 4 develops an average for the same quarters in the three-year period. For example, the first quarters of the three years are added together and divided by three. A seasonal factor is then derived by dividing that average by the general average for all 12 quarters ($\frac{33,350}{12}$, or 2,779). For example, this first quarter seasonal factor is $\frac{2,266.7}{2,779} = 0.82$. These are entered in column 5. Note that the seasonal factors are identical for similar quarters in each year.

Step 2. Deseasonalize the original data. To remove the seasonal effect on the data, we divide the original data by the seasonal factor. This step is called the deseasonalization of demand and is shown in column 6 of Exhibit 3.11.

Step 3. Develop a least squares regression line for the deseasonalized data. The purpose here is to develop an equation for the trend line Y, which we then modify with the seasonal factor. The procedure is the same as we used before:

$$Y = a + bt$$

where

y_d = Deseasonalized demand (see Exhibit 3.11)
t = Quarter
Y = Demand computed using the regression equation $Y = a + bt$
a = Y intercept
b = Slope of the line

The least squares calculations using columns 1, 7, and 8 of Exhibit 3.11 are shown in the lower section of the exhibit. The final deseasonalized equation for our data is $Y = 554.9 + 342.2t$. This straight line is shown in Exhibit 3.12.

Step 4. Project the regression line through the period to be forecast. Our purpose is to forecast periods 13 through 16. We start by solving the equation for Y at each of these periods (shown in step 5, column 3).

Step 5. Create the final forecast by adjusting the regression line by the seasonal factor. Recall that the Y equation has been deseasonalized. We now reverse the procedure by multiplying the quarterly data we derived by the seasonal factor for that quarter:

PERIOD	QUARTER	Y FROM REGRESSION LINE	SEASONAL FACTOR	FORECAST (Y × SEASONAL FACTOR)
13	1	5,003.5	0.82	4,102.87
14	2	5,345.7	1.10	5,880.27
15	3	5,687.9	0.97	5,517.26
16	4	6,030.1	1.12	6,753.71

Our forecast is now complete.

Error Range When a straight line is fitted through data points and then used for forecasting, errors can come from two sources. First, there are the usual errors similar to the standard deviation of any set of data. Second, there are errors that arise because the line

Excel:
Forecasting

exhibit 3.12   Straight Line Graph of Deseasonalized Equation

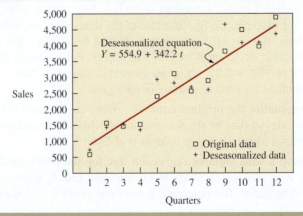

Prediction Intervals for Linear Trend	exhibit 3.13

is wrong. Exhibit 3.13 shows this error range. Instead of developing the statistics here, we will briefly show why the range broadens. First, visualize that one line is drawn that has some error such that it slants too steeply upward. Standard errors are then calculated for this line. Now visualize another line that slants too steeply downward. It also has a standard error. The total error range for this analysis consists of errors resulting from both lines, as well as all other possible lines. We included this exhibit to show how the error range widens as we go further into the future.

Forecast Errors

In using the term **forecast error**, we are referring to the difference between what actually occurred and what was forecast. In statistics, these errors are called *residuals*. As long as the forecast value is within the confidence limits, as we discuss later under the heading "Measurement of Error," this is not really an error since it is what we expected. But common usage refers to the difference as an error.

Demand for a product is generated through the interaction of a number of factors too complex to describe accurately in a model. Therefore, all forecasts certainly contain some error. In discussing forecast errors, it is convenient to distinguish between *sources of error* and the *measurement of error.*

Forecast error
The difference between actual demand and what was forecast.

Sources of Error

Errors can come from a variety of sources. One common source that many forecasters are unaware of is projecting past trends into the future. For example, when we talk about statistical errors in regression analysis, we are referring to the deviations of observations from our regression line. It is common to attach a confidence band (that is, statistical control limits) to the regression line to reduce the unexplained error. But when we then use this regression line as a forecasting device by projecting it into the future, the error may not be correctly defined by the projected confidence band. This is because the confidence interval is based on past data; it may not hold for projected data points and therefore cannot be used with the same confidence. In fact, experience has shown that the actual errors tend to be greater than those predicted from forecast models.

Errors can be classified as bias or random. *Bias errors* occur when a consistent mistake is made. Sources of bias include the failure to include the right variables; the use of the wrong relationships among variables; employing of the wrong trend line; a mistaken shift in the seasonal demand from where it normally occurs; and the existence of some undetected secular trend. *Random errors* can be defined as those that cannot be explained by the forecast model being used.

Measurement of Error

Several common terms used to describe the degree of error are *standard error, mean squared error* (or *variance*), and *mean absolute deviation.* In addition, tracking signals may be used to indicate any positive or negative bias in the forecast.

Standard error is discussed in the section on linear regression in this chapter. Because the standard error is the square root of a function, it is often more convenient to use than the function itself. This is called the mean squared error, or variance.

Mean absolute deviation (MAD) The average forecast error using absolute values of the error of each past forecast.

The **mean absolute deviation (MAD)** was in vogue in the past but subsequently was ignored in favor of standard deviation and standard error measures. In recent years, MAD has made a comeback because of its simplicity and usefulness in obtaining tracking signals. MAD is the average error in the forecasts, using absolute values. It is valuable because MAD, like the standard deviation, measures the dispersion of some observed value from some expected value.

MAD is computed using the differences between the actual demand and the forecast demand without regard to sign. It equals the sum of the absolute deviations divided by the number of data points, or, stated in equation form,

$$\text{MAD} = \frac{\sum_{t=1}^{n} |A_t - F_t|}{n} \qquad \text{[3.11]}$$

where

t = Period number
A_t = Actual demand for the period t
F_t = Forecast demand for the period t
n = Total number of periods
$\| $ = A symbol used to indicate the absolute value disregarding positive and negative signs

When the errors that occur in the forecast are normally distributed (the usual case), the mean absolute deviation relates to the standard deviation as

$$1 \text{ standard deviation} = \sqrt{\frac{\pi}{2}} \times \text{MAD, or approximately 1.25 MAD}$$

Mean absolute percent error (MAPE) The mean absolute deviation divided by the average demand; the average error expressed as a percentage of demand.

Conversely,

1 MAD is approximately 0.8 standard deviation

The standard deviation is the larger measure. If the MAD of a set of points was found to be 60 units, then the standard deviation would be approximately 75 units. In the usual statistical manner, if control limits were set at plus or minus 3 standard deviations (or ±3.75 MADs), then 99.7 percent of the points would fall within these limits.

An additional measure of error that is often useful is the **mean absolute percent error (MAPE)**. This measure gauges the error relative to the average demand. For example, if the MAD is 10 units and the average demand is 20 units, the error is large and significant, but relatively insignificant on an average demand of 1,000 units. MAPE is calculated by taking the MAD and dividing by the average demand

$$\text{MAPE} = \frac{\text{MAD}}{\text{Average demand}} \qquad [3.12]$$

This is a useful measure because it is an estimate of how much error to expect with a forecast. So if the MAD were 10 and the average demand 20, the MAPE would be 50 percent ($\frac{10}{20} = .50$). In the case of an average demand of 1,000 units, the MAPE would be only 1 percent ($\frac{10}{1,000} = .01$).

A **tracking signal** is a measurement that indicates whether the forecast average is keeping pace with any genuine upward or downward changes in demand. When a forecast is consistently low or high, it is referred to as a *biased* forecast. Exhibit 3.14 shows a normal distribution with a mean of 0 and a MAD equal to 1. Thus, if we compute the tracking signal and find it equal to minus 2, we can see that the forecast model is providing forecasts that are quite a bit above the mean of the actual occurrences.

A tracking signal (TS) can be calculated using the arithmetic sum of forecast deviations divided by the mean absolute deviation

Tracking signal
A measure that indicates whether the forecast average is keeping pace with any genuine upward or downward changes in demand.

$$\text{TS} = \frac{\text{RSFE}}{\text{MAD}} \qquad [3.13]$$

where

RSFE = The running sum of forecast errors, considering the nature of the error. (For example, negative errors cancel positive errors and vice versa.)

MAD = The average of all the forecast errors (disregarding whether the deviations are positive or negative). It is the average of the absolute deviations.

A Normal Distribution with Mean = 0 and MAD = 1   **exhibit 3.14**

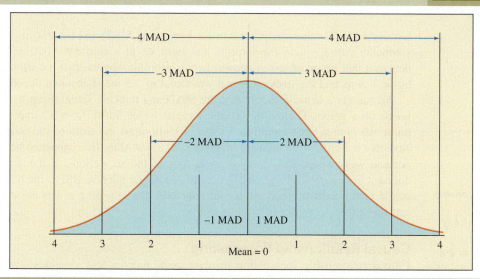

| exhibit 3.15 | Computing the Mean Absolute Deviation (MAD), the Running Sum of Forecast Errors (RSFE), and the Tracking Signal (TS) from Forecast and Actual Data |

Excel:
Forecasting

MONTH	DEMAND FORECAST	ACTUAL	DEVIATION	RSFE	ABS. DEV.	SUM OF ABS. DEV.	MAD*	TS = $\frac{RSFE^\dagger}{MAD}$
1	1,000	950	−50	−50	50	50	50	−1
2	1,000	1,070	+70	+20	70	120	60	.33
3	1,000	1,100	+100	+120	100	220	73.3	1.64
4	1,000	960	−40	+80	40	260	65	1.2
5	1,000	1,090	+90	+170	90	350	70	2.4
6	1,000	1,050	+50	+220	50	400	66.7	3.3

*Overall, MAD = 400 ÷ 6 = 66.7. For all 6 months, the average demand is 1,036.7. Given this, the MAPE = 66.7/1,036.7 = 6.43%.

†Overall, TS = $\frac{RSFE}{MAD}$ = $\frac{220}{66.7}$ = 3.3 MADs. For all 6 months, the average demand is 1,036.7.

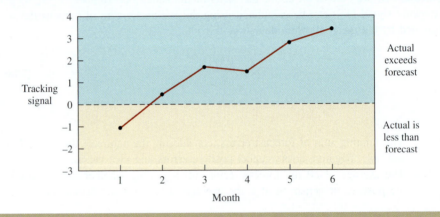

Exhibit 3.15 illustrates the procedure for computing MAD and the tracking signal for a six-month period where the forecast had been set at a constant 1,000 and the actual demands that occurred are as shown. In this example, the forecast, on average, was off by 66.7 units and the tracking signal was equal to 3.3 mean absolute deviations.

We can get a better feel for what the MAD and tracking signal mean by plotting the points on a graph. Though this is not completely legitimate from a sample-size standpoint, we plotted each month in Exhibit 3.15 to show the drift of the tracking signal. Note that it drifted from minus 1 MAD to plus 3.3 MADs. This happened because actual demand was greater than the forecast in four of the six periods. If the actual demand does not fall below the forecast to offset the continual positive RSFE, the tracking signal would continue to rise and we would conclude that assuming a demand of 1,000 is a bad forecast.

Causal relationship forecasting
Forecasting using independent variables other than time to predict future demand.

Causal Relationship Forecasting

Causal relationship forecasting involves using independent variables other than time to predict future demand. To be of value for the purpose of forecasting, any independent variable must be a leading indicator. For example, we can expect that an extended period of rain will increase sales of umbrellas and raincoats. The rain causes the sale of rain gear. This is a causal relationship, where one occurrence causes another. If the causing element is known far enough in advance, it can be used as a basis for forecasting.

The following shows one example of a forecast using a causal relationship.

Example 3.5: Forecasting Using a Causal Relationship

The Carpet City Store in Carpenteria has kept records of its sales (in square yards) each year, along with the number of permits for new houses in its area.

	NUMBER OF HOUSING STARTS	
YEAR	PERMITS	SALES (IN SQ. YDS.)
1	18	13,000
2	15	12,000
3	12	11,000
4	10	10,000
5	20	14,000
6	28	16,000
7	35	19,000
8	30	17,000
9	20	13,000

Carpet City's operations manager believes forecasting sales is possible if housing starts are known for that year. First, the data are plotted in Exhibit 3.16, with

x = Number of housing start permits
y = Sales of carpeting

Causal Relationship: Sales to Housing Starts   **exhibit 3.16**

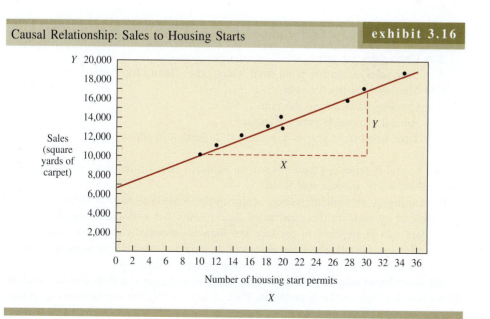

Excel:
Forecasting

Because the points appear to be in a straight line, the manager decides to use the linear relationship $Y = a + bx$.

SOLUTION

An easy way to solve this problem is to use the SLOPE and INTERCEPT functions in Excel. Given the data in the table, the SLOPE is equal to 344.2211 and the INTERCEPT is equal to 6,698.492.

The manager interprets the slope as the average number of square yards of carpet sold for each new house built in the area. The forecasting equation is therefore

$$Y = 6,698.492 + 344.2211x$$

Now suppose that there are 25 permits for houses to be built next year. The sales forecast would therefore be

$$6,698.492 + 344.2211(25) = 15,304.02 \text{ square yards}$$

In this problem, the lag between filing the permit with the appropriate agency and the new home owner coming to Carpet City to buy carpet makes a causal relationship feasible for forecasting. •

Multiple Regression Analysis

Another forecasting method is multiple regression analysis, in which a number of variables are considered, together with the effects of each on the item of interest. For example, in the home furnishings field, the effects of the number of marriages, housing starts, disposable income, and the trend can be expressed in a multiple regression equation as

$$S = A + B_m(M) + B_h(H) + B_i(I) + B_t(T)$$

where

S = Gross sales for year
A = Base sales, a starting point from which other factors have influence
M = Marriages during the year
H = Housing starts during the year
I = Annual disposable personal income
T = Time trend (first year = 1, second = 2, third = 3, and so forth)

B_m, B_h, B_i, and B_t represent the influence on expected sales of the numbers of marriages and housing starts, income, and trend.

Forecasting by multiple regression is appropriate when a number of factors influence a variable of interest—in this case, sales. Its difficulty lies with collecting all the additional data that is required to produce the forecast, especially data that comes from outside the firm. Fortunately, standard computer programs for multiple regression analysis are available, relieving the need for tedious manual calculation.

Microsoft Excel supports the time series analysis techniques described in this section. These functions are available under the Data Analysis tools for exponential smoothing, moving averages, and regression.

QUALITATIVE TECHNIQUES IN FORECASTING

Qualitative forecasting techniques generally take advantage of the knowledge of experts and require much judgment. These techniques typically involve processes that are well defined to those participating in the forecasting exercise. For example, in the case of forecasting the demand for new fashion merchandise in a retail store, the firm can include a combination of typical customers to express preferences and store managers who understand product mix and store volumes, where they view the merchandise and run through a series of exercises designed to bring the group to a consensus estimate. The point is that these are not wild guesses as to the expected demand, but rather involve a well-thought-out and structured decision-making approach.

LO3–3 Apply qualitative techniques to forecast demand.

These techniques are most useful when the product is new or there is little experience with selling into a new region. Here such information as knowledge of similar products, the habits of customers in the area, and how the product will be advertised and introduced may be important to estimate demand successfully. In some cases, it may even be useful to consider industry data and the experience of competing firms in making estimates of expected demand.

The following are samples of qualitative forecasting techniques.

Market Research

Firms often hire outside companies that specialize in *market research* to conduct this type of forecasting. You may have been involved in market surveys through a marketing class. Certainly, you have not escaped telephone calls asking you about product preferences, your income, habits, and so on.

Market research is used mostly for product research in the sense of looking for new product ideas, likes and dislikes about existing products, which competitive products within a particular class are preferred, and so on. Again, the data collection methods are primarily surveys and interviews.

Panel Consensus

In a *panel consensus,* the idea that two heads are better than one is extrapolated to the idea that a panel of people from a variety of positions can develop a more reliable forecast than a narrower group. Panel forecasts are developed through open meetings with a free exchange of ideas from all levels of management and individuals. The difficulty with this open style is that lower-level employees are intimidated by higher levels of management. For example, a salesperson in a particular product line may have a good estimate of future product demand but may not speak up to refute a much different estimate given by the vice president of marketing. The Delphi technique (which we discuss shortly) was developed to try to correct this impairment to free exchange.

When decisions in forecasting are at a broader, higher level (as when introducing a new product line or concerning strategic product decisions such as new marketing areas), the term *executive judgment* is generally used. The term is self-explanatory: a higher level of management is involved.

Historical Analogy

In trying to forecast demand for a new product, an ideal situation would be where an existing product or generic product could be used as a model. There are many ways to classify such analogies—for example, complementary products, substitutable or competitive products, and products as a function of income. Again, you have surely gotten a deluge of mail advertising products in a category similar to a product purchased via catalog, the Internet, or mail order. If you buy a DVD through the mail, you will receive more mail about new DVDs and DVD players. A causal relationship would be that demand for compact discs is caused by demand for DVD players. An analogy would be forecasting the demand for digital videodisc players by analyzing the historical demand for VCRs. The products are in the same general category of electronics and may be bought by consumers at similar rates. A simpler example would be toasters and coffeemakers. A firm that already produces toasters and wants to produce coffeemakers could use the toaster history as a likely growth model.

The Delphi Method

As we mentioned under panel consensus, a statement or opinion of a higher-level person will likely be weighted more than that of a lower-level person. The worst case is where lower-level people feel threatened and do not contribute their true beliefs. To prevent this problem, the *Delphi method* conceals the identity of the individuals participating in the study. Everyone has the same weight. Procedurally, a moderator creates a questionnaire and distributes it to participants. Their responses are summed and given back to the entire group, along with a new set of questions.

The step-by-step procedure for the Delphi method is:

1. Choose the experts to participate. There should be a variety of knowledgeable people in different areas.
2. Through a questionnaire (or e-mail), obtain forecasts (and any premises or qualifications for the forecasts) from all participants.
3. Summarize the results, and redistribute them to the participants along with appropriate new questions.
4. Summarize again, refining forecasts and conditions, and again develop new questions.
5. Repeat step 4 if necessary. Distribute the final results to all participants.

The Delphi technique can usually achieve satisfactory results in three rounds. The time required is a function of the number of participants, how much work is involved for them to develop their forecasts, and their speed in responding.

Collaborative Planning, Forecasting, and Replenishment (CPFR)
An Internet tool to coordinate forecasting, production, and purchasing in a firm's supply chain.

LO3–4 Apply collaborative techniques to forecast demand.

WEB-BASED FORECASTING: COLLABORATIVE PLANNING, FORECASTING, AND REPLENISHMENT (CPFR)

Collaborative Planning, Forecasting, and Replenishment (CPFR) is a Web-based tool used to coordinate demand forecasting, production and purchase planning, and inventory replenishment between supply chain trading partners. CPFR is being used as a means of integrating all members of an *n*-tier supply chain, including manufacturers, distributors, and retailers. As depicted in Exhibit 3.17, the ideal point of collaboration utilizing CPFR is the retail-level demand forecast, which is successively used to synchronize forecasts, production, and replenishment plans upstream through the supply chain.

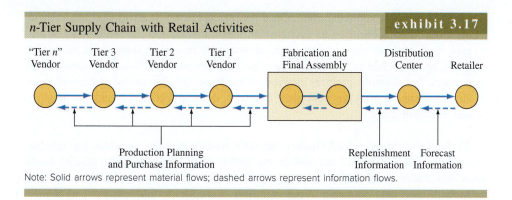

n-Tier Supply Chain with Retail Activities   **exhibit 3.17**

"Tier *n*"   Tier 3   Tier 2   Tier 1   Fabrication and   Distribution
Vendor   Vendor   Vendor   Vendor   Final Assembly   Center   Retailer

Production Planning   Replenishment   Forecast
and Purchase Information   Information   Information

Note: Solid arrows represent material flows; dashed arrows represent information flows.

Although the methodology is applicable to any industry, CPFR applications to date have largely focused on the food, apparel, and general merchandise industries. The potential benefits of sharing information for enhanced planning visibility in any supply chain are enormous. Various estimates for cost savings attributable to improved supply chain coordination have been proposed, including $30 billion annually in the food industry alone.

CPFR's objective is to exchange selected internal information on a shared Web server in order to provide for reliable, longer-term future views of demand in the supply chain. CPFR uses a cyclic and iterative approach to derive consensus supply chain forecasts. It consists of the following five steps:

Step 1. Creation of a front-end partnership agreement. This agreement specifies (1) objectives (e.g., inventory reductions, lost sales elimination, lower product obsolescence) to be gained through collaboration, (2) resource requirements (e.g., hardware, software, performance metrics) necessary for the collaboration, and (3) expectations of confidentiality concerning the prerequisite trust necessary to share sensitive company information, which represents a major implementation obstacle.

Step 2. Joint business planning. Typically, partners create partnership strategies, design a joint calendar identifying the sequence and frequency of planning activities to follow that affect product flows, and specify exception criteria for handling planning variances between the trading partners' demand forecasts.

Step 3. Development of demand forecasts. Forecast development may follow preexisting company procedures. Retailers should play a critical role as shared *point-of-sale (POS)* data permit the development of more accurate and timely expectations (compared with extrapolated warehouse withdrawals or aggregate store orders) for both retailers and vendors. Given the frequency of forecast generation and the potential for vast numbers of items requiring forecast preparation, a simple forecast procedure such as a moving average is commonly used within CPFR. Simple techniques are easily used in conjunction with expert knowledge of promotional or pricing events to modify forecast values accordingly.

Step 4. Forecast sharing. Retailer (order forecasts) and vendor (sales forecasts) then electronically post their latest forecasts for a list of products on a shared server. The server examines pairs of corresponding forecasts and issues an exception notice for any forecast pair where the difference exceeds a preestablished safety margin (e.g., 5 percent). If the safety margin is exceeded, planners from both firms may collaborate electronically to derive a consensus forecast.

Step 5. Inventory replenishment. Once the corresponding forecasts are in agreement, the order forecast becomes an actual order, which commences the replenishment process. Each of these steps is then repeated iteratively in a continuous cycle, at varying times, by individual products and the calendar of events established between trading partners. For example, partners may review the front-end partnership agreement annually, evaluate the joint business plans quarterly, develop forecasts weekly to monthly, and replenish daily.

The early exchange of information between trading partners provides for reliable, longer-term future views of demand in the supply chain. The forward visibility based upon information sharing leads to a variety of benefits within supply chain partnerships.

As with most new corporate initiatives, there is skepticism and resistance to change. One of the largest hurdles hindering collaboration is the lack of trust over complete information sharing between supply chain partners. The conflicting objective between the profit-maximizing vendor and the cost-minimizing customer gives rise to adversarial supply chain relationships. Sharing sensitive operating data may enable one trading partner to take advantage of the other. Similarly, there is the potential loss of control as a barrier to implementation. Some companies are rightfully concerned about the idea of placing strategic data such as financial reports, manufacturing schedules, and inventory values online. Companies open themselves to security breaches. The front-end partnership agreements, nondisclosure agreements, and limited information access may help overcome these fears.

CONCEPT CONNECTIONS

LO3–1 Understand how forecasting is essential to supply chain planning.

Forecasts are essential to every business organization. It is important to consider the purpose of the forecast before selecting the technique.

- Strategic forecasts are typically longer term and usually involve forecasting demand for a group of products.
- Tactical forecasts would cover only a short period of time, at most a few weeks in the future, and would typically be for individual items.

Forecasts are used in many different problems studied in this book.

Strategic forecasts Medium- and long-term forecasts used to make decisions related to strategy and estimating aggregate demand.

Tactical forecasts Short-term forecasts used as input for making day-to-day decisions related to meeting demand.

LO3–2 Evaluate demand using quantitative forecasting models.

In this chapter, the focus is on time series analysis techniques. With a time series analysis, past demand data are used to predict future demand.

- Demand can be broken down or "decomposed" into basic elements, such as trend, seasonality, and random variation (there are other elements, but these are the ones considered in this chapter).
- Four different time series models are evaluated: simple moving average, weighted moving average, exponential smoothing, and linear regression.
- Trend and seasonal components are analyzed for these problems.

- Causal relationship forecasting is different from time series (but commonly used) since it uses data other than past demand in making the forecast.
- The quality of a forecast is measured based on its error. Various measures exist, including the average error, percentage of error, and bias. Bias occurs when a forecast is consistently higher or lower than actual demand.

Time series analysis   A type of forecast in which data relating to past demand are used to predict future demand.

Moving average   A forecast based on average past demand.

Weighted moving average   A forecast made with past data where more recent data are given more significance than older data.

Exponential smoothing   A time series forecasting technique in which each increment of past demand data is decreased by $(1 - \alpha)$.

Smoothing constant alpha (α)   The parameter in the exponential smoothing equation that controls the speed of reaction to differences between forecasts and actual demand.

Smoothing constant delta (δ)   An additional parameter used in an exponential smoothing equation that includes an adjustment for trend.

Linear regression forecasting   A forecasting technique that assumes that past data and future projections fall around a straight line.

Decomposition   The process of identifying and separating time series data into fundamental components such as trend and seasonality.

Forecast error   The difference between actual demand and what was forecast.

Mean absolute deviation (MAD)   The average forecast error using absolute values of the error of each past forecast.

Mean absolute percent error (MAPE)   The mean absolute deviation divided by the average demand; the average error expressed as a percentage of demand.

Tracking signal   A measure that indicates whether the forecast average is keeping pace with any genuine upward or downward changes in demand.

Causal relationship forecasting   Forecasting using independent variables other than time to predict future demand.

Forecasting formulas

$$F_t = \frac{A_{t-1} + A_{t-2} + A_{t-3} + \cdots + A_{t-n}}{n} \tag{3.1}$$

$$F_t = w_1 A_{t-1} + w_2 A_{t-2} + \cdots + w_n A_{t-n} \tag{3.2}$$

$$F_t = F_{t-1} + \alpha(A_{t-1} - F_{t-1}) \tag{3.3}$$

$$F_t = \text{FIT}_{t-1} + \alpha(A_{t-1} - \text{FIT}_{t-1}) \tag{3.4}$$

$$T_t = T_{t-1} + \delta(F_t - \text{FIT}_{t-1}) \tag{3.5}$$

$$\text{FIT}_t = F_t + T_t \tag{3.6}$$

$$Y_t = a + bt \tag{3.7}$$

$$a = \bar{y} - b\bar{t} \tag{3.8}$$

$$b = \frac{\Sigma ty - n\bar{t} \cdot \bar{y}}{\Sigma t^2 - n\bar{t}^2} \tag{3.9}$$

$$S_{yt} = \sqrt{\frac{\sum\limits_{i=1}^{n}(y_i - Y_i)^2}{n-2}}$$ [3.10]

$$MAD = \frac{\sum\limits_{t=1}^{n}|A_t - F_t|}{n}$$ [3.11]

$$MAPE = \frac{MAD}{\text{Average demand}}$$ [3.12]

$$TS = \frac{RSFE}{MAD}$$ [3.13]

LO3-3 **Apply qualitative techniques to forecast demand.**

- Qualitative techniques depend more on judgment or the opinions of experts and can be useful when past demand data are not available.
- These techniques typically involve a structured process so that experience can be acquired and accuracy assessed.

LO3-4 **Apply collaborative techniques to forecast demand.**

- Collaboration between supply chain partners, such as the manufacturer and the retailer selling a product, can be useful.
- Typically, Web-based technology is used to derive a forecast that is a consensus of all the participants. There are often great benefits to all participants due to the sharing of information and future planning visibility offered through the system.

Collaborative Planning, Forecasting, and Replenishment (CPFR)   An Internet tool to coordinate forecasting, production, and purchasing in a firm's supply chain.

SOLVED PROBLEMS

Excel:
Forecasting

SOLVED PROBLEM 1

Sunrise Baking Company markets doughnuts through a chain of food stores. It has been experiencing overproduction and underproduction because of forecasting errors. The following data are its demand in dozens of doughnuts for the past four weeks. Doughnuts are made for the following day; for example, Sunday's doughnut production is for Monday's sales, Monday's production is for Tuesday's sales, and so forth. The bakery is closed Saturday, so Friday's production must satisfy demand for both Saturday and Sunday.

	4 WEEKS AGO	3 WEEKS AGO	2 WEEKS AGO	LAST WEEK
Monday	2,200	2,400	2,300	2,400
Tuesday	2,000	2,100	2,200	2,200
Wednesday	2,300	2,400	2,300	2,500
Thursday	1,800	1,900	1,800	2,000
Friday	1,900	1,800	2,100	2,000
Saturday	(closed on Saturday)			
Sunday	2,800	2,700	3,000	2,900

Make a forecast for this week on the following basis:

a. Daily, using a simple four-week moving average.

b. Daily, using a weighted moving average with weights of 0.40, 0.30, 0.20, and 0.10 (most recent to oldest week).

c. Sunrise is also planning its purchases of ingredients for bread production. If bread demand had been forecast for last week at 22,000 loaves and only 21,000 loaves were actually demanded, what would Sunrise's forecast be for this week using exponential smoothing with $\alpha = 0.10$?

d. Suppose, with the forecast made in c, this week's demand actually turns out to be 22,500. What would the new forecast be for the next week?

Solution

a. Simple moving average, four-week.

$$\text{Monday} \quad \frac{2{,}400 + 2{,}300 + 2{,}400 + 2{,}200}{4} = \frac{9{,}300}{4} = 2{,}325 \text{ doz.}$$

$$\text{Tuesday} \quad = \frac{8{,}500}{4} = 2{,}125 \text{ doz.}$$

$$\text{Wednesday} \quad = \frac{9{,}500}{4} = 2{,}375 \text{ doz.}$$

$$\text{Thursday} \quad = \frac{7{,}500}{4} = 1{,}875 \text{ doz.}$$

$$\text{Friday} \quad = \frac{7{,}800}{4} = 1{,}950 \text{ doz.}$$

$$\text{Saturday and Sunday} \quad = \frac{11{,}400}{4} = 2{,}850 \text{ doz.}$$

b. Weighted average with weights of .40, .30, .20, and .10.

	(.10)		(.20)		(.30)		(.40)		
Monday	220	+	480	+	690	+	960	=	2,350
Tuesday	200	+	420	+	660	+	880	=	2,160
Wednesday	230	+	480	+	690	+	1,000	=	2,400
Thursday	180	+	380	+	540	+	800	=	1,900
Friday	190	+	360	+	630	+	800	=	1,980
Saturday and Sunday	280	+	540	+	900	+	1,160	=	2,880

c. Exponentially smoothed forecast for bread demand

$$F_t = F_{t-1} + \alpha(A_{t-1} - F_{t-1})$$
$$= 22{,}000 + 0.10(21{,}000 - 22{,}000)$$
$$= 22{,}000 - 100 = 21{,}900 \text{ loaves}$$

d. Exponentially smoothed forecast

$$F_{t+1} = 21{,}900 + .10(22{,}500 - 21{,}900)$$
$$= 21{,}900 + .10(600) = 21{,}960 \text{ loaves}$$

SOLVED PROBLEM 2

Given the following information, make a forecast for May using exponential smoothing with trend and linear regression.

MONTH	JANUARY	FEBRUARY	MARCH	APRIL
Demand	700	760	780	790

For exponential smoothing with trend, assume that the previous forecast (for April) including trend (FIT) was 800 units, and the previous trend component (T) was 50 units. Also, alpha(α) = .3 and delta(δ) = .1.

For linear regression, use the January through April demand data to fit the regression line. Use the Excel regression functions SLOPE and INTERCEPT to calculate these values.

Solution

Exponential smoothing with trend

Use the following three steps to update the forecast each period:

1. Forecast without Trend $F_t = \text{FIT}_{t-1} + \alpha(A_{t-1} - \text{FIT}_{t-1})$
2. Update Trend estimate $T_t = T_{t-1} + \delta(F_t - \text{FIT}_{t-1})$
3. New Forecast including Trend $\text{FIT}_t = F_t + T_t$

$$\text{Given} \quad \text{FIT}_{April} = 800$$
$$\text{and } T_{April} = 50$$
$$\text{Then} \quad F_{May} = 800 + .3(790 - 800) = 797$$
$$T_{May} = 50 + .1(797 - 800) = 49.7$$
$$\text{FIT}_{May} = 797 + 49.7 = 846.7$$

Linear regression

1. Set up the problem and calculate the slope and intercept as shown here.
2. Forecast using linear regression

$$Y_t = a + bt$$

where a is the "Slope" and b is the "Intercept" and t for May is 5 (the index for month 5).

$$\text{Then} \quad F_{May} = 685 + 29(5) = 830$$

	A	B	C	D	E
1	Month	Demand			
2	1	700			
3	2	760			
4	3	780			
5	4	790			
6	Intercept	685	=INTERCEPT(B2:B5,A2:A5)		
7	Slope	29	=SLOPE(B2:B5,A2:A5)		
8					

SOLVED PROBLEM 3

Here are quarterly data for the past two years. From these data, prepare a forecast for the upcoming year using decomposition.

Excel:
Forecasting

PERIOD	ACTUAL		PERIOD	ACTUAL
1	300		5	416
2	540		6	760
3	885		7	1,191
4	580		8	760

Solution

(Note that the values you obtain may be slightly different due to rounding. The values given here were obtained using an Excel spreadsheet.)

(1) PERIOD x	(2) ACTUAL y	(3) PERIOD AVERAGE	(4) SEASONAL FACTOR	(5) DESEASONALIZED DEMAND y_d
1	300	358	0.527	568.99
2	540	650	0.957	564.09
3	885	1,038	1.529	578.92
4	580	670	0.987	587.79
5	416		0.527	789.01
6	760		0.957	793.91
7	1,191		1.529	779.08
8	760		0.987	770.21
Total	5,432	2,716	8.0	
Average	679	679	1	

Column 3 is seasonal average. For example, the first-quarter average is

$$\frac{300 + 416}{2} = 358$$

Column 4 is the quarter average (column 3) divided by the overall average (679). Column 5 is the actual data divided by the seasonal index. To determine t^2 and ty, we can construct a table as follows:

PERIOD t	DESEASONALIZED DEMAND (y_d)	t^2	ty_d
1	568.99	1	569.0
2	564.09	4	1,128.2
3	578.92	9	1,736.7
4	587.79	16	2,351.2
5	789.01	25	3,945.0
6	793.91	36	4,763.4
7	779.08	49	5,453.6
8	770.21	64	6,161.7
Sums	36	5,432	204	26,108.8
Average	4.5	679		

Now we calculate regression results for deseasonalized data.

$$b = \frac{(26108.8) - (8)(4.5)(679)}{(204) - (8)(4.5)^2} = 39.64$$

$$a = \bar{y}_d - b\bar{t}$$

$$a = 679 - 39.64(4.5) = 500.6$$

Therefore, the deseasonalized regression results are

$$Y = 500.6 + 39.64t$$

PERIOD	TREND FORECAST		SEASONAL FACTOR		FINAL FORECAST
9	857.4	×	0.527	=	452.0
10	897.0	×	0.957	=	858.7
11	936.7	×	1.529	=	1,431.9
12	976.3	×	0.987	=	963.4

SOLVED PROBLEM 4

**Excel:
Forecasting**

A specific forecasting model was used to forecast demand for a product. The forecasts and the corresponding demand that subsequently occurred are shown below. Use the MAD, tracking signal technique, and MAPE to evaluate the accuracy of the forecasting model.

	ACTUAL	FORECAST
October	700	660
November	760	840
December	780	750
January	790	835
February	850	910
March	950	890

Solution

Evaluate the forecasting model using the MAD, the tracking signal, and MAPE.

	ACTUAL DEMAND	FORECAST DEMAND	ACTUAL DEVIATION	CUMULATIVE DEVIATION (RSFE)	TRACKING SIGNAL	ABSOLUTE DEVIATION
October	700	660	40	40	1.00	40
November	760	840	−80	−40	0.67	80
December	780	750	30	−10	0.20	30
January	790	835	−45	−55	1.13	45
February	850	910	−60	−115	2.25	60
March	950	890	60	−55	1.05	60
Average demand = 805					Total dev. = 315	

$$\text{MAD} = \frac{315}{6} = 52.5$$

$$\text{Tracking signal} = \frac{-55}{52.5} = -1.05$$

$$\text{MAPE} = \frac{52.5}{805} = 6.52\%$$

There is not enough evidence to reject the forecasting model, so we accept its recommendations.

DISCUSSION QUESTIONS

LO3–1

1. Why is forecasting necessary in OSCM?
2. It is a common saying that the only thing certain about a forecast is that it will be wrong. What is meant by this?

LO3–2

3. From the choice of the simple moving average, weighted moving average, exponential smoothing, and linear regression analysis, which forecasting technique would you consider the most accurate? Why?
4. All forecasting methods using exponential smoothing, adaptive smoothing, and exponential smoothing including trend require starting values to get the equations going. How would you select the starting value for, say, F_{t-1}?
5. How is a seasonal index computed from a regression line analysis?
6. Discuss the basic differences between the mean absolute deviation and mean absolute percent error.
7. What implications do forecast errors have for the search for ultrasophisticated statistical forecasting models?
8. Causal relationships are potentially useful for which component of a time series?

LO3–3

9. Let's say you work for a company that makes prepared breakfast cereals like corn flakes. Your company is planning to introduce a new hot breakfast product made from whole grains that would require some minimal preparation by the consumer. This would be a completely new product for the company. How would you propose forecasting initial demand for this product?

LO3–4

10. How has the development of the Internet affected the way companies forecast in support of their supply chain planning process?
11. What sorts of risks do you see in reliance on the Internet in the use of Collaborative Planning, Forecasting, and Replenishment (CPFR)?

OBJECTIVE QUESTIONS

LO3–1

1. What is the term for forecasts used for making day-to-day decisions about meeting demand?
2. What category of forecasting techniques uses managerial judgment in lieu of numerical data?

LO3–2

3. Given the following history, use a three-quarter moving average to forecast the demand for the third quarter of this year. Note, the 1st quarter is Jan, Feb, and Mar; 2nd quarter Apr, May, Jun; 3rd quarter Jul, Aug, Sep; and 4th quarter Oct, Nov, Dec.

	JAN	FEB	MAR	APR	MAY	JUN	JUL	AUG	SEP	OCT	NOV	DEC
Last year	100	125	135	175	185	200	150	140	130	200	225	250
This year	125	135	135	190	200	190						

4. Here are the data for the past 21 months for actual sales of a particular product:

	LAST YEAR	THIS YEAR		LAST YEAR	THIS YEAR
January	300	275	July	400	350
February	400	375	August	300	275
March	425	350	September	375	350
April	450	425	October	500	
May	400	400	November	550	
June	460	350	December	500	

Develop a forecast for the fourth quarter using a three-quarter, weighted moving average. Weight the most recent quarter 0.5, the second most recent 0.25, and the third 0.25. Do the problem using quarters, as opposed to forecasting separate months.

5. The following table contains the number of complaints received in a department store for the first six months of operation:

MONTH	COMPLAINTS	MONTH	COMPLAINTS
January	36	April	90
February	45	May	108
March	81	June	144

If a three-month moving average is used to smooth this series, what would have been the forecast for May?

6. The following tabulations are actual sales of units for six months and a starting forecast in January.
    a. Calculate forecasts for the remaining five months using simple exponential smoothing with $\alpha = 0.2$.
    b. Calculate MAD for the forecasts.

	ACTUAL	FORECAST
January	100	80
February	94	
March	106	
April	80	
May	68	
June	94	

7. The following table contains the demand from the last 10 months:

MONTH	ACTUAL DEMAND	MONTH	ACTUAL DEMAND
1	31	6	36
2	34	7	38
3	33	8	40
4	35	9	40
5	37	10	41

    a. Calculate the single exponential smoothing forecast for these data using an α of 0.30 and an initial forecast (F_1) of 31.
    b. Calculate the exponential smoothing with trend forecast for these data using an α of 0.30, a δ of 0.30, an initial trend forecast (T_1) of 1, and an initial exponentially smoothed forecast (F_1) of 30.
    c. Calculate the mean absolute deviation (MAD) for each forecast. Which is best?

8. Actual demand for a product for the past three months was

Three months ago	400 units
Two months ago	350 units
Last month	325 units

    a. Using a simple three-month moving average, make a forecast for this month.
    b. If 300 units were actually demanded this month, what would your forecast be for next month?
    c. Using simple exponential smoothing, what would your forecast be for this month if the exponentially smoothed forecast for three months ago was 450 units and the smoothing constant was 0.20?

9. Assume an initial starting F_t of 300 units, a trend (T_t) of eight units, an alpha of 0.30, and a delta of 0.40. If actual demand turned out to be 288, calculate the forecast for the next period.

10. The number of cases of merlot wine sold by the Connor Owen winery in an eight-year period is as follows:

YEAR	CASES OF MERLOT WINE	YEAR	CASES OF MERLOT WINE
1	270	5	358
2	356	6	500
3	398	7	410
4	456	8	376

Using an exponential smoothing model with an alpha value of 0.20, estimate the smoothed value calculated as of the end of year 8. Use the average demand for years 1 through 3 as your initial forecast, and then smooth the forecast forward to year 8.

11. Not all the items in your office supply store are evenly distributed as far as demand is concerned, so you decide to forecast demand to help plan your stock. Past data for legal-sized yellow tablets for the month of August are

Week 1	300	Week 3	600
Week 2	400	Week 4	700

a. Using a three-week moving average, what would you forecast the next week to be?

b. Using exponential smoothing with $\alpha = 0.20$, if the exponential forecast for week 3 was estimated as the average of the first two weeks [(300 + 400)/2 = 350], what would you forecast week 5 to be?

12. Assume that your stock of sales merchandise is maintained based on the forecast demand. If the distributor's sales personnel call on the first day of each month, compute your forecast sales by each of the three methods requested here.

	ACTUAL
June	140
July	180
August	170

a. Using a simple three-month moving average, what is the forecast for September?

b. Using a weighted moving average, what is the forecast for September with weights of 0.20, 0.30, and 0.50 for June, July, and August, respectively?

c. Using single exponential smoothing and assuming that the forecast for June had been 130, forecast sales for September with a smoothing constant alpha of 0.30.

13. Historical demand for a product is as follows:

	DEMAND
April	60
May	55
June	75
July	60
August	80
September	75

a. Using a simple four-month moving average, calculate a forecast for October.

b. Using single exponential smoothing with $\alpha = 0.2$ and a September forecast = 65, calculate a forecast for October.

c. Using simple linear regression, calculate the trend line for the historical data. Let's say the X axis is April = 1, May = 2, and so on, while the Y axis is demand.

d. Calculate a forecast for October using your regression formula.

14. Demand for stereo headphones and MP3 players for joggers has caused Nina Industries to grow almost 50 percent over the past year. The number of joggers continues to expand, so Nina expects demand for headsets to also expand, because, as yet, no safety laws have been passed to prevent joggers from wearing them. Demand for the players for last year was as follows:

MONTH	DEMAND (UNITS)	MONTH	DEMAND (UNITS)
January	4,200	July	5,300
February	4,300	August	4,900
March	4,000	September	5,400
April	4,400	October	5,700
May	5,000	November	6,300
June	4,700	December	6,000

a. Using linear regression analysis, what would you estimate demand to be for each month next year? Using a spreadsheet, follow the general format in Exhibit 3.8. Compare your results to those obtained by using the forecast spreadsheet function.

b. To be reasonably confident of meeting demand, Nina decides to use three standard errors of estimate for safety. How many additional units should be held to meet this level of confidence?

15. Historical demand for a product is

	DEMAND
January	12
February	11
March	15
April	12
May	16
June	15

a. Using a weighted moving average with weights of 0.60, 0.30, and 0.10, find the July forecast.

b. Using a simple three-month moving average, find the July forecast.

c. Using single exponential smoothing with $\alpha = 0.2$ and a June forecast = 13, find the July forecast. Make whatever assumptions you wish.

d. Using simple linear regression analysis, calculate the regression equation for the preceding demand data.

e. Using the regression equation in d, calculate the forecast for July.

16. The tracking signals computed using past demand history for three different products are as follows. Each product used the same forecasting technique.

	TS 1	TS 2	TS 3
1	−2.70	1.54	0.10
2	−2.32	−0.64	0.43
3	−1.70	2.05	1.08
4	−1.10	2.58	1.74
5	−0.87	−0.95	1.94
6	−0.05	−1.23	2.24
7	0.10	0.75	2.96
8	0.40	−1.59	3.02
9	1.50	0.47	3.54
10	2.20	2.74	3.75

Discuss the tracking signals for each and what the implications are.

17. Here are the actual tabulated demands for an item for a nine-month period (January through September). Your supervisor wants to test two forecasting methods to see which method was better over this period.

Month	Actual	Month	Actual
January	110	June	180
February	130	July	140
March	150	August	130
April	170	September	140
May	160		

  a. Forecast April through September using a three-month moving average.
  b. Use simple exponential smoothing with an alpha of 0.3 to estimate April through September, using the average of January through March as the initial forecast for April.
  c. Use MAD to decide which method produced the better forecast over the six-month period.

18. A particular forecasting model was used to forecast a six-month period. Here are the forecasts and actual demands that resulted:

	Forecast	Actual
April	250	200
May	325	250
June	400	325
July	350	300
August	375	325
September	450	400

  Find the tracking signal and state whether you think the model being used is giving acceptable answers.

19. Harlen Industries has a simple forecasting model: Take the actual demand for the same month last year and divide that by the number of fractional weeks in that month. This gives the average weekly demand for that month. This weekly average is used as the weekly forecast for the same month this year. This technique was used to forecast eight weeks for this year, which are shown below along with the actual demand that occurred.

  The following eight weeks show the forecast (based on last year) and the demand that actually occurred:

Week	Forecast Demand	Actual Demand	Week	Forecast Demand	Actual Demand
1	140	137	5	140	180
2	140	133	6	150	170
3	140	150	7	150	185
4	140	160	8	150	205

  a. Compute the MAD of forecast errors.
  b. Using the RSFE, compute the tracking signal.
  c. Based on your answers to parts (*a*) and (*b*), comment on Harlen's method of forecasting.

20. In this problem, you are to test the validity of your forecasting model. Here are the forecasts for a model you have been using and the actual demands that occurred:

Week	Forecast	Actual
1	800	900
2	850	1,000
3	950	1,050
4	950	900
5	1,000	900
6	975	1,100

Use the method stated in the text to compute MAD and tracking signal. Then decide whether the forecasting model you have been using is giving reasonable results.

21. The following table shows predicted product demand using your particular forecasting method along with the actual demand that occurred:

FORECAST	ACTUAL
1,500	1,550
1,400	1,500
1,700	1,600
1,750	1,650
1,800	1,700

a. Compute the tracking signal using the mean absolute deviation and running sum of forecast errors.
b. Discuss whether your forecasting method is giving good predictions.

22. Your manager is trying to determine what forecasting method to use. Based upon the following historical data, calculate the following forecast and specify what procedure you would utilize.

MONTH	ACTUAL DEMAND	MONTH	ACTUAL DEMAND
1	62	7	76
2	65	8	78
3	67	9	78
4	68	10	80
5	71	11	84
6	73	12	85

a. Calculate the simple three-month moving average forecast for periods 4–12.
b. Calculate the weighted three-month moving average using weights of 0.50, 0.30, and 0.20 for periods 4–12.
c. Calculate the single exponential smoothing forecast for periods 2–12 using an initial forecast (F_1) of 61 and an α of 0.30.
d. Calculate the exponential smoothing with trend component forecast for periods 2–12 using an initial trend forecast (T_1) of 1.8, an initial exponential smoothing forecast (F_1) of 60, an α of 0.30, and a δ of 0.30.
e. Calculate the mean absolute deviation (MAD) for the forecasts made by each technique in periods 4–12. Which forecasting method do you prefer?

23. After using your forecasting model for six months, you decide to test it using MAD and a tracking signal. Here are the forecast and actual demands for the six-month period:

PERIOD	FORECAST	ACTUAL
May	450	500
June	500	550
July	550	400
August	600	500
September	650	675
October	700	600

a. Find the tracking signal.
b. Decide whether your forecasting routine is acceptable.

24. Zeus Computer Chips, Inc. used to have major contracts to produce the Centrino-type chips. The market has been declining during the past three years because of the quad-core chips, which it cannot produce, so Zeus has the

unpleasant task of forecasting next year. The task is unpleasant because the firm has not been able to find replacement chips for its product lines. Here is the demand over the past 12 quarters:

TWO YEARS AGO		LAST YEAR		THIS YEAR	
I	4,800	I	3,500	I	3,200
II	3,500	II	2,700	II	2,100
III	4,300	III	3,500	III	2,700
IV	3,000	IV	2,400	IV	1,700

Use the decomposition technique to forecast the demand for the next four quarters.

25. The sales data for two years are as follows. Data are aggregated with two months of sales in each "period."

MONTHS	SALES	MONTHS	SALES
January–February	109	January–February	115
March–April	104	March–April	112
May–June	150	May–June	159
July–August	170	July–August	182
September–October	120	September–October	126
November–December	100	November–December	106

a. Plot the data.
b. Fit a simple linear regression model to the sales data.
c. In addition to the regression model, determine multiplicative seasonal index factors. A full cycle is assumed to be a full year.
d. Using the results from parts (*b*) and (*c*), prepare a forecast for the next year.

26. The following table shows the past two years of quarterly sales information. Assume that there are both trend and seasonal factors and that the seasonal cycle is one year. Use time series decomposition to forecast quarterly sales for the next year.

QUARTER LAST YEAR	SALES	QUARTER THIS YEAR	SALES
I	215	I	160
II	240	II	195
III	205	III	150
IV	190	IV	140

27. Tucson Machinery, Inc. manufactures numerically controlled machines, which sell for an average price of $0.5 million each. Sales for these NCMs for the past two years were as follows:

QUARTER LAST YEAR	QUANTITY (UNITS)	QUARTER THIS YEAR	QUANTITY (UNITS)
I	12	I	16
II	18	II	24
III	26	III	28
IV	16	IV	18

a. Find a line using regression in Excel.
b. Find the trend and seasonal factors.
c. Forecast sales for next year.

28. Use regression analysis on deseasonalized demand to forecast next summer's demand, given the following historical demand data:

YEAR	SEASON	ACTUAL DEMAND
2 years ago	Spring	205
	Summer	140
	Fall	375
	Winter	575
Last year	Spring	475
	Summer	275
	Fall	685
	Winter	965

29. Here are earnings per share for two companies by quarter from the first quarter three years ago through the second quarter of this year. Forecast earnings per share for the rest of this year and next year. Use exponential smoothing to forecast the third period of this year, and the time series decomposition method to forecast the last two quarters of this year and all four quarters of next year. (It is much easier to solve this problem on a computer spreadsheet so you can see what is happening.)

		EARNINGS PER SHARE	
	QUARTER	COMPANY A	COMPANY B
3 years ago	I	$1.67	$0.17
	II	2.35	0.24
	III	1.11	0.26
	IV	1.15	0.34
2 years ago	I	1.56	0.25
	II	2.04	0.37
	III	1.14	0.36
	IV	0.38	0.44
Last year	I	0.29	0.33
	II	−0.18 (loss)	0.40
	III	−0.97 (loss)	0.41
	IV	0.20	0.47
This year	I	−1.54 (loss)	0.30
	II	0.38	0.47

a. For the exponential smoothing method, choose the first quarter of three years ago as the beginning forecast. Make two forecasts: one with $\alpha = 0.10$ and one with $\alpha = 0.30$.

b. Using the MAD method of testing the forecasting model's performance, plus actual data from three years ago through the second quarter of this year, how well did the model perform?

c. Using the decomposition of a time series method of forecasting, forecast earnings per share for the last two quarters of this year and all four quarters of next year. Is there a seasonal factor in the earnings?

d. Using your forecasts, comment on each company.

30. Mark Price, the new productions manager for Speakers and Company, needs to find out which variable most affects the demand for their line of stereo speakers. He is uncertain whether the unit price of the product or the effects of increased marketing are the main drivers in sales and wants to use regression analysis to figure out which factor drives more demand for its particular market. Pertinent information was collected by an extensive marketing project that lasted

over the past 12 years (year 1 is data from 12 years ago) and was reduced to the data that follow:

YEAR	SALES/UNIT (THOUSANDS)	PRICE/ UNIT	ADVERTISING ($000)
1	400	280	600
2	700	215	835
3	900	211	1,100
4	1,300	210	1,400
5	1,150	215	1,200
6	1,200	200	1,300
7	900	225	900
8	1,100	207	1,100
9	980	220	700
10	1,234	211	900
11	925	227	700
12	800	245	690

a. Perform a regression analysis based on these data using Excel. Answer the following questions based on your results.

b. Which variable, price or advertising, has a larger effect on sales and how do you know?

c. Predict average yearly speaker sales for Speakers and Company based on the regression results if the price was $300 per unit and the amount spent on advertising (in thousands) was $900.

31. Sales by quarter for last year and the first three quarters of this year were as follows:

	QUARTER			
	I	II	III	IV
Last year	$23,000	$27,000	$18,000	$9,000
This year	19,000	24,000	15,000	

Using a procedure that you develop that captures the change in demand from last year to this year and also the seasonality in demand, forecast expected sales for the fourth quarter of this year.

32. The following are sales revenues for a large utility company for years 1 through 11. Forecast revenue for years 12 through 15. Because we are forecasting four years into the future, you will need to use linear regression as your forecasting method.

YEAR	REVENUE (MILLIONS)	YEAR	REVENUE (MILLIONS)
1	$4,865.9	7	$5,094.4
2	5,067.4	8	5,108.8
3	5,515.6	9	5,550.6
4	5,728.8	10	5,738.9
5	5,497.7	11	5,860.0
6	5,197.7		

LO3–3 33. What forecasting technique makes use of written surveys or telephone interviews?

34. Which qualitative forecasting technique was developed to ensure that the input from every participant in the process is weighted equally?

35. When forecasting demand for new products, sometimes firms will use demand data from similar existing products to help forecast demand for the new product. What technique is this an example of?

LO3-4   36. Often, firms will work with their partners across the supply chain to develop forecasts and execute production and distribution between the partners. What technique does this describe?
37. How many steps are there in collaborative planning, forecasting, and replenishment (CPFR)?
38. What is the first step in CPFR?

ANALYTICS EXERCISE: FORECASTING SUPPLY CHAIN DEMAND— STARBUCKS CORPORATION (LO3-2)

As we discussed at the beginning of the chapter, Starbucks has a large, global supply chain that must efficiently supply over 17,000 stores. Although the stores might appear to be very similar, they are actually very different. Depending on the location of the store, its size, and the profile of the customers served, Starbucks management configures the store offerings to take maximum advantage of the space available and customer preferences.

Starbucks' actual distribution system is much more complex, but for the purpose of our exercise let's focus on a single item that is currently distributed through five distribution centers in the United States. Our item is a logo-branded coffeemaker that is sold at some of the larger retail stores. The coffeemaker has been a steady seller over the years due to its reliability and rugged construction. Starbucks does not consider this a seasonal product, but there is some variability in demand. Demand for the product over the past 13 weeks is shown in the following table.

The demand at the distribution centers (DCs) varies between about 40 units on average per week in Atlanta and 48 units in Dallas. The current quarter's data are pretty close to the demand shown in the table.

Management would like you to experiment with some forecasting models to determine what should be used in a new system to be implemented. The new system is programmed to use one of two forecasting models: simple moving average or exponential smoothing.

WEEK	1	2	3	4	5	6	7	8	9	10	11	12	13	AVERAGE
Atlanta	33	45	37	38	55	30	18	58	47	37	23	55	40	40
Boston	26	35	41	40	46	48	55	18	62	44	30	45	50	42
Chicago	44	34	22	55	48	72	62	28	27	95	35	45	47	47
Dallas	27	42	35	40	51	64	70	65	55	43	38	47	42	48
LA	32	43	54	40	46	74	40	35	45	38	48	56	50	46
Total	162	199	189	213	246	288	245	204	236	257	174	248	229	222

Excel:
Starbucks
Data

Questions

1. Consider using a simple moving average model. Experiment with models using five weeks' and three weeks' past data. The past data in each region are given below (week −1 is the week before week 1 in the table, −2 is two weeks before week 1, etc.). Evaluate the forecasts that would have been made over the 13 weeks using the overall (at the end of the 13 weeks) mean absolute deviation, mean absolute percent error, and tracking signal as criteria.

2. Next, consider using a simple exponential smoothing model. In your analysis, test two alpha values, 0.2 and 0.4. Use the same criteria for evaluating the model as in part 1. When using an alpha value of 0.2, assume that the forecast for week 1 is the past three-week average (the average demand for periods −3, −2, and −1). For the model using an alpha of 0.4, assume that the forecast for week 1 is the past five-week average.

3. Starbucks is considering simplifying the supply chain for their coffeemaker. Instead of stocking the coffeemaker in all five distribution centers, they are considering only supplying it from a single location. Evaluate this option by analyzing how accurate the forecast would be based on the demand aggregated across all regions. Use the model that you think is best from your analysis of parts 1 and 2. Evaluate your new forecast using mean absolute deviation, mean absolute percent error, and the tracking signal.

4. What are the advantages and disadvantages of aggregating demand from a forecasting view? Are there other things that should be considered when going from multiple DCs to a DC?

WEEK	−5	−4	−3	−2	−1
Atlanta	45	38	30	58	37
Boston	62	18	48	40	35
Chicago	62	22	72	44	48
Dallas	42	35	40	64	43
LA	43	40	54	46	35
Total	254	153	244	252	198

PRACTICE EXAM

1. This is a type of forecast used to make long-term decisions, such as where to locate a warehouse or how many employees to have in a plant next year.
2. This is the type of demand that is most appropriate for using forecasting models.
3. This is a term used for actually influencing the sale of a product or service.
4. These are the six major components of demand.
5. This type of analysis is most appropriate when the past is a good predictor of the future.
6. This is identifying and separating time series data into components of demand.
7. If the demand in the current week was 102 units and we had forecast it to be 125, what would be next week's forecast using an exponential smoothing model with an alpha of 0.3?
8. Assume you are using exponential smoothing with an adjustment for trend. Demand is increasing at a very steady rate of about five units per week. Would you expect your alpha and delta parameters to be closer to one or zero?
9. Your forecast is, on average, incorrect by about 10 percent. The average demand is 130 units. What is the MAD?
10. If the tracking signal for your forecast was consistently positive, you could then say this about your forecasting technique.
11. What would you suggest to improve the forecast described in question 10?
12. You know that sales are greatly influenced by the amount your firm advertises in the local paper. What forecasting technique would you suggest trying?
13. What forecasting tool is most appropriate when closely working with customers dependent on your products?

Answers to Practice Exam 1. Strategic forecast 2. Independent demand 3. Demand management 4. Average demand for the period, trend, seasonal elements, cyclical elements, random variation, and autocorrelation 5. Time series analysis 6. Decomposition 7. 118 units 8. Zero 9. 13 10. Biased, consistently too low 11. Add a trend component. 12. Causal relationship forecasting (using regression) 13. Collaborative Planning, Forecasting, and Replenishment (CPFR)

CHAPTER 4

STRATEGIC CAPACITY MANAGEMENT

Learning Objectives

LO4–1 Explain what capacity management is and why it is strategically important.

LO4–2 Exemplify how to plan capacity.

LO4–3 Evaluate capacity alternatives using decision trees.

LO4–4 Compare capacity planning in services to capacity planning in manufacturing.

CAPACITY MANAGEMENT IN OPERATIONS
AND SUPPLY CHAIN MANAGEMENT

SHOULDICE HOSPITAL: HERNIA SURGERY INNOVATION

In July 1945, Shouldice Hospital, with a staff consisting of a nurse, a secretary, and a cook, opened its doors to its waiting patients. In a single operating room, Dr. Shouldice repaired two hernias per day using an innovative surgical treatment that he developed during World War II. His new surgical approach shortened patient recovery time from three weeks of hospitalization to only three days. As requests for this surgery increased, Dr. Shouldice extended the facilities, located in Toronto, by eventually buying three adjacent buildings and increasing the staff accordingly. In 1953, he purchased a country estate in Thornhill, where a new hospital was built.

Today all surgery takes place in Thornhill. Repeated development has culminated in the present 90-bed facility. Shouldice Hospital has been dedicated to the repair of hernias for over 70 years, using the "Shouldice Technique." The "formula," although not a secret, extends beyond the skill of surgeons and their ability to perform to the Shouldice standard. Shouldice Hospital is a total environment. Study the capacity problems with this special type of hospital in the case at the end of the chapter.

Source: Summarized from www.shouldice.com

CAPACITY MANAGEMENT IN OPERATIONS AND SUPPLY CHAIN MANAGEMENT

LO4–1 Explain what capacity management is and why it is strategically important.

A dictionary definition of capacity is "the ability to hold, receive, store, or accommodate." In a general business sense, it is most frequently viewed as the amount of output that a system is capable of achieving over a specific period of time. In a service setting, this might be the number of customers that can be handled between noon and 1:00 P.M. In manufacturing, this might be the number of automobiles that can be produced in a single shift.

When looking at capacity, operations managers need to look at both resource inputs *and* product outputs. For planning purposes, real (or effective) capacity depends on what is to be produced. For example, a firm that makes multiple products inevitably can produce more of one kind than of another with a given level of resource inputs. Thus, while the managers of an automobile factory may state that their facility has 6,000 production hours available per year, they are also thinking that these hours can be used to make either 150,000 two-door models or 120,000 four-door models (or some mix of the two- and four-door models). This reflects their knowledge of what their current technology and labor force inputs can produce and the product mix that is to be demanded from these resources.

An operations management view also emphasizes the time dimension of capacity. That is, capacity must also be stated relative to some period of time. This is evidenced in the common distinction drawn between long-range, intermediate-range, and short-range capacity planning.

Capacity planning is generally viewed in three time durations:

Long range—greater than one year. Where productive resources (such as buildings, equipment, or facilities) take a long time to acquire or dispose of, long-range capacity planning requires top management participation and approval.

Intermediate range—monthly or quarterly plans for the next 6 to 18 months. Here, capacity may be varied by such alternatives as hiring, layoffs, new tools, minor equipment purchases, and subcontracting.

Short range—less than one month. This is tied into the daily or weekly scheduling process and involves making adjustments to eliminate the variance between planned and actual output. This includes alternatives such as overtime, personnel transfers, and alternative production routings.

In this chapter, our focus is on capacity planning related to the long-term decisions. These involve the purchase of highly capital-intensive items, such as buildings, equipment, and other assets. The medium-term capacity-related decisions are considered as part of the aggregate operations planning decisions, which are the topic of Chapter 8. Short-term capacity planning is discussed in the context of the different types of processes covered in the book: manufacturing in Chapter 6, service in Chapter 7, and material requirements planning in Chapter 9.

Although there is no one person with the job title "capacity manager," there are several managerial positions charged with the effective use of capacity. *Capacity* is a relative term. In an operations management context, it may be defined as *the amount of resource inputs available relative to output requirements over a particular period of time.*

Strategic capacity planning
Finding the overall capacity level of capital-intensive resources to best support the firm's long-term strategy.

The objective of **strategic capacity planning** is to provide an approach for determining the overall capacity level of capital-intensive resources—facilities, equipment, and overall labor force size—that best supports the company's long-term competitive strategy. The capacity level selected has a critical impact on the firm's response rate, its cost structure, its inventory policies, and its management and staff support requirements. If capacity is inadequate, a company may lose customers through slow service or by allowing competitors to enter the market. If capacity is excessive, a company may have to reduce prices to stimulate demand, underutilize its workforce, carry excess inventory, or seek additional and less profitable products to stay in business.

Capacity Planning Concepts

The term **capacity** implies an attainable rate of output, for example, 480 cars per day, but says nothing about how long that rate can be sustained. Thus, we do not know if this 480 cars per day is a one-day peak or a six-month average. To avoid this problem, the concept of **best operating level** is used. This is the level of capacity for which process was designed and thus is the volume of output at which average unit cost is minimized. Determining this minimum is difficult because it involves a complex trade-off between the allocation of fixed overhead costs and the cost of overtime, equipment wear, defect rates, and other costs.

An important measure is the **capacity utilization rate**, which reveals how close a firm is to its best operating level:

$$\text{Capacity utilization rate} = \frac{\text{Capacity used}}{\text{Best operating level}} \qquad [4.1]$$

So, for example, if our plant's *best operating level* was 500 cars per day and the plant was currently operating at 480 cars per day, the *capacity utilization rate* would be 96 percent.

$$\text{Capacity utilization rate} = \frac{480}{500} = .96 \text{ or } 96\%$$

The capacity utilization rate is expressed as a percentage and requires that the numerator and denominator be measured in the same units and time periods (such as machine hours/day, barrels of oil/day, or dollars of output/day).

Economies and Diseconomies of Scale

The basic notion of **economies of scale** is that as a plant gets larger and volume increases, the average cost per unit of output drops. This is partially due to lower operating and capital cost, because a piece of equipment with twice the capacity of another piece typically does not cost twice as much to purchase or operate. Plants also gain efficiencies when they become large enough to fully utilize dedicated resources (people and equipment) for information technology, material handling, and administrative support.

At some point, the size of a plant becomes too large and

© PATRICK HERTZOG/Getty Images

Capacity
The output that a system is capable of achieving over a period of time.

Best operating level
Output level where average unit cost is minimized.

Capacity utilization rate
Measure of how close the firm's current output rate is to its best operating level (percent).

Economies of scale
Idea that as the plant gets larger and volume increases, the average cost per unit drops. At some point, the plant gets too large and cost per unit increases.

diseconomies of scale become a problem. These diseconomies may surface in many different ways. For example, maintaining the demand required to keep the large facility busy may require significant discounting of the product. U.S. automobile manufacturers continually face this problem. Another typical example involves using a few large-capacity pieces of equipment. Minimizing equipment downtime is essential in this type of operation. M&M Mars, for example, has highly automated, high-volume equipment to make M&M's. A single packaging line moves 2.6 million M&M's each hour. Even though direct labor to operate the equipment is very low, the labor required to maintain the equipment is high.

In many cases, the size of a plant may be influenced by factors other than the internal equipment, labor, and other capital expenditures. A major factor may be the cost to transport raw materials and finished product to and from the plant. A cement factory, for example, would have a difficult time serving customers more than a few hours from its plant. Similarly, automobile companies such as Ford, Honda, Nissan, and Toyota have found it advantageous to locate plants within specific international markets. The anticipated size of these intended markets will largely dictate the size and capacity of the plants.

Jaguar, the luxury automobile producer, recently found they had too many plants. Jaguar was employing 8,560 workers in three plants that produced 126,122 cars, about 15 cars per employee. In comparison, Volvo's plant in Torslanda, Sweden, was more than twice as productive, building 158,466 cars with 5,472 workers, or 29 cars per employee. By contrast, BMW AG's Mini unit made 174,000 vehicles at a single British plant with just 4,500 workers, or 39 cars per employee.

Capacity Focus

Focused factory
A facility designed around a limited set of production objectives. Typically the focus would relate to a specific product or product group.

The concept of a **focused factory** holds that a production facility works best when it focuses on a fairly limited set of production objectives. This means, for example, that a firm should not expect to excel in every aspect of manufacturing performance: cost, quality, delivery speed and reliability, changes in demand, and flexibility to adapt to new products. Rather, it should select a limited set of tasks that contribute the most to corporate objectives. Typically, the focused factory would produce a specific product or related group of products. A focused factory allows capacity to be focused on producing those specific items.

Plant within a plant (PWP)
An area in a larger facility that is dedicated to a specific production objective (for example, product group). This can be used to operationalize the focused factory concept.

The capacity focus concept can be operationalized through the mechanism of **plant within a plant**—or **PWP**. A focused factory (Exhibit 4.1) may have several PWPs, each of which may have separate suborganizations, equipment and process policies, workforce management policies, production control methods, and so forth for different products—even if they are made under the same roof. This, in effect, permits finding the best operating level for each department of the organization and thereby carries the focus concept down to the operating level.

Capacity Flexibility

Capacity flexibility means having the ability to rapidly increase or decrease production levels, or to shift production capacity quickly from one product or service to another. Such flexibility is achieved through flexible plants, processes, and workers, as well as through strategies that use the capacity of other organizations. Increasingly, companies are taking the idea of flexibility into account as they design their supply chains. Working with suppliers, they can build capacity into their whole systems.

Focused Factories—Plant-Within-Plant

exhibit 4.1

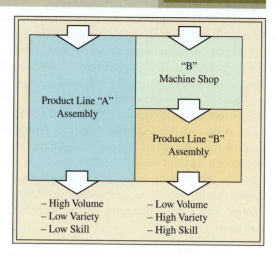

THIS COMPANY NEEDS TO PRODUCE TWO DIFFERENT PRODUCTS. PRODUCT "A" IS HIGH VOLUME AND STANDARD (THERE IS NO VARIATION IN HOW IT IS MADE). PRODUCT "B" IS LOW VOLUME AND NEEDS TO BE CUSTOMIZED TO EACH ORDER. THIS PLANT IS DIVIDED INTO THREE DISTINCT AREAS THAT OPERATE INDEPENDENTLY. THE PRODUCT LINE "A" AREA IS A HIGH-VOLUME ASSEMBLY LINE DESIGNED TO PRODUCE "A". "B" MACHINE SHOP IS AN AREA WHERE CUSTOM PARTS ARE MADE FOR PRODUCT "B". ASSEMBLY "B" IS WHERE PRODUCT "B" IS ASSEMBLED BASED ON EACH CUSTOMER ORDER. THIS FACTORY, WITH ITS PLANTS WITHIN A PLANT CAN OPERATE MORE EFFICIENTLY THAN IF BOTH PRODUCTS WERE MADE WITH A SINGLE COMMON PRODUCTION PROCESS.

Flexible Plants Perhaps the ultimate in plant flexibility is the *zero-changeover-time* plant. Using movable equipment, knockdown walls, and easily accessible and reroutable utilities, such a plant can quickly adapt to change. An analogy to a familiar service business captures the flavor well: a plant with equipment that is easy to install and easy to tear down and move—like the Ringling Bros.–Barnum and Bailey Circus in the old tent-circus days.

Flexible Processes Flexible processes are epitomized by flexible manufacturing systems on the one hand and simple, easily set up equipment on the other. Both of these technological approaches permit rapid low-cost switching from one product to another, enabling what are sometimes referred to as **economies of scope**. (By definition, economies of scope exist when multiple products can be combined and produced at one facility at a lower cost than they can be produced separately.)

Economies of scope
When multiple products can be produced at lower cost in combination than they can be separately.

Flexible Workers Flexible workers have multiple skills and the ability to switch easily from one kind of task to another. They require broader training than specialized workers and need managers and staff support to facilitate quick changes in their work assignments.

CAPACITY PLANNING

Considerations in Changing Capacity

Many issues must be considered when adding or decreasing capacity. Three important ones are maintaining system balance, frequency of capacity additions or reductions, and use of external capacity.

LO4–2 Exemplify how to plan capacity.

Maintaining System Balance In a perfectly balanced plant with three production stages, the output of stage 1 provides the exact input requirement for stage 2. Stage 2's output provides the exact input requirement for stage 3, and so on. In practice, however, achieving such a "perfect" design is usually both impossible and undesirable. One reason is that the best operating levels for each stage generally differ. For instance, department 1 may operate most efficiently over a range of 90 to 110 units per month, whereas department 2, the next stage in the process, is most efficient at 75 to 85 units per month, and department 3 works best over a range of 150 to 200 units per month. Another reason is that variability in product demand and the processes themselves may lead to imbalance.

There are various ways of dealing with imbalance. One is to add capacity to stages that are bottlenecks. This can be done by temporary measures, such as scheduling overtime, leasing equipment, or purchasing additional capacity through subcontracting. A second way is through the use of buffer inventories in front of the bottleneck stage to ensure that it always has something to work on. A third approach involves duplicating or increasing the facilities of one department on which another is dependent. All these approaches are increasingly being applied to supply chain design. This supply planning also helps reduce imbalances for supplier partners and customers.

Frequency of Capacity Additions   There are two types of costs to consider when adding capacity: the cost of upgrading too frequently and that of upgrading too infrequently. Upgrading capacity too frequently is expensive. Direct costs include removing and replacing old equipment and training employees on the new equipment. In addition, the new equipment must be purchased, often for considerably more than the selling price of the old. Finally, there is the opportunity cost of idling the plant or service site during the changeover period.

Conversely, upgrading capacity too infrequently is also expensive. Infrequent expansion means that capacity is purchased in larger chunks. Any excess capacity that is purchased must be carried as overhead until it is utilized. (Exhibit 4.2 illustrates frequent versus infrequent capacity expansion.)

exhibit 4.2   Frequent versus Infrequent Capacity Expansion

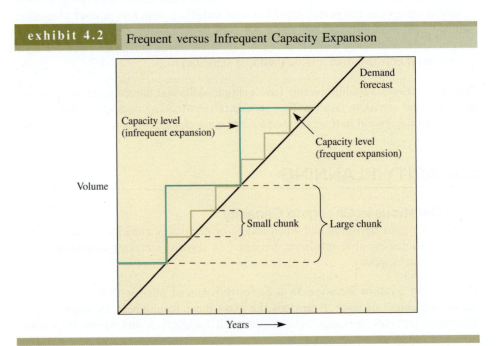

External Sources of Operations and Supply Capacity

In some cases, it may be cheaper not to add capacity at all, but rather to use some existing external source of capacity. Two common strategies used by organizations are outsourcing and sharing capacity. An example of outsourcing is Dell Computer using a Chinese company to assemble its notebook computers. An example of sharing capacity is two domestic airlines flying different routes with different seasonal demands exchanging aircraft (suitably repainted) when one's routes are heavily used and the other's are not. A new twist is airlines sharing routes—using the same flight number even though the airline company may change through the route. Outsourcing is covered in more depth in Chapter 13.

© Lou Linwei/Alamy

Decreasing Capacity

Although we normally think in terms of expansions, shedding capacity in response to decreased demand can create significant problems for a firm. Temporary strategies such as scheduling fewer hours or scheduling an extended shutdown period are often used. More permanent reductions in capacity would typically require the sale of equipment or possibly even the liquidation of entire facilities.

Determining Capacity Requirements

In determining capacity requirements, we must address the demands for individual product lines, individual plant capabilities, and allocation of production throughout the plant network. Typically, this is done according to the following steps:

1. Use forecasting techniques (see Chapter 3) to predict sales for individual products within each product line.
2. Calculate equipment and labor requirements to meet product line forecasts.
3. Project labor and equipment availabilities over the planning horizon.

Often the firm then decides on some **capacity cushion** that will be maintained between the projected requirements and the actual capacity. A capacity cushion is an amount of capacity in excess of expected demand. For example, if the expected annual demand on a facility is $10 million in products per year and the design capacity is $12 million per year, it has a 20 percent capacity cushion. A 20 percent capacity cushion equates to an 83 percent utilization rate (100%/120%).

When a firm's design capacity is less than the capacity required to meet its demand, it is said to have a negative capacity cushion. If, for example, a firm has a demand of $12 million in products per year but can produce only $10 million per year, it has a negative capacity cushion of 16.7 percent.

We now apply these three steps to an example.

Capacity cushion
Capacity in excess of expected demand.

Example 4.1: Determining Capacity Requirements

The Stewart Company produces two brands of salad dressings: Paul's and Newman's. Each is available in bottles and single-serving plastic bags. Management would like to determine equipment and labor requirements for their packing operation for the next five years. The demand for the two flavors and for each packaging option is given in this table. The company has three machines that

Excel:
Capacity

can package 150,000 bottles each year (each machine has two operators). It also has five machines that can package 250,000 plastic bags per year (each of these machines has three operators). Will the company have enough packaging capacity to meet future demand?

	YEAR				
	1	2	3	4	5
Paul's					
Bottles (000s)	60	100	150	200	250
Plastic bags (000s)	100	200	300	400	500
Newman's					
Bottles (000s)	75	85	95	97	98
Plastic bags (000s)	200	400	600	650	680

SOLUTION

Step 1. Use forecasting techniques to predict sales for individual products within each product line. The marketing department, which is now running a promotional campaign for Newman's dressing, provided the forecast demand values (in thousands) given in the table above for the next five years. The campaign is expected to continue for the next two years. The table of expected future demand is presented above.

Step 2. Calculate equipment and labor requirements to meet product line forecasts. Currently, three machines that can package up to 150,000 bottles each per year are available. Each machine requires two operators and can produce bottles of both Newman's and Paul's dressings. Six bottle machine operators are available. Also, five machines that can package up to 250,000 plastic bags each per year are available. Three operators are required for each machine, which can produce plastic bags of both Newman's and Paul's dressings. Currently, 15 plastic bag machine operators are available.

Total product line forecasts can be calculated from the preceding table by adding the yearly demand for bottles and plastic bags as follows:

	YEAR				
	1	2	3	4	5
Bottles (000s)	135	185	245	297	348
Plastic bags (000s)	300	600	900	1,050	1,180

We can now calculate equipment and labor requirements for the current year (year 1). Because the total available capacity for packaging bottles is 450,000/year (3 machines × 150,000 each), we will be using 135/450 = 0.3 of the available capacity for the current year, or 0.3 × 3 = 0.9 machine. Similarly, we will need 300/1,250 = 0.24 of the available capacity for plastic bags for the current year, or 0.24 × 5 = 1.2 machines. The total number of crew required to support our forecast demand for the first year will equal the crew required for the bottle machine plus the crew required for the plastic bag machine.

The labor requirement for year 1's bottle operation is

$$0.9 \text{ bottle machine} \times 2 \text{ operators} = 1.8 \text{ operators}$$
$$1.2 \text{ bag machines} \times 3 \text{ operators} = 3.6 \text{ operators}$$

Step 3. Project labor and equipment availabilities over the planning horizon. We repeat the preceding calculations for the remaining years:

	YEAR				
	1	2	3	4	5
Bottle Operation					
Percentage capacity utilized	30	41	54.4	66	77.3
Machine requirement	.9	1.23	1.63	1.98	2.32
Labor requirement	1.8	2.46	3.26	3.96	4.64
Plastic Bag Operation					
Percentage capacity utilized	24	48	72	84	94
Machine requirement	1.2	2.4	3.6	4.2	4.7
Labor requirement	3.6	7.2	10.8	12.6	14.1

A positive capacity cushion exists for all five years because the available capacity for both operations always exceeds the expected demand. The Stewart Company can now begin to develop the intermediate-range sales and operations plan for the two production lines. •

USING DECISION TREES TO EVALUATE CAPACITY ALTERNATIVES

A convenient way to lay out the steps of a capacity problem is through the use of decision trees. The tree format helps not only in understanding the problem but also in finding a solution. A *decision tree* is a schematic model of the sequence of steps in a problem and the conditions and consequences of each step. In recent years, a few commercial software packages have been developed to assist in the construction and analysis of decision trees. These packages make the process quick and easy.

LO4–3 Evaluate capacity alternatives using decision trees.

  Decision trees are composed of decision nodes with branches extending to and from them. Usually squares represent decision points and circles represent chance events. Branches from decision points show the choices available to the decision maker; branches from chance events show the probabilities for their occurrence.

  In solving decision tree problems, we work from the end of the tree backward to the start of the tree. As we work back, we calculate the expected values at each step. In calculating the expected value, the time value of money is important if the planning horizon is long.

  Once the calculations are made, we prune the tree by eliminating from each decision point all branches except the one with the highest payoff. This process continues to the first decision point, and the decision problem is thereby solved.

  We now demonstrate an application of capacity planning for Hackers Computer Store.

Example 4.2: Decision Trees

The owner of Hackers Computer Store is considering what to do with his business over the next five years. Sales growth over the past couple of years has been good, but sales could grow substantially if a major proposed electronics firm is built in his area. Hackers' owner sees three options. The first is to enlarge his current store, the second is to locate at a new site, and the third is to simply wait and do nothing. The process of expanding or moving would take little time, and, therefore, the store would not lose revenue. If nothing were done the first year and strong growth occurred, then the decision to expand could be reconsidered. Waiting longer than one year would allow competition to move in and would make expansion no longer feasible.

The assumptions and conditions are as follows:

1. Strong growth as a result of the increased population of computer fanatics from the new electronics firm has a 55 percent probability.
2. Strong growth with a new site would give annual returns of $195,000 per year. Weak growth with a new site would mean annual returns of $115,000.
3. Strong growth with an expansion would give annual returns of $190,000 per year. Weak growth with an expansion would mean annual returns of $100,000.
4. At the existing store with no changes, there would be returns of $170,000 per year if there is strong growth and $105,000 per year if growth is weak.
5. Expansion at the current site would cost $87,000.
6. The move to the new site would cost $210,000.
7. If growth is strong and the existing site is enlarged during the second year, the cost would still be $87,000.
8. Operating costs for all options are equal.

SOLUTION

We construct a decision tree to advise Hackers' owner on the best action. Exhibit 4.3 shows the decision tree for this problem. There are two decision points (shown with the square nodes) and three chance occurrences (round nodes).

The values of each alternative outcome shown on the right of the diagram in Exhibit 4.4 are calculated as follows:

**Excel:
Decision Trees**

ALTERNATIVE	REVENUE	COST	VALUE
Move to new location, strong growth	$195,000 × 5 yrs	$210,000	$765,000
Move to new location, weak growth	$115,000 × 5 yrs	$210,000	$365,000
Expand store, strong growth	$190,000 × 5 yrs	$87,000	$863,000
Expand store, weak growth	$100,000 × 5 yrs	$87,000	$413,000
Do nothing now, strong growth, expand next year	$170,000 × 1 yr + $190,000 × 4 yrs	$87,000	$843,000
Do nothing now, strong growth, do not expand next year	$170,000 × 5 yrs	$0	$850,000
Do nothing now, weak growth	$105,000 × 5 yrs	$0	$525,000

Working from the rightmost alternatives, which are associated with the decision of whether to expand, we see that the alternative of doing nothing has a higher value than the expansion alternative. We therefore eliminate the expansion in the second year alternatives. What this means is that if we do nothing in the first year and we experience strong growth, then in the second year it makes no sense to expand.

Now we can calculate the expected values associated with our current decision alternatives. We simply multiply the value of the alternative by its probability and sum the values. The expected value for the alternative of moving now is $585,000. The expansion alternative has an expected value of $660,500, and doing nothing now has an expected value of $703,750. Our analysis indicates that our best decision is to do nothing (both now and next year)!

Due to the five-year time horizon, it may be useful to consider the time value of the revenue and cost streams when solving this problem. If we assume a 16 percent interest rate, the first alternative outcome (move now, strong growth) has a discounted revenue valued at

Decision Tree for Hackers Computer Store Problem

exhibit 4.3

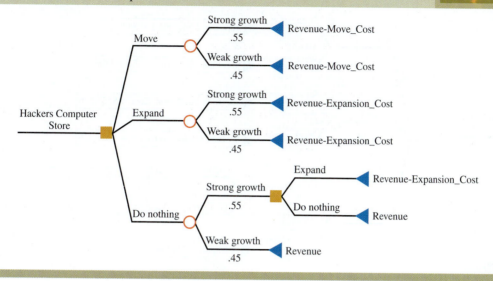

Decision Tree Analysis

exhibit 4.4

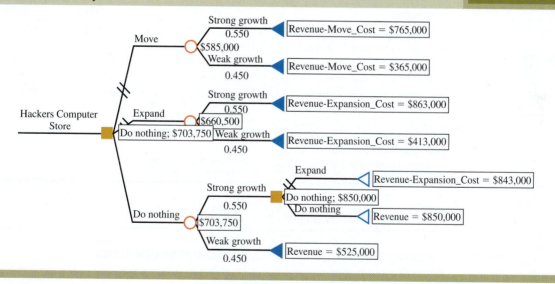

$428,487 (195,000 × 3.274293654) minus the $210,000 cost to move immediately. Exhibit 4.5 shows the analysis considering the discounted flows. Details of the calculations are given below. The present value table in Appendix C can be used to look up the discount factors. In order to make our calculations agree with those completed by Excel (in Excel, calculate the discount factor = $(1 + \text{interest rate})^{(-\text{years})}$), we have used discount factors that are calculated to 10 digits of precision. The only calculation that is a little tricky is the one for revenue when we do nothing now and expand at the beginning of next year. In this case, we have a revenue stream of $170,000 the first year, followed by four years at $190,000. The first part of the calculation (170,000 × .862068966)

exhibit 4.5 Decision Tree Analysis Using Net Present Value Calculations

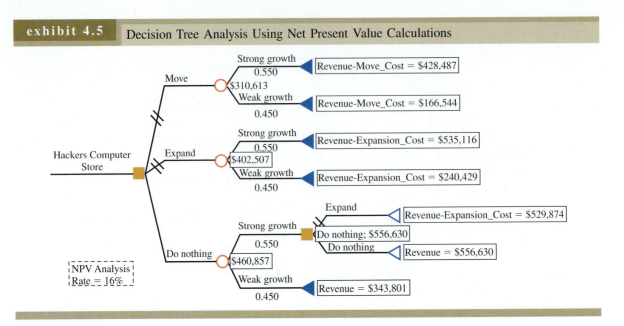

discounts the first-year revenue to the present. The next part (190,000 × 2.798180638) discounts the next four years to the start of year two. We then discount this four-year stream to the present value.

ALTERNATIVE	REVENUE	COST	VALUE
Move to new location, strong growth	$195,000 × 3.274293654	$210,000	$428,487
Move to new location, weak growth	$115,000 × 3.274293654	$210,000	$166,544
Expand store, strong growth	$190,000 × 3.274293654	$87,000	$535,116
Expand store, weak growth	$100,000 × 3.274293654	$87,000	$240,429
Do nothing now, strong growth, expand next year	$170,000 × .862068966 + $190,000 × 2.798180638 × .862068966	$87,000 × .862068966	$529,874
Do nothing now, strong growth, do not expand next year	$170,000 × 3.274293654	$0	$556,630
Do nothing now, weak growth	$105,000 × 3.274293654	$0	$343,801.

PLANNING SERVICE CAPACITY

LO4–4 Compare capacity planning in services to capacity planning in manufacturing.

Capacity Planning in Services versus Manufacturing

Although capacity planning in services is subject to many of the same issues as manufacturing capacity planning, and facility sizing can be done in much the same way, there are several important differences. Service capacity is more time- and location-dependent, it is subject to more volatile demand fluctuations, and utilization directly impacts service quality.

Time Unlike goods, services cannot be stored for later use. As such, in the services realm, managers must consider time as one of their supplies. The capacity must be available to produce a service when it is needed. For example, a customer cannot be given a seat that went unoccupied on a previous airline flight if the current flight is full. Nor can the customer purchase a seat on a particular day's flight and take it home to be used at some later date.

Location In face-to-face settings, the service capacity must be located near the customer. In manufacturing, production takes place, and then the goods are distributed to the customer. With services, however, the opposite is true. The capacity to deliver the service must first be distributed to the customer (either physically or through some communications medium, such as the telephone), then the service can be produced. A hotel room or rental car that is available in another city is not much use to the customer—it must be where the customer is when that customer needs it.

Volatility of Demand The volatility of demand on a service delivery system is much higher than that on a manufacturing production system for three reasons. First, as just mentioned, services cannot be stored. This means that inventory cannot smooth the demand as in manufacturing. The second reason is that the customers interact directly with the production system—and these customers often have different needs, will have different levels of experience with the process, and may require a different number of transactions. This contributes to greater variability in the processing time required for each customer and hence greater variability in the minimum capacity needed. The third reason for the greater volatility in service demand is that it is directly affected by consumer behavior. Influences on customer behavior ranging from the weather to a major event can directly affect the demand for different services. Go to any restaurant near your campus during spring break and it will probably be almost empty. This behavioral effect can be seen over even shorter time frames, such as the lunch-hour rush at a bank's drive-through window. Because of this volatility, service capacity is often planned in increments as small as 10 to 30 minutes, as opposed to the one-week increments more common in manufacturing.

Capacity Utilization and Service Quality

Planning capacity levels for services must consider the day-to-day relationship between service utilization and service quality. Exhibit 4.6 shows a service situation using waiting line terms (arrival rates and service rates). The term *arrival rate* refers to the average number of customers that come to a facility during a specific period of time. The *service rate* is the average number of customers that can be processed over the same period of time when the facility is operating at maximum capacity. The best operating point is near 70 percent of the maximum capacity. This is enough to keep servers busy but allows enough time to

Relationship between the Rate of Service Utilization (ρ) and Service Quality **exhibit 4.6**

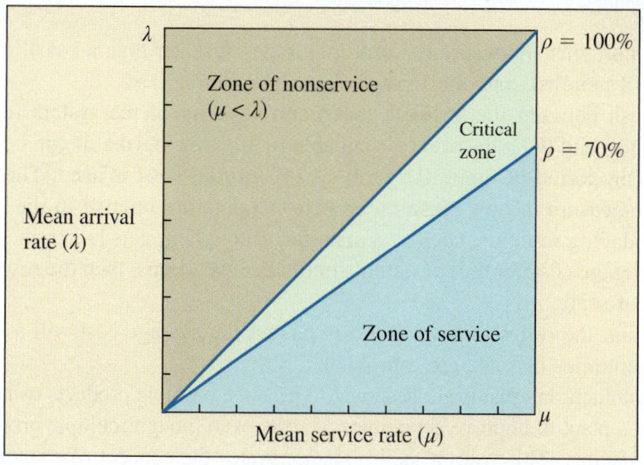

© Tom Dahlin/Getty Images

serve customers individually and keep enough capacity in reserve so as not to create too many managerial headaches. In the critical zone, customers are processed through the system, but service quality declines. Above the critical zone, where customers arrive at a rate faster than they can be served, the line builds up and it is likely that many customers may never be served. (Details related to how waiting lines operate relative to capacity are presented in Chapter 7 in the section "Waiting Line Models.")

The optimal utilization rate is very context-specific. Low rates are appropriate when both the degree of uncertainty and the stakes are high. For example, hospital emergency rooms and fire departments should aim for low utilization because of the high level of uncertainty and the life-or-death nature of their activities. Relatively predictable services such as commuter trains or service facilities without customer contact (for example, postal sorting operations) can plan to operate much nearer to 100 percent utilization. Interestingly, there is a third group for which high utilization is desirable. All sports teams like sellouts, not only because of the virtually 100 percent contribution margin of each customer, but because a full house creates an atmosphere that pleases customers, motivates the home team to perform better, and boosts future ticket sales. Stage performances and bars share this phenomenon. On the other hand, many airline passengers feel that a flight is too crowded when the seat next to theirs is occupied. Airlines capitalize on this response to sell more business-class seats.

CONCEPT CONNECTIONS

LO4–1 **Explain what capacity management is and why it is strategically important.**

- An operations and supply chain management view of capacity emphasizes the time dimension of capacity.
- Three time horizons are generally used: long range (greater than a year), intermediate range (next 6 to 18 months), and short range (less than a month).
- To distinguish between the absolute maximum capacity of the system (the highest output rate attainable) and the rate that is sustainable by the system (that it can be run at efficiently and for a long period of time), the term *best operating level* is used. The utilization of the system is a measure of how close the system is operating relative to the best level.
- When a producing resource, such as a manufacturing plant, gets larger and volume increases while the average cost per unit of output simultaneously drops, then the resource is exhibiting economies of scale.
- At some point, the resource may be too large and the average cost will start to rise. This is when diseconomies of scale are a problem.
- Focused manufacturing plants are designed to produce multiple products using a concept called plant within a plant to improve economies of scale even though multiple products are produced in the same facility. This type of facility demonstrates the concept of economies of scope.
- Having capacity flexibility is often important to meeting the needs of a firm's customers.

Strategic capacity planning   Determining the overall capacity level of capital-intensive resources that best supports the company's long-range competitive strategy.

Capacity   The amount of output that a system is capable of achieving over a specific period of time.

Best operating level   The level of capacity for which the process was designed and the volume of output at which average unit cost is minimized.

Capacity utilization rate   Measures how close a firm's current output is to its best operating level.

Economies of scale   The notion that as a plant gets larger and volume increases, the average cost per unit drops. At some point, the plant gets too large and costs per unit begin to increase.

Focused factory   A facility with a fairly limited set of production objectives. Typically, the focus would relate to a specific product or product group.

Plant within a plant (PWP)   A concept that can be used to operationalize a focused factory by designating a specific area in a larger plant.

Economies of scope   When multiple products can be produced at a lower cost in combination than they can be separately.

$$\text{Capacity utilization rate} = \frac{\text{Capacity used}}{\text{Best operating level}} \qquad [4.1]$$

LO4–2   **Exemplify how to plan capacity.**

- From a strategic, long-term view, capacity additions or reductions come in chunks (fixed amounts). For example, an additional machine of a certain type is added to the existing pool of machines. Issues involve how frequently and how much capacity is added or removed over time.

Capacity cushion   Capacity in excess of expected demand.

LO4–3   **Evaluate capacity alternatives using decision trees.**

- A useful technique for analyzing capacity problems is the decision tree.
- With this format, the sequences of decisions are organized like branches in a tree.
- The potential consequences of the decisions are enumerated and evaluated based on their probability of occurrence and corresponding expected value.

LO4–4   **Compare capacity planning in services to capacity planning in manufacturing.**

- Often, services require that capacity be available immediately and that it be near where the customer resides. For example, a bank needs automated teller machines (ATMs) close to where customers want immediate cash, and enough of them so customers will not have to wait in long lines.
- Also, firms that offer services often need to deal with dramatic changes in customer demand over time (for example, the lunch-hour rush at a bank's drive-through window).

SOLVED PROBLEM

LO4–3

E-Education is a new start-up that develops and markets MBA courses offered over the Internet. The company is currently located in Chicago and employs 150 people. Due to strong growth, the company needs additional office space. The company has the option of leasing additional space at its current location in Chicago for the next two years, but after that will need to move to a new building. Another option the company is considering is moving the entire operation to a small Midwest town immediately. A third option is for the company to lease a new building in Chicago immediately. If the company chooses the first option and leases new space at its current location, it can, at the end of two years, either lease a new building in Chicago or move to the small Midwest town.

The following are some additional facts about the alternatives and current situation:

1. The company has a 75 percent chance of surviving the next two years.
2. Leasing the new space for two years at the current location in Chicago would cost $750,000 per year.
3. Moving the entire operation to a Midwest town would cost $1 million. Leasing space would run only $500,000 per year.
4. Moving to a new building in Chicago would cost $200,000, and leasing the new building's space would cost $650,000 per year.
5. The company can cancel the lease at any time.
6. The company will build its own building in five years, if it survives.
7. Assume all other costs and revenues are the same no matter where the company is located.

What should E-Education do?

Solution

Step 1: Construct a decision tree that considers all of E-Education's alternatives. The following shows the tree that has decision points (with the square nodes) followed by chance occurrences (round nodes). In the case of the first decision point, if the company survives, two additional decision points need consideration.

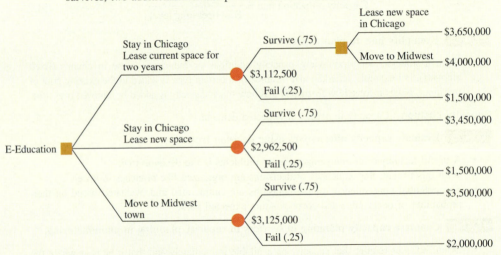

Step 2: Calculate the values of each alternative as follows:

ALTERNATIVE	CALCULATION	VALUE
Stay in Chicago, lease current space for two years, survive, lease new building in Chicago	(750,000) × 2 + 200,000 + (650,000) × 3 =	$3,650,000
Stay in Chicago, lease current space for two years, survive, move to Midwest	(750,000) × 2 + 1,000,000 + (500,000) × 3 =	$4,000,000
Stay in Chicago, lease current space for two years, fail	(750,000) × 2 =	$1,500,000
Stay in Chicago, lease new building in Chicago, survive	200,000 + (650,000) × 5 =	$3,450,000
Stay in Chicago, lease new building in Chicago, fail	200,000 + (650,000) × 2 =	$1,500,000
Move to Midwest, survive	1,000,000 + (500,000) × 5 =	$3,500,000
Move to Midwest, fail	1,000,000 + (500,000) × 2 =	$2,000,000

Working from our rightmost alternatives, the first two alternatives end in decision nodes. If we fail after the first two years, represented by the third alternative, the cost is only $1,500,000. The expected value of the first option of staying in Chicago and leasing space for the first two years is .75 × 3,650,000 + .25 × 1,500,000 = $3,112,500.

The second option, staying in Chicago and leasing a new building now, has an expected value of .75 × 3,450,000 + .25 × 1,500,000 = $2,962,500.

Finally, the third option of moving to the Midwest immediately has an expected value of .75 × 3,500,000 + .25 × 2,000,000 = $3,125,000.

From this, it looks like the best alternative is to stay in Chicago and lease a new building immediately.

DISCUSSION QUESTIONS

LO4–1

1. What capacity problems are encountered when a new drug is introduced to the market?

2. List some practical limits to economies of scale. In other words, when should a plant stop growing?

3. What are some capacity balance problems faced by the following organizations or facilities?
   a. An airline terminal
   b. A university computing lab
   c. A clothing manufacturer

4. At first glance, the concepts of the focused factory and capacity flexibility may seem to contradict each other. Do they really?

LO4–2

5. Management may choose to build up capacity in anticipation of demand or in response to developing demand. Cite the advantages and disadvantages of both approaches.

6. What is capacity balance? Why is it hard to achieve? What methods are used to deal with capacity imbalances?

7. What are some reasons for a plant to maintain a capacity cushion? How about a negative capacity cushion?

LO4–3

8. Will the use of decision tree analysis guarantee the best decision for a firm? Why or why not? If not, why bother using it?

9. Consider the example in Exhibit 4.5. Can you think of anything else you might do with that example that would be helpful to the ultimate decision maker?

LO4–4

10. What are some major capacity considerations in a hospital? How do they differ from those of a factory?

11. Refer to Exhibit 4.6. Why is it that the critical zone begins at a utilization rate of about 70 percent in a typical service operation? Draw upon your own experiences as either a customer or a server in common service establishments.

OBJECTIVE QUESTIONS

LO4–1

1. A manufacturing shop is designed to operate most efficiently at an output of 550 units per day. In the past month, the plant produced 490 units. What was its capacity utilization rate last month?

2. A company has a factory that is designed so that it is *most efficient* (average unit cost is minimized) when producing 15,000 units of output each month. However, it has an absolute maximum output capability of 17,250 units per month, and can produce as little as 7,000 units per month without corporate headquarters shifting production to another plant. If the factory produces 10,925 units in October, what is the *capacity utilization rate* in October for this factory?

3. Hoosier Manufacturing operates a production shop that is designed to have the lowest unit production cost at an output rate of 100 units per hour. In the month of July, the company operated the production line for a total of 175 hours and produced 16,900 units of output. What was its capacity utilization rate for the month?

LO4–2

4. AlwaysRain Irrigation, Inc. would like to determine capacity requirements for the next four years. Currently, two production lines are in place for making bronze and plastic sprinklers. Three types of sprinklers are available in both bronze and plastic: 90-degree nozzle sprinklers, 180-degree nozzle sprinklers, and 360-degree nozzle sprinklers. Management has forecast demand for the next four years as follows:

	YEARLY DEMAND			
	1 (IN 000s)	2 (IN 000s)	3 (IN 000s)	4 (IN 000s)
Plastic 90	32	44	55	56
Plastic 180	15	16	17	18
Plastic 360	50	55	64	67
Bronze 90	7	8	9	10
Bronze 180	3	4	5	6
Bronze 360	11	12	15	18

Both production lines can produce all the different types of nozzles. The bronze machines needed for the bronze sprinklers require two operators and can produce up to 12,000 sprinklers. The plastic injection molding machine needed for the plastic sprinklers requires four operators and can produce up to 200,000 sprinklers. Three bronze machines and only one injection molding machine are available. What are the capacity requirements for the next four years? (Assume that there is no learning.)

5. Suppose that AlwaysRain Irrigation's marketing department will undertake an intense ad campaign for the bronze sprinklers, which are more expensive but also more durable than the plastic ones. Forecast demand for the next four years is

	YEARLY DEMAND			
	1 (IN 000s)	2 (IN 000s)	3 (IN 000s)	4 (IN 000s)
Plastic 90	32	44	55	56
Plastic 180	15	16	17	18
Plastic 360	50	55	64	67
Bronze 90	11	15	18	23
Bronze 180	6	5	6	9
Bronze 360	15	16	17	20

What are the capacity implications of the marketing campaign (assume no learning)?

6. In anticipation of the ad campaign, AlwaysRain bought an additional bronze machine. Will this be enough to ensure that adequate capacity is available?

7. Suppose that operators have enough training to operate both the bronze machines and the injection molding machine for the plastic sprinklers. Currently, AlwaysRain has 10 such employees. In anticipation of the ad campaign described in problem 5, management approved the purchase of two additional bronze machines. What are the labor requirement implications?

LO4–3

8. Expando, Inc. is considering the possibility of building an additional factory that would produce a new addition to its product line. The company is currently considering two options. The first is a small facility that it could build at a cost of $6 million. If demand for new products is low, the company expects to receive $10 million in discounted revenues (present value of future revenues) with the small facility. On the other hand, if demand is high, it expects $12 million in discounted revenues using the small facility. The second option is to build a large factory at a cost of $9 million. Were demand to be low, the company would expect $10 million in discounted revenues with the large plant. If demand is high, the company estimates that the discounted revenues would be $14 million. In either case, the probability of demand being high is .40, and the probability of it being low is .60. Not constructing a new factory would result in no additional revenue being generated because the current factories cannot produce these new products. Construct a decision tree to help Expando make the best decision.

9. A builder has located a piece of property that she would like to buy and eventually build on. The land is currently zoned for four homes per acre, but she is planning to request new zoning. What she builds depends on approval of zoning requests and your analysis of this problem to advise her. With her input and your help, the decision process has been reduced to the following costs, alternatives, and probabilities:

Cost of land: $2 million.
Probability of rezoning: .60.
If the land is rezoned, there will be additional costs for new roads, lighting, and so on, of $1 million.

If the land is rezoned, the contractor must decide whether to build a shopping center or 1,500 apartments that the tentative plan shows would be possible. If she builds a shopping center, there is a 70 percent chance that she can sell the shopping center to a large department store chain for $4 million over her construction cost, which excludes the land; and there is a 30 percent chance that she can sell it to an insurance company for $5 million over her construction cost (also excluding the land). If, instead of the shopping center, she decides to build the 1,500 apartments, she places probabilities on the profits as follows: There is a 60 percent chance that she can sell the apartments to a real estate investment corporation for $3,000 each over her construction cost; there is a 40 percent chance that she can get only $2,000 each over her construction cost. (Both exclude the land cost.)

If the land is not rezoned, she will comply with the existing zoning restrictions and simply build 600 homes, on which she expects to make $4,000 over the construction cost on each one (excluding the cost of land).

Draw a decision tree of the problem and determine the best solution and the expected net profit.

LO4–4 10. Owners of a local restaurant are concerned about their ability to provide quality service as they continue to grow and attract more customers. They have collected data from Friday and Saturday nights, their busiest times of the week. During these time periods, about 75 customers arrive per hour for service. Given the number of tables and chairs, and the typical time it takes to serve a customer, the owners estimate they can serve, on average, about 100 customers per hour. During these nights, are they in the *zone of service*, the *critical zone*, or the *zone of nonservice*?

11. Owners of the restaurant in the prior problem anticipate that in one year their demand will double as long as they can provide good service to their customers. How much will they have to increase their service capacity to stay out of the critical zone?

CASE: SHOULDICE HOSPITAL—A CUT ABOVE

"Shouldice Hospital, the house that hernias built, is a converted country estate which gives the hospital 'a country club' appeal."
A quote from *American Medical News*

Shouldice Hospital in Canada is widely known for one thing—hernia repair! In fact, that is the only operation it performs, and it performs a great many of them. Over the past two decades this small 90-bed hospital has averaged 7,000 operations annually. Last year, it had a record year and performed nearly 7,500 operations. Patients' ties to Shouldice do not end when they leave the hospital. Every year, the gala Hernia Reunion dinner (with complimentary hernia inspection) draws in over 1,000 former patients, some of whom have been attending the event for over 30 years.

A number of notable features in Shouldice's service delivery system contribute to its success: (1) Shouldice accepts only patients with uncomplicated external hernias, and uses a superior technique developed for this type of hernia by Dr. Shouldice during World War II. (2) Patients are subject to early ambulation, which promotes healing. (Patients literally walk off the operating table and engage in light exercise throughout their stay, which lasts only three days.) (3) Its country club atmosphere, gregarious nursing staff, and built-in socializing make a surprisingly pleasant experience out of an inherently unpleasant medical problem. Regular times are set aside for tea, cookies, and socializing. All patients are paired up with a roommate with a similar background and interests.

The Production System

The medical facilities at Shouldice consist of five operating rooms, a patient recovery room, a laboratory, and six examination rooms. Shouldice performs, on average, 150 operations per week, with patients generally staying at the hospital for three days. Although operations are performed only five days a week, the remainder of the hospital is in operation continuously to attend to recovering patients.

An operation at Shouldice Hospital is performed by one of the 12 full-time surgeons assisted by one of seven part-time assistant surgeons. Surgeons generally take about one hour to prepare for and perform each hernia operation, and they operate on four patients per day. The surgeons' day ends at 4 P.M., although they can expect to be on call every 14th night and every 10th weekend.

The Shouldice Experience

Each patient undergoes a screening exam prior to setting a date for his or her operation. Patients in the Toronto area are encouraged to walk in for the diagnosis. Examinations are done between 9 A.M. and 3:30 P.M. Monday through Friday, and between 10 A.M. and 2 P.M. on Saturday. Out-of-town patients are mailed a medical information questionnaire (also available over the Internet), which is used for the diagnosis. A small percentage of the patients who are overweight or otherwise represent an undue medical risk are refused treatment. The remaining patients receive confirmation cards with the scheduled dates for their operations. A patient's folder is transferred to the reception desk once an arrival date is confirmed.

Patients arrive at the clinic between 1 and 3 P.M. the day before their surgery. After a short wait, they receive a brief preoperative examination. They are then sent to an admissions clerk to complete any necessary paperwork. Patients are next directed to one of the two nurses' stations for blood and urine tests and then are shown to their rooms. They spend the remaining time before orientation getting settled and acquainting themselves with their roommates.

Orientation begins at 5 P.M., followed by dinner in the common dining room. Later in the evening, at 9 P.M., patients gather in the lounge area for tea and cookies. Here, new patients can talk with patients who have already had their surgery. Bedtime is between 9:30 and 10 P.M.

On the day of the operation, patients with early operations are awakened at 5:30 A.M. for preoperative sedation. The first operations begin at 7:30 A.M. Shortly before an operation starts, the patient is administered a local anesthetic, leaving him or her alert and fully aware of the proceedings. At the conclusion of the operation, the patient is invited to walk from the operating table to a nearby wheelchair, which is waiting to return the patient to his or her room. After a brief period of rest, the patient is encouraged to get up and start exercising. By 9 P.M. that day, he or she is in the lounge having cookies and tea and talking with new, incoming patients.

The skin clips holding the incision together are loosened, and some even removed, the next day. The remainder are removed the following morning just before the patient is discharged.

When Shouldice Hospital started, the average hospital stay for hernia surgery was three weeks. Today, many institutions push "same day surgery" for a variety of reasons. Shouldice Hospital firmly believes that this is not in the best interests of patients and is committed to its three-day process. Shouldice's postoperative rehabilitation program is designed to enable the patient to resume normal activities with minimal interruption and discomfort. Shouldice patients frequently return to work in a few days; the average total time off is eight days.

"It is interesting to note that approximately 1 out of every 100 Shouldice patients is a medical doctor."

Future Plans

The management of Shouldice is thinking of expanding the hospital's capacity to serve considerable unsatisfied demand. To this effect, the vice president is seriously considering two options. The first involves adding one more day of operations (Saturday) to the existing five-day schedule, which would increase capacity by 20 percent. The second option is to add another floor of rooms to the hospital, increasing the number of beds by 50 percent. This would require more aggressive scheduling of the operating rooms.

The administrator of the hospital, however, is concerned about maintaining control over the quality of the service delivered. He thinks the facility is already getting very good utilization. The doctors and the staff are happy with their jobs, and the patients are satisfied with the service. According to him, further expansion of capacity might make it hard to maintain the same kind of working relationships and attitudes.

Questions

Exhibit 4.7 is a room-occupancy table for the existing system. Each row in the table follows the patients who checked in on a given day. The columns indicate the number of patients in the hospital on a given day. For example, the first row of the table shows that 30 people checked in on Monday and were in the hospital for Monday, Tuesday, and Wednesday. By summing the columns of the table for Wednesday, we see that there are 90 patients staying in the hospital that day.

1. How well is the hospital currently utilizing its beds?
2. Develop a similar table to show the effects of adding operations on Saturday. (Assume that 30 operations would still be performed each day.) How would this affect the utilization of the bed capacity? Is this capacity sufficient for the additional patients?
3. Now look at the effect of increasing the number of beds by 50 percent. How many operations could the hospital perform per day before running out of bed capacity?

Operations with 90 Beds (30 patients per day)

exhibit 4.7

CHECK-IN DAY	BEDS REQUIRED						
	MONDAY	TUESDAY	WEDNESDAY	THURSDAY	FRIDAY	SATURDAY	SUNDAY
Monday	30	30	30				
Tuesday		30	30	30			
Wednesday			30	30	30		
Thursday				30	30	30	
Friday							
Saturday							
Sunday	30	30					30
Total	60	90	90	90	60	30	30

Excel:
Shouldice
Hospital

(Assume operations are performed five days per week, with the same number performed on each day.) How well would the new resources be utilized relative to the current operation? Could the hospital really perform this many operations? Why? (*Hint:* Look at the capacity of the 12 surgeons and the five operating rooms.)

4. Although financial data are sketchy, an estimate from a construction company indicates that adding bed capacity would cost about $100,000 per bed. In addition, the rate charged for the hernia surgery varies between about $900 and $2,000 (U.S. dollars), with an average rate of $1,300 per operation. The surgeons are paid a flat $600 per operation. Due to all the uncertainties in government health care legislation, Shouldice would like to justify any expansion within a five-year time period.

PRACTICE EXAM

1. The level of capacity for which a process was designed and at which it operates at minimum cost.
2. A facility has a maximum capacity of 4,000 units per day using overtime and skipping the daily maintenance routine. At 3,500 units per day, the facility operates at a level where average cost per unit is minimized. Currently, the process is scheduled to operate at a level of 3,000 units per day. What is the capacity utilization rate?
3. The concept that relates to gaining efficiency through the full utilization of dedicated resources, such as people and equipment.
4. A facility that limits its production to a single product or a set of very similar products.
5. When multiple (usually similar) products can be produced in a facility less expensively than a single product.
6. The ability to serve more customers than expected.
7. In considering a capacity expansion we have two alternatives. The first alternative is expected to cost $1,000,000 and has an expected profit of $500,000 over the next three years. The second alternative has an expected cost of $800,000 and an expected profit of $450,000 over the next three years. Which alternative should we select, and what is the expected value of the expansion? Assume a 10 percent interest rate.
8. In a service process such as the checkout counter in a discount store, what is a good target percent for capacity utilization?

CHAPTER 4A:

LEARNING CURVES

Learning Objectives

LO4A–1 Understand what a learning curve is and where learning curves are applicable.
LO4A–2 Plot and analyze learning curves.

THE LEARNING CURVE

LO4A–1
Understand what a learning curve is and where learning curves are applicable.

Learning curve
A line displaying the relationship between the cumulative number of units produced and the time or cost to produce the unit.

A well-known concept is the learning curve. A **learning curve** is a line displaying the relationship between unit production, time and cost, and the cumulative number of units produced. As plants produce more, they gain experience in the best production methods, which reduce their costs of production in a predictable manner. Every time a plant's cumulative production doubles, its production costs decline by a specific percentage depending on the nature of the business. Exhibit 4A.1 demonstrates the effect of a learning curve on the production costs of hamburgers.

The learning curve percentage varies across industries. To apply this concept to the restaurant industry, consider a hypothetical fast-food chain that has produced 5 million hamburgers. Given a current variable cost of $0.55 per burger, what will the cost per burger be when cumulative production reaches 10 million burgers? If the firm has a 90 percent learning curve, costs will fall to 90 percent of $0.55, or $0.495, when accumulated production reaches 10 million. At 1 billion hamburgers, the variable cost drops to less than $0.25.

---

exhibit 4A.1   The Learning Curve

a. Costs per unit produced fall by a specific percentage each time cumulative production doubles. This relationship can be expressed through a linear scale, as shown in this graph of a 90 percent learning curve:

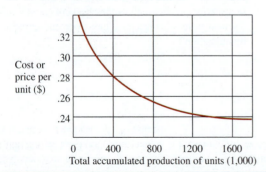

b. It can also be expressed through logarithms:

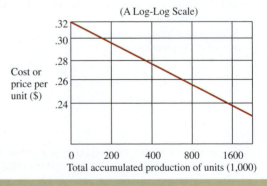

Learning Curves Plotted as Times and Numbers of Units

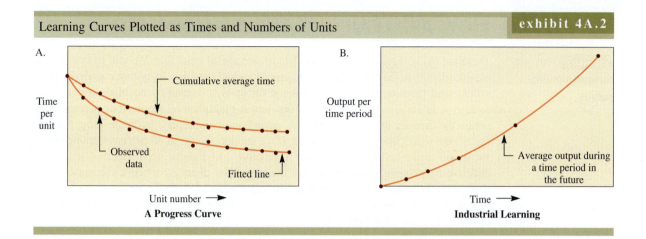

A Progress Curve

Industrial Learning

Note that sales volume becomes an important issue in achieving cost savings. If firm A serves twice as many hamburgers daily as firm B, it will accumulate "experience" twice as fast.

Learning curve theory is based on three assumptions:

1. The amount of time required to complete a given task or unit of a product will be less each time the task is undertaken.
2. The unit time will decrease at a decreasing rate.
3. The reduction in time will follow a predictable pattern.

Each of these assumptions was found to hold true in the airplane industry, where learning curves were first applied. In this application, it was observed that, as output doubled, there was a 20 percent reduction in direct production worker-hours per unit between doubled units. Thus, if it took 100,000 hours for Plane 1, it would take 80,000 hours for Plane 2, 64,000 hours for Plane 4, and so forth. Because the 20 percent reduction meant that, say, Unit 4 took only 80 percent of the production time required for Unit 2, the line connecting the coordinates of output and time was referred to as an "80 percent learning curve." (By convention, the percentage learning rate is used to denote any given exponential learning curve.)

A learning curve may be developed from an arithmetic tabulation, by logarithms, or by some other curve-fitting method, depending on the amount and form of the available data.

There are two ways to think about the improved performance that comes with learning curves: time per unit (as in Exhibit 4A.2A) or units of output per time period (as in 4A.2B). *Time per unit* shows the decrease in time required for each successive unit. *Cumulative average time* shows the cumulative average performance times as the total number of units increases. Time per unit and cumulative average times are also called *progress curves,* or *product learning,* and are useful for complex products or products with a longer cycle time. *Units of output per time period* is also called *industry learning* and is generally applied to high-volume production (short cycle time).

Note in Exhibit 4A.2A that the cumulative average curve does not decrease as fast as the time per unit because the time is being averaged. For example, if the times for Units 1, 2, 3, and 4 were 100, 80, 70, and 64, they would be plotted that way on the time per unit graph, but would be plotted as 100, 90, 83.3, and 78.5 on the cumulative average time graph.

HOW ARE LEARNING CURVES MODELED?

LO4A–2 Plot and analyze learning curves.

There are many ways to analyze past data to fit a useful trend line. We will use the simple exponential curve first as an arithmetic procedure and then as a logarithmic analysis. In an arithmetical tabulation approach, a column for units is created by doubling, row by row, as 1, 2, 4, 8, 16. . . . The time for the first unit is multiplied by the learning percentage to obtain the time for the second unit. The second unit is multiplied by the learning percentage for the fourth unit, and so on. Thus, if we are developing an 80 percent learning curve, we would arrive at the figures listed in column 2 of Exhibit 4A.3. Because it is often desirable for planning purposes to know the cumulative direct labor hours, column 4, which lists this information, is also provided. The calculation of these figures is straightforward; for example, for Unit 4, cumulative average direct labor hours would be found by dividing cumulative direct labor hours by 4, yielding the figure given in column 4.

Exhibit 4A.4A shows three curves with different learning rates: 90 percent, 80 percent, and 70 percent. Note that if the cost of the first unit was $100, the 30th unit would cost $59.63 at the 90 percent rate and $17.37 at the 70 percent rate. Differences in learning rates can have dramatic effects.

In practice, learning curves are plotted using a graph with logarithmic scales. The unit curves become linear throughout their entire range, and the cumulative curve becomes linear after the first few units. The property of linearity is desirable because it facilitates extrapolation and permits a more accurate reading of the cumulative curve. This type of scale is an option in Microsoft Excel. Simply generate a regular scatter plot in your spreadsheet and then select each axis and format the axis with the logarithmic option. Exhibit 4A.4B shows the 80 percent unit cost curve and average cost curve on a logarithmic scale. Note that the cumulative average cost is essentially linear after the eighth unit.

Although the arithmetic tabulation approach is useful, direct logarithmic analysis of learning curve problems is generally more efficient because it does not require a complete enumeration of successive time–output combinations. Moreover, where such data are not available, an analytical model that uses logarithms may be the most convenient way of obtaining output estimates.

exhibit 4A.3	Unit, Cumulative, and Cumulative Average Direct Labor Worker-Hours Required for an 80 Percent Learning Curve

Excel:
Learning Curves

(1) UNIT NUMBER	(2) UNIT DIRECT LABOR HOURS	(3) CUMULATIVE DIRECT LABOR HOURS	(4) CUMULATIVE AVERAGE DIRECT LABOR HOURS
1	100,000	100,000	100,000
2	80,000	180,000	90,000
4	64,000	314,210	78,553
8	51,200	534,591	66,824
16	40,960	892,014	55,751
32	32,768	1,467,862	45,871
64	26,214	2,392,447	37,382
128	20,972	3,874,384	30,269
256	16,777	6,247,572	24,405

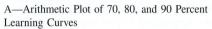

Learning Curve Plots

A—Arithmetic Plot of 70, 80, and 90 Percent
Learning Curves

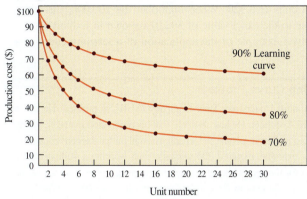

B—Logarithmic Plot of an 80 Percent
Learning Curve

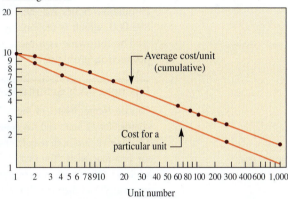

Logarithmic Analysis The normal form of the learning curve equation is

$$Y_x = Kx^n \qquad\qquad [4A.1]$$

where

- x = Unit number
- Y_x = Number of direct labor hours required to produce the xth unit
- K = Number of direct labor hours required to produce the first unit
- n = log b/log 2 where b = Learning percentage

We can solve this mathematically or by using a table, as shown in the next section. Mathematically, to find the labor-hour requirement for the eighth unit in our example (Exhibit 4A.3), we would substitute as follows:

$$Y_8 = (100{,}000)(8)^n$$

Using logarithms:

$$Y_8 = 100{,}000(8)^{\log 0.8/\log 2}$$

$$= 100{,}000(8)^{-0.322} = \frac{100{,}000}{(8)^{0.322}}$$

$$= \frac{100{,}000}{1.9534} = 51{,}193$$

Therefore, it would take 51,193 hours to make the eighth unit. Your answers may vary slightly due to rounding. (See the spreadsheet "Learning Curves.")

Excel:
Learning
Curves

Learning Curve Tables When the learning percentage is known, the tables in Exhibit 4A.5 can be easily used to calculate estimated labor hours for a specific unit or for cumulative groups of units. We need only multiply the initial unit labor hour figure by the appropriate tabled value.

Excel:
Learning Curves

To illustrate, suppose we want to double-check the figures in Exhibit 4A.3 for unit and cumulative labor hours for Unit 16. From Exhibit 4A.5, the unit improvement factor for Unit 16 at 80 percent is .4096. This multiplied by 100,000 (the hours for Unit 1) gives 40,960, the same as in Exhibit 4A.3. From Exhibit 4A.6, the cumulative improvement factor for cumulative hours for the first 16 units is 8.920. When multiplied by 100,000, this gives 892,000, which is reasonably close to the exact value of 892,014 shown in Exhibit 4A.3.

The following is a more involved example of the application of a learning curve to a production problem.

Example 4A.1: Sample Learning Curve Problem

Captain Nemo, owner of the Suboptimum Underwater Boat Company (SUB), is puzzled. He has a contract for 11 boats and has completed 4 of them. He has observed that his production manager, young Mr. Overick, has been reassigning more and more people to torpedo assembly after the construction of the first four boats. The first boat, for example, required 225 workers, each working a 40-hour week, while 45 fewer workers were required for the second boat. Overick has told them that "this is just the beginning" and that he will complete the last boat in the current contract with only 100 workers!

Overick is banking on the learning curve, but has he gone overboard?

SOLUTION

Because the second boat required 180 workers, a simple exponential curve shows that the learning percentage is 80 percent (180 ÷ 225). To find out how many workers are required for the 11th boat, we look up unit 11 for an 80 percent improvement ratio in Exhibit 4A.5 and multiply this value by the number required for the first sub. By interpolating between unit 10 and unit 12, we find the improvement ratio is equal to .4629 (note, the "Learning Curves" spreadsheet can be used to find the improvement ratio or it can be calculated directly from equation 4A.1). This yields 104.15 workers (.4629 interpolated from table × 225). Thus, Overick's estimate missed the boat by four people. •

Example 4A.2: Estimating Cost Using Learning Curves

SUB has produced the first unit of a new line of minisubs at a cost of 500,000. Exactly $200,000 of this is for materials and $300,000 for labor. SUB has agreed to accept a 10 percent profit, based on cost, and it is willing to contract on the basis of a 70 percent learning curve. What will be the contract price for three minisubs?

SOLUTION

Cost of first sub		$ 500,000
Cost of second sub		
Materials	$200,000	
Labor: $300,000 × .70	210,000	410,000
Cost of third sub		
Materials	200,000	
Labor: $300,000 × .5682	170,460	370,460
Total cost		1,280,460
Markup: $1,280,460 × .10		128,046
Selling price		$1,408,506

If the operation is interrupted, then some relearning must occur. How far to go back up the learning curve can be estimated in some cases. •

Learning Curve Tables

Learning Curves: Table of Unit Values							exhibit 4A.5	
	UNIT IMPROVEMENT FACTOR							
UNIT	60%	65%	70%	75%	80%	85%	90%	95%
1	1.0000	1.0000	1.0000	1.0000	1.0000	1.0000	1.0000	1.0000
2	.6000	.6500	.7000	.7500	.8000	.8500	.9000	.9500
3	.4450	.5052	.5682	.6338	.7021	.7729	.8462	.9219
4	.3600	.4225	.4900	.5625	.6400	.7225	.8100	.9025
5	.3054	.3678	.4368	.5127	.5956	.6857	.7830	.8877
6	.2670	.3284	.3977	.4754	.5617	.6570	.7616	.8758
7	.2383	.2984	.3674	.4459	.5345	.6337	.7439	.8659
8	.2160	.2746	.3430	.4219	.5120	.6141	.7290	.8574
9	.1980	.2552	.3228	.4017	.4930	.5974	.7161	.8499
10	.1832	.2391	.3058	.3846	.4765	.5828	.7047	.8433
12	.1602	.2135	.2784	.3565	.4493	.5584	.6854	.8320
14	.1430	.1940	.2572	.3344	.4276	.5386	.6696	.8226
16	.1290	.1785	.2401	.3164	.4096	.5220	.6561	.8145
18	.1188	.1659	.2260	.3013	.3944	.5078	.6445	.8074
20	.1099	.1554	.2141	.2884	.3812	.4954	.6342	.8012
22	.1025	.1465	.2038	.2772	.3697	.4844	.6251	.7955
24	.0961	.1387	.1949	.2674	.3595	.4747	.6169	.7904
25	.0933	.1353	.1908	.2629	.3548	.4701	.6131	.7880
30	.0815	.1208	.1737	.2437	.3346	.4505	.5963	.7775
35	.0728	.1097	.1605	.2286	.3184	.4345	.5825	.7687
40	.0660	.1010	.1498	.2163	.3050	.4211	.5708	.7611
45	.0605	.0939	.1410	.2060	.2936	.4096	.5607	.7545
50	.0560	.0879	.1336	.1972	.2838	.3996	.5518	.7486
60	.0489	.0785	.1216	.1828	.2676	.3829	.5367	.7386
70	.0437	.0713	.1123	.1715	.2547	.3693	.5243	.7302
80	.0396	.0657	.1049	.1622	.2440	.3579	.5137	.7231
90	.0363	.0610	.0987	.1545	.2349	.3482	.5046	.7168
100	.0336	.0572	.0935	.1479	.2271	.3397	.4966	.7112
120	.0294	.0510	.0851	.1371	.2141	.3255	.4830	.7017
140	.0262	.0464	.0786	.1287	.2038	.3139	.4718	.6937
160	.0237	.0427	.0734	.1217	.1952	.3042	.4623	.6869
180	.0218	.0397	.0691	.1159	.1879	.2959	.4541	.6809
200	.0201	.0371	.0655	.1109	.1816	.2887	.4469	.6757
250	.0171	.0323	.0584	.1011	.1691	.2740	.4320	.6646
300	.0149	.0289	.0531	.0937	.1594	.2625	.4202	.6557
350	.0133	.0262	.0491	.0879	.1517	.2532	.4105	.6482
400	.0121	.0241	.0458	.0832	.1453	.2454	.4022	.6419
450	.0111	.0224	.0431	.0792	.1399	.2387	.3951	.6363
500	.0103	.0210	.0408	.0758	.1352	.2329	.3888	.6314
600	.0090	.0188	.0372	.0703	.1275	.2232	.3782	.6229
700	.0080	.0171	.0344	.0659	.1214	.2152	.3694	.6158
800	.0073	.0157	.0321	.0624	.1163	.2086	.3620	.6098
900	.0067	.0146	.0302	.0594	.1119	.2029	.3556	.6045
1,000	.0062	.0137	.0286	.0569	.1082	.1980	.3499	.5998
1,200	.0054	.0122	.0260	.0527	.1020	.1897	.3404	.5918
1,400	.0048	.0111	.0240	.0495	.0971	.1830	.3325	.5850
1,600	.0044	.0102	.0225	.0468	.0930	.1773	.3258	.5793
1,800	.0040	.0095	.0211	.0446	.0895	.1725	.3200	.5743
2,000	.0037	.0089	.0200	.0427	.0866	.1683	.3149	.5698
2,500	.0031	.0077	.0178	.0389	.0806	.1597	.3044	.5605
3,000	.0027	.0069	.0162	.0360	.0760	.1530	.2961	.5530

Excel:
Learning
Curves

Excel:
Learning
Curves

Learning Curves: Table of Cumulative Values

	UNIT IMPROVEMENT FACTOR							
UNIT	60%	65%	70%	75%	80%	85%	90%	95%
1	1.000	1.000	1.000	1.000	1.000	1.000	1.000	1.000
2	1.600	1.650	1.700	1.750	1.800	1.850	1.900	1.950
3	2.045	2.155	2.268	2.384	2.502	2.623	2.746	2.872
4	2.405	2.578	2.758	2.946	3.142	3.345	3.556	3.774
5	2.710	2.946	3.195	3.459	3.738	4.031	4.339	4.662
6	2.977	3.274	3.593	3.934	4.299	4.688	5.101	5.538
7	3.216	3.572	3.960	4.380	4.834	5.322	5.845	6.404
8	3.432	3.847	4.303	4.802	5.346	5.936	6.574	7.261
9	3.630	4.102	4.626	5.204	5.839	6.533	7.290	8.111
10	3.813	4.341	4.931	5.589	6.315	7.116	7.994	8.955
12	4.144	4.780	5.501	6.315	7.227	8.244	9.374	10.62
14	4.438	5.177	6.026	6.994	8.092	9.331	10.72	12.27
16	4.704	5.541	6.514	7.635	8.920	10.38	12.04	13.91
18	4.946	5.879	6.972	8.245	9.716	11.41	13.33	15.52
20	5.171	6.195	7.407	8.828	10.48	12.40	14.61	17.13
22	5.379	6.492	7.819	9.388	11.23	13.38	15.86	18.72
24	5.574	6.773	8.213	9.928	11.95	14.33	17.10	20.31
25	5.668	6.909	8.404	10.19	12.31	14.80	17.71	21.10
30	6.097	7.540	9.305	11.45	14.02	17.09	20.73	25.00
35	6.478	8.109	10.13	12.72	15.64	19.29	23.67	28.86
40	6.821	8.631	10.90	13.72	17.19	21.43	26.54	32.68
45	7.134	9.114	11.62	14.77	18.68	23.50	29.37	36.47
50	7.422	9.565	12.31	15.78	20.12	25.51	32.14	40.22
60	7.941	10.39	13.57	17.67	22.87	29.41	37.57	47.65
70	8.401	11.13	14.74	19.43	25.47	33.17	42.87	54.99
80	8.814	11.82	15.82	21.09	27.96	36.80	48.05	62.25
90	9.191	12.45	16.83	22.67	30.35	40.32	53.14	69.45
100	9.539	13.03	17.79	24.18	32.65	43.75	58.14	76.59
120	10.16	14.11	19.57	27.02	37.05	50.39	67.93	90.71
140	10.72	15.08	21.20	29.67	41.22	56.78	77.46	104.7
160	11.21	15.97	22.72	32.17	45.20	62.95	86.80	118.5
180	11.67	16.79	24.14	34.54	49.03	68.95	95.96	132.1
200	12.09	17.55	25.48	36.80	52.72	74.79	105.0	145.7
250	13.01	19.28	28.56	42.05	61.47	88.83	126.9	179.2
300	13.81	20.81	31.34	46.94	69.66	102.2	148.2	212.2
350	14.51	22.18	33.89	51.48	77.43	115.1	169.0	244.8
400	15.14	23.44	36.26	55.75	84.85	127.6	189.3	277.0
450	15.72	24.60	38.48	59.80	91.97	139.7	209.2	309.0
500	16.26	25.68	40.58	63.68	98.85	151.5	228.8	340.6
600	17.21	27.67	44.47	70.97	112.0	174.2	267.1	403.3
700	18.06	29.45	48.04	77.77	124.4	196.1	304.5	465.3
800	18.82	31.09	51.36	84.18	136.3	217.3	341.0	526.5
900	19.51	32.60	54.46	90.26	147.7	237.9	376.9	587.2
1,000	20.15	31.01	57.40	96.07	158.7	257.9	412.2	647.4
1,200	21.30	36.59	62.85	107.0	179.7	296.6	481.2	766.6
1,400	22.32	38.92	67.85	117.2	199.6	333.9	548.4	884.2
1,600	23.23	41.04	72.49	126.8	218.6	369.9	614.2	1,001
1,800	24.06	43.00	76.85	135.9	236.8	404.9	678.8	1,116
2,000	24.83	44.84	80.96	144.7	254.4	438.9	742.3	1,230
2,500	26.53	48.97	90.39	165.0	296.1	520.8	897.0	1,513
3,000	27.99	52.62	98.90	183.7	335.2	598.9	1,047	1,791

Managerial Considerations in Using Learning Curves Managers should be aware of the following factors when using and interpreting learning curves.

1. **Individual learning and incentives.** Extensive research indicates a rather obvious fact: To enhance worker learning, there must be adequate incentives for the worker and the organization. (It should be noted, however, that the concept of incentives may be broadened to include any of the positive or negative administrative options available to managers.)

2. **Learning on new jobs versus old jobs.** The newer the job, the greater will be the improvement in labor hours and cost. Conversely, when production has been under way for a long time, improvement will be less discernible. For example, for an 80 percent learning curve situation, the improvement between the first and second units will be 20 percent. However, if the product has been manufactured for 50 years, it will take another 50 years to reduce labor hours by 20 percent.

3. **Improvement comes from working smarter, not harder.** While incentives must be included to motivate the individual worker, most improvement in output comes from better methods and effective support systems rather than simply increased worker effort, assuming that yearly production volume remains the same.

4. **Built-in production bias through suggesting any learning rate.** If a manager expects an 80 percent improvement factor, he or she may treat this percentage as a goal rather than as an unbiased measure of actual learning. In short, it may be a "self-fulfilling prophecy." This, however, is not necessarily undesirable. What is wrong with setting a target improvement factor and then attempting to control production to achieve it?

5. **Preproduction versus postproduction adjustments.** The amount of learning shown by the learning curve depends both on the initial unit(s) of output and on the learning percentage. If there is much preproduction planning, experimentation, and adjustment, the early units will be produced more rapidly than if improvements are made after the first few units—other things being equal. In the first case, therefore, the apparent learning will be less than in the second case, even though subsequent "actual" learning may be the same in each instance.

6. **Changes in indirect labor and supervision.** Learning curves represent direct labor output, but if the mix of indirect labor and supervision changes, it is likely that the productivity of direct labor will be altered. We expect, for example, that more supervisors, repairpersons, and material handlers would speed up production, whereas a reduction in their numbers would slow it down.

7. **Changes in purchasing practices, methods, and organization structure.** Obviously, significant adjustments in any of these factors will affect the production rate and, hence, the learning curve. Likewise, the institution of preventive maintenance programs, zero-defect programs, and other schemes designed to improve efficiency or product quality generally would have some impact on the learning phenomenon.

8. **Contract phase-out.** Though not relevant to all contract situations, the point should be made that the learning curve may begin to turn upward as a contract nears completion. This may result from transferring trained workers to other projects, nonreplacement of worn tooling, and reduced attention to efficiency on the part of management.

CONCEPT CONNECTIONS

LO4A–1 Understand what a learning curve is and where learning curves are applicable.

- A learning curve maps the relationship between unit production time and the cumulative number of units produced.
- These curves are useful for estimating the time required to produce a product and to estimate cost.
- It is particularly useful for large-scale, capital- and labor-intensive products, such as airplanes.
- The fundamental idea is that as output doubles, there is a fixed percentage reduction in the time needed to produce each unit.
- Learning can be due to improvements as people repeat a process and gain skill. Learning can also come from bigger picture improvements in a firm's administration, equipment and technology, and product design.

Learning curve　A line displaying the relationship between unit production time and the cumulative number of units produced.

Individual learning　Improvement that results when people repeat a process and gain skill or efficiency from their own experience.

Organizational learning　Improvement that comes both from experience and from changes in administration, equipment, and product design.

LO4A–2 Plot and analyze learning curves.

- Learning curves can be analyzed using graphs or by mathematically using the learning curve equations.
- When a spreadsheet is not available, learning curve tables are used to simplify the calculations so they can be done with a calculator.
- The most common calculations are made to estimate the time to make a particular unit in the future, and also the cumulative time to make a number of units in the future.

$$Y_x = Kx^n \qquad [4A.1]$$

SOLVED PROBLEMS

SOLVED PROBLEM 1

LO4A–2

A job applicant is being tested for an assembly-line position. Management feels that steady-state times have been approximately reached after 1,000 performances. Regular assembly-line workers are expected to perform the task within four minutes.

- a. If the job applicant performed the first test operation in 10 minutes and the second one in 9 minutes, should this applicant be hired?
- b. What is the expected time that the job applicant would take to finish the 10th unit?

Solution

- a. Learning rate = 9 minutes/10 minutes = 90%
  From Exhibit 4A.5, the time for the 1,000th unit is .3499 × 10 minutes = 3.499 minutes. Yes, hire the person.
- b. From Exhibit 4A.5, unit 10 at 90% is .7047. Therefore, the time for the 10th unit = .7047 × 10 = 7.047 minutes.

SOLVED PROBLEM 2

Boeing Aircraft collected the following cost data on the first eight units of their new business jet.

UNIT NUMBER	COST ($ MILLIONS)	UNIT NUMBER	COST ($ MILLIONS)
1	$100	5	$60
2	83	6	57
3	73	7	53
4	62	8	51

  a. Estimate the learning curve for the new business jet.
  b. Estimate the average cost for the first 1,000 units of the jet.
  c. Estimate the cost to produce the 1,000th jet.

Solution

  a. First, estimate the learning curve rate by calculating the average learning rate with each doubling of production.

$$\text{Units 1 to 2} = 83/100 = 83\%$$
$$\text{Units 2 to 4} = 62/83 = 74.7\%$$
$$\text{Units 4 to 8} = 51/62 = 82.3\%$$
$$\text{Average} = (83 + 74.7 + 82.3)/3 = 80\%$$

  b. The average cost of the first 1,000 units can be estimated using Exhibit 4A.6. The cumulative improvement factor for the 1,000th unit at 80 percent learning is 158.7. The cost to produce the first 1,000 units is

$$\$100M \times 158.7 = \$15,870M$$

The average cost for each of the first 1,000 units is

$$\$15,870M/1,000 = \$15.9M$$

  c. To estimate the cost to produce the 1,000th unit, use Exhibit 4A.5.
The unit improvement factor for the 1,000th unit at 80 percent is .1082.
The cost to produce the 1,000th unit is

$$\$100M \times .1082 = \$10.28M$$

DISCUSSION QUESTIONS

LO4A–1 1. How might the following business specialists use learning curves: accountants, marketers, financial analysts, personnel managers, and computer programmers?
  2. What relationship is there between learning curves and productivity measurement?
  3. What relationship is there between learning curves and capacity analysis?
  4. Do you think learning curve analysis has an application in a service business like a restaurant? Why or why not?

LO4A–2 5. As shown in the chapter, the effect of learning in a *given* system eventually flattens out over time. At that point in the life of a system, learning still exists, though its effect continues to diminish. Beyond that point, is it impossible to significantly reduce the time to produce a unit? What would it take to do that?
  6. The learning curve phenomenon has been shown in practice to be widely applicable. Once a company has established a learning rate for a process, they can use it to predict future system performance. Would there be any reason to reevaluate the process's learning rate once it has been initially established?
  7. As a manager, which learning percentage would you prefer (other things being equal), 110 percent or 60 percent? Explain.

OBJECTIVE QUESTIONS

LO4A-1
1. Firm A typically sees a learning percentage of 85 percent in its processes. Firm B has a learning percentage of 80 percent. Which firm has the faster learning rate?

2. Company Z is just starting to make a brand new product it has never made before. It has completed two units so far. The first unit took 12 hours to complete and the next unit took 11 hours. Based only on this information, what would be the estimate of the learning percentage in this process?

3. Omega Technology is starting production of a new supercomputer for use in large research universities. It has just completed the first unit, which took 120 labor hours to produce. Based on its experience, it estimates its learning percentage to be 80 percent. How many labor hours should it expect the second unit to require to manufacture?

LO4A-2
4. You've just completed a pilot run of 10 units of a major product and found the processing time for each unit was as follows:

UNIT NUMBER	TIME (HOURS)	UNIT NUMBER	TIME (HOURS)
1	970	6	250
2	640	7	220
3	420	8	207
4	380	9	190
5	320	10	190

 a. According to the pilot run, what would you estimate the learning rate to be?
 b. Based on (a), how much time would it take for the next 190 units, assuming no loss of learning?
 c. How much time would it take to make the 1,000th unit?

5. Jack Simpson, contract negotiator for Nebula Airframe Company, is currently involved in bidding on a follow-up government contract. In gathering cost data from the first three units, which Nebula produced under a research and development contract, he found that the first unit took 2,000 labor hours, the second took 1,800 labor hours, and the third took 1,692 hours.

   In a contract for three more units, how many labor hours should Simpson plan for?

6. Lazer Technologies Inc. (LTI) has produced a total of 20 high-power laser systems that could be used to destroy any approaching enemy missiles or aircraft. The 20 units have been produced, funded in part as private research within the research and development arm of LTI, but the bulk of the funding came from a contract with the U.S. Department of Defense (DoD).

   Testing of the laser units has shown that they are effective defense weapons, and through redesign to add portability and easier field maintenance, the units could be truck-mounted.

   DoD has asked LTI to submit a bid for 100 units.

   The 20 units that LTI has built so far cost the following amounts and are listed in the order in which they were produced:

UNIT NUMBER	COST ($ MILLIONS)	UNIT NUMBER	COST ($ MILLIONS)
1	$12	11	$3.9
2	10	12	3.5
3	6	13	3.0
4	6.5	14	2.8
5	5.8	15	2.7
6	6	16	2.7
7	5	17	2.3
8	3.6	18	3.0
9	3.6	19	2.9
10	4.1	20	2.6

   a. Based on past experience, what is the learning rate?

   b. What bid should LTI submit for the total order of 100 units, assuming that learning continues?

   c. What is the cost expected to be for the last unit under the learning rate you estimated?

7. Johnson Industries received a contract to develop and produce four high-intensity long-distance receiver/transmitters for cellular telephones. The first took 2,000 labor hours and $39,000 worth of purchased and manufactured parts; the second took 1,500 labor hours and $37,050 in parts; the third took 1,450 labor hours and $31,000 in parts; and the fourth took 1,275 labor hours and $31,492 in parts.

   Johnson was asked to bid on a follow-on contract for another dozen receiver/transmitter units. Ignoring any forgetting factor effects, what should Johnson estimate time and parts costs to be for the dozen units? (*Hint:* There are two learning curves—one for labor and one for parts.)

8. Lambda Computer Products competed for and won a contract to produce two prototype units of a new type of computer that is based on laser optics rather than on electronic binary bits.

   The first unit produced by Lambda took 5,000 hours to produce and required $250,000 worth of material, equipment usage, and supplies. The second unit took 3,500 hours and used $200,000 worth of materials, equipment usage, and supplies. Labor is $30 per hour.

   a. Lambda was asked to present a bid for 10 additional units as soon as the second unit was completed. Production would start immediately. What would this bid be?

   b. Suppose there was a significant delay between the contracts. During this time, personnel and equipment were reassigned to other projects. Explain how this would affect the subsequent bid.

9. Honda Motor Company has discovered a problem in the exhaust system of one of its automobile lines and has voluntarily agreed to make the necessary modifications to conform with government safety requirements. Standard procedure is for the firm to pay a flat fee to dealers for each modification completed.

   Honda is trying to establish a fair amount of compensation to pay dealers and has decided to choose a number of randomly selected mechanics and observe their performance and learning rate. Analysis demonstrated that the average learning rate was 90 percent, and Honda then decided to pay a $60 fee for each repair (3 hours × $20 per flat-rate hour).

   Southwest Honda, Inc., has complained to Honda Motor Company about the fee. Six mechanics, working independently, have completed two modifications each. All took 9 hours on the average to do the first unit and 6.3 hours to do the second. Southwest refuses to do any more unless Honda allows at least 4.5 hours. The dealership expects to perform the modification to approximately 300 vehicles.

   What is your opinion of Honda's allowed rate and the mechanics' performance?

10. United Research Associates (URA) had received a contract to produce two units of a new cruise missile guidance control. The first unit took 4,000 hours to complete and cost $30,000 in materials and equipment usage. The second took 3,200 hours and cost $21,000 in materials and equipment usage. Labor cost is charged at $18 per hour.

   The prime contractor has now approached URA and asked to submit a bid for the cost of producing another 20 guidance controls.

   a. What will the last unit cost to build?

   b. What will be the average time for the 20 missile guidance controls?

   c. What will the average cost be for guidance control for the 20 in the contract?

CHAPTER 5

PROJECTS

Learning Objectives

LO5–1 Explain what projects are and how projects are organized.

LO5–2 Evaluate projects using earned value management.

LO5–3 Analyze projects using network-planning models.

LO5–4 Exemplify how network-planning models and earned value management are implemented in commercial software packages.

CAN A 15-STORY HOTEL BE BUILT IN LESS THAN A WEEK?

A Chinese construction company recently built a 15-story hotel in just six days. To show this was not a fluke, it then built a 30-story hotel in only 15 days! The company believes it can construct buildings that are 150 stories tall using the same high-speed techniques. Using these techniques, construction takes less than one-third the time it would take on a normal schedule.

The company uses many workers during the short construction period; and detailed schedules coordinate the many teams working simultaneously and around the clock on the building. Materials are prefabricated ahead of time in a factory. Premade modules are carried to the construction site on large trucks where they are placed in the steel structure with cranes. Special inspection and review processes are used to eliminate these delays in the construction process.

CHINESE WORKERS MANUFACTURE STEEL FRAMES TO BE USED TO BUILD THE 15-STORY NEW ARK HOTEL, WHICH WAS BUILT IN SIX DAYS.

WHAT IS PROJECT MANAGEMENT?

"The high-impact project is the gem . . . the fundamental nugget . . . the fundamental atomic particle from which the new white collar world will be constructed and/or reconstructed. Projects should be, well, WOW!"

—Tom Peters

Although most of the material in this chapter focuses on the technical aspects of project management (structuring project networks and calculating the critical path), as we saw in the opening vignette, the management aspects are equally important. Success in project management is very much an activity that requires careful control of critical resources. We spend much of the time in this book focused on the management of nonhuman resources such as machines and material; for projects, however, the key resource is often our employees' time. Human resources are often the most expensive, and those people involved in projects that are critical to the success of the firm are often the most valuable managers, consultants, and engineers.

At the highest levels in an organization, management often involves juggling a portfolio of projects. There are many different types of projects, ranging from the development of totally new products, revisions to old products, new marketing plans, and a vast array of projects for better serving customers and reducing costs.

LO5–1 Explain what projects are and how they are organized.

exhibit 5.1	Types of Development Projects

	More ←——— Change ———→ Less		
	Breakthrough Projects	Platform Projects	Derivative Projects
Product Change	New core product	Addition to product family	Product enhancement
Process Change	New core process	Process upgrade	New machine
Research & Development	New core technology	Technology upgrade	New software
Alliance & Partnership	Outsource major activity	Select new partner	Select carrier

Most companies deal with projects individually—pushing each through the pipeline as quickly and cost-effectively as possible. Many of these same companies are very good at applying the techniques described in this chapter in a manner in which myriad tasks are executed flawlessly, yet the projects do not just deliver the expected results. Worse, what often happens is that the projects consuming the most resources have the least connection to the firm's strategy.

The vital big-picture decision is what mix of projects is best for the organization. A firm should have the right mix of projects that best supports a company's strategy. Projects should be selected from the following types: derivative (incremental changes such as new product packaging or no-frills versions), breakthrough (major changes that create entirely new markets), and platform (fundamental improvements to existing products). Projects can be categorized in four major areas: product change, process change, research and development, and alliance and partnership (see Exhibit 5.1).

In this chapter, we only scratch the surface in our introduction to the topic of project management. Professional project managers are individuals skilled at not only the technical aspects of calculating such things as early start and early finish time but also, just as important, at motivating people. In addition, the ability to resolve conflicts as key decision points occur in the project is a critical skill. Without a doubt, leading successful projects is the best way to prove your promotability to the people who make promotion decisions. Virtually all project work is teamwork, and leading a project involves leading a team. Your success at leading a project will spread quickly through the individuals in the team. As organizations flatten (through reengineering, downsizing, outsourcing), more will depend on projects and project leaders to get work done, work that previously was handled within departments.

A **project** may be defined as a series of related jobs usually directed toward some major output and requiring a significant period of time to perform. **Project management** can be defined as planning, directing, and controlling resources (people, equipment, material) to meet the technical, cost, and time constraints of the project.

Although projects are often thought to be one-time occurrences, the fact is that many projects can be repeated or transferred to other settings or products. The result will be another project output. A contractor building houses or a firm producing low-volume

Project
A series of related jobs usually directed toward some major output and requiring a significant period of time to perform.

Project management
Planning, directing, and controlling resources (people, equipment, material) to meet the technical, cost, and time constraints of a project.

products such as supercomputers, locomotives, or jet airliners can effectively consider these as projects.

Organizing the Project Team

Before the project starts, senior management must decide which of three organizational structures will be used to tie the project to the parent firm: pure project, functional project, or matrix project. We next discuss the strengths and weaknesses of the three main forms.

Pure Project When innovation and speed are the priorities, a small project-focused team is used. In this case, team members are assigned solely to the team for the duration of the project. This **pure project** (nicknamed *skunkworks*) structure is where a self-contained team works full time on the project.

Pure project
A structure for organizing a project where a self-contained team works full time on the project.

Advantages
- The project manager has full authority over the project.
- Team members report to one boss. They do not have to worry about dividing loyalty between functional-area managers.
- Lines of communication are shortened. Decisions are made quickly.
- Team pride, motivation, and commitment are high.

Disadvantages
- Duplication of resources. Equipment and people are not shared across projects.
- Organizational goals and policies are ignored, as team members are often both physically and psychologically removed from headquarters.
- The organization falls behind in its knowledge of new technology due to weakened functional divisions.
- Because team members have no functional area home, they often worry about "life after the project," and so project termination is frequently delayed.

Functional Project At the other end of the project organization spectrum is the **functional project**, housing the project within a functional division.

Functional project
A structure where team members are assigned from the functional units of the organization. The team members remain a part of their functional units and typically are not dedicated to the project.

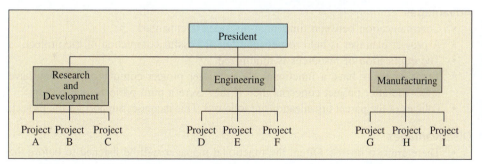

Advantages
- A team member can work on several projects.
- Technical expertise is maintained within the functional area even if individuals leave the project or organization.
- The functional area is a home after the project is completed. Functional specialists can advance vertically.

• A critical mass of specialized functional-area experts creates synergistic solutions to a project's technical problems.

Disadvantages
• Aspects of the project that are not directly related to the functional area get short-changed.
• The motivation of team members is often weak.
• The needs of the client are secondary and are responded to slowly.

Matrix project
A structure that blends the functional and pure project structures. Each project uses people from different functional areas. A dedicated project manager decides what tasks need to be performed and when, but the functional managers control which people to use.

Matrix Project The classic specialized organizational form, the "**matrix project**," attempts to blend properties of functional and pure project structures. Each project utilizes people from different functional areas. The project manager (PM) decides what tasks and when they will be performed, but the functional managers control which people and technologies are used. If the matrix form is chosen, different projects (rows of the matrix) borrow resources from functional areas (columns). Senior management must then decide whether a weak, balanced, or strong form of a matrix is to be used. This establishes whether project managers have little, equal, or more authority than the functional managers with whom they negotiate for resources.

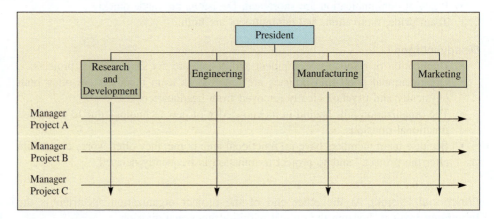

Advantages
• Communication between functional divisions is enhanced.
• A project manager is held responsible for successful completion of the project.
• The duplication of resources is minimized.
• Team members have a functional "home" after project completion, so they have fewer life-after-project concerns than if they were a pure project organization.
• Policies of the parent organization are followed. This increases support for the project.

Disadvantages
• There are two bosses. Often, the functional manager will be listened to before the project manager. After all, who can promote you or give you a raise?
• It is doomed to failure unless the PM has strong negotiating skills.
• Suboptimization is a danger, as PMs hoard resources for their own project, thus harming other projects.

Note that regardless of which of the three major organizational forms is used, the project manager is the primary contact point with the customer. Communication and flexibility are greatly enhanced because one person is responsible for successful completion of the project.

Organizing Project Tasks

A project starts out as a *statement of work (SOW)*. The SOW may be a written description of the objectives to be achieved, with a brief statement of the work to be done and a proposed schedule specifying the start and completion dates. It also could contain performance measures in terms of budget and completion steps (milestones) and the written reports to be supplied.

A *task* is a further subdivision of a project. It is usually not longer than several months in duration and is performed by one group or organization. A *subtask* may be used if needed to further subdivide the project into more meaningful pieces.

A *work package* is a group of activities combined to be assignable to a single organizational unit. It still falls into the format of all project management; the package provides a description of what is to be done, when it is to be started and completed, the budget, measures of performance, and specific events to be reached at points in time. These specific events are called **project milestones**. Typical milestones might be the completion of the design, the production of a prototype, the completed testing of the prototype, and the approval of a pilot run.

Project milestone
A specific event in a project.

The **work breakdown structure (WBS)** defines the hierarchy of project tasks, subtasks, and work packages. Completion of one or more work packages results in the completion of a subtask; completion of one or more subtasks results in the completion of a task; and, finally, the completion of all tasks is required to complete the project. A representation of this structure is shown in Exhibit 5.2.

Work breakdown structure (WBS)
The hierarchy of project tasks, subtasks, and work packages.

Exhibit 5.3 shows the WBS for an optical scanner project. The WBS is important in organizing a project because it breaks the project down into manageable pieces. The number of levels will vary depending on the project. How much detail or how many levels to use depends on the following:

- The level at which a single individual or organization can be assigned responsibility and accountability for accomplishing the work package.
- The level at which budget and cost data will be collected during the project.

An Example of a Work Breakdown Structure	**exhibit 5.2**

exhibit 5.3	Work Breakdown Structure, Large Optical Scanner Design

Level 1	2	3	4		
X				1	Optical simulator design
	X			1.1	Optical design
		X		1.1.1	Telescope design/fab
		X		1.1.2	Telescope/simulator optical interface
		X		1.1.3	Simulator zoom system design
		X		1.1.4	Ancillary simulator optical component specification
	X			1.2	System performance analysis
		X		1.2.1	Overall system firmware and software control
			X	1.2.1.1	Logic flow diagram generation and analysis
			X	1.2.1.2	Basic control algorithm design
		X		1.2.2	Far beam analyzer
		X		1.2.3	System inter- and intra-alignment method design
		X		1.2.4	Data recording and reduction requirements
	X			1.3	System integration
	X			1.4	Cost analysis
		X		1.4.1	Cost/system schedule analysis
		X		1.4.2	Cost/system performance analysis
	X			1.5	Management
		X		1.5.1	System design/engineering management
		X		1.5.2	Program management
	X			1.6	Long lead item procurement
		X		1.6.1	Large optics
		X		1.6.2	Target components
		X		1.6.3	Detectors

There is not a single correct WBS for any project, and two different project teams might develop different WBSs for the same project. Some experts have referred to project management as an art rather than a science, because there are so many different ways that a project can be approached. Finding the correct way to organize a project depends on experience with the particular task.

Activities are defined within the context of the work breakdown structure and are pieces of work that consume time. Activities do not necessarily require the expenditure of effort by people, although they often do. For example, waiting for paint to dry may be an activity in a project. Activities are identified as part of the WBS. From our sample project in Exhibit 5.3, activities would include telescope design and fabrication (1.1.1), telescope/simulator optical interface (1.1.2), and data recording (1.2.4). Activities need to be defined in such a way that when they are all completed, the project is done.

Activities
Pieces of work within a project that consume time. The completion of all the activities of a project marks the end of the project.

LO5–2 Evaluate projects using earned value management.

Gantt chart
Shows in a graphic manner the amount of time involved and the sequence in which activities can be performed. Often referred to as a **bar chart.**

MANAGING PROJECTS

We now look at how projects are actually managed while they are being completed. Charts and various types of standard forms are useful because their visual presentation are easily understood. Computer programs are available to quickly generate the charts, and we discuss these later in the chapter.

Exhibit 5.4A is a sample **Gantt chart**, sometimes referred to as a *bar chart*, showing both the amount of time involved and the sequence in which activities can be performed. The chart is named after Henry L. Gantt, who won a presidential citation for his application of this type of chart to shipbuilding during World War I. In the example in Exhibit 5.4A, "long lead procurement" and "manufacturing schedules" are independent activities and can occur simultaneously. All other activities must be done in the sequence from

Sample of Graphic Project Reports   exhibit 5.4

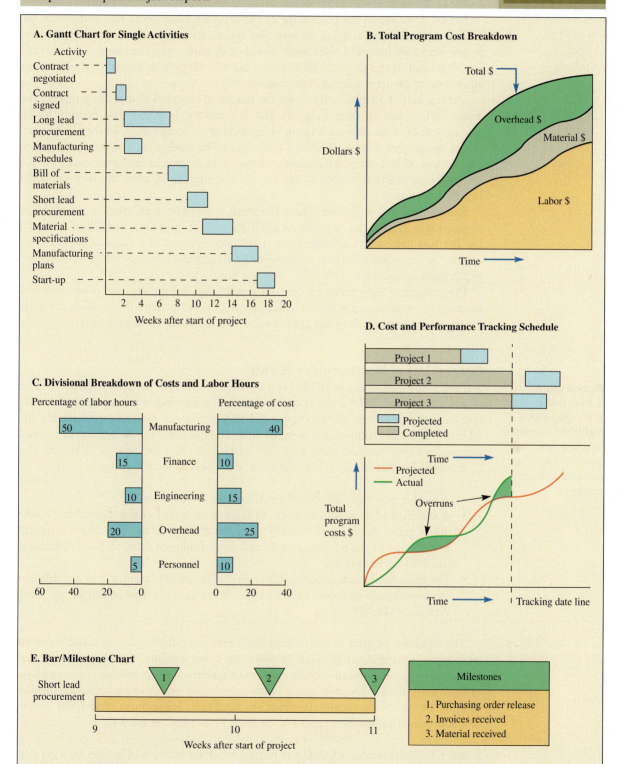

top to bottom. Exhibit 5.4B graphs the amounts of money spent on labor, material, and overhead. Its value is its clarity in identifying sources and amounts of cost.

Exhibit 5.4C shows the percentage of the project's labor hours that come from the various areas of manufacturing, finance, and so on. These labor hours are related to the proportion of the project's total labor cost. For example, manufacturing is responsible for 50 percent of the project's labor hours, but this 50 percent has been allocated just 40 percent of the total labor dollars charged.

The top half of Exhibit 5.4D shows the degree of completion of these projects. The dotted vertical line signifies today. Project 1, therefore, is already late because it still has work to be done. Project 2 is not being worked on temporarily, so there is a space before the projected work. Project 3 continues to be worked on without interruption. The bottom of Exhibit 5.4D compares actual total costs and projected costs. As we see, two cost overruns occurred, and the current cumulative costs are over projected cumulative costs.

Exhibit 5.4E is a milestone chart. The three milestones mark specific points in the project where checks can be made to see if the project is on time and where it should be. The best place to locate milestones is at the completion of a major activity. In this exhibit, the major activities completed were "purchase order release," "invoices received," and "material received."

Other standard reports can be used for a more detailed presentation comparing cost to progress (such as cost schedule status report—CSSR) or reports providing the basis for partial payment (such as the earned value report, which we discuss next).

Earned Value Management (EVM)

Earned value management (EVM) is a technique for measuring project progress in an objective manner. EVM has the ability to combine measurements of scope, schedule, and cost in a project. When properly applied, EVM provides a method for evaluating the relative success of a project at a point in time. The measures can be applied to projects focused on either "revenue generation" or "cost," depending on the type of project.

Essential features of any EVM implementation include the following:

- A project plan that identifies the activities to be accomplished.
- A valuation of each activity work. In the case of a project that generates revenue, this is called the Planned Value (PV) of the activity. In the case where a project is evaluated based on cost, this is called the Budgeted Cost of Work Scheduled (BCWS) for the activity.
- The predefined "earning or costing rules" (also called "metrics") to quantify the accomplishment of work, called Earned Value (EV) or Budgeted Cost of Work Performed (BCWP).

The terminology used in the features is general since the valuations could be based on either a value measure (revenue or profit) or a cost measure. EVM implementations for large or complex projects include many more features, such as indicators and forecasts of cost performance (overbudget or underbudget) and schedule performance (behind schedule or ahead of schedule). However, the most basic requirement of an EVM system is that it quantifies progress using PV (or BCWS) and EV (or BCWP).

Project Tracking without EVM It is helpful to see an example of project tracking that does not include earned value performance management. Consider a project that has been

Earned Value Management Charts

exhibit 5.5

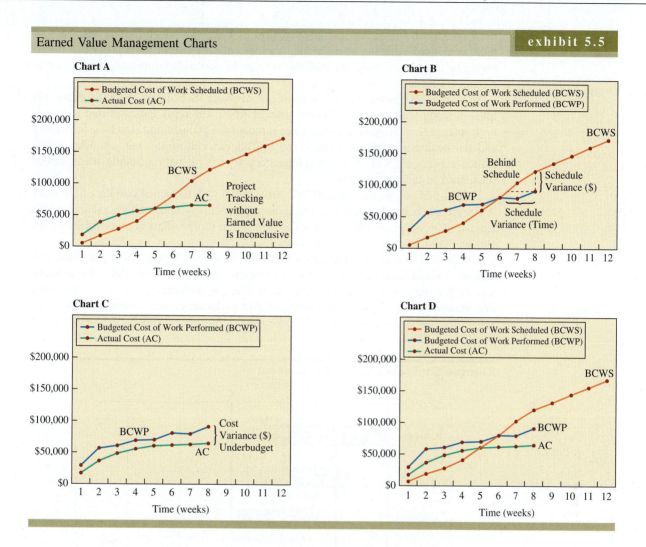

planned in detail, including a time-phased spend plan for all elements of work. This is a case where the project is evaluated based on cost. Exhibit 5.5A shows the cumulative cost budget for this project as a function of time (the blue line, labeled BCWS). It also shows the cumulative actual cost of the project (red line) through week 8. To those unfamiliar with EVM, it might appear that this project was overbudget through week 4 and then underbudget from week 6 through week 8. However, what is missing from this chart is any understanding of how much work has been accomplished during the project. If the project was actually completed at week 8, then the project would be well underbudget and far ahead of schedule. If, on the other hand, the project is only 10 percent complete at week 8, then the project is significantly overbudget and behind schedule. A method is needed to measure technical performance objectively and quantitatively, and that is what EVM accomplishes.

Project Tracking with EVM Consider the same project, except this time the project plan includes predefined methods of quantifying the accomplishment of work. At the end of each week, the project manager identifies every detailed element of work that has been completed, and sums the Budgeted Cost of Work Performed (BCWP) for each of these completed elements by estimating the percent complete of the activity and multiplying by the activity budgeted cost. BCWP may be accumulated monthly, weekly, or as progress is made.

Exhibit 5.5B shows the Budgeted Cost of Work Scheduled (BCWS) curve (in orange) along with the BCWP curve from chart C. The chart indicates that technical performance (i.e., progress) started more rapidly than planned, but slowed significantly and fell behind schedule at week 7 and 8. This chart illustrates the schedule performance aspect of EVM. It is complementary to critical path schedule management (described in the next section).

Exhibit 5.5C shows the same BCWP curve (blue) with the actual cost data from chart A (in green). It can be seen that the project was actually underbudget, relative to the amount of work accomplished, since the start of the project. This is a much better conclusion than might be derived from chart A.

Exhibit 5.5D shows all three curves together—which is a typical EVM line chart. The best way to read these three-line charts is to identify the BCWS curve first, then compare it to BCWP (for schedule performance) and AC (for cost performance). It can be seen from this illustration that a true understanding of cost performance and schedule performance *relies first on measuring technical performance objectively*. This is the *foundational principle* of EVM.

Example 5.1: Earned Value Management

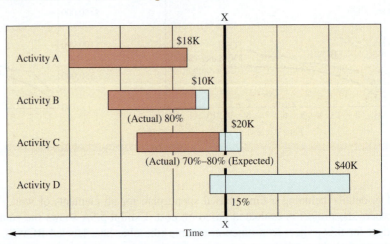

The figure above illustrates how to determine the Budgeted Cost of Work Scheduled by summing the dollar values (in $1,000s) of the work scheduled for accomplishment at the end of period *X*. The Budgeted Cost of Work Performed is determined by summing the earned value for the work actually accomplished, shown in red shading.

SOLUTION

From the diagram, the budgeted cost of all the project work is the following: Activity A − $18K, B − $10K, C − $20K, D − $40K. This is the cost of each activity when it is 100 percent completed.

The project is currently at day *X* According to the diagram, 100 percent of activity A should be completed, and it is; 100 percent of activity B should be completed, but only 80 percent is; 80 percent of activity C should be completed, but only 70 percent is; and 15 percent of activity D should be finished, but it has not started.

Step 1: Calculate the Budgeted Cost of Work Scheduled (BCWS) given the current state of the project. This is the value or cost of the project that is expected, given the project is at time X:

Activity A − 100% of $18K = $18K
Activity B − 100% of $10K = $10K
Activity C − 80% of $20K = $16K
Activity D − 15% of $40K = $6K

BCWS = $18K + $10K + $16K + $6K = $50K

Step 2: Calculate the Budgeted Cost of Work Performed (BCWP) given the current state of the project. This is the actual value or cost of the project to date, given the project is at time X:

Activity A − 100% of $18K = $18K
Activity B − 80% of $10K = $8K
Activity C − 70% of $20K = $14K
Activity D − 0% of $40K = $0

BCWP = $18K + $8K + $14K + $0K = $40K

Step 3: Obtain the Actual Cost (AC) of the work performed. This would need to be obtained from accounting records for the project. Assume that the actual cost for this project to date is $45K.

AC = $45K (Data from Acct. System)

Step 4: Calculate key performance measures for the project:

Schedule Variance: This is the difference between the Budgeted Cost of Work Performed (BCWP) and the Budgeted Cost of Work Scheduled (BCWS) for the project:

Schedule Variance = BCWP − BCWS
Schedule Variance = $40K − $50K = −$10K

Greater than 0 is generally good, because it implies that the project is ahead of schedule.

Schedule Performance Index: This is the ratio of the BCWP versus the BCWS for the project:

Schedule Performance Index = BCWP/BCWS
Schedule Performance Index = $40K − $50K = 0.8

Greater than 1 is generally good, because it implies that the project is ahead of schedule.

Cost Variance: This is the difference between BCWP and the Actual Cost (AC):

Cost Variance = BCWP − AC
Cost Variance = $40K − $45K = −5K

Greater than zero is generally good as it implies underbudget.

Cost Performance Index: This is the ratio of the BCWP versus the AC for the project to date:

Cost Performance Index = BCWP/AC
Cost Performance Index = $40K/$45K = 0.89

<1 means the cost of completing the work is higher than planned, which is bad;
=1 means the cost of completing the work is right on plan, which is good;
>1 means the cost of completing the work is lower than planned, which is usually good.

That means the project is spending about $1.13 for every $1.00 of budgeted work accomplished. This is not very good as the project is overbudget and tasks are not being completed on time or on budget. A Schedule Performance Index and a Cost Performance Index greater than one are desirable. •

NETWORK-PLANNING MODELS

The two best-known network-planning models were developed in the 1950s. The Critical Path Method (CPM) was developed for scheduling maintenance shutdowns at chemical processing plants owned by DuPont. Since maintenance projects are performed often in this industry, reasonably accurate time estimates for activities are available. CPM is based on the assumptions that project activity times can be estimated accurately and that they do not vary. The Program Evaluation and Review Technique (PERT) was developed for the U.S. Navy's Polaris missile project. This was a massive project involving over 3,000 contractors. Because most of the activities had never been done before, PERT was developed to handle uncertain time estimates. As years passed, features that distinguished CPM from PERT have diminished, so in our treatment here we just use the term *CPM*.

In a sense, the CPM techniques illustrated here owe their development to the widely used predecessor, the Gantt chart. Although the Gantt chart is able to relate activities to time in a usable fashion for small projects, the interrelationship of activities, when displayed in this form, becomes extremely difficult to visualize and to work with for projects that include more than about 25 activities.

Critical path
The sequence(s) of activities in a project that form(s) the longest chain in terms of their time to complete.

The **critical path** of activities in a project is the sequence of activities that form the longest chain in terms of their time to complete. If any one of the activities in the critical path is delayed, then the entire project is delayed. It is possible and it often happens that there are multiple paths of the same length through the network, so there are multiple critical paths. Determining scheduling information about each activity in the project is the major goal of CPM techniques. The techniques calculate when an activity must start and end, together with whether the activity is part of the critical path.

Critical Path Method (CPM)

Here is a procedure for scheduling a project. In this case, a single time estimate is used because we are assuming that the activity times are known. A very simple project will be scheduled to demonstrate the basic approach.

Consider that you have a group assignment that requires a decision on whether you should invest in a company. Your instructor has suggested that you perform the analysis in the following four steps:

A Select a company.
B Obtain the company's annual report and perform a ratio analysis.
C Collect technical stock price data and construct charts.
D Individually review the data and make a team decision on whether to buy the stock.

NEW ZEALAND'S TE APITI WIND FARM PROJECT CONSTRUCTED THE LARGEST WIND FARM IN THE SOUTHERN HEMISPHERE, WITHIN ONE YEAR FROM COMMISSION TO COMPLETION, ON TIME AND WITHIN BUDGET. EMPLOYING EFFECTIVE PROJECT MANAGEMENT AND USING THE CORRECT TOOLS AND TECHNIQUES, THE MERIDIAN ENERGY COMPANY PROVIDED A VIABLE OPTION FOR RENEWABLE ENERGY IN NEW ZEALAND AND ACTS AS A BENCHMARK FOR LATER WIND FARM PROJECTS.

© Chris Ratcliffe/Bloomberg/Getty Images

Determine the "critical path" for a project.

Your group of four people decides that the project can be divided into four activities as suggested by the instructor. You decide that all the team members should be involved in selecting the company and that it should take one week to complete this activity. You will meet at the end of the week to decide what company the group will consider. During this meeting, you will split your group in half: two people will be responsible for the annual report and ratio analysis, and the other two will collect the technical data and construct the charts. Your group expects it to take two weeks to get the annual report and perform the ratio analysis, and a week to collect the stock price data and generate the charts. You agree that the two groups can work independently. Finally, you agree to meet as a team to make the purchase decision. Before you meet, you want to allow one week for each team member to review all the data.

This is a simple project, but it will serve to demonstrate the approach. The following are the appropriate steps:

1. **Identify each activity to be done in the project and estimate how long it will take to complete each activity.** This is simple, given the information from your instructor. We identify the activities as follows: A(1), B(2), C(1), D(1). The number is the expected duration of the activity.

2. **Determine the required sequence of activities and construct a network reflecting the precedence relationships.** An easy way to do this is to first identify the **immediate predecessors** associated with an activity. The immediate predecessors are the activities that need to be completed immediately before an activity. Activity A needs to be completed before activities B and C can start. B and C need to be completed before D can start. The following table reflects what we know so far:

Immediate predecessors Activities that need to be completed immediately before another activity.

ACTIVITY	DESIGNATION	IMMEDIATE PREDECESSORS	TIME (WEEKS)
Select company	A	None	1
Obtain annual report and perform ratio analysis	B	A	2
Collect stock price data and perform technical analysis	C	A	1
Review data and make a decision	D	B and C	1

Here is a diagram that depicts these precedence relationships:

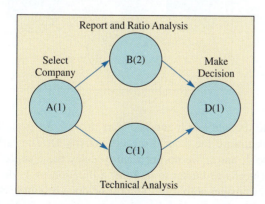

3. **Determine the critical path.** Consider each sequence of activities that runs from the beginning to the end of the project. For our simple project there are two paths: A–B–D and A–C–D. The critical path is the path where the sum of the activity times is the longest. A–B–D has a duration of four weeks and A–C–D has a duration of three weeks. The critical path, therefore, is A–B–D. If any activity along the critical path is delayed, then the entire project will be delayed.

4. **Determine the early start/finish and late start/finish schedule.** To schedule the project, find when each activity needs to start and when it needs to finish.

Slack time
The time that an activity can be delayed without delaying the entire project; the difference between the late and early start times of an activity.

For some activities in a project, there may be some leeway regarding when an activity can start and finish. This is called the **slack time** in an activity. For each activity in the project, we calculate four points in time: the early start, early finish, late start, and late finish times. The early start and early finish are the earliest times that the activity can start and be finished. Similarly, the late start and late finish are the latest times the activities can start and finish without delaying the project. The difference between the late start time and early start time is the slack time. To help keep all of this straight, we place these numbers in special places around the nodes that represent each activity in our network diagram, as shown here.

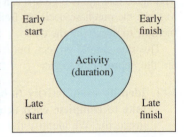

To calculate numbers, start from the beginning of the network and work to the end, calculating the early start and early finish numbers. Start counting with the current period, designated as period 0. Activity A has an early start of 0 and an early finish of 1. Activity B's early start is A's early finish or 1. Similarly, C's early start is 1. The early finish for B is 3, and the early finish for C is 2. Now consider activity D. D cannot start until both B and C are done. Because B cannot be done until 3, D cannot start until that time. The early start for D, therefore, is 3, and the early finish is 4. Our diagram now looks like this.

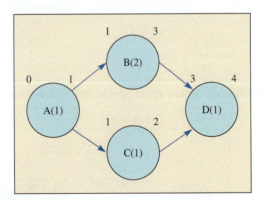

To calculate the late finish and late start times, start from the end of the network and work toward the front. Consider activity D. The earliest that it can be done is at time 4; and if we do not want to delay the completion of the project, the late finish needs to be set to 4. With a duration of 1, the latest that D can start is 3. Now consider activity C. C must be done by time 3 so that D can start, so C's late finish time is 3 and its late start time is 2. Notice the difference between the early and late start and finish times: This activity has one week of slack time. Activity B must be done by time 3 so that D can start, so its late finish time is 3 and late start time is 1. There is no slack in B. Finally, activity A must be done so that B and C can start. Because B must start earlier than C, and A must get done in time for B to start, the late finish time for A is 1. Finally, the late start time for A is 0. Notice there is no slack in activities A, B, and D. The final network looks like this. (Hopefully, the stock your investment team has chosen is a winner!)

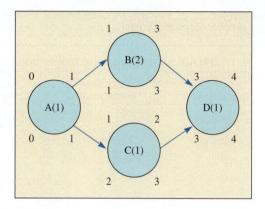

Example 5.2: Critical Path Method

Many firms that have tried to enter the notebook computer market have failed. Suppose your firm believes there is a big demand in this market because existing products have not been designed correctly. They are too heavy, too large, or too small to have standard-sized keyboards. Your intended computer will be small enough to carry inside a jacket pocket if need be. The ideal size will be no larger than 5 inches × 9½ inches × 1 inch with a folding keyboard. It should weigh no more than 15 ounces and have an LCD display, a solid state drive, and a wireless bluetooth connection. This should appeal to traveling businesspeople, but it could have a much wider market, including students. It should be priced in the $175–$200 range.

The project, then, is to design, develop, and produce a prototype of this small computer. In the rapidly changing computer industry, it is crucial to hit the market with a product of this sort in less than a year. Therefore, the project team has been allowed approximately eight months (35 weeks) to produce the prototype.

Excel: Project Management

SOLUTION

The first charge of the project team is to develop a project network chart and determine if the prototype computer can be completed within the 35-week target. Let's follow the steps in the development of the network.

1. **Activity identification.** The project team decides that the following activities are the major components of the project: design of the computer, prototype construction, prototype testing, methods specification (summarized in a report), evaluation studies of automatic assembly equipment, an assembly equipment study report, and a final report summarizing all aspects of the design, equipment, and methods.

2. **Activity sequencing and network construction.** On the basis of discussion with staff, the project manager develops the precedence table and sequence network shown in Exhibit 5.6. When constructing a network, take care to ensure that the activities are in the proper order and that the logic of their relationships is maintained. For example, it would be illogical to have a situation where Event A precedes Event B, B precedes C, and C precedes A.

3. **Critical path determination.** The critical path is the longest sequence of connected activities through the network and is defined as the path with zero slack time. This network has four different paths: A–C–F–G, A–C–E–G, A–B–D–F–G, and A–B–D–E–G. The lengths of these paths are 38, 35, 38, and 35 weeks. Note that this project has two different critical

exhibit 5.6 **CPM Network for Computer Design Project**

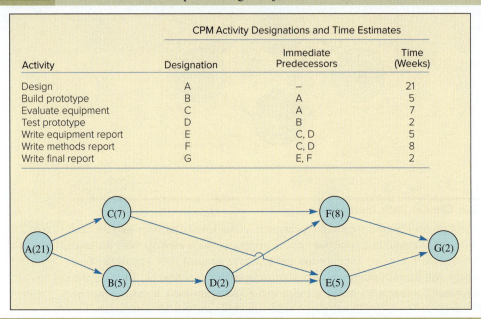

CPM Activity Designations and Time Estimates

Activity	Designation	Immediate Predecessors	Time (Weeks)
Design	A	–	21
Build prototype	B	A	5
Evaluate equipment	C	A	7
Test prototype	D	B	2
Write equipment report	E	C, D	5
Write methods report	F	C, D	8
Write final report	G	E, F	2

paths; this might indicate that this would be a fairly difficult project to manage. Calculating the early start and late start schedules gives additional insight into how difficult this project might be to complete on time. •

Early start schedule
A project schedule that lists all activities by their early start times.

Late start schedule
A project schedule that lists all activities by their late start times. This schedule may create savings by postponing purchases of material and other costs associated with the project.

Early Start and Late Start Schedules An **early start schedule** is one that lists all of the activities by their early start times. For activities not on the critical path, there is slack time between the completion of each activity and the start of the next activity. The early start schedule completes the project and all its activities as soon as possible.

A **late start schedule** lists the activities to start as late as possible without delaying the completion date of the project. One motivation for using a late start schedule is that savings are realized by postponing purchases of materials, the use of labor, and other costs until necessary. These calculations are shown in Exhibit 5.7. From this, we see that the only activity that has slack is activity E. This certainly would be a fairly difficult project to complete on time.

CPM with Three Activity Time Estimates

If a single estimate of the time required to complete an activity is not reliable, the best procedure is to use three time estimates. These three times not only allow us to estimate the activity time but also let us obtain a probability estimate for completion time for the entire network. Briefly, the procedure is as follows: The estimated activity time is calculated using a weighted average of a minimum, maximum, and most likely time estimate. The expected completion time of the network is computed using the procedure described above. Using estimates of variability for the activities on the critical path, the probability of completing the project by particular times can be

CPM Network for Computer Design Project   **exhibit 5.7**

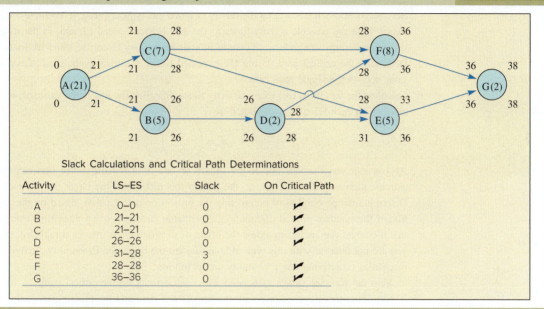

Slack Calculations and Critical Path Determinations

Activity	LS–ES	Slack	On Critical Path
A	0–0	0	✔
B	21–21	0	✔
C	21–21	0	✔
D	26–26	0	✔
E	31–28	3	
F	28–28	0	✔
G	36–36	0	✔

estimated. (Note that the probability calculations are a distinguishing feature of the classic PERT approach.)

Example 5.3: Three Time Estimates

We use the same information as in Example 5.2, with the exception that activities have three time estimates.

SOLUTION

1. Identify each activity to be done in the project.
2. Determine the sequence of activities and construct a network reflecting the precedence relationships.
3. The three estimates for an activity time are:

    a = Optimistic time: the minimum reasonable period of time in which the activity can be completed. (There is only a small probability, typically assumed to be 1 percent, that the activity can be completed in less time.)

    m = Most likely time: the best guess of the time required. Since m would be the time thought most likely to appear, it is also the mode of the beta distribution discussed in step 4.

    b = Pessimistic time: the maximum reasonable period of time the activity would take to be completed. (There is only a small probability, typically assumed to be 1 percent, that it would take longer.)

    Typically, this information is gathered from those people who are to perform the activity.
4. Calculate the expected time (ET) for each activity. The formula for this calculation is

$$ET = \frac{a + 4m + b}{6}$$ [5.1]

This is based on the beta statistical distribution and weights the most likely time (m) four times more than either the optimistic time (a) or the pessimistic time (b). The beta distribution is extremely flexible. It can take on the variety of forms that typically arise; it has finite end points (which limit the possible activity times to the area between a and b); and, in the simplified version, it permits straightforward computation of the activity mean and standard deviation.

5. Determine the critical path. Using the expected times, a critical path is calculated in the same way as the single time case.

6. Calculate the variances (σ^2) of the activity times. Specifically, this is the variance, σ^2, associated with each ET and is computed as

$$\sigma^2 = \left(\frac{b-a}{6}\right)^2 \qquad\qquad [5.2]$$

As you can see, the variance is the square of one-sixth the difference between the two extreme time estimates. Of course, the greater this difference, the larger the variance.

7. Determine the probability of completing the project on a given date, based on the application of the standard normal distribution. A valuable feature of using three time estimates is that it enables the analyst to assess the effect of uncertainty on project completion time. (If you are not familiar with this type of analysis, see the box titled Probability Analysis.) The mechanics of deriving this probability are as follows:

   a. Sum the variance values associated with each activity on the critical path.

   b. Substitute this figure, along with the project due date and the project expected completion time, into the Z transformation formula. This formula is

$$Z = \frac{D-T}{\sqrt{\Sigma \sigma_{cp}^2}} \qquad\qquad [5.3]$$

where

$$D = \text{Desired completion date for the project}$$
$$T_E = \text{Expected completion time for the project}$$
$$\Sigma\sigma_{cp}^2 = \text{Sum of the variances along the critical path}$$

   c. Calculate the value of Z, which is the number of standard deviations (of a standard normal distribution) that the project due date is from the expected completion time.

   d. Using the value of Z, find the probability of meeting the project due date (using a table of normal probabilities such as Appendix E). The *expected completion time* is the starting time plus the sum of the activity times on the critical path.

Following the steps just outlined, we developed Exhibit 5.8, showing expected times and variances. The project network was created the same way we did previously. The only difference is that the activity times are weighted averages. We determine the critical path as before, using these values as if they were single numbers. The difference between the single time estimate and the three times (optimistic, most likely, and pessimistic) is in computing the probabilities of completion. Exhibit 5.9 shows the network and critical path.

Because there are two critical paths in the network, we must decide which variances to use in arriving at the probability of meeting the project due date. A conservative approach dictates using the critical path with the largest total variance to focus management's attention on the activities most likely to exhibit broad variations. On this basis, the variances associated with activities A, C, F, and G would be used to find the probability of completion. Thus $\Sigma\sigma_{cp}^2 = 9 + 2.7778 + 0.1111 + 0 = 11.8889$. Suppose management asks for the probability of completing the project in 35 weeks. D, then, is 35. The expected completion time was found to be 38. Substituting into the Z equation and solving, we obtain

$$Z = \frac{D-T_E}{\sqrt{\Sigma\sigma_{cp}^2}} = \frac{35-38}{\sqrt{11.8889}} = -0.87$$

Activity Expected Times and Variances

exhibit 5.8

ACTIVITY	ACTIVITY DESIGNATION	TIME ESTIMATES a	m	b	EXPECTED TIMES (ET) $\dfrac{a + 4m + b}{6}$	ACTIVITY VARIANCES (σ^2) $\left(\dfrac{b - a}{6}\right)^2$
Design	A	10	22	28	21	9
Build prototype	B	4	4	10	5	1
Evaluate equipment	C	4	6	14	7	2.7778
Test prototype	D	1	2	3	2	0.1111
Write report	E	1	5	9	5	1.7778
Write methods report	F	7	8	9	8	0.1111
Write final report	G	2	2	2	2	0

Excel: Project Management

Computer Design Project with Three Time Estimates

exhibit 5.9

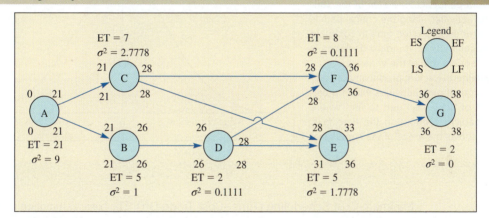

Looking at Appendix E, we see that a Z value of -0.87 yields a probability of 0.1922, which means that the project manager has only about a 19 percent chance of completing the project in 35 weeks. Note that this probability is really the probability of completing the critical path A–C–F–G. Because there is another critical path and other paths that might become critical, the probability of completing the project in 35 weeks is actually less than 0.19. •

Time–Cost Models and Project Crashing

In practice, project managers are as much concerned with the cost to complete a project as with the time to complete the project. For this reason, **time–cost models** have been devised. These models—extensions of the basic critical path method—attempt to develop a minimum-cost schedule for an entire project and to control expenditures during the project.

Time–cost models
Extension of the critical path models that considers the trade-off between the time required to complete an activity and cost. This is often referred to as "crashing" the project.

Probability Analysis

The three-time-estimate approach introduces the ability to consider the probability that a project will be completed within a particular amount of time. The assumption needed to make this probability estimate is that the activity duration times are independent random variables. If this is true, the central limit theorem can be used to find the mean and the variance of the sequence of activities that form the critical path. The central limit theorem says that the sum of a group of independent, identically distributed random variables approaches a normal distribution as the number of random variables increases. In the case of project management problems, the random variables are the actual times for the activities in the project. (Recall that the time for each activity is assumed to be independent of other activities and to follow a beta statistical distribution.) For this, the expected time to complete the critical path activities is the sum of the activity times.

Likewise, because of the assumption of activity time independence, the sum of the variances of the activities along the critical path is the variance of the expected time to complete the path. Recall that the standard deviation is equal to the square root of the variance.

To determine the actual probability of completing the critical path activities within a certain amount of time, we need to find where on our probability distribution the time falls. Appendix E shows the areas of the cumulative standard normal distribution for different values of Z. Z measures the number of standard deviations either to the right or to the left of zero in the distribution. The values correspond to the cumulative probability associated with each value of Z. For example, the first value in the table, -4.00, has a $G(z)$ equal to 0.00003. This means that the probability associated with a Z value of -4.0 is only 0.003 percent. Similarly, a Z value of 1.50 has a $G(z)$ equal to 0.93319 or 93.319 percent. The Z values are calculated using equation 5.3, given in step 7b of the "Three Time Estimates" example solution. These cumulative probabilities also can be obtained by using the NORMSDIST (Z) function built into Microsoft Excel.

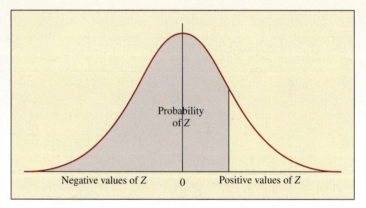

Minimum-Cost Scheduling (Time–Cost Trade-Off) The basic assumption in minimum-cost scheduling, also known as "crashing," is that there is a relationship between activity completion time and the cost of a project. Crashing refers to the compression or shortening of the time to complete the project. It costs money to expedite an activity, and these costs are termed *activity direct costs* and add to the project direct cost. Some may be worker-related, such as overtime work, hiring more workers, and transferring workers from other jobs; others are resource-related, such as buying or leasing additional or more efficient equipment and drawing on additional support facilities.

The costs associated with sustaining the project are termed *project indirect costs*: overhead, facilities, and resource opportunity costs, and, under certain contractual situations, penalty costs or lost incentive payments. Because *activity direct costs and project indirect costs* are opposing costs dependent on time, the scheduling problem is essentially one of finding the project duration that minimizes their sum, or in other words, finding the optimum point in a time–cost trade-off.

The procedure for project crashing consists of the following five steps. It is explained by using the simple four-activity network shown in Exhibit 5.10. Assume that the indirect costs remain constant at $10 per day if the project takes eight days or less and then increases at the rate of $5 per day.

Example of Time–Cost Trade-Off Procedure

exhibit 5.10

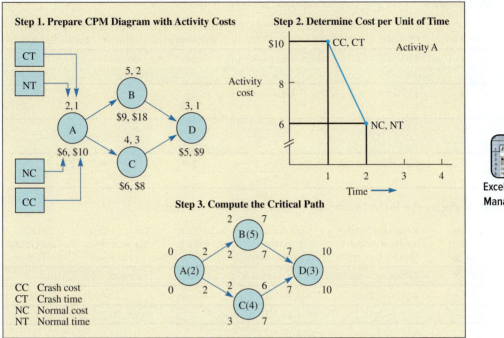

Excel: Project Management

1. **Prepare a CPM-type network diagram.** For each activity, this diagram should list:
   a. Normal cost (NC): the lowest expected activity costs. (These are the lesser of the cost figures shown under each node in Exhibit 5.10.)
   b. Normal time (NT): the time associated with each normal cost.
   c. Crash time (CT): the shortest possible activity time.
   d. Crash cost (CC): the cost associated with each crash time.
2. **Determine the cost per unit of time (assume days) to expedite each activity.** The relationship between activity time and cost may be shown graphically by plotting CC and CT coordinates and connecting them to the NC and NT coordinates by a concave, convex, or straight line—or some other form, depending on the actual cost structure of activity performance, as in Exhibit 5.10. For activity A, we assume a linear relationship between time and cost. This assumption is common in practice and helps us derive the cost per day to expedite because this value may be found directly by taking the slope of the line using the formula Slope = (CC − NC) ÷ (NT − CT). (When the assumption of linearity cannot be made, the cost of expediting must be determined graphically for each day the activity may be shortened.)

   The calculations needed to obtain the cost of expediting the remaining activities are shown in Exhibit 5.11A.
3. **Compute the critical path.** For the simple network we have been using, this schedule would take 10 days. The critical path is A–B–D.
4. **Shorten the critical path at the least cost.** The easiest way to proceed is to start with the normal schedule, find the critical path, and reduce the path time by one day using the lowest-cost activity. Then recompute and find the new critical path

exhibit 5.11

A. Calculating Cost per Day to Expedite Each Activity

ACTIVITY	CC − NC	NT − CT	$\dfrac{CC - NC}{NT - CT}$	COST PER DAY TO EXPEDITE	MAXIMUM NUMBER OF DAYS ACTIVITY MAY BE SHORTENED
A	$10 − $6	2 − 1	$\dfrac{\$10 - \$6}{2 - 1}$	$4	1
B	$18 − $9	5 − 2	$\dfrac{\$18 - \$9}{5 - 2}$	$3	3
C	$8 − $6	4 − 3	$\dfrac{\$8 - \$6}{4 - 3}$	$2	1
D	$9 − $5	3 − 1	$\dfrac{\$9 - \$5}{3 - 1}$	$2	2

B. Reducing the Project Completion Time One Day at a Time

CURRENT CRITICAL PATH(S)	REMAINING NUMBER OF DAYS ACTIVITY MAY BE SHORTENED	COST PER DAY TO EXPEDITE EACH ACTIVITY	LEAST-COST ACTIVITY TO EXPEDITE	TOTAL COST OF ALL ACTIVITIES IN NETWORK	PROJECT COMPLETION TIME
ABD	All activity times and costs are normal.			$26	10
ABD	A−1, B−3, D−2	A−4, B−3, D−2	D	28	9
ABD	A−1, B−3, D−1	A−4, B−3, D−2	D	30	8
ABD	A−1, B−3	A−4, B−3	B	33	7
ABD ACD	A−1, B−2, C−1	A−4, B−3, C−2	A*	37	6
ABD ACD	B−2, C−1	B−3, C−2	B&C†	42	5
ABD ACD	B−1	B−3	B+	45	5

*To reduce the critical path by one day, reduce either A alone or B and C together at the same time (either B or C by itself just modifies the critical path without shortening it).
†B and C must be crashed together to reduce the path by one day.
+Crashing activity B does not reduce the length of the project, so this additional cost would not be incurred.

and reduce it by one day also. Repeat this procedure until the time of completion is satisfactory, or until there can be no further reduction in the project completion time. Exhibit 5.11B shows the reduction of the network one day at a time.

Working through Exhibit 5.11B might initially seem difficult. In the first line, all activities are at their normal time, and costs are at their lowest value. The critical path is A–B–D, cost for completing the project is $26, and the project completion time is 10 days.

The goal in line two is to reduce the project completion time by one day. We know it is necessary to reduce the time for one or more of the activities on the critical path. In the second column, we note that activity A can be reduced one day (from two to one day), activity B can be reduced three days (from five to two days), and activity D can be reduced two days (from three to one day). The next column tracks the cost to reduce each of the activities by a single day. For example, for activity A, it normally costs $6 to complete in two days. It could be completed in one day at a cost of $10, a $4 increase. So we indicate the cost to expedite activity A by one day is $4. For activity B, it normally costs $9 to complete in five days. It could be completed in two days at a cost of $18. Our cost to reduce B by three days is $9, or $3 per day. For C, it normally costs $5 to complete in three days. It could be completed in one day at a cost of $9; a two-day reduction would cost $4 ($2 per day). The least expensive alternative for a one-day reduction in time is to expedite activity D at a cost of $2. Total cost for the network goes up to $28 and the project completion time is reduced to nine days.

Our next iteration starts in line three, where the goal is to reduce the project completion time to eight days. The nine-day critical path is A–B–D. We could shorten activity A by one day, B by three days, and D by one day (note D has already been reduced from three to two days). Cost to reduce each activity by one day is the same as in line two. Again, the least expensive activity to reduce is D. Reducing activity D from two to one day results in the total cost for all activities in the network going up to $30 and the project completion time coming down to eight days.

Line four is similar to line three, but now only A and B are on the critical path and can be reduced. B is reduced, which takes our cost up $3 to $33 and reduces the project completion time to seven days.

In line five (actually our fourth iteration in solving the problem), activities A, B, C, and D are all critical. D cannot be reduced, so our only options are activities A, B, and C. Note that B and C are in parallel, so it does not help to reduce B without reducing C. Our options are to reduce A alone at a cost of $4 or B and C together at a cost of $5 ($3 for B and $2 for C), so we reduce A in this iteration.

In line six, we take the B and C option that was considered in line five. Finally, in line seven, our only option is to reduce activity B. Since B and C are in parallel and we cannot reduce C, there is no value in reducing B alone. We can reduce the project completion time no further.

5. **Plot project direct, indirect, and total-cost curves and find the minimum-cost schedule.** Exhibit 5.12 shows the indirect cost plotted as a constant $10 per day for up to eight days and increasing $5 per day thereafter (as was stated initially with the example). The direct costs are plotted from Exhibit 5.11B, and the total project cost is shown as the total of the two costs.

Summing the values for direct and indirect costs for each day yields the project total cost curve. As you can see, this curve is at its minimum with an eight-day schedule, which costs $40 ($30 direct + $10 indirect).

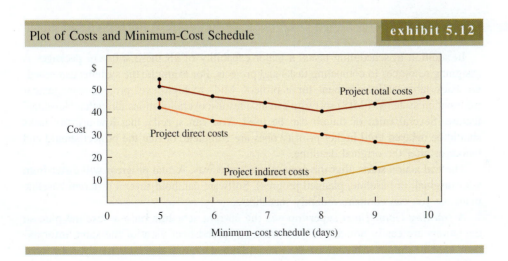

Plot of Costs and Minimum-Cost Schedule   **exhibit 5.12**

PROJECT MANAGEMENT INFORMATION SYSTEMS

LO5–4 Exemplify how network-planning models and earned value management are implemented in commercial software packages.

Interest in the techniques and concepts of project management has exploded in the past 10 years. This has resulted in a parallel increase in project management software offerings. Now there are over 100 companies offering project management software. For the most up-to-date information about software available, check out the Website of the Project Management Institute (**www.pmi.org**). Two of the leading companies are Microsoft, with Microsoft Project, and Primavera, with Primavera Project Planner.

The Microsoft Project program comes with an excellent online tutorial, which is one reason for its overwhelming popularity with project managers tracking mid-sized projects. This package is compatible with the Microsoft Office Suite, which opens all the communications and Internet integration capabilities that Microsoft offers. The program includes features for scheduling, allocating and leveling resources, and controlling costs and producing presentation-quality graphics and reports.

For managing very large projects or programs having several projects, Primavera Project Planner is often the choice. Primavera was the first major vendor of this type of software and has possibly the most sophisticated capability.

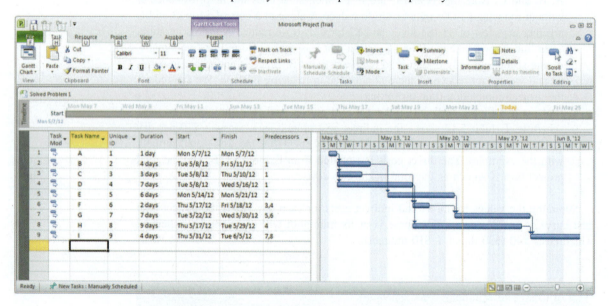

In addition to scheduling tasks, a major capability of all these software packages is assigning resources to competing tasks and projects. For example, the systems can schedule back labor and equipment for a project. Mid- to high-level project management information systems (PMIS) software can also resolve overallocations through a "leveling" feature. Several rules of thumb can be used. You can specify that low-priority tasks should be delayed until higher-priority ones are complete, or that the project should end before or after the original deadline.

The real action starts after the project gets under way. Actual progress will differ from your original, or baseline, planned progress. Software can hold several different baseline plans, so you can compare monthly snapshots.

A *tracking Gantt chart* superimposes the current schedule onto a baseline plan so deviations are easily noticed. If you prefer, a spreadsheet view of the same information can be output. Deviations between planned start/finish and newly scheduled start/finish also appear, and a "slipping filter" can be applied to highlight or output only those tasks that are scheduled to finish at a later date than the planned baseline. Management by exception also can be applied to find deviations between budgeted costs and actual costs.

CONCEPT CONNECTIONS

LO5–1 Explain what projects are and how projects are organized.

- Projects can be categorized into four major types: product change, process change, research and development, and alliance and partnerships.
- Even though some projects are often thought to be one-time occurrences, they are sometimes repeated.
- The project team can be organized in different ways. The most common are pure project, where the team works full time on the project; functional project, where team members stay in their functional group and work on many different projects at the same time; and matrix project, which blends the pure project and functional project structures.
- The activities of the projects are organized according to the work breakdown structure, which groups them into subtasks and work packages. Completion of a work package results in the completion of a subtask, and completion of all of the subtasks is required to complete the project.

Project   A series of related jobs usually directed toward some major output and requiring a significant period of time to perform.

Project management   Planning, directing, and controlling resources (people, equipment, material) to meet the technical, cost, and time constraints of a project.

Pure project   A structure for organizing a project where a self-contained team works full time on the project.

Functional project   A structure where team members are assigned from the functional units of the organization. The team members remain a part of their functional units and typically are not dedicated to the project.

Matrix project   A structure that blends the functional and pure project structure. Each project uses people from different functional areas. A dedicated project manager decides what tasks need to be performed and when, but the functional managers control which people to use.

Project milestone   A specific event in a project.

Work breakdown structure (WBS)   The hierarchy of project tasks, subtasks, and work packages.

Activities   Pieces of work within a project that consume time. The completion of all the activities of a project marks the end of the project.

LO5–2 Evaluate projects using earned value management.

- A key aspect to managing a project is understanding the current status of its activities.
- Simple graphical techniques are often augmented with standard reports that give a detailed analysis of the work completed together with what is left to be done.
- Earned value management (EVM) is a technique commonly used for measuring project progress.

Gantt chart   Shows in a graphic manner the amount of time involved and the sequence in which activities can be performed. This chart is often referred to as a bar chart.

Earned value management (EVM)   Technique that combines measures of scope, schedule, and cost for evaluating project progress.

LO5–3 Analyze projects using network-planning models.

- The critical path method (CPM) is the most widely used approach to scheduling projects. There are a number of variations on the basic approach.
- The goal is to find the earliest time that the entire project can be completed.
- The techniques also identify what activities are critical, meaning that there cannot be delays without delaying the earliest time that the project can be completed.
- The three techniques studied in the chapter are the following: CPM with a single activity time, CPM with three activity time estimates, and time–cost models with project crashing.

Critical path   The sequence of activities in a project that forms the longest chain in terms of their time to complete. This path contains zero slack time. It is possible for there to be multiple critical paths in a project. Techniques used to find the critical path are called CPM, or critical path method, techniques.

Immediate predecessor   Activity that needs to be completed immediately before another activity.

Slack time   The time that an activity can be delayed; without delaying the entire project; the difference between the late and early start times of an activity.

Early start schedule   A project schedule that lists all activities by their early start times.

Late start schedule   A project schedule that lists all activities by their late start times. This schedule may create savings by postponing purchases of material and other costs associated with the project.

Time–cost models   Extension of the critical path models that considers the trade-off between the time required to complete an activity and the cost. This is often referred to as "crashing" the project.

$$ET = \frac{a + 4m + b}{6} \qquad \text{[5.1]}$$

$$\sigma^2 = \left(\frac{b - a}{6}\right)^2 \qquad \text{[5.2]}$$

$$Z = \frac{D - T}{\sqrt{\Sigma \sigma_{cp}^2}} \qquad \text{[5.3]}$$

LO5–4 Exemplify how network-planning models and earned value management are implemented in commercial software packages.

- The techniques and concepts described in this chapter are implemented in commercially available software packages.
- Two of the most common packages are Microsoft Project and Primavera Project Planner.
- These packages are capable of managing multiple projects at the same time and can help resolve resource usage conflicts of competing projects.

SOLVED PROBLEMS

Excel:
Ch5_Solved
Problems

LO5–2 SOLVED PROBLEM 1

You have been asked to calculate the Cost Performance Index for a project using earned value management techniques. It is currently day 20 of the project and the following summarizes the current status of the project:

ACTIVITY	EXPECTED COST	ACTIVITY DURATION	EXPECTED START DATE	EXPECTED COMPLETION DATE	EXPECTED % COMPLETE	ACTUAL % COMPLETE	ACTUAL COST TO DATE
Start-up	$100,000	10 days	0	10	100%	100%	$105,000
Construction	325,000	14 days	8	22	12/14 = 85.714%	90%	280,000
Finishing	50,000	12 days	18	30	2/12 = 16.667%	25%	2,500

Calculate the Schedule Variance, Schedule Performance Index, and Cost Performance Index for the project.

Solution

Step 1: Calculate Budgeted Cost of the Work Scheduled (BCWS) to date:

Start-up is 100 percent complete and we are beyond the expected completion date, so budgeted cost is $100,000 for this activity.

Would expect Construction to be 85.714 percent complete and cost $278,571 to date.
Would expect Finishing to be 16.667 percent complete at a cost of $8,333 to date.

$$\text{Budgeted Cost of Work Scheduled} = \$100,000 + \$278,571 + \$8,333 = \$386,904$$

Step 2: Calculate the Budgeted Cost of the Work Performed (BCWP) to date:

Start-up is 100 percent complete, so budgeted cost is $100,000.
Construction is actually only 90 percent complete, so budgeted cost for this much of the activity is (325,000 × .9) = $292,500.

Finishing is now 25 percent complete, so budgeted cost is ($50,000 × .25) = $12,500.

$$\text{Budgeted Cost of Work Performed} = \$100,000 + \$292,500 + \$12,500 = \$405,000$$

Step 3: Actual Cost (AC) of the project to date is $105,000 + $280,000 + $2,500 = $387,500.

Step 4: Calculate performance measures:

$$\text{Schedule Variance} = \$405,000 - \$386,904 = \$18,096$$

$$\text{Schedule Performance Index} = \$405,000/\$386,904 = 1.05$$

$$\text{Cost Performance Index} = \$405,000/\$387,500 = 1.05$$

The project looks good since it is both ahead of schedule and below the budgeted cost.

LO5–3 **SOLVED PROBLEM 2**

A project has been defined to contain the following list of activities, along with their required times for completion:

ACTIVITY	TIME (DAYS)	IMMEDIATE PREDECESSORS
A	1	—
B	4	A
C	3	A
D	7	A
E	6	B
F	2	C, D
G	7	E, F
H	9	D
I	4	G, H

Excel:
Ch5_Solved
Problems

a. Draw the critical path diagram.

b. Show the early start, early finish, late start, and late finish times.

c. Show the critical path.

d. What would happen if activity F was revised to take four days instead of two?

Solution

The answers to *a, b,* and *c* are shown in the following diagram.

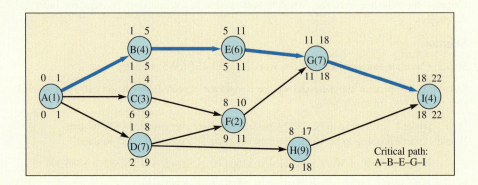

PATH	LENGTH (DAYS)
A-B-E-G-I	**22 (critical path)**
A-C-F-G-I	17
A-D-F-G-I	21
A-D-H-I	21

d. New critical path: A–D–F–G–I. Time of completion is 23 days.

LO5–3 SOLVED PROBLEM 3

A project has been defined to contain the following activities, along with their time estimates for completion:

	TIME ESTIMATES (WEEKS)			
ACTIVITY	*a*	*m*	*b*	IMMEDIATE PREDECESSOR
A	1	4	7	—
B	2	6	7	A
C	3	4	6	D
D	6	12	14	A
E	3	6	12	D
F	6	8	16	B, C
G	1	5	6	E, F

a. Calculate the expected time and the variance for each activity.

b. Draw the critical path diagram.

c. Show the early start, early finish times, and late start, late finish times.

d. Show the critical path.

e. What is the probability that the project can be completed in 34 weeks?

Solution

a.

ACTIVITY	EXPECTED TIME $\dfrac{a + 4m + b}{6}$	ACTIVITY VARIANCE $\left(\dfrac{b - a}{6}\right)^2$
A	4.00	1
B	5.50	0.6944
C	4.17	0.2500
D	11.33	1.7778
E	6.50	2.2500
F	9.00	2.7778
G	4.50	0.6944

b.

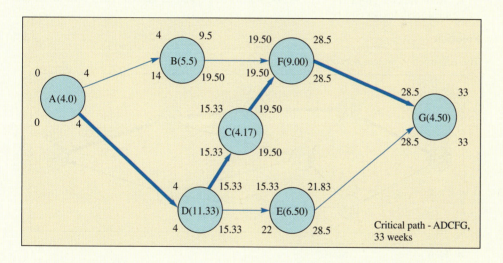

c. Shown on diagram.

d. Shown on diagram.

PATH	LENGTH (WEEKS)
A-B-F-G	23
A-D-C-F-G	**33 critical path**
A-D-E-G	26.33

$$Z = \frac{D - T_E}{\sqrt{\Sigma \sigma_{cp}^2}} = \frac{34 - 33}{\sqrt{1 + 1.7778 + .25 + 2.7778 + .6944}} = \frac{1}{2.5495} = .3922$$

Look up that value in Appendix E and we see that there is about a 65 percent chance of completing the project by that date.

LO5-3 **SOLVED PROBLEM 4**

Here are the precedence requirements, normal and crash activity times, and normal and crash costs for a construction project:

		REQUIRED TIME (WEEKS)		COST	
ACTIVITY	PRECEDING ACTIVITIES	NORMAL	CRASH	NORMAL	CRASH
A	—	4	2	$10,000	$11,000
B	A	3	2	6,000	9,000
C	A	2	1	4,000	6,000
D	B	5	3	14,000	18,000
E	B, C	1	1	9,000	9,000
F	C	3	2	7,000	8,000
G	E, F	4	2	13,000	25,000
H	D, E	4	1	11,000	18,000
I	H, G	6	5	20,000	29,000

a. What are the critical path and the estimated completion time?

b. To shorten the project by three weeks, which tasks would be shortened and what would the final total project cost be?

Solution

The construction project network is shown below:

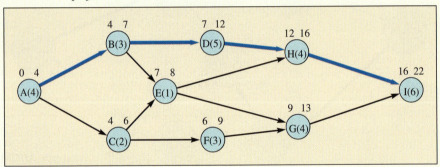

a.

PATH	LENGTH
A-B-D-H-I	22 critical path
A-B-E-H-I	18
A-B-E-G-I	18
A-C-E-H-I	17
A-C-E-G-I	17
A-C-F-G-I	19

Normal completion time is 22 weeks.

ACTIVITY	CRASH COST	NORMAL COST	NORMAL TIME	CRASH TIME	COST PER WEEK	WEEKS
A	$11,000	$10,000	4	2	$ 500	2
B	9,000	6,000	3	2	3,000	1
C	6,000	4,000	2	1	2,000	1
D	18,000	14,000	5	3	2,000	2
E	9,000	9,000	1	1		0
F	8,000	7,000	3	2	1,000	1
G	25,000	13,000	4	2	6,000	2
H	18,000	11,000	4	1	2,333	3
I	29,000	20,000	6	5	9,000	1

(1) 1st week: CP = A–B–D–H–I. A is least expensive at $500. Critical path stays the same.
(2) 2nd week: A is still the least expensive at $500. Critical path stays the same.
(3) 3rd week: Because A is no longer available, the choices are B (at $3,000), D (at $2,000), H (at $2,333), or I (at $9,000). Therefore, choose D at $2,000.

The total project cost if shortened by three weeks is

A	$11,000
B	6,000
C	4,000
D	16,000
E	9,000
F	7,000
G	13,000
H	11,000
I	20,000
	$97,000

DISCUSSION QUESTIONS

LO5–1
1. What was the most complex project you have been involved in? Give examples of the following as they pertain to the project: the work breakdown structure, tasks, subtasks, and work package. Were you on the critical path? Did it have a good project manager?
2. What are some reasons project scheduling is not done well?

LO5–2
3. Discuss the graphic presentations in Exhibit 5.4. Are there any other graphic outputs you would like to see if you were project manager?
4. Why is it important to use *earned value management (EVM)* in the overall management of projects? Compare to the use of baseline and current schedules only.
5. Consider the EVM charts in Exhibit 5.5. Are there any other measures you might want to use in the management of a project? What are some controllable variables that may affect the costs being tracked?

LO5–3
6. Which characteristics must a project have for critical path scheduling to be applicable? What types of projects have been subjected to critical path analysis?
7. What are the underlying assumptions of minimum-cost scheduling? Are they equally realistic?
8. "Project control should always focus on the critical path." Comment.
9. Why would subcontractors for a government project want their activities on the critical path? Under what conditions would they try to avoid being on the critical path?

LO5–4
10. What do you think might be some barriers to the successful, effective use of the project management software packages discussed in the chapter?

OBJECTIVE QUESTIONS

LO5–1
1. What are the three types of projects based on the amount of change involved?
2. What are the four major categories of projects based on the type of change involved?

3. Match the following characteristics with their relevant project team organizational structures:

   ___ The project is housed within a functional division of the firm.   A. Pure project
   ___ A project manager leads personnel from different functional areas.   B. Functional project
   ___ Personnel work on a dedicated project team.   C. Matrix project
   ___ A team member reports to two bosses.
   ___ Team pride, motivation, and commitment are high.
   ___ Team members can work on several projects.
   ___ Duplication of resources is minimized.

4. What is the term for a group of project activities that are assigned to a single organizational unit?

LO5–2

5. Your project to obtain charitable donations is now 30 days into a planned 40-day project. The project is divided into 3 activities. The first activity is designed to solicit individual donations. It is scheduled to run the first 25 days of the project and to bring in $25,000. Even though we are 30 days into the project, we still see that we have only 90 percent of this activity complete. The second activity relates to company donations and is scheduled to run for 30 days starting on day 5 and extending through day 35. We estimate that, even though we should have 83 percent (25/30) of this activity complete, it is actually only 50 percent complete. This part of the project was scheduled to bring in $150,000 in donations. The final activity is for matching funds. This activity is scheduled to run the last 10 days of the project and has not started. It is scheduled to bring in an additional $50,000. So far, $175,000 has actually been brought in on the project.

Calculate the Schedule Variance, Schedule Performance Index, and Cost (actually value in this case) Performance Index. How is the project going? (*Hint:* Note that this problem is different since revenue rather than cost is the relevant measure. Use care in how the measures are interpreted.)

6. A project to build a new bridge seems to be going very well since the project is well ahead of schedule and costs seem to be running very low. A major milestone has been reached where the first two activities have been totally completed and the third activity is 60 percent complete. The planners were expecting to be only 50 percent through the third activity at this time. The first activity involves prepping the site for the bridge. It was expected that this would cost $1,420,000 and it was done for only $1,300,000. The second activity was the pouring of concrete for the bridge. This was expected to cost $10,500,000 but was actually done for $9,000,000. The third and final activity is the actual construction of the bridge superstructure. This was expected to cost a total of $8,500,000. To date, they have spent $5,000,000 on the superstructure.

Calculate the Schedule Variance, Schedule Performance Index, and Cost Performance Index for the project to date. How is the project going?

LO5–3

7. The following activities are part of a project to be scheduled using CPM:

ACTIVITY	IMMEDIATE PREDECESSOR	TIME (WEEKS)
A	—	6
B	A	3
C	A	7
D	C	2
E	B, D	4
F	D	3
G	E, F	7

   a. Draw the network.
   b. What is the critical path?
   c. How many weeks will it take to complete the project?
   d. How much slack does activity B have?
8. Schedule the following activities using CPM:

ACTIVITY	IMMEDIATE PREDECESSOR	TIME (WEEKS)
A	—	1
B	A	4
C	A	3
D	B	2
E	C, D	5
F	D	2
G	F	2
H	E, G	3

   a. Draw the network.
   b. What is the critical path?
   c. How many weeks will it take to complete the project?
   d. Which activities have slack, and how much?
9. The R&D department is planning to bid on a large project for the development of a new communication system for commercial planes. The accompanying table shows the activities, times, and sequences required:

ACTIVITY	IMMEDIATE PREDECESSOR	TIME (WEEKS)
A	—	3
B	A	2
C	A	4
D	A	4
E	B	6
F	C, D	6
G	D, F	2
H	D	3
I	E, G, H	3

   a. Draw the network diagram.
   b. What is the critical path?
   c. Suppose you want to shorten the completion time as much as possible, and you have the option of shortening any or all of B, C, D, and G each one week. Which would you shorten?
   d. What is the new critical path and earliest completion time?
10. The following represents a project that should be scheduled using CPM:

ACTIVITY	IMMEDIATE PREDECESSORS	*a*	*m*	*b*
A	—	1	3	5
B	—	1	2	3
C	A	1	2	3
D	A	2	3	4
E	B	3	4	11
F	C, D	3	4	5
G	D, E	1	4	6
H	F, G	2	4	5

The "TIMES (DAYS)" heading spans the *a*, *m*, *b* columns.

    a. Draw the network.

    b. What is the critical path?

    c. What is the expected project completion time?

    d. What is the probability of completing this project within 16 days?

11. There is an 82 percent chance the project below can be completed in *X* weeks or less. What is *X*?

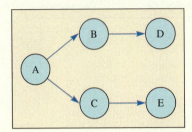

ACTIVITY	MOST OPTIMISTIC	MOST LIKELY	MOST PESSIMISTIC
A	2	5	11
B	3	3	3
C	1	3	5
D	6	8	10
E	4	7	10

12. The following table represents a plan for a project:

		TIMES (DAYS)		
JOB NO.	PREDECESSOR JOB(S)	*a*	*m*	*b*
1	—	2	3	4
2	1	1	2	3
3	1	4	5	12
4	1	3	4	11
5	2	1	3	5
6	3	1	2	3
7	4	1	8	9
8	5, 6	2	4	6
9	8	2	4	12
10	7	3	4	5
11	9, 10	5	7	8

    a. Construct the appropriate network diagram.

    b. Indicate the critical path.

    c. What is the expected completion time for the project?

    d. You can accomplish any one of the following at an additional cost of $1,500:

        (1) Reduce job 5 by two days.

        (2) Reduce job 3 by two days.

        (3) Reduce job 7 by two days.

        If you will save $1,000 for each day that the earliest completion time is reduced, which action, if any, would you choose?

    e. What is the probability that the project will take more than 30 days to complete?

13. A construction project is broken down into the following 10 activities:

ACTIVITY	IMMEDIATE PREDECESSOR	TIME (WEEKS)
1	—	4
2	1	2
3	1	4
4	1	3
5	2, 3	5
6	3	6
7	4	2
8	5	3
9	6, 7	5
10	8, 9	7

a. Draw the network diagram.

b. Find the critical path.

c. If activities 1 and 10 cannot be shortened, but activities 2 through 9 can be shortened to a minimum of one week each at a cost of $10,000 per week, which activities would you shorten to cut the project by four weeks?

14. Here is a CPM network with activity times in weeks:

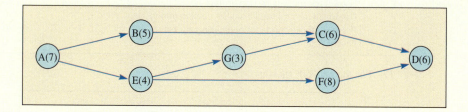

a. Determine the critical path.

b. How many weeks will the project take to complete?

c. Suppose F could be shortened by two weeks and B by one week. How would this affect the completion date?

15. Here is a network with the activity times shown in days:

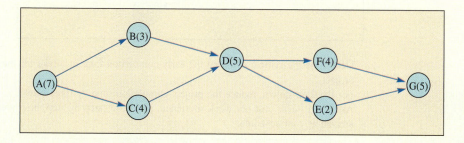

a. Find the critical path.

b. The following table shows the normal times and the crash times, along with the associated costs for each activity.

ACTIVITY	NORMAL TIME	CRASH TIME	NORMAL COST	CRASH COST
A	7	6	$7,000	$ 8,000
B	3	2	5,000	7,000
C	4	3	9,000	10,200
D	5	4	3,000	4,500
E	2	1	2,000	3,000
F	4	2	4,000	7,000
G	5	4	5,000	8,000

If the project is to be shortened by four days, show which activities, in order of reduction, would be shortened and the resulting cost.

16. The home office billing department of a chain of department stores prepares monthly inventory reports for use by the stores' purchasing agents. Given the following information, use the critical path method to determine:

a. How long the total process will take.

b. Which jobs can be delayed without delaying the early start of any subsequent activity.

	JOB AND DESCRIPTION	IMMEDIATE PREDECESSORS	TIME (HOURS)
A	Start	—	0
B	Get computer printouts of customer purchases	A	10
C	Get stock records for the month	A	20
D	Reconcile purchase printouts and stock records	B, C	30
E	Total stock records by department	B, C	20
F	Determine reorder quantities for coming period	E	40
G	Prepare stock reports for purchasing agents	D, F	20
H	Finish	G	0

17. For the network shown:

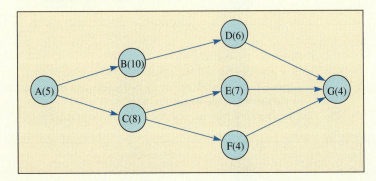

a. Determine the critical path and the early completion time in weeks for the project.
b. For the data shown, reduce the project completion time by three weeks. Assume a linear cost per week shortened, and show, step by step, how you arrived at your schedule.

ACTIVITY	NORMAL TIME	NORMAL COST	CRASH TIME	CRASH COST
A	5	$ 7,000	3	$13,000
B	10	12,000	7	18,000
C	8	5,000	7	7,000
D	6	4,000	5	5,000
E	7	3,000	6	6,000
F	4	6,000	3	7,000
G	4	7,000	3	9,000

18. The following CPM network has estimates of the normal time in weeks listed for the activities:

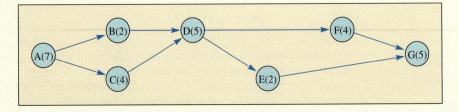

a. Identify the critical path.
b. What is the length of time to complete the project?
c. Which activities have slack, and how much?

d. Here is a table of normal and crash times and costs. Which activities would you shorten to cut two weeks from the schedule in a rational fashion? What would be the incremental cost? Is the critical path changed?

ACTIVITY	NORMAL TIME	CRASH TIME	NORMAL COST	CRASH COST
A	7	6	$7,000	$ 8,000
B	2	1	5,000	7,000
C	4	3	9,000	10,200
D	5	4	3,000	4,500
E	2	1	2,000	3,000
F	4	2	4,000	7,000
G	5	4	5,000	8,000

19. Bragg's Bakery is building a new automated bakery in downtown Sandusky. Here are the activities that need to be completed to get the new bakery built and the equipment installed.

ACTIVITY	PREDECESSOR	NORMAL TIME (WEEKS)	CRASH TIME (WEEKS)	EXPEDITING COST/WEEK
A	—	9	6	$3,000
B	A	8	5	3,500
C	A	15	10	4,000
D	B, C	5	3	2,000
E	C	10	6	2,500
F	D, E	2	1	5,000

a. Draw the project diagram.
b. What is the normal project length?
c. What is the project length if all activities are crashed to their minimum?
d. Bragg's loses $3,500 in profit per week for every week the bakery is not completed. How many weeks will the project take if we are willing to pay crashing cost as long as it is less than $3,500?

20. Assume the network and data that follow:

ACTIVITY	NORMAL TIME (WEEKS)	NORMAL COST	CRASH TIME (WEEKS)	CRASH COST	IMMEDIATE PREDECESSORS
A	2	$ 50	1	$ 70	—
B	4	80	2	160	A
C	8	70	4	110	A
D	6	60	5	80	A
E	7	100	6	130	B
F	4	40	3	100	D
G	5	100	4	150	C, E, F

a. Construct the network diagram.
b. Indicate the critical path when normal activity times are used.
c. Compute the minimum total direct cost for each project duration based on the cost associated with each activity. Consider durations of 13, 14, 15, 16, 17, and 18 weeks.
d. If the indirect costs for each project duration are $400 (18 weeks), $350 (17 weeks), $300 (16 weeks), $250 (15 weeks), $200 (14 weeks), and $150 (13 weeks), what is the total project cost for each duration? Indicate the minimum total project cost duration.

21. What feature in project management information systems can be used to resolve over-allocation of project resources?

22. What was the first major project management information system that is now commonly used for managing very large projects?

23. What type of chart compares the current project schedule with the original baseline schedule so that deviations from the original plan can be easily noticed?

ANALYTICS EXERCISE: PRODUCT DESIGN PROJECT

You work for Nokia in its global cell phone group. You have been made project manager for the design of a new cell phone. Your supervisors have already scoped the project, so you have a list showing the work breakdown structure, and this includes major project activities. You must plan the project schedule and calculate project duration. Your boss wants the schedule on his desk tomorrow morning!

You have been given the information in Exhibit 5.13. It includes all the activities required in the project and the duration of each activity. Also, dependencies between the activities have been identified. Remember that the preceding activity must be fully completed before work on the following activity can be started.

Your project is divided into five major subprojects. Subproject "P" involves developing specifications for the new cell phone. Here, decisions related to such things as

battery life, size of the phone, and features need to be made. These details are based on how a customer uses the cell phone. These user specifications are redefined in terms that have meaning to the subcontractors that will actually make the new cell phone in subproject "S" supplier specifications. These involve engineering details for how the product will perform.

The individual components that make up the product are the focus of subproject "D." Subproject "I" brings all the components together, and a working prototype is built and tested.

Finally, in subproject "V," suppliers are selected and contracts are negotiated.

1. Draw a project network that includes all the activities.
2. Calculate the start and finish times for each activity and determine the minimum number of weeks for

| exhibit 5.13 | Work Breakdown Structure and Activities for the Cell Phone Design Project |

MAJOR SUBPROJECTS/ACTIVITIES	ACTIVITY IDENTIFICATION	DEPENDENCY	DURATION (WEEKS)
Product specifications (P)			
Market research	P1	—	2
Overall product specifications	P2	P1	4
Hardware	P3	P2	5
Software	P4	P3	5
Supplier specifications (S)			
Hardware	S1	P4	5
Software	S2	P4	6
Product design (D)			
Battery	D1	S1	1
Display	D2	S1	2
Camera	D3	S1	1
Outer cover	D4	D1, D2, D3	4
Product integration (I)			
Hardware	I1	D4	3
User interface	I2	D2	4
Software coding	I3	I2	4
Prototype testing	I4	I1, I3	4
Subcontracting (V)			
Suppliers selection	V1	S1, S2	10
Contract negotiation	V2	I4, V1	2

completing the project. Find the activities that are on the critical path for completing the project in the shortest time.

3. Identify slack in the activities not on the project critical path.

4. Your boss would like you to study the impact of making two changes to how the project is organized. The first change involves using dedicated teams that would work strictly in parallel on the activities in each subproject. For example, in subproject P (product specifications) the team would work on P1, P2, P3, and P4 all in parallel. In other words, there would be no precedence relationships within a subproject—all tasks within a subproject would be worked on at the same time and each would take the same amount of time as originally specified. With this new design, all the subprojects would be done sequentially with P done first, then S, D, I, and finally V. What would be the expected

impact on how long it would take to complete the project if this change were made?

5. The second change your boss would like you to consider would be to select the suppliers during subproject P and have them work directly with the dedicated teams as described in step 4. This would involve adding an additional activity to subproject P called supplier selection and contract negotiation (P5) with a duration of 12 weeks. This new activity would be done in parallel with P1, P2, P3, and P4. Subprojects S and V would be eliminated from the project. What would be the expected impact on how long it would take to complete the project if this additional change were made?

6. Evaluate the impact of making these changes using criteria other than just the time to complete the project. Do you think it would be in Nokia's best interest to try to make these changes in how it runs this and future cell phone design projects?.

PRACTICE EXAM

1. A project structured where a self-contained team works full time on the project.

2. Specific events that upon completion mark important progress toward completing a project.

3. This defines the hierarchy of project tasks, subtasks, and work packages.

4. Pieces of work in a project that consume time to complete.

5. A chart that shows both the time and sequence for completing the activities in a project.

6. Activities that in sequence form the longest chain in a project.

7. The difference between the late and early start time for an activity.

8. When activities are scheduled with probabilistic task times.

9. The procedure used to reduce project completion time by trading off time versus cost.

10. A key assumption related to the resources needed to complete activities when using the critical path method.

Answers to Practice Exam 1. Pure project or skunkworks   2. Milestones   3. Work breakdown structure   4. Activities   5. Gantt chart   6. Critical path(s)   7. Slack   8. The Program Evaluation and Review Technique (PERT)   9. Crashing   10. Resources are always available.

CHAPTER 6

MANUFACTURING PROCESSES

Learning Objectives

LO6–1 Understand what a manufacturing process is.

LO6–2 Understand production process mapping and Little's law.

LO6–3 Explain how manufacturing processes are organized.

LO6–4 Understand how to design and analyze an assembly line.

THREE-DIMENSIONAL PRINTING—THE TECHNOLOGY COULD BE USED TO MAKE PARTS THAT PERFORM BETTER AND COST LESS

The technology for printing three-dimensional objects has existed for decades, but its application has been largely limited to novelty items and specialized custom fabrication, such as making personalized prosthetics. The technology has now improved to the point where these printers can make intricate objects out of durable materials, including ceramics and metals (such as titanium and aluminum), with a resolution on the scale of tens of micrometers.

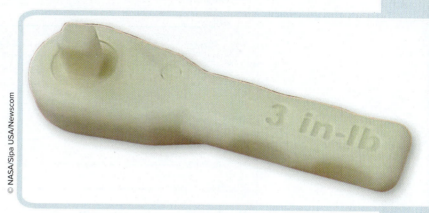

THIS RATCHET WRENCH WAS MADE USING A 3-D PRINTER ON THE INTERNATIONAL SPACE STATION IN ABOUT FOUR HOURS.

PRODUCTION PROCESSES

In this chapter, we consider how processes used to make tangible goods are designed. Production processes are used to make everything that we buy ranging from the apartment building in which we live to the ink pens with which we write. The high-level view of what is required to make something can be divided into three simple steps. The first step is sourcing the parts we need, followed by actually making the item, and then sending the item to the customer. As discussed in Chapter 1, a supply chain view of this may involve a complex series of players where subcontractors feed suppliers, suppliers feed manufacturing plants, manufacturing plants feed warehouses, and, finally, warehouses feed retailers. Depending on the item being produced, the supply chain can be very long with subcontractors and manufacturing plants spread out over the globe (such as an automobile or computer manufacturer) or short where parts are sourced and the product is made locally (such as a house builder).

Consider Exhibit 6.1, which illustrates the Source step where parts are procured from one or more suppliers, the Make step where manufacturing takes place, and the Deliver step where the product is shipped to the customer. Depending on the strategy of the firm, the capabilities of manufacturing, and the needs of customers,

LO6–1 Understand what a manufacturing process is.

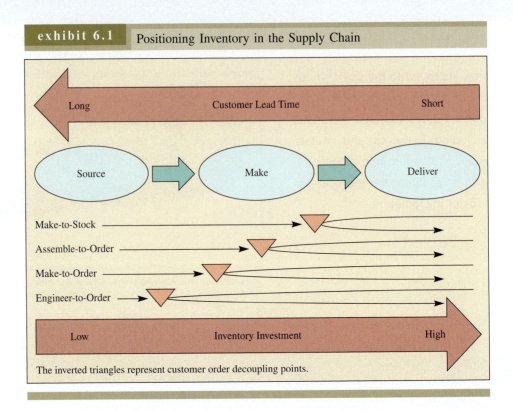

exhibit 6.1   Positioning Inventory in the Supply Chain

The inverted triangles represent customer order decoupling points.

Lead time
The time needed
to respond to a
customer order.

**Customer order
decoupling point**
Where inventory is
positioned in the
supply chain.

Make-to-stock
A production
environment where
the customer is
served "on-demand"
from finished goods
inventory.

these activities are organized to minimize cost while meeting the competitive priorities necessary to attract customer orders. For example, in the case of consumer products such as DVDs or clothes, customers normally want these products "on-demand" for quick delivery from a local department store. As a manufacturer of these products, we build them ahead of time in anticipation of demand and ship them to the retail stores where they are carried in inventory until they are sold. At the other end of the spectrum are custom products, such as military airplanes, that are ordered with very specific uses in mind and that need to be designed and then built to the design. In the case of an airplane, the time needed to respond to a customer order, called the **lead time**, could easily be years, compared to only a few minutes for the DVD.

A key concept in production processes is the **customer order decoupling point**, which determines where inventory is positioned to allow processes or entities in the supply chain to operate independently. For example, if a product is stocked at a retailer, the customer pulls the item from the shelf and the manufacturer never sees a customer order. Inventory acts as a buffer to separate the customer from the manufacturing process. Selection of decoupling points is a strategic decision that determines customer lead times and can greatly impact inventory investment. The closer this point is to the customer, the quicker the customer can be served. Typically, there is a trade-off where quicker response to customer demand comes at the expense of greater inventory investment because finished goods inventory is more expensive than raw material inventory. An item in finished goods inventory typically contains all the raw materials needed to produce the item. So, from a cost view it includes the cost of the material plus the cost to fabricate the finished item.

Positioning of the customer order decoupling point is important in understanding production environments. Firms that serve customers from finished goods inventory are known as **make-to-stock** firms. Those that combine a number of pre-assembled modules to meet a customer's specifications are called **assemble-to-order** firms. Those that make the customer's product from raw materials, parts, and components are **make-to-order** firms. An **engineer-to-order** firm will work with the customer to design the product, and then make it from purchased materials, parts, and components. Of course, many firms serve a combination of these environments and a few will have all simultaneously. Depending on the environment and the location of the customer order decoupling point, one would expect inventory concentrated in finished goods, work-in-process (this is inventory in the manufacturing process), manufacturing raw material, or at the supplier, as shown in Exhibit 6.1.

The essential issue in satisfying customers in the make-to-stock environment is to balance the level of finished inventory against the level of service to the customer. Examples of products produced by these firms include televisions, clothing, and packaged food products. If unlimited inventory were possible and free, the task would be trivial. Unfortunately, that is not the case. Providing more inventory increases costs, so a trade-off between the costs of the inventory and the level of customer service must be made. The trade-off can be improved by better estimates (or knowledge) of customer demand, by more rapid transportation alternatives, by speedier production, and by more flexible manufacturing. Many make-to-stock firms invest in **lean manufacturing** programs in order to achieve higher service levels for a given inventory investment. Regardless of the trade-offs involved, the focus in the make-to-stock environment is on providing finished goods where and when the customers want them.

In the assemble-to-order environment, a primary task is to define a customer's order in terms of alternative components and options since it is these components that are carried in inventory. A good example is the way Dell Computer makes its desktop computers. The number of combinations that can be made may be nearly infinite (although some might not be feasible). One of the capabilities required for success in the assemble-to-order environment is an engineering design that enables as much flexibility as possible in combining components, options, and modules into finished products. Similar to make-to-stock, many assemble-to-order companies have applied lean manufacturing principles to dramatically decrease the time required to assemble finished goods. By doing so, they are delivering customers' orders so quickly that they appear to be make-to-stock firms from the perspective of the customer.

When assembling-to-order, there are significant advantages from moving the customer order decoupling point from finished goods to components. The number of finished products is usually substantially greater than the number of components that are combined to produce the finished product. Consider, for example, a computer for which there are four processor alternatives, three hard disk drive choices, four DVD alternatives, two speaker systems, and four monitors available. If all combinations of these 17 components

Assemble-to-order
A production environment where pre-assembled components, subassemblies, and modules are put together in response to a specific customer order.

Make-to-order
A production environment where the product is built directly from raw materials and components in response to a specific customer order.

Engineer-to-order
Here the firm works with the customer to design the product, which is then made from purchased material, parts, and components.

Lean manufacturing
To achieve high customer service with minimum levels of inventory investment.

CONFIGURING A DELL COMPUTER.

© AP Images/Liu Zheng/ColorChinaPhoto

are valid, they can be combined into a total of 384 different final configurations. This can be calculated as follows:

If N_i is the number of alternatives for component i, the total number of combinations of n components (given all are viable) is

$$\text{Total number of combinations} = N_1 \times N_2 \times \cdots \times N_n \qquad [6.1]$$

$$\text{Or } 384 = 4 \times 3 \times 4 \times 2 \times 4 \text{ for this example.}$$

It is much easier to manage and forecast the demand for 17 components than for 384 computers.

In the make-to-order and engineer-to-order environments, the customer order decoupling point could be in either raw materials at the manufacturing site or possibly even with the supplier inventory. Boeing's process for making commercial aircraft is an example of make-to-order. The need for engineering resources in the engineer-to-order case is somewhat different than make-to-order because engineering determines what materials will be required and what steps will be required in manufacturing. Depending on how similar the products are, it might not even be possible to pre-order parts. Rather than inventory, the emphasis in these environments may be more toward managing the capacity of critical resources, such as engineering and construction crews. Lockheed Martin's Satellite division uses an engineer-to-order strategy.

PRODUCTION PROCESS MAPPING AND LITTLE'S LAW

LO6–2 Understand production process mapping and Little's law.

Next, we look at how to quickly develop a high-level map of a supply chain process, which can be useful to understand how material flows and where inventory is held. The approach used here should be the first step in analyzing the flow of material through a production process. This idea will be further developed in "Value Stream Mapping" in Chapter 12.

Consider a simple system that might be typical of many make-to-stock companies. As shown in Exhibit 6.2, material is purchased from a set of suppliers and initially staged in raw material inventory. The material is used in a manufacturing process where the product is fabricated (different types of manufacturing processes are discussed in the next

exhibit 6.2   Make-to-Stock Process Map

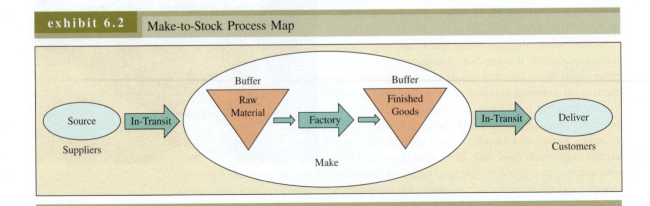

section, "How Production Processes Are Organized"). After fabrication, the product is put into finished goods inventory and from here it is shipped according to orders received from customers.

Focusing on the Make part of the process, it is useful to analyze how this step operates using performance measures that relate to the inventory investment and also how quickly material flows through the process. A simplified way of thinking about material in a process is that it is in one of two states. The first state is where material is moving or "in-transit." The second state is material that is sitting in inventory and acting as a "buffer" waiting to be used.

In the first state, material is moving in the process. This is material that is in-transit between entities in the process; for example, between the vendor and the raw material inventory at the manufacturer. Material that is in a manufacturing process in a factory can also be considered in-transit. Actually, we refer to this material as "work-in-process" inventory. In the second state, material is held in a storage area and waits until it is needed. In the case of raw material inventory, the need is dependent on the factory usage of the item. This "buffer" inventory allows different entities in the process to operate relatively independently.

A common measure is the **total average value of inventory** in the process. From an accounting view, this would be the sum of the value (at cost) of the raw material, work-in-process, and finished goods inventory. This is commonly tracked in accounting systems and reported in the firm's financial statements. Although useful for accounting purposes, these measures are not particularly useful for evaluating the performance of a process. Consider the total average value of inventory. What is better, a firm that has $2 million worth of inventory on average or one that has $4 million? This depends greatly on the size of the firm, the type of strategy being used (make-to-order or make-to-stock, for example), and the relative cost of the product being produced.

A better measure than the total value of inventory is **inventory turn**, which is the cost of goods sold divided by the average inventory value. Because inventory turn scales the amount of inventory by dividing by the cost of goods sold, this provides a relative measure that has some comparability, at least across similar firms. For two similar consumer products manufacturers, an inventory turn of six times per year is certainly much better than a firm turning inventory two times per year. A measure directly related is **days-of-supply**, which is the inverse of inventory turn scaled to days. For example, if a firm turns inventory six times per year, the days of supply is equal to one-sixth times per year, or approximately every 61 days (this is calculated as 1/6 year × 365 days/year = 60.8 days).

Simple systems can be analyzed quickly using a principle known as **Little's law**. Little's law says there is a long-term relationship between the inventory, throughput, and flow time of a production system in steady state. The relationship is

$$\text{Inventory} = \text{Throughput rate} \times \text{Flow time} \qquad [6.2]$$

Throughput is the long-term average rate that items are flowing through the process. **Flow time** is the time that it takes a unit to flow through the process from beginning to end. Consider the factory process in Exhibit 6.2. Raw material is brought into the factory and is transformed and then stored in finished goods inventory. The analysis assumes that the process is operating in "steady state," meaning that over a long enough period of time the amount that is produced by the factory is equal to the amount shipped to customers. The throughput rate of the process is equal to average demand, and the process is not producing any excess or shortage. If this were not true and the amount produced by the manufacturing process was greater than demand, for example, the finished goods inventory

Total average value of inventory
The total investment in inventory at the firm, which includes raw material, work-in-process, and finished goods.

Inventory turn
An efficiency measure where the cost of goods sold is divided by the total average value of inventory.

Days-of-supply
A measure of the number of days of supply of an item.

Little's law
Mathematically relates inventory, throughput, and flow time.

Throughput
The average rate (e.g., units/day) that items flow through a process.

Flow time
The time it takes one unit to completely flow through a process.

would build over time. So if demand averages 1,000 units per day and if it takes 20 days for a unit to flow through the factory, then the expected work-in-process in the factory would be 20,000 units.

We can think of Little's law as a relationship between units and time. Inventory is measured in pieces, flow time in days, and throughput in pieces per day. Therefore, if we divide inventory by throughput, we get flow time. For example, 20,000 units divided by 1,000 units per day is 20 days. We can also take inventory and divide by flow time and get throughput rate. Here, 20,000 units divided by 20 days is equal to 1,000 units a day. This conversion is useful when diagnosing a plant's performance.

To appreciate a major limitation, suppose that a process has just started with no inventory on-hand. Some of the initial production will be used to fill the system, thus limiting initial throughput. In this case, Little's law will not hold, but after the process has been operating for a while, and there is inventory at every step, the process stabilizes, and then the relationship holds.

Little's law is actually much more general than a simple way to convert between units. It can be applied to single workstations, multistep production lines, factories, or even entire supply chains. Further, it applies to processes with variability in the arrival rate (or demand rate) and processing time. It can be applied to single or multiple product systems. It even applies to nonproduction systems where inventory represents people, financial orders, or other entities.

For our factory, it is common for accounting systems to capture average work-in-process in terms of the value (at cost) of the inventory that is being worked on in the factory. For our example, say that work-in-process averages $200,000 and that each unit is valued at a cost of $10.00. This would imply that there are 20,000 units in the factory (calculated $200,000 ÷ $10.00 per unit = 20,000 units).

The following example shows how these concepts can be applied to quickly analyze simple processes.

Example 6.1: Car Batteries

An automobile company assembles cars in a plant and purchases batteries from a vendor in China. The average cost of each battery is $45. The automobile company takes ownership of the batteries when they arrive at the plant. It takes exactly 12 hours to make a car in the plant and the plant assembles 200 cars per 8-hour shift (currently the plant operates one shift per day). Each car uses one battery. The company holds, on average, 8,000 batteries in raw material inventory at the plant as a buffer. Assignment: Find the total number of batteries in the plant on average (in work-in-process at the plant and in raw material inventory). How much are these batteries worth? How many days of supply are held in raw material inventory on average?

SOLUTION

We can split this into two inventories: work-in-process and raw material. For the work-in-process, Little's law can be directly applied to find the amount of work-in-process inventory:

$$Inventory = Throughput \times Flow\ time$$

Throughput is the production rate of the plant, 200 cars per 8-hour shift or 25 cars per hour. Since we use one battery per car, our throughput rate for the batteries is 25 per hour. Flow time is 12 hours, so the work-in-process is

Work-in-process inventory = 25 batteries/hour × 12 hours = 300 batteries

We know from the problem that there are 8,000 batteries in raw material inventory, so the total number of batteries in the pipeline on average is

$$\text{Total inventory} = 8{,}000 + 300 = 8{,}300 \text{ batteries}$$

These batteries are worth $8{,}300 \times \$45 = \$373{,}500$.

The days of supply in raw material inventory is equal to the "flow time" for a battery in raw material inventory (or the average amount of time that a battery spends in raw material inventory). Here, we need to assume that the batteries are used in the same order they arrive. Rearrange our Little's law formula to

$$\textit{Flow time} = \textit{Inventory/Throughput}$$

So, Flow time = 8,000 batteries/(200 batteries/day) = 40 days, which represents a 40-day supply of inventory. ●

In the next section, we look at how the production processes are organized in different environments. This is largely dependent on the variety of products being produced and on the volume. How a company produces airplanes is very different when compared to building computers or making ink pens.

HOW PRODUCTION PROCESSES ARE ORGANIZED

Process selection refers to the strategic decision of selecting which kind of production processes to use to produce a product or provide a service. For example, in the case of Toshiba notebook computers, if the volume is very low, we may just have a worker manually assemble each computer by hand. In contrast, if the volume is higher, setting up an assembly line is appropriate.

The format by which a facility is arranged is defined by the general pattern of work flow; there are five basic structures (project, workcenter, manufacturing cell, assembly line, and continuous process).

In a **project layout**, the product (by virtue of its bulk or weight) remains in a fixed location. Manufacturing equipment is moved to the product rather than vice versa. Construction sites (houses and bridges) and movie shooting lots are examples of this format. Items produced with this type of layout are typically managed using the project management techniques described in Chapter 5. Areas on the site will be designated for various purposes, such as material staging, subassembly construction, site access for heavy equipment, and a management area.

A **workcenter** layout, sometimes referred to as a job shop, is where similar equipment or functions are grouped together, such as all drilling machines in one area and all stamping machines in another. A part being worked on travels, according to the established sequence of operations, from workcenter to workcenter, where the proper machines are located for each operation.

A **manufacturing cell** layout is a dedicated area where products that are similar in processing requirements are produced. These cells are designed to perform a specific set of processes, and the cells are dedicated to a limited range of products. A firm may have many different cells in a production area, each set up to produce a single product or a similar group of products efficiently, but typically at lower volume levels. These cells typically are scheduled to produce "as needed" in response to current customer demand.

LO6–3 Explain how manufacturing processes are organized.

Project layout
For large or massive products produced in a specific location, labor, material, and equipment are moved to the product rather than vice versa.

Workcenter
A process with great flexibility to produce a variety of products, typically at lower volume levels.

Manufacturing cell
Dedicated area where a group of similar products are produced.

Assembly line
Area where an item is produced through a fixed sequence of workstations, designed to achieve a specific production rate.

An **assembly line** is where work processes are arranged according to the progressive steps by which the product is made. These steps are defined so that a specific production rate can be achieved. The path for each part is, in effect, a straight line. Discrete products are made by moving from workstation to workstation at a controlled rate, following the sequence needed to build the product. Examples include the assembly of toys, appliances, and automobiles. These are typically used in high-volume items where the specialized process can be justified.

Continuous process
A process that converts raw materials into finished product in one contiguous process.

A **continuous process** is similar to an assembly line in that production follows a predetermined sequence of steps, but the flow is continuous such as with liquids, rather than discrete. Such structures are usually highly automated and, in effect, constitute one integrated "machine" that may operate 24 hours a day to avoid expensive shutdowns and start-ups. Conversion and processing of undifferentiated materials such as petroleum, chemicals, and drugs are good examples.

Product–process matrix
A framework depicting when the different production process types are typically used depending on product volume and how standardized the product is.

The relationship between layout structures is often depicted on a **product–process matrix** similar to the one shown in Exhibit 6.3. Two dimensions are shown. The horizontal dimension relates to the volume of a particular product or group of standardized products. Standardization is shown on the vertical axis and refers to variations in the product that is produced. These variations are measured in terms of geometric differences, material differences, and so on. Standardized products are highly similar from a manufacturing processing point of view, whereas low standardized products require different processes.

Exhibit 6.3 shows the processes approximately on a diagonal. In general, it can be argued that it is desirable to design processes along the diagonal. For example, if we produce nonstandard products at relatively low volumes, workcenters should be used. A highly standardized product (commodity) produced at high volumes should be produced using an assembly line or a continuous process, if possible. As a result of the advanced manufacturing technology available today, we see that some of the layout structures span relatively large areas of the product–process matrix. For example, manufacturing cells can be used for a very wide range of applications, and this has become a popular layout structure that often is employed by manufacturing engineers.

exhibit 6.3	Product–Process Matrix: Framework Describing Layout Strategies

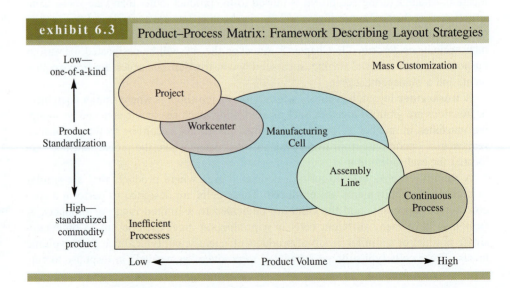

Designing a Production System

There are many techniques available to determine the actual layouts of the production process. This section gives a quick overview of how the problems are addressed. For each of the layout types, descriptions are given of how the layouts are represented and the main criteria used. The next section takes an in-depth look at the assembly-line balancing problem.

Project Layout In developing a project layout, visualize the product as the hub of a wheel, with materials and equipment arranged concentrically around the production point in the order of use and movement difficulty. Thus, in building commercial aircraft, for example, rivets used throughout construction would be placed close to or in the fuselage; heavy engine parts, which must travel to the fuselage only once, would be placed at a more distant location; and cranes would be set up close to the fuselage because of their constant use.

In a project layout, a high degree of task ordering is common. To the extent that this task ordering, or precedence, determines production stages, a project layout may be developed by arranging materials according to their assembly priority. This procedure would be expected in making a layout for a large machine tool, such as a stamping machine, where manufacturing follows a rigid sequence; assembly is performed from the ground up, with parts being added to the base in almost a building-block fashion.

Workcenters The most common approach to developing this type of layout is to arrange workcenters in a way that optimizes the movement of material. A workcenter

AN EXAMPLE OF A PROJECT LAYOUT.

© Digital Vision/Getty Images RF

A WORKCENTER.

© David Parker/Science Source

A MANUFACTURING CELL.

© William Taufic/Flirt/Corbis

sometimes is referred to as a department and is focused on a particular type of operation. Examples include a workcenter for drilling holes, one for performing grinding operations, and a painting area. The workcenters in a low-volume toy factory might consist of shipping and receiving, plastic molding and stamping, metal forming, sewing, and painting. Parts for the toys are fabricated in these workcenters and then sent to the assembly workcenter, where they are put together. In many installations, optimal placement often means placing workcenters with large amounts of interdepartmental traffic adjacent to each other.

Manufacturing Cells A manufacturing cell is formed by allocating dissimilar machines to cells that are designed to work on products that have similar shapes and processing requirements. Manufacturing cells are widely used in metal fabricating, computer chip manufacture, and assembly work.

The process used to develop a manufacturing cell is depicted in Exhibit 6.4. It can be broken down into three distinct steps:

1. Group parts into families that follow a common sequence of steps. This requires classifying parts by using some type of coding system. In practice, this can often be quite complex and can require a computerized system. For the purpose of the example shown in Exhibit 6.4A, four "part families" have already been defined and are identified by unique arrow designs. This part of the exhibit shows the routing of parts when a conventional workcenter-based layout is used. Here, parts are routed through the individual workcenters to be produced.
2. Next, dominant flow patterns are identified for each part family. This will be used as the basis for reallocating equipment to the manufacturing cells (see Exhibit 6.4B).
3. Finally, machines and the associated processes are physically regrouped into cells (see Exhibit 6.4C). Often, there will be parts that cannot be associated with a family and specialized machinery that cannot be placed in any single cell because of its general use. These unattached parts and machinery are placed in a "remainder cell."

Development of Manufacturing Cell

exhibit 6.4

A. Original workcenter layout

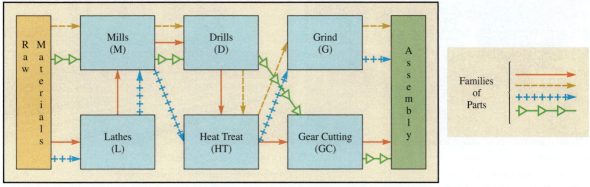

Source: Adapted from D. Fogarty and T. Hoffman, *Production and Inventory Management* (Cincinnati: South-Western Publishing, 1983), p. 472.

B. Routing matrix based upon flow of parts

Raw Materials	Part Family	Lathes	Mills	Drills	Heat Treating	Grinders	Gear Cutting	To	Assembly
	--→		X	X	X	X		--→	
	▷▷→		X	X			X	▷▷→	
	—→	X	X	X	X		X	—→	
	++▶	X	X		X	X		++▶	

C. Reallocating machines to form cells according to part family processing requirements

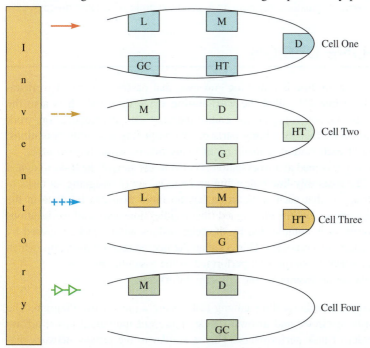

AN ASSEMBLY LINE.
© Jeff Kowalsky/Bloomberg/Getty Images

AN EXAMPLE OF A CONTINUOUS PROCESS.
© Andrew Holt/Photographer's Choice/Getty Images

Assembly-Line and Continuous Process Layouts

An assembly line is a layout design for the special purpose of building a product by going through a progressive set of steps. The assembly steps are done in areas referred to as "stations," and typically the stations are linked by some form of material handling device. In addition, usually there is some form of pacing by which the amount of time allowed at each station is managed. Rather than develop the process for designing assembly at this time, we will devote the entire next section of this chapter to the topic of assembly-line design since these designs are used so often by manufacturing firms around the world. A continuous or flow process is similar to an assembly line except that the product continuously moves through the process. Often, the item being produced by the continuous process is a liquid or chemical that actually "flows" through the system; this is the origin of the term. A gasoline refinery is a good example of a flow process.

 **LO6–4** Understand how to design and analyze an assembly line.

Workstation cycle time
The time between successive units coming off the end of an assembly line.

Assembly-line balancing
The problem of assigning tasks to a series of workstations so that the required cycle time is met and idle time is minimized.

Precedence relationship
The required order in which tasks must be performed in an assembly process.

ASSEMBLY-LINE DESIGN

The most common assembly line is a moving conveyor that passes a series of workstations in a uniform time interval called the **workstation cycle time** (which is also the time between successive units coming off the end of the line). At each workstation, work is performed on a product either by adding parts or by completing assembly operations. The work performed at each station is made up of many bits of work, termed *tasks*.

The total work to be performed at a workstation is equal to the sum of the tasks assigned to that workstation. The **assembly-line balancing** problem is one of assigning all tasks to a series of workstations so that each workstation has no more than can be done in the workstation cycle time and so that the unassigned (that is, idle) time across all workstations is minimized. The problem is complicated by the relationships among tasks imposed by product design and process technologies. This is called the **precedence relationship**, which specifies the order in which tasks must be performed in the assembly process.

The steps in balancing an assembly line are straightforward:

1. Specify the sequential relationships among tasks using a precedence diagram. The diagram consists of circles and arrows. Circles represent individual tasks; arrows indicate the order of task performance. This is similar to the project network diagram in Chapter 5.

2. Determine the required workstation cycle time (C), using the formula

$$C = \frac{\text{Production time per day}}{\text{Required output per day (in units)}} \qquad [6.3]$$

3. Determine the theoretical minimum number of workstations (N_t) required to satisfy the workstation cycle time constraint using the formula (note that this must be rounded up to the next highest integer)

$$N_t = \frac{\text{Sum of task times } (T)}{\text{Cycle time } (C)} \qquad [6.4]$$

4. Select a primary rule by which tasks are to be assigned to workstations and a secondary rule to break ties. For example, the primary rule might be the longest task time, and the secondary rule, the task with the longest number of following tasks. In this case, for the tasks that can be assigned, pick the one with the longest task time. If there is a tie, pick the one that has the greatest number of following tasks.

5. Assign tasks, one at a time, to the first workstation until the sum of the task times is equal to the workstation cycle time or no other tasks are feasible because of time or sequence restrictions. Every time a task is assigned, re-create the list of tasks that are feasible to assign and then pick one based on the rule defined in 4. Repeat the process for Workstation 2, Workstation 3, and so on until all tasks are assigned.

6. Evaluate the efficiency of the balance derived using the formula

$$\text{Efficiency} = \frac{\text{Sum of task times } (T)}{\text{Actual number of workstations } (N_a) \times \text{Workstation cycle time } (C)} \qquad [6.5]$$

Here, we assume there is one worker per workstation. When, for some reason, the number of workstations does not equal the number of workers, we would usually substitute the number of workers for number of workstations.

7. If efficiency is unsatisfactory, rebalance using a different decision rule.

Example 6.2: Assembly-Line Balancing

The Model J Wagon is to be assembled on a conveyor belt. Five hundred wagons are required per day. Production time per day is 420 minutes, and the assembly steps and times for the wagon are given in Exhibit 6.5A. Assignment: Find the balance that minimizes the number of workstations, subject to cycle time and precedence constraints.

SOLUTION

1. Draw a precedence diagram. Exhibit 6.5B illustrates the sequential relationships identified in Exhibit 6.6A. (The length of the arrows has no meaning.)

2. Determine workstation cycle time. Here we have to convert to seconds because our task times are in seconds.

$$C = \frac{\text{Production time per day}}{\text{Output per day}} = \frac{60 \text{ sec.} \times 420 \text{ min.}}{500 \text{ wagons}} = \frac{25,200}{500} = 50.4$$

exhibit 6.5

A. Assembly Steps and Times for Model J Wagon

TASK	TASK TIME (IN SECONDS)	DESCRIPTION	TASKS THAT MUST PRECEDE
A	45	Position rear axle support and hand fasten four screws to nuts.	—
B	11	Insert rear axle.	A
C	9	Tighten rear axle support screws to nuts.	B
D	50	Position front axle assembly and hand fasten with four screws to nuts.	—
E	15	Tighten front axle assembly screws.	D
F	12	Position rear wheel #1 and fasten hubcap.	C
G	12	Position rear wheel #2 and fasten hubcap.	C
H	12	Position front wheel #1 and fasten hubcap.	E
I	12	Position front wheel #2 and fasten hubcap.	E
J	8	Position wagon handle shaft on front axle assembly and hand fasten bolt and nut.	F, G, H, I
K	9	Tighten bolt and nut.	J
	195		

B. Precedence Graph for Model J Wagon

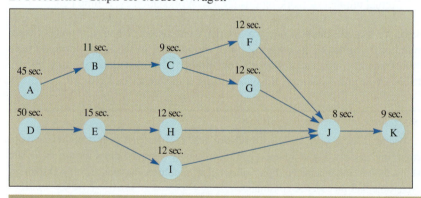

3. Determine the theoretical minimum number of workstations required (the actual number may be greater):

$$N_t = \frac{T}{C} = \frac{195 \text{ sec.}}{50.4 \text{ sec.}} = 3.87 = 4 \text{ (rounded up)}$$

4. Select assignment rules. In general, the strategy is to use a rule assigning tasks that either have many followers or are of long duration because they effectively limit the balance achievable. In this case, we use the following as our primary rule:

a. Prioritize tasks in order of the largest number of following tasks.

TASK	NUMBER OF FOLLOWING TASKS
A	6
B or D	5
C or E	4
F, G, H, or I	2
J	1
K	0

Our secondary rule, to be invoked where ties exist from our primary rule, is:

b. Prioritize tasks in order of longest task time (shown in Exhibit 6.6). Note that D should be assigned before B, and E assigned before C, due to this tiebreaking rule.

exhibit 6.6

A. Balance Made According to Largest-Number-of-Following-Tasks Rule

	TASK	TASK TIME (IN SECONDS)	REMAINING UNASSIGNED TIME (IN SECONDS)	FEASIBLE REMAINING TASKS	TASK WITH MOST FOLLOWERS	TASK WITH LONGEST OPERATION TIME
Station 1	A	45	5.4 idle	None		
Station 2	D	50	0.4 idle	None		
Station 3	B	11	39.4	C, E	C, E	E
	E	15	24.4	C, H, I	C	
	C	9	15.4	F, G, H, I	F, G, H, I	F, G, H, I
	F*	12	3.4 idle	None		
Station 4	G	12	38.4	H, I	H, I	H, I
	H*	12	26.4	I		
	I	12	14.4	J		
	J	8	6.4 idle	None		
Station 5	K	9	41.4 idle	None		

*Denotes task arbitrarily selected where there is a tie between longest operation times.

B. Precedence Graph for Model J Wagon

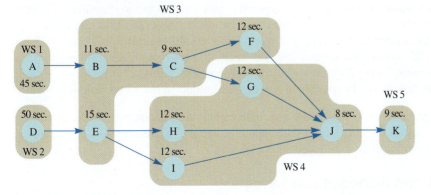

C. Efficiency Calculation

$$\text{Efficiency} = \frac{T}{N_aC} = \frac{195}{(5)(50.4)} = .77, \text{ or } 77\%$$

5. Make task assignments to form Workstation 1, Workstation 2, and so forth until all tasks are assigned. The actual assignment is given in Exhibit 6.6A and is shown graphically in Exhibit 6.6B. To understand this, it is best to trace through the task assignments in sequence in Exhibit 6.6A. See that when an assignment is made, the feasible, remaining assignments are updated along with the priority rules. It is important to meet precedence and cycle time requirements as the assignments are made.

6. Calculate the efficiency. This is shown in Exhibit 6.6C.

7. Evaluate the solution. An efficiency of 77 percent indicates an imbalance or idle time of 23 percent (1.0–.77) across the entire line. From Exhibit 6.6A we can see that there are 57 total seconds of idle time, and the "choice" job is at Workstation 5.

Is a better balance possible? In this case, yes. Try balancing the line with rule b and breaking ties with rule a. (This will give you a feasible four-station balance.) •

Splitting Tasks

Often, the longest required task time defines the shortest possible workstation cycle time for the production line. This task time is the lower time bound unless it is possible to split the task into two or more workstations.

Consider the following illustration. Suppose that an assembly line contains the following task times in seconds: 40, 30, 15, 25, 20, 18, 15. The line runs for $7\frac{1}{2}$ hours per day and demand for output is 750 per day.

The workstation cycle time required to produce 750 per day is 36 seconds [($7\frac{1}{2}$ hours × 60 minutes × 60 seconds)/750]. Our problem is that we have one task that takes 40 seconds. How do we deal with this task?

There are several ways that we may be able to accommodate the 40-second task in a 36-second cycle. Possibilities are

1. **Split the task.** Can we split the task so that complete units are processed in two workstations?

2. **Share the task.** Can the task somehow be shared so an adjacent workstation does part of the work? This differs from the split task in the first option because the adjacent station acts to assist, not to do some units containing the entire task.

3. **Use parallel workstations.** It may be necessary to assign the task to two workstations that would operate in parallel.

4. **Use a more skilled worker.** Because this task exceeds the workstation cycle time by just 11 percent, a faster worker may be able to meet the 36-second time.

5. **Work overtime.** Producing at a rate of one every 40 seconds would create 675 per day, 75 short of the needed 750. The amount of overtime required to produce the additional 75 is 50 minutes (75 × 40 seconds/60 seconds).

6. **Redesign.** It may be possible to redesign the product to reduce the task time slightly.

Other possibilities to reduce the task time include an equipment upgrade, a roaming helper to support the line, a change of materials, and multiskilled workers to operate the line as a team rather than as independent workers.

Flexible and U-Shaped Line Layouts

As we saw in the preceding example, assembly-line balances frequently result in unequal workstation times. Flexible line layouts such as those shown in Exhibit 6.7 are a common way of dealing with this problem. In our toy company example, the U-shaped line with work-sharing at the bottom of the figure could help resolve the imbalance.

Flexible Line Layouts

exhibit 6.7

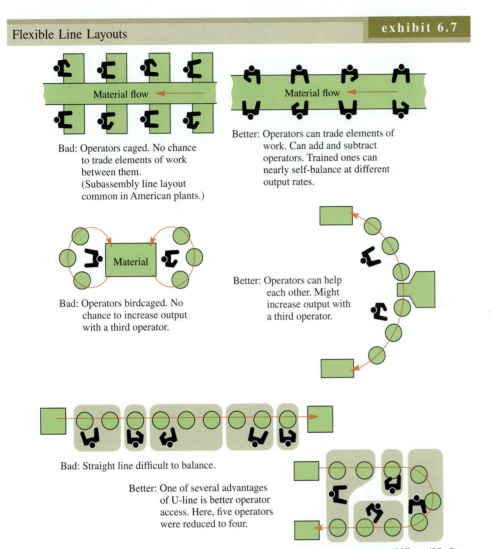

Bad: Operators caged. No chance to trade elements of work between them. (Subassembly line layout common in American plants.)

Better: Operators can trade elements of work. Can add and subtract operators. Trained ones can nearly self-balance at different output rates.

Bad: Operators birdcaged. No chance to increase output with a third operator.

Better: Operators can help each other. Might increase output with a third operator.

Bad: Straight line difficult to balance.

Better: One of several advantages of U-line is better operator access. Here, five operators were reduced to four.

Source: R. W. Hall, *Attaining Manufacturing Excellence* (Homewood, IL: Dow Jones-Irwin, 1987), p. 125. Copyright © 1987 McGraw-Hill Companies Inc.

CONCEPT CONNECTIONS

LO6–1 **Understand what a manufacturing process is.**

- Manufacturing processes are used to make tangible items.
- At a high level, these processes can be divided into three steps: (1) sourcing the parts needed, (2) making the item, and (3) sending the item to the customer.
- To allow parts of the process to operate independently, inventory is strategically positioned in the process. These places in the process are called decoupling points. Positioning the decoupling points has an impact on how fast a customer can be served, the flexibility the firm has in responding to specific customer requests, and many other trade-offs.

Lead time   The time needed to respond to a customer order.

Customer order decoupling point   Where inventory is positioned in the supply chain.

Make-to-stock   A production environment where the customer is served "on-demand" from finished goods inventory.

Assemble-to-order   A production environment where pre-assembled components, subassemblies, and modules are put together in response to a specific customer order.

Make-to-order   A production environment where the product is built directly from raw materials and components in response to a specific customer order.

Engineer-to-order   Here the firm works with the customer to design the product, which is then made from purchased material, parts, and components.

Lean manufacturing   To achieve high customer service with minimum levels of inventory investment.

$$\text{Total number of combinations} = N_1 \times N_2 \times \cdots \times N_n \qquad [6.1]$$

LO6–2 Understand production process mapping and Little's law.

- Process mapping is the drawing of a diagram that depicts the material flow and inventory in a process.
- Material in a process is in one of two states. The first state is where material is moving or "in-transit" and the second is when material is sitting in inventory and acting as a "buffer" waiting to be used. Material that is in a manufacturing process in a factory can be consider in-transit and is referred to as "work-in-process."
- Little's law is a mathematical relationship between units in inventory and time.

Total average value of inventory   The total investment in inventory at the firm, which includes raw materials, work-in-process, and finished goods.

Inventory turn   An efficiency measure where the cost of goods sold is divided by the total average value of inventory.

Days-of-supply   A measure of the number of days of supply of an item.

Little's law   Mathematically relates inventory, throughput, and flow time.

Throughput   The average rate (e.g., units/day) that items flow through a process.

Flow time   The time it takes one unit to completely flow through a process.

$$\text{Inventory} = \text{Throughput rate} \times \text{Flow time} \qquad [6.2]$$

LO6–3 Explain how manufacturing processes are organized.

- Manufacturing layouts are designed based on the nature of the product, the volume needed to meet demand, and the cost of equipment.
- The trade-offs are depicted in the product–process matrix, which depicts the type of layout relative to product volume and the relative standardization of the product. Break-even analysis, which is discussed in Chapter 6A, is useful for understanding the cost trade-offs between alternative equipment choices.

Project layout   For large or massive products produced in a specific location, labor, material, and equipment are moved to the product rather than vice versa.

Workcenter   A process with great flexibility to produce a variety of products, typically at lower volume levels.

Manufacturing cell   A dedicated area where a group of similar products are produced.

Assembly line   Area where an item is produced through a fixed sequence of workstations, designed to achieve a specific production rate.

Continuous process   A process that converts raw materials into finished product in one contiguous process.

Product–process matrix   A framework depicting when the different production process types are typically used, depending on product volume and how standardized the product is.

Project layout   The product, because of its sheer bulk or weight, remains fixed in a location. Equipment is moved to the product rather than vice versa.

Workcenters   Often referred to as a job shop, a process structure suited for low-volume production of a great variety of nonstandard products. Workcenters sometimes are referred to as departments and are focused on a particular type of operation.

Manufacturing cell   An area where simple items that are similar in processing requirements are produced.

Continuous process   An often automated process that converts raw materials into a finished product in one contiguous process.

LO6–4   **Understand how to design and analyze an assembly line.**

- The assembly-line design is centered on defining the work content of workstations that are typically spaced along the line. This technique is called assembly-line balancing.
- The workstations need to be defined so that efficiency is maximized while meeting maximum cycle times and precedence constraints.

Workstation cycle time   The time between successive units coming off the end of an assembly line.

Assembly-line balancing   The problem of assigning tasks to a series of workstations so that the required cycle time is met and idle time is minimized.

Precedence relationship   The required order in which tasks must be performed in an assembly process.

$$C = \frac{\text{Production time per day}}{\text{Required output per day (in units)}} \qquad [6.3]$$

$$N_t = \frac{\text{Sum of task times } (T)}{\text{Cycle time } (C)} \qquad [6.4]$$

$$\text{Efficiency} = \frac{\text{Sum of task times } (T)}{\text{Actual number of workstations } (N_a) \times \text{Workstation cycle time } (C)} \qquad [6.5]$$

SOLVED PROBLEMS

LO6–2   SOLVED PROBLEM 1

Suppose we schedule shipments to our customers so that we expect each shipment to wait for two days in finished goods inventory (in essence, we add two days to the expected ship date). We do this to protect against system variability and ensure a high on-time delivery service. If we ship approximately 2,000 units each day, how many units do we expect to have in finished goods inventory by allowing this extra time? If the item is valued at $4.50 each, what is the expected value of this inventory?

Solution

Using Little's law, the expected finished goods inventory is

$$\text{Inventory} = 2,000 \text{ units per day} \times 2 \text{ days} = 4,000 \text{ units}$$

This would be valued at 4,000 units × $4.50 per unit = $18,000.

LO6–4 **SOLVED PROBLEM 2**

The following tasks must be performed on an assembly line in the sequence and times specified:

TASK	TASK TIME (SECONDS)	TASKS THAT MUST PRECEDE
A	50	—
B	40	—
C	20	A
D	45	C
E	20	C
F	25	D
G	10	E
H	35	B, F, G

a. Draw the schematic diagram.

b. What is the theoretical minimum number of stations required to meet a forecast demand of 400 units per eight-hour day?

c. Use the longest-task-time rule and balance the line in the minimum number of stations to produce 400 units per day.

Solution

a.

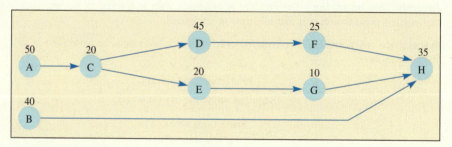

b. The theoretical minimum number of stations to meet $D = 400$ is

$$N_t = \frac{T}{C} = \frac{245 \text{ seconds}}{\left(\dfrac{60 \text{ seconds} \times 480 \text{ minutes}}{400 \text{ units}}\right)} = \frac{245}{72} = 3.4 \text{ stations}$$

c.

	TASK	TASK TIME (SECONDS)	REMAINING UNASSIGNED TIME	FEASIBLE REMAINING TASK
Station 1	A	50	22	C
	C	20	2	None
Station 2	D	45	27	E, F
	F	25	2	None
Station 3	B	40	32	E
	E	20	12	G
	G	10	2	None
Station 4	H	35	37	None

LO6–4 **SOLVED PROBLEM 3**

The manufacturing engineers at Suny Manufacturing were working on a new remote-controlled toy monster truck. They hired a production consultant to help them determine the best type of production process to meet the forecasted demand for this new product. The consultant recommended that they use an assembly line. He told the manufacturing engineers that the line must be able to produce 600 monster trucks per day to meet the demand forecast. The workers in the plant work eight hours per day. The task information for the new monster truck is given below:

TASK	TASK TIME (SECONDS)	TASK THAT MUST PRECEDE
A	28	—
B	13	—
C	35	B
D	11	A
E	20	C
F	6	D, E
G	23	F
H	25	F
I	37	G
J	11	G, H
K	27	I, J
Total	236	

a. Draw the schematic diagram.
b. What is the required cycle time to meet the forecasted demand of 600 trucks per day based on an eight-hour workday?
c. What is the theoretical minimum number of workstations, given the answer in part *b*?
d. Use longest task time with alphabetical order as the tie breaker, and balance the line in the minimum number of stations to produce 600 trucks per day.
e. Use the largest number of following tasks, and as a tie breaker use the shortest task time, to balance the line in the minimum number of stations to produce 600 trucks per day.

Solution

a.

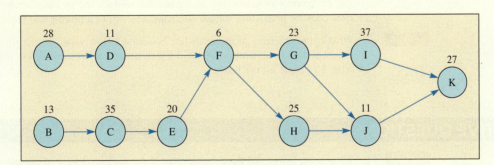

b. $C = \dfrac{\text{Production time per day}}{\text{Output per day}} = \dfrac{60 \text{ seconds} \times 480 \text{ minutes}}{600 \text{ trucks}} = \dfrac{28,800}{600} = 48 \text{ seconds}$

c. $N_t = \dfrac{T}{C} = \dfrac{236 \text{ seconds}}{48 \text{ seconds}} = 4.92 = 5 \text{ (rounded up)}$

d.

	FEASIBLE TASKS	TASK	TASK TIME (SECONDS)	REMAINING UNASSIGNED TIME
Station 1	A, B	A	28	20
	B, D	B	13	7
Station 2	C, D	C	35	13
	D	D	11	2
Station 3	E	E	20	28
	F	F	6	22
Station 4	G, H	H	25	23
	G	G	23	0
Station 5	I, J	I	37	11
	J	J	11	0
Station 6	K	K	27	21

e. Solution same as above.

DISCUSSION QUESTIONS

LO6–1

1. What is meant by a process? Describe its important features.
2. What is a *customer order decoupling point*? Why is it important?
3. What's the relationship between the design of a manufacturing process and the firm's strategic competitive dimensions (Chapter 2)?

LO6–2

4. What is meant by *manufacturing process flow*?
5. Why is it that reducing the number of moves, delays, and storages in a manufacturing process is a good thing? Can they be completely eliminated?

LO6–3

6. What does the product–process matrix tell us? How should the kitchen of a Chinese restaurant be structured?
7. It has been noted that during World War II Germany made a critical mistake by having its formidable Tiger tanks produced by locomotive manufacturers, while the less formidable U.S. Sherman tank was produced by American car manufacturers. Use the product–process matrix to explain that mistake and its likely result.
8. How does the production volume affect the selection of a process and profitability?

LO6–4

9. What is the objective of assembly-line balancing? How would you deal with the situation where one worker, although trying hard, is 20 percent slower than the other 10 people on the line?

OBJECTIVE QUESTIONS

LO6–1

1. What is the first of the three simple steps in the high-level view of manufacturing?
2. The customer order decoupling point determines the position of what in the supply chain?
3. Dell Computer's primary consumer business takes orders from customers for specific configurations of desktop and laptop computers. Customers must select from a certain model line of computer and choose from available parts, but within those constraints may customize the computer as they desire. Once the order is received, Dell assembles the computer as ordered and delivers it to the customer. What type of manufacturing process is described here?

4. What term is used to mean manufacturing designed to achieve high customer satisfaction with minimum levels of inventory investment?

LO6–2

5. You are in a line at the bank drive-through and 10 cars are in front of you. You estimate that the clerk is serving 1 car about every five minutes. How long do you expect to wait in line?

6. A firm has redesigned its production process so that it now takes 10 hours for a unit to be made. Using the old process, it took 15 hours to make a unit. If the process makes one unit each hour on average and each unit is worth $1,500, what is the reduction in work-in-process value?

7. The Avis Company is a car rental company and is located three miles from the Los Angeles airport (LAX). Avis is dispatching a bus from its offices to the airport every 2 minutes. The average traveling time (a round trip) is 20 minutes.
   a. How many Avis buses are traveling to and from the airport?
   b. The branch manager wants to improve the service and suggests dispatching buses every 0.5 minute. She argues that this will reduce the average traveling time from the airport to Avis's offices to 2.5 minutes. Is she correct? If your answer is negative, then what will the average traveling time be?

8. Safety regulations require that the time between airplane takeoffs (on the same runway) will be at least 3 minutes. When taking off, the run time of an airplane on the runway is 45 seconds. Planes wait, on average, 4 minutes and 15 seconds for takeoff. On average, there are 15 planes taking off per hour. How many planes are either on the runway or waiting to take off?

9. In Children's Hospital in Seattle, there are, on average, 60 births per week. Mothers and babies stay, on average, two days before they leave the hospital. In Swedish Hospital (also in Seattle), the average number of births per week is 210. Mothers and children stay in the hospital two days, on average.
   a. How many new mothers are staying in Children's Hospital?
   b. How many new mothers are staying in Swedish Hospital?
   c. The directors of the two hospitals are negotiating unifying the children wards of the two hospitals. They believe that by doing so they will be able to reduce the number of new mothers staying in the hospital. Are they correct? How many new mothers will stay, on average, in the unified ward?
       You may assume that the average number of births and the lengths of stay of the new mothers will not change.

10. A call center employs 1,000 agents. Every month, 50 employees leave the company and 50 new employees are hired.
    a. How long, on average, does an agent work for this call center?
        Suppose the cost of hiring and training a new agent is $1,000. The manager of this call center believes that increasing agents' salaries would keep them working longer at the company. The manager wants to increase the average time that an agent works for the call center to 24 months, or two years.
    b. If an agent works for the call center for 24 months on average, how much can the company save on hiring and training costs over a year? (*Hint:* First determine the current annual cost for hiring and training, then determine the new annual cost for hiring and training.)

11. Money Laundry has 10 washers and 15 dryers. All orders are first sent to wash and then to dry. It takes, on average, 30 minutes to wash one order and 40 minutes to dry.
    a. What is the capacity of the washing stage?
    b. What is the capacity of the drying stage?
    c. Identify the bottleneck(s). Briefly explain.
    d. What is the capacity of Money Laundry? Briefly explain.
    e. If Money Laundry would like to increase the capacity by buying one more machine, should they buy a washer or a dryer? Why?

The manager, Mr. Money, decided not to buy a machine. He still has 10 washers and 15 dryers. The manager estimates that, on average, Money Laundry receives eight orders every hour. The manager also finds that, on average, there are five orders in the washing stage and seven orders in the drying stage.

f. What is the utilization of washers, on average?

g. What is the utilization of dryers, on average?

h. On average, how long does it take an order to finish the washing process from the time the order is received?

i. On average, how long does it take an order to finish the drying process from the time the order finishes the washing process?

j. On average, how long does an order stay in Money Laundry?

LO6–3 12. How would you characterize the most important difference for the following issues when comparing a workcenter (job shop) and an assembly line?

ISSUE	WORKCENTER (JOB SHOP)	ASSEMBLY LINE
Number of setups (job changeovers)		
Labor content of product		
Flexibility		

13. The product–process matrix is a convenient way of characterizing the relationship between product volumes (one-of-a-kind to continuous) and the processing system employed by a firm at a particular location. In the box presented below, describe the nature of the intersection between the type of shop (column) and process dimension (row).

	WORKCENTER	ASSEMBLY LINE
Engineering emphasis		
General workforce skill		
Facility layout		
WIP inventory level		

14. For each of the following variables, explain the differences (in general) as one moves from a workcenter to an assembly-line environment.

a. Throughput time (time to convert raw material into product)

b. Capital/labor intensity

c. Bottlenecks

LO6–4 15. An assembly line is to operate eight hours per day with a desired output of 240 units per day. The following table contains information on this product's task times and precedence relationships:

TASK	TASK TIME (SECONDS)	IMMEDIATE PREDECESSOR
A	60	—
B	80	A
C	20	A
D	50	A
E	90	B, C
F	30	C, D
G	30	E, F
H	60	G

a. Draw the precedence diagram.

b. What is the workstation cycle time required to produce 240 units per day?

c. Balance this line using the longest task time.

d. What is the efficiency of your line balance, assuming it is running at the cycle time from part (*b*)?

16. The desired daily output for an assembly line is 360 units. This assembly line will operate 450 minutes per day. The following table contains information on this product's task times and precedence relationships:

TASK	TASK TIME (SECONDS)	IMMEDIATE PREDECESSOR
A	30	—
B	35	A
C	30	A
D	35	B
E	15	C
F	65	C
G	40	E, F
H	25	D, G

a. Draw the precedence diagram.

b. What is the workstation cycle time required to produce 360 units per day?

c. Balance this line using the largest number of following tasks. Use the longest task time as a secondary criterion.

d. What is the efficiency of your line balance, assuming it is running at the cycle time 17 from part (*b*)?

17. Some tasks and the order in which they must be performed according to their assembly requirements are shown in the following table. These are to be combined into workstations to create an assembly line. The assembly line operates 7½ hours per day. The output requirement is 1,000 units per day.

TASK	PRECEDING TASKS	TIME (SECONDS)
A	—	15
B	A	24
C	A	6
D	B	12
E	B	18
F	C	7
G	C	11
H	D	9
I	E	14
J	F, G	7
K	H, I	15
L	J, K	10

a. What is the workstation cycle time required to produce 1,000 units per day?

b. Balance the line using the longest task time based on the 1,000-unit forecast, stating which tasks would be done in each workstation.

c. For (*b*), what is the efficiency of your line balance, assuming it is running at the cycle time from part (*a*)?

d. After production was started, Marketing realized that it understated demand and must increase output to 1,100 units. What action would you take? Be specific and quantitative in your answer.

18. An assembly line is to be designed to operate 7½ hours per day and supply a steady demand of 300 units per day. Here are the tasks and their performance times:

TASK	PRECEDING TASKS	PERFORMANCE TIME (SECONDS)	TASK	PRECEDING TASKS	PERFORMANCE TIME (SECONDS)
A	—	70	G	D	60
B	—	40	H	E	50
C	—	45	I	F	15
D	A	10	J	G	25
E	B	30	K	H, I	20
F	C	20	L	J, K	25

a. Draw the precedence diagram.
b. What is the workstation cycle time required to produce 300 units per day?
c. What is the theoretical minimum number of workstations?
d. Assign tasks to workstations using the longest operating time.
e. What is the efficiency of your line balance, assuming it is running at the cycle time from part (b)?
f. Suppose demand increases by 10 percent. How would you react to this? Assume that you can operate only 7½ hours per day.

19. The following tasks are to be performed on an assembly line:

TASK	SECONDS	TASKS THAT MUST PRECEDE
A	20	—
B	7	A
C	20	B
D	22	B
E	15	C
F	10	D
G	16	E, F
H	8	G

The workday is seven hours long. The demand for completed product is 750 per day.
a. Find the cycle time required to produce 750 units per day.
b. What is the theoretical number of workstations?
c. Draw the precedence diagram.
d. Balance the line using sequential restrictions and the longest-operating-time rule.
e. What is the efficiency of the line balanced as in part (d), assuming it is running at the cycle time from part (a)?
f. Suppose that demand rose from 750 to 800 units per day. What would you do? Show any amounts or calculations.
g. Suppose that demand rose from 750 to 1,000 units per day. What would you do? Show any amounts or calculations.

20. The Sun River beverage company is a regional producer of teas, exotic juices, and energy drinks. With an interest in healthier lifestyles, there has been an increase in demand for its sugar-free formulation.

The final packing operation requires 13 tasks. Sun River bottles its sugar-free product 5 hours a day, 5 days a week. Each week, there is a demand for 3,000 bottles of this product. Using the data below, solve the assembly-line balancing problem and calculate the efficiency of your solution, assuming the line runs at the cycle time required to meet demand. Use the longest task time for your decision criteria. Use the largest number of following tasks as a secondary criterion.

TASK	PRECEDING TIME (MINUTES)	TASKS THAT MUST FOLLOW
1	0.1	—
2	0.1	1
3	0.1	2
4	0.2	2
5	0.1	2
6	0.2	3, 4, 5
7	0.1	1

TASK	PRECEDING TIME (MINUTES)	TASKS THAT MUST FOLLOW
8	0.15	7
9	0.3	8
10	0.5	9
11	0.2	6
12	0.2	10, 11
13	0.1	12

21. Consider the following tasks, times, and predecessors for an assembly of set-top cable converter boxes:

TASK ELEMENT	TIME (MINUTES)	ELEMENT PREDECESSOR
A	1	—
B	1	A
C	2	B
D	1	B
E	3	C, D
F	1	A
G	1	F
H	2	G
I	1	E, H

Given a cycle time of four minutes, develop two alternative layouts. Use the longest task time rule and the largest number of following tasks as a secondary criterion. What is the efficiency of your layouts, assuming the 4-minute cycle time?

ADVANCED PROBLEM

22. Francis Johnson's plant needs to design an efficient assembly line to make a new product. The assembly line needs to produce 15 units per hour, and there is room for only four workstations. The tasks and the order in which they must be performed are shown in the following table. Tasks cannot be split, and it would be too expensive to duplicate any task.

TASK	TASK TIME (MINUTES)	IMMEDIATE PREDECESSOR
A	1	—
B	2	—
C	3	—
D	1	A, B, C
E	3	C
F	2	E
G	3	E

a. Draw the precedence diagram.
b. What is the workstation cycle time required to produce 15 units per hour?
c. Balance the line so that only four workstations are required. Use whatever method you feel is appropriate.
d. What is the efficiency of your line balance, assuming the cycle time from part (*b*)?

ANALYTICS EXERCISE: DESIGNING A MANUFACTURING PROCESS

Toshiba's Notebook Computer Assembly Line

Toshihiro Nakamura, manufacturing engineering section manager, is examining the prototype assembly process sheet (shown in Exhibit 6.8) for the newest subnotebook computer model. With every new model introduced, management felt that the assembly line had to increase productivity and lower costs, usually resulting in changes to the assembly process. When a new model is designed, considerable attention is directed toward reducing the number of components and simplifying parts production and assembly requirements. This new computer was a marvel of high-tech, low-cost innovation and should give Toshiba an advantage during the upcoming fall/winter selling season.

Production of the subnotebook is scheduled to begin in 10 days. Initial production for the new model is to be 150 units per day, increasing to 250 units per day the following week (management thought that eventually production would reach 300 units per day). Assembly lines at the plant normally are staffed by 10 operators who work at a 14.4-meter-long

assembly line. The line is organized in a straight line with workers shoulder to shoulder on one side. The line can accommodate up to 12 operators if there is a need. The line normally operates for 7.5 hours a day (employees work from 8:15 A.M. to 5:00 P.M. and regular hours include one hour of unpaid lunch and 15 minutes of scheduled breaks). It is possible to run one, two, or three hours of overtime, but employees need at least three days' notice for planning purposes.

The Assembly Line

At the head of the assembly line, a computer displays the daily production schedule, consisting of a list of model types and corresponding lot sizes scheduled to be assembled on the line. The models are simple variations of hard disk size, memory, and battery power. A typical production schedule includes seven or eight model types in lot sizes varying from 10 to 100 units. The models are assembled sequentially: All the units of the first model are assembled, followed by all the units of the second, and so on. This computer screen also indicates how far along the assembly line is in completing its

exhibit 6.8	Notebook Computer Assembly Process Sheet

TASK	TASK TIME (SECONDS)	TASKS THAT MUST PRECEDE
1. Assemble cover.	75	None
2. Install LCD in cover.	61	Task 1
3. Prepare base assembly.	24	None
4. Install M-PCB in base.	36	Task 3
5. Install CPU.	22	Task 4
6. Install backup batteries and test.	39	Task 4
7. Install Accupoint pointing device and wrist rest.	32	Task 4
8. Install speaker and microphone.	44	Task 4
9. Install auxiliary printed circuit board (A-PCB) on M-PCB.	29	Task 4
10. Prepare and install keyboard.	26	Task 9
11. Prepare and install digital video drive (DVD) and hard disk drive (HDD).	52	Task 10
12. Install battery pack.	7	Task 11
13. Insert memory card.	5	Task 12
14. Start software load.	11	Tasks 2, 5, 6, 7, 8, 13
15. Software load (unattended).	310	Task 14
16. Test video display.	60	Task 15
17. Test keyboard.	60	Task 16

| Engineers' Initial Design of the Assembly Line | | | **exhibit 6.9** |

ASSEMBLY LINE POSITION	TASKS	WORKSTATION NUMBER	LABOR TIME (SECONDS)
1	1. Assemble cover. (75)	1	75
2	2. Install LCD in cover. (61) 3. Prepare base assembly. (24)	2	61 + 24 = 85
3	4. Install main printed circuit board (M-PCB) in base. (36) 5. Install CPU. (22) 6. Install backup batteries and test. (39)	3	36 + 22 + 39 = 97
4	7. Install Accupoint pointing device and wrist rest. (32) 8. Install speaker and microphone. (44) 9. Install auxiliary printed circuit board (A-PCB) on M-PCB.	4	32 + 44 + 29 = 105
5	10. Prepare and install keyboard. (26) 11. Prepare and install digital video drive (DVD) and hard disk drive (HDD). (52) 12. Install battery pack. (7) 13. Insert memory card. (5) 14. Start software load. (11) 15. Software load. (19)	5	26 + 52 + 7 + 5 + 11 = 101
6	Continue software load. (120)		
7	Continue software load. (120)		
8	Continue software load. (51)		
9	16. Test video display. (60) 17. Test keyboard. (60)	6	120
10	Empty.		
11	Empty.		
12	Empty.		

daily schedule, which serves as a guide for the material handlers who supply parts to the assembly lines.

The daily schedules are shared with the nearby Fujihashi Parts Collection and Distribution Center. Parts are brought from Fujihashi to the plant within two hours of when they are needed. The material supply system is very tightly coordinated and works well.

The assembly line consists of a 14.4-meter conveyor belt that carries the computers, separated at 1.2-meter intervals by white stripes on the belt. Workers stand shoulder to shoulder on one side of the conveyor and work on the units as they move by. In addition to the assembly workers, a highly skilled worker, called a "supporter," is assigned to each line. The supporter moves along the line, assisting workers who are falling behind and replacing workers who need to take a break. Supporters also make decisions about what to do when problems are encountered during the assembly process (such as a defective part). The line speed and the number of workers vary from day to day, depending on production demand and

the workers' skills and availability. Although the assembly line has 12 positions, often they are not all used.

Exhibit 6.9 provides details of how the engineers who designed the new subnotebook computer felt that the new line should be organized. These engineers designed the line assuming that one notebook would be assembled every two minutes by six line workers.

In words, the following is a brief description of what is done at each workstation:

Workstation 1: The first operator lays out the major components of a computer between two white lines on the conveyor. The operator then prepares the cover for accepting the LCD screen by installing fasteners and securing a cable.

Workstation 2: The second operator performs two different tasks. First, the LCD screen is installed in the cover. This task needs to be done after the cover is assembled (task 1). A second independent task done by the operator is the preparation of the base so that the main printed circuit board (M-PCB) can be installed.

Workstation 3: Here the M-PCB is installed in the base. After this is done, the central processing unit (CPU) and backup batteries are installed and tested.

Workstation 4: The Accupoint pointing device (touchpad) and wrist rest are installed, the speaker and microphone is installed, and the auxiliary printed circuit board (A-PCB) is installed. These are all independent tasks that can be done after the M-PCB is installed.

Workstation 5: Here, tasks are performed in a sequence. First, the keyboard is installed, followed by the DVD and hard disk drive (HDD). The battery pack is then installed, followed by the memory card. The computer is then powered up and a program started that loads software that can be used to test the computer. Actually loading the software takes 310 seconds, and this is done while the computer travels through positions 6, 7, and 8 on the assembly line. Computers that do not work are sent to a rework area where they are fixed. Only about 1 percent of the computers fail to start, and these are usually quickly repaired by the "supporter."

Workstation 6: The video display and keyboard are tested in this workstation.

After assembly, the computers are moved to a separate burn-in area that is separate from the assembly line. Here, computers are put in racks for a 24-hour, 25°C "burn-in" of the circuit components. After burn-in, the computer is tested again, software is installed, and the finished notebook computer is packaged and placed on pallets for shipment to Toshiba distribution centers around the world.

Tweaking the Initial Assembly-Line Design

From past experience, Toshihiro has found that the initial assembly-line design supplied by the engineers often needs to be tweaked. Consider the following questions that Toshihiro is considering:

1. What is the daily capacity of the assembly line designed by the engineers? Assume that the assembly line has a computer at every position when it is started at the beginning of the day.
2. When the assembly line designed by the engineers is running at maximum capacity, what is the efficiency of the line relative to its use of labor? Assume that the "supporter" is not included in efficiency calculations.
3. How should the line be redesigned to operate at the initial 250 units per day target, assuming that no overtime will be used? What is the efficiency of your new design?
4. What about running the line at 300 units per day? If overtime were used with the engineers' initial design, how much time would the line need to be run each day?
5. Design a new assembly line that can produce 300 units per day without using overtime.
6. What other issues might Toshihiro consider when bringing the new assembly line up to speed?

PRACTICE EXAM

1. A firm that makes predesigned products directly to fill customer orders has this type of production environment.
2. A point where inventory is positioned to allow the production process to operate independently of the customer order delivery process.
3. A firm that designs and builds products from scratch according to customer specifications would have this type of production environment.
4. If a production process makes a unit every two hours and it takes 42 hours for the unit to go through the entire process, then the expected work-in-process is equal to this.
5. A finished goods inventory contains, on average, 10,000 units. Demand averages 1,500 units per week. Given that the process runs 50 weeks a year, what is the expected inventory turn for the inventory?

Assume that each item held in inventory is valued at about the same amount.

6. This is a production layout where similar products are made. Typically, it is scheduled on an as-needed basis in response to current customer demand.
7. The relationship between how different layout structures are best suited depending on volume and product variety characteristics is depicted using this type of graph.
8. A firm is using an assembly line and needs to produce 500 units during an eight-hour day. What is the required cycle time in seconds?
9. What is the efficiency of an assembly line that has 25 workers and a cycle time of 45 seconds? Each unit produced on the line has 16 minutes of work that needs to be completed based on a time study completed by engineers at the factory.

Answers to Practice Exam 1. Make-to-order 2. Customer order decoupling point 3. Engineer-to-order
4. 21 units = 42/2 5. 7.5 turns = (1,500 × 50)/10,000 6. Manufacturing cell 7. Product–process matrix
8. 57.6 seconds = (8 × 60 × 60)/500 9. 85% = (16 × 60)/(25 ×45)

CHAPTER 6A

BREAK-EVEN ANALYSIS

The choice of which specific equipment to use in a process often can be based on an analysis of cost trade-offs. There is often a trade-off between more and less specialized equipment. Less specialized equipment is referred to as "general purpose," meaning it can be used easily in many different ways if it is set up in the proper manner. More specialized equipment, referred to as "special purpose," is often available as an alternative to a general-purpose machine. For example, if we need to drill holes in a piece of metal, the general-purpose option may be to use a simple hand drill. An alternative special-purpose drill is a drill press. Given the proper setup, the drill press can drill holes much quicker than the hand drill can. The trade-offs involve the cost of the equipment (the manual drill is inexpensive, and the drill press expensive), the setup time (the manual drill is quick, while the drill press takes some time), and the time per unit (the manual drill is slow, and the drill press quick).

A standard approach to choosing among alternative processes or equipment is *break-even analysis*. A break-even chart visually presents alternative profits and losses due to the number of units produced or sold. The choice obviously depends on anticipated demand. The method is most suitable when processes and equipment entail a large initial investment and fixed cost, and when variable costs are reasonably proportional to the number of units produced.

Example 6A.1: Break-Even Analysis

Suppose a manufacturer has identified the following options for obtaining a machined part: It can buy the part at $200 per unit (including materials); it can make the part on a numerically controlled semiautomatic lathe at $75 per unit (including materials); or it can make the part on a machining center at $15 per unit (including materials). There is negligible fixed cost if the item is purchased; a semiautomatic lathe costs $80,000; and a machining center costs $200,000.

The total cost for each option is

$$\text{Purchase cost} = \$200 \times \text{Demand}$$

$$\text{Produce-using-lathe cost} = \$80{,}000 + \$75 \times \text{Demand}$$

$$\text{Produce-using-machining-center cost} = \$200{,}000 + \$15 \times \text{Demand}$$

SOLUTION

Whether we approach the solution to this problem as cost minimization or profit maximization really makes no difference as long as the revenue function is the same for all alternatives. Exhibit 6A.1 shows the break-even point for each process. If demand is expected to be more than 2,000 units (point A), the machine center is the best choice because this would result in the lowest total cost. If demand is between 640 (point B) and 2,000 units, the semiautomatic lathe is the cheapest. If demand is less than 640 (between 0 and point B), the most economical course is to buy the product.

The break-even point A calculation is

$$\$80{,}000 + \$75 \times \text{Demand} = \$200{,}000 + \$15 \times \text{Demand}$$

$$\text{Demand (point A)} = 120{,}000/60 = 2{,}000 \text{ units}$$

Excel:
Break-Even
Analysis

exhibit 6A.1 Break-Even Chart of Alternative Processes

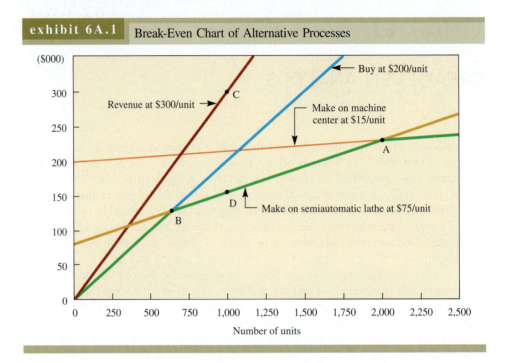

The break-even point B calculation is

$$\$200 \times \text{Demand} = \$80,000 + \$75 \times \text{Demand}$$

$$\text{Demand (point B)} = 80,000/125 = 640 \text{ units}$$

Consider the effect of revenue, assuming the part sells for $300 each. As Exhibit 6A.1 shows, profit (or loss) is the vertical distance between the revenue line and the alternative process cost at a given number of units. At 1,000 units, for example, maximum profit is the difference between the $300,000 revenue (point C) and the semiautomatic lathe cost of $155,000 (point D). For this quantity, the semiautomatic lathe is the cheapest alternative available. The optimal choices for both minimizing cost and maximizing profit are the lowest segments of the lines: origin to B, to A, and to the right side of Exhibit 6A.1, as shown in green. •

SOLVED PROBLEMS

SOLVED PROBLEM 1

An automobile manufacturer is considering a change in an assembly line that should save money by reducing labor and material cost. The change involves the installation of four new robots that will automatically install windshields. The cost of the four robots, including installation and initial programming, is $400,000. Current practice is to amortize the initial cost of the robots over two years on a straight-line basis. The process engineer estimates that one full-time technician will be needed to monitor, maintain, and reprogram the robots on an ongoing basis. This person will cost approximately $60,000 per year. Currently, the company uses four full-time employees on this job and each makes about $52,000 per year. One of these employees is a material handler, and this person will still be needed with the new process. To complicate matters, the process engineer estimates that the robots will apply the windshield sealing material in a manner that will result in a savings of $0.25 per windshield installed. How many automobiles need to be produced over the next two years to make the new robots an attractive investment? Due to the relatively short horizon, do not consider the time value of money.

Solution

The cost of the current process over the next two years is just the cost of the four full-time employees.

$$\$52,000/\text{employee} \times 4 \text{ employees} \times 2 \text{ years} = \$416,000$$

The cost of the new process over the next two years, assuming the robot is completely costed over that time, is

$$(\$52,000/\text{material handler} + \$60,000/\text{technician}) \times 2 + \$400,000/\text{robots} - \$0.25 \times \text{autos}$$

Equating the two alternatives

$$\$416,000 = \$624,000 - \$0.25 \times \text{autos}$$

Solving for the break-even point

$$-\$208,000/-\$0.25 = 832,000 \text{ autos}$$

This indicates that, to break even, 832,000 autos would need to be produced with the robots over the next two years.

SOLVED PROBLEM 2

A contract manufacturer makes a product for a customer that consists of two items, a cable with standard RCA connectors and a cable with a mini-plug, which are then packaged together as the final product (each product sold contains one RCA and one mini-plug cable). The manufacturer makes both cables on the same assembly line and can only make one type at a time: Either it can make RCA cables or it can make mini-plug cables. There is a setup time when switching from one cable to the other. The assembly line costs $500/hour to operate, and this rate is charged whether it is being set up or actually making cables.

Current plans are to make 100 units of the RCA cable, then 100 units of the mini-plug cable, then 100 units of the RCA cable, then 100 units of the mini-plug cable, and so on, where the setup and run times for each cable are given below.

COMPONENT	SETUP/CHANGEOVER TIME	RUN TIME/UNIT
RCA cable	5 minutes	0.2 minute
Mini-plug cable	10 minutes	0.1 minute

Assume the packaging of the two cables is totally automated and takes only two seconds per unit of the final product and is done as a separate step from the assembly line. Since the packaging step is quick and the time required does not depend on the assembly-line batch size, its cost does not vary and need not be considered in the analysis.

What is the average hourly output in terms of the number of units of packaged product (which includes one RCA cable and one mini-plug cable)? What is the average cost per unit for assembling the product? If the batch size were changed from 100 to 200 units, what would be the impact on the assembly cost per unit?

Solution

The average hourly output rate when the batch size is 100 units is calculated by first calculating the total time to produce a batch of cable. The time consists of the setup time plus the run time for a batch

$$5 + 10 + 0.2(100) + 0.1(100) = 15 + 30 = 45 \text{ minutes/100 units}$$

So if we can produce 100 units in 45 minutes, we need to calculate how many units can be produced in 60 minutes. We can find this with the following ratio:

$$45/100 = 60/X$$

Solving for X

$$X = 133.3 \text{ units/hour}$$

The cost per unit is then

$$\$500/133.3 = \$3.75/\text{unit}$$

If the batch size were increased to 200 units

$$5 + 10 + 0.2(200) + 0.1(200) = 15 + 60 = 75 \text{ minutes/200 units}$$
$$75/200 = 60/X$$
$$X = 160/\text{hour}$$
$$\$500/160 = \$3.125/\text{unit}$$

OBJECTIVE QUESTIONS

1. A book publisher has fixed costs of $300,000 and variable costs per book of $8. The book sells for $23 per copy.
   a. How many books must be sold to break even?
   b. If the fixed cost increased, would the new break-even point be higher or lower?
   c. If the variable cost per unit decreased, would the new break-even point be higher or lower?
2. A manufacturing process has a fixed cost of $150,000 per month. Each unit of product being produced contains $25 worth of material and takes $45 of labor. How many units are needed to break even if each completed unit has a value of $90?
3. Assume a fixed cost of $900.00, a variable cost of $4.50, and a selling price of $5.50.
   a. What is the break-even point?
   b. How many units must be sold to make a profit of $500.00?
   c. How many units must be sold to average $0.25 profit per unit? $0.50 profit per unit? $1.50 profit per unit?
4. Aldo Redondo drives his own car on company business. His employer reimburses him for such travel at the rate of 36 cents per mile. Aldo estimates that his fixed costs per year such as taxes, insurance, and depreciation are $2,052.00. The direct or variable costs such as gas, oil, and maintenance average about 14.4 cents per mile. How many miles must he drive to break even?

5. A firm is selling two products, chairs and bar stools, each at $50 per unit. Chairs have a variable cost of $25, and bar stools $20. Fixed cost for the firm is $20,000.

   a. If the sales mix is 1:1 (one chair sold for every bar stool sold), what is the break-even point in dollars of sales? In units of chairs and bar stools?

   b. If the sales mix changes to 1:4 (one chair sold for every four bar stools sold), what is the break-even point in dollars of sales? In units of chairs and bar stools?

6. Owen Conner works part time packaging software for a local distribution company in Indiana. The annual fixed cost is $10,000.00 for this process, direct labor is $3.50 per package, and material is $4.50 per package. The selling price will be $12.50 per package. How much revenue do we need to take in before breaking even? What is the break-even point in units?

CHAPTER 7

SERVICE PROCESSES

Learning Objectives

LO7–1 Understand the characteristics of service processes.

LO7–2 Analyze simple service systems.

LO7–3 Understand waiting line (queuing) analysis.

PAYING WITH A WAVE OF YOUR PHONE

Futurists have long predicted that shoppers at retail stores would soon pay with the waving of a cellphone instead of credit cards. Starbucks, in its stores in the United States, has done this for many years using a special Starbucks card app where customers hold their smartphone in front of a scanner at the cash register. The money is then deducted from their Starbucks account, which they load with credit cards or PayPal funds.

A much more convenient approach from Apple Computer called Apple Pay now allows this to be done at virtually any store. All users have to do is position their iPhone near a reader at the store and hold their finger on the touch ID. A special "near field" antenna, built into the iPhone, connects and completes the transaction. A quick vibration and beep lets the user know the checkout is complete.

Paying with these quick cellphone apps simplifies and quickens the transaction and could reduce waiting in line for everyone.

© PHILIPPE HUGUEN/Getty Images

THE NATURE OF SERVICES

A service is an output of a process that is intangible, meaning that it does not have physical dimensions that can be weighed or measured. Unlike a product innovation, services cannot be patented, so a company with a new concept must expand rapidly before competitors copy its procedures.

LO7–1 Understand the characteristics of service processes.

Services typically require some degree of interaction with the customer. The interaction may be brief, but it must exist for the service to be complete. Often, the interaction differs depending on the needs of the customer. In addition, the service typically is time-dependent, with the customer demanding the service quickly or at a specific time.

Every service has a **service package**, which is defined as a bundle of goods and services that is provided in some environment. This bundle consists of five features:

Service package
A bundle of goods and services that is provided in some environment.

1. *Supporting facility:* The physical resources that must be in place before a service can be offered. Examples are a golf course, a ski lift, an airline, and an auto repair facility.
2. *Facilitating goods:* The material purchased or consumed by the buyer or the items provided to the customer. Examples are golf clubs, skis, beverages, and auto parts.
3. *Information:* Operations data or information that is provided to the customer to enable efficient and customized services. Examples include tee-off times, weather reports, medical records, seat preferences, and parts availability.

4. *Explicit services:* The benefits that are readily observable by the senses and that consist of the essential or intrinsic features of the service. Examples are response time of an ambulance, air conditioning in a hotel room, and a smooth-running car after a tune-up.
5. *Implicit services:* Psychological benefits that the customer may sense only vaguely, or the extrinsic features of the service. Examples are the status of a degree from an Ivy League school, the privacy of a loan office, and worry-free auto repair.

An Operational Classification of Services

Service organizations are generally classified according to who the customer is (for example, individuals or other businesses) and the service they provide (financial services, health services, transportation services, and so on). These groupings, though useful in presenting aggregate economic data, are not particularly appropriate for OSCM purposes because they tell us little about the process. Manufacturing, by contrast, has fairly evocative terms to classify production activities (such as assembly lines and continuous processes); when applied to a manufacturing setting, they readily convey the essence of the process. Although it is possible to describe services in these same terms, we need one additional item of information to reflect the fact that the customer is involved in the production system. That item, which we believe operationally distinguishes one service system from another in its production function, is the extent of customer contact in the creation of the service.

Customer contact refers to the physical presence of the customer in the system, and *creation of the service* refers to the work process involved in providing the service itself. *Extent of contact* here may be roughly defined as the percentage of time the customer must be in the system relative to the total time it takes to perform the customer service. Generally speaking, the greater the percentage of contact time between the service system and the customer, the greater the degree of interaction between the two during the production process.

High and low degree of customer contact
A concept that relates to the physical presence of the customer in the system.

From this conceptualization, it follows that service systems with a **high degree of customer contact** are more difficult to control and more difficult to rationalize than those with a **low degree of customer contact**. In high-contact systems, the customer can affect the time of demand, the exact nature of the service, and the quality, or perceived quality, of service because the customer is involved in the process.

There can be a tremendous diversity of customer influence and, hence, system variability within high-contact service systems. For example, a bank branch offers both simple services such as cash withdrawals that take just a minute or so and complicated services such as loan application preparation that can take in excess of an hour. Moreover, these activities may range from being self-service through an ATM, to coproduction where bank personnel and the customer work as a team to develop the loan application.

Designing Service Organizations

In designing service organizations, we must remember one distinctive characteristic of services: We cannot inventory services. Unlike manufacturing, where we can build up inventory during slack periods for peak demand and thus maintain a relatively stable level of employment and production planning, in services we must (with a few exceptions) meet demand as it arises. Consequently, in services, capacity becomes a dominant issue. Think about the many service situations you find yourself in—for example, eating in a restaurant or going to a Saturday night movie. Generally speaking, if the restaurant or the theater is full, you will decide to go someplace else. So, an important design parameter in services is "What capacity should we aim for?" Too much capacity

Mayo Clinic Design Improves the Patient–Provider Experience

Mayo Clinic invited IDEO to help turn an internal medicine wing into a laboratory for improving the patient–provider experience. The team devised a simple and flexible design that allows for more informative, comfortable, and guided interactions among staff and patients. There are four areas through which patients proceed: Service Home Base, Visitor-Facing Hub, Preparation Service area, and Innovation Central.

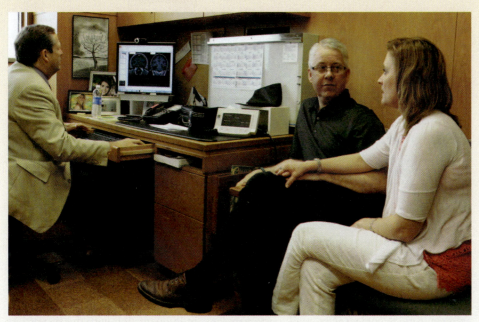

© Dan Browning/Corbis Wire/Corbis

generates excessive costs. Insufficient capacity leads to lost customers. In these situations, of course, we seek the assistance of marketing to influence demand. This is one reason why we have discount airfares, hotel specials on weekends, and so on. This is also a good illustration of why it is difficult to separate the operations management functions from marketing in services.

Waiting line models, which are discussed in this chapter, provide a powerful mathematical tool for analyzing many common service situations. Questions such as how many tellers we should have in a bank or how many computer servers we need in an Internet service operation can be analyzed with these models. These models can be easily implemented using spreadsheets.

Structuring the Service Encounter: Service–System Design Matrix

Service encounters can be configured in a number of different ways. The service–system design matrix in Exhibit 7.1 identifies six common alternatives.

The top of the matrix shows the degree of customer/server contact: the *buffered core,* which is physically separated from the customer; the *permeable system,* which is penetrable

exhibit 7.1	Service–System Design Matrix

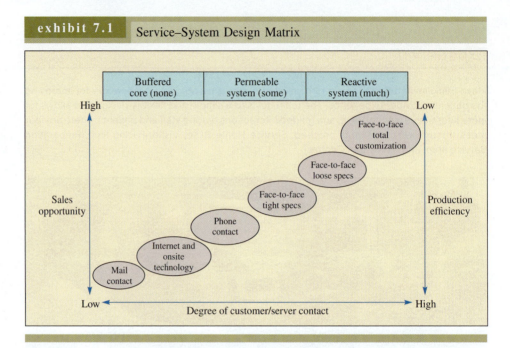

by the customer via phone or face-to-face contact; and the *reactive system,* which is both penetrable and reactive to the customer's requirements. The left side of the matrix shows what we believe to be a logical marketing opportunity—namely, that the greater the amount of contact, the greater the sales opportunity at the time when the service is delivered; the right side shows the impact on production efficiency as the customer exerts more influence on the operation.

The entries within the matrix list the ways in which service can be delivered. At one extreme, service contact is by mail; customers have little interaction with the system. At the other extreme, customers "have it their way" through face-to-face contact. The remaining four entries in the exhibit contain varying degrees of interaction.

As one would guess, production efficiency decreases as the customer has more contact (and therefore more influence) on the system. To offset this, the face-to-face contact provides high sales opportunity to sell additional products. Conversely, low contact, such as mail, allows the system to work more efficiently because the customer is unable to significantly affect (or disrupt) the system. However, there is relatively little opportunity for additional product sales.

There can be some shifting in the positioning of each entry. For our first example, consider the "Internet and onsite technology" entry in the matrix. The Internet clearly buffers the company from the customer, but interesting opportunities are available to provide relevant information and services to the customer. Because the Website can be programmed to intelligently react to the inputs of the customer, significant opportunities for new sales may be possible. In addition, the system can be made to interface with real employees when the customer needs assistance that goes beyond the programming of the Web site. The Internet is truly a revolutionary technology when applied to the services that need to be provided by a company.

Another example of shifting in the positioning of an entry can be shown with the "face-to-face tight specs" entry in Exhibit 7.1. This entry refers to those situations where there is little variation in the service process—neither customer nor server has much

Characteristics of Workers, Operations, and Innovations Relative to the Degree of Customer/Server Contact					**exhibit 7.2**	

Degree of customer/server contact

Low ←————————————————————————————→ High

	Mail	Internet	Phone	Face-to-face tight specs	Face-to-face loose specs	Face-to-face total customization
Worker requirements	Clerical skills	Helping skills	Verbal skills	Procedural skills	Trade skills	Diagnostic skills
Focus of operations	Paper handling	Demand management	Scripting calls	Flow control	Capacity management	Client mix
Technological innovations	Office automation	Routing methods	Computer databases	Electronic aids	Self-serve	Client/worker teams

discretion in creating the service. Fast-food restaurants and Disneyland come to mind. Face-to-face loose specs refers to situations where the service process is generally understood but there are options in how it will be performed or in the physical goods that are part of it. A full-service restaurant and a car sales agency are examples. Face-to-face total customization refers to service encounters whose specifications must be developed through some interaction between the customer and server. Legal and medical services are of this type, and the degree to which the resources of the system are mustered for the service determines whether the system is reactive, possibly to the point of even being proactive, or merely permeable. Examples would be the mobilization of an advertising firm's resources in preparation for an office visit by a major client, or an operating team scrambling to prepare for emergency surgery.

Exhibit 7.2 extends the design matrix. It shows the changes in workers, operations, and types of technical innovations as the degree of customer/service system contact changes. For worker requirements, the relationships between mail contact and clerical skills, Internet technology and helping skills, and phone contact and verbal skills are self-evident. Face-to-face tight specs require procedural skills in particular, because the worker must follow the routine in conducting a generally standardized, high-volume process. Face-to-face loose specs frequently call for trade skills (bank teller, draftsperson, maître d', dental hygienist) to finalize the design for the service. Face-to-face total customization tends to call for diagnostic skills of the professional to ascertain the needs or desires of the client.

Virtual Service: The New Role of the Customer
The service–system design matrix was developed from the perspective of the production system's utilization of company resources. With the advent of virtual services through the Internet, we need to account not just for a customer's interactions with a business, but for his or her interaction with other customers as well. As suggested by Brigham Young University professor Scott Sampson, we have two categories of contact: *pure virtual customer contact* where companies such as eBay and Second Life enable customers to interact with one another in an open environment; and *mixed virtual and actual customer contact* where customers interact with one another in a server-moderated environment such as product discussion groups, YouTube, and Wikipedia are examples of these groups. In these environments, the operations management challenge is to keep the technology functioning and up to date and to provide a policing function through monitoring the encounters that take place.

LO7–2 Analyze simple service systems.

Service blueprint
A flowchart of a process emphasizing what is visible and what is not visible to the customer.

SERVICE BLUEPRINTING AND FAIL-SAFING

Just as is the case with manufacturing process design, the standard tool for service process design is the flowchart. In services, the flowchart is called a **service blueprint** to emphasize the importance of process design. A unique feature of the service blueprint is the distinction made between the high customer contact aspects of the service (the parts of the process that the customer sees) and those activities that the customer does not see. This distinction is made with a "line of visibility" on the flowchart.

Exhibit 7.3 (shown here and continuing on the next page) is a blueprint of a typical automobile service operation. Each activity that makes up a typical service encounter

exhibit 7.3   Fail-Safing an Automotive Service Operation

FAILURE: CUSTOMER FORGETS THE NEED FOR SERVICE. POKA-YOKE: SEND AUTOMATIC REMINDERS WITH A 5 PERCENT DISCOUNT.

FAILURE: CUSTOMER CANNOT FIND SERVICE AREA, OR DOES NOT FOLLOW PROPER FLOW. POKA-YOKE: CLEAR AND INFORMATIVE SIGNAGE DIRECTING CUSTOMERS.

FAILURE: CUSTOMER HAS DIFFICULTY COMMUNICATING PROBLEM. POKA-YOKE: JOINT INSPECTION— SERVICE ADVISER REPEATS HIS/HER UNDERSTANDING OF THE PROBLEM FOR CONFIRMATION OR ELABORATION BY THE CUSTOMER.

FAILURE: CUSTOMER DOES NOT UNDERSTAND THE NECESSARY SERVICE. POKA-YOKE: PREPRINTED MATERIAL FOR MOST SERVICES, DETAILING WORK AND REASONS, AND POSSIBLY SHOWING A GRAPHIC REPRESENTATION.

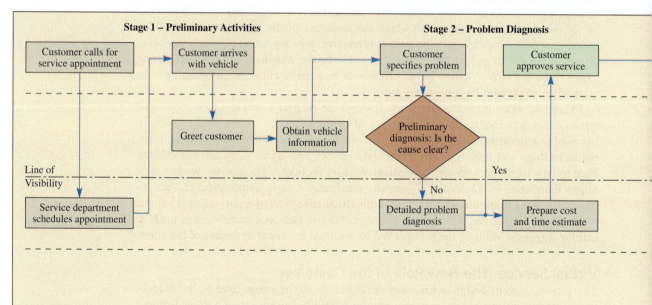

FAILURE: CUSTOMER ARRIVAL UNNOTICED. POKA-YOKE: USE A MOTION-ACTIVATED ALARM TO SIGNAL ARRIVALS.

FAILURE: CUSTOMERS NOT SERVED IN ORDER OF ARRIVAL. POKA-YOKE: PLACE NUMBERED MARKERS ON CARS AS THEY ARRIVE. FAILURE: VEHICLE INFORMATION INCORRECT AND PROCESS IS TIME-CONSUMING. POKA-YOKE: MAINTAIN CUSTOMER DATABASE AND PRINT FORMS WITH HISTORICAL INFORMATION.

FAILURE: INCORRECT DIAGNOSIS OF THE PROBLEM. POKA-YOKE: HIGH-TECH CHECKLISTS, SUCH AS EXPERT SYSTEMS AND DIAGNOSTIC EQUIPMENT.

FAILURE: INCORRECT ESTIMATE. POKA-YOKE: CHECKLISTS ITEMIZING COSTS BY COMMON REPAIR TYPES.

is mapped into the flowchart. To better show the entity that controls the activities, levels are shown in the flowchart. The top level consists of activities that are under the control of the customer. Next are those activities performed by the service manager in handling the customer. The third level is the repair activities performed in the garage; the lowest level is the internal accounting activity.

Basic blueprinting describes the features of the service design but does not provide any direct guidance on how to make the process conform to that design. An approach to this problem is the application of **poka-yokes**—procedures that block the inevitable mistake from becoming a service defect. Poka-yokes (roughly translated from the Japanese as "avoid mistakes") are common in factories and consist of such things as fixtures

Poka-yokes
Procedures that prevent mistakes from becoming defects.

FAILURE: CUSTOMER NOT LOCATED.
POKA-YOKE: ISSUE BEEPERS TO CUSTOMERS WHO WISH TO LEAVE FACILITY.

FAILURE: BILL IS ILLEGIBLE.
POKA-YOKE: GIVE TOP COPY TO CUSTOMER OR JUST A PLAIN PAPER BILL.

FAILURE: FEEDBACK NOT OBTAINED.
POKA-YOKE: CUSTOMER SATISFACTION POSTCARD GIVEN TO CUSTOMER WITH KEYS TO VEHICLE.

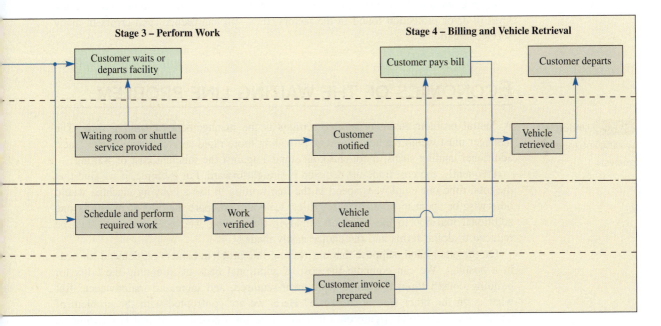

FAILURE: SERVICE SHUTTLE IS INCONVENIENT.
POKA-YOKE: SEATING IN AVAILABLE SHUTTLES IS ALLOCATED WHEN SCHEDULING APPOINTMENTS. LACK OF FREE SPACE INDICATES THAT CUSTOMERS NEEDING SHUTTLE SERVICE SHOULD BE SCHEDULED FOR ANOTHER TIME.
FAILURE: PARTS ARE NOT IN STOCK.
POKA-YOKE: LIMIT SWITCHES ACTIVATE SIGNAL LAMPS WHEN PART LEVEL FALLS BELOW ORDER POINT.

FAILURE: VEHICLE NOT CLEANED CORRECTLY.
POKA-YOKE: PERSON RETRIEVING VEHICLE INSPECTS, ORDERS A TOUCH-UP IF NECESSARY, AND REMOVES FLOOR MAT IN PRESENCE OF CUSTOMER.

FAILURE: VEHICLE TAKES TOO LONG TO ARRIVE.
POKA-YOKE: WHEN CASHIER ENTERS CUSTOMER'S NAME TO PRINT THE BILL, INFORMATION IS ELECTRONICALLY SENT TO RUNNERS WHO RETRIEVE VEHICLE WHILE THE CUSTOMER IS PAYING.

to ensure that parts can be attached only in the right way, electronic switches that automatically shut off equipment if a mistake is made, the kitting of parts prior to assembly to make sure the right quantities are used, and checklists to ensure that the right sequence of steps is followed.

There are many applications of poka-yokes to services as well. These can be classified into warning methods, physical or visual contact methods, and what we call the *Three Ts*—the Task to be done (Was the car fixed right?), the Treatment accorded to the customer (Was the service manager courteous?), and the Tangible or environmental features of the service facility (Was the waiting area clean and comfortable?). Finally (unlike in manufacturing), service poka-yokes often must be applied to fail-safing the actions of the customer as well as the service worker.

Poka-yoke examples include height bars at amusement parks; indented trays used by surgeons to ensure that no instruments are left in the patient; chains to configure waiting lines; take-a-number systems; turnstiles; beepers on ATMs to warn people to take their cards out of the machine; beepers at restaurants to make sure customers do not miss their table calls; mirrors on telephones to ensure a "smiling voice"; reminder calls for appointments; locks on airline lavatory doors that activate lights inside; small gifts in comment card envelopes to encourage customers to provide feedback about a service; and pictures of what "a clean room" looks like for kindergarten children.

Exhibit 7.3 illustrates how a typical automobile service operation might be fail-safed using poka-yokes. As a final comment, although these procedures cannot guarantee the level of error protection found in the factory, they still can reduce such errors in many service situations.

ECONOMICS OF THE WAITING LINE PROBLEM

LO7–3 Understand waiting line (queuing) analysis.

A central problem in many service settings is the management of waiting time. The manager must weigh the added cost of providing more rapid service (more traffic lanes, additional landing strips, more checkout stands) against the inherent cost of waiting.

Frequently, the cost trade-off decision is straightforward. For example, if we find that the total time our employees spend in the line waiting to use a copying machine would otherwise be spent in productive activities, we could compare the cost of installing one additional machine to the value of employee time saved. The decision could then be reduced to dollar terms and the choice easily made.

On the other hand, suppose that our waiting line problem centers on demand for beds in a hospital. We can compute the cost of additional beds by summing the costs for building construction, additional equipment required, and increased maintenance. But what is on the other side of the scale? Here, we are confronted with the problem of trying to place a dollar figure on a patient's need for a hospital bed that is unavailable. While we can estimate lost hospital income, what about the human cost arising from this lack of adequate hospital care?

The Practical View of Waiting Lines

Before we proceed with a technical presentation of waiting line theory, it is useful to look at the intuitive side of the issue to see what it means. Exhibit 7.4 shows arrivals at a service facility (such as a bank) and service requirements at that facility (such as tellers and loan officers). One important variable is the number of arrivals over the hours that the service system is open. From the service delivery viewpoint, customers demand

exhibit 7.4

Arrival and Service Profiles

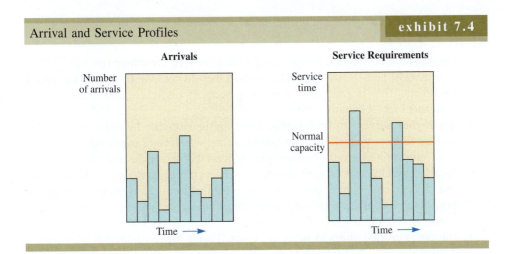

varying amounts of service, often exceeding normal capacity. We can control arrivals in a variety of ways. For example, we can have a short line (such as a drive-in at a fast-food restaurant with only several spaces), we can establish specific hours for specific customers, or we can run specials. For the server, we can affect service time by using faster or slower servers, faster or slower machines, different tooling, different material, different layout, faster setup time, and so on.

The essential point is waiting lines are *not* a fixed condition of a productive system but are to a very large extent within the control of the system management and design.

Useful suggestions for managing queues based on research in the banking industry are the following:

- **Segment the customers.** If a group of customers need something that can be done very quickly, give them a special line so that they do not have to wait for the slower customers. This is commonly done at grocery stores where checkout lines are designated for "12 items or less."
- **Train your servers to be friendly.** Greeting the customer by name or providing another form of special attention can go a long way toward overcoming the negative feeling of a long wait. Psychologists suggest that servers be told when to invoke specific friendly actions such as smiling when greeting customers, taking orders, and giving change (for example, in a convenience store). Tests using such specific behavioral actions have shown significant increases in the perceived friendliness of the servers in the eyes of the customer.
- **Inform your customers of what to expect.** This is especially important when the waiting time will be longer than normal. Tell them why the waiting time is longer than usual and what you are doing to alleviate the wait.
- **Try to divert the customer's attention when waiting.** Providing music, a video, or some other form of entertainment may help distract the customers from the fact that they are waiting.
- **Encourage customers to come during slack periods.** Inform customers of times when they usually would not have to wait; also tell them when the peak periods are—this may help smooth the load.

The Queuing System

Queuing system
A process where customers wait in line for service.

The **queuing system** consists essentially of three major components: (1) the source population and the way customers arrive at the system, (2) the servicing system, and (3) the condition of the customers exiting the system (back to source population or not?), as seen in Exhibit 7.5. The following sections discuss each of these areas.

exhibit 7.5   Components of a Queuing System

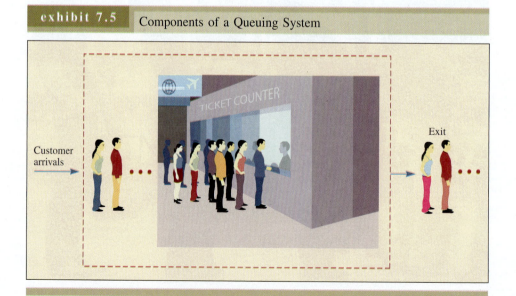

Customer Arrivals Arrivals at a service system may be drawn from a *finite* or an *infinite* population. The distinction is important because the analyses are based on different premises and require different equations for their solution.

Finite Population. A *finite population* refers to the limited-size customer pool that will use the service and, at times, form a line. The reason this finite classification is important is that when a customer leaves its position as a member of the population (due to a machine breaking down and requiring service, for example), the size of the user group is reduced by one, which reduces the probability of the next occurrence. Conversely, when a customer is serviced and returns to the user group, the population increases and the probability of a user requiring service also increases. This finite class of problems requires a separate set of formulas from that of the infinite population case.

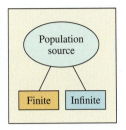

As an example, consider a group of six machines maintained by one repairperson. In this case, the machines are the customers of the repairperson. When one machine breaks down, the source population is reduced to five, and the chance of one of the remaining five breaking down and needing repair is certainly less than when six machines were operating. If two machines are down with only four operating, the probability of another breakdown is again changed. Conversely, when a machine is repaired and returned to service, the machine population increases, thus raising the probability of the next breakdown.

Infinite Population. An *infinite population* is large enough in relation to the service system so that the population size caused by subtractions or additions to the population (a customer needing service or a serviced customer returning to the population) does not significantly affect the system probabilities. If, in the preceding finite explanation, there were 100 customer machines instead of 6, then if 1 or 2 machines broke down, the probabilities for the next breakdowns would not be very different and the assumption could be made without a great deal of error that the population (for all practical purposes) was infinite. Nor would the formulas for "infinite" queuing problems cause much error if applied to a physician with 1,000 patients or a department store with 10,000 customers.

Distribution of Arrivals When describing a waiting system, we need to define the manner in which customers or the waiting units are arranged for service.

Waiting line formulas generally require an **arrival rate**, or the number of units per period (such as an average of one every six minutes). A *constant* arrival distribution is periodic, with exactly the same time between successive arrivals. In productive systems, the only arrivals that truly approach a constant interval period are those subject to machine control. Much more common are *variable* (random) arrival distributions.

In observing arrivals at a service facility, we can look at them from two viewpoints: First, we can analyze the time between successive arrivals to see if the times follow some statistical distribution. Usually, we assume that the time between arrivals is exponentially distributed. Second, we can set some time length (T) and try to determine how many arrivals might enter the system within T. We typically assume that the number of arrivals per time unit is Poisson distributed.

Exponential Distribution. In the first case, when arrivals at a service facility occur in a purely random fashion, a plot of the interarrival times yields an **exponential distribution** such as that shown in Exhibit 7.6. The probability function is

$$f(t) = \lambda e^{-\lambda t} \qquad [7.1]$$

where λ is the mean number of arrivals per time period.

Arrival rate
The expected number of customers that arrive each period.

Exponential distribution
A probability distribution associated with the time between arrivals.

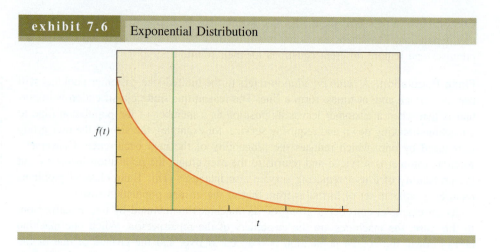

exhibit 7.6   Exponential Distribution

The cumulative area beneath the curve in Exhibit 7.6 is the summation of equation 7.1 over its positive range, which is $e^{-\lambda t}$. This integral allows us to compute the probabilities of arrivals within a specified time. For example, for the case of one arrival per minute to a waiting line ($\lambda = 1$), the following table can be derived either by solving $e^{-\lambda t}$ or by using Appendix D. Column 2 shows the probability that it will be more than t minutes until the next arrival. Column 3 shows the probability of the next arrival within t minutes (computed as 1 minus column 2).

(1)	(2)	(3)
	PROBABILITY THAT THE NEXT ARRIVAL WILL OCCUR IN	PROBABILITY THAT THE NEXT ARRIVAL WILL OCCUR IN
t	t MINUTES OR MORE (FROM	t MINUTES OR LESS
(MINUTES)	APPENDIX D OR SOLVING e^{-t})	[1 − COLUMN (2)]
0	100%	0%
0.5	61%	39%
1.0	37%	63%
1.5	22%	78%
2.0	14%	86%

Poisson Distribution. In the second case, where one is interested in the number of arrivals during some time period T, the distribution appears as in Exhibit 7.7 and is obtained by finding the probability of exactly n arrivals during T. If the arrival process is random, the distribution is the **Poisson**, and the formula is

Poisson distribution
Probability distribution for the number of arrivals during each time period.

$$P_T(n) = \frac{(\lambda T)^n\, e^{-\lambda T}}{n!}$$ [7.2]

Equation 7.2 shows the probability of exactly n arrivals in time T. For example, if the mean arrival rate of units into a system is three per minute ($\lambda = 3$) and we want to find the probability that exactly five units will arrive within a one-minute period ($n = 5$, $T = 1$), we have

$$P_1(5) = \frac{(3 \times 1)^5 e^{-3 \times 1}}{5!} = \frac{3^5 e^{-3}}{120} = 2.025 e^{-3} = 0.101$$

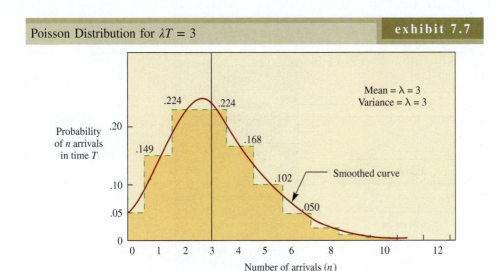

exhibit 7.7

Poisson Distribution for $\lambda T = 3$

That is, there is a 10.1 percent chance that there will be five arrivals in any one-minute interval.

Although often shown as a smoothed curve, as in Exhibit 7.7, the Poisson is a discrete distribution. (The curve becomes smoother as n becomes large.) The distribution is discrete because in our example, n refers to the number of arrivals in a system, and this must be an integer. (For example, there cannot be 1.5 arrivals.)

Also note that the exponential and Poisson distributions can be derived from one another. The mean and variance of the Poisson are equal and denoted by λ. The mean of the exponential is $1/\lambda$ and its variance is $1/\lambda^2$. (Remember that the time between arrivals is exponentially distributed and the number of arrivals per unit of time is Poisson distributed.)

Other arrival characteristics include arrival patterns, size of arrival units, and degree of patience. (See Exhibit 7.8.)

- **Arrival patterns.**   The arrivals at a system are far more controllable than is generally recognized. Barbers may decrease their Saturday arrival rate (and supposedly shift it to other days of the week) by charging an extra $1 for adult haircuts or charging adult prices for children's haircuts. Department stores run sales during the off-season or hold one-day-only sales in part for purposes of control. Airlines offer excursion and off-season rates for similar reasons. The simplest of all arrival-control devices is the posting of business hours.

    Some service demands are clearly uncontrollable, such as emergency medical demands on a city's hospital facilities. But even in these situations, arrivals at emergency rooms in specific hospitals are controllable to some extent by, say, keeping ambulance drivers in the service region informed of the status of their respective host hospitals.

- **Size of arrival units.**   A *single arrival* may be thought of as one unit. (A unit is the smallest number handled.) A single arrival on the floor of the New York Stock Exchange (NYSE) is 100 shares of stock; a single arrival at an egg-processing plant might be a dozen eggs or a flat of 2½ dozen; a single arrival at a restaurant is a single person.

    A *batch arrival* is some multiple of the unit, such as a block of 1,000 shares on the NYSE, a case of eggs at the processing plant, or a party of five at a restaurant.

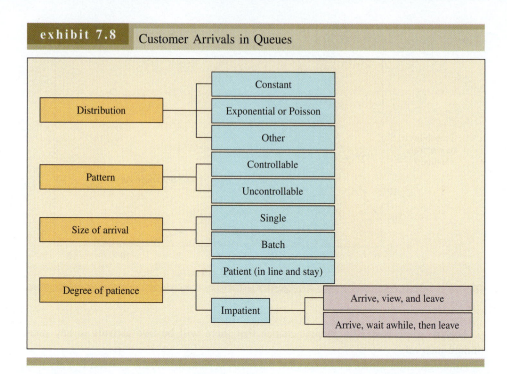

exhibit 7.8   Customer Arrivals in Queues

- **Degree of patience.**   A *patient* arrival is one who waits as long as necessary until the service facility is ready to serve him or her. (Even if arrivals grumble and behave impatiently, the fact that they wait is sufficient to label them as patient arrivals for purposes of waiting line theory.)

   There are two classes of *impatient* arrivals. Members of the first class arrive, survey both the service facility and the length of the line, and then decide to leave. Those in the second class arrive, view the situation, join the waiting line, and then, after some period of time, depart. The behavior of the first type is termed *balking*, while the second is termed *reneging*. To avoid balking and reneging, companies that provide high service levels typically try to target server utilization levels (the percentage of time busy) at no more than 70 to 80 percent.

Waiting Lines and Servers

The queuing system consists primarily of the waiting line(s) and the available number of servers. Here, we discuss issues pertaining to waiting line characteristics and management, line structure, and service rate. Factors to consider with waiting lines include the line length, number of lines, and queue discipline.

Length.   In a practical sense, an infinite line is simply one that is very long in terms of the capacity of the service system. Examples of *infinite potential length* are a line of vehicles backed up for miles at a bridge crossing and customers who must form a line around the block as they wait to purchase tickets at a theater.

   Gas stations, loading docks, and parking lots have *limited line capacity* caused by legal restrictions or physical space characteristics. This complicates the waiting line problem not only in service system utilization and waiting line computations but also in the shape of the actual arrival distribution. The arrival denied entry into the line because of lack of space may rejoin the population for a later try or may seek service elsewhere. Either action makes an obvious difference in the finite population case.

Number of lines.   A single line or single file is, of course, one line only. The term *multiple lines* refers to the single lines that form in front of two or more servers or to single lines that converge at some central redistribution point. The disadvantage of multiple lines in a busy facility is that arrivals often shift lines if several previous services have been of short duration or if those customers currently in other lines appear to require a short service time.

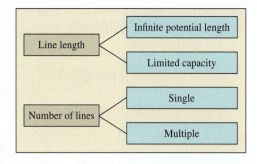

Queue discipline.   A queue discipline is a priority rule or set of rules for determining the order of service to customers in a waiting line. The rules selected can have a dramatic effect on the system's overall performance. The number of customers in line, the average waiting time, the range of variability in waiting time, and the efficiency of the service facility are just a few of the factors affected by the choice of priority rules.

Probably the most common priority rule is first come, first served (FCFS). This rule states that customers in line are served on the basis of their chronological arrival; no other characteristics have any bearing on the selection process. This is popularly accepted as the fairest rule, although in practice it discriminates against the arrival requiring a short service time.

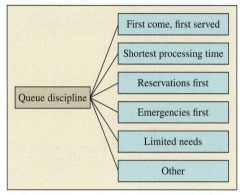

Reservations first, emergencies first, highest-profit customer first, largest orders first, best customers first, longest waiting time in line, and soonest promised date are other examples of priority rules. There are two major practical problems in using any rule: One is ensuring that customers know and follow the rule. The other is ensuring that a system exists to enable employees to manage the line (such as take-a-number systems).

Service Time Distribution Another important feature of the waiting structure is the time the customer or unit spends with the server once the service has started. Waiting line formulas generally specify **service rate** as the capacity of the server in number of units per time period (such as 12 completions per hour) and *not* as service time, which might average five minutes each. A constant service time rule states that each service takes exactly the same time. As in constant arrivals, this characteristic is generally limited to machine-controlled operations.

Service rate
The number of customers a server can handle during a given time period.

When service times are random, they can be approximated by the exponential distribution. When using the exponential distribution as an approximation of the service times, we will refer to μ as the average number of units or customers that can be served per time period.

Line Structures As Exhibit 7.9 shows, the flow of items to be serviced may go through a single line, multiple lines, or some mixture of the two. The choice of format depends partly on the volume of customers served and partly on the restrictions imposed by sequential requirements governing the order in which service must be performed.

1. **Single channel, single phase.**   This is the simplest type of waiting line structure, and straightforward formulas are available to solve the problem for standard distribution patterns of arrival and service. When the distributions are nonstandard, the problem is easily solved by computer simulation. A typical example of a single-channel, single-phase situation is the one-person barbershop.

exhibit 7.9   Line Structures

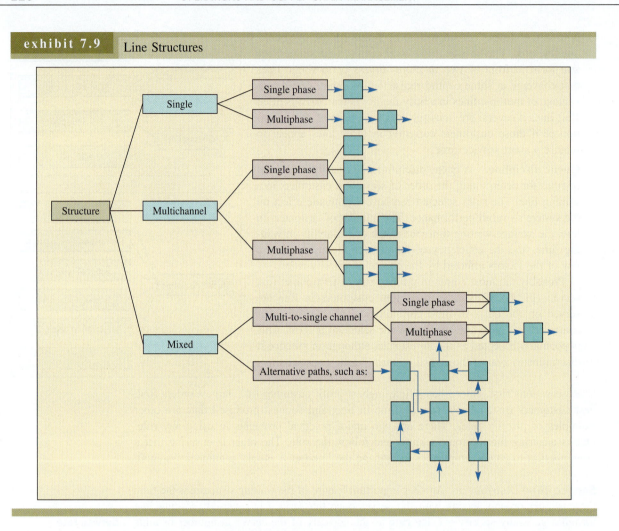

2. **Single channel, multiphase.** A car wash is an illustration because a series of services (vacuuming, wetting, washing, rinsing, drying, window cleaning, and parking) is performed in a fairly uniform sequence. A critical factor in the single-channel case with service in series is the amount of buildup of items allowed in front of each service, which in turn constitutes separate waiting lines.

3. **Multichannel, single phase.** Tellers' windows in a bank and checkout counters in high-volume department stores exemplify this type of structure. The difficulty with this format is that the uneven service time given each customer results in unequal speed or flow among the lines. This results in some customers being served before others who arrived earlier, as well as in some degree of line shifting. Varying this structure to ensure the servicing of arrivals in chronological order would require forming a single line, from which, as a server becomes available, the next customer in the queue is assigned.

   The major problem of this structure is that it requires rigid control of the line to maintain order and to direct customers to available servers. In some instances, assigning numbers to customers in order of their arrival helps alleviate this problem.

4. **Multichannel, multiphase.** This case is similar to the preceding one except that two or more services are performed in sequence. The admission of patients in a hospital follows this pattern because a specific sequence of steps is usually followed:

initial contact at the admissions desk, filling out forms, making identification tags, obtaining a room assignment, escorting the patient to the room, and so forth. Because several servers are usually available for this procedure, more than one patient at a time may be processed.

5. **Mixed.**   Under this general heading, we consider two subcategories: (1) multiple-to-single channel structures and (2) alternative path structures. Under (1), we find either lines that merge into one for single-phase service, as at a bridge crossing where two lanes merge into one, or lines that merge into one for multiphase service, such as subassembly lines feeding into a main line. Under (2), we encounter two structures that differ in directional flow requirements. The first is similar to the multichannel–multiphase case, except that (a) there may be switching from one channel to the next after the first service has been rendered and (b) the number of channels and phases may vary—again—after performance of the first service.

Exiting the Queuing System   Once a customer is served, two exit fates are possible: (1) The customer may return to the source population and immediately become a competing candidate for service again or (2) there may be a low probability of reservice. The first case can be illustrated by a customer machine that has been routinely repaired and returned to duty but may break down again; the second can be illustrated by a customer machine that has been overhauled or modified and has a low probability of reservice over the near future. In a lighter vein, we might refer to the first as the "recurring-common-cold case" and to the second as the "appendectomy-only-once case."

It should be apparent that when the population source is finite, any change in the service performed on customers who return to the population modifies the arrival rate at the service facility. This, of course, alters the characteristics of the waiting line under study and necessitates reanalysis of the problem.

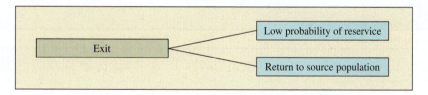

Waiting Line Models

In this section, we present three sample waiting line problems followed by their solutions. Each has a slightly different structure (see Exhibit 7.10) and solution equation (see Exhibit 7.11). There are more types of models than these three, but the formulas and solutions become quite complicated, and those problems are generally solved using computer simulation. Also, in using these formulas, keep in mind that they are steady-state formulas derived on the assumption that the process under study is ongoing. Thus, they may provide inaccurate results when applied to processes where the arrival rates and/or service rates change over time. The Excel spreadsheet QueueModels.xls included on the book Website can be used to solve these problems.

Excel:
Queue_
Models

Here is a quick preview of our three problems to illustrate each of the three waiting line models in Exhibits 7.10 and 7.11.

Problem 1: Customers in line.   A bank wants to know how many customers are waiting for a drive-in teller, how long they have to wait, the utilization of the teller, and what the service rate would have to be so that 95 percent of the time there will not be more than three cars in the system at any time.

exhibit 7.10 Properties of Some Specific Waiting Line Models

Model	Layout	Service Phase	Source Population	Arrival Pattern	Queue Discipline	Service Pattern	Permissible Queue Length	Typical Example
1. Simple System	Single channel	Single	Infinite	Poisson	FCFS	Exponential	Unlimited	Drive-in teller at bank; one-lane toll bridge
2. Constant Service Time System	Single channel	Single	Infinite	Poisson	FCFS	Constant	Unlimited	Roller coaster rides in amusement park
3. Multichannel System	Multichannel	Single	Infinite	Poisson	FCFS	Exponential	Unlimited	Parts counter in auto agency

exhibit 7.11 Notations for Equations

INFINITE QUEUING NOTATION: MODELS 1–3

λ = Arrival rate

μ = Service rate

$\frac{1}{\mu}$ = Average service time

$\frac{1}{\lambda}$ = Average time between arrivals

ρ = Ratio of total arrival rate to service rate for a single server $\left(\frac{\lambda}{\mu}\right)$

L_q = Average number waiting in line

L_s = Average number in system (including any being served)

W_q = Average time waiting in line

W_s = Average total time in system (including time to be served)

n = Number of units in the system

S = Number of identical service channels

P_n = Probability of exactly n units in system

P_w = Probability of waiting in line

EQUATIONS FOR SOLVING THREE MODEL PROBLEMS

Model 1

$$L_q = \frac{\lambda^2}{\mu(\mu - \lambda)} \qquad W_q = \frac{L_q}{\lambda} \qquad P_n = \left(1 - \frac{\lambda}{\mu}\right)\left(\frac{\lambda}{\mu}\right)^n \qquad P_0 = \left(1 - \frac{\lambda}{\mu}\right)$$

$$L_s = \frac{\lambda}{\mu - \lambda} \qquad W_s = \frac{L_s}{\lambda} \qquad \rho = \frac{\lambda}{\mu}$$ [7.3]

Model 2

$$L_q = \frac{\lambda^2}{2\mu(\mu - \lambda)} \qquad W_q = \frac{L_q}{\lambda}$$

$$L_s = L_q + \frac{\lambda}{\mu} \qquad W_s = \frac{L_s}{\lambda}$$ [7.4]

Model 3

$$L_s = L_q + \frac{\lambda}{\mu} \qquad W_s = \frac{L_s}{\lambda}$$

$$W_q = \frac{L_q}{\lambda} \qquad P_w = L_q\left(\frac{S\mu}{\lambda} - 1\right)$$ [7.5]

Problem 2: Equipment selection. A franchise for Robot Car Wash must decide which equipment to purchase out of a choice of three. Larger units cost more but wash cars faster. To make the decision, costs are related to revenue.

Problem 3: Determining the number of servers.   An auto agency parts department must decide how many clerks to employ at the counter. More clerks cost more money, but there is a savings because mechanics wait less time.

Example 7.1: Customers in Line

Western National Bank is considering opening a drive-through window for customer service. Management estimates that customers will arrive at the rate of 15 per hour. The teller who will staff the window can service customers at the rate of 1 every three minutes or 20 per hour.

Part 1   Assuming Poisson arrivals and exponential service, find

1. Utilization of the teller.
2. Average number in the waiting line.
3. Average number in the system.
4. Average waiting time in line.
5. Average waiting time in the system, including service.

SOLUTION—PART 1

Excel:
Queue

1. The average utilization of the teller is (using Model 1—Simple System)

$$\rho = \frac{\lambda}{\mu} = \frac{15}{20} = 75 \text{ percent}$$

2. The average number in the waiting line is

$$L_q = \frac{\lambda^2}{\mu(\mu - \lambda)} = \frac{(15)^2}{20(20 - 15)} = 2.25 \text{ customers}$$

3. The average number in the system is

$$L_s = \frac{\lambda}{\mu - \lambda} = \frac{15}{20 - 15} = 3 \text{ customers}$$

4. Average waiting time in line is

$$W_q = \frac{L_q}{\lambda} = \frac{2.25}{15} = 0.15 \text{ hour, or 9 minutes}$$

5. Average waiting time in the system is

$$W_s = \frac{L_s}{\lambda} = \frac{3}{15} = 0.2 \text{ hour, or 12 minutes}$$

Part 2   Because of limited space availability and a desire to provide an acceptable level of service, the bank manager would like to ensure, with 95 percent confidence, that no more than three cars will be in the system at any time. What is the present level of service for the three-car limit? What level of teller use must be attained and what must be the service rate of the teller to ensure the 95 percent level of service?

SOLUTION—PART 2

The present level of service for three or fewer cars is the probability that there are 0, 1, 2, or 3 cars in the system. From Model 1, Exhibit 7.11,

$$P_n = \left(1 - \frac{\lambda}{\mu}\right)\left(\frac{\lambda}{\mu}\right)^n$$

at $n = 0$, $P_0 = (1 - 15/20)$ $(15/20)^0 = 0.250$
at $n = 1$, $P_1 = (1/4)$ $(15/20)^1 = 0.188$
at $n = 2$, $P_2 = (1/4)$ $(15/20)^2 = 0.141$
at $n = 3$, $P_3 = (1/4)$ $(15/20)^3 = \underline{0.105}$
                            0.684   or   68.4 percent

The probability of having more than three cars in the system is 1.0 minus the probability of three or fewer cars $(100 - 68.4 = 31.6$ percent).

For a 95 percent service level of three or fewer cars, this states that $P_0 + P_1 + P_2 + P_3 = 95$ percent.

$$0.95 = \left(1 - \frac{\lambda}{\mu}\right)\left(\frac{\lambda}{\mu}\right)^0 + \left(1 - \frac{\lambda}{\mu}\right)\left(\frac{\lambda}{\mu}\right)^1 + \left(1 - \frac{\lambda}{\mu}\right)\left(\frac{\lambda}{\mu}\right)^2 + \left(1 - \frac{\lambda}{\mu}\right)\left(\frac{\lambda}{\mu}\right)^3$$

$$0.95 = \left(1 - \frac{\lambda}{\mu}\right)\left[1 + \frac{\lambda}{\mu} + \left(\frac{\lambda}{\mu}\right)^2 + \left(\frac{\lambda}{\mu}\right)^3\right]$$

We can solve this by trial and error for values of λ/μ. If $\lambda/\mu = 0.50$,

$$0.95 \stackrel{?}{=} 0.5(1 + 0.5 + 0.25 + 0.125)$$
$$0.95 \neq 0.9375$$

With $\lambda/\mu = 0.45$,

$$0.95 \stackrel{?}{=} (1 - 0.45)(1 + 0.45 + 0.203 + 0.091)$$
$$0.95 \neq 0.96$$

With $\lambda/\mu = 0.47$,

$$0.95 \stackrel{?}{=} (1 - 0.47)(1 + 0.47 + 0.221 + 0.104) = 0.9512$$
$$0.95 \approx 0.95135$$

Therefore, with the utilization $\rho = \lambda/\mu$ of 47 percent, the probability of three or fewer cars in the system is 95 percent.

To find the rate of service required to attain this 95 percent service level, we simply solve the equation $\lambda/\mu = 0.47$, where $\lambda =$ number of arrivals per hour. This gives $\mu = 32$ per hour. That is, the teller must serve approximately 32 people per hour (a 60 percent increase over the original 20-per-hour capability) for 95 percent confidence that not more than three cars will be in the system. Perhaps service may be speeded up by modifying the method of service, adding another teller, or limiting the types of transactions available at the drive-through window. Note that with the condition of 95 percent confidence that three or fewer cars will be in the system, the teller will be idle 53 percent of the time. •

Example 7.2: Equipment Selection

The Robot Company franchises combination gas and car wash stations throughout the United States. Robot gives a free car wash for a gasoline fill-up or, for a wash alone, charges $5. Past experience shows that the number of customers that have car washes following fill-ups is about the same as for a wash alone. The average profit on a gasoline fill-up is about $7.00, and the cost of the car wash to Robot is $1. Robot stays open 14 hours per day.

Robot has three power units and drive assemblies, and a franchisee must select the unit preferred. Unit 1 can wash cars at the rate of one every five minutes and is leased for $120 per day. Unit 2, a larger unit, can wash cars at the rate of one every four minutes but costs $160 per day. Unit 3, the largest, costs $220 per day and can wash a car in three minutes.

The franchisee estimates that customers will not wait in line more than five minutes for a car wash. A longer time will cause Robot to lose the gasoline sales as well as the car wash sale.

If the estimate of customer arrivals resulting in washes is 10 per hour, which wash unit should be selected?

Excel:
Queue

SOLUTION

Using Unit I, calculate the average waiting time of customers in the wash line (μ for Unit 1 = 12 per hour). From the Model 2—Constant Service Time System equations (Exhibit 7.11),

$$L_q = \frac{\lambda^2}{2\mu(\mu - \lambda)} = \frac{10^2}{2(12)(12 - 10)} = 2.08333$$

$$W_q = \frac{L_q}{\lambda} = \frac{2.08333}{10} = 0.208 \text{ hour, or } 12\tfrac{1}{2} \text{ minutes}$$

For Unit 2 at 15 per hour,

$$L_q = \frac{10^2}{2(15)(15 - 10)} = 0.667$$

$$W_q = \frac{0.667}{10} = 0.0667 \text{ hour, or 4 minutes}$$

If waiting time is the only criterion, Unit 2 should be purchased. But before we make the final decision, we must look at the profit differential between both units.

With Unit 1, some customers would balk and renege because of the $12\tfrac{1}{2}$-minute wait. And, although this greatly complicates the mathematical analysis, we can gain some estimate of lost sales with Unit 1 by increasing $W_q = 5$ minutes or $\tfrac{1}{12}$ hour (the average length of time customers will wait) and solving for λ. This would be the effective arrival rate of customers:

$$W_q = \frac{L_q}{\lambda} = \left(\frac{\lambda^2/2\mu(\mu - \lambda)}{\lambda} \right)$$

$$W_q = \frac{\lambda}{2\mu(\mu - \lambda)}$$

$$\lambda = \frac{2W_q\mu^2}{1 + 2W_q\mu} = \frac{2(\tfrac{1}{12})(12)^2}{1 + 2(\tfrac{1}{12})(12)} = 8 \text{ per hour}$$

Therefore, because the original estimate of λ was 10 per hour, an estimated 2 customers per hour will be lost. Lost profit of 2 customers per hour × 14 hours × $\tfrac{1}{2}$($7 fill-up profit + $4 wash profit) = $154 per day.

Because the additional cost of Unit 2 over Unit 1 is only $40 per day, the loss of $154 profit obviously warrants installing Unit 2.

The original five-minute maximum wait constraint is satisfied by Unit 2. Therefore, Unit 3 is not considered unless the arrival rate is expected to increase. •

Example 7.3: Determining the Number of Servers

In the service department of the Glenn-Mark Auto Agency, mechanics requiring parts for auto repair or service present their request forms at the parts department counter. The parts clerk fills a request while the mechanic waits. Mechanics arrive in a random (Poisson) fashion at the rate of 40 per hour, and a clerk can fill requests at the rate of 20 per hour (exponential). If the cost for a parts clerk is $30.00 per hour and the cost for a mechanic is $60.00 per hour, determine the optimum number of clerks to staff the counter. (Because of the high arrival rate, an infinite source may be assumed.)

SOLUTION

Excel:
Queue

First, assume that three clerks will be used because having only one or two clerks would create infinitely long lines (since $\lambda = 40$ and $\mu = 20$). The equations for Model 3—Multichannel System from Exhibit 7.11 will be used here. But first we need to obtain the average number in line using the table of Exhibit 7.12. Using the table and values $\lambda/\mu = 2$ and $S = 3$, we obtain $L_q = 0.8888$ mechanic.

At this point, we see that we have an average of 0.8888 mechanic waiting all day. For an eight-hour day at $60.00 per hour, there is a loss of a mechanic's time worth 0.8888 mechanic × $60.00 per hour × 8 hours = $426.62.

Our next step is to reobtain the waiting time if we add another parts clerk. We then compare the added cost of the additional employee with the time saved by the mechanics. Again, using the table of Exhibit 7.12 but with $S = 4$, we obtain

$L_q = 0.1730$ mechanic in line

$0.1730 \times \$60.00 \times 8$ hours $= \$83.04$ cost of a mechanic waiting in line

Value of mechanics' time saved is $426.62 − $83.04	= $343.62
Cost of an additional parts clerk is 8 hours × $30.00	= $240.00
Cost of reduction by adding fourth clerk	= $103.62

This problem could be expanded to consider the addition of runners to deliver parts to mechanics; the problem then would be to determine the optimal number of runners. This, however, would have to include the added cost of lost time caused by errors in parts receipts. For example, a mechanic would recognize a wrong part at the counter and obtain an immediate correction, whereas the parts runner might not. •

Computer Simulation of Waiting Lines

Some waiting line problems that seem simple on first impression turn out to be extremely difficult or impossible to solve. Throughout this chapter, we have been treating waiting line situations that are independent; that is, either the entire system consists of a single phase, or else each service that is performed in a series is independent. (This could happen if the output of one service location is allowed to build up in front of the next one so that this, in essence, becomes a calling population for the next service.) When a series of services is performed in sequence where the output rate of one becomes the input rate of the next, we can no longer use the simple formulas. This is also true for any problem where conditions do not meet the requirements of the equations, as specified in Exhibit 7.10. The technique best suited to solving this type of problem is computer simulation.

Some common examples where similation is used are the following:

- Simulation of trucking or airline systems. Here, planned schedules can be simulated to better understand the impact of traffic and different types of randomly occurring interruptions.
- Simulation of factory production systems. Here, the impact of such things as machine setups, breakdowns, or working productivity variations can be analyzed.

Expected Number of People Waiting in Line (L_q) for Various Values of S and λ/M

exhibit 7.12

Excel

λ/μ	M	L_q	P_0	λ/μ	M	L_q	P_0	λ/μ	M	L_q	P_0
0.15	1	0.026	0.850		3	0.024	0.425		4	0.080	0.180
	2	0.001	0.860		4	0.003	0.427		5	0.017	0.182
0.20	1	0.050	0.800	0.90	1	8.100	0.100	1.80	2	7.674	0.053
	2	0.002	0.818		2	0.229	0.379		3	0.532	0.146
0.25	1	0.083	0.750		3	0.030	0.403		4	0.105	0.162
	2	0.004	0.778		4	0.004	0.406		5	0.023	0.165
0.30	1	0.129	0.700	0.95	1	18.050	0.050	1.90	2	17.587	0.026
	2	0.007	0.739		2	0.277	0.356		3	0.688	0.128
0.35	1	0.188	0.650		3	0.037	0.383		4	0.136	0.145
	2	0.011	0.702		4	0.005	0.386		5	0.030	0.149
0.40	1	0.267	0.600	1.00	2	0.333	0.333		6	0.007	0.149
	2	0.017	0.667		3	0.045	0.364	2.00	3	0.889	0.111
0.45	1	0.368	0.550		4	0.007	0.367		4	0.174	0.130
	2	0.024	0.633	1.10	2	0.477	0.290		5	0.040	0.134
	3	0.002	0.637		3	0.066	0.327		6	0.009	0.135
0.50	1	0.500	0.500		4	0.011	0.332	2.10	3	1.149	0.096
	2	0.033	0.600	1.20	2	0.675	0.250		4	0.220	0.117
	3	0.003	0.606		3	0.094	0.294		5	0.052	0.121
0.55	1	0.672	0.450		4	0.016	0.300		6	0.012	0.122
	2	0.045	0.569		5	0.003	0.301	2.20	3	1.491	0.081
	3	0.004	0.576	1.30	2	0.951	0.212		4	0.277	0.105
0.60	1	0.900	0.400		3	0.130	0.264		5	0.066	0.109
	2	0.059	0.538		4	0.023	0.271		6	0.016	0.111
	3	0.006	0.548		5	0.004	0.272	2.30	3	1.951	0.068
0.65	1	1.207	0.350	1.40	2	1.345	0.176		4	0.346	0.093
	2	0.077	0.509		3	0.177	0.236		5	0.084	0.099
	3	0.008	0.521		4	0.032	0.245		6	0.021	0.100
0.70	1	1.633	0.300		5	0.006	0.246	2.40	3	2.589	0.056
	2	0.098	0.481	1.50	2	1.929	0.143		4	0.431	0.083
	3	0.011	0.495		3	0.237	0.211		5	0.105	0.089
0.75	1	2.250	0.250		4	0.045	0.221		6	0.027	0.090
	2	0.123	0.455		5	0.009	0.223		7	0.007	0.091
	3	0.015	0.471	1.60	2	2.844	0.111	2.50	3	3.511	0.045
0.80	1	3.200	0.200		3	0.313	0.187		4	0.533	0.074
	2	0.152	0.429		4	0.060	0.199		5	0.130	0.080
	3	0.019	0.447		5	0.012	0.201		6	0.034	0.082
0.85	1	4.817	0.150	1.70	2	4.426	0.081		7	0.009	0.082
	2	0.187	0.404		3	0.409	0.166	2.60	3	4.933	0.035

(Continued)

exhibit 7.12 Expected Number of People Waiting in Line (L_q) for Various Values of S and λ/M (*Contd.*)

λ/μ	M	L_q	P_0	λ/μ	M	L_q	P_0	λ/μ	M	L_q	P_0
	4	0.658	0.065	3.40	4	3.906	0.019		9	0.019	0.018
	5	0.161	0.072		5	0.737	0.029	4.10	5	2.703	0.011
	6	0.043	0.074		6	0.209	0.032		6	0.668	0.015
	7	0.011	0.074		7	0.063	0.033		7	0.212	0.016
2.70	3	7.354	0.025		8	0.019	0.033		8	0.070	0.016
	4	0.811	0.057	3.50	4	5.165	0.015		9	0.023	0.017
	5	0.198	0.065		5	0.882	0.026	4.20	5	3.327	0.009
	6	0.053	0.067		6	0.248	0.029		6	0.784	0.013
	7	0.014	0.067		7	0.076	0.030		7	0.248	0.014
2.80	3	12.273	0.016		8	0.023	0.030		8	0.083	0.015
	4	1.000	0.050		9	0.007	0.030		9	0.027	0.015
	5	0.241	0.058	3.60	4	7.090	0.011		10	0.009	0.015
	6	0.066	0.060		5	1.055	0.023	4.30	5	4.149	0.008
	7	0.018	0.061		6	0.295	0.026		6	0.919	0.012
2.90	3	27.193	0.008		7	0.019	0.027		7	0.289	0.130
	4	1.234	0.044		8	0.028	0.027		8	0.097	0.013
	5	0.293	0.052		9	0.008	0.027		9	0.033	0.014
	6	0.081	0.054	3.70	4	10.347	0.008		10	0.011	0.014
	7	0.023	0.055		5	1.265	0.020	4.40	5	5.268	0.006
3.00	4	1.528	0.038		6	0.349	0.023		6	1.078	0.010
	5	0.354	0.047		7	0.109	0.024		7	0.337	0.012
	6	0.099	0.049		8	0.034	0.025		8	0.114	0.012
	7	0.028	0.050		9	0.010	0.025		9	0.039	0.012
	8	0.008	0.050	3.80	4	16.937	0.005		10	0.013	0.012
3.10	4	1.902	0.032		5	1.519	0.017	4.50	5	6.862	0.005
	5	0.427	0.042		6	0.412	0.021		6	1.265	0.009
	6	0.120	0.044		7	0.129	0.022		7	0.391	0.010
	7	0.035	0.045		8	0.041	0.022		8	0.134	0.011
	8	0.010	0.045		9	0.013	0.022		9	0.046	0.011
3.20	4	2.386	0.027	3.90	4	36.859	0.002		10	0.015	0.011
	5	0.513	0.037		5	1.830	0.015	4.60	5	9.289	0.004
	6	0.145	0.040		6	0.485	0.019		6	1.487	0.008
	7	0.043	0.040		7	0.153	0.020		7	0.453	0.009
	8	0.012	0.041		8	0.050	0.020		8	0.156	0.010
3.30	4	3.027	0.023		9	0.016	0.020		9	0.054	0.010
	5	0.615	0.033	4.00	5	2.216	0.013		10	0.018	0.010
	6	0.174	0.036		6	0.570	0.017	4.70	5	13.382	0.003
	7	0.052	0.037		7	0.180	0.018		6	1.752	0.007
	8	0.015	0.037		8	0.059	0.018		7	0.525	0.008

Expected Number of People Waiting in Line (L_q) for Various Values of S and λ/M (*Contd.*)   **exhibit 7.12**

λ/μ	M	L_q	P_0	λ/μ	M	L_q	P_0	λ/μ	M	L_q	P_0
	8	0.181	0.009	5.20	6	4.301	0.003		7	1.944	0.003
	9	0.064	0.009		7	1.081	0.005		8	0.631	0.003
	10	0.022	0.009		8	0.368	0.005		9	0.233	0.004
4.80	5	21.641	0.002		9	0.135	0.005		10	0.088	0.004
	6	2.071	0.006		10	0.049	0.005		11	0.033	0.004
	7	0.607	0.008		11	0.018	0.006		12	0.012	0.004
	8	0.209	0.008	5.30	6	5.303	0.003	5.70	6	16.446	0.001
	9	0.074	0.008		7	1.249	0.004		7	2.264	0.002
	10	0.026	0.008		8	0.422	0.005		8	0.721	0.003
4.90	5	46.566	0.001		9	0.155	0.005		9	0.266	0.003
	6	2.459	0.005		10	0.057	0.005		10	0.102	0.003
	7	0.702	0.007		11	0.021	0.005		11	0.038	0.003
	8	0.242	0.007		12	0.007	0.005		12	0.014	0.003
	9	0.087	0.007	5.40	6	6.661	0.002	5.80	6	26.373	0.001
	10	0.031	0.007		7	1.444	0.004		7	2.648	0.002
	11	0.011	0.007		8	0.483	0.004		8	0.823	0.003
5.00	6	2.938	0.005		9	0.178	0.004		9	0.303	0.003
	7	0.810	0.006		10	0.066	0.004		10	0.116	0.003
	8	0.279	0.006		11	0.024	0.005		11	0.044	0.003
	9	0.101	0.007		12	0.009	0.005		12	0.017	0.003
	10	0.036	0.007	5.50	6	8.590	0.002	5.90	6	56.300	0.000
	11	0.013	0.007		7	1.674	0.003		7	3.113	0.002
5.10	6	3.536	0.004		8	0.553	0.004		8	0.939	0.002
	7	0.936	0.005		9	0.204	0.004		9	0.345	0.003
	8	0.321	0.006		10	0.077	0.004		10	0.133	0.003
	9	0.117	0.006		11	0.028	0.004		11	0.051	0.003
	10	0.042	0.006		12	0.010	0.004		12	0.019	0.003
	11	0.015	0.006	5.60	6	11.519	0.001				

CONCEPT CONNECTIONS

LO7–1 **Understand the characteristics of service processes.**

- A service is the output of a process that is intangible.
- Services cannot be patented.
- Services can be conveniently classified according to the degree of "contact" or physical presence of the customer in the system.
- In some processes, the customer need not be present at all. For example, when a customer order is processed from an online transaction.

- In other processes, the customer is directly involved. For example, when a tooth is removed at a dentist's office.
- Service systems differ from manufacturing systems in that typically services cannot be placed in inventory for later use. The process is the product.
- The service–system design matrix explores the trade-offs between sales opportunity, efficiency, and characteristics of the workers in service processes.
- Virtual services, offered through the Internet, often enable customers to interact directly with one another in an open or moderated environment.

Service package   A bundle of goods and services that is provided in some environment.

High and low degree of customer contact   The physical presence of the customer in the system and the percentage of time the customer must be in the system relative to the total time it takes to perform the service.

LO7–2   **Analyze simple service systems.**

- Service blueprints are a special type of flowchart that places special emphasis on identifying the high customer contact and low customer contact aspects of a service.
- The distinction is made using a "line of visibility" on the flowchart.

Service blueprint   A flowchart of a process emphasizing what is visible and what is not visible to the customer.

Poka-yokes   Procedures that prevent mistakes in the execution of processes, thus reducing defects.

- Queuing theory is the mathematical analysis of the waiting line.
- A waiting line (or queuing) system consists of three major parts: (1) the customers arriving to the system, (2) the servicing of the customers, and (3) how customers exit the system.
- Queuing theory assumes that customers arrive according to a Poisson arrival distribution and are served according to an exponential service time distribution. These are specific probability distributions that often match well with actual situations.
- There are many different waiting line models; three are studied in this chapter.
  - Model 1 is useful for simple situations where there is a single line of customers who arrive according to a Poisson distribution, and who are processed by a single server that serves each customer in the order they came according to an exponential distribution (for example, an automated teller machine).
  - Model 2 is similar to Model 1 with the difference being that it takes exactly the same time to serve each customer, there is no service variability (for example, a robot making the same part over and over again).
  - Model 3 is like Model 1, but two or more servers are available (for example, a bank lobby with multiple tellers).

Queuing system   A process where customers wait in line for service.

Arrival rate   The expected number of customers that arrive during each period.

Exponential distribution   A probability distribution associated with the time between arrivals.

Poisson distribution   Probability distribution for the number of arrivals during each time period.

Service rate   The number of customers a server can handle during a given time period.

Exponential distribution

$$f(t) = \lambda e^{-\lambda t} \qquad [7.1]$$

Poisson distribution

$$P_T(n) = \frac{(\lambda T)^n e^{-\lambda T}}{n!} \qquad [7.2]$$

Model 1 (See Exhibit 7.11.)

$$L_q = \frac{\lambda^2}{\mu(\mu - \lambda)} \qquad W_q = \frac{L_q}{\lambda} \qquad P_n = \left(1 - \frac{\lambda}{\mu}\right)\left(\frac{\lambda}{\mu}\right)^n \qquad P_0 = \left(1 - \frac{\lambda}{\mu}\right)$$

$$L_s = \frac{\lambda}{\mu - \lambda} \qquad W_s = \frac{L_s}{\lambda} \qquad \rho = \frac{\lambda}{\mu} \qquad\qquad [7.3]$$

Model 2

$$L_q = \frac{\lambda^2}{2\mu(\mu - \lambda)} \qquad W_q = \frac{L_q}{\lambda}$$

$$L_s = L_q + \frac{\lambda}{\mu} \qquad W_s = \frac{L_s}{\lambda} \qquad\qquad [7.4]$$

Model 3

$$L_s = L_q + \frac{\lambda}{\mu} \qquad W_s = \frac{L_s}{\lambda}$$

$$W_q = \frac{L_q}{\lambda} \qquad P_w = L_q\left(\frac{S\mu}{\lambda} - 1\right) \qquad\qquad [7.5]$$

SOLVED PROBLEMS

SOLVED PROBLEM 1

Quick Lube Inc. operates a fast lube and oil change garage. On a typical day, customers arrive at the rate of three per hour, and lube jobs are performed at an average rate of one every 15 minutes. The mechanics operate as a team on one car at a time.

Assuming Poisson arrivals and exponential service, find:

Excel:
Queue

   a. The utilization of the lube team.
   b. The average number of cars in line.
   c. The average time a car waits before it is lubed.
   d. The total time it takes to go through the system (that is, waiting in line plus lube time).

Solution

$\lambda = 3, \mu = 4$

   a. Utilization $\rho = \dfrac{\lambda}{\mu} = \dfrac{3}{4} = 75$ percent.

   b. $L_q = \dfrac{\lambda^2}{\mu(\mu - \lambda)} = \dfrac{3^2}{4(4 - 3)} = \dfrac{9}{4} = 2.25$ cars in line.

   c. $W_q = \dfrac{L_q}{\lambda} = \dfrac{2.25}{3} = .75$ hour, or 45 minutes.

   d. $W_s = \dfrac{L_s}{\lambda} = \dfrac{\lambda}{\mu - \lambda}/\lambda = \dfrac{3}{4 - 3}/3 = 1$ hour (waiting + lube).

Excel:

Queue

SOLVED PROBLEM 2

American Vending Inc. (AVI) supplies vended food to a large university. Because students often kick the machines out of anger and frustration, management has a constant repair problem. The machines break down on an average of three per hour, and the breakdowns are distributed in a Poisson manner. Downtime costs the company $250/hour per machine, and each maintenance worker gets $40 per hour. One worker can service machines at an average rate of five per hour, distributed exponentially; two workers working together can service seven per hour, distributed exponentially; and a team of three workers can repair eight per hour, distributed exponentially.

What is the optimal maintenance crew size for servicing the machines?

Solution

Case I—One worker:

λ = 3/hour Poisson, μ = 5/hour exponential

There is an average number of broken machines in the system of

$$L_s = \frac{\lambda}{\mu - \lambda} = \frac{3}{5 - 3} = \frac{3}{2} = 1.5 \text{ machines}$$

Downtime cost is $250.00 × 1.5 = $375.00 per hour; repair cost is $40.00 per hour; and total cost per hour for 1 worker is $375.00 + $40.00 = $415.00.

$$
\begin{array}{ll}
\text{Downtime } (1.5 \times \$250.00) = & \$375.00 \\
\text{Labor } (1 \text{ worker} \times \$40.00) = & \underline{\$40.00} \\
& \underline{\$415.00}
\end{array}
$$

Case II—Two workers:

λ = 3, μ = 7

$$L_s = \frac{\lambda}{\mu - \lambda} = \frac{3}{7 - 3} = .75 \text{ machine}$$

$$
\begin{array}{ll}
\text{Downtime } (.75 \times \$250.00) = & \$187.50 \\
\text{Labor } (2 \text{ workers} \times \$40.00) = & \underline{\$80.00} \\
& \underline{\$267.50}
\end{array}
$$

Case III—Three workers:

λ = 3, μ = 8

$$L_s = \frac{\lambda}{\mu - \lambda} = \frac{3}{8 - 3} = \frac{3}{5} = .60 \text{ machine}$$

$$
\begin{array}{ll}
\text{Downtime } (.60 \times \$250.00) = & \$150.00 \\
\text{Labor } (3 \text{ workers} \times \$40.00) = & \underline{\$120.00} \\
& \underline{\$270.00}
\end{array}
$$

Comparing the costs for one, two, or three workers, we see that Case II with two workers is the optimal decision.

DISCUSSION QUESTIONS

`LO7–1`

1. What is the service package of your college or university?
2. Some suggest that customer expectation is the key to service success. Give an example from your own experience to support or refute this assertion.
3. Where would you place a drive-in church, a campus food vending machine, and a bar's automatic mixed drink machine on the service–system design matrix?

LO7–2   4. Why should a manager of a bank home office be evaluated differently from a manager of a bank branch?

5. Identify the high-contact and low-contact operations of the following services:
   a. A dental office
   b. An airline
   c. An accounting office
   d. An automobile agency
   e. Amazon.com

LO7–3   6. Distinguish between a *channel* and a *phase*.

7. In what way might the first-come, first-served rule be unfair to the customer waiting for service in a bank or hospital?

8. Define, in a practical sense, what is meant by an *exponential service time*.

9. For which of the following would you expect the exponential distribution to be a good approximation of service times?
   a. Buying an airline ticket at the airport
   b. Riding a merry-go-round at a carnival
   c. Checking out of a hotel
   d. Completing a midterm exam in your OSCM class

10. A Poisson distribution might be a good approximation for which of the following?
   a. Runners crossing the finish line in the Boston Marathon
   b. Arrival times of the students in your OSCM class
   c. Arrival times of the school bus at your stop

11. What is the major cost trade-off that must be made in managing waiting line situations?

12. Which assumptions are necessary to employ the formulas given for Model 1?

OBJECTIVE QUESTIONS

LO7–1   1. What is the term used for the bundle of goods and services that are provided in some environment by every service operation?

2. Are service operations with a high degree of customer contact more or less difficult to control than those with a low degree of customer contact?

3. List at least three significant ways in which service systems differ from manufacturing systems.

4. A ride at an amusement park is an example of a service operation where there is direct contact between the customer and server, but little variation in the service process: Neither the customer nor server has much discretion in how the service will be provided. As shown in the service–system design matrix, which type of service is being delivered?

5. As the degree of customer contact increases in a service operation, what generally happens to the efficiency of the operation?

6. As the degree of customer contact increases in a service system, what worker skills would be more important, clerical skills or diagnostic skills?

7. An important difference between service and manufacturing operations is that customers introduce far more variability into the operations in a service system. Name at least three of the basic types of variation that customers bring to a service system.

LO7–2   8. Flowcharts are a common process design and analysis tool used in both manufacturing and services. What is a key feature on flowcharts used in service operations that differentiates between the front-office and back-office aspects of the system?

9. What are the Three Ts relevant to poka-yokes in service systems?

LO7–3

10. The *exponential distribution* is often used to model what in a queuing system?

11. If the average time between customer arrivals is eight minutes, what is the hourly arrival rate?

12. How much time, on average, would a server need to spend on a customer to achieve a service rate of 20 customers per hour?

13. What is the term used for the situation where a potential customer arrives at a service operation and decides to leave upon seeing a long line?

14. What is the most commonly used priority rule for setting queue discipline, likely because it is seen as the most fair?

15. Students arrive at the Administrative Services Office at an average of one every 15 minutes, and their requests take, on average, 10 minutes to be processed. The service counter is staffed by only one clerk, Judy Gumshoes, who works eight hours per day. Assume Poisson arrivals and exponential service times.
    a. What percentage of time is Judy idle?
    b. How much time, on average, does a student spend waiting in line?
    c. How long is the (waiting) line on average?
    d. What is the probability that an arriving student (just before entering the Administrative Services Office) will find at least one other student waiting in line?

16. Burrito King (a new fast-food franchise opening up nationwide) has successfully automated burrito production for its drive-up fast-food establishments. The Burro-Master 9000 requires a constant 45 seconds to produce a batch of burritos. It has been estimated that customers will arrive at the drive-up window according to a Poisson distribution at an average of one every 50 seconds. To help determine the amount of space needed for the line at the drive-up window, Burrito King would like to know the expected average time in the system, the average line length (in cars), and the average number of cars in the system (both in line and at the window).

17. The Bijou Theater shows vintage movies. Customers arrive at the theater line at the rate of 100 per hour. The ticket seller averages 30 seconds per customer, which includes placing validation stamps on customers' parking lot receipts and punching their frequent watcher cards. (Because of these added services, many customers don't get in until after the feature has started.)
    a. What is the average customer time in the system?
    b. What would be the effect on customer time in the system of having a second ticket taker doing nothing but validations and card punching, thereby cutting the average service time to 20 seconds?
    c. Would system waiting time be less than you found in (b) if a second window was opened with each server doing all three tasks?

18. To support National Heart Week, the Heart Association plans to install a free blood pressure testing booth in El Con Mall for the week. Previous experience indicates that, on average, 10 persons per hour request a test. Assume arrivals are Poisson distributed from an infinite population. Blood pressure measurements can be made at a constant time of five minutes each. Assume the queue length can be infinite with the FCFS discipline.
    a. What average number in line can be expected?
    b. What average number of persons can be expected to be in the system?
    c. What is the average amount of time that a person can expect to spend in line?
    d. On average, how much time will it take to measure a person's blood pressure, including their waiting time?
    e. On weekends, the arrival rate can be expected to increase to over 12 per hour. What effect will this have on the number in the waiting line?

19. A cafeteria serving line has a coffee urn from which customers serve themselves. Arrivals at the urn follow a Poisson distribution at the rate of three per minute. In serving themselves, customers take about 15 seconds, exponentially distributed.

a. How many customers would you expect to see, on average, at the coffee urn?

b. How long would you expect it to take to get a cup of coffee?

c. What percentage of time is the urn being used?

d. What is the probability that three or more people are in the cafeteria?

e. If the cafeteria installs an automatic vendor that dispenses a cup of coffee at a constant time of 15 seconds, how does this change your answers to (*a*) and (*b*)?

20. L. Winston Martin (an allergist) has an excellent system for handling his regular patients who come in just for allergy injections. Patients arrive for an injection and fill out a name slip, which is then placed in an open slot that passes into another room staffed by up to three nurses. The specific injections for a patient are prepared, and the patient is called through a speaker system into the room to receive the injection. At certain times during the day, patient load drops and only one nurse is needed to administer the injections.

    Let's focus on the simpler case of the two—namely, when there is one nurse. Also, assume that patients arrive in a Poisson fashion and the service rate of the nurse is exponentially distributed. During this slower period, patients arrive with an interarrival time of approximately three minutes. It takes the nurse an average of two minutes to prepare the patients' serum and administer the injection.

    a. What is the average number you would expect to see in Dr. Martin's facilities?

    b. How long would it take for a patient to arrive, get an injection, and leave?

    c. What is the probability that there will be three or more patients on the premises?

    d. What is the utilization of the nurse?

    e. Assume three nurses are available. Each takes an average of two minutes to prepare the patients' serum and administer the injection. What is the average total time of a patient in the system?

21. Benny the Barber owns a one-chair shop. At barber college, they told Benny that his customers would exhibit a Poisson arrival distribution and that he would provide an exponential service distribution. His market survey data indicate that customers arrive at a rate of two per hour. It will take Benny an average of 20 minutes to give a haircut. Based on these figures, find the following:

    a. The average number of customers waiting.

    b. The average time a customer waits.

    c. The average time a customer is in the shop.

    d. The average utilization of Benny's time.

22. Bobby, another enterprising barber, is thinking about advertising in the local newspaper since he is idle 45 percent of the time. Currently, customers arrive, on average, every 40 minutes. What does the arrival rate need to be for Bobby to be busy 85 percent of the time?

23. Customers enter the camera department of a store at an average rate of six per hour. The department is staffed by one employee, who takes an average of six minutes to serve each arrival. Assume this is a simple Poisson arrival, exponentially distributed service time situation.

    a. As a casual observer, how many people would you expect to see in the camera department (excluding the clerk)? How long would a customer expect to spend in the camera department (total time)?

    b. What is the utilization of the clerk?

    c. What is the probability that there are more than two people in the camera department (excluding the clerk)?

    d. Another clerk has been hired for the camera department who also takes an average of six minutes to serve each arrival. How long would a customer expect to spend in the department now?

24. An office employs several clerks who create documents, and one operator who enters the document information in a computer system. The group creates documents at a rate of 25 per hour. The operator can enter the information with

an average exponentially distributed time of two minutes. Assume the population is infinite, arrivals are Poisson, and queue length is infinite with the FCFS discipline.

a. Calculate the percentage utilization of the operator.

b. Calculate the average number of documents in the system.

c. Calculate the average time in the system.

d. Calculate the probability of four or more documents being in the system.

e. If another clerk were added, the document origination rate would increase to 30 per hour. What would the expected average number of documents in the system become? Show why.

25. A study-aid desk staffed by a graduate student has been established to answer students' questions and help in working problems in your OSCM course. The desk is staffed eight hours per day. The dean wants to know how the facility is working. Statistics show that students arrive at a rate of four per hour and the distribution is approximately Poisson. Assistance time averages 10 minutes, distributed exponentially. Assume population and line length can be infinite and queue discipline is FCFS.

a. Calculate the percentage utilization of the graduate student.

b. Calculate the average number of students in the system, excluding the graduate student service.

c. Calculate the average time in the system.

d. Calculate the probability of four or more students being in line or being served.

e. Before a test, the arrival of students increases to six per hour, on average. What will the new average line length be?

26. At a border inspection station, vehicles arrive at a rate of 10 per hour in a Poisson distribution. For simplicity in this problem, assume there is only one lane and one inspector, who can inspect vehicles at the rate of 12 per hour in an exponentially distributed fashion.

a. What is the average length of the waiting line?

b. What is the average time that a vehicle must wait to get through the system?

c. What is the utilization of the inspector?

d. What is the probability that when you arrive there will be three or more vehicles ahead of you?

27. During the campus Spring Fling, the bumper car amusement attraction has a problem with cars becoming disabled and needing repair. Repair personnel can be hired at the rate of $20 per hour, but they work only as one team. So, if one person is hired, he or she works alone; two or three people work together on the same repair.

One repairer can fix cars in an average time of 30 minutes. Two repairers take 20 minutes, and three take 15 minutes. While these cars are down, lost income is $40 per hour. Cars tend to break down at the rate of two per hour.

How many repairers should be hired?

28. A toll tunnel has decided to experiment with the use of a debit card for the collection of tolls. Initially, only one lane will be used. Cars are estimated to arrive at this experimental lane at the rate of 750 per hour. It will take exactly four seconds to verify the debit card.

a. How much time would you expect a customer to wait in line, pay with a debit card, and leave?

b. How many cars would you expect to see in the system?

29. A local fast-food restaurant wants to analyze its drive-thru window. At this time, the only information known is the average number of customers in the system (4.00) and the average time a customer spends at the restaurant (1.176 minutes). What are the arrival rate and the service rate?

ANALYTICS EXERCISE: PROCESSING CUSTOMER ORDERS

Analyzing a Taco Bell Restaurant

The following scenario was written by a reporter who became a Taco Bell worker for a few hours to experience what it's like to work in the drive-thru window at one of the most high-tech, quick-serve restaurant chains in the world. As you read, visualize how you could analyze a Taco Bell using the queuing models we discussed in this chapter. After the scenario, we will give you some hints related to how you can model the Quick Service (QS) restaurant and then we will ask you a series of questions related to your model.

It must always be, "Hi, how are you today?" Never, "Hi, how are you?" "Hi, how's it going?" or "Welcome to Taco Bell." Never, "What will it be today?" or, even worse, "What do you want?" Every Taco Bell Service Champion memorizes the order script before his first shift. The folks who work the drive-thru windows at the Taco Bell here in Tustin, California, about 35 miles south of Los Angeles, and everywhere else, are called Service Champions. Those who work the food production line are called Food Champions.

You think you know it—"Hi, how are you today?" It seems easy enough. And you follow that with, "You can order when you're ready," never "Can I take your order?" The latter puts pressure on the driver, who might be a distracted teenager busy texting her friend or a soccer mom with a half-dozen kids in the van. "They don't need the additional pressure of a disembodied voice demanding to know their order," explains Mike Harkins. Harkins, 49, is vice-president of One System Operations for Taco Bell, which means he spends all day, every day, thinking about the kitchen and the drive-thru.

He has been prepping me for my debut at the window. Getting ready, I wash my hands, scrubbing for the mandated 20 seconds; slide on rubber gloves; and don the three-channel headset that connects me to the ordering station out in the lot, as well as to my fellow Champions. I take my place at the window. I hear the ding indicating a customer has pulled into the loop around the restaurant, and I immediately ask, "Hi, how's it going?"

It gets worse from there. As a Service Champion, my job is to say my lines, input the order into the proprietary point of sale (POS) system, prepare and make drinks like Limeade Sparklers and Frutista Freezes, collect bills or credit cards, and make change. I input Beefy Crunch Burritos, Volcano Burritos, Chalupas, and Gorditas. My biggest worry is that someone will order a Crunchwrap Supreme, a fast-food marvel made up of two kinds of tortillas, beef, cheese, lettuce, tomatoes, and sauces, all scooped, folded, and assembled into a handheld, multiple-food-group package, which then gets grilled for 27 seconds. This actually doubles the time it takes to prepare a normal order. An order for a Crunchwrap Supreme, the most complex item on the menu, sometimes requires the Service Champion to take up position on the food production line to complete it in anything like the 164 seconds that Taco Bell averages for each customer, from driving up to the ordering station to pulling away from the pick-up window.

Above me on the wall, a flat-screen display shows the average time of the last five cars at either the order station or the pick-up window, depending on which is slowest. If the number is red, as it is now, that means one, or both, of the waits is exceeding 50 seconds, the target during peak periods. It now shows 53 seconds, on its way to 60, 70 . . . and then I stop looking. The high-pitched ding that announces each new customer becomes steady, unrelenting, and dispiriting—85 cars will roll through over the peak lunch rush. And I keep blowing the order script.

I fall behind so quickly and completely that restaurant manager Amanda Mihal, a veteran of 12 years in the QSR business (Quick Serve Restaurant, the acronym for an industry that makes acronyms for everything), has to step in. "You'll get it," Amanda says as she fixes an order that I have managed to screw up. "Eventually."

Every Taco Bell has two food production lines, one dedicated to the drive-thru and the other to servicing the walk-up counter. Working those lines is no easier than wearing the headset. The back of the restaurant has been engineered so that the Steamers, Stuffers, and Expeditors, the names given to the Food Champions who work the pans, take as few footsteps as possible during a shift. There are three prep areas: the hot holding area, the cold holding area, and the wrapping expediting area. The Stuffer in the hot holding area stuffs the meat into the tortillas, ladling beef with Taco Bell's proprietary tool, the BPT, or beef portioning tool. The steps for scooping the beef have been broken down into another acronym, SST, for stir, scoop, and tap. Flour tortillas must be cooked on one side for 15 seconds and the other for five.

When I take my place on the line and start to prepare burritos, tacos, and chalupas—they won't let me near a Crunchwrap Supreme—it is immediately clear that this has been engineered to make the process as simple as possible. The real challenge is the wrapping. Taco Bell once had 13 different wrappers for its products. That has been cut to six by labeling the corners of each wrapper differently. The paper, designed to slide off a stack in single sheets, has to be angled with the name of the item being made at the upper corner. The tortilla is placed in the middle of the paper and the item assembled from there until you fold the whole thing up in the wrapping expediting area next to the grill. "We had so many wrappers before, half a dozen stickers; it was all costing us seconds," says Harkins. In repeated attempts, I never get the proper item name into the proper place. And my burritos just do not hold together.

With me on the line are Carmen Franco, 60, and Ricardo Alvarez, 36. The best Food Champions can prepare about 100 burritos, tacos, chalupas, and gorditas in less than half an hour, and they have the 78-item menu memorized. Franco and Alvarez are a precise and frighteningly fast team. Ten orders at a time are displayed on a screen above the line, five drive-thrus and five walk-ins. Franco is a blur of motion as she slips out wrapping paper and tortillas, stirs, scoops, and taps, then slides the items down the line while looking up at the screen. The top Food Champions have an ability to scan through the next five orders and identify those that require more preparation steps, such as Grilled Stuffed Burritos and Crunchwrap Supremes, and set those up before returning to simpler tacos and burritos. When Alvarez is bogged down, Franco slips around him, and slides Crunchwrap Supremes into their boxes.

At the drive-thru window in Tustin, I would have shaken off the headset many orders ago had it not been for manager Mihal's support, but I'm hanging in there. After a while, I do begin to detect a pleasing, steady rhythm to the system, the transaction, the delivery of the food. Each is a discrete, predictable, scripted interaction. When the order is input correctly, the customer drives up to the window, the money is paid, the Frutista Freeze or Atomic Bacon Bombers (a test item specific to this Taco Bell) handed over, and you send people on their way with a smile and a "Thank you for coming to Taco Bell," you feel a moment of accomplishment. And so does Harkins, for it has all gone exactly as he has planned.

Then a ding in my headset.

"Um, hello?"

Idiot, I think to myself, I've blown the script again.

Source: Karl Taro Greenfeld, *Bloomberg Businessweek*, Features Section, May 5, 2011.

Modeling the Restaurant

In the scenario, they indicate that it takes about 164 seconds, on average, to serve a customer during the busy lunch-hour period. Put yourself in the seat of your car getting food at the FS restaurant. Let's assume you are using the drive-through window and that you will pick up the food and take it home to eat with some friends.

You drive into the restaurant lot and notice there is a line of cars that has formed at the order kiosk. You wait for your turn to talk to the Customer Service Champion so that you can place your order. The menu is sitting there in clear view, so you can see exactly what you want. Soon it is your turn and you quickly place your order, learn what the bill will be, and move your car to the line at the drive-through window. While waiting, you get your money out and count out the exact change you will need. After a short time, it's your turn at the window and you give the Service Champion your money, take your drink and food, and carefully drive out of the parking lot.

Think about what happened at the restaurant. First, you waited in two lines. The first was at the order kiosk and the second at the drive-through window. Next, consider the work that the restaurant needed to complete to process your order. The Service Champion took your order and entered it in the POS system, prepared your drink, and then when the food was ready, collected your money, and delivered your drink and food. One of the Food Champions prepared your food using information from a screen that shows orders as they are entered by the Service Champion.

The total time it takes between when you arrive at the restaurant until you leave is made up of the following elements:

1. The service time for the Service Champion to process your order
2. The service time for the Food Champion to prepare your order
3. The waiting while the Service Champion and Food Champion served other customers

To model this using the queuing models in the chapter, assume that you have two totally independent service processes. The first process is the Service Champion and the second is the Food Champion. Each process has potentially a different mean service time per customer. The Service Champion must serve each customer and they arrive at a particular rate. The Food Champion prepares the individual items on the order such as a burrito, taco, chalupa, or gorditas taco. As the orders are taken, each individual item appears on a monitor telling the Food Champion what should be made next. The average time for a customer to run through the system is the sum of the average service times (time to take the order by the Service Champion and time to make the order by the Food Champion) plus the sum of the expected waiting times for the two processes. This assumes that these processes operate totally independent of each other, which might not be exactly true. But we leave that to a later discussion.

Assume that the queues in front of each process are large, meaning that there is plenty of room for cars in the line before and after the order kiosk. Also, assume there is a single Service Champion and two Food Champions each operating independently and working just on the drive-through orders. Also, assume that the arrival pattern is Poisson, customers are handled first come, first served, and the service pattern is exponential.

Given this, answer the following questions:

1. Draw a diagram of the process using the format in Exhibit 7.3.
2. Consider a base case where a customer arrives every 40 seconds and the Customer Service Champion can handle 120 customers per hour. There are two Food Champions, each capable of handling 100 orders per hour. How long should it take to be served by the restaurant (from the time a customer enters the kiosk queue until her food is delivered)? Use queuing models to estimate this.
3. On average, how busy are the Customer Service Champions and the two Food Champions?
4. On average, how many cars do you expect to have in the drive-through line? (Include those waiting to place orders and those waiting for food.)
5. If the restaurant runs a sale and the customer arrival rate increases by 20 percent, how would this change the total time expected to serve a customer? How would this change the average number of cars in the drive-through line?
6. Currently, relatively few customers (less than 0.5 percent) order the Crunchwrap Supreme. What would happen if the restaurant ran the sale, demand jumped on the Crunchwrap Supreme, and 30 percent of the orders were for this item? Take a quantitative approach to answering this question. Assume that the Customer Service Champion never helps the Food Champions and that these two processes remain independent.
7. For the type of analysis done in this case, what are the key assumptions? What would be the impact on our analysis if these assumptions were not true?
8. Could this type of analysis be used for other service-type businesses? Give examples to support your answer.

PRACTICE EXAM

1. Service systems can be generally categorized according to this characteristic that relates to the customer.
2. A framework that relates to the customer service system encounter.
3. This is the key feature that distinguishes a service blueprint from a normal flowchart.
4. This is done to make a system mistake-proof.
5. The queuing models assume that customers are served in what order?
6. Consider two queuing systems identical except for the service time distribution. In the first system, the service time is random and distributed according to a Poisson distribution. The service time is constant in the second system. How would the waiting time differ in the two systems?
7. What is the average utilization of the servers in a system that has three servers? On average, 15 customers arrive every 15 minutes. It takes a server exactly three minutes to wait on each customer.
8. What is the expected waiting time for the system described in question 7?
9. Firms that desire high service levels where customers have short wait times should target server utilization levels at no more than this percent.
10. In most cases, if a firm increases its service capacity by 10 percent, it would expect waiting times to be reduced by what percent? Assume customer arrivals and service times are random.

CHAPTER 8

SALES AND OPERATIONS PLANNING

Learning Objectives

LO8–1 Understand what sales and operations planning is and how it coordinates manufacturing, logistics, service, and marketing plans.

LO8–2 Construct and evaluate aggregate plans that employ different strategies for meeting demand.

LO8–3 Explain yield management and why it is an important strategy.

Let's eavesdrop on an executive staff meeting at the Acme Widget Company. The participants are not happy campers.

President:	This shortage situation is terrible. When will we ever get our act together? Whenever business gets good, we run out of product and our customer service is lousy.
VP Operations:	I'll tell you when. When we start to get some decent forecasts from the Sales Department . . .
VP Sales (interrupting):	Wait a minute. We forecasted this upturn.
VP Operations:	. . . In time to do something about it? Yeah, we got the revised forecast four days after the start of the month. By then it was too late.

VP Sales:	I could have told you months ago. All you had to do was ask.
VP Finance:	I'd like to be in on those conversations. We've been burned more than once by building inventories for a business upturn that doesn't happen. Then we get stuck with tons of inventory and run out of cash.

And the beat goes on. Back orders, dissatisfied customers, high inventories, late shipments, finger-pointing, cash-flow problems, demand and supply out of balance, missing the business plan. This is the norm in many companies.

It does not, however, have to be that way. Today, many companies are using a business process called sales and operations planning (S&OP) to help avoid such problems. To learn what it is, and how to make it work, read on.

Source: Adapted from Thomas F. Wallace, *Sales and Operations Planning: The How-To Handbook* (Cincinnati, OH: T. F. Wallace & Co., 2000), p. 3. Copyright © 2000 Thomas Wallace.

Aggregate operations plan
A plan for labor and production for the intermediate term with the objective to minimize the cost of resources needed to meet demand.

LO8–1 Understand what sales and operations planning is and how it coordinates manufacturing, logistics, service, and marketing plans.

In this chapter, we focus on the **aggregate operations plan**, which translates annual and quarterly business plans into broad labor and output plans for the intermediate term (3 to 18 months). The objective of the aggregate operations plan is to minimize the cost of resources required to meet demand over that period.

WHAT IS SALES AND OPERATIONS PLANNING?

Sales and operations planning is a process that helps firms provide better customer service, lower inventory, shorten customer lead times, stabilize production rates, and give top management a handle on the business. The process is designed to coordinate the key business activities related to marketing and sales with the operations and supply chain activities that are required to meet demand over time. Depending on the situation, business activities may include the timing of newspaper advertisements, volume discounting of discontinued items, and major direct sales channel promotions, for example. The process is designed to help a company get demand and supply in balance and keep them in balance over time. The process requires teamwork among sales, distribution and logistics, operations, finance, and product development.

The sales and operations planning process consists of a series of meetings, finishing with a high-level meeting where key intermediate-term decisions are made. The end goal is an agreement between various departments on the best course of action to achieve the optimal balance between supply and demand. The idea is to put the operational plan in line with the business plan.

This balance must occur at an aggregate level and also at the detailed individual product level. By *aggregate,* we mean at the level of major groups of products. Over time, we need to ensure that we have enough total capacity. Since demand is often quite dynamic, it is important that we monitor our expected needs 3 to 18 months or further in the future. When planning this far into the future, it is difficult to know exactly how many of a particular product we will need, but we should be able to know how a larger group of similar products should sell. The term *aggregate* refers to this group of products. Given that we have enough aggregate capacity, our individual product schedulers, working within aggregate capacity constraints, can handle the daily and weekly launching of individual product orders to meet short-term demand.

Overview of Sales and Operations Planning Activities

Sales and operations planning
The process that companies use to keep demand and supply in balance by coordinating manufacturing, distribution, marketing, and financial plans.

Exhibit 8.1 positions sales and operations planning relative to other major operations planning activities. The term **sales and operations planning** was coined by companies to refer to the process that helps firms keep demand and supply in balance. In operations management, this process traditionally was called *aggregate planning.* The new terminology is meant to capture the importance of cross-functional work. Typically, this activity requires an integrated effort with cooperation from sales, distribution and logistics, operations, finance, and product development.

Within sales and operations planning, marketing develops a sales plan that extends through the next 3 to 18 months. This sales plan typically is stated in units of aggregate product groups and often is tied into sales incentive programs and other marketing activities. The operations side develops an operations plan as an output of the process, which is discussed in depth in this chapter. By focusing on aggregate product and sales volumes, the marketing and operations functions are able to develop plans for the way demand will be met. This is a particularly difficult task when there are significant changes in demand over time as a result of market trends or other factors.

exhibit 8.1

Overview of Major Operations and Supply Chain Planning Activities

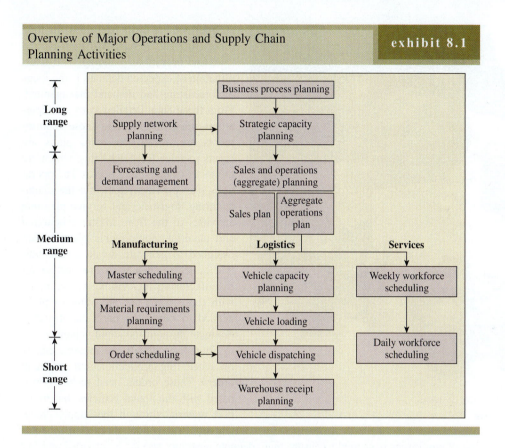

Aggregation on the supply side is done by product families, and on the demand side it is done by groups of customers. Individual product production schedules and matching customer orders can be handled more readily as a result of the sales and operations planning process. Typically, sales and operations planning occurs on a monthly cycle. Sales and operations planning links a company's strategic plans and business plan to its detailed operations and supply processes. These detailed processes include manufacturing, logistics, and service activities, as shown in Exhibit 8.1.

In Exhibit 8.1, the time dimension is shown as long, intermediate, and short range. **Long-range planning** generally is done annually, focusing on a horizon greater than one year. **Intermediate-range planning** usually covers a period from 3 to 18 months, with time increments that are weekly, monthly, or sometimes quarterly. **Short-range planning** covers a period from one day to six months, with daily or weekly time increments.

Long-range planning activities are done in two major areas. The first is the design of the manufacturing and service processes that produce the products of the firm, and the second is the design of the logistics activities that deliver products to the customer. Process planning deals with determining the specific technologies and procedures required to produce a product or service. Strategic capacity planning deals with determining the long-term capabilities (such as size and scope) of the production systems. Similarly, from a logistics point of view, supply network planning determines how the product will be distributed to the customer on the outbound side, with decisions relating to the location of warehouses and the types of transportation systems to be used. On the inbound side, supply network planning involves decisions relating to outsourcing production, selection of parts and component suppliers, and related decisions.

Long-range planning
One year or more.

Intermediate-range planning
3 to 18 months.

Short-range planning
A day to six months.

THE PRODUCT FAMILY OF CANON CAMERAS.

© Yoshikazu Tsuno/AFP/Getty Images

Intermediate-term activities include forecasting and demand management and sales and operations planning. The determination of expected demand is the focus of forecasting and demand management. From these data, detailed sales and operations plans for meeting these requirements are made. The sales plans are inputs to sales force activities, which are the focus of marketing books. The operations plan provides input into the manufacturing, logistics, and service planning activities of the firm. Master scheduling and material requirements planning are designed to generate detailed schedules that indicate when parts are needed for manufacturing activities. Coordinated with these plans are the logistics plans needed to move the parts and finished products through the supply chain.

Short-term details are focused mostly on scheduling production and shipment orders. These orders need to be coordinated with the actual vehicles that transport material through the supply chain. On the service side, short-term scheduling of employees is needed to ensure that adequate customer service is provided and fair worker schedules are maintained.

The Aggregate Operations Plan

The aggregate operations plan is concerned with setting production rates by product group or other broad categories for the intermediate term (3 to 18 months). Note again from Exhibit 8.1 that the aggregate plan precedes the master schedule. *The main purpose of the aggregate plan is to specify the optimal combination of production rate, workforce level, and inventory on-hand.* **Production rate** refers to the number of units completed per unit of time (such as per hour or per day). **Workforce level** is the number of workers needed for production (production = production rate × workforce level). **Inventory on-hand** is unused inventory carried over from the previous period.

Here is a formal statement of the aggregate planning problem: Given the demand forecast F_t for each period t in the planning horizon that extends over T periods, determine the production level P_t, inventory level I_t, and workforce level W_t for periods $t = 1, 2, \ldots, T$ that minimize the relevant costs over the planning horizon.

The form of the aggregate plan varies from company to company. In some firms, it is a formalized report containing planning objectives and the planning premises on which it is based. In other companies, particularly smaller ones, the owner may make simple calculations of workforce needs that reflect a general staffing strategy.

The process by which the plan itself is derived also varies. One common approach is to derive it from the corporate annual plan, as shown in Exhibit 8.1. A typical corporate plan contains a section on manufacturing that specifies how many units in each major product

Production rate
Number of units completed per unit of time.

Workforce level
Number of workers needed in a period.

Inventory on-hand
Inventory carried from the previous period.

line need to be produced over the next 12 months to meet the sales forecast. The planner takes this information and attempts to determine how best to meet these requirements with available resources. Alternatively, some organizations combine output requirements into equivalent units and use this as the basis for the aggregate plan. For example, a division of General Motors may be asked to produce a certain number of cars of all types at a particular facility. The production planner would then take the average labor hours required for all models as a basis for the overall aggregate plan. Refinements to this plan, specifically model types to be produced, would be reflected in shorter-term production plans.

Another approach is to develop the aggregate plan by simulating various master production schedules and calculating corresponding capacity requirements to see if adequate labor and equipment exist at each work center. If capacity is inadequate, additional requirements for overtime, subcontracting, extra workers, and so forth are specified for each product line and combined into a rough-cut plan. This plan is then modified by cut-and-try or mathematical methods to derive a final and (one hopes) lower-cost plan.

Production Planning Environment

Exhibit 8.2 illustrates the internal and external factors that constitute the production planning environment. In general, the external environment is outside the production planner's direct control, but in some firms, demand for the product can be managed. Through close cooperation between marketing and operations, promotional activities and price cutting can be used to build demand during slow periods. Conversely, when demand is strong, promotional activities can be curtailed and prices raised to maximize the revenues from those products or services that the firm has the capacity to provide. The current practices in managing demand will be discussed later in the section titled "Yield Management."

Complementary products may work for firms facing cyclical demand fluctuations. For instance, lawnmower manufacturers will have strong demand for spring and summer, but weak demand during fall and winter. Demands on the production system can be smoothed out by producing a complementary product with high demand during fall and winter, and low demand during spring and summer (for instance, snowmobiles, snowblowers, or

Required Inputs to the Production Planning System	exhibit 8.2

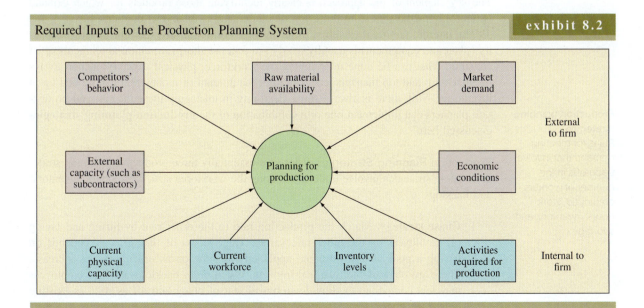

WATER SKIS AND SNOW SKIS ARE EXAMPLES OF COMPLEMENTARY PRODUCTS.

(Left): © Kelly Redinger/Design Pics RF, (Right): © RF/Corbis

leafblowers). With services, cycles are more often measured in hours than months. Restaurants with strong demand during lunch and dinner will often add a breakfast menu to increase demand during the morning hours.

But even so, there are limits to how much demand can be controlled. Ultimately, the production planner must live with the sales projections and orders promised by the marketing function, leaving the internal factors as variables that can be manipulated in deriving a production plan. A new approach to facilitate managing these internal factors is termed *accurate response*. This entails the refined measurement of historical demand patterns blended with expert judgment to determine when to begin production of particular items. The key element of the approach is clearly identifying those products for which demand is relatively predictable from those for which demand is relatively unpredictable.

The internal factors themselves differ in their controllability. Current physical capacity (plant and equipment) is usually nearly fixed in the short run; union agreements often constrain what can be done in changing the workforce; physical capacity cannot always be increased; and top management may limit the amount of money that can be tied up in inventories. Still, there is always some flexibility in managing these factors, and production planners can implement one or a combination of the **production planning strategies** discussed here.

Production planning strategies
Plans for meeting demand that involve trade-offs in the number of workers employed, work hours, inventory, and shortages.

Production Planning Strategies There are essentially three production planning strategies. These strategies involve trade-offs among the workforce size, work hours, inventory, and backlogs.

1. **Chase strategy.** Match the production rate to the order rate by hiring and laying off employees as the order rate varies. The success of this strategy depends on having a pool of easily trained applicants to draw on as order volumes increase. There are obvious motivational impacts. When order backlogs are low, employees may feel compelled to slow down out of fear of being laid off as soon as existing orders are completed.

2. **Stable workforce—variable work hours.** Vary the output by varying the number of hours worked through flexible work schedules or overtime. By varying the number of work hours, you can match production quantities to orders. This strategy provides workforce continuity and avoids many of the emotional and tangible costs of hiring and firing associated with the chase strategy.
3. **Level strategy.** Maintain a stable workforce working at a constant output rate. Shortages and surpluses are absorbed by fluctuating inventory levels, order backlogs, and lost sales. Employees benefit from stable work hours at the cost of potentially decreased customer service levels and increased inventory costs. Another concern is the possibility of inventoried products becoming obsolete.

When just one of these variables is used to absorb demand fluctuations, it is termed a **pure strategy**; two or more used in combination constitute a **mixed strategy**. As you might suspect, mixed strategies are more widely applied in industry.

Pure strategy
A simple strategy that uses just one option, such as hiring and firing workers, for meeting demand.

Subcontracting In addition to these strategies, managers also may choose to subcontract some portion of production. This strategy is similar to the chase strategy, but hiring and laying off are translated into subcontracting and not subcontracting. Some level of subcontracting can be desirable to accommodate demand fluctuations. However, unless the relationship with the supplier is particularly strong, a manufacturer can lose some control over schedule and quality.

Mixed strategy
A more complex strategy that combines options for meeting demand.

Relevant Costs

Four costs are relevant to the aggregate production plan. These relate to the production cost itself, as well as the cost to hold inventory and to have unfilled orders. More specifically, these are

1. **Basic production costs.** These are the fixed and variable costs incurred in producing a given product type in a given time period. Included are direct and indirect labor costs and regular as well as overtime compensation.
2. **Costs associated with changes in the production rate.** Typical costs in this category are those involved in hiring, training, and laying off personnel. Hiring temporary help is a way of avoiding these costs.
3. **Inventory holding costs.** A major component is the cost of capital tied up in inventory. Other components are storing, insurance, taxes, spoilage, and obsolescence.
4. **Backordering costs.** Usually, these are very hard to measure and include costs of expediting, loss of customer goodwill, and loss of sales revenues resulting from backordering.

Budgets To receive funding, operations managers are generally required to submit annual, and sometimes quarterly, budget requests. The aggregate plan is key to the success of the budgeting process. Recall that the goal of the aggregate plan is to minimize the total production-related costs over the planning horizon by determining the optimal combination of workforce levels and inventory levels. Thus, the aggregate plan provides justification for the requested budget amount. Accurate medium-range planning increases the likelihood of (1) receiving the requested budget and (2) operating within the limits of the budget.

In the next section, we provide an example of medium-range planning in a manufacturing setting. This example illustrates the trade-offs associated with different production planning strategies.

AGGREGATE PLANNING TECHNIQUES

Companies commonly use simple cut-and-try charting and graphic methods to develop aggregate plans. A cut-and-try approach involves costing out various production planning alternatives and selecting the one that is best. Elaborate spreadsheets are developed to facilitate the decision process. Sophisticated approaches involving linear programming and simulation are often incorporated into these spreadsheets. In the following, we demonstrate a spreadsheet approach to evaluate four strategies for meeting demand for the JC Company. Later we discuss more sophisticated approaches using linear programming (see Appendix A).

A Cut-and-Try Example: The JC Company

A firm with pronounced seasonal variation normally plans production for a full year to capture the extremes in demand during the busiest and slowest months. But we can illustrate the general principles involved with a shorter horizon. Suppose we wish to set up a production plan for the JC Company's Chinese manufacturing plant for the next six months. We are given the following information:

DEMAND AND WORKING DAYS							
	JANUARY	FEBRUARY	MARCH	APRIL	MAY	JUNE	TOTALS
Demand forecast	1,800	1,500	1,100	900	1,100	1,600	8,000
Number of working days	22	19	21	21	22	20	125

COSTS	
Materials	$100.00/unit
Inventory holding cost	$1.50/unit/month
Marginal cost of stockout	$5.00/unit/month
Marginal cost of subcontracting	$20.00/unit ($120.00 subcontracting cost less $100.00 material savings)
Hiring and training cost	$200.00/worker
Layoff cost	$250.00/worker
Labor hours required	5/unit
Straight-time cost (first eight hours each day)	$4.00/hour
Overtime cost (time and a half)	$6.00/hour

INVENTORY	
Beginning inventory	400 units
Safety stock	25% of month demand

In solving this problem, we can exclude the material costs. We could have included this $100.00 cost in all our calculations, but if we assume that a $100.00 cost is common to each demanded unit, then we need only concern ourselves with the marginal costs. Because the subcontracting cost is $120.00, our marginal cost that does not include materials is $20.00.

Note that many costs are expressed in a different form than typically found in the accounting records of a firm. Therefore, do not expect to obtain all these costs directly from such records, but obtain them indirectly from management personnel, who can help interpret the data.

Aggregate Production Planning Requirements						exhibit 8.3
	JANUARY	FEBRUARY	MARCH	APRIL	MAY	JUNE
Beginning inventory	400	450	375	275	225	275
Demand forecast	1,800	1,500	1,100	900	1,100	1,600
Safety stock (.25 × Demand forecast)	450	375	275	225	275	400
Production requirement (Demand forecast + Safety stock − Beginning inventory)	1,850	1,425	1,000	850	1,150	1,725
Ending inventory (Beginning inventory + Production requirement − Demand forecast)	450	375	275	225	275	400

Excel:
Aggregate
Planning

Inventory at the beginning of the first period is 400 units. Because the demand forecast is imperfect, the JC Company has determined that a *safety stock* (buffer inventory) should be established to reduce the likelihood of stockouts. For this example, assume the safety stock should be one-quarter of the demand forecast. (Chapter 11 covers this topic in depth.)

Before investigating alternative production plans, it is often useful to convert demand forecasts into *production requirements,* which take into account the safety stock estimates. In Exhibit 8.3, note that these requirements implicitly assume that the safety stock is never actually used, so that the ending inventory each month equals the safety stock for that month. For example, the January safety stock of 450 (25 percent of January demand of 1,800) becomes the inventory at the end of January. The production requirement for January is demand plus safety stock minus beginning inventory (1,800 + 450 − 400 = 1,850).

Now we must formulate alternative production plans for the JC Company. Using a spreadsheet, we investigate four different plans with the objective of finding the one with the lowest total cost.

Plan 1. Produce to exact monthly production requirements using a regular eight-hour day by varying workforce size.

Plan 2. Produce to meet expected average demand over the next six months by maintaining a constant workforce. This constant number of workers is calculated by finding the average number of workers required each day over the horizon. Take the total production requirements and multiply by the time required for each unit. Then divide by the total time that one person works over the horizon [(8,000 units × 5 hours per unit) ÷ (125 days × 8 hours per day) = 40 workers]. Inventory is allowed to accumulate, with shortages filled from next month's production by backordering. Negative beginning inventory balances indicate that demand is backordered. In some cases, sales may be lost if demand is not met. The lost sales can be shown with a negative ending inventory balance followed by a zero beginning inventory balance in the next period. Notice that in this plan we use our safety stock in January, February, March, and June to meet expected demand.

Plan 3. Produce to meet the minimum expected demand (April) using a constant workforce on regular time. Subcontract to meet additional output requirements. The number of workers is calculated by locating the minimum monthly production requirement and determining how many workers would be needed for that month [(850 units × 5 hours per unit) ÷ (21 days × 8 hours per day) = 25 workers] and subcontracting any monthly difference between requirements and production.

Plan 4.   Produce to meet expected demand for all but the first two months using a constant workforce on regular time. Use overtime to meet additional output requirements. The number of workers is more difficult to compute for this plan, but the goal is to finish June with an ending inventory as close as possible to the June safety stock. By trial and error it can be shown that a constant workforce of 38 workers is the closest approximation.

The next step is to calculate the cost of each plan. This requires the series of simple calculations shown in Exhibit 8.4. Note that the headings in each row are different for each plan because each is a different problem requiring its own data and calculations.

The final step is to tabulate and graph each plan and compare their costs. From Exhibit 8.5 we can see that using subcontractors resulted in the lowest cost (Plan 3). Exhibit 8.6 shows the effects of the four plans. This is a cumulative graph illustrating the expected results on the total production requirement.

Note that we have made one other assumption in this example: The plan can start with any number of workers with no hiring or layoff cost. This usually is the case because an aggregate plan draws on existing personnel, and we can start the plan that way. However, in an actual application, the availability of existing personnel transferable from other areas of the firm may change the assumptions.

Plan 1 is the S-curve when we chase demand by varying workforce. Plan 2 has the highest average production rate (the line representing cumulative demand has the greatest slope). Using subcontracting in Plan 3 results in it having the lowest production rate. Limits on the amount of overtime available results in Plan 4 being similar to Plan 2.

Each of these four plans focused on one particular cost, and the first three were simple pure strategies. Obviously, there are many other feasible plans, some of which would use a combination of workforce changes, overtime, and subcontracting. The problems at the end of this chapter include examples of such mixed strategies. In practice, the final plan chosen would come from searching a variety of alternatives and future projections beyond the six-month planning horizon we have used.

Keep in mind that the cut-and-try approach does not guarantee finding the minimum-cost solution. However, spreadsheet programs, such as Microsoft Excel, can perform cut-and-try cost estimates in seconds and have elevated this kind of what-if analysis to a fine art. More sophisticated programs can generate much better solutions without the user having to intercede, as in the cut-and-try method.

Aggregate Planning Applied to Services:
Tucson Parks and Recreation Department

Charting and graphic techniques are also useful for aggregate planning in service applications. The following example shows how a city's parks and recreation department could use the alternatives of full-time employees, part-time employees, and subcontracting to meet its commitment to provide a service to the city.

Tucson Parks and Recreation Department has an operation and maintenance budget of $9,760,000. The department is responsible for developing and maintaining open space, all public recreational programs, adult sports leagues, golf courses, tennis courts, pools, and so forth. There are 336 full-time-equivalent employees (FTEs). Of these, 216 are full-time permanent personnel who provide the administration and year-round maintenance to all areas. The remaining 120 FTE positions are staffed with part-timers; about three-quarters of them are used during the summer, and the remaining quarter in the fall, winter, and spring seasons. The three-fourths (or 90 FTE positions) show up as approximately 800 part-time summer jobs: lifeguards, baseball umpires, and instructors in

Costs of Four Production Plans

exhibit 8.4

Excel:
Aggregate
Planning

PRODUCTION PLAN 1: EXACT PRODUCTION; VARY WORKFORCE

	JANUARY	FEBRUARY	MARCH	APRIL	MAY	JUNE	TOTAL
Production requirement (from Exhibit 8.3)	1,850	1,425	1,000	850	1,150	1,725	
Production hours required (Production requirement × 5 hr./unit)	9,250	7,125	5,000	4,250	5,750	8,625	
Working days per month	22	19	21	21	22	20	
Hours per month per worker (Working days × 8 hr./day)	176	152	168	168	176	160	
Workers required (Production hours required/Hours per month per worker)	53	47	30	25	33	54	
New workers hired (assuming opening workforce equal to first month's requirement of 53 workers)	0	0	0	0	8	21	
Hiring cost (New workers hired × $200)	$0	$0	$0	$0	$1,600	$4,200	$5,800
Workers laid off	0	6	17	5	0	0	
Layoff cost (Workers laid off × $250)	$0	$1,500	$4,250	$1,250	$0	$0	$7,000
Straight-time cost (Production hours required × $4)	$37,000	$28,500	$20,000	$17,000	$23,000	$34,500	$160,000
						Total cost	$172,800

PRODUCTION PLAN 2: CONSTANT WORKFORCE; VARY INVENTORY AND STOCKOUT

	JANUARY	FEBRUARY	MARCH	APRIL	MAY	JUNE	TOTAL
Beginning inventory	400	8	−276	−32	412	720	
Working days per month	22	19	21	21	22	20	
Production hours available (Working days per month × 8 hr./day × 40 workers)*	7,040	6,080	6,720	6,720	7,040	6,400	
Actual production (Production hours available/5 hr./unit)	1,408	1,216	1,344	1,344	1,408	1,280	
Demand forecast (from Exhibit 8.3)	1,800	1,500	1,100	900	1,100	1,600	
Ending inventory (Beginning inventory + Actual production − Demand forecast)	8	−276	−32	412	720	400	
Shortage cost (Units short × $5)	$0	$1,380	$160	$0	$0	$0	$1,540
Safety stock (from Exhibit 8.3)	450	375	275	225	275	400	
Units excess (Ending inventory − Safety stock) only if positive amount	0	0	0	187	445	0	
Inventory cost (Units excess × $1.50)	$0	$0	$0	$281	$668	$0	$948
Straight-time cost (Production hours available × $4)	$28,160	$24,320	$26,880	$26,880	$28,160	$25,600	$160,000
						Total cost	$162,488

*(Sum of production requirement in Exhibit 8.3 × 5 hr./unit)/(Sum of production hours available × 8 hr./day) = (8,000 × 5)/(125 × 8) = 40.

(continued)

exhibit 8.4   Costs of Four Production Plans (*Concluded*)

PRODUCTION PLAN 3: CONSTANT LOW WORKFORCE; SUBCONTRACT

	JANUARY	FEBRUARY	MARCH	APRIL	MAY	JUNE	TOTAL
Production requirement (from Exhibit 8.3)	1,850	1,425	1,000	850	1,150	1,725	
Working days per month	22	19	21	21	22	20	
Production hours available (Working days × 8 hr./day × 25 workers)*	4,400	3,800	4,200	4,200	4,400	4,000	
Actual production (Production hours available/5 hr. per unit)	880	760	840	840	880	800	
Units subcontracted (Production requirement − Actual production)	970	665	160	10	270	925	
Subcontracting cost (Units subcontracted × $20)	$19,400	$13,300	$3,200	$200	$5,400	$18,500	$60,000
Straight-time cost (Production hours available × $4)	$17,600	$15,200	$16,800	$16,800	$17,600	$16,000	$100,000
						Total cost	$160,000

*Minimum production requirement. In this example, April is minimum of 850 units. Number of workers required for April is $(850 \times 5)/(21 \times 8) = 25$.

PRODUCTION PLAN 4: CONSTANT WORKFORCE; OVERTIME

	JANUARY	FEBRUARY	MARCH	APRIL	MAY	JUNE	TOTAL
Beginning inventory	400	0	0	177	554	792	
Working days per month	22	19	21	21	22	20	
Production hours available (Working days × 8 hr./day × 38 workers)*	6,688	5,776	6,384	6,384	6,688	6,080	
Regular shift production (Production hours available/5 hr./unit)	1,338	1,155	1,277	1,277	1,338	1,216	
Demand forecast (from Exhibit 8.3)	1,800	1,500	1,100	900	1,100	1,600	
Units available before overtime (Beginning inventory + Regular shift production − Demand forecast). This number has been rounded to the nearest integer.	−62	−345	177	554	792	408	
Units overtime	62	375	0	0	0	0	
Overtime cost (Units overtime × 5 hr./unit × $6/hr.)	$1,860	$10,350	$0	$0	$0	$0	$12,210
Safety stock (from Exhibit 8.3)	450	375	275	225	275	400	
Units excess (Units available before overtime − Safety stock) only if positive amount	0	0	0	329	517	8	
Inventory cost (Units excessive × $1.50)	$0	$0	$0	$494	$776	$12	$1,281
Straight-time cost (Production hours available × $4)	$26,752	$23,104	$25,536	$25,536	$26,752	$24,320	$152,000
						Total cost	$165,491

*Workers determined by trial and error. See text for explanation.

Comparison of Four Plans

exhibit 8.5

Excel:
Aggregate
Planning

COSTS	PLAN 1: EXACT PRODUCTION; VARY WORKFORCE	PLAN 2: CONSTANT WORKFORCE; VARY INVENTORY AND STOCKOUT	PLAN 3: CONSTANT LOW WORKFORCE; SUBCONTRACT	PLAN 4: CONSTANT WORKFORCE; OVERTIME
Hiring	$ 5,800	$ 0	$ 0	$ 0
Layoff	7,000	0	0	0
Excess inventory	0	948	0	1,281
Shortage	0	1,540	0	0
Subcontract	0	0	60,000	0
Overtime	0	0	0	12,210
Straight time	160,000	160,000	100,000	152,000
	$172,800	$162,488	$160,000	$165,491

Four Plans for Satisfying a Production Requirement over the Number of Production Days Available

exhibit 8.6

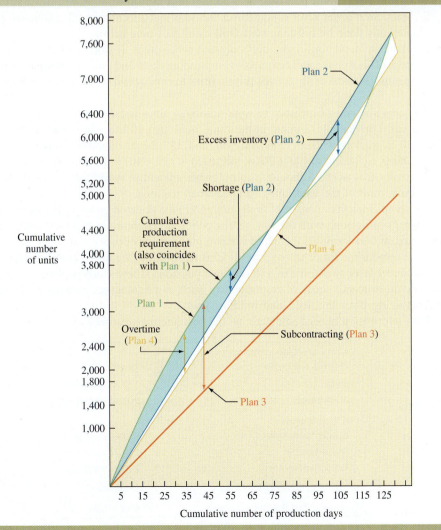

Cumulative number of production days

summer programs for children. Eight hundred part-time jobs came from 90 FTEs because many last for only a month or two, while the FTEs are a year long.

Currently, the only parks and recreation work subcontracted amounts to less than $100,000. This is for the golf and tennis pros and for grounds maintenance at the libraries and veterans' cemetery.

Because of the nature of city employment, the probable bad public image, and civil service rules, the option to hire and fire full-time help daily or weekly to meet seasonal demand is out of the question. However, temporary part-time help is authorized and traditional. Also, it is virtually impossible to have regular (full-time) staff for all the summer jobs. During the summer months, the approximately 800 part-time employees are staffing many programs that occur simultaneously, prohibiting level scheduling over a normal 40-hour week. A wider variety of skills are required (such as umpires, coaches, lifeguards, and teachers of ceramics, guitar, karate, belly dancing, and yoga) than can be expected from full-time employees.

Three options are open to the department in its aggregate planning:

1. The present method, which is to maintain a medium-level full-time staff and schedule work during off-seasons (such as rebuilding baseball fields during the winter months) and to use part-time help during peak demands.
2. Maintain a lower level of staff over the year and subcontract all additional work presently done by full-time staff (still using part-time help).
3. Maintain an administrative staff only and subcontract all work, including part-time help. (This would entail contracts to landscaping firms and pool maintenance companies as well as to newly created private firms to employ and supply part-time help.)

The common unit of measure of work across all areas is full-time-equivalent jobs or employees. For example, assume in the same week that 30 lifeguards worked 20 hours each, 40 instructors worked 15 hours each, and 35 baseball umpires worked 10 hours each. This is equivalent to $(30 \times 20) + (40 \times 15) + (35 \times 10) = 1,550 \div 40 = 38.75$ FTE positions for that week. Although a considerable amount of workload can be shifted to off-season, most of the work must be done when required.

Full-time employees consist of three groups: (1) the skeleton group of key department personnel coordinating with the city, setting policy, determining budgets, measuring performance, and so forth; (2) the administrative group of supervisory and office personnel who are responsible for or whose jobs are directly linked to the direct-labor workers; and (3) the direct-labor workforce of 116 full-time positions. These workers physically maintain the department's areas of responsibility, such as cleaning up, mowing golf greens and ballfields, trimming trees, and watering grass.

Cost information needed to determine the best alternative strategy is

Full-time direct-labor employees	
Average wage rate	$8.90 per hour
Fringe benefits	17% of wage rate
Administrative costs	20% of wage rate
Part-time employees	
Average wage rate	$8.06 per hour
Fringe benefits	11% of wage rate
Administrative costs	25% of wage rate
Subcontracting all full-time jobs	$3.2 million
Subcontracting all part-time jobs	$3.7 million

exhibit 8.7

Actual Demand Requirement for Full-Time Direct Employees and Full-Time-Equivalent (FTE) Part-Time Employees

	JAN.	FEB.	MAR.	APR.	MAY	JUNE	JULY	AUG.	SEPT.	OCT.	NOV.	DEC.	TOTAL
Days	22	20	21	22	21	20	21	21	21	23	18	22	252
Full-time employees	66	28	130	90	195	290	325	92	45	32	29	60	
Full-time days*	1,452	560	2,730	1,980	4,095	5,800	6,825	1,932	945	736	522	1,320	28,897
Full-time-equivalent part-time employees	41	75	72	68	72	302	576	72	0	68	84	27	
FTE days	902	1,500	1,512	1,496	1,512	6,040	12,096	1,512	0	1,564	1,512	594	30,240

*Full-time days are derived by multiplying the number of days in each month by the number of workers.

Monthly Requirement for Full-Time Direct-Labor Employees (Other Than Key Personnel) and Full-Time-Equivalent Part-Time Employees

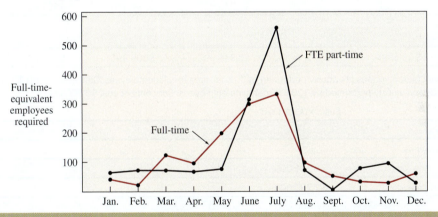

Excel:
Aggregate
Planning

June and July are the peak demand seasons in Tucson. Exhibit 8.7 shows the high requirements for June and July personnel. The part-time help reaches 576 FTE positions (although, in actual numbers, this is approximately 800 different employees). After a low fall and winter staffing level, the demand shown as "full-time direct" reaches 130 in March (when grounds are reseeded and fertilized) and then increases to a high of 325 in July. The present method levels this uneven demand over the year to an average of 116 full-time year-round employees by early scheduling of work. As previously mentioned, no attempt is made to hire and lay off full-time workers to meet this uneven demand.

Exhibit 8.8 shows the cost calculations for all three alternatives and compares the total costs for each alternative. From this analysis, it appears that the department is already using the lowest-cost alternative (Alternative 1).

exhibit 8.8	Three Possible Plans for the Parks and Recreation Department

Alternative 1: Maintain 116 full-time regular direct workers. Schedule work during off-seasons to level workload throughout the year. Continue to use 120 full-time-equivalent (FTE) part-time employees to meet high demand periods.

COSTS	DAYS PER YEAR (EXHIBIT 8.7)	HOURS (EMPLOYEES × DAYS × 8 HOURS)	WAGES (FULL-TIME, $8.90; PART-TIME, $8.06)	FRINGE BENEFITS (FULL-TIME, 17%; PART-TIME, 11%)	ADMINISTRATIVE COST (FULL-TIME, 20%; PART-TIME, 25%)
116 full-time regular employees	252	233,856	$2,081,318	$353,824	$416,264
120 part-time employees	252	241,920	$1,949,875	$214,486	$487,469
Total cost = $5,503,236			$4,031,193	$568,310	$903,733

Alternative 2: Maintain 50 full-time regular direct workers and the present 120 FTE part-time employees. Subcontract jobs releasing 66 full-time regular employees. Subcontract cost, $2,200,000.

COSTS	DAYS PER YEAR (EXHIBIT 8.7)	HOURS (EMPLOYEES × DAYS × 8 HOURS)	WAGES (FULL-TIME, $8.90; PART-TIME, $8.06)	FRINGE BENEFITS (FULL-TIME, 17%; PART-TIME, 11%)	ADMINISTRATIVE COST (FULL-TIME, 20%; PART-TIME, 25%)	SUBCONTRACT COST
50 full-time employees	252	100,800	$897,120	$152,510	$179,424	
120 FTE part-time employees	252	241,920	$1,949,875	$214,486	$487,469	
Subcontracting cost						$2,200,000
Total cost = $6,080,884			$2,846,995	$366,996	$666,893	$2,200,000

Alternative 3: Subcontract all jobs previously performed by 116 full-time regular employees. Subcontract cost $3,200,000. Subcontract all jobs previously performed by 120 FTE part-time employees. Subcontract cost $3,700,000.

COST	SUBCONTRACT COST
0 full-time employees	
0 part-time employees	
Subcontract full-time jobs	$3,200,000
Subcontract part-time jobs	$3,700,000
Total cost	$6,900,000

Excel:
Aggregate
Planning

Yield management
Given limited capacity, the process of allocating it to customers at the right price and time to maximize profit.

YIELD MANAGEMENT

Why is it that the guy sitting next to you on the plane paid half the price you paid for your ticket? Why was a hotel room you booked more expensive when you booked it six months in advance than when you checked in without a reservation (or vice versa)? The answers lie in the practice known as yield management. **Yield management** can be defined as the process of allocating the right type of capacity to the right type of customer at the right price and time to maximize revenue or yield. Yield management can be a powerful approach to making demand more predictable, which is important to aggregate planning.

Yield management has existed as long as there has been limited capacity for serving customers. However, its widespread scientific application began with American Airlines' computerized reservation system (SABRE), introduced in the mid-1980s. The system allowed the airline to change ticket prices on any routes instantaneously as a function of forecast demand. Peoples' Express, a no-frills, low-cost competitor airline, was one of the most famous victims of American's yield management system. Basically, the system enabled hour-by-hour updating on competing routes so that American could match or better prices wherever Peoples' Express was flying. The president of Peoples' Express realized that the game was lost when his mother flew on American to Peoples' hub for a lower price than Peoples' could offer!

MANY HOTEL CHAINS USE PRICELINE TO SELL EXCESS CAPACITY AT A DISCOUNT.

© NetPhotos/Alamy

From an operational perspective, yield management is most effective when

1. Demand can be segmented by customer.
2. Fixed costs are high and variable costs are low.
3. Inventory is perishable.
4. Product can be sold in advance.
5. Demand is highly variable.

LO8–3 Explain yield management and why it is an important strategy.

Hotels illustrate these five characteristics well. They offer one set of rates during the week for the business traveler and another set during the weekend for the vacationer. The variable costs associated with a room (such as cleaning) are low in comparison to the cost of adding rooms to the property. Available rooms cannot be transferred from night to night, and blocks of rooms can be sold to conventions or tours. Finally, potential guests may cut short their stay or not show up at all.

Most organizations (such as airlines, rental car agencies, cruise lines, and hotels) manage yield by establishing decision rules for opening or closing rate classes as a function of expected demand and available supply. The methodologies for doing this can be quite sophisticated. A common approach is to forecast demand over the planning horizon and then use marginal analysis to determine the rates that will be charged if demand is forecast as being above or below set control limits around the forecast mean.

Operating Yield Management Systems

A number of interesting issues arise in managing yield. One is that pricing structures must appear logical to the customer and justify the different prices. Such justification, commonly called *rate fences,* may have either a physical basis (such as a room with a view) or a nonphysical basis (like unrestricted access to the Internet). Pricing also should relate to addressing specific capacity problems. If capacity is sufficient for peak demand, price reductions stimulating off-peak demand should be the focus. If capacity is insufficient, offering deals to customers who arrive during nonpeak periods (or creating alternative service locations) may enhance revenue generation.

A second issue is handling variability in arrival or starting times, duration, and time between customers. This entails employing maximally accurate forecasting methods (the greater the accuracy in forecasting demand, the more likely yield management will succeed); coordinated policies on overbooking, deposits, and no-show or cancellation penalties; and well-designed service processes that are reliable and consistent.

A third issue relates to managing the service process. Some strategies include scheduling additional personnel to meet peak demand; increasing customer self-service; creating adjustable capacity; utilizing idle capacity for complementary services; and cross-training employees to create reserves for peak periods.

The fourth and perhaps most critical issue is training workers and managers to work in an environment where overbooking and price changes are standard occurrences that directly impact the customer. Companies have developed creative ways of mollifying overbooked customers. A golf course company offers $100 putters to players who have been overbooked at a popular tee time. Airlines, of course, frequently give overbooked passengers free tickets for other flights.

CONCEPT CONNECTIONS

LO8–1 Understand what sales and operations planning is and how it coordinates manufacturing, logistics, service, and marketing plans.

- The output of the sales and operation planning process is the aggregate plan.
- The aggregate plan is a high-level operational plan that can be executed by the operations and supply chain functions.
- The process brings together marketing and sales, distribution and logistics, operations, finance, and product development to agree on the best plan to match supply with demand.
- The input into the process is the sales plan developed by marketing.
- Typically, aggregation is done by product families and by groups of customers, and the plan is completed using these aggregate supply and demand quantities.
- Outputs of the plan are planned production rates, aggregate labor requirements, and expected finished good levels.
- Cost minimization is typically a major driver when finding a plan.

Aggregate operations plan   A plan for labor and production for the intermediate term with the objective to minimize the cost of resources needed to meet the demand.

Sales and operations planning   The process that companies use to keep demand and supply in balance by coordinating manufacturing, distribution, marketing, and financial plans.

Long-range planning   One year or more.

Intermediate-range planning   3 to 18 months.

Short-range planning   A day to six months.

Production rate   Number of units completed per unit of time.

Workforce level   Number of workers needed in a period.

Inventory on-hand   Inventory carried from the previous period.

Production planning strategies   Plans for meeting demand that involve trade-offs in the number of workers employed, work hours, inventory, and shortages.

Pure strategy   A simple strategy that uses just one option, such as hiring and firing workers, for meeting demand.

Mixed strategy   A more complex strategy that combines options for meeting demand.

LO8–2 Construct and evaluate aggregate plans that employ different strategies for meeting demand.

- Companies commonly use simple cut-and-try (trial-and-error) techniques for analyzing aggregate planning problems. Sophisticated mathematical programming techniques can also be used.
- Strategies vary greatly depending on the situation faced by the company. Plans are typically evaluated based on cost, but it is important to consider the feasibility of the plan (that overtime is not excessive, for example).

LO8–3 Explain yield management and why it is an important strategy.

- Yield management occurs when a firm adjusts the price of its product or service in order to influence demand. Usually, it is done to make future demand more predictable, which is important to successful sales and operations planning.
- This practice is commonly used in the airline, hotel, casino, and auto retail industries, for example.
- Policies that involve overbooking, requiring deposits, and no-show or cancellation penalties are coordinated with the different pricing scheme.

Yield management   Given limited capacity, the process of allocating it to customers at the right price and time to maximize profit.

SOLVED PROBLEM

LO8–2 Jason Enterprises (JE) produces video telephones for the home market. Quality is not quite as good as it could be at this point, but the selling price is low and Jason can study market response while spending more time on R&D.

At this stage, however, JE needs to develop an aggregate production plan for the six months from January through June. You have been commissioned to create the plan. The following information should help:

Excel:
Aggregate
Planning
Solved
Problem

DEMAND AND WORKING DAYS

	JANUARY	FEBRUARY	MARCH	APRIL	MAY	JUNE	TOTALS
Demand forecast	500	600	650	800	900	800	4,250
Number of working days	22	19	21	21	22	20	125

COSTS

Materials	$100.00/unit
Inventory holding cost	$10.00/unit/month
Marginal cost of stock out	$20.00/unit/month
Marginal cost of subcontracting	$100.00/unit ($200 subcontracting cost less $100 material savings)
Hiring and training cost	$50.00/worker
Layoff cost	$100.00/worker
Labor hours required	4/unit
Straight-time cost (first eight hours each day)	$12.50/hour
Overtime cost (time and a half)	$18.75/hour

INVENTORY

Beginning inventory	200 units
Safety stock required	0% of month demand

What is the cost of each of the following production strategies?

a. Produce exactly to meet demand; vary workforce (assuming opening workforce equal to first month's requirements).

b. Constant workforce; vary inventory and allow shortages only (assuming a workforce of 10).

c. Constant workforce of 10; use subcontracting.

Solution

AGGREGATE PRODUCTION PLANNING REQUIREMENTS

	JANUARY	FEBRUARY	MARCH	APRIL	MAY	JUNE	TOTAL
Beginning inventory	200	0	0	0	0	0	
Demand forecast	500	600	650	800	900	800	
Safety stock (0.0 × Demand forecast)	0	0	0	0	0	0	
Production requirement (Demand forecast + Safety stock − Beginning inventory)	300	600	650	800	900	800	
Ending inventory (Beginning inventory + Production requirement − Demand forecast)	0	0	0	0	0	0	

PRODUCTION PLAN 1: EXACT PRODUCTION; VARY WORKFORCE

	JANUARY	FEBRUARY	MARCH	APRIL	MAY	JUNE	TOTAL
Production requirement	300	600	650	800	900	800	
Production hours required (Production requirement × 4 hr./unit)	1,200	2,400	2,600	3,200	3,600	3,200	
Working days per month	22	19	21	21	22	20	
Hours per month per worker (Working days × 8 hr./day)	176	152	168	168	176	160	
Workers required (Production hours required/Hours per month per worker)	7	16	15	19	20	20	
New workers hired (assuming opening workforce equal to first month's requirement of 7 workers)	0	9	0	4	1	0	
Hiring cost (New workers hired × $50)	$0	$450	$0	$200	$50	$0	$700
Workers laid off	0	0	1	0	0	0	
Layoff cost (Workers laid off × $100)	$0	$0	$100	$0	$0	$0	$100
Straight-time cost (Production hours required × $12.50)	$15,000	$30,000	$32,500	$40,000	$45,000	$40,000	$202,500
						Total Cost	$203,300

PRODUCTION PLAN 2: CONSTANT WORKFORCE; VARY INVENTORY AND STOCK OUT

	JANUARY	FEBRUARY	MARCH	APRIL	MAY	JUNE	TOTAL
Beginning inventory	200	140	−80	−310	−690	−1150	
Working days per month	22	19	21	21	22	20	
Production hours available (Working days per month × 8 hr./day × 10 workers)*	1,760	1,520	1,680	1,680	1,760	1,600	
Actual production (Production hours available/4 hr./unit)	440	380	420	420	440	400	
Demand forecast	500	600	650	800	900	800	
Ending inventory (Beginning inventory + Actual production − Demand forecast)	140	−80	−310	−690	−1,150	−1,550	
Shortage cost (Units short × $20)	$0	$1,600	$6,200	$13,800	$23,000	$31,000	$75,600
Safety stock	0	0	0	0	0	0	
Units excess (Ending inventory − Safety stock; only if positive amount)	140	0	0	0	0	0	
Inventory cost (Units excess × $10)	$1,400	$0	$0	$0	$0	$0	$1,400
Straight-time cost (Production hours available × $12.50)	$22,000	$19,000	$21,000	$21,000	$22,000	$20,000	$125,000
							Total cost $202,000

*Assume a constant workforce of 10.

PRODUCTION PLAN 3: CONSTANT WORKFORCE; SUBCONTRACT

	JANUARY	FEBRUARY	MARCH	APRIL	MAY	JUNE	TOTAL
Production requirement	300	460[†]	650	800	900	800	
Working days per month	22	19	21	21	22	20	
Production hours available (Working days × 8 hr./day × 10 workers)*	1,760	1,520	1,680	1,680	1,760	1,600	
Actual production (Production hours available/4 hr. per unit)	440	380	420	420	440	400	
Units subcontracted (Production requirements − Actual production)	0	80	230	380	460	400	
Subcontracting cost (Units subcontracted × $100)	$0	$8,000	$23,000	$38,000	$46,000	$40,000	$155,000
Straight-time cost (Production hours available × $12.50)	$22,000	$19,000	$21,000	$21,000	$22,000	$20,000	$125,000
							Total cost $280,000

*Assume a constant workforce of 10.
[†]600 − 140 units of beginning inventory in February.

SUMMARY

PLAN DESCRIPTION	HIRING	LAYOFF	SUBCONTRACT	STRAIGHT TIME	SHORTAGE	EXCESS INVEN-TORY	TOTAL COST
1. Exact production; vary workforce	$700	$100		$202,500			$203,300
2. Constant workforce; vary inventory and shortages				$125,000	$75,600	$1,400	$202,000
3. Constant workforce; subcontract			$155,000	$125,000			$280,000

DISCUSSION QUESTIONS

LO8–1
1. What are the basic controllable variables of a production planning problem? What are the four major costs?
2. Distinguish between pure and mixed strategies in production planning.

LO8–2
3. What are the major differences between aggregate planning in manufacturing and aggregate planning in services?
4. How does forecast accuracy relate, in general, to the practical application of the aggregate planning models discussed in the chapter?
5. In what way does the time horizon chosen for an aggregate plan determine whether it is the best plan for the firm?

LO8–3
6. Define yield management. How does it differ from the pure strategies in production planning?
7. How would you apply yield management concepts to a barbershop? A soft drink vending machine?

OBJECTIVE QUESTIONS

LO8–1
1. Major operations and supply planning activities can be grouped into categories based on the relevant time range of the activity. Into what time range category does sales and operations planning fit?
2. What category of planning covers a period from a day to six months, with daily or weekly time increments?
3. In the agriculture industry, migrant workers are commonly employed to pick crops ready for harvest. They are hired as needed and are laid off once the crops are picked. The realities of the industry make this approach necessary. Which production planning strategy best describes this approach?
4. What is the term for a more complex production strategy that combines approaches from more than one basic strategy?
5. List at least three of the four costs relevant to the aggregate production plan.
6. Which of the four costs relevant to aggregate production planning is the most difficult to accurately measure?

LO8–2

7. Develop a production plan and calculate the annual cost for a firm whose demand forecast is: fall, 10,000; winter, 8,000; spring, 7,000; summer, 12,000. Inventory at the beginning of fall is 500 units. At the beginning of fall you currently have 30 workers, but you plan to hire temporary workers at the beginning of summer and lay them off at the end of summer. In addition, you have negotiated with the union an option to use the regular workforce on overtime during winter or spring if overtime is necessary to prevent stock-outs at the end of those quarters. Overtime is *not* available during the fall. Relevant costs are hiring, $100 for each temp; layoff, $200 for each worker laid off; inventory holding, $5 per unit-quarter; backorder, $10 per unit; straight time, $5 per hour; overtime, $8 per hour. Assume that the worker productivity is 0.5 unit per worker hour, with eight hours per day and 60 days per season.

8. Plan production for a four-month period: February through May. For February and March, you should produce to exact demand forecast. For April and May, you should use overtime and inventory with a stable workforce; *stable* means that the number of workers needed for March will be held constant through May. However, government constraints put a maximum of 5,000 hours of overtime labor per month in April and May (zero overtime in February and March). If demand exceeds supply, then backorders occur. There are 100 workers on January 31. You are given the following demand forecast: February, 80,000; March, 64,000; April, 100,000; May, 40,000. Productivity is four units per worker hour, eight hours per day, 20 days per month. Assume zero inventory on February 1. Costs are: hiring, $50 per new worker; layoff, $70 per worker laid off; inventory holding, $10 per unit-month; straight-time labor, $10 per hour; overtime, $15 per hour; backorder, $20 per unit. Find the total cost of this plan.

9. Plan production for the next year. The demand forecast is: spring, 20,000; summer, 10,000; fall, 15,000; winter, 18,000. At the beginning of spring, you have 70 workers and 1,000 units in inventory. The union contract specifies that you may lay off workers only once a year, at the beginning of summer. Also, you may hire new workers only at the end of summer to begin regular work in the fall. The number of workers laid off at the beginning of summer and the number hired at the end of summer should result in planned production levels for summer and fall that equal the demand forecasts for summer and fall, respectively. If demand exceeds supply, use overtime in spring only, which means that backorders could occur in winter. You are given these costs: hiring, $100 per new worker; layoff, $200 per worker laid off; holding, $20 per unit-quarter; backorder cost, $8 per unit; straight-time labor, $10 per hour; overtime, $15 per hour. Productivity is 0.5 unit per worker hour, eight hours per day, 50 days per quarter. Find the total cost.

10. DAT, Inc., needs to develop an aggregate plan for its product line. Relevant data are

Production time	1 hour per unit	Beginning inventory	500 units
Average labor cost	$10 per hour	Safety stock	One-half month
Workweek	5 days, 8 hours each day	Shortage cost	$20 per unit per month
Days per month	Assume 20 workdays per month	Carrying cost	$5 per unit per month

The forecast for next year is

JAN.	FEB.	MAR.	APR.	MAY	JUNE	JULY	AUG.	SEPT.	OCT.	NOV.	DEC.
2,500	3,000	4,000	3,500	3,500	3,000	3,000	4,000	4,000	4,000	3,000	3,000

Management prefers to keep a constant workforce and production level, absorbing variations in demand through inventory excesses and shortages. Demand not met is carried over to the following month.

Develop an aggregate plan that will meet the demand and other conditions of the problem. Do not try to find the optimum; just find a good solution and state the procedure you might use to test for a better solution. Make any necessary assumptions.

11. Old Pueblo Engineering Contractors creates six-month "rolling" schedules, which are recomputed monthly. For competitive reasons (it would need to divulge proprietary design criteria, methods, and so on), Old Pueblo does not subcontract. Therefore, its only options to meet customer requirements are (1) work on regular time; (2) work on overtime, which is limited to 30 percent of regular time; (3) do customers' work early, which would cost an additional $5 per hour per month; and (4) perform customers' work late, which would cost an additional $10 per hour per month penalty, as provided by their contract.

Old Pueblo has 25 engineers on its staff at an hourly rate of $30. The overtime rate is $45. Customers' hourly requirements for the six months from January to June are

JANUARY	FEBRUARY	MARCH	APRIL	MAY	JUNE
5,000	4,000	6,000	6,000	5,000	4,000

Develop an aggregate plan using a spreadsheet. Assume 20 working days in each month.

12. Alan Industries is expanding its product line to include three new products: A, B, and C. These are to be produced on the same production equipment, and the objective is to meet the demands for the three products using overtime where necessary. The demand forecast for the next four months, in hours required to make each product, is

PRODUCT	APRIL	MAY	JUNE	JULY
A	800	600	800	1,200
B	600	700	900	1,100
C	700	500	700	850

Because the products deteriorate rapidly, there is a high loss in quality and, consequently, a high carrying cost when a product is made and carried in inventory to meet future demand. Each hour's production carried into future months costs $3 per production hour for A, $4 for Model B, and $5 for Model C.

Production can take place either during regular working hours or during overtime. Regular time is paid at $4 when working on A, $5 for B, and $6 for C. The overtime premium is 50 percent of the regular time cost per hour.

The number of production hours available for regular time and overtime is

	APRIL	MAY	JUNE	JULY
Regular time	1,500	1,300	1,800	2,000
Overtime	700	650	900	1,000

Set up the problem in a spreadsheet and an optimal solution using the Excel Solver. Appendix A describes how to use the Excel Solver.

13. Shoney Video Concepts produces a line of video streaming servers that are linked to computers for storing movies. These devices have very fast access and large storage capacity.

Shoney is trying to determine a production plan for the next 12 months. The main criterion for this plan is that the employment level is to be held constant over the period. Shoney is continuing in its R&D efforts to develop new applications and prefers not to prompt any adverse feelings from the local workforce. For the same reason, all employees should put in full workweeks, even if that is not the lowest-cost alternative. The demand forecast for servers for the next 12 months is

Month	Forecast Demand	Month	Forecast Demand
January	600	July	200
February	800	August	200
March	900	September	300
April	600	October	700
May	400	November	800
June	300	December	900

Manufacturing cost is $200 per server, equally divided between materials and labor. Inventory storage cost is $5 per month. A shortage of servers results in lost sales and is estimated to cost an overall $20 per unit short.

The inventory on-hand at the beginning of the planning period is 200 units. Ten labor hours are required per DVD player. The workday is eight hours.

Develop an aggregate production schedule for the year using a constant workforce. For simplicity, assume 22 working days each month except July, when the plant closes down for three weeks' vacation (leaving seven working days). Assume that total production capacity is greater than or equal to total demand.

14. Develop a production schedule to produce the exact production requirements by varying the workforce size for the following problem. Use the example in the chapter as a guide (Plan 1).

The monthly forecasts for Product X for January, February, and March are 1,000, 1,500, and 1,200, respectively. Safety stock policy recommends that half of the forecast for that month be defined as safety stock. There are 22 working days in January, 19 in February, and 21 in March. Beginning inventory is 500 units.

Manufacturing cost is $200 per unit, storage cost is $3 per unit per month, standard pay rate is $6 per hour, overtime rate is $9 per hour, cost of stock out is $10 per unit per month, marginal cost of subcontracting is $10 per unit, hiring and training cost is $200 per worker, layoff cost is $300 per worker, and worker productivity is 0.1 unit per hour. Assume that you start off with 50 workers and that they work 8 hours per day.

15. Helter Industries, a company that produces a line of women's bathing suits, hires temporaries to help produce its summer product demand. For the current four-month rolling schedule, there are three temps on staff and 12 full-time employees. The temps can be hired when needed and can be used as needed, whereas the full-time employees must be paid whether they are needed or not. Each full-time employee can produce 205 suits, while each part-time employee can produce 165 suits per month.

Demand for bathing suits for the next four months is as follows:

May	June	July	August
3,200	2,800	3,100	3,000

Beginning inventory in May is 403 bathing suits. Bathing suits cost $40 to produce and carrying cost is 24 percent per year.

Develop an aggregate plan that uses the 12 full-time employees each month and a minimum number of temporary employees. Assume that all employees will produce at their full potential each month. Calculate the inventory carrying cost associated with your plan using planned end-of-month levels.

LO8–3

16. The widespread scientific application of yield management began within what industry?
17. Under what type of demand is yield management most effective?
18. In a yield managment system, pricing differences must appear logical and justified to the customer. What is the basis for this justification commonly called?
19. The essence of yield management is the ability to manage what?

ANALYTICS EXERCISE: DEVELOPING AN AGGREGATE PLAN—BRADFORD MANUFACTURING

The Situation

You are the operations manager for a manufacturing plant that produces pudding food products. One of your important responsibilities is to prepare an aggregate plan for the plant. This plan is an important input into the annual budget process. The plan provides information on production rates, manufacturing labor requirements, and projected finished goods inventory levels for the next year.

You make those little boxes of pudding mix on packaging lines in your plant. A packaging line has a number of machines that are linked by conveyors. At the start of the line, the pudding is mixed; it is then placed in small packets. These packets are inserted into the small pudding boxes, which are collected and placed in cases that hold 48 boxes of pudding. Finally, 160 cases are collected and put on a pallet. The pallets are staged in a shipping area from which they are sent to four distribution centers. Over the years, the technology of the packaging lines has improved so that all the different flavors can be made in relatively small batches with no setup time to switch between flavors. The plant has 15 of these lines, but currently only 10 are being used. Six employees are required to run each line.

The demand for this product fluctuates from month to month. In addition, there is a seasonal component, with peak sales before Thanksgiving, Christmas, and Easter each year. To complicate matters, at the end of the first quarter of each year the marketing group runs a promotion in which special deals are made for large purchases. Business is going well, and the company has been experiencing a general increase in sales.

The plant sends product to four large distribution warehouses strategically located in the United States. Trucks move product daily. The amounts shipped are based on maintaining target inventory levels at the warehouses. These targets are calculated based on anticipated weeks of supply at each warehouse. Current targets are set at two weeks of supply.

In the past, the company has had a policy of producing very close to what it expects sales to be because of limited capacity for storing finished goods. Production capacity has been adequate to support this policy.

A sales forecast for next year has been prepared by the marketing department. The forecast is based on quarterly sales quotas, which are used to set up an incentive program for the salespeople. Sales are mainly to the large U.S. retail grocers.

The pudding is shipped to the grocers from the distribution warehouses based on orders taken by the salespeople.

Your immediate task is to prepare an aggregate plan for the coming year. The technical and economic factors that must be considered in this plan are shown next.

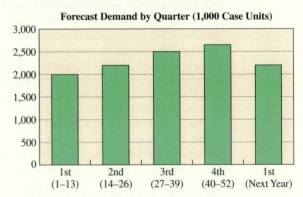

Forecast Demand by Quarter (1,000 Case Units)

Technical and Economic Information

1. The plant runs 5 days each week, and currently is running 10 lines with no overtime. Each line requires six people to run. For planning purposes, the lines are run for 7.5 hours each normal shift. Employees, though, are paid for eight hours' work. It is possible to run up to two hours of overtime each day, but it must be scheduled for a week at a time, and all the lines must run overtime when it is scheduled. Workers are paid $20.00/hour during a regular shift and $30.00/hour on overtime. The standard production rate for each line is 450 cases/hour.

2. The marketing forecast for demand is as follows: Q1—2,000; Q2—2,200; Q3—2,500; Q4—2,650; and Q1 (next year)—2,200. These numbers are in 1,000-case units. Each number represents a 13-week forecast.

3. Management has instructed manufacturing to maintain a two-week safety stock supply of pudding inventory in the warehouses. The two-week supply should be based on future expected sales. The following are ending inventory target levels to comply with the safety stock requirement for each quarter: Q1—338; Q2—385; Q3—408; Q4—338.

4. Inventory carrying cost is estimated by accounting to be $1.00 per case per year. This means that if a case of pudding is held in inventory for an entire year, the cost to just carry that case in inventory is $1.00. If a case is carried for only one week, the cost is $1.00/52, or $0.01923. The cost is proportional to the time carried in inventory. There are 200,000 cases in inventory at the beginning of Q1 (this is 200 cases in the 1,000-case units that the forecast is given in).

5. If a stock out occurs, the item is backordered and shipped at a later date. The cost when a backorder occurs is $2.40 per case due to the loss of goodwill and the high cost of emergency shipping.

6. The human resource group estimates that it costs $5,000 to hire and train a new production employee. It costs $3,000 to lay off a production worker.

7. Make the following assumptions in your cost calculations:
   • Inventory costs are based on inventory in excess of the safety stock requirement.
   • Backorder costs are incurred on the negative deviation from the planned safety stock requirement, even though planned inventory may be positive.
   • Overtime must be used over an entire quarter and should be based on hours per day over that time.

Questions

1. Prepare an aggregate plan for the coming year, assuming that the sales forecast is perfect. Use the spreadsheet "Bradford Manufacturing." In the spreadsheet, an area has been designated for your aggregate plan solution. Supply the number of packaging lines to run and the number of overtime hours for each quarter. You will need to set up the cost calculations in the spreadsheet.

   You may want to try using the Excel Solver to find a lowcost solution. Remember that your final solution needs an integer number of lines and an integer number of overtime hours for each quarter. (Solutions that require 8.9134 lines and 1.256 hours of overtime are not feasible.)

   It is important that your spreadsheet calculations are set up so that any values in the number of lines and overtime hours rows evaluates correctly. Your spreadsheet will be evaluated based on this.

2. Find a solution to the problem that goes beyond just minimizing cost. Prepare a short write-up that describes the process you went through to find your solution and that justifies why you think it is a good solution.

PRACTICE EXAM

1. Term used to refer to the process a firm uses to balance supply and demand.

2. When doing aggregate planning, these are the three general operations–related variables that can be adjusted.

3. A strategy where the production rate is set to match expected demand.

4. When overtime is used to meet demand and avoid the costs associated with hiring and firing.

5. A strategy that uses inventory and backorders as part of the strategy to meet demand.

6. Sometimes a firm may choose to have all or part of the work done by an outside vendor. This is the term used for the approach.

7. If expected demand during the next four quarters is 150, 125, 100, and 75 thousand units, and each worker can produce 1,000 units per quarter, how many workers should be used if a level strategy is being employed?

8. Given the data from question 7, how many workers would be needed for a chase strategy?

9. In a service setting, what general operations–related variable is not available compared to a production setting?

10. The practice of allocating capacity and manipulating demand to make it more predictable.

CHAPTER 9

MATERIAL REQUIREMENTS PLANNING

Learning Objectives

LO9–1 Explain what material requirements planning (MRP) is.

LO9–2 Understand how the MRP system is structured.

LO9–3 Analyze an MRP problem.

LO9–4 Evaluate and compare MRP lot-sizing techniques.

INSIDE THE IPAD

So what does it cost for Apple Computer to build an iPad?

A good estimate can be made by taking one apart and evaluating the cost of each component. There are many analysts who look at this each time a new model iPad is introduced. Looking at many of these reports, an estimate of the major costs for a iPad 3 with 64GB of memory is the following:

Memory $80

Touchscreen and display $130

Processor $23

Cameras $12

Wi-Fi and sensors $15

Battery and power management $42

Other items $50

Box and charger $6

Manufacturing cost $10

So, for a total cost of about $368 Apple can build an iPad that it sells for about $700. Of course, this does not include the cost to transport the iPad and other support costs, but a profit of $332 is not bad.

© McGraw-Hill Education/Mark Dierker, photographer

UNDERSTANDING MATERIAL REQUIREMENTS PLANNING

Enterprise resource planning (ERP) is a computer system that integrates application programs in accounting, sales, manufacturing, and the other functions in a firm. This integration is accomplished through a database shared by all the application programs. Current ERP vendors have set new standards in information integration that can significantly benefit a company. When implemented correctly, ERP links all areas of the business. Manufacturing knows about new orders as soon as they are entered into the system. Sales knows the exact status of a customer order. Purchasing knows what manufacturing needs to the minute, and the accounting system is updated as all relevant transactions occur. The potential benefits of ERP are huge.

The operations and supply functions in an ERP system include many applications. In Exhibit 9.1, we see a diagram that depicts typical operations and supply chain functions.

- In sales and distribution (SD), products or services are sold to customers. All the details of shipping to the customer and invoices are handled in these modules.

Enterprise resource planning (ERP)
A computer system that integrates application programs in accounting, sales, manufacturing, and the other functions in a firm.

exhibit 9.1   Operations and Supply Integration Overview

exhibit 9.1   Operations and Supply Integration Overview

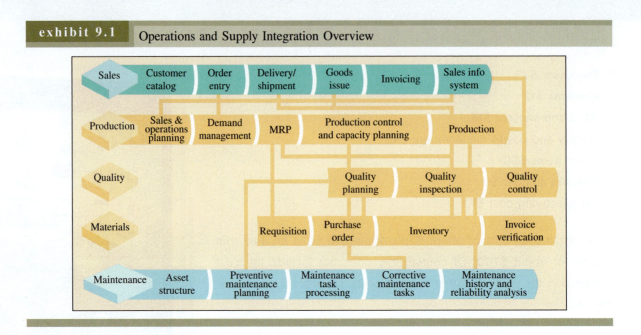

- Production planning (PP) supports both discrete and process manufacturing processes and includes the material requirements planning (MRP) application, which is the topic of this chapter.
- Quality management (QM) plans and implements procedures for inspection and quality assurance. It is integrated with the procurement and production processes so that the user can identify inspection points both for incoming materials and for products during the manufacturing process.
- Material management (MM) covers all tasks within the supply chain, including purchasing, vendor evaluation, invoice verification, and material use planning. It also includes inventory and warehouse management.
- Plant maintenance (PM) supports the activities associated with planning and performing repairs and preventive maintenance. Completion and cost reports are available and maintenance activities can be managed and measured.

LO9–1 Explain what material requirements planning (MRP) is.

Material requirements planning (MRP) The logic for determining the number of parts, components, and materials needed to produce a product.

Our emphasis here is on **material requirements planning (MRP)**, which is the key piece of logic that ties the production functions together from a material planning and control view. MRP has been installed almost universally in manufacturing firms, even those considered small companies. The reason is that MRP is a logical, easily understandable approach to the problem of determining the number of parts, components, and materials needed to produce each end item. MRP also provides the schedule specifying when each of these items should be ordered or produced.

MRP is based on dependent demand. Dependent demand is caused by the demand for a higher-level item. Tires, wheels, and engines are dependent demand items based on the demand for automobiles, for example.

Determining the number of dependent demand items needed is essentially a straightforward multiplication process. If one part A takes five parts of B to make it, then five parts of A require 25 parts of B. The basic difference in independent demand covered in Chapter 11 and dependent demand covered in this chapter is as follows: If part A is

WHEELS ARE DEPENDENT DEMAND ITEMS BASED ON THE ASSEMBLY LINE PRODUCTION RATE.

© Xu Xiaolin/Encyclopedia/Corbis

sold outside the firm, the amount of part A that we sell is uncertain. We need to create a forecast using past data or do something like a market analysis. Part A is an independent item. However, part B is a dependent part and its use depends on part A. The number of B needed is simply the number of A times five. As a result of this type of multiplication, the requirements of other dependent demand items tend to become more and more lumpy as we go further down into the product creation sequence. Lumpiness means that the requirements tend to bunch or lump rather than having an even dispersal. This is also caused by the way manufacturing is done. When manufacturing occurs in lots (or batches), items needed to produce the lot are withdrawn from inventory in quantities (perhaps all at once) rather than one at a time.

Where MRP Can Be Used

MRP is most valuable in industries where a number of products are made in batches using the same productive equipment. The list in Exhibit 9.2 includes examples of different industry types and the expected benefit from MRP. As you can see in the exhibit, MRP is most valuable to companies involved in assembly operations and least valuable to those in fabrication. One more point to note: MRP does not work well in companies that produce a low number of units annually. Especially for companies producing complex, expensive products requiring advanced research and design, experience has shown that lead times tend to be too long and too uncertain, and the product configuration too complex. Such companies need the control features that network scheduling techniques offer. These project management methods are covered in Chapter 5.

Master Production Scheduling

Generally, the **master production schedule (MPS)** deals with end items (typically finished goods items sold to customers) and is a major input to the MRP process. If the end item is quite large or expensive, however, the master schedule may schedule major subassemblies or components instead.

All production systems have limited capacity and limited resources. This presents a challenging job for the master scheduler. Although the aggregate plan provides the

Master production schedule (MPS)
A time-phased plan specifying how many end items the firm plans to build, and when.

exhibit 9.2	**Industry Applications and Expected Benefits of MRP**	

INDUSTRY TYPE	EXAMPLES	EXPECTED BENEFITS
Assemble-to-stock	Combines multiple component parts into a finished product, which is then stocked in inventory to satisfy customer demand. Examples: watches, tools, appliances.	High
Make-to-stock	Items are manufactured from purchased materials rather than assembled from parts. These are standard stock items carried in anticipation of customer demand. Examples: piston rings, electrical switches.	Low
Assemble-to-order	A final assembly is made from standard options that the customer chooses. Examples: trucks, generators, motors.	High
Make-to-order	Items are manufactured from purchased materials to customer order. These are generally industrial orders. Examples: bearings, gears, fasteners.	Low
Engineer-to-order	Items are fabricated or assembled completely to customer specification. Examples: turbine generators, heavy machine tools.	High
Process	Includes industries such as foundries, rubber and plastics, specialty paper, chemicals, paint, drug, food processors.	Medium

general range of production each week by product group, the master scheduler must specify exactly what is to be produced for each individual item within the group. These decisions are made while responding to pressures from various functional areas such as the sales department (meet the customer's promised due date), finance (minimize inventory), management (maximize productivity and customer service, minimize resource needs), and manufacturing (have level schedules and minimize setup time).

To determine an acceptable, feasible schedule to be released to the shop, trial master production schedules are run through the MRP program, which is described in the next section. The resulting planned order releases (the detailed production schedules) are checked to make sure that resources are available and that the completion times are reasonable. What appears to be a feasible master schedule may turn out to require excessive resources once the required materials, parts, and components from lower levels are determined. If this does happen (the usual case), the master production schedule is then modified with these limitations and the MRP program is run again. To ensure good master scheduling, the master scheduler (the human being) must

- Include all demands from product sales, warehouse replenishment, spares, and interplant requirements.
- Never lose sight of the aggregate plan.
- Be involved with customer order promising.
- Be visible to all levels of management.
- Objectively trade off manufacturing, marketing, and engineering conflicts.
- Identify and communicate all problems.

The upper portion of Exhibit 9.3 shows an aggregate plan for the total number of mattresses planned per month, without regard for mattress type. The lower portion shows a master production schedule specifying the exact type of mattress and the quantity planned for production by week. In month 1, for example, a total of 900 mattresses are scheduled: 600 Model 327s, 200 Model 538s, and 100 Model 749s. The next level down (not shown) would be the MRP program that develops detailed schedules showing when cotton batting, springs, and hardwood are needed to make the mattresses.

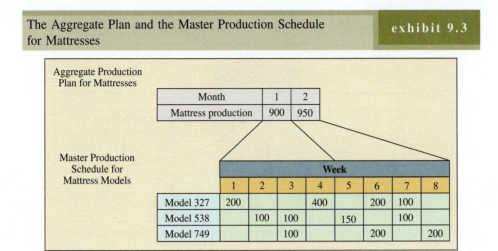

The Aggregate Plan and the Master Production Schedule for Mattresses — exhibit 9.3

To again summarize the planning sequence, the aggregate operations plan, discussed in Chapter 8, specifies product groups. It does not specify exact items. The next level down in the planning process is the master production schedule (MPS). The MPS is the time-phased plan specifying how many end items the firm plans to build, and when. For example, the aggregate plan for a furniture company may specify the total volume of mattresses it plans to produce over the next month or next quarter. The MPS goes the next step down and identifies the exact size mattresses and their qualities and styles. All of the mattresses sold by the company would be specified by the MPS. The MPS also states period by period (usually weekly) how many of these mattress types are needed, and when.

Still further down the disaggregation process is the MRP program, which calculates and schedules all raw materials, parts, and supplies needed to make the mattress specified by the MPS.

Time Fences

The question of flexibility within a master production schedule depends on several factors: production lead time, commitment of parts and components to a specific end item, the relationship between the customer and vendor, the amount of excess capacity, and the reluctance or willingness of management to make changes.

The purpose of time fences is to maintain a reasonably controlled flow through the production system. Unless some operating rules are established and adhered to, the system could be chaotic and filled with overdue orders and constant expediting.

Exhibit 9.4 shows an example of a master production schedule time fence. Management defines *time fences* as periods of time having some specified level of opportunity for the customer to make changes. (The customer may be the firm's own marketing department, which may be considering product promotions, broadening variety, or the like.) Note in the exhibit that, for the next eight weeks, this particular master schedule is frozen. Each firm has its own time fences and operating rules. Under these rules, *frozen* could be defined as anything from absolutely no changes in one company to only the most minor of changes in another. *Slushy* may allow changes in specific products within a product group so long as parts are available. *Liquid* may allow almost any

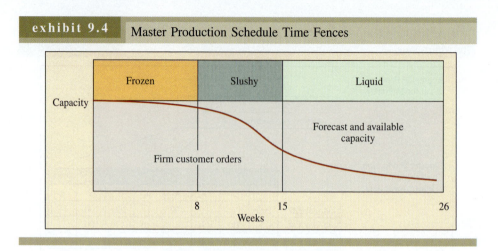

exhibit 9.4 Master Production Schedule Time Fences

variations in products, with the provisions that capacity remains about the same and that there are no long lead time items involved.

Available to promise
A feature of MRP systems that identifies the difference between the number of units currently included in the master schedule and the actual (firm) customer orders.

Some firms use a feature known as **available to promise** for items that are master scheduled. This feature identifies the difference between the number of units currently included in the master schedule and firm customer orders. For example, assume the master schedule indicates that 100 units of Model 538 mattress are going to be made during week seven. If firm customer orders now only indicate that 65 of those mattresses have actually been sold, the sales group has another 35 mattresses "available to promise" for delivery during that week. This can be a powerful tool for coordinating sales and production activities.

MATERIAL REQUIREMENTS PLANNING SYSTEM STRUCTURE

LO9–2 Understand how the MRP system is structured.

The material requirements planning portion of manufacturing activities most closely interacts with the master schedule, bill-of-materials file, inventory records file, and output reports as shown in Exhibit 9.5.

Each facet of Exhibit 9.5 is detailed in the following sections, but essentially the MRP system works as follows: the master production schedule states the number of items to be produced during specific time periods. A *bill-of-materials* file identifies the specific materials used to make each item and the correct quantities of each. The inventory records file contains data such as the number of units on-hand and on-order. These three sources—master production schedule, bill-of-materials file, and inventory records file—become the data sources for the material requirements program, which expands the production schedule into a detailed order scheduling plan for the entire production sequence.

Demand for Products

Product demand for end items comes primarily from two main sources. The first is known customers who have placed specific orders, such as those generated by sales personnel, or from interdepartment transactions. These orders usually carry promised

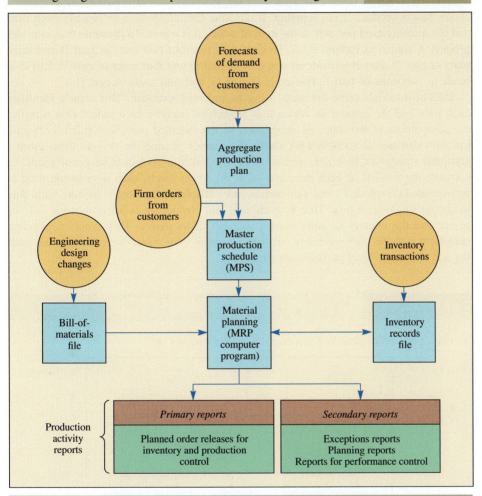

Overall View of the Inputs to a Standard Material Requirements Planning Program and the Reports Generated by the Program   exhibit 9.5

delivery dates. There is no forecasting involved in these orders—simply add them up. The second source is the aggregate production plan (described in Chapter 8). The aggregate plan reflects the firm's strategy for meeting demand in the future. The strategy is implemented through the detailed master production schedule.

In addition to the demand for end products, customers also order specific parts and components either as spares or for service and repair. These demands are not usually part of the master production schedule; instead, they are fed directly into the material requirements planning program at the appropriate levels. That is, they are added in as a gross requirement for that part or component.

Bill-of-Materials

The **bill-of-materials (BOM)** file contains the complete product description, listing not only the materials, parts, and components but also the sequence in which the product is

Bill-of-materials (BOM)

The complete product description, listing the materials, parts, and components, and also the sequence in which the product is created.

created. This BOM file is one of the three main inputs to the MRP program. (The other two are the master schedule and the inventory records file.)

The BOM file is often called the *product structure file* or *product tree* because it shows how a product is put together. It contains the information to identify each item and the quantity used per unit of the item of which it is a part. To illustrate this, consider product A shown in Exhibit 9.6A. Product A is made of two units of part B and three units of part C. Part B is made of one unit of part D and four units of part E. Part C is made of two units of part F, five units of part G, and four units of part H.

Bills-of-materials often list parts using an indented structure. This clearly identifies each item and the manner in which it is assembled because each indentation signifies the components of the item. A comparison of the indented parts in Exhibit 9.6B with the item structure in Exhibit 9.6A shows the ease of relating the two displays. From a computer standpoint, however, storing items in indented parts lists is very inefficient. To compute the amount of each item needed at the lower levels, each item would need to be expanded ("exploded") and summed. A more efficient procedure is to store parts data in simple single-level lists. That is, each item and component is listed showing only its parent and the number of units needed per unit of its parent. This avoids duplication because it includes each assembly only once. Exhibit 9.6B shows both the indented parts list and the single-level parts list for Product A.

exhibit 9.6

A. Bill-of-Materials (Product Structure Tree) for Product A

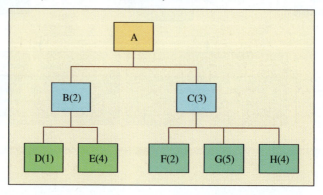

B. Parts List in an Indented Format and in a Single-Level List

INDENTED PARTS LIST			SINGLE-LEVEL PARTS LIST		
A			A		
	B(2)				B(2)
					C(3)
		D(1)	B		
		E(4)			D(1)
	C(3)				E(4)
		F(2)	C		
		G(5)			F(2)
		H(4)			G(5)
					H(4)

Product L Hierarchy in (A) Expanded to the Lowest Level of Each Item in (B)   exhibit 9.7

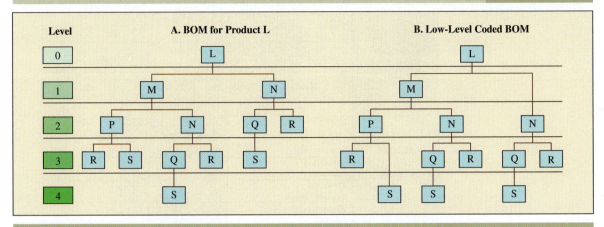

A *modular* bill-of-materials is the term for a buildable item that can be produced and stocked as a subassembly. It is also a standard item with no options within the module. Many end items that are large and expensive are better scheduled and controlled as modules (or subassemblies). It is particularly advantageous to schedule subassembly modules when the same subassemblies appear in different end items. For example, a manufacturer of cranes can combine booms, transmissions, and engines in a variety of ways to meet a customer's needs. Using a modular bill-of-materials simplifies the scheduling and control and also makes it easier to forecast the use of different modules. Another benefit in using modular bills is that if the same item is used in a number of products, then the total inventory investment can be minimized.

A *super* bill-of-materials includes items with fractional options. (A super bill can specify, for example, 0.3 of a part. What that means is that 30 percent of the units produced contain that part and 70 percent do not.) Modular and super bills-of-materials are often referred to as planning bills-of-materials since they simplify the planning process.

Low-Level Coding If all identical parts occur at the same level for each end product, the total number of parts and materials needed for a product can be computed easily. Consider product L shown in Exhibit 9.7A. Notice that item N, for example, occurs both as an input to L and as an input to M. Item N, therefore, needs to be lowered to level 2 (Exhibit 9.7B) to bring all Ns to the same level. If all identical items are placed at the same level, it becomes a simple matter for the computer to scan across each level and summarize the number of units of each item required.

Inventory Records

The inventory records file can be quite lengthy. Exhibit 9.8 shows the variety of information contained in the inventory records. The MRP program accesses the *status* segment of the record according to specific time periods (called *time buckets* in MRP slang). These records are accessed as needed during the program run.

As we will see, the MRP program performs its analysis from the top of the product structure downward, calculating requirements level by level. There are times, however,

exhibit 9.8 | The Inventory Status Record for an Item in Inventory

Item master data segment	Part no.		Description		Lead time		Std. cost	Safety stock
	Order quantity		Setup	Cycle		Last year's usage		Class
	Scrap allowance		Cutting data		Pointers		Etc.	

Inventory status segment		Allocated		Control balance	Period								Totals
					1	2	3	4	5	6	7	8	
	Gross requirements												
	Scheduled receipts												
	Projected available balance												
	Planned order releases												

SUBSIDIARY DATA	Order details	
	Pending action	
	Counters	
	Keeping track	

when it is desirable to identify the parent item that caused the material requirement. For example, we may want to know what subassemblies are generating the requirement for a part that we order from a supplier. The MRP program allows the creation of a *peg record* file either separately or as part of the inventory record file. Pegging requirements allows us to retrace a material requirement upward in the product structure through each level, identifying each parent item that created the demand.

Inventory Transactions File　The inventory status file is kept up to date by posting inventory transactions as they occur. These changes occur because of stock receipts and disbursements, scrap losses, wrong parts, canceled orders, and so forth.

The MRP Computer Program

The material requirements planning program operates using information from the inventory records, the master schedule, and the bill-of-materials. The process of calculating the exact requirements for each item managed by the system is often referred to as the "explosion" process. Working from the top level downward in the bill-of-materials, requirements from parent items are used to calculate the requirements for component items. Consideration is taken of current on-hand balances and orders that are scheduled for receipt in the future.

The following is a general description of the MRP explosion process:

1. The requirements for level 0 items, typically referred to as "end items," are retrieved from the master schedule. These requirements are referred to as "gross requirements" by the MRP program. Typically, the gross requirements are scheduled in weekly time buckets.

2. Next, the program uses the current on-hand balance together with the schedule of orders that will be received in the future to calculate the "net requirements." Net requirements are the amounts that are needed week by week in the future over and above what is currently on-hand or committed to through an order already released and scheduled.

3. Using net requirements, the program calculates when orders should be received to meet these requirements. This can be a simple process of just scheduling orders to arrive according to the exact net requirements or a more complicated process where requirements are combined for multiple periods. This schedule of when orders should arrive is referred to as "planned-order receipts."

4. Since there is typically a lead time associated with each order, the next step is to find a schedule for when orders are actually released. Offsetting the "planned-order receipts" by the required lead time does this. This schedule is referred to as the "planned-order release."

5. After these four steps have been completed for all the level zero items, the program moves to level 1 items.

6. The gross requirements for each level 1 item are calculated from the planned-order release schedule for the parents of each level 1 item. Any additional independent demand also needs to be included in the gross requirements.

7. After the gross requirements have been determined, net requirements, planned-order receipts, and planned-order releases are calculated as described in steps 2–4 above.

8. This process is then repeated for each level in the bill-of-materials.

The process of doing these calculations is much simpler than the description, as you will see in the example that follows. Typically, the explosion calculations are performed each week or whenever changes have been made to the master schedule. Some MRP programs have the option of generating immediate schedules, called *net change* schedules. **Net change systems** are "activity" driven and requirements and schedules are updated whenever a transaction is processed that has an impact on the item. Net change enables the system to reflect in "real time" the exact status of each item managed by the system.

Net change systems An MRP system that calculates the impact of a change in the MRP data (the inventory status, BOM, or master schedule) immediately.

AN EXAMPLE USING MRP

Ampere, Inc., produces a line of electric meters installed in residential buildings by electric utility companies to measure power consumption. Meters used on single-family homes are of two basic types for different voltage and amperage ranges. In addition to complete meters, some subassemblies are sold separately for repair or for change-overs to a different voltage or power load. The problem for the MRP system is to determine a production schedule to identify each item, the period it is needed, and the appropriate quantities. The schedule is then checked for feasibility, and the schedule is modified if necessary.

LO9–3 Analyze an MRP problem.

Forecasting Demand

Demand for the meters and components originates from two sources: regular customers that place firm orders in advance based on the needs of their projects; and other, typically smaller, customers that buy these items as needed. The smaller customer requirements were forecast using one of the usual techniques described in Chapter 3 and past demand

exhibit 9.9	Future Requirements for Meters A and B and Subassembly D Stemming from Specific Customer Orders and from Forecasts

	METER A		METER B		SUBASSEMBLY D	
MONTH	KNOWN	FORECAST	KNOWN	FORECAST	KNOWN	FORECAST
3	1,000	250	410	60	200	70
4	600	250	300	60	180	70
5	300	250	500	60	250	70

exhibit 9.10	A Master Schedule to Satisfy Demand Requirements as Specified in Exhibit 9.9

	Week								
	9	10	11	12	13	14	15	16	17
Meter A	1,250				850				550
Meter B	470				360				560
Subassembly D	270				250				320

data. Exhibit 9.9 shows the requirements for meters A and B and subassembly D for a three-month period (months three through five). There are some "other parts" used to make the meters. In order to keep our example manageable, we are not including them in this example.

Developing a Master Production Schedule

For the meter and component requirements specified in Exhibit 9.9, assume that the quantities to satisfy the known and random demands must be available during the first week of the month. This assumption is reasonable because management (in our example) prefers to produce meters in a single batch each month rather than a number of batches throughout the month.

Exhibit 9.10 shows the trial master schedule that we use under these conditions, with demand for months 3, 4, and 5 listed in the first week of each month, or as weeks 9, 13, and 17. For brevity, we will work with demand through week 9. The schedule we develop should be examined for resource availability, capacity availability, and so on, and then revised and run again. We will stop with our example at the end of this one schedule, however.

Bill-of-Materials (Product Structure)

The product structure for meters A and B is shown in Exhibit 9.11A in the typical way using low-level coding, in which each item is placed at the lowest level at which it appears in the structure hierarchy. Meters A and B consist of a common subassembly C and some parts that include part D. To keep things simple, we will focus on only one of the parts, part D, which is a transformer.

exhibit 9.11

A. Product Structure for Meters A and B

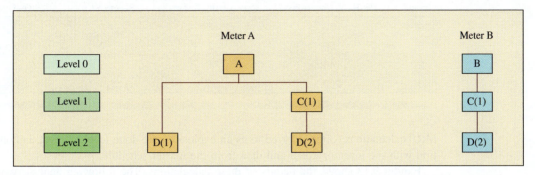

B. Indented Parts List for Meter A and Meter B, with the Required Number of Items per Unit of Parent Listed in Parentheses

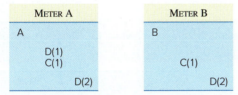

This exhibit shows the subassemblies and parts that make up the meters and displays the numbers of units required per unit of parent in parentheses.

From the product structure, notice that part D (the transformer) is used in subassembly C (which is used in both meters A and B). In the case of meter A, an additional part D (transformer) is needed. The "2" in parentheses next to D when used to make a C indicates that two Ds are required for every C that is made. The product structure, as well as the indented parts list in Exhibit 9.11B, indicates how the meters are actually made. First subassembly C is made, and potentially these are carried in inventory. In a final assembly process, meters A and B are put together, and in the case of meter A, an additional part D is used.

Inventory Records

The inventory records data would be similar to those appearing in Exhibit 9.8. As shown earlier in the chapter, additional data such as vendor identity, cost, and lead time also would be included in these data. For this example, the pertinent data include the on-hand inventory at the start of the program run, safety stock requirements, and the current status of orders that have already been released (see Exhibit 9.12). Safety stock is a minimum amount of inventory that we always want to keep on-hand for an item. For example, for subassembly C, we never want the inventory to get below 5 units. We also see that we have an order for 10 units of meter B that is scheduled for receipt at the beginning of week 5. Another order for 100 units of part D (the transformer) is scheduled to arrive at the beginning of week 4.

Performing the MRP Calculations

Conditions are now set to perform the MRP calculations: End-item requirements have been presented in the master production schedule, while the status of inventory and the order lead times are available, and we also have the pertinent product structure data. The

exhibit 9.12

exhibit 9.12 Number of Units On-Hand and Lead Time Data That Would Appear on the Inventory Record File

ITEM	ON-HAND INVENTORY	LEAD TIME (WEEKS)	SAFETY STOCK	ON-ORDER
A	50	2	0	
B	60	2	0	10 (Week 5)
C	40	1	5	
D	200	1	20	100 (Week 4)

MRP calculations (often referred to as an explosion) are done level by level, in conjunction with the inventory data and data from the master schedule.

Exhibit 9.13 shows the details of these calculations. The following analysis explains the logic in detail. We will limit our analysis to the problem of meeting the gross requirements for 1,250 units of meter A, 470 units of meter B, and 270 units of transformer D, all in week 9.

exhibit 9.13 Material Requirements Planning Schedule for Meters A and B, and Subassemblies C and D

Item		Week 4	Week 5	Week 6	Week 7	Week 8	Week 9
A LT = 2 weeks On hand = 50 Safety stock = 0 Order qty = lot-for-lot	Gross requirements						1,250
	Scheduled receipts						
	Projected available balance	50	50	50	50	50	0
	Net requirements						1,200
	Planned-order receipts						1,200
	Planned-order releases				1,200		
B LT = 2 weeks On hand = 60 Safety stock = 0 Order qty = lot-for-lot	Gross requirements						470
	Scheduled receipts		10				
	Projected available balance	60	70	70	70	70	0
	Net requirements						400
	Planned-order receipts						400
	Planned-order releases				400		
C LT = 1 week On hand = 40 Safety stock = 5 Order qty = 2,000	Gross requirements				400+ 1,200		
	Scheduled receipts						
	Projected available balance	35	35	35	435	435	435
	Net requirements				1,565		
	Planned-order receipts				2,000		
	Planned-order releases			2,000			
D LT = 1 week On hand = 200 Safety stock = 20 Order qty = 5,000	Gross requirements			4,000	1,200		270
	Scheduled receipts	100					
	Projected available balance	280	280	1,280	80	80	4,810
	Net requirements			3,720			190
	Planned-order receipts			5,000			5,000
	Planned-order releases		5,000			5,000	

An MRP record is kept for each item managed by the system. The record contains *gross requirements, scheduled receipts, projected available balance, net requirements, planned-order receipts*, and *planned-order releases* data. *Gross requirements* are the total amount required for a particular item. These requirements can be from external customer demand and also from demand calculated due to manufacturing requirements. *Scheduled receipts* represent orders that have already been released and that are scheduled to arrive as of the beginning of the period. Once the paperwork on an order has been released, what was prior to that event's "planned" order now becomes a *scheduled receipt*. *Projected available balance* is the amount of inventory expected as of the end of a period. This can be calculated as follows:

$$\begin{array}{c}\text{Projected}\\\text{available}\\\text{balance}_t\end{array} = \begin{array}{c}\text{Projected}\\\text{available}\\\text{balance}_{t-1}\end{array} - \begin{array}{c}\text{Gross}\\\text{requirements}_t\end{array} + \begin{array}{c}\text{Scheduled}\\\text{receipts}_t\end{array} + \begin{array}{c}\text{Planned-}\\\text{order}\\\text{receipts}_t\end{array}$$

One thing that needs to be considered is the initial projected available balance. In the case where safety stock is needed, the on-hand balance needs to be reduced by the safety stock. So, projected available balance in period zero is on-hand minus the safety stock.

A *net requirement* is the amount needed when the *projected available* balance plus the *scheduled receipts* in a period are not sufficient to cover the *gross requirement*. The *planned-order receipt* is the amount of an order that is required to meet a net requirement in the period. Finally, the *planned-order release* is the planned-order receipt offset by the lead time.

Beginning with meter A, the projected available balance is 50 units and there are no net requirements until week 9. In week 9, an additional 1,200 units are needed to cover the demand of 1,250 generated from the order scheduled through the master schedule. The order quantity is designated "lot-for-lot," which means that we can order the exact quantity needed to meet net requirements. An order, therefore, is planned for receipt of 1,200 units for the beginning of week 9. Since the lead time is two weeks, this order must be released at the beginning of week 7.

Meter B is similar to A, although an order for 10 units is scheduled for receipt in period 5. We project that 70 units will be available at the end of week 5. There is a net requirement for 400 additional units to meet the gross requirement of 470 units in week 9. This requirement is met with an order for 400 units that must be released at the beginning of week 7.

Item C is the subassembly used in both meters A and B. We need additional Cs only when either A or B is being made. Our analysis of A indicates that an order for 1,200 will be released in week 7. An order for 400 Bs also will be released in week 7, so the total demand for C is 1,600 units in week 7. The projected available balance is the 40 units on-hand minus the safety stock of 5 units we have specified, or 35 units. In week 7, the net requirement is 1,565 units. The order policy for C indicates an order quantity of 2,000 units, so an order receipt for 2,000 is planned for week 7. This order needs to be released in week 6 due to the one-week lead time. Assuming this order is actually processed in the future, the projected available balance is 435 units in weeks 7, 8, and 9.

Item D, the transformer, has demand from three different sources. The demand in week 6 is due to the requirement to put Ds into subassembly C. In this case, two Ds are needed for every C, or 4,000 units (the product structure indicates this two-to-one relationship). In the seventh week, 1,200 Ds are needed for the order for 1,200 As that are scheduled to be released in week 7. Another 270 units are needed in week 9 to meet the independent demand that is scheduled through the master schedule. The projected available balance at the end of week 4 is 280 units (200 on-hand plus the scheduled receipt of 100 units minus the safety stock of 20 units) and 280 units in week 5. There is a net requirement for an additional 3,720 units in week 6, so we plan to receive an order for 5,000 units (the order quantity). This results in a projected balance of 1,280 in week 6 and 80 in week 7 since 1,200 are used to meet demand. Eighty units are projected to be available in week 8. Due to the demand for 270 in week 9, a net requirement of 190 units in week 9 results in planning the receipt of an additional 5,000-unit order in week 9.

Example 9.1: MRP Explosion Calculations

Juno Lighting makes special lights that are popular in new homes. Juno expects demand for two popular lights to be the following over the next eight weeks.

	WEEK							
	1	2	3	4	5	6	7	8
VH1-234	34	37	41	45	48	48	48	48
VH2-100	104	134	144	155	134	140	141	145

A key component in both lights is a socket that the bulb is screwed into in the base fixture. Each light has one of these sockets. Given the following information, plan the production of the lights and purchases of the socket.

	VH1-234	VH2-100	LIGHT SOCKET
On-hand	85	358	425
Q	200 (the production lot size)	400 (the production lot size)	500 (purchase quantity)
Lead time	1 week	1 week	3 weeks
Safety stock	0 units	0 units	20 units

SOLUTION

		WEEK							
ITEM		1	2	3	4	5	6	7	8
VH1-234	Gross requirement	34	37	41	45	48	48	48	48
Q = 200	Scheduled receipts								
LT = 1	Projected available balance	51	14	173	128	80	32	184	136
OH = 85	Net requirements			27				16	
SS = 0	Planned-order receipts			200				200	
	Planned-order releases		200				200		
VH2-100	Gross requirement	104	134	144	155	134	140	141	145
Q = 400	Scheduled receipts								
LT = 1	Projected available balance	254	120	376	221	87	347	206	61
OH = 358	Net requirements			24			53		
SS = 0	Planned-order receipts			400			400		
	Planned-order releases	400		400					
Socket	Gross requirement		600			400	200		
Q = 500	Scheduled receipts	500							
LT = 3	Projected available balance	905	305	305	305	405	205	205	205
OH = 425	Net requirements					95			
SS = 20	Planned-order receipts					500			
	Planned-order releases	500							

The best way to proceed is to work period by period by focusing on the projected available balance calculation. Whenever the available balance goes below zero, a net requirement is generated. When this happens, plan an order receipt to meet the requirement. For example, for VH1 we start with 85 units in inventory and need 34 to meet week 1 production requirements. This brings our available balance at the end of week 1 to 51 units. Another 37 units are used during week 2, dropping inventory to 14. In week 3, our projected balance drops to 0 and we have a net requirement of 27 units that needs to be covered with an order scheduled to be received in week 3. Since the lead time is one week, this order needs to be released in week 2. Week 4 projected available balance is 128, calculated by taking the 200 units that are received in week 3 and subtracting the week 3 net requirement of 27 units and the 45 units needed for week 4.

Since sockets are used in both VH1 and VH2, the gross requirements come from the planned-order releases for these items: 600 are needed in week 2 (200 for VH1s and 400 for VH2s), 400 in week 5, and 200 in week 6. The projected available balance is the beginning inventory of 425 plus the scheduled receipts of 500 units minus the 20 units of safety stock. •

LOT SIZING IN MRP SYSTEMS

The determination of lot sizes in an MRP system is a complicated and difficult problem. Lot sizes are the part quantities issued in the planned-order receipt and planned-order release sections of an MRP schedule. For parts produced in-house, lot sizes are the production quantities of batch sizes. For purchased parts, these are the quantities ordered from the supplier. Lot sizes generally meet part requirements for one or more periods.

LO9–4 Evaluate and compare MRP lot-sizing techniques.

Most lot-sizing techniques deal with how to balance the setup or order costs and holding costs associated with meeting the net requirements generated by the MRP planning process. Many MRP systems have options for computing lot sizes based on some of the more commonly used techniques. The use of lot-sizing techniques increases the complexity of running MRP schedules in a plant. In an attempt to save setup costs, the inventory generated with the larger lot sizes needs to be stored, making the logistics in the plant much more complicated.

Next, we explain four lot-sizing techniques using a common example. The lot-sizing techniques presented are lot-for-lot (L4L), economic order quantity (EOQ), least total cost (LTC), and least unit cost (LUC).

Consider the following MRP lot-sizing problem; the net requirements are shown for eight scheduling weeks:

Cost per item	$10.00
Order or setup cost	$47.00
Inventory carrying cost/week	0.5%

WEEKLY NET REQUIREMENTS							
1	2	3	4	5	6	7	8
50	60	70	60	95	75	60	55

Lot-for-Lot

Lot-for-lot (L4L) is the most common technique. It

- Sets planned orders to exactly match the net requirements.
- Produces exactly what is needed each week with none carried over into future periods.
- Minimizes carrying cost.
- Does not take into account setup costs or capacity limitations.

exhibit 9.14   Lot-for-Lot Run Size for an MRP Schedule

(1) WEEK	(2) NET REQUIREMENTS	(3) PRODUCTION QUANTITY	(4) ENDING INVENTORY	(5) HOLDING COST	(6) SETUP COST	(7) TOTAL COST
1	50	50	0	$0.00	$47.00	$ 47.00
2	60	60	0	0.00	47.00	94.00
3	70	70	0	0.00	47.00	141.00
4	60	60	0	0.00	47.00	188.00
5	95	95	0	0.00	47.00	235.00
6	75	75	0	0.00	47.00	282.00
7	60	60	0	0.00	47.00	329.00
8	55	55	0	0.00	47.00	376.00

Exhibit 9.14 shows the lot-for-lot calculations. The net requirements are given in column 2. Because the logic of lot-for-lot says the production quantity (column 3) will exactly match the required quantity (column 2), there will be no inventory left at the end (column 4). Without any inventory to carry over into the next week, there is zero holding cost (column 5). However, lot-for-lot requires a setup cost each week (column 6). Incidentally, there is a setup cost each week because this is a work center where a variety of items are worked on each week. This is not a case where the work center is committed to one product and sits idle when it is not working on that product (in which case only one setup would result). Lot-for-lot causes high setup costs.

Economic Order Quantity

In Chapter 11, we discuss the EOQ model that explicitly balances setup and holding costs (see Chapter 11 for the details). In an EOQ model, either fairly constant demand must exist or safety stock must be kept to provide for demand variability. The EOQ model uses an estimate of total annual demand, the setup or order cost, and the annual holding cost. EOQ was not designed for a system with discrete time periods such as MRP. The lot-sizing techniques used for MRP assume that part requirements are satisfied at the start of the period. Holding costs are then charged only to the ending inventory for the period, not to the average inventory as in the case of the EOQ model. EOQ assumes that parts are used continuously during the period. The lot sizes generated by EOQ do not always cover the entire number of periods. For example, the EOQ might provide the requirements for 4.6 periods. Using the same data as in the lot-for-lot example, the economic order quantity is calculated as follows:

$$\text{Annual demand based on the 8 weeks} = D = \frac{525}{8} \times 52 = 3{,}412.5 \text{ units}$$

$$\text{Annual holding cost} = H = 0.5\% \times \$10 \times 52 \text{ weeks} = \$2.60 \text{ per unit}$$

$$\text{Setup cost} = S = \$47 \text{ (given)}$$

$$EOQ = \sqrt{\frac{2DS}{H}} = \sqrt{\frac{2(3{,}412.5)(\$47)}{\$2.60}} = 351 \text{ units}$$

Economic Order Quantity Run Size for an MRP Schedule   **exhibit 9.15**

WEEK	NET REQUIREMENTS	PRODUCTION QUANTITY	ENDING INVENTORY	HOLDING COST	SETUP COST	TOTAL COST
1	50	351	301	$15.05	$47.00	$ 62.05
2	60	0	241	12.05	0.00	74.10
3	70	0	171	8.55	0.00	82.65
4	60	0	111	5.55	0.00	88.20
5	95	0	16	0.80	0.00	89.00
6	75	351	292	14.60	47.00	150.60
7	60	0	232	11.60	0.00	162.20
8	55	0	177	8.85	0.00	171.05

Exhibit 9.15 shows the MRP schedule using an EOQ of 351 units. The EOQ lot size in week 1 is enough to meet requirements for weeks 1 through 5 and a portion of week 6. Then, in week 6 another EOQ lot is planned to meet the requirements for weeks 6 through 8. Notice that the EOQ plan leaves some inventory at the end of week 8 to carry forward into week 9.

Least Total Cost

The least total cost method (LTC) is a dynamic lot-sizing technique that calculates the order quantity by comparing the carrying cost and the setup (or ordering) costs for various lot sizes and then selects the lot in which these are most nearly equal.

The top half of Exhibit 9.16 shows the least cost lot size results. The procedure to compute least total cost lot sizes is to compare order costs and holding costs for various numbers of weeks. For example, costs are compared for producing in week 1 to cover the requirements for week 1; producing in week 1 for weeks 1 and 2; producing in week 1 to cover weeks 1, 2, and 3; and so on. The correct selection is the lot size where the ordering costs and holding costs are approximately equal. In Exhibit 9.16, the best lot size is 335 because a $38 carrying cost and a $47 ordering cost are closer than $56.75 and $47 ($9 versus $9.75). This lot size covers requirements for weeks 1 through 5. Unlike EOQ, the lot size covers only whole numbers of periods.

Based on the week 1 decision to place an order to cover five weeks, we are now located in week 6, and our problem is to determine how many weeks into the future we can provide for from here. Exhibit 9.16 shows that holding and ordering costs are closest in the quantity that covers requirements for weeks 6 through 8. Notice that the holding and ordering costs here are far apart. This is because our example extends only to week 8. If the planning horizon were longer, the lot size planned for week 6 would likely cover more weeks into the future beyond week 8. This brings up one of the limitations of both LTC and LUC (discussed below). Both techniques are influenced by the length of the planning horizon. The bottom half of Exhibit 9.16 shows the final run size and total cost.

Least Unit Cost

The least unit cost method is a dynamic lot-sizing technique that adds the ordering and inventory carrying cost for each trial lot size and divides by the number of units in each

| exhibit 9.16 | Least Total Cost Run Size for an MRP Schedule |

WEEKS	QUANTITY ORDERED	CARRYING COST	ORDER COST	TOTAL COST	
1	50	$ 0.00	$47.00	$ 47.00	
1–2	110	3.00	47.00	50.00	
1–3	180	10.00	47.00	57.00	
1–4	240	19.00	47.00	66.00	1st order
1–5	335	38.00	47.00	85.00	← Least total cost
1–6	410	56.75	47.00	103.75	
1–7	470	74.75	47.00	121.75	
1–8	525	94.00	47.00	141.00	
6	75	0.00	47.00	47.00	
6–7	135	3.00	47.00	50.00	2nd order
6–8	190	8.50	47.00	55.50	← Least total cost

WEEK	NET REQUIREMENTS	PRODUCTION QUANTITY	ENDING INVENTORY	HOLDING COST	SETUP COST	TOTAL COST
1	50	335	285	$14.25	$47.00	$ 61.25
2	60	0	225	11.25	0.00	72.50
3	70	0	155	7.75	0.00	80.25
4	60	0	95	4.75	0.00	85.00
5	95	0	0	0.00	0.00	85.00
6	75	190	115	5.75	47.00	137.75
7	60	0	55	2.75	0.00	140.50
8	55	0	0	0.00	0.00	140.50

lot size, picking the lot size with the lowest unit cost. The top half of Exhibit 9.17 calculates the unit cost for ordering lots to meet the needs of weeks 1 through 8. Note that the minimum occurred when the quantity 410, ordered in week 1, was sufficient to cover weeks 1 through 6. The lot size planned for week 7 covers through the end of the planning horizon.

The least unit cost run size and total cost are shown in the bottom half of Exhibit 9.17.

Choosing the Best Lot Size

Using the lot-for-lot method, the total cost for the eight weeks is $376; the EOQ total cost is $171.05; the least total cost method is $140.50; and the least unit cost is $153.50. The lowest cost was obtained using the least total cost method of $140.50. If there were more than eight weeks, the lowest cost could differ.

The advantage of the least unit cost method is that it is a more complete analysis and would take into account ordering or setup costs that might change as the order size increases. If the ordering or setup costs remain constant, the lowest total cost method is more attractive because it is simpler and easier to compute; yet it would be just as accurate under that restriction.

| | | | | | | exhibit 9.17 |

Least Unit Cost Run Size for an MRP Schedule

WEEKS	QUANTITY ORDERED	CARRYING COST	ORDER COST	TOTAL COST	UNIT COST	
1	50	$ 0.00	$47.00	$47.00	$0.9400	
1–2	110	3.00	47.00	50.00	0.4545	
1–3	180	10.00	47.00	57.00	0.3167	
1–4	240	19.00	47.00	66.00	0.2750	
1–5	335	38.00	47.00	85.00	0.2537	1st order
1–6	410	56.75	47.00	103.75	0.2530 ← Least unit cost	
1–7	470	74.75	47.00	121.75	0.2590	
1–8	525	94.00	47.00	141.00	0.2686	
?	60	0.00	47.00	47.00	0.7833	2nd order
7–8	115	2.75	47.00	49.75	0.4326 ← Least unit cost	

WEEK	NET REQUIREMENTS	PRODUCTION QUANTITY	ENDING INVENTORY	HOLDING COST	SETUP COST	TOTAL COST
1	50	410	360	$18.00	$47.00	$ 65.00
2	60	0	300	15.00	0.00	80.00
3	70	0	230	11.50	0.00	91.50
4	60	0	170	8.50	0.00	100.00
5	95	0	75	3.75	0.00	103.75
6	75	0	0	0	0.00	103.75
7	60	115	55	2.75	47.00	153.50
8	55	0	0	0	0.00	$153.50

CONCEPT CONNECTIONS

LO9–1 **Explain what material requirements planning (MRP) is.**

- An enterprise resource planning (ERP) system integrates application programs in accounting, sales, manufacturing, and the other functions in a firm. MRP is typically an application within the ERP system.
- MRP is the logic that calculates the number of parts, components, and other materials needed to produce a product.
- MRP determines detailed schedules that show exactly what is needed over time.
- MRP is most useful in industries where standard products are made in batches from common components and parts.
- The master production schedule (MPS) is a plan that specifies what will be made by a production system in the future.
- The items scheduled in the MPS are referred to as "end items" and represent the products that drive the requirements for the MRP system.
- The MPS is a plan for meeting all the demands for the end items, including customer demand, the demand for replacements, and any other demands that might exist.
- Often, "time fences" are used in the MPS to make the schedules calculated by the MRP system stable and ensure their feasibility. When the MPS is based on forecast demand, rather than actual demand, a feature known as "available to promise" is often used that

identifies the difference between the number of units included in the MPS and current actual customer orders (these may be different since the forecast may be different from actual customer demand). This can be useful for coordinating sales and production activities.

Enterprise resource planning (ERP)   A computer system that integrates application programs in accounting, sales, manufacturing, and the other functions of the firm.

Material requirements planning (MRP)   The logic for determining the number of parts, components, and materials needed to produce a product.

Master production schedule (MPS)   A time-phased plan specifying how many and when the firm plans to build each end item.

Available to promise   A feature of MRP systems that identifies the difference between the number of units currently included in the master schedule and the actual (firm) customer orders.

LO9–2   Understand how the MRP system is structured.

- The MRP system uses three sources of information
  - Demand comes from the master schedule.
  - The bill-of-materials identifies exactly what is needed to make each end item.
  - The current inventory status of the items managed by the system (units currently on-hand, expected receipts in the future, and how long it takes to replenish an item).
- Using the three sources of information, the MRP system produces schedules for each item it manages.
- The MRP system can be updated in real time or periodically, depending on the application.

Bill-of-materials (BOM)   The complete product description, listing the materials, parts, and components, and also the sequence in which the product is created.

Net change systems   An MRP system that calculates the impact of a change in the MRP data (the inventory status, BOM, or master schedule) immediately.

LO9–3   Analyze an MRP problem.

- The logic used by MRP is often referred to as explosion calculations, since the requirements shown in the MPS are "exploded" into detailed schedules for each item managed by the system.
- The basic logic is that the projected available balance in this period is calculated by taking the balance from the last period, subtracting the gross requirements from this period, and adding in scheduled and planned receipts.

LO9–4   Evaluate and compare MRP lot-sizing techniques.

- Lot sizes are the production (or purchasing) quantities used by the MRP system.
- Lot-for-lot is the simplest case and is when the system schedules exactly what is needed in each period.
- When setup cost is significant or other constraints force different quantities, lot-for-lot might not be the best method to use.
- Lot-size techniques are used to balance the fixed and variable costs that vary according to the production lot size.

SOLVED PROBLEMS

Excel:
Ch9_Solved_Problem

LO9–3   **SOLVED PROBLEM 1**

Product X is made of two units of Y and three of Z. Y is made of one unit of A and two units of B. Z is made of two units of A and four units of C.

Lead time for X is one week; Y, two weeks; Z, three weeks; A, two weeks; B, one week; and C, three weeks.

a. Draw the bill-of-materials (product structure tree).

b. If 100 units of X are needed in week 10, develop a planning schedule showing when each item should be ordered and in what quantity. Assume we have no inventory in any of the items to start.

Solution

a.

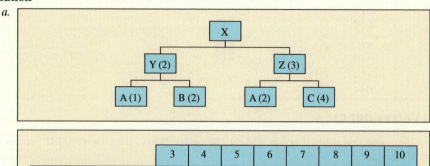

b. The orders are circled.

SOLVED PROBLEM 2

Product M is made of two units of N and three of P. N is made of two units of R and four units of S. R is made of one unit of S and three units of T. P is made of two units of T and four units of U.

a. Show the bill-of-materials (product structure tree).

b. If 100 Ms are required, how many units of each component are needed?

c. Show both a single-level parts list and an indented parts list.

Solution

a.

b. M = 100   S = 800 + 400 = 1,200

   N = 200   T = 600 + 1,200 = 1,800

   P = 300   U = 1,200

   R = 400

c.

SINGLE-LEVEL PARTS LIST		INDENTED PARTS LIST		
M		M		
	N (2)		N(2)	
	P (3)			R(2)
N				S (1)
	R (2)			T (3)
	S (4)			S (4)
R			P (3)	
	S (1)			T (2)
	T (3)			U (4)
P				
	T (2)			
	U (4)			

SOLVED PROBLEM 3

Given the product structure diagram, and the data given below, complete the MRP records for parts A, B, and C.

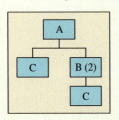

ITEM		WEEK					
		1	2	3	4	5	6
A	Gross requirements	5	15	18	8	12	22
LT = 1 week	Scheduled receipts						
On-hand = 21	Projected available balance						
Safety stock = 0	Net requirements						
Order quantity = 20	Planned-order receipts						
	Planned-order releases						
B	Gross requirements						
LT = 2 weeks	Scheduled receipts	32					
On-hand = 20	Projected available balance						
Safety stock = 0	Net requirements						
Order quantity = 40	Planned-order receipts						
	Planned-order releases						
C	Gross requirements						
LT = 1 week	Scheduled receipts						
On-hand = 70	Projected available balance						
Safety Stock = 10	Net requirements						
Order quantity = lot-for-lot	Planned-order receipts						
	Planned-order releases						

Solution

ITEM		WEEK					
		1	2	3	4	5	6
A	Gross requirements	5	15	18	8	12	22
LT = 1 week	Scheduled receipts						
On-hand = 21	Projected available balance	16	1	3	15	3	1
Safety stock = 0	Net requirements			17	5		19
Order quantity = 20	Planned-order receipts			20	20		20
	Planned-order releases		20	20		20	
B	Gross requirements			40	40		40
LT = 2 weeks	Scheduled receipts	32					
On-hand = 20	Projected available balance	52	12	12	12	12	12
Safety stock = 0	Net requirements			28		28	
Order quantity = 40	Planned-order receipts			40		40	
	Planned-order releases	40		40			
C	Gross requirements	40	20	60		20	
LT = 1 week	Scheduled receipts						
On-hand = 70	Projected available balance	20	0	0	0	0	0
Safety Stock = 10	Net requirements			60		20	
Order quantity = lot-for-lot	Planned-order receipts			60		20	
	Planned-order releases		60		20		

Notes:

1. For item A, start by calculating the projected available balance through week 2. In week 3, there is a net requirement for 17 units, so we plan to receive an order for 20 units. Projected available balance for week 3 is three units and a net requirement for five in week 4, so we plan another order to be received in week 4. Projected available balance for week 4 is 15 units, with three in week 5 and a net requirement for 19 in week 6. We need to plan one more order for receipt in week 6.

2. The gross requirements for B are based on two times the planned order releases for A. We need to account for the scheduled receipt in week 1 of 32 units, resulting in a projected available balance of 52 at the end of week 1.

3. The gross requirements for C are based on the planned order releases for items A and B, since C is used in both items. The projected available balance is calculated by subtracting out the safety stock since this inventory is kept in reserve. In week 1, for example, projected available balance is 70 units on-hand − 40 units gross requirements − 10 units safety stock = 20 units.

LO9–4 SOLVED PROBLEM 4

Consider the following data relevant to an MRP lot-sizing problem:

Item cost per unit	$25
Setup cost	$100
Inventory carrying cost per year	20.8%

WEEKLY NET REQUIREMENTS							
1	2	3	4	5	6	7	8
105	80	130	50	0	200	125	100

Use the four lot-sizing rules in the chapter to propose an MRP schedule under each rule. Assume there is no beginning inventory.

Solution

Lot-for-Lot

The lot-for-lot rule is very commonly used because it is so simple and intuitive. The planned-order quantities are equal to the net requirements each week.

WEEK	REQUIREMENTS NET	PRODUCTION QUANTITY	ENDING INVENTORY	HOLDING COST	SETUP COST	TOTAL COST
1	105	105	0	$0.00	$100.00	$100.00
2	80	80	0	0.00	100.00	200.00
3	130	130	0	0.00	100.00	300.00
4	50	50	0	0.00	100.00	400.00
5	0	0	0	0.00	100.00	500.00
6	200	200	0	0.00	100.00	600.00
7	125	125	0	0.00	100.00	700.00
8	100	100	0	0.00	100.00	800.00

Economic Order Quantity

We need *D, S,* and *H* in the EOQ formula. We will estimate annual demand based on average weekly demand over these 8 weeks.

$$D = \text{Annual demand} = \frac{105 + 80 + 130 + 50 + 0 + 200 + 125 + 100}{8} \times 52 = 5,135$$

$$H = \text{Annual holding cost} = .208 \times \$25.00 = \$5.20$$

$$S = \text{Setup cost} = \$100 \text{ (given)}$$

$$EOQ = \sqrt{\frac{2DS}{H}} = \sqrt{\frac{2(5135)(100)}{5.20}} = 444$$

In computing holding costs per week, divide H by 52. Weekly holding cost is $0.10 per unit. We can now develop an order schedule based on EOQ lot sizing.

WEEK	NET REQUIREMENTS	PRODUCTION QUANTITY	ENDING INVENTORY	HOLDING COST	SETUP COST	TOTAL COST
1	105	444	339	$33.90	$100.00	$133.90
2	80	0	259	25.90	0.00	159.80
3	130	0	129	12.90	0.00	172.70
4	50	0	79	7.90	0.00	180.60
5	0	0	79	7.90	0.00	188.50
6	200	444	323	32.30	100.00	320.80
7	125	0	198	19.80	0.00	340.60
8	100	0	98	9.80	0.00	350.40

Least Total Cost (LTC)

Similar to the example in Exhibit 9.16, we can create the following table comparing costs for ordering 1 through 8 weeks' demand in the first order.

WEEKS	NET REQUIREMENTS	PRODUCTION QUANTITY	HOLDING COST	SETUP COST	TOTAL COST
1	105	105	$ 0.00	$100.00	$100.00
1–2	80	185	8.00	100.00	108.00
1–3	130	315	34.00	100.00	134.00
1–4	50	365	49.00	100.00	149.00
1–5	0	365	49.00	100.00	149.00
1–6	**200**	**565**	**149.00**	**100.00**	**249.00**
1–7	125	690	224.00	100.00	324.00
1–8	100	790	294.00	100.00	394.00
7	125	125	0.00	100.00	100.00
7–8	**100**	**225**	**10.00**	**100.00**	**110.00**

For the first order, the difference between holding and setup costs is least when ordering for weeks 1 through 6, so the first order should be for 565 units, enough for weeks 1–6. For the second order, we need to consider only weeks 7 and 8. The difference between holding and setup costs is least when placing a second order to cover demand during weeks 7–8, so the second order should be for 225 units. Note that as we move through time and net requirements for weeks 9 and beyond become known, we would revisit the second order based on those new requirements. It is likely that the best second order will end up being for more than just weeks 7 and 8. For now, we can develop an order schedule based on the data we have available.

WEEK	NET REQUIREMENTS	PRODUCTION QUANTITY	ENDING INVENTORY	HOLDING COST	SETUP COST	TOTAL COST
1	105	565	460	$46.00	$100.00	$146.00
2	80	0	380	38.00	0.00	184.00
3	130	0	250	25.00	0.00	209.00
4	50	0	200	20.00	0.00	229.00
5	0	0	200	20.00	0.00	249.00
6	200	0	0	0.00	0.00	249.00
7	125	225	100	10.00	100.00	359.00
8	100	0	0	0.00	0.00	359.00

Least Unit Cost (LUC)

The LUC method uses calculations from the LTC method, dividing each option's total cost by the order quantity to determine a unit cost. Most of the following table is copied from the LTC method, with one additional column to calculate the unit costs.

WEEK	NET REQUIREMENTS	PRODUCTION QUANTITY	HOLDING COST	SETUP COST	TOTAL COST	UNIT COST
1	105	105	$ 0.00	$100.00	$100.00	$0.9524
1–2	80	185	8.00	100.00	108.00	0.5838
1–3	130	315	34.00	100.00	134.00	0.4254
1–4	**50**	**365**	**49.00**	**100.00**	**149.00**	**0.4082**
1–5	**0**	**365**	**49.00**	**100.00**	**149.00**	**0.4082**
1–6	200	565	149.00	100.00	249.00	0.4407
1–7	125	690	224.00	100.00	324.00	0.4696
1–8	100	790	294.00	100.00	394.00	0.4987
6	200	200	0.00	100.00	100.00	0.5000
6–7	125	325	12.50	100.00	112.50	0.3462
6–8	**100**	**425**	**32.50**	**100.00**	**132.50**	**0.3118**

For the first order, the least unit cost results from ordering enough to cover weeks 1 through 5, so our first order would be for 365 units. (This example can be a bit tricky—we have to use a little common sense.) Ordering for weeks 1–4 has the same low unit cost because there is no demand for week 5. We will say we are ordering for weeks 1–5 so that we don't place an unnecessary order in week 5 to cover demand for weeks 5–8. For the second order, the lowest unit cost comes from ordering for weeks 6–8, so we would plan for an order of 425 units. As with the LTC example, our second order might change as we learn net requirements for weeks 9 and beyond. Based on these orders, we can now develop an order schedule based on LUC.

WEEK	NET REQUIREMENTS	PRODUCTION QUANTITY	ENDING INVENTORY	HOLDING COST	SETUP COST	TOTAL COST
1	105	365	260	$26.00	$100.00	$126.00
2	80	0	180	18.00	0.00	144.00
3	130	0	50	5.00	0.00	149.00
4	50	0	0	0.00	0.00	149.00
5	0	0	0	0.00	0.00	149.00
6	200	425	225	22.50	100.00	271.50
7	125	0	100	10.00	0.00	281.50
8	100	0	0	0.00	0.00	281.50

Best Lot Size Method

Based on the data we have available, the total costs for each lot-sizing method are lot-for-lot, $800.00; EOQ, $350.40; LTC, $359.00; and LUC, $281.50. The relatively high setup cost in this example makes lot-for-lot an unwise choice. LUC has the lowest total cost by a significant margin. It works so well here because it minimizes holding costs across the planning horizon.

DISCUSSION QUESTIONS

LO9–1
1. What do we mean when we say that MRP is based on dependent demand?
2. Discuss the importance of the master production schedule in an MRP system.
3. Explain the need for *time fences* in the master production schedule.

LO9–2
4. "MRP just prepares shopping lists. It does not do the shopping or cook the dinner." Comment.
5. What are the sources of demand in an MRP system? Are these dependent or independent, and how are they used as inputs to the system?
6. State the types of data that would be carried in the bill-of-materials file and the inventory record file.

LO9–3
7. Discuss the meaning of MRP terms such as *planned-order release and scheduled order receipt*.
8. Why is the MRP process referred to as an "explosion"?
9. Many practitioners currently update MRP weekly or biweekly. Would it be more valuable if it were updated daily? Discuss.
10. Should safety stock be necessary in an MRP system with dependent demand? If so, why? If not, why do firms carry it anyway?

11. Contrast the significance of the term *lead time* in the traditional EOQ context and in an MRP system.

LO9–4

12. Planning orders using a lot-for-lot (L4L) technique is commonly done because it is simple and intuitive. It also helps minimize holding costs because you are only ordering what is needed when it is needed. So far, it sounds like a good idea. Are there any disadvantages to this approach?

13. What is meant when we say that the least total cost (LTC) and least unit cost (LUC) methods are dynamic lot-sizing techniques?

OBJECTIVE QUESTIONS

LO9–1

1. Match the industry type to the expected benefits from an MRP system as High, Medium, or Low.

INDUSTRY TYPE	EXPECTED BENEFIT (HIGH, MEDIUM, OR LOW)
Assemble-to-stock	
Assemble-to-order	
Make-to-stock	
Make-to-order	
Engineer-to-order	
Process	

2. MRP is based on what type of demand?

3. Which scheduling process drives requirements in the MRP process?

4. What term is used to identify the difference between the number of units of an item listed on the master schedule and the number of firm customer orders?

LO9–2

5. What are the three primary data sources used by the MRP system?

6. What is another common name for the bill-of-materials?

7. What is the process used to ensure that all of the needs for a particular item are calculated at the same time in the MRP process?

8. What is the MRP term for the time periods used in planning?

LO9–3

Note: For these problems, to simplify data handling to include the receipt of orders that have actually been placed in previous periods, the following six-level scheme can be used. (A number of different techniques are used in practice, but the important issue is to keep track of what is on-hand, what is expected to arrive, what is needed, and what size orders should be placed.) One way to calculate the numbers is as follows:

	WEEK
Gross requirements	
Scheduled receipts	
Projected available balance	
Net requirements	
Planned-order receipt	
Planned-order release	

9. Semans is a manufacturer that produces bracket assemblies. Demand for bracket assemblies (X) is 130 units. The following is the BOM in indented form:

ITEM	DESCRIPTION	USAGE
X	Bracket assembly	1
A	Wall board	4
B	Hanger subassembly	2
D	Hanger casting	3
E	Ceramic knob	1
C	Rivet head screw	3
F	Metal tong	4
G	Plastic cap	2

Below is a table indicating current inventory levels:

Item	X	A	B	C	D	E	F	G
Inventory	25	16	60	20	180	160	1,000	100

    a. Using Excel, create the MRP using the information provided.

    b. What are the net requirements of each item in the MPS?

10. In the following MRP planning schedule for item J, indicate the correct net requirements, planned-order receipts, and planned-order releases to meet the gross requirements. Lead time is one week.

	WEEK NUMBER					
ITEM J	0	1	2	3	4	5
Gross requirements			75		50	70
On-hand	40					
Net requirements						
Planned-order receipt						
Planned-order release						

11. Assume that product Z is made of two units of A and four units of B. A is made of three units of C and four of D. D is made of two units of E.

    Lead times for purchase or fabrication of each unit to final assembly are: Z takes two weeks; A, B, C, and D take one week each; and E takes three weeks.

    Fifty units are required in period 10. (Assume that there is currently no inventory on-hand of any of these items.)

    a. Show the bill-of-materials (product structure tree).

    b. Develop an MRP planning schedule showing gross and net requirements and order release and order receipt dates.

12. One unit of A is made of three units of B, one unit of C, and two units of D. B is composed of two units of E and one unit of D. C is made of one unit of B and two units of E. E is made of one unit of F.

    Items B, C, E, and F have one-week lead times; A and D have lead times of two weeks.

    Assume that lot-for-lot (L4L) lot sizing is used for items A, B, and F; lots of size 50, 50, and 200 are used for Items C, D, and E, respectively. Items C, E, and F have on-hand (beginning) inventories of 10, 50, and 150, respectively; all other items have zero beginning inventory. We are scheduled to receive 10 units of A in week 2, 50 units of E in week 1, and also 50 units of F in week 1. There are no other scheduled receipts. If 30 units of A are required in week 8, use the low-level-coded bill-of-materials to find the necessary planned-order releases for all components.

13. One unit of A is made of two units of B, three units of C, and two units of D. B is composed of one unit of E and two units of F. C is made of two units of F and one unit of D. E is made of two units of D. Items A, C, D, and F have one-week lead times; B and E have lead times of two weeks. Lot-for-lot (L4L) lot sizing is used for items A, B, C, and D; lots of size 50 and 180 are used for items E and F, respectively. Item C has an on-hand (beginning) inventory of 15; D has an on-hand inventory of 50; all other items have zero beginning inventories. We are scheduled to receive 20 units of item E in week 2; there are no other scheduled receipts.

    Construct simple and low-level-coded bill-of-materials (product structure tree) and indented and summarized parts lists.

    If 20 units of A are required in week 8, use the low-level-coded bill-of-materials to find the necessary planned-order releases for all components.

14. One unit of A is made of one unit of B and one unit of C. B is made of four units of C and one unit each of E and F. C is made of two units of D and one unit of E. E is made of three units of F. Item C has a lead time of one week;

items A, B, E, and F have two-week lead times; and item D has a lead time of three weeks. Lot-for-lot (L4L) lot sizing is used for items A, D, and E; lots of size 50, 100, and 50 are used for items B, C, and F, respectively. Items A, C, D, and E have on-hand (beginning) inventories of 20, 50, 100, and 10, respectively; all other items have zero beginning inventory. We are scheduled to receive 10 units of A in week 1, 100 units of C in week 1, and 100 units of D in week 3; there are no other scheduled receipts. If 50 units of A are required in week 10, use the low-level-coded bill-of-materials (product structure tree) to find the necessary planned-order releases for all components.

15. One unit of A is made of two units of B and one unit of C. B is made of three units of D and one unit of F. C is composed of three units of B, one unit of D, and four units of E. D is made of one unit of E. Item C has a lead time of one week; items A, B, E, and F have two-week lead times; and item D has a lead time of three weeks. Lot-for-lot (L4L) lot sizing is used for items C, E, and F; lots of size 20, 40, and 160 are used for items A, B, and D, respectively. Items A, B, D, and E have on-hand (beginning) inventories of 5, 10, 100, and 100, respectively; all other items have zero beginning inventories. We are scheduled to receive 10 units of A in week 3, 20 units of B in week 7, 40 units of F in week 5, and 60 units of E in week 2; there are no other scheduled receipts. If 20 units of A are required in week 10, use the low-level-coded bill-of-materials (product structure tree) to find the necessary planned order releases for all components.

16. One unit of A is composed of two units of B and three units of C. Each B is composed of one unit of F. C is made of one unit of D, one unit of E, and two units of F. Items A, B, C, and D have 20, 50, 60, and 25 units of on-hand inventory, respectively. Items A, B, and C use lot-for-lot (L4L) as their lot-sizing technique, while D, E, and F require multiples of 50, 100, and 100, respectively, to be purchased. B has scheduled receipts of 30 units in period 1. No other scheduled receipts exist. Lead times are one period for items A, B, and D, and two periods for items C, E, and F. Gross requirements for A are 20 units in period 1, 20 units in period 2, 60 units in period 6, and 50 units in period 8. Find the planned order releases for all items.

17. Each unit of A is composed of one unit of B, two units of C, and one unit of D. C is composed of two units of D and three units of E. Items A, C, D, and E have on-hand inventories of 20, 10, 20, and 10 units, respectively. Item B has a scheduled receipt of 10 units in period 1, and C has a scheduled receipt of 50 units in period 1. Lot-for-lot (L4L) lot sizing is used for items A and B. Item C requires a minimum lot size of 50 units. D and E are required to be purchased in multiples of 100 and 50, respectively. Lead times are one period for items A, B, and C, and two periods for items D and E. The gross requirements for A are 30 in period 2, 30 in period 5, and 40 in period 8. Find the planned-order releases for all items.

18. Product A is an end item and is made from two units of B and four of C. B is made of three units of D and two of E. C is made of two units of F and two of E.

    A has a lead time of one week. B, C, and E have lead times of two weeks, and D and F have lead times of three weeks.
    a. Show the bill-of-materials (product structure tree).
    b. If 100 units of A are required in week 10, develop the MRP planning schedule, specifying when items are to be ordered and received. There are currently no units of inventory on-hand.

19. Audio Products, Inc., produces two AM/FM/CD players for cars. The radio/CD units are identical, but the mounting hardware and finish trim differ. The standard model fits intermediate and full-sized cars, and the sports model fits small sports cars.

    Audio Products handles the production in the following way. The chassis (radio/CD unit) is assembled in Mexico and has a manufacturing lead time of two weeks. The mounting hardware is purchased from a sheet steel company and has a three-week lead time. The finish trim is purchased as prepackaged units consisting of knobs and various trim pieces from a Taiwan electronics company with offices in Los Angeles. Trim packages have a two-week lead time. Final assembly time may be disregarded because adding the trim package and mounting are performed by the customer.

Audio Products supplies wholesalers and retailers, which place specific orders for both models up to eight weeks in advance. These orders, together with enough additional units to satisfy the small number of individual sales, are summarized in the following demand schedule:

	WEEK							
MODEL	1	2	3	4	5	6	7	8
Standard model				300				400
Sports model					200			100

There are currently 50 radio/CD units on-hand but no trim packages or mounting hardware.

Prepare a material requirements plan to meet the demand schedule exactly. Specify the gross and net requirements, on-hand amounts, and the planned order release and receipt periods for the radio/CD chassis, the standard trim and sports car model trim, and the standard mounting hardware and the sports car mounting hardware.

LO9–4 20. The MRP gross requirements for item A are shown here for the next 10 weeks. Lead time for A is three weeks and setup cost is $10. There is a carrying cost of $0.01 per unit per week. Beginning inventory is 90 units.

	WEEK									
	1	2	3	4	5	6	7	8	9	10
Gross requirements	30	50	10	20	70	80	20	60	200	50

Use the least total cost or the least unit cost lot-sizing method to determine when and for what quantity the first order should be released.

21. The MRP gross requirements for item X are shown here for the next 10 weeks. Lead time for A is two weeks, and setup cost is $9. There is a carrying cost of $0.02 per unit per week. Beginning inventory is 70 units.

	WEEK									
	1	2	3	4	5	6	7	8	9	10
Gross requirements	20	10	15	45	10	30	100	20	40	150

Use the least total cost or the least unit cost lot-sizing method to determine when and for what quantity the first order should be released.

22. Product A consists of two units of subassembly B, three units of C, and one unit of D. B is composed of four units of E and three units of F. C is made of two units of H and three units of D. H is made of five units of E and two units of G.
a. Construct a simple bill-of-materials (product structure tree).
b. Construct a product structure tree using low-level coding.
c. Construct an indented parts list.
d. To produce 100 units of A, determine the number of units of B, C, D, E, F, G, and H required.

ANALYTICS EXERCISE: AN MRP EXPLOSION—BRUNSWICK MOTORS

Recently, Phil Harris, the production control manager at Brunswick, read an article on time-phased requirements planning. He was curious about how this technique might work in scheduling Brunswick's engine assembly operations and decided to prepare an example to illustrate the use of time-phased requirements planning.

Phil's first step was to prepare a master schedule for one of the engine types produced by Brunswick: the Model 1000 engine. This schedule indicates the number of units of the Model 1000 engine to be assembled each week during the last 12 weeks and is shown on the next page. Next, Phil decided to simplify his requirements planning example by considering only two of the many components that are needed to complete the assembly of the Model 1000 engine. These two components, the gear box and the input shaft, are shown in the product structure diagram shown below. Phil noted that the gear box is assembled by the Subassembly Department and subsequently is sent to the main engine assembly line. The input shaft is one of several component parts manufactured by Brunswick that are needed to produce a gear box subassembly. Thus, levels 0, 1, and 2 are included in the product structure diagram to indicate the three manufacturing stages that are involved in producing an engine: the Engine Assembly Department, the Subassembly Department, and the Machine Shop.

The manufacturing lead times required to produce the gear box and input shaft components are also indicated in the bill-of-materials diagram. Note that two weeks are required to produce a batch of gear boxes and that all the gear boxes must be delivered to the assembly line parts stockroom before Monday morning of the week in which they are to be used. Likewise, it takes three weeks to produce a lot of input shafts,

and all the shafts needed for the production of gear boxes in a given week must be delivered to the Subassembly Department stockroom before Monday morning of that week.

In preparing the MRP example, Phil planned to use the worksheets shown on the next page and to make the following assumptions:

1. Seventeen gear boxes are on-hand at the beginning of week 1, and five gear boxes are currently on order to be delivered at the start of week 2.
2. Forty input shafts are on-hand at the start of week 1, and 22 are scheduled for delivery at the beginning of week 2.

Assignment

1. Initially, assume that Phil wants to minimize his inventory requirements. Assume that each order will be only for what is required for a single period. Using the following forms, calculate the net requirements and planned order releases for the gear boxes and input shafts. Assume that lot sizing is done using lot-for-lot.
2. Phil would like to consider the costs that his accountants are currently using for inventory carrying and setup for the gear boxes and input shafts. These costs are as follows:

PART	COST
Gear Box	Setup = $90/order
	Inventory carrying cost = $2/unit/week
Input Shaft	Setup = $45/order
	Inventory carrying cost = $1/unit/week

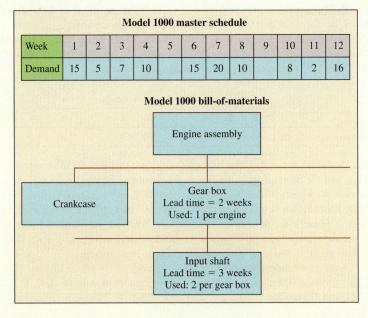

Model 1000 master schedule

Week	1	2	3	4	5	6	7	8	9	10	11	12
Demand	15	5	7	10		15	20	10		8	2	16

Model 1000 bill-of-materials

Engine assembly

Crankcase

Gear box
Lead time = 2 weeks
Used: 1 per engine

Input shaft
Lead time = 3 weeks
Used: 2 per gear box

Given the cost structure, evaluate the cost of the schedule from (1). Assume inventory is valued at the end of each week.

3. Find a better schedule by reducing the number of orders and carrying some inventory. What are the cost savings with this new schedule?

Engine assembly master schedule

Week	1	2	3	4	5	6	7	8	9	10	11	12
Quantity												

Gear box requirements

Week	1	2	3	4	5	6	7	8	9	10	11	12
Gross requirements												
Scheduled receipts												
Projected available balance												
Net requirements												
Planned-order release												

Input shaft requirements

Week	1	2	3	4	5	6	7	8	9	10	11	12
Gross requirements												
Scheduled receipts												
Projected available balance												
Net requirements												
Planned-order release												

PRACTICE EXAM

1. Term used for a computer system that integrates application programs for the different functions in a firm.
2. Logic used to calculate the needed parts, components, and other materials needed to produce an end item.
3. This drives the MRP calculations and is a detailed plan for how we expect to meet demand.
4. Period of time during which a customer has a specified level of opportunity to make changes.
5. This identifies the specific materials used to make each item and the correct quantities of each.
6. If an item is used in two places in a bill-of-materials, say level 3 and level 4, what low-level code would be assigned to the item?
7. One unit of part C is used in item A and in item B. Currently, we have 10 As, 20 Bs, and 100 Cs in inventory. We want to ship 60 As and 70 Bs. How many additional Cs do we need to purchase?
8. These are orders that have already been released and are to arrive in the future.
9. This is the total amount required for a particular item.
10. This is the amount needed after considering what we currently have in inventory and what we expect to arrive in the future.
11. The planned-order receipt and planned-order release are offset by this amount of time.
12. These are the part quantities issued in the planned-order release section of an MRP report.
13. The term for ordering exactly what is needed each period without regard to economic considerations.
14. None of the techniques for determining order quantity consider this important noneconomic factor that could make the order quantity infeasible.

Quality Management and Six Sigma

GE SIX SIGMA SUPPLY CHAIN PROCESSES

General Electric (GE) has been a major advocate of Six Sigma for over 20 years. Jack Welch, the legendary and now retired CEO, declared that "the big myth is that Six Sigma is about quality control and statistics. It is that—but it's much more. Ultimately, it drives leadership to be better by providing tools to think through tough issues. At Six Sigma's core is an idea that can turn a company inside out, focusing the organization outward on the customer." GE's commitment to quality centers on Six Sigma. Six Sigma is defined on the GE Website as follows:

© Bloomberg/Getty Images

> First, what is Six Sigma? First, what it is not. It is not a secret society, a slogan or a cliché. Six Sigma is a highly disciplined process that helps us focus on developing and delivering near-perfect products and services. Why "Sigma"? The word is a statistical term that measures how far a given process deviates from perfection. The central idea behind Six Sigma is that if you can measure how many "defects" you have in a process, you can systematically figure out how to eliminate them and get as close to "zero defects" as possible. To achieve Six Sigma Quality, a process must produce no more than 3.4 defects per million opportunities. An "opportunity" is defined as a chance for nonconformance, or not meeting the required specifications. This means we need to be nearly flawless in executing our key processes.

At its core, Six Sigma revolves around a few key concepts.

Critical to Quality:	Attributes most important to the customer
Defect:	Failing to deliver what the customer wants
Process Capability:	What your process can deliver
Variation:	What the customer sees and feels
Stable Operations:	Ensuring consistent, predictable processes to improve what the customer sees and feels
Design for Six Sigma:	Designing to meet customer needs and process capability

TOTAL QUALITY MANAGEMENT

LO10–1 Explain the scope of total quality management in a firm.

Total quality management (TQM)
Managing the entire organization so that it excels on all dimensions of products and services that are important to the customer.

Malcolm Baldrige National Quality Award
An award established by the U.S. Department of Commerce given annually to companies that excel in quality.

Total quality management (TQM) may be defined as managing the entire organization so that it excels on all dimensions of products and services that are important to the customer. It has two fundamental operational goals, namely

- Careful design of the product or service.
- Assurance that the organization's systems can consistently produce the design.

These two goals can be achieved only if the entire organization is oriented toward them—hence, the term *total* quality management. TQM became a national concern in the United States in the 1980s primarily as a response to Japanese quality superiority in manufacturing automobiles and other durable goods such as room air conditioners. A widely cited study of Japanese and U.S. air-conditioning manufacturers showed that the best-quality American products had *higher* average defect rates than those of the poorest Japanese manufacturers. So severe was the quality shortfall in the United States that improving it throughout industry became a national priority, with the Department of Commerce establishing the **Malcolm Baldrige National Quality Award** in 1987 to help companies review and structure their quality programs. Also gaining major attention at this time was the requirement that suppliers demonstrate that they are measuring and documenting their quality practices according to specified criteria, called ISO standards, if they wished to compete for international contracts. We will have more to say about this later.

The philosophical leaders of the quality movement, notably Philip Crosby, W. Edwards Deming, and Joseph M. Juran—the so-called Quality Gurus—had slightly different definitions of what quality is and how to achieve it (see Exhibit 10.1), but they all had the same general message: To achieve outstanding quality requires quality leadership from senior management, a customer focus, total involvement of the workforce, and continuous improvement based upon rigorous analysis of processes. Later in the chapter, we will discuss how these precepts are applied in the latest approach to TQM—Six Sigma. We will now turn to some fundamental concepts that underlie any quality effort: quality specifications and quality costs.

Baldrige Quality Award

The Baldrige Quality Award is given to organizations that have demonstrated outstanding quality in their products and processes. The award program is administered by the National Institute of Standards and Technology, an agency of the U.S. Department of Commerce. Up to 18 awards total may be given annually in these categories: manufacturing, service, small business, education, health care, and not-for-profit.

Candidates for the award must submit an application of up to 50 pages that details the approach, deployment, and results of their quality activities under seven major categories: Leadership, Strategic Planning, Customer and Market Focus, Information and Analysis, Human Resource Focus, Process Management, and Business Results. These applications are scored on total points out of 1,000 by examiners and judges. Those who score above roughly 650 are selected for site visits. Winners selected from this group are then honored at an annual meeting in Washington, D.C. A major benefit to all applicants is feedback from the examiners, which is essentially an audit of their practices. Many states have used the Baldrige Criteria as the basis of their own quality award programs. A report, *Building on Baldrige: American Quality for the 21st Century,* by the private Council on Competitiveness, said, "More than any other program, the Baldrige Quality Award is responsible for making quality a national priority and disseminating best practices across the United States."

	CROSBY	DEMING	JURAN
Definition of quality	Conformance to requirements	A predictable degree of uniformity and dependability at low cost and suited to the market	Fitness for use (satisfies customer's needs)
Degree of senior management responsibility	Responsible for quality	Responsible for 94% of quality problems	Less than 20% of quality problems are due to workers
Performance standard/ motivation	Zero defects	Quality has many "scales"; use statistics to measure performance in all areas; critical of zero defects	Avoid campaigns to do perfect work
General approach	Prevention, not inspection	Reduce variability by continuous improvement; cease mass inspection	General management approach to quality, especially human elements
Structure	14 steps to quality improvement	14 points for management	10 steps to quality improvement
Statistical process control (SPC)	Rejects statistically acceptable levels of quality (wants 100% perfect quality)	Statistical methods of quality control must be used	Recommends SPC but warns that it can lead to tool-driver approach
Improvement basis	A process, not a program; improvement goals	Continuous to reduce variation; eliminate goals without methods	Project-by-project team approach; set goals
Teamwork	Quality improvement teams; quality councils	Employee participation in decision making; break down barriers between departments	Team and quality circle approach
Costs of quality	Cost of nonconformance; quality is free	No optimum; continuous improvement	Quality is not free; there is not an optimum
Purchasing and goods received	State requirements; supplier is extension of business; most faults due to purchasers themselves	Inspection too late; sampling allows defects to enter system; statistical evidence and control charts required	Problems are complex; carry out formal surveys
Vendor rating	Yes, quality audits useless	No, critical of most systems	Yes, but help supplier improve

The Quality Gurus Compared — exhibit 10.1

Quality Specifications and Quality Costs
Fundamental to any quality program is the determination of quality specifications and the costs of achieving (or *not* achieving) those specifications.

Developing Quality Specifications The quality specifications of a product or service derive from decisions and actions made relative to the quality of its design and the quality of its conformance to that design.

Design quality refers to the inherent value of the product in the marketplace and is thus a strategic decision for the firm. The dimensions of quality are listed in Exhibit 10.2. These dimensions refer to features of the product or service that relate directly to design issues.

A firm designs a product or service with certain performance characteristics and features based on what an intended market expects. Materials and manufacturing process

Design quality
The inherent value of the product in the marketplace.

exhibit 10.2 — The Dimensions of Design Quality

DIMENSION	MEANING
Performance	Primary product or service characteristics
Features	Added touches, bells and whistles, secondary characteristics
Reliability/durability	Consistency of performance over time, probability of failing, useful life
Serviceability	Ease of repair
Aesthetics	Sensory characteristics (sound, feel, look, and so on)
Perceived quality	Past performance and reputation

attributes can greatly impact the reliability and durability of a product. Here, the company attempts to design a product or service that can be produced or delivered at reasonable cost. The serviceability of the product may have a great impact on the cost of the product or service to the customer after the initial purchase is made. It also may impact the warranty and repair cost to the firm. Aesthetics may greatly impact the desirability of the product or service, in particular consumer products. Especially when a brand name is involved, the design often represents the next generation of an ongoing stream of products or services. Consistency in the relative performance of the product compared to the state of the art, for example, may have a great impact on how the quality of the product is perceived. This may be very important to the long-run success of the product or service.

Conformance quality refers to the degree to which the product or service design specifications are met. The activities involved in achieving conformance are of a tactical, day-to-day nature. It should be evident that a product or service can have high design quality but low conformance quality, and vice versa.

Conformance quality
The degree to which the product or service design specifications are met.

J.D. Power and Associates Initial Quality Study of New Cars

J.D. Power and Associates uses concepts similar to those discussed in this section to measure the quality of new automobiles during the first 90 days of ownership. The study is run each year on newly designed vehicles produced by manufacturers from around the world. Each year, results from the study are published at www.jdpower.com. The study captures problems experienced by owners in two distinct categories—design-related problems and defects and malfunctions. The following is a list of their measures:

Powertrain Quality—Design: This score is based on problems with the engine or transmission, as well as problems that affect the driving experience (i.e., ride smoothness, responsiveness of the steering system and brakes, and handling/stability).

Body and Interior Quality—Design: This score is based on problems with the front-/rear-end styling, the appearance of the interior and exterior, and the sound of the doors when closing.

Features and Accessories Quality—Design: This score is based on problems with the seats, stereo/navigation system, heater, air conditioner, and sunroof.

Overall Quality—Mechanical: This score is based on problems that have caused a complete breakdown or malfunction of any component, feature, or item (i.e., components that stop working or trim pieces that break or come loose).

Body and Interior Quality—Mechanical: This score is based on problems with wind noise, water leaks, poor interior fit/finish, paint imperfection, and squeaks/rattles.

Features and Accessories Quality—Mechanical: This score is based on problems with the seats, windshield wipers, navigation system, rear-seat entertainment system, heater, air conditioner, stereo system, sunroof, and trip computer.

Source: www.jdpower.com.

Examples of Dimensions of Quality		exhibit 10.3

	MEASURES	
DIMENSION	PRODUCT EXAMPLE: LASER PRINTER	SERVICE EXAMPLE: CHECKING ACCOUNT AT A BANK
Performance	Pages per minute Print density	Time to process customer requests
Features	Multiple paper trays Color capability	Automatic bill paying
Reliability/ durability	Mean time between failures Estimated time to obsolescence Expected life of major components	Variability of time to process requests Keeping pace with industry trends
Serviceability	Availability of authorized repair centers Number of copies per print cartridge Modular design	Online reports Ease of getting updated information
Aesthetics	Control button layout Case style Courtesy of dealer	Appearance of bank lobby Courtesy of teller
Perceived quality	Brand name recognition Rating in *Consumer Reports*	Endorsed by community leaders

Quality at the source is frequently discussed in the context of conformance quality. This means that the person who does the work takes responsibility for making sure that his or her output meets specifications. Where a product is involved, achieving the quality specifications is typically the responsibility of manufacturing management; in a service firm, it is usually the responsibility of the location operations manager. Exhibit 10.3 shows two examples of the **dimensions of quality**. One is a laser printer that meets the pages-per-minute and print density standards; the second is a checking account transaction in a bank.

Both quality of design and quality of conformance should provide products that meet the customer's objectives for those products. This is often termed the product's *fitness for use*, and it entails identifying the dimensions of the product (or service) that the customer wants (i.e., the voice of the customer) and developing a quality control program to ensure that these dimensions are met.

Cost of Quality Although few can quarrel with the notion of prevention, management often needs hard numbers to determine how much prevention activities will cost. This issue was recognized by Joseph Juran, who wrote about it in 1951 in his *Quality Control Handbook*. Today, **cost of quality (COQ)** analyses are common in industry and constitute one of the primary functions of QC departments.

There are a number of definitions and interpretations of the term *cost of quality*. From the purist's point of view, it means all of the costs attributable to the production of quality that is not 100 percent perfect. A less stringent definition considers only those costs that are the difference between what can be expected from excellent performance and the current costs that exist.

Quality at the source
Making the person who does the work responsible for ensuring that specifications are met.

Dimensions of quality
Criteria by which quality is measured.

Cost of quality (COQ)
Expenditures related to achieving product or service quality, such as the costs of prevention, appraisal, internal failure, and external failure.

How significant is the cost of quality? It has been estimated at between 15 and 20 percent of every sales dollar—the cost of reworking, scrapping, repeated service, inspections, tests, warranties, and other quality-related items. It is generally believed that the correct cost for a well-run quality management program should be under 2.5 percent.

Three basic assumptions justify an analysis of the costs of quality: (1) failures occur, (2) prevention is cheaper, and (3) performance can be measured.

The costs of quality are generally classified into four types:

- **Appraisal costs.** Costs of the inspection, testing, and other tasks to ensure that the product or process is acceptable.
- **Prevention costs.** The sum of all the costs to prevent defects, such as the costs to identify the cause of the defect, to implement corrective action to eliminate the cause, to train personnel, to redesign the product or system, and to purchase new equipment or make modifications.
- **Internal failure costs.** Costs for defects incurred within the system: scrap, rework, repair.
- **External failure costs.** Costs for defects that pass through the system: customer warranty replacements, loss of customers or goodwill, handling complaints, and product repair.

Exhibit 10.4 illustrates the type of report that might be submitted to show the various costs by categories. Prevention is the most important influence. A rule of thumb says that for every dollar you spend in prevention, you can save $10 in failure and appraisal costs.

Often, increases in productivity occur as a by-product of efforts to reduce the cost of quality. A bank, for example, set out to improve quality and reduce the cost of quality

Quality Cost Report		exhibit 10.4
	CURRENT MONTH'S COST	PERCENTAGE OF TOTAL
Prevention costs		
Quality training	$ 2,000	1.3%
Reliability consulting	10,000	6.5
Pilot production runs	5,000	3.3
Systems development	8,000	5.2
Total prevention	$ 25,000	16.3%
Appraisal costs		
Materials inspection	6,000	3.9
Supplies inspection	3,000	2.0
Reliability testing	5,000	3.3
Laboratory testing	25,000	16.3
Total appraisal	$ 39,000	25.5%
Internal failure costs		
Scrap	15,000	9.8
Repair	18,000	11.8
Rework	12,000	7.8
Downtime	6,000	3.9
Total internal failure	$ 51,000	33.3%
External failure costs		
Warranty costs	14,000	9.2
Out-of-warranty repairs and replacement	6,000	3.9
Customer complaints	3,000	2.0
Product liability	10,000	6.5
Transportation losses	5,000	3.3
Total external failure	$ 38,000	24.8%
Total quality costs	$153,000	100.0%

and found that it had also boosted productivity. The bank developed this productivity measure for the loan processing area: the number of tickets processed divided by the resources required (labor cost, computer time, ticket forms). Before the quality improvement program, the productivity index was 0.2661 [2,080/($11.23 × 640 hours + $0.05 × 2,600 forms + $500 for systems costs)]. After the quality improvement project was completed, labor time fell to 546 hours and the number of forms rose to 2,100, for a change in the index to 0.3106 [2,100/($11.23 × 546 hours + $0.05 × 2,600 forms + $500 for system costs)], an increase in productivity of over 16 percent.

ISO 9000 AND ISO 14000

ISO 9000 and ISO 14000 are international standards for quality management and assurance. The standards are designed to help companies document that they are maintaining an efficient quality system. The standards were originally published in 1987 by the International Organization for Standardization (ISO), a specialized international agency

LO10–2 Illustrate globally recognized quality benchmarks.

ISO 9000

Formal standards for quality certification developed by the International Organization for Standardization.

recognized by affiliates in more than 160 countries. **ISO 9000** has become an international reference for quality management requirements in business-to-business dealing, and ISO 14000 is primarily concerned with environmental management.

The idea behind the standards is that defects can be prevented through the planning and application of *best practices* at every stage of business—from design through manufacturing and then installation and servicing. These standards focus on identifying criteria by which any organization, regardless of whether it is manufacturing- or service-oriented, can ensure that product leaving its facility meets the requirements of its customers. These standards ask a company first to document and implement its systems for quality management and then to verify, by means of an audit conducted by an independent accredited third party, the compliance of those systems with the requirements of the standards.

The ISO 9000 standards are based on seven quality management principles. These principles focus on business processes related to different areas in the firm. These areas include (1) customer focus, (2) leadership, (3) involvement of people, (4) process approach, (5) continual improvement, (6) factual approach to decision making, and (7) mutually beneficial supplier relationships. The ISO documents provide detailed requirements for meeting the standards and describe standard tools that are used for improving quality in the firm. These documents are intended to be generic and applicable to any organization producing products or services.

The ISO 14000 family of standards on environmental management addresses the need to be environmentally responsible. The standards define a three-pronged approach for dealing with environmental challenges. The first is the definition of more than 350 international standards for monitoring the quality of air, water, and soil. For many countries, these standards serve as the technical basis for environmental regulation. The second part of ISO 14000 is a strategic approach: defining the requirements of an environmental management system that can be implemented using the monitoring tools. Finally, the environmental standard encourages the inclusion of environmental aspects in product design and encourages the development of profitable environment-friendly products and services.

In addition to the generic ISO 9000 and ISO 14000 standards, many other specific standards have been defined. The following are some examples:

- QS-9000 is a quality management system developed by Chrysler, Ford, and General Motors for suppliers of production parts, materials, and services to the automotive industry.
- ISO/TS 16949, developed by the International Automotive Task Force, aligns existing American, German, French, and Italian automotive quality standards within the global automotive industry.
- ISO 14001 environmental standards are applied by automobile suppliers as a requirement from Ford and General Motors.
- ANSI/ASQ Z1.4-2003 provides methods for collecting, analyzing, and interpreting data for inspection by attributes, while Z1.9-2003 relates to inspection by variables.
- TL 9000 defines the telecommunications quality system requirements for the design, development, production, delivery, installation, and maintenance of products and services in the telecommunications industry.

New ISO documents are being developed on an ongoing basis. ISO 26000, which offers guidance on socially responsible behavior, has recently been adopted. The standard encourages organizations to discuss the social responsibility issues and possible actions with relevant stakeholders. Although not a strict "standard," the document argues that being socially responsible is a requirement for both public and private sector organizations.

The ISO standards provide accepted global guidelines for quality. Although certification is not required, many companies have found it is essential to be competitive in the global markets. Consider the situation where you need to purchase parts for your firm and several suppliers offer similar parts at similar prices. Assume that one of these firms has been ISO 9000–certified and the others have not. From whom would you purchase? There is no doubt that the ISO 9000–certified company would have the inside track in your decision making. Why? Because ISO 9000 specifies the way the supplier firm operates as well as its quality standards, delivery times, service levels, and so on.

There are three forms of certification:

- First party: A firm audits itself against ISO 9000 standards.
- Second party: A customer audits its supplier.
- Third party: A "qualified" national or international standards or certifying agency serves as an auditor.

The best certification of a firm is through a third party. Once passed by the third-party audit, a firm is certified and may be registered and recorded as having achieved ISO 9000 status and it becomes a part of a registry of certified companies. This third-party certification also has legal advantages in the European Community. For example, a manufacturer is liable for injury to a user of the product.

The firm, however, can free itself from any liability by showing that it has used the appropriate standards in its production process and carefully selected its suppliers as part of its purchasing requirements. For this reason, there is strong motivation to choose ISO 9000–certified suppliers.

External Benchmarking for Quality Improvement

The quality improvement approaches described so far are more or less inward looking. They seek to make improvements by analyzing in detail the current practices of the company itself. **External benchmarking**, however, goes outside the organization to examine what industry competitors and excellent performers outside of the industry are doing. Benchmarking typically involves the following steps:

External benchmarking Looking outside the company to examine what excellent performers inside and outside the company's industry are doing in the way of quality.

Identify processes needing improvement. Identify a firm that is the world leader in performing the process. For many processes, this may be a company that is not in the same industry. Examples would be Procter & Gamble using L.L.Bean as the benchmark in evaluating its order entry system, or ICL (a large British computer maker) benchmarking Marks and Spencer (a large UK department store) to improve its distribution system. A McKinsey study cited a firm that measured pit stops on a motor racing circuit as a benchmark for worker changes on its assembly line. *Contact the managers of that company and make a personal visit to interview managers and workers.* Many companies select a team of workers from that process as part of the team of visitors.

Analyze data. This entails looking at gaps between what your company is doing and what the benchmarking company is doing. There are two aspects of the study: One is comparing the actual processes; the other is comparing the performance of these processes according to a set of measures. The processes are often described using flowcharts and subjective evaluations of how workers relate to the process. In some cases, companies even permit video recording.

SIX SIGMA QUALITY

LO10–3
Understand the Six Sigma approach to improving quality and productivity.

Six Sigma
A statistical term to describe the quality goal of no more than 3.4 defects out of every million units. Also refers to a quality improvement philosophy and program.

Defects per million opportunities (DPMO)
A metric used to describe the variability of a process.

Six Sigma refers to the philosophy and methods companies such as General Electric and Motorola use to eliminate defects in their products and processes. A defect is simply any component that does not fall within the customer's specification limits. Each step or activity in a company represents an opportunity for defects to occur and Six Sigma programs seek to reduce the variation in the processes that lead to these defects. Indeed, Six Sigma advocates see variation as the enemy of quality, and much of the theory underlying Six Sigma is devoted to dealing with this problem. A process that is in Six Sigma control will produce no more than two defects out of every billion units. Often, this is stated as 3.4 defects per million units, which is true if the process is only running somewhere within 1.5 sigma of the target specification.

One of the benefits of Six Sigma thinking is that it allows managers to readily describe the performance of a process in terms of its variability and to compare different processes using a common metric. This metric is **defects per million opportunities (DPMO)**. This calculation requires three pieces of data:

1. **Unit.** The item produced or being serviced.
2. **Defect.** Any item or event that does not meet the customer's requirements.
3. **Opportunity.** A chance for a defect to occur.

A straightforward calculation is made using the following formula:

$$DPMO = \frac{\text{Number of defects}}{\text{Number of opportunities for error per unit} \times \text{Number of units}} \times 1{,}000{,}000$$

Example 10.1

The customers of a mortgage bank expect to have their mortgage applications processed within 10 days of filing. This would be called a *critical customer requirement,* or CCR, in Six Sigma terms. Suppose all defects are counted (loans in a monthly sample taking more than 10 days to process), and it is determined that there are 150 loans in the 1,000 applications processed last month that don't meet this customer requirement. Thus, the DPMO = 150/1,000 × 1,000,000, or 150,000 loans out of every million processed that fail to meet a CCR. Put differently, it means that only 850,000 loans out of a million are approved within time expectations. Statistically, 15 percent of the loans are defective and 85 percent are correct. This is a case where all the loans processed in less than 10 days meet our criteria. Often, there are upper and lower customer requirements rather than just a single upper requirement as we have here.

DMAIC
An acronym for the **D**efine, **M**easure, **A**nalyze, **I**mprove, and **C**ontrol improvement methodology followed by companies engaging in Six Sigma programs.

In the following section, we describe the Six Sigma process cycle and tools commonly used in Six Sigma projects.

Six Sigma Methodology

While Six Sigma's methods include many of the statistical tools that were employed in other quality movements, here they are employed in a systematic project-oriented fashion through the define, measure, analyze, improve, and control (**DMAIC**) cycle. The overarching focus of the methodology is understanding and achieving what the customer wants, since that is seen as the key to profitability of a production process. In fact, to get across this point, some use the DMAIC as an acronym for "Dumb Managers Always Ignore Customers."

A standard approach to Six Sigma projects is the DMAIC methodology described below:

1. Define (D)
   - Identify customers and their priorities.
   - Identify a project suitable for Six Sigma efforts based on business objectives as well as customer needs and feedback.
   - Identify CTQs (critical-to-quality characteristics) that the customer considers to have the most impact on quality.
2. Measure (M)
   - Determine how to measure the process and how it is performing.
   - Identify the key internal processes that influence CTQs and measure the defects currently generated relative to those processes.
3. Analyze (A)
   - Determine the most likely causes of defects.
   - Understand why defects are generated by identifying the key variables that are most likely to create process variation.
4. Improve (I)
   - Identify means to remove the causes of defects.
   - Confirm the key variables and quantify their effects on the CTQs.
   - Identify the maximum acceptance ranges of the key variables and a system for measuring deviations of the variables.
   - Modify the process to stay within an acceptable range.
5. Control (C)
   - Determine how to maintain the improvements.
   - Put tools in place to ensure that the key variables remain within the maximum acceptance ranges under the modified process.

Source: S. Walleck, D. O'Halloran, and C. Leader, "Benchmarking World-Class Performance," *McKinsey Quarterly,* no. 1 (1991), p. 7.

Analytical Tools for Six Sigma

The analytical tools of Six Sigma have been used for many years in traditional quality improvement programs. What makes their application to Six Sigma unique is the integration of these tools in a corporatewide management system. The tools common to all quality efforts are flowcharts, run charts, Pareto charts, histograms, checksheets, cause-and-effect diagrams, and control charts. Examples of these, along with an opportunity flow diagram, are shown in Exhibit 10.5, arranged according to DMAIC categories where they commonly appear.

Flowcharts. There are many types of flowcharts. The one shown in Exhibit 10.5 depicts the process steps as part of a SIPOC (supplier, input, process, output, customer) analysis. SIPOC, in essence, is a formalized input-output model, used in the define stage of a project.

Run charts. They depict trends in data over time, and thereby help companies understand the magnitude of a problem at the define stage.

Pareto charts. These charts help break down a problem into the relative contributions of its components. They are based on the common empirical finding that a large percentage of problems are due to a small percentage of causes. In the example, 80 percent of customer complaints are due to late deliveries, which are 20 percent of the causes listed.

exhibit 10.5   Analytical Tools for Six Sigma and Continuous Improvement

Define

Flowchart of Major Steps in a Process

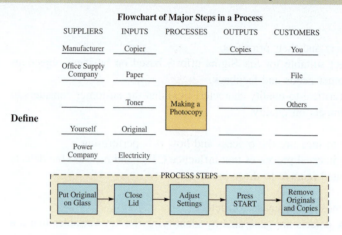

Measure

Run Chart
Average monthly volume of deliveries
(per shop)

1,951 deliveries

Pareto Chart
Types of customer complaints
Total = 2520 October–December
(across 6 shops)

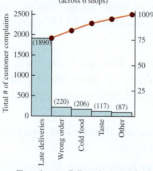

Illustration note: Delivery time was defined
by the total time from when the order was
placed to when the customer received it.

DATA COLLECTION FORMS

Checksheets are basic forms that help standardize data collection
by providing specific spaces where people should record data.

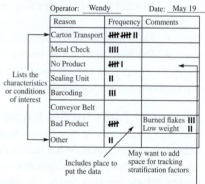

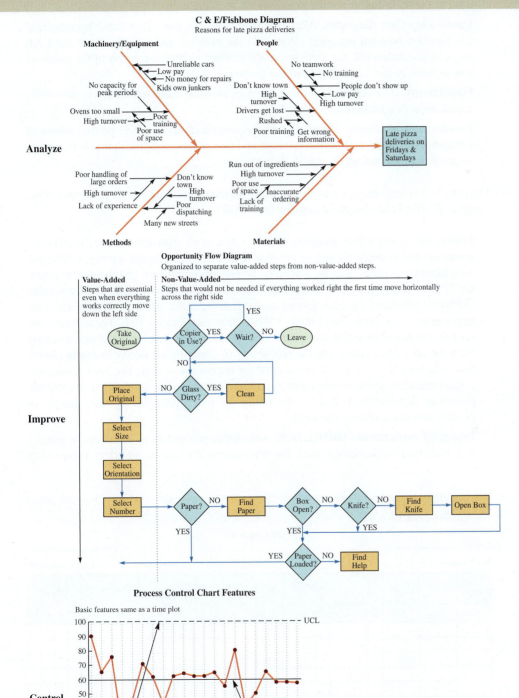

C & E/Fishbone Diagram
Reasons for late pizza deliveries

Analyze

Machinery/Equipment
- Unreliable cars
- Low pay
- No money for repairs
- Kids own junkers
- No capacity for peak periods
- Ovens too small
- High turnover
- Poor training
- Poor use of space

People
- No teamwork
- No training
- Don't know town
- People don't show up
- High turnover
- Low pay
- High turnover
- Drivers get lost
- Rushed
- Poor training
- Get wrong information

Late pizza deliveries on Fridays & Saturdays

Methods
- Poor handling of large orders
- High turnover
- Lack of experience
- Don't know town
- High turnover
- Poor dispatching
- Many new streets

Materials
- Run out of ingredients
- High turnover
- Poor use of space
- Lack of training
- Inaccurate ordering

Opportunity Flow Diagram
Organized to separate value-added steps from non-value-added steps.

Improve

Value-Added
Steps that are essential even when everything works correctly move down the left side

Non-Value-Added
Steps that would not be needed if everything worked right the first time move horizontally across the right side

Take Original → Copier in Use? → YES → Wait? → NO → Leave
YES (Wait? → YES)
NO
Glass Dirty? → YES → Clean
Place Original ← NO
Select Size
Select Orientation
Select Number → Paper? → NO → Find Paper → Box Open? → NO → Knife? → NO → Find Knife → Open Box
YES
Paper Loaded? → NO → Find Help
YES

Process Control Chart Features

Basic features same as a time plot

Control

UCL — 100
LCL — 20

J A S O N D J F M A M J J A S O N D J F M

Control limits (calculated from data) added to plot

Centerline usually average instead of median

Checksheets. These are basic forms that help standardize data collection. They are used to create histograms such as shown on the Pareto chart.

Cause-and-effect diagrams. Also called *fishbone diagrams,* they show hypothesized relationships between potential causes and the problem under study. Once the C&E diagram is constructed, the analysis would proceed to find out which of the potential causes were in fact contributing to the problem.

Opportunity flow diagram. This is used to separate value-added from non-value-added steps in a process.

Process control charts. These are time-sequenced charts showing plotted values of a statistic, including a centerline average and one or more control limits. It is used to assure that processes are in statistical control.

Other tools that have seen extensive use in Six Sigma projects are failure mode and effect analysis (FMEA) and design of experiments (DOE).

Failure mode and effect analysis. This is a structured approach to identify, estimate, prioritize, and evaluate the risk of possible failures at each stage of a process. It begins with identifying each element, assembly, or part of the process and listing the potential failure modes, potential causes, and effects of each failure. A risk priority number (RPN) is calculated for each failure mode. It is an index used to measure the rank importance of the items listed in the FMEA chart. See Exhibit 10.6. These conditions include the probability that the failure takes place (occurrence), the damage resulting from the failure (severity), and the probability of detecting the failure in-house (detection). High RPN items should be targeted for improvement first. The FMEA suggests a recommended action to eliminate the failure condition by assigning a responsible person or department to resolve the failure by redesigning the system, design, or process and recalculating the RPN.

Design of experiments (DOE). DOE, sometimes referred to as *multivariate testing,* is a statistical methodology used for determining the cause-and-effect relationship

exhibit 10.6   FMEA Form

FMEA Analysis

Project: _____   Date: _____(original)

Team: _____   _____ (revised)

Item or Process Step	Potential Failure Mode	Potential Effects of Failure	Severity	Potential Cause(s)	Occurrence	Current Controls	Detection	RPN	Recommended Action	Responsibility and Target Date	"After" → Action Taken	Severity	Occurrence	Detection	RPN
Total Risk Priority Number:										"After" Risk Priority Number:					

between process variables (Xs) and the output variable (Y). In contrast to standard statistical tests, which require changing each individual variable to determine the most influential one, DOE permits experimentation with many variables simultaneously by carefully selecting a subset of them.

STATISTICAL QUALITY CONTROL

This section on **statistical quality control (SQC)** covers the quantitative aspects of quality management. In general, SQC is a number of different techniques designed to evaluate quality from a conformance view; that is, how well are we doing at meeting the specifications that have been set during the design of the parts or services that we are providing? Managing quality performance using SQC techniques usually involves periodic sampling of a process and analysis of these data using statistically derived performance criteria.

As you will see, SQC can be applied to logistics, manufacturing, and service processes. Here are some examples of situations where SQC can be applied:

- How many paint defects are there in the finish of a car? Have we improved our painting process by installing a new sprayer?
- How long does it take to execute market orders in our Web-based trading system? Has the installation of a new server improved the service? Does the performance of the system vary over the trading day?
- How well are we able to maintain the dimensional tolerance on our three-inch ball bearing assembly? Given the variability of our process for making this ball bearing, how many defects would we expect to produce per million bearings that we make?
- How long does it take for customers to be served from our drive-through window during the busy lunch period?

Processes that provide goods and services usually exhibit some variation in their output. This variation can be caused by many factors, some of which we can control and others that are inherent in the process. Variation that is caused by factors that can be clearly identified and possibly even managed is called **assignable variation**. For example, variation caused by workers not being equally trained or by improper machine adjustment is assignable variation. Variation that is inherent in the process itself is called **common variation**. Common variation is often referred to as *random variation* and may be the result of the type of equipment used to complete a process, for example.

As the title of this section implies, this material requires an understanding of very basic statistics. Recall from your study of statistics involving numbers that are normally distributed the definition of the mean and standard deviation. The mean ($\overline{X}$) is just the average value of a set of numbers. Mathematically this is

$$\overline{X} = \frac{\sum_{i=1}^{n} x_i}{n}$$ [10.1]

where:

x_i = Observed value
n = Total number of observed values

LO10–4 Illustrate process variation and explain how to measure it.

Statistical quality control (SQC)
A number of different techniques designed to evaluate quality from a conformance view.

Assignable variation
Deviation in the output of a process that can be clearly identified and managed.

Common variation
Deviation in the output of a process that is random and inherent in the process itself.

The standard deviation is

$$\sigma = \sqrt{\frac{\sum_{i=1}^{n}(x_i - \overline{X})^2}{n}}$$

[10.2]

In monitoring a process using SQC, samples of the process output would be taken and sample statistics calculated. The distribution associated with the samples should exhibit the same kind of variability as the actual distribution of the process, although the actual variance of the sampling distribution would be less. This is good because it allows the quick detection of changes in the actual distribution of the process. The purpose of sampling is to find when the process has changed in some nonrandom way, so that the reason for the change can be quickly determined.

In SQC terminology, *sigma* (or the symbol σ) is often used to refer to the sample standard deviation. As you will see in the examples, sigma is calculated in a few different ways, depending on the underlying theoretical distribution (i.e., a normal distribution or a Poisson distribution).

Understanding and Measuring Process Variation

It is generally accepted that as variation is reduced, quality is improved. Sometimes that knowledge is intuitive. If a commuter train is always on time, schedules can be planned more precisely. If clothing sizes are consistent, time can be saved by ordering from a catalog. But rarely are such things thought about in terms of the value of low variability. When engineering a mechanical device such as an automobile, the knowledge is better defined. Pistons must fit cylinders, doors must fit openings, electrical components must be compatible, and tires must be able to handle the required load—otherwise quality will be unacceptable and customers will be dissatisfied.

However, engineers also know that it is impossible to have zero variability. For this reason, designers establish specifications that define not only the target value of something but also acceptable limits about the target. For example, if the target value of a

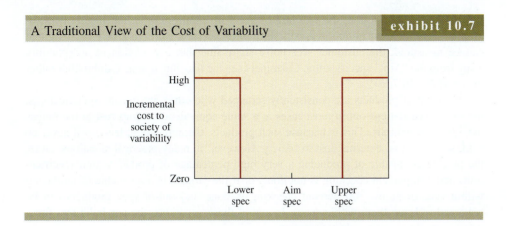

A Traditional View of the Cost of Variability   **exhibit 10.7**

dimension is 10 inches, the design specifications might then be 10.00 inches ± 0.02 inch. This would tell the manufacturing department that, while it should aim for exactly 10 inches, anything between 9.98 and 10.02 inches is OK. These design limits are often referred to as the **upper and lower specification limits**.

A traditional way of interpreting such a specification is that any part that falls within the allowed range is equally good, whereas any part falling outside the range is totally bad. This is illustrated in Exhibit 10.7. (Note that the cost is zero over the entire specification range, and then there is a quantum leap in cost once the limit is violated.)

Genichi Taguchi (1924–2012), a noted quality expert from Japan who developed a methodology for applying statistics to improve the quality of manufactured goods, pointed out that the traditional view illustrated in Exhibit 10.7 is nonsense for two reasons:

1. From the customer's view, there is often practically no difference between a product just inside specifications and a product just outside. Conversely, there is a far greater difference in the quality of a product that is at the target and the quality of one that is near a limit.
2. As customers get more demanding, there is pressure to reduce variability. However, Exhibit 10.7 does not reflect this logic.

Taguchi suggests that a more correct picture of the loss is shown in Exhibit 10.8. Notice that in this graph the cost is represented by a smooth curve. There are dozens of

Upper and lower specification limits The range of values in a measure associated with a process that is allowable given the intended use of the product or service.

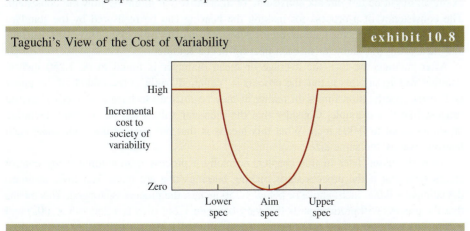

Taguchi's View of the Cost of Variability   **exhibit 10.8**

illustrations of this notion: the meshing of gears in a transmission, the speed of photographic film, the temperature in a workplace or department store. In nearly anything that can be measured, the customer sees not a sharp line, but a gradation of acceptability away from the "Aim" specification. Customers see the loss function as Exhibit 10.8 rather than Exhibit 10.7.

Of course, if products are consistently scrapped when they are outside specifications, the loss curve flattens out in most cases at a value equivalent to scrap cost in the ranges outside specifications. This is because such products, theoretically at least, will never be sold, so there is no external cost to society. However, in many practical situations, either the process is capable of producing a very high percentage of product within specifications and 100 percent checking is not done, or if the process is not capable of producing within specifications, 100 percent checking is done and out-of-spec products can be reworked to bring them within specs. In any of these situations, the parabolic loss function is usually a reasonable assumption.

Process Capability

Taguchi argues that being within specification is not a yes/no decision, but rather a continuous function. The Motorola quality experts, on the other hand, argue that the process used to produce a good or deliver a service should be so good that the probability of generating a defect should be very, very low. Motorola made process capability and product design famous by adopting Six Sigma limits. When a part is designed, certain dimensions are specified to be within the upper and lower specification limits.

As a simple example, assume engineers are designing a bearing for a rotating shaft—say an axle for the wheel of a car. There are many variables involved for both the bearing and the axle—for example, the width of the bearing, the size of the rollers, the size of the axle, the length of the axle, how it is supported, and so on. The designer specifies limits for each of these variables to ensure that the parts will fit properly. Suppose that initially a design is selected and the diameter of the bearing is set at 1.250 inches ± 0.005 inch. This means that acceptable parts may have a diameter that varies between 1.245 and 1.255 inches (which are the lower and upper specification limits).

Next, consider the process in which the bearing will be made. Consider that many different processes for making the bearing are available. Usually there are trade-offs that need to be considered when designing a process for making a part. The process, for example, might be fast but not consistent, or alternatively it might be slow but consistent. The consistency of a process for making the bearing can be measured by the standard deviation of the diameter measurement. A test can be run by making, say, 100 bearings and measuring the diameter of each bearing in the sample.

After running the test, the average or mean diameter is found to be 1.250 inches. Another way to say this is that the process is "centered" right in the middle of the upper and lower specification limits. In reality, it may be difficult to have a perfectly centered process like this example. Consider that the diameter values have a standard deviation or sigma equal to 0.002 inch. What this means is that the process does not make each bearing exactly the same size.

As is discussed later in this chapter, normally a process is monitored using control charts such that if the process starts making bearings that are more than three standard deviations (± 0.006 inch) above or below 1.250 inches, the process is stopped. This means that the process will produce parts that vary between 1.244 (this is $1.250 - 3 \times .002$) and 1.256 (this is $1.250 + 3 \times .002$) inches. The 1.244 and 1.256 are referred to as the upper and lower process limits. Be careful not to get the terminology confused here. The "process" limits relate to how consistent the process is for making the bearing. The goal in managing the process is to keep it within plus or minus three standard deviations of the process mean. The "specification" limits are related to the design of the part. Recall that, from a design view, acceptable parts have a diameter between 1.245 and 1.255 inches (which are the lower and upper specification limits).

As can be seen, process limits are slightly greater than the specification limits given by the designer. This is not good, because the process will produce some parts that do not meet specifications. Companies with Six Sigma processes insist that a process making a part be capable of operating so that the design specification limits are six standard deviations away from the process mean. For the bearing process, how small would the process standard deviation need to be for it to be Six Sigma capable? Recall that the design specification was 1.250 inches plus or minus 0.005 inch. Consider that the 0.005 inch must relate to the variation in the process. Divide 0.005 inch by 6, which equals 0.00083, to determine the process standard deviation for a Six Sigma process. So, for the process to be Six Sigma capable, the mean diameter produced by the process would need to be exactly 1.250 inches and the process standard deviation would need to be less than or equal to 0.00083 inch.

We can imagine that some of you are really confused at this point with the whole idea of Six Sigma. Why doesn't the company, for example, just check the diameter of each bearing and throw out the ones with a diameter less than 1.245 or greater than 1.255? This could certainly be done, and for many, many parts 100 percent testing is done. The problem is for a company that is making thousands of parts each hour, testing each critical dimension of each part made can be very expensive. For the bearing, there could easily be 10 or more additional critical dimensions in addition to the diameter. These would all need to be checked. Using a 100 percent testing approach, the company would spend more time testing than it takes to actually make the part! This is why a company uses small samples to periodically check that the process is in statistical control. We discuss exactly how this statistical sampling works later in the chapter.

We say that a process is *capable* when the mean and standard deviation of the process are operating such that the upper and lower control limits are acceptable relative to the upper and lower specification limits. Consider diagram A in Exhibit 10.9. This represents the distribution of the bearing diameter dimension in our original process. The average or mean value is 1.250 and the lower and upper design specifications are 1.245 and 1.255, respectively. Process control limits are plus and minus three standard deviations (1.244 and 1.256). Notice that there is a probability (the yellow areas) of producing defective parts.

If the process can be improved by reducing the standard deviation associated with the bearing diameter, the probability of producing defective parts can be reduced. Diagram B in Exhibit 10.9 shows a new process where the standard deviation has been reduced to 0.00083 (the area outlined in green). Even though we cannot see it in the diagram, there is some probability that a defect could be produced by this new process, but that probability is very, very small.

Suppose that the central value or mean of the process shifts away from the mean. Exhibit 10.10 shows the mean shifted one standard deviation closer to the upper specification limit. This, of course, causes a slightly higher number of expected defects, but we can see that this is still very, very good. The *capability index* is used to measure how well our process is capable of producing relative to the design specifications. A description of how to calculate this index is in the next section.

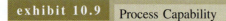

exhibit 10.9 Process Capability

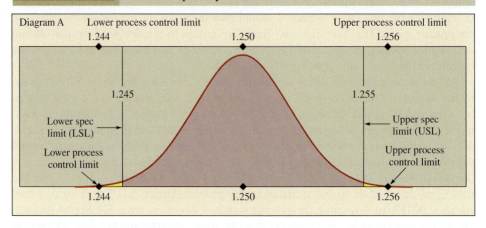

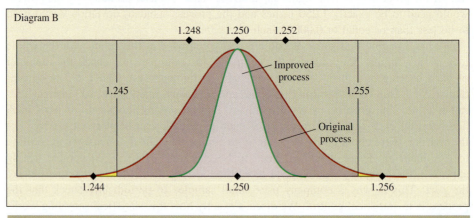

exhibit 10.10 Process Capability with a Shift in the Process Mean

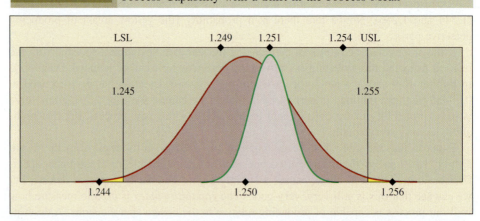

Capability Index (C_{pk}) The **capability index (C_{pk})** shows how well the parts being produced fit into the range specified by the design specification limits. If the specification limits are larger than the three sigma allowed in the process, then the mean of the process can be allowed to drift off-center before readjustment, and a high percentage of good parts will still be produced.

Referring to Exhibits 10.9 and 10.10, the capability index (C_{pk}) is the position of the mean and tails of the process relative to design specifications. The more off-center, the greater the chance to produce defective parts.

Because the process mean can shift in either direction, the direction of shift and its distance from the design specification set the limit on the process capability. The direction of shift is toward the smaller number.

Formally stated, the capability index (C_{pk}) is calculated as the smaller of the two numbers as follows:

$$C_{pk} = \min\left[\frac{\overline{\overline{X}} - LSL}{3\sigma} \quad \text{or} \quad \frac{USL - \overline{\overline{X}}}{3\sigma} \right] \qquad [10.3]$$

Working with our example in Exhibit 10.10, let's assume our process is centered at 1.251 and $\sigma = 0.00083$ (σ is the symbol for standard deviation).

$$C_{pk} = \min\left[\frac{1.251 - 1.245}{3(.00083)} \quad \text{or} \quad \frac{1.255 - 1.251}{3(.00083)} \right]$$

$$= \min\left[\frac{.006}{.00249} \quad \text{or} \quad \frac{.004}{.00249} \right]$$

$$C_{pk} = \min[2.4 \quad \text{or} \quad 1.6]$$

$C_{pk} = 1.6$, which is the smaller number. This is a pretty good capability index since few defects will be produced by this process.

This tells us that the process mean has shifted to the right similar to Exhibit 10.10, but parts are still well within design specification limits.

At times, it is useful to calculate the actual probability of producing a defect. Assuming that the process is producing with a consistent standard deviation, this is a fairly straightforward calculation, particularly when we have access to a spreadsheet. The approach to use is to calculate the probability of producing a part outside the lower and upper design specification limits given the mean and standard deviation of the process.

Working with our example, where the process is not centered, with a mean of 1.251 inches, $\sigma = .00083$, LSL = 1.245, and USL = 1.255, we first need to calculate the Z score associated with the upper and lower specification limits. Recall from your study of statistics that the Z score is the standard deviation either to the right or to the left of zero in a probability distribution.

$$Z_{LSL} = \frac{LSL - \overline{\overline{X}}}{\sigma} \qquad Z_{USL} = \frac{USL - \overline{\overline{X}}}{\sigma}$$

For our example,

$$Z_{LSL} = \frac{1.245 - 1.251}{.00083} = -7.2289 \qquad Z_{USL} = \frac{1.255 - 1.251}{.00083} = 4.8193$$

Capability index (C_{pk})
The ratio of the range of values allowed by the design specifications divided by the range of values produced by the process.

Excel: SPC

An easy way to get the probabilities associated with these Z values is to use the NORM.S.DIST function built into Excel (you also can use the table in Appendix E). The format for this function is NORM.S.DIST(Z), where Z is the Z value calculated above. Excel returns the following values. (We have found that you might get slightly different results from those given here, depending on the version of Excel you are using.)

$$\text{NORM.S.DIST}(-7.2289) = 2.43461\text{E-}13 \quad \text{and} \quad \text{NORM.S.DIST}(4.8193) = .99999928$$

Interpreting this information requires understanding exactly what the NORM.S.DIST function is providing. NORM.S.DIST is giving the cumulative probability to the left of the given Z value. Since $Z = -7.2289$ is the number of standard deviations associated with the lower specification limit, the fraction of parts that will be produced lower than this is 2.43461E-13. This number is in scientific notation and that E-13 at the end means we need to move the decimal over 13 places to get the real fraction defective. So the fraction defective is .00000000000024361, which is a very small number! Similarly, we see that approximately .99999928 of our parts will be below our upper specification limit. What we are really interested in is the fraction that will be above this limit since these are the defective parts. This fraction defective above the upper spec is $1 - .99999928 = .00000082$ of our parts.

Adding these two fraction defective numbers together we get .00000082000024361. We can interpret this to mean that we expect only about .82 parts per million to be defective. Clearly, this is a great process. You will discover as you work the problems at the end of the chapter that this is not always the case.

Example 10.2

Excel:
Ch10_SPC

The quality assurance manager is assessing the capability of a process that puts pressurized grease in an aerosol can. The design specifications call for an average of 60 pounds per square inch (psi) of pressure in each can, with an upper specification limit of 65 psi and a lower specification limit of 55 psi. A sample is taken from production and it is found that the cans average 61 psi, with a standard deviation of 2 psi. What is the capability of the process? What is the probability of producing a defect?

SOLUTION

Step 1—Interpret the data from the problem

$$\text{LSL} = 55 \quad \text{USL} = 65 \quad \overline{\overline{X}} = 61 \quad \sigma = 2$$

Step 2—Calculate the C_{pk}

$$C_{pk} = \min\left[\frac{\overline{\overline{X}} - \text{LSL}}{3\sigma}, \frac{\text{USL} - \overline{\overline{X}}}{3\sigma}\right]$$

$$C_{pk} = \min\left[\frac{61 - 55}{3(2)}, \frac{65 - 61}{3(2)}\right]$$

$$C_{pk} = \min\left[1, .6667\right] = .6667$$

This is not a very good capability index. We see why this is true in step 3.

Step 3—Calculate the probability of producing a defective can:
Probability of a can with less than 55 psi

$$Z = \frac{X - \bar{\bar{X}}}{\sigma} = \frac{55 - 61}{2} = -3$$

NORM.S.DIST(−3) = 0.001349898

Probability of a can with more than 65 psi

$$Z = \frac{X - \bar{\bar{X}}}{\sigma} = \frac{65 - 61}{2} = 2$$

1 − NORM.S.DIST(2) = 1 − 0.977249868 = 0.022750132

Probability of a can with less than 55 psi or more than 65 psi

Probability = 0.001349898 + 0.022750132 = .024100030

Or approximately 2.4 percent of the cans will be defective. •

The following table is a quick reference for the fraction of defective units for various design specification limits (expressed in standard deviations). This table assumes that the standard deviation is constant and that the process is centered exactly between the design specification limits.

Design Limits	C_{pk}	Defective Parts	Fraction Defective
±1σ	.333	317 per thousand	.3173
±2σ	.667	45 per thousand	.0455
±3σ	1.0	27 per thousand	.0027
±4σ	1.333	63 per million	.000063
±5σ	1.667	574 per billion	.000000574
±6σ	2.0	2 per billion	.000000002

Motorola's design specification limit of Six Sigma with a shift of the process off the mean by 1.5σ ($C_{pk} = 1.5$) gives 3.4 defects per million. If the mean is exactly in the center ($C_{pk} = 2$), then 2 defects per *billion* are expected, as the table above shows.

STATISTICAL PROCESS CONTROL PROCEDURES

LO10–5 Analyze process quality using statistics.

Process control is concerned with monitoring quality *while the product or service is being produced*. Typical objectives of process control plans are to provide timely information on whether currently produced items are meeting design specifications and to detect shifts in the process that signal that future products may not meet specifications. **Statistical process control (SPC)** involves testing a random sample of output from a process to determine whether the process is producing items within a preselected range.

The examples given so far have all been based on quality characteristics (or *variables*) that are measurable, such as the diameter or weight of a part. **Attributes** are quality characteristics that are classified as either conforming or not conforming to specification. Goods or services may be observed to be either good or bad, or functioning or malfunctioning. For example, a lawnmower either runs or it doesn't; it attains a certain level of torque and horsepower or it doesn't. This type of measurement is known as sampling by

Statistical process control (SPC)
Techniques for testing a random sample of output from a process to determine whether the process is producing items within a prescribed range.

Attributes
Quality characteristics that are classified as either conforming or not conforming to specification.

attributes. Alternatively, a lawnmower's torque and horsepower can be measured as an amount of deviation from a set standard. This type of measurement is known as sampling by variables. The following section describes some standard approaches to controlling processes: first, an approach useful for attribute measures and then an approach for variable measures. Both of these techniques result in the construction of control charts. Exhibit 10.11 shows some examples for how control charts can be analyzed to understand how a process is operating.

exhibit 10.11   Process Control Chart Evidence for Investigation

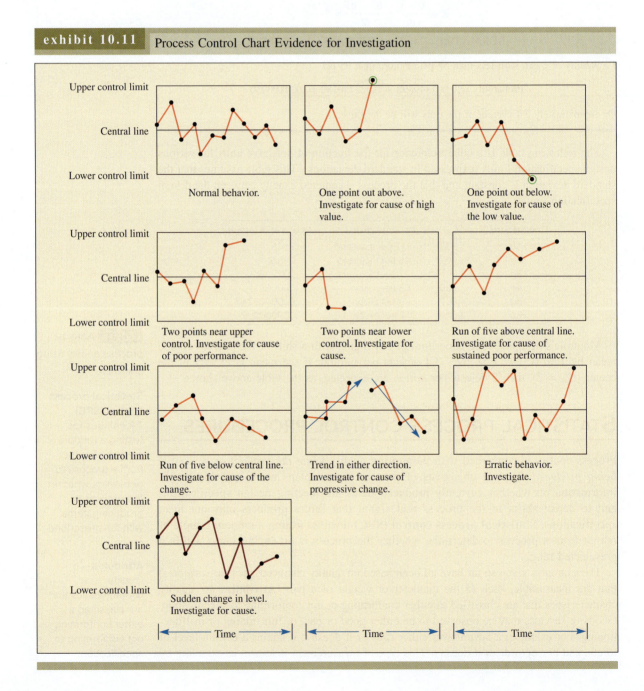

Process Control with Attribute Measurements: Using *p*-Charts

Measurement by attributes means taking samples and using a single decision—the item is good or it is bad. Because it is a yes or no decision, we can use simple statistics to create a *p*-chart with an upper process control limit (UCL) and a lower process control limit (LCL). We can draw these control limits on a graph and then plot the fraction defective of each individual sample tested. The process is assumed to be working correctly when the samples, which are taken periodically during the day, continue to stay between the control limits.

$$\bar{p} = \frac{\text{Total number of defective units from all samples}}{\text{Number of samples} \times \text{Sample size}} \quad [10.4]$$

$$S_p = \sqrt{\frac{\bar{p}(1 - \bar{p})}{n}} \quad [10.5]$$

$$\text{UCL} = \bar{p} + zs_p \quad [10.6]$$

$$\text{LCL} = \bar{p} - zs_p \text{ or 0 if less than 0} \quad [10.7]$$

where $\bar{p}$ is the fraction defective, s_p is the standard deviation, n is the sample size, and z is the number of standard deviations for a specific confidence. Typically, $z = 3$ (99.7 percent confidence) or $z = 2.58$ (99 percent confidence) is used.

Size of the Sample The size of the sample must be large enough to allow counting of the attribute. For example, if we know that a machine produces 1 percent defective units, then a sample size of five would seldom capture a bad unit. A rule of thumb when setting up a *p*-chart is to make the sample large enough to expect to count the attribute twice in each sample. So an appropriate sample size if the defective rate were approximately 1 percent would be 200 units. One final note: In the calculations shown in equations 10.4 through 10.7, the assumption is that the sample size is fixed. The calculation of the standard deviation depends on this assumption. If the sample size varies, the standard deviation and upper and lower process control limits should be recalculated for each sample.

Example 10.3: Process Control Chart Design

An insurance company wants to design a control chart to monitor whether insurance claim forms are being completed correctly. The company intends to use the chart to see if improvements in the design of the form are effective. To start the process, the company collected data on the number of incorrectly completed claim forms over the past 10 days. The insurance company processes thousands of these forms each day, and due to the high cost of inspecting each form, only a small representative sample was collected each day. The data and analysis are shown in Exhibit 10.12.

SOLUTION

To construct the control chart, first calculate the overall fraction defective from all samples. This sets the centerline for the control chart.

$$\bar{p} = \frac{\text{Total number of defective units from all samples}}{\text{Number of samples} \times \text{Sample size}} = \frac{91}{3,000} = .03033$$

| exhibit 10.12 | Insurance Company Claim Form | | |

SAMPLE	NUMBER INSPECTED	NUMBER OF FORMS COMPLETED INCORRECTLY	FRACTION DEFECTIVE
1	300	10	0.03333
2	300	8	0.02667
3	300	9	0.03000
4	300	13	0.04333
5	300	7	0.02333
6	300	7	0.02333
7	300	6	0.02000
8	300	11	0.03667
9	300	12	0.04000
10	300	8	0.02667
Totals	3,000	91	0.03033
Sample standard deviation			0.00990

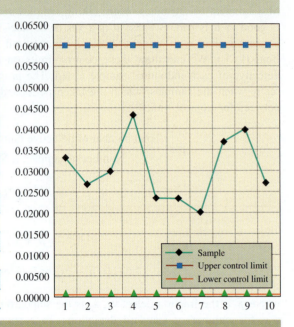

Excel:
SPC

Next, calculate the sample standard deviation:

$$s_p = \sqrt{\frac{\bar{p}(1 - \bar{p})}{n}} = \sqrt{\frac{.03033(1 - .03033)}{300}} = .0099$$

Finally, calculate the upper and lower process control limits. A z-value of 3 gives 99.7 percent confidence that the process is within these limits.

$$\text{UCL} = \bar{p} + 3s_p = .03033 + 3(.00990) = .06003$$

$$\text{LCL} = \bar{p} - 3s_p = .03033 - 3(.00990) = .00063$$

The calculations in Exhibit 10.12, including the control chart, are included in the spreadsheet SPC.xls. •

Process Control with Attribute Measurements: Using c-Charts

In the case of the p-chart, the item was either good or bad. There are times when the product or service can have more than one defect. For example, a board sold at a lumber yard may have multiple knotholes and, depending on the quality grade, may or may not be defective. When it is desired to monitor the number of defects per unit, the c-chart is appropriate.

The underlying distribution for the c-chart is the Poisson, which is based on the assumption that defects occur randomly on each unit. If c is the number of defects for a particular unit, then $\bar{c}$ is the average number of defects per unit, and the standard deviation is $\sqrt{\bar{c}}$. For the purposes of our control chart, we use the normal approximation to the Poisson distribution and construct the chart using the following control limits.

$$\bar{c} = \text{Average number of defects per unit} \qquad [10.8]$$

$$s_c = \sqrt{\bar{c}} \qquad [10.9]$$

$$\text{UCL} = \bar{c} + z\sqrt{\bar{c}} \qquad [10.10]$$

$$\text{LCL} = \bar{c} - z\sqrt{\bar{c}} \text{ or 0 if less than 0} \qquad [10.11]$$

Just as with the *p*-chart, typically $z = 3$ (99.7 percent confidence) or $z = 2.58$ (99 percent confidence) is used.

Example 10.4

The owners of a lumber yard want to design a control chart to monitor the quality of 2 × 4 boards that come from their supplier. For their medium-quality boards, they expect an average of four knotholes per 8-foot board. Design a control chart for use by the person receiving the boards using three-sigma (standard deviation) limits.

SOLUTION

For this problem, $\bar{c} = 4$, $s_c = \sqrt{\bar{c}} = 2$

$$\text{UCL} = \bar{c} + z\sqrt{\bar{c}} = 4 + 3(2) = 10$$

$\text{LCL} = \bar{c} - z\sqrt{\bar{c}} = 4 - 3(2) = -2 \rightarrow 0$ (Zero is used since it is not possible to have a negative number of defects.) •

Process Control with Variable Measurements:
Using $\bar{X}$- and *R*-Charts

$\bar{X}$- and *R*- (range) charts are widely used in statistical process control.

In attribute sampling, we determine whether something is good or bad, fits or doesn't fit—it is a go/no-go situation. In **variables** sampling, however, we measure the actual weight, volume, number of inches, or other variable measurements, and we develop control charts to determine the acceptability or rejection of the process based on those measurements. For example, in attribute sampling, we might decide that if something is over 10 pounds, we will reject it, and under 10 pounds, we will accept it. In variable sampling, we measure a sample and may record weights of 9.8 pounds or 10.2 pounds. These values are used to create or modify control charts and to see whether they fall within the acceptable limits.

Variables Quality characteristics that are measured in actual weight, volume, inches, centimeters, or other measure.

There are four main issues to address in creating a control chart: the size of the samples, number of samples, frequency of samples, and control limits.

Size of Samples For industrial applications in process control involving the measurement of variables, it is preferable to keep the sample size small. There are two main reasons. First, the sample needs to be taken within a reasonable length of time; otherwise, the process might change while the samples are taken. Second, the larger the sample, the more it costs to take.

CONTROL CHECK OF CAR AXLE AT DANA
CORPORATION RESEARCH AND DEVELOPMENT
CENTER.

© Jim West/Alamy

Sample sizes of four or five units seem to be the preferred numbers. The *means* of samples of this size have an approximately normal distribution, no matter what the distribution of the parent population looks like. Sample sizes greater than five give narrower process control limits and thus more sensitivity. For detecting finer variations of a process, it may be necessary, in fact, to use larger sample sizes. However, when sample sizes exceed 15 or so, it would be better to use $\overline{X}$-charts with standard deviation σ rather than $\overline{X}$-charts with the range R, as we use in Example 10.4.

Number of Samples Once the chart has been set up, each sample taken can be compared to the chart and a decision can be made about whether the process is acceptable. To set up the charts, however, prudence and statistics suggest that 25 or so sample sets be analyzed.

Frequency of Samples How often to take a sample is a trade-off between the cost of sampling (along with the cost of the unit if it is destroyed as part of the test) and the benefit of adjusting the system. Usually, it is best to start off with frequent sampling of a process and taper off as confidence in the process builds. For example, one might start with a sample of five units every half hour and end up feeling that one sample per day is adequate.

Control Limits Standard practice in statistical process control for variables is to set control limits three standard deviations above the mean and three standard deviations below. This means that 99.7 percent of the sample means are expected to fall within these process control limits (i.e., within a 99.7 percent confidence interval). Thus, if one sample mean falls outside this obviously wide band, we have strong evidence that the process is out of control.

How to Construct $\overline{X}$- and *R*-Charts

If the standard deviation of the process distribution is known, the $\overline{X}$-chart may be defined:

$$\text{UCL}_{\overline{X}} = \overline{\overline{X}} + zS_{\overline{X}} \quad \text{and} \quad \text{LCL}_{\overline{X}} = \overline{\overline{X}} - zS_{\overline{X}} \qquad [10.12]$$

where

$S_{\overline{X}} = s/\sqrt{n} =$ Standard deviation of sample means
$s =$ Standard deviation of the process distribution
$n =$ Sample size
$\overline{\overline{X}} =$ Average of sample means or a target value set for the process
$z =$ Number of standard deviations for a specific confidence level (typically, $z = 3$)

An $\overline{X}$-chart is simply a plot of the means of the samples that were taken from a process. $\overline{\overline{X}}$ is the average of the means.

In practice, the standard deviation of the process is not known. For this reason, an approach that uses actual sample data is commonly used. This practical approach is described in the next section.

An R-chart is a plot of the average of the range within each sample. The range is the difference between the highest and the lowest numbers in that sample. R values provide an easily calculated measure of variation used like a standard deviation. $\overline{R}$ is the average of the range of each sample. More specifically defined, these are

$$\overline{X} = \frac{\sum_{i=1}^{n} X_i}{n} \qquad \text{[Same as 10.1]}$$

where

$\overline{X}$ = Mean of the sample
i = Item number
n = Total number of items in the sample

$$\overline{\overline{X}} = \frac{\sum_{j=1}^{m} \overline{X}_j}{m} \qquad \text{[10.13]}$$

where

$\overline{\overline{X}}$ = The average of the means of the samples
j = Sample number
m = Total number of samples

$$\overline{R} = \frac{\sum_{j=1}^{m} R_j}{m} \qquad \text{[10.14]}$$

where

R_j = Difference between the highest and lowest measurement in the sample
$\overline{R}$ = Average of the measurement differences R for all samples

E. L. Grant and R. Leavenworth computed a table (Exhibit 10.13) that allows us to easily compute the upper and lower control limits for both the $\overline{X}$-chart and the R-chart. These are defined as

$$\text{Upper control limit for } \overline{X} = \overline{\overline{X}} + A_2\overline{R} \qquad \text{[10.15]}$$
$$\text{Lower control limit for } \overline{X} = \overline{\overline{X}} - A_2\overline{R} \qquad \text{[10.16]}$$
$$\text{Upper control limit for } R = D_4\overline{R} \qquad \text{[10.17]}$$
$$\text{Lower control limit for } R = D_3\overline{R} \qquad \text{[10.18]}$$

Example 10.5: $\overline{X}$- and R-Charts

We would like to create $\overline{X}$- and R-charts for a process. Exhibit 10.14 shows measurements for all 25 samples. The last two columns show the average of the sample $\overline{X}$, and the range, R.

Excel:
SPC

exhibit 10.13 Factor for Determining from $\bar{R}$ the Three-Sigma Control Limits for $\bar{X}$- and R-Charts

NUMBER OF OBSERVATIONS IN EACH SAMPLE n	FACTOR FOR $\bar{X}$-CHART A_2	FACTORS FOR R-CHART	
		LOWER CONTROL LIMIT D_3	UPPER CONTROL LIMIT D_4
2	1.88	0	3.27
3	1.02	0	2.57
4	0.73	0	2.28
5	0.58	0	2.11
6	0.48	0	2.00
7	0.42	0.08	1.92
8	0.37	0.14	1.86
9	0.34	0.18	1.82
10	0.31	0.22	1.78
11	0.29	0.26	1.74
12	0.27	0.28	1.72
13	0.25	0.31	1.69
14	0.24	0.33	1.67
15	0.22	0.35	1.65
16	0.21	0.36	1.64
17	0.20	0.38	1.62
18	0.19	0.39	1.61
19	0.19	0.40	1.60
20	0.18	0.41	1.59

Upper control limit for $\bar{X}$ = $UCL_{\bar{X}}$ = $\bar{\bar{X}} + A_2\bar{R}$
Lower control limit for $\bar{X}$ = $LCL_{\bar{X}}$ = $\bar{\bar{X}} - A_2\bar{R}$
Upper control limit for R = UCL_R = $D_4\bar{R}$
Lower control limit for R = LCL_R = $D_3\bar{R}$

Note: All factors are based on the normal distribution.

Values for A_2, D_3, and D_4 were obtained from Exhibit 10.13.

$$\text{Upper control limit for } \bar{X} = \bar{\bar{X}} + A_2\bar{R} = 10.21 + .58(.60) = 10.56$$
$$\text{Lower control limit for } \bar{X} = \bar{\bar{X}} - A_2\bar{R} = 10.21 - .58(.60) = 9.86$$
$$\text{Upper control limit for } R = D_4\bar{R} = 2.11(.60) = 1.27$$
$$\text{Lower control limit for } R = D_3\bar{R} = 0(.60) = 0$$

SOLUTION

Exhibit 10.15 shows the $\bar{X}$-chart and R-chart with a plot of all the sample means and ranges of the samples. All the points are well within the control limits, although sample 23 is close to the $\bar{X}$ lower control limit and samples 13 through 17 are above the target. •

exhibit 10.14

Measurements in Samples of Five from a Process

Excel:
SPC

SAMPLE NUMBER	EACH UNIT IN SAMPLE					AVERAGE $\bar{X}$	RANGE R
1	10.60	10.40	10.30	9.90	10.20	10.28	.70
2	9.98	10.25	10.05	10.23	10.33	10.17	.35
3	9.85	9.90	10.20	10.25	10.15	10.07	.40
4	10.20	10.10	10.30	9.90	9.95	10.09	.40
5	10.30	10.20	10.24	10.50	10.30	10.31	.30
6	10.10	10.30	10.20	10.30	9.90	10.16	.40
7	9.98	9.90	10.20	10.40	10.10	10.12	.50
8	10.10	10.30	10.40	10.24	10.30	10.27	.30
9	10.30	10.20	10.60	10.50	10.10	10.34	.50
10	10.30	10.40	10.50	10.10	10.20	10.30	.40
11	9.90	9.50	10.20	10.30	10.35	10.05	.85
12	10.10	10.36	10.50	9.80	9.95	10.14	.70
13	10.20	10.50	10.70	10.10	9.90	10.28	.80
14	10.20	10.60	10.50	10.30	10.40	10.40	.40
15	10.54	10.30	10.40	10.55	10.00	10.36	.55
16	10.20	10.60	10.15	10.00	10.50	10.29	.60
17	10.20	10.40	10.60	10.80	10.10	10.42	.70
18	9.90	9.50	9.90	10.50	10.00	9.96	1.00
19	10.60	10.30	10.50	9.90	9.80	10.22	.80
20	10.60	10.40	10.30	10.40	10.20	10.38	.40
21	9.90	9.60	10.50	10.10	10.60	10.14	1.00
22	9.95	10.20	10.50	10.30	10.20	10.23	.55
23	10.20	9.50	9.60	9.80	10.30	9.88	.80
24	10.30	10.60	10.30	9.90	9.80	10.18	.80
25	9.90	10.30	10.60	9.90	10.10	10.16	.70
						$\bar{\bar{X}} = 10.21$	$\bar{R} = .60$

exhibit 10.15

$\bar{X}$-Chart and $\bar{R}$-Chart

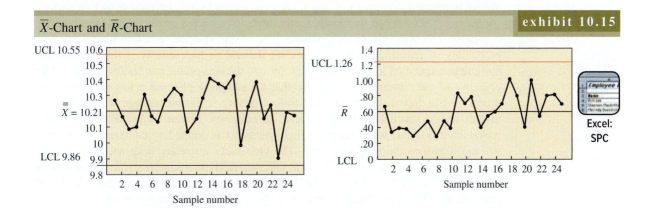

Excel:
SPC

ACCEPTANCE SAMPLING

LO10–6 Analyze the quality of batches of items using statistics.

Design of a Single Sampling Plan for Attributes

Acceptance sampling is performed on goods that already exist to determine what percentage of products conform to specifications. These products may be items received from another company and evaluated by the receiving department, or they may be components that have passed through a processing step and are evaluated by company personnel either in production or later in the warehousing function. Whether inspection should be done at all is addressed in the following example.

Acceptance sampling is executed through a sampling plan. In this section, we illustrate the planning procedures for a single sampling plan—that is, a plan in which the quality is determined from the evaluation of one sample. (Other plans may be developed using two or more samples.)

Example 10.6: Costs to Justify Inspection

Total (100 percent) inspection is justified when the cost of a loss incurred by not inspecting is greater than the cost of inspection. For example, suppose a faulty item results in a $10 loss and the average percentage defective of items in the lot is 3 percent.

SOLUTION

If the average percentage of defective items in a lot is 3 percent, the expected cost of faulty items is $0.03 \times \$10$, or $0.30 each. Therefore, if the cost of inspecting each item is less than $0.30, the economic decision is to perform 100 percent inspection. Not all defective items will be removed, however, because inspectors will pass some bad items and reject some good ones.

The purpose of a sampling plan is to test the lot to either (1) find its quality or (2) ensure that the quality is what it is supposed to be. Thus, if a quality control supervisor already knows the quality (such as the 0.03 given in the example), he or she does not sample for defects. Either all of them must be inspected to remove the defects or none of them should be inspected, and the rejects pass into the process. The choice simply depends on the cost to inspect and the cost incurred by passing a reject. •

A single sampling plan is defined by n and c, where n is the number of units in the sample and c is the acceptance number. The size of n may vary from one up to all the items in the lot (usually denoted as N) from which it is drawn. The acceptance number c denotes the maximum number of defective items that can be found in the sample before the lot is rejected. Values for n and c are determined by the interaction of four factors (AQL, α, LTPD, and β) that quantify the objectives of the product's producer and its consumer. The objective of the producer is to ensure that the sampling plan has a low probability of rejecting good lots. Lots are defined as high quality if they contain no more than a specified level of defectives, termed the *acceptable quality level (AQL)*. The objective of the consumer is to ensure that the sampling plan has a low probability of accepting bad lots. Lots are defined as low quality if the percentage of defectives is greater than a specified amount, termed *lot tolerance percent defective (LTPD)*. The probability associated with rejecting a high-quality lot is denoted by the Greek letter alpha (α) and is termed the *producer's risk*. The probability associated with accepting a low-quality lot is denoted by the letter beta (β) and is termed the *consumer's risk*. The selection of particular values for AQL, α, LTPD, and β is an economic decision based on a cost trade-off or, more typically, on company policy or contractual requirements.

ALUMINUM SHEETS
ARE EXAMINED UNDER
QUALITY CONTROL
LIGHTS ON THE
ALUMINUM PRODUCTION
LINE AT THE ALCOA
SZÉKESFEHÉRVÁR,
HUNGARY, EXTRUSION
PLANT.

© Charles Thatcher/Getty Images

The following example, using an excerpt from a standard acceptance sampling table, illustrates how the four parameters—AQL, α, LTPD, and β—are used in developing a sampling plan.

Example 10.7: Values of *n* and *c*

Hi-Tech Industries manufactures Z-Band radar scanners used to detect speed traps. The printed circuit boards in the scanners are purchased from an outside vendor. The vendor produces the boards to an AQL of 2 percent defectives and is willing to run a 5 percent risk (α) of having lots of this level or fewer defectives rejected. Hi-Tech considers lots of 8 percent or more defectives (LTPD) unacceptable and wants to ensure that it will accept such poor-quality lots no more than 10 percent of the time (β). A large shipment has just been delivered. What values of *n* and *c* should be selected to determine the quality of this lot?

SOLUTION

The parameters of the problem are AQL = 0.02, α = 0.05, LTPD = 0.08, and β = 0.10. We can use Exhibit 10.16 to find *c* and *n*.

First, divide LTPD by AQL (0.08 ÷ 0.02 = 4). Then, find the ratio in column 2 that is equal to or just greater than that amount (4). This value is 4.057, which is associated with *c* = 4.

Finally, find the value in column 3 that is in the same row as *c* = 4, and divide that quantity by AQL to obtain *n* (1.970 ÷ 0.02 = 98.5).

The appropriate sampling plan is *c* = 4, *n* = 99. Ninety-nine scanners will be inspected and if more than four defective units are found, the lot will be rejected. •

Excerpt from a Sampling Plan Table for α = 0.05, β = 0.10   **exhibit 10.16**

c	LTPD/AQL	*n* * AQL	*c*	LTPD/AQL	*n* * AQL
0	44.890	0.052	5	3.549	2.613
1	10.946	0.355	6	3.206	3.286
2	6.509	0.818	7	2.957	3.981
3	4.890	1.366	8	2.768	4.695
4	4.057	1.970	9	2.618	5.426

Operating Characteristic Curves

While a sampling plan such as the one just described meets our requirements for the extreme values of good and bad quality, we cannot readily determine how well the plan discriminates between good and bad lots at intermediate values. For this reason, sampling plans are generally displayed graphically through the use of operating characteristic (OC) curves. These curves, which are unique for each combination of n and c, simply illustrate the probability of accepting lots with varying percentages of defectives. The procedure we have followed in developing the plan, in fact, specifies two points on an OC curve: one point defined by AQL and $1 - \alpha$ and the other point defined by LTPD and β. Curves for common values of n and c can be computed or obtained from available tables.

Shaping the OC Curve   A sampling plan discriminating perfectly between good and bad lots has an infinite slope (vertical) at the selected value of AQL. In Exhibit 10.17, any percentage defective to the left of 2 percent would always be accepted, and those to the right, always rejected. However, such a curve is possible only with complete inspection of all units and thus is not a possibility with a true sampling plan.

An OC curve should be steep in the region of most interest (between the AQL and the LTPD), which is accomplished by varying n and c. If c remains constant, increasing the sample size n causes the OC curve to be more vertical. While holding n constant, decreasing c (the maximum number of defective units) also makes the slope more vertical, moving closer to the origin.

exhibit 10.17   Operating Characteristic Curve for AQL = 0.02, α = 0.05, LTPD = 0.08, β = 0.10

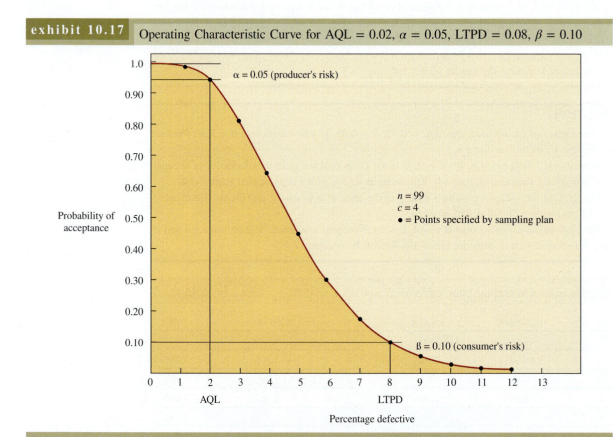

The Effects of Lot Size The size of the lot that the sample is taken from has relatively little effect on the quality of protection. Consider, for example, that samples—all of the same size: 20 units—are taken from different lots ranging from a lot size of 200 units to a lot size of infinity. If each lot is known to have 5 percent defectives, the probability of accepting the lot based on the sample of 20 units ranges from about 0.34 to about 0.36. This means that as long as the lot size is several times the sample size, it makes little difference how large the lot is. It seems a bit difficult to accept, but statistically (on average in the long run), whether we have a carload or box full, we'll get about the same answer. It just seems that a carload should have a larger sample size. Of course, this assumes that the lot is randomly chosen and that defects are randomly spread through the lot.

CONCEPT CONNECTIONS

LO10–1 Explain the scope of total quality management in a firm.

- Total quality management is a comprehensive approach to quality with a focus on what is important to the customer.
- There are two aspects of quality to consider: (1) the careful design of the product or service and (2) assurance that the firm's processes can consistently produce or deliver the design.
- Specific features of the design relate to what the intended market for the products expects and its inherent value.
- Processes are designed so that specific design specifications such as size, surface, finish, or delivery speed are consistently met when the product is produced or service delivered.
- Costs related to quality include the expenses related to inspection, rework, and repair or warranty.

Total quality management (TQM)   Managing the entire organization so that it excels on all dimensions of products and services that are important to the customer.

Malcolm Baldrige National Quality Award   An award established by the U.S. Department of Commerce given annually to companies that excel in quality.

Design quality   The inherent value of the product in the marketplace.

Conformance quality   The degree to which the product or service design specifications are met.

Quality at the source   Making the person who does the work responsible for ensuring that specifications are met.

Dimensions of quality   Criteria by which quality is measured.

Cost of quality (COQ)   Expenditures related to achieving product or service quality such as the costs of prevention, appraisal, internal failure, and external failure.

LO10–2 Illustrate globally recognized quality benchmarks.

- The International Organization for Standardization (ISO) has developed specifications that define best-quality practices and are accepted internationally.
- ISO 9000 relates to manufacturing and business-to-business processes.
- ISO 14000 is concerned with environmental management.
- External benchmarking is a useful approach for seeking ways to make innovative improvement.

ISO 9000   Formal standards for quality certification developed by the International Organization of Standardization.

External benchmarking   Looking outside the company to examine what excellent performers inside and outside the company's industry are doing in the way of quality.

Understand the Six Sigma approach to improving quality and productivity.

- Six Sigma is a philosophy and set of tools developed to measure and reduce defects.
- Six Sigma projects are completed in five steps: (1) define, (2) measure, (3) analyze, (4) improve, and (5) control.
- There is a comprehensive set of analysis tools that can be used in Six Sigma projects and many of these use statistics to analyze performance data.

Six Sigma A statistical term to describe the quality goal of no more than 3.4 defects out of every million units. Also refers to a quality improvement philosophy and program.

Defects per million opportunities (DPMO) A metric used to describe the variability of a process.

DMAIC An acronym for the **D**efine, **M**easure, **A**nalyze, **I**mprove, and **C**ontrol improvement methodology followed by companies engaging in Six Sigma programs.

LO10–4 **Illustrate process variation and explain how to measure it.**

- Variation is inherent in all processes and can be caused by many factors.
- Variation caused by identifiable factors is called assignable variation and can possibly be managed.
- Variation inherent in a process is called common or random variation.
- Statistical quality control (SQC) involves sampling output from a process and using statistics to find when the process has changed in a nonrandom way.
- When a product or service is designed, specification limits are assigned relative to critical parameters.
- The capability index of a process measures its ability to consistently produce within specifications limits.

Statistical quality control (SQC) A number of different techniques designed evaluate quality from a conformance view.

Assignable variation Deviation in the output of a process that can be clearly identified and managed.

Common variation Deviation in the output of a process that is random and inherent in the process itself.

Upper and lower specification limits The range of values in a measure associated with a process that is allowable given the intended use of the product or service.

Capability index (C_{pk}) The ratio of the range of values allowed by the design specifications divided by the range of values produced by the process.

Mean or average

$$\overline{X} = \frac{\sum_{i=1}^{n} x_i}{n}$$ [10.1]

Standard deviation

$$\sigma = \sqrt{\frac{\sum_{i=1}^{n} (x_i - \overline{X})^2}{n}}$$ [10.2]

Capability index

$$C_{pk} = \min\left[\frac{\overline{\overline{X}} - \text{LSL}}{3\sigma}, \frac{\text{USL} - \overline{\overline{X}}}{3\sigma}\right]$$ [10.3]

LO10–5 **Analyze process quality using statistics.**

- Statistical process control involves monitoring the quality of a process as it is operating.
- Control charts are used to visually monitor the status of a process over time.
- Attributes are characteristics that can be evaluated as either conforming or not conforming to the design specifications.
- *P*-charts and *c*-charts are used to monitor attribute characteristics.
- $\overline{X}$- and *R*-charts are used when the characteristic is a variable measure.

Statistical process control (SPC)   Techniques for testing a random sample of output from a process to determine whether the process is producing items within a prescribed range.

Attributes   Quality characteristics that are classified as either conforming or not conforming to specifications.

Variables   Quality characteristics that are measured in actual weight, volume, inches, centimeters, or other measure units.

Process control charts using attribute measurements

$$\bar{p} = \frac{\text{Total number of defective units from all samples}}{\text{Number of samples} \times \text{Sample size}} \qquad [10.4]$$

$$s_p = \sqrt{\frac{\bar{p}(1 - \bar{p})}{n}} \qquad [10.5]$$

$$\text{UCL} = \bar{p} + zs_p \qquad [10.6]$$

$$\text{LCL} = \bar{p} - zs_p \text{ or } 0 \text{ if less than } 0 \qquad [10.7]$$

$$\bar{c} = \text{Average number of defects per unit} \qquad [10.8]$$

$$s_c = \sqrt{\bar{c}} \qquad [10.9]$$

$$\text{UCL} = \bar{c} + z\sqrt{\bar{c}} \qquad [10.10]$$

$$\text{LCL} = \bar{c} + z\sqrt{\bar{c}} \text{ or } 0 \text{ if less than } 0 \qquad [10.11]$$

Process control $\overline{X}$- and *R*-charts

$$\text{UCL}_{\overline{X}} = \overline{\overline{X}} + zS_{\overline{X}} \quad \text{and} \quad \text{LCL}_{\overline{X}} = \overline{\overline{X}} - zS_{\overline{X}} \qquad [10.12]$$

$$\overline{\overline{X}} = \frac{\sum_{j=1}^{m} \overline{X}_j}{m} \qquad [10.13]$$

$$\overline{R} = \frac{\sum_{j=1}^{m} R_j}{m} \qquad [10.14]$$

$$\text{Upper control limit for } \overline{X} = \overline{\overline{X}} + A_2\overline{R} \qquad [10.15]$$

$$\text{Lower control limit for } \overline{X} = \overline{\overline{X}} - A_2\overline{R} \qquad [10.16]$$

$$\text{Upper control limit for } R = D_4\overline{R} \qquad [10.17]$$

$$\text{Lower control limit for } R = D_3\overline{R} \qquad [10.18]$$

LO10–6 Analyze the quality of batches of items using statistics.

- Acceptance sampling is used to evaluate if a batch of parts, as received in an order from a supplier for example, conforms to specification limits.
- An acceptance sampling plan is defined by a sample size and the number of acceptable defects in the sample.
- Since the plan is defined using statistics, there is the possibility that a bad lot will be accepted. This is called the consumer's risk.
- There is also the possibility that a good lot will be rejected. This is called the producer's risk.

SOLVED PROBLEMS

LO10–4 SOLVED PROBLEM 1

HVAC Manufacturing produces parts and materials for the heating, ventilation, and air conditioning industry. One of its facilities produces metal ductwork in various sizes for the home construction market. One particular product is 6-inch-diameter round metal ducting. It is a simple product, but the diameter of the finished ducting is critical. If it is too small or large, contractors will have difficulty fitting the ducting into other parts of the system. The target diameter is 6 inches exactly, with an acceptable tolerance of ± 0.03 inch. Anything produced outside specifications is considered defective. The line supervisor for this product has data showing that the actual diameter of finished product is 5.99 inches with a standard deviation of 0.01 inch.

- a. What is the current capability index of this process? What is the probability of producing a defective unit in this process?
- b. The line supervisor thinks he will be able to adjust the process so that the mean diameter of output is the same as the target diameter, without any change in the process variation. What would the capability index be if he is successful? What would be the probability of producing a defective unit in this adjusted process?
- c. Through better training of employees and investment in equipment upgrades, the company could produce output with a mean diameter equal to the target and a standard deviation of 0.005 inch. What would the capability index be if this were to happen? What would be the probability of producing a defective unit in this case?

Solution

a. $\overline{\overline{X}} = 5.99$ $\text{LSL} = 6.00 - .03 = 5.97$ $\text{USL} = 6.00 + .03 = 6.03$ $\sigma = .01$

$$C_{pk} = \min \left[\frac{5.99 - 5.97}{.03} \quad \text{or} \quad \frac{6.03 - 5.99}{.03} \right] = \min [.667 \text{ or } 1.333] = 0.667$$

This process is not what would be considered capable. The capability index is based on the LSL, showing that the process mean is lower than the target.

To find the probability of a defective unit, we need to find the Z-scores of the LCL and USL with respect to the current process:

$$Z_{\text{LSL}} = \frac{\text{LSL} - \overline{\overline{X}}}{\sigma} = \frac{5.97 - 5.99}{.01} = -2.00 \quad \text{NORM.S.DIST}(-2.00) = .02275$$

2.275 percent of the output will be too small.

$$Z_{\text{LSL}} = \frac{\text{USL} - \overline{\overline{X}}}{\sigma} = \frac{6.03 - 5.99}{.01} = 4.00 \quad \text{NORM.S.DIST}(4.00) = .999968$$

The probability of too large a unit is $1 - .999968 = .000032$, so $.0032$ percent of output will be too small.

The probability of producing a defective unit is $.02275 + .000032 = .022782$, so 2.2782 percent of output will be defective. As a numerical example, 22,782 out of every million units will be defective.

b. $\overline{\overline{X}} = 6.00$ $LSL = 6.00 - .03 = 5.97$ $USL = 6.00 + .03 = 6.03$ $\sigma = .01$

$$C_{pk} = \min \left[\frac{6.00 - 5.97}{.03} \quad \text{or} \quad \frac{6.03 - 6.00}{.03} \right] = \min [1.00 \text{ or } 1.00] = 1.00$$

$$Z_{LSL} = \frac{LSL - \overline{\overline{X}}}{\sigma} = \frac{5.97 - 6.00}{.01} = -3.00 \quad \text{NORM.S.DIST}(-3.00) = .00135$$

Only 0.135 percent of the output will be too small.

$$Z_{USL} = \frac{USL - \overline{\overline{X}}}{\sigma} = \frac{6.03 - 6.00}{.01} = 3.00 \quad \text{NORM.S.DIST}(3.00) = .99865$$

The probability of too large a unit is $1- .99865 = .00135$, so 0.135 percent of the output will be too large.

The probability of producing a defective unit is $.00135 + .00135 = .0027$, so 0.27 percent of the output will be defective. As a numerical example, 2,700 out of every million units will be defective. That's about a 90 percent reduction in defective output just from adjusting the process mean!

Because the process is exactly centered on the target and the specification limits are three standard deviations away from the process mean, this adjusted process has a $C_{pk} = 1.00$. In order to do any better than that, we would need to reduce the variation in the process, as shown in part (c).

c. $\overline{\overline{X}} = 6.00$ $LSL = 6.00 - .03 = 5.97$ $USL = 6.00 + .03 = 6.03$ $\sigma = .005$

$$C_{pk} = \min \left[\frac{6.00 - 5.97}{.015} \quad \text{or} \quad \frac{6.03 - 6.00}{.015} \right] = \min [2.00 \text{ or } 2.00] = 2.00$$

We have doubled the process capability index by cutting the standard deviation of the process in half. What will be the effect on the probability of defective output?

$$Z_{LSL} = \frac{LSL - \overline{\overline{X}}}{\sigma} = \frac{5.97 - 6.00}{.005} = -6.00 \quad \text{NORM.S.DIST}(-6.00) = 0.0000000009866$$

$$Z_{USL} = \frac{USL - \overline{\overline{X}}}{\sigma} = \frac{6.03 - 6.00}{.005} = 6.00 \quad \text{NORM.S.DIST}(6.00) = 0.9999999990134$$

Following earlier logic, the probability of producing a defective unit in this case is just 0.000000001973, a very small probability indeed! Using the earlier numerical example, this would result in only .001973 defective units out of every million. By cutting the process standard deviation in half, we could gain far more than a 50 percent reduction in defective output—in this case, essentially eliminating defective units due to the diameter of the ducting. This example demonstrates the power and importance of Six Sigma quality concepts.

LO10–5 SOLVED PROBLEM 2

Completed forms from a particular department of an insurance company were sampled daily to check the performance quality of that department. To establish a tentative norm for the department, one sample of 100 units was collected each day for 15 days, with these results:

Excel:
Ch10_SPC

SAMPLE	SAMPLE SIZE	NUMBER OF FORMS WITH ERRORS	SAMPLE	SAMPLE SIZE	NUMBER OF FORMS WITH ERRORS
1	100	4	9	100	4
2	100	3	10	100	2
3	100	5	11	100	7
4	100	0	12	100	2
5	100	2	13	100	1
6	100	8	14	100	3
7	100	1	15	100	1
8	100	3			

a. Develop a *p*-chart using a 95 percent confidence interval ($z = 1.96$).
b. Plot the 15 samples collected.
c. What comments can you make about the process?

Solution

a. $\bar{P} = \dfrac{46}{15(100)} = .0307$

$$s_p = \sqrt{\frac{\bar{p}(1 - \bar{p})}{n}} = \sqrt{\frac{.0307(1 - .0307)}{100}} = \sqrt{.0003} = .017$$

$\text{UCL} = \bar{p} + 1.96 s_p = .031 + 1.96(.017) = .064$

$\text{LCL} = \bar{p} - 1.96 s_p = .031 - 1.96(.017) = -.00232$ or zero

b. The defectives are plotted below.

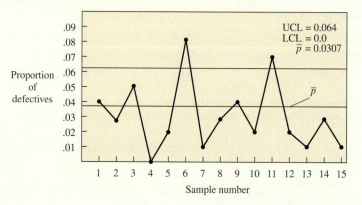

c. Of the 15 samples, 2 were out of the control limits. Because the control limits were established as 95 percent, or 1 out of 20, we would say that the process is out of control. It needs to be examined to find the cause of such widespread variation.

LO10–6 SOLVED PROBLEM 3

Management is trying to decide whether part A, which is produced with a consistent 3 percent defective rate, should be inspected. If it is not inspected, the 3 percent defectives will go through a product assembly phase and have to be replaced later. If all part A's are inspected, one-third of the defectives will be found, thus raising the quality to 2 percent defectives.

a. Should the inspection be done if the cost of inspecting is $0.01 per unit and the cost of replacing a defective in the final assembly is $4.00?
b. Suppose the cost of inspecting is $0.05 per unit rather than $0.01. Would this change your answer in (*a*)?

Solution

Should part A be inspected?

.03 defective with no inspection.

.02 defective with inspection.

a. This problem can be solved simply by looking at the opportunity for 1 percent improvement.

Benefit = .01($4.00) = $0.04

Cost of inspection = $0.01

Therefore, inspect and save $0.03 per unit.

b. A cost of $0.05 per unit to inspect would be $0.01 greater than the savings, so inspection should not be performed.

DISCUSSION QUESTIONS

LO10–1
1. Is the goal of Six Sigma realistic for services such as Blockbuster On Demand or Redbox DVD kiosks?
2. "If line employees are required to work on quality improvement activities, their productivity will suffer." Discuss.
3. "You don't inspect quality into a product; you have to build it in." Discuss the implications of this statement.
4. "Before you build quality in, you must think it in." How do the implications of this statement differ from those in question 3?

LO10–2
5. Is certification under the ISO standards in this chapter necessary for competing in the modern market? What should companies consider when deciding whether or not to become certified?
6. Do you see any relationship between the ISO standards mentioned in this chapter and the competitive strategy concepts mentioned earlier in the text?

LO10–3
7. Business writer Tom Peters has suggested that in making process changes, we should "Try it, test it, and get on with it." How does this square with the DMAIC/continuous improvement philosophy?
8. Develop a cause-and-effect (fishbone) diagram to address everything that impacts your grade in this course. How much is under your control?

LO10–4
9. The capability index allows for some drifting of the process mean. Discuss what this means in terms of product quality output.
10. In an agreement between a supplier and a customer, the supplier must ensure that all parts are within specification before shipment to the customer. What is the effect on the cost of quality to the customer?
11. In the situation described in question 10, what would be the effect on the cost of quality to the supplier?

LO10–5
12. Discuss the purposes of and differences between p-charts and $\overline{X}$- and R-charts.
13. The application of control charts is straightforward in manufacturing processes when you have tangible goods with physical characteristics you can easily measure on a numerical scale. Quality control is also important in service businesses, but you are generally not going to want to measure the physical characteristics of your customers! Do you think control charts have a place in service businesses? Discuss how you might apply them to specific examples.

LO10–6
14. Discuss the trade-off between achieving a zero AQL (acceptable quality level) and a positive AQL (such as an AQL of 2 percent).
15. The cost of performing inspection sampling moves inversely to the cost of quality failures. We can reduce the cost of quality failures by increased levels of inspection, but that of course would increase the cost of inspection. Can you think of any methods to reduce the cost of quality failures without increasing a company's cost of inspection? Think specifically in terms of material purchased from vendors.

OBJECTIVE QUESTIONS

LO10–1

1. What is the name of the national quality award given by the government of the United States?
2. Match the quality "guru" with the specific aspects of their teachings. Use C for Crosby, D for Deming, and J for Juran.

_____ Defined quality as "fitness for use."
_____ Defined quality as "conformance to requirements."
_____ Set the performance standard as "zero defects."
_____ Defined 14 points for management to follow.
_____ Emphasized a general management approach to quality, especially the human elements.
_____ Rejected the concept of statistically acceptable levels of quality.
_____ Stated that less than 20 percent of quality problems are due to workers.
_____ Recommended continuous improvement to reduce variations.

3. What is the term that means making the person who does the work responsible for ensuring that specifications are met?
4. What are the four general categories of quality costs?
5. What term means managing the entire organization so that it excels on all dimensions of products and services that are important to customers?

LO10–2

6. Which international standard has recently been developed to address the socially responsible behavior of firms?
7. Which industry-specific standard has been developed by automakers for suppliers of parts, materials, and services to the automotive industry?
8. What is it called when a firm looks externally and examines other companies for examples of best practices?

LO10–3

9. A manager states that her process is really working well. Out of 1,500 parts, 1,477 were produced free of a particular defect and passed inspection. Based on Six Sigma theory, how would you rate this performance, other things being equal?
10. The following table lists all costs of quality incurred by Sam's Surf Shop last year. What was Sam's appraisal cost for quality last year?

Annual inspection costs	$ 155,000
Annual cost of scrap materials	286,000
Annual rework cost	34,679
Annual cost of quality training	456,000
Annual warranty cost	1,546,000
Annual testing cost	543,000

11. Below is a table of data collected over a six-month period in a local grocery store. Construct a Pareto analysis of the data and determine the percentage of total complaints represented by the two most common categories.

All Other	71
Checker	59
General	58
Service Level	55
Policy/Procedures	40
Price Marking	45
Product Quality	87
Product Request	105
Checkout Queue	33
Stock Condition	170

12. A common problem that many drivers encounter is a car that will not start. Create a fishbone diagram to assist in the diagnosis of the potential causes of this problem.

13. A manufacturing company has been inspecting units of output from a process. Each product inspected is evaluated on five criteria. If the unit does not meet standards for the criteria, it counts as a defect for the unit. Each unit could have as few as zero defects, and as many as five. After inspecting 2,000 units, they discovered 33 defects. What is the DPMO measure for this process?

14. What is the term for a flowchart that is used to separate value-added from non-value-added steps in a process?

15. What does the acronym DMAIC stand for?

16. A customer call center is evaluating customer satisfaction surveys to identify the most prevalent quality problems in their process. Specific customer complaints have been analyzed and grouped into eight different categories. Every instance of a complaint adds to the count in its category. Which Six Sigma analytical tool would be most helpful to management here?

LO10–4 17. A company currently using an inspection process in its material receiving department is trying to install an overall cost reduction program. One possible reduction is the elimination of one inspection position. This position tests material that has a defective content on the average of 0.04. By inspecting all items, the inspector is able to remove all defects. The inspector can inspect 50 units per hour. The hourly rate including fringe benefits for this position is $9. If the inspection position is eliminated, defects will go into product assembly and will have to be replaced later at a cost of $10 each when they are detected in final product testing.
   a. Should this inspection position be eliminated?
   b. What is the cost to inspect each unit?
   c. Is there benefit (or loss) from the current inspection process? How much?

18. A metal fabricator produces connecting rods with an outer diameter that has a $1 \pm .01$ inch specification. A machine operator takes several sample measurements over time and determines the sample mean outer diameter to be 1.002 inches with a standard deviation of .003 inch.
   a. Calculate the process capability index for this example.
   b. What does this figure tell you about the process?

19. Output from a process contains 0.02 defective unit. Defective units that go undetected into final assemblies cost $25 each to replace. An inspection process, which would detect and remove all defectives, can be established to test these units. However, the inspector, who can test 20 units per hour, is paid $8 per hour, including fringe benefits. Should an inspection station be established to test all units?
   a. What is the cost to inspect each unit?
   b. What is the benefit (or loss) from the inspection process?

20. There is a 3 percent error rate at a specific point in a production process. If an inspector is placed at this point, all the errors can be detected and eliminated. However, the inspector is paid $8 per hour and can inspect units in the process at the rate of 30 per hour.
   If no inspector is used and defects are allowed to pass this point, there is a cost of $10 per unit to correct the defect later on.
   Should an inspector be hired?

21. Design specifications require that a key dimension on a product measure 100 ± 10 units. A process being considered for producing this product has a standard deviation of four units.
   a. What can you say (quantitatively) regarding the process capability?
   b. Suppose the process average shifts to 92. Calculate the new process capability.
   c. What can you say about the process after the shift? Approximately what percentage of the items produced will be defective?

22. C-Spec, Inc., is attempting to determine whether an existing machine is capable of milling an engine part that has a key specification of 4 ± .003 inch. After a trial run on this machine, C-Spec has determined that the machine has a sample mean of 4.001 inches with a standard deviation of .002 inch.
    a. Calculate the C_{pk} for this machine.
    b. Should C-Spec use this machine to produce this part? Why?

LO10–5 23. Ten samples of 15 parts each were taken from an ongoing process to establish a p-chart for control. The samples and the number of defectives in each are shown in the following table:

SAMPLE	n	NUMBER OF DEFECTIVE ITEMS IN THE SAMPLE	SAMPLE	n	NUMBER OF DEFECTIVE ITEMS IN THE SAMPLE
1	15	3	6	15	2
2	15	1	7	15	0
3	15	0	8	15	3
4	15	0	9	15	1
5	15	0	10	15	0

a. Develop a p-chart for 95 percent confidence (1.96 standard deviation).
b. Based on the plotted data points, what comments can you make?

24. A shirt manufacturer buys cloth by the 100-yard roll from a supplier. For setting up a control chart to manage the irregularities (e.g., loose threads and tears), the following data were collected from a sample provided by the supplier.

SAMPLE	1	2	3	4	5	6	7	8	9	10
IRREGULARITIES	3	5	2	6	5	4	6	3	4	5

a. Using these data, set up a c-chart with $z = 2$.
b. Suppose the next five rolls from the supplier had three, two, five, three, and seven irregularities. Is the supplier process under control?

25. Resistors for electronic circuits are manufactured on a high-speed automated machine. The machine is set up to produce a large run of resistors of 1,000 ohms each.

   To set up the machine and to create a control chart to be used throughout the run, 15 samples were taken with four resistors in each sample. The complete list of samples and their measured values are as follows:

SAMPLE NUMBER	READINGS (IN OHMS)			
1	1,010	991	985	986
2	995	996	1,009	994
3	990	1,003	1,015	1,008
4	1,015	1,020	1,009	998
5	1,013	1,019	1,005	993
6	994	1,001	994	1,005
7	989	992	982	1,020
8	1,001	986	996	996
9	1,006	989	1,005	1,007
10	992	1,007	1,006	979
11	996	1,006	997	989
12	1,019	996	991	1,011
13	981	991	989	1,003
14	999	993	988	984
15	1,013	1,002	1,005	992

Develop an $\bar{X}$-chart and an R-chart and plot the values. From the charts, what comments can you make about the process? (Use three-sigma control limits, as in Exhibit 10.13.)

26. You are the newly appointed assistant administrator at a local hospital, and your first project is to investigate the quality of the patient meals put out by the food-service department. You conducted a 10-day survey by submitting a simple questionnaire to the 400 patients with each meal, asking that they simply check off that the meal was either satisfactory or unsatisfactory. For simplicity in this problem, assume that the response was 1,000 returned questionnaires from the 1,200 meals each day. The results are as follows:

	NUMBER OF UNSATISFACTORY MEALS	SAMPLE SIZE
December 1	74	1,000
December 2	42	1,000
December 3	64	1,000
December 4	80	1,000
December 5	40	1,000
December 6	50	1,000
December 7	65	1,000
December 8	70	1,000
December 9	40	1,000
December 10	75	1,000
	600	10,000

a. Construct a p-chart based on the questionnaire results, using a confidence interval of 95.5 percent, which is two standard deviations.
b. What comments can you make about the results of the survey?

27. The state and local police departments are trying to analyze crime rates so they can shift their patrols from decreasing-rate areas to areas where rates are increasing. The city and county have been geographically segmented into areas containing 5,000 residences. The police recognize that not all crimes and offenses are reported: People do not want to become involved, consider the offenses too small to report, are too embarrassed to make a police report, or do not take the time, among other reasons. Every month, because of this, the police are contacting by phone a random sample of 1,000 of the 5,000 residences for data on crime. (Respondents are guaranteed anonymity.) Here are the data collected for the past 12 months for one area:

MONTH	CRIME INCIDENCE	SAMPLE SIZE	CRIME RATE
January	7	1,000	0.007
February	9	1,000	0.009
March	7	1,000	0.007
April	7	1,000	0.007
May	7	1,000	0.007
June	9	1,000	0.009
July	7	1,000	0.007
August	10	1,000	0.010
September	8	1,000	0.008
October	11	1,000	0.011
November	10	1,000	0.010
December	8	1,000	0.008

Construct a *p*-chart for 95 percent confidence (1.96) and plot each of the months. If the next three months show crime incidences in this area as

$$January = 10 \text{ (out of 1,000 sampled)}$$
$$February = 12 \text{ (out of 1,000 sampled)}$$
$$March = 11 \text{ (out of 1,000 sampled)}$$

what comments can you make regarding the crime rate?

28. Some citizens complained to city council members that there should be equal protection under the law against the occurrence of crimes. The citizens argued that this equal protection should be interpreted as indicating that high-crime areas should have more police protection than low-crime areas. Therefore, police patrols and other methods for preventing crime (such as street lighting or cleaning up abandoned areas and buildings) should be used proportionately to crime occurrence.

    In a fashion similar to problem 11, the city has been broken down into 20 geographic areas, each containing 5,000 residences. The 1,000 sampled from each area showed the following incidence of crime during the past month:

AREA	NUMBER OF CRIMES	SAMPLE SIZE	CRIME RATE
1	14	1,000	0.014
2	3	1,000	0.003
3	19	1,000	0.019
4	18	1,000	0.018
5	14	1,000	0.014
6	28	1,000	0.028
7	10	1,000	0.010
8	18	1,000	0.018
9	12	1,000	0.012
10	3	1,000	0.003
11	20	1,000	0.020
12	15	1,000	0.015
13	12	1,000	0.012
14	14	1,000	0.014
15	10	1,000	0.010
16	30	1,000	0.030
17	4	1,000	0.004
18	20	1,000	0.020
19	6	1,000	0.006
20	30	1,000	0.030
	300		

Suggest a reallocation of crime protection effort, if indicated, based on a *p*-chart analysis. To be reasonably certain in your recommendation, select a 95 percent confidence level (i.e., $Z = 1.96$).

29. The following table contains the measurements of the key length dimension from a fuel injector. These samples of size five were taken at one-hour intervals.

SAMPLE NUMBER	OBSERVATIONS				
	1	2	3	4	5
1	.486	.499	.493	.511	.481
2	.499	.506	.516	.494	.529
3	.496	.500	.515	.488	.521
4	.495	.506	.483	.487	.489
5	.472	.502	.526	.469	.481
6	.473	.495	.507	.493	.506
7	.495	.512	.490	.471	.504
8	.525	.501	.498	.474	.485

(*continued*)

	OBSERVATIONS				
SAMPLE NUMBER	1	2	3	4	5
9	.497	.501	.517	.506	.516
10	.495	.505	.516	.511	.497
11	.495	.482	.468	.492	.492
12	.483	.459	.526	.506	.522
13	.521	.512	.493	.525	.510
14	.487	.521	.507	.501	.500
15	.493	.516	.499	.511	.513
16	.473	.506	.479	.480	.523
17	.477	.485	.513	.484	.496
18	.515	.493	.493	.485	.475
19	.511	.536	.486	.497	.491
20	.509	.490	.470	.504	.512

Construct a three-sigma $\bar{X}$-chart and R-chart (use Exhibit 10.13) for the length of the fuel injector. What can you say about this process?

LO10–6 30. In the past, Alpha Corporation has not performed incoming quality control inspections but has taken the word of its vendors. However, Alpha has been having some unsatisfactory experience recently with the quality of purchased items and wants to set up sampling plans for the receiving department to use.

For a particular component, X, Alpha has a lot tolerance percentage defective of 10 percent. Zenon Corporation, from which Alpha purchases this component, has an acceptable quality level in its production facility of 3 percent for component X. Alpha has a consumer's risk of 10 percent and Zenon has a producer's risk of 5 percent.

a. When a shipment of product X is received from Zenon Corporation, what sample size should the receiving department test?

b. What is the allowable number of defects in order to accept the shipment?

31. Large-scale integrated (LSI) circuit chips are made in one department of an electronics firm. These chips are incorporated into analog devices that are then encased in epoxy. The yield is not particularly good for LSI manufacture, so the AQL specified by that department is 0.15, while the LTPD acceptable by the assembly department is 0.40.

a. Develop a sampling plan.

b. Explain what the sampling plan means; that is, how would you tell someone to do the test?

ANALYTICS EXERCISE: QUALITY MANAGEMENT—TOYOTA

Case Part A: Toyota—Under-the-Radar Recall Responses

After a bruising series of recalls in 2010, Toyota Motor Corp. has quietly implemented a number of new quality and safety-related reforms to its operations, even as it denies its vehicles are prone to defective parts or engineering flaws. Toyota admits that the number of recalls has increased but insists that it is because the company now tags vehicles even for issues that it had not previously considered problematic as part of its new effort to appease customers. It claims this improvement contrasts with its slow response in the past, which had hurt its reputation.

Executives admit they were lax in instituting companywide programs to police repairs at dealerships and didn't grasp how some car owners were driving their cars in potentially hazardous ways, such as using after-market floor mats piled up under the gas pedal. Company engineers never envisioned that kind of problem when they designed and produced cars, and mechanics at dealers didn't bother to report it up the chain of command.

"We had a top-down, bureaucratic system with lots of check-lists that weren't taken seriously by regular employees because their hearts weren't in it," said Shinzo Kobuki, a Toyota senior managing director in charge of overseeing advanced research and safety. "Even with our suppliers, we rated their ability to meet strict scheduling deadlines ahead of their ability to meet strict quality and safety guidelines. Now the opposite is true."

Toru Sakuragi, chief executive of SC-Abeam Automotive Consulting, a Tokyo-based automotive research/consulting firm, says Toyota has been caught between a need to cut costs to overcome the strong yen and the need to improve quality to prevent recalls. "They are now pursuing both strategies, but they are essentially at odds with one another," said Mr. Sakuragi. It remains to be seen if Toyota's actions are sufficient to prevent a recurrence of the missteps that tarnished its image as it recalled some 10 million vehicles worldwide. Importantly, the company's soul searching has amounted to a mere slap on the wrist for its senior-most officials, in the form of a 20 percent pay cut for just three months last summer. And Toyota denies any culpability for structural defects or systematic cover-ups.

A RECALLED TOYOTA GAS PEDAL IS POSED NEXT TO A RECALLED TOYOTA AVALON. TOYOTA ISSUED THE PARTS TO FIX STICKY GAS PEDALS, BUT THE 4.2 MILLION CUSTOMERS AFFECTED HAD TO WAIT UNTIL TECHNICIANS WERE TRAINED.

© A3250/_Oliver Berg/dpa/Corbis

To some extent, the Japanese automaker was vindicated by the announcement from the U.S. National Highway Traffic Safety Board that many of the reported accidents involving Toyota models resulted not from gremlins in electronic control systems, but "pedal misapplication"—or driver error. Yet the company still faces hundreds of lawsuits stemming from unintended acceleration-related accidents, including some from seven major insurers who filed separate but identical complaints in Los Angeles County Superior Court blaming defects in Toyota vehicles for the crashes.

For its part, Toyota says it has found no defects or safety issues with new model cars that have undergone enhanced checks ahead of their debut to the marketplace. In the final stage of its recent Camry review, Toyota concentrated on fine-tuning things such as the level of vibration in the steering wheel to ease perceived quality gaps. These changes forced a delay in the car's debut by several weeks.

New Initiatives

The Japanese automaker has launched, unannounced, several low-profile initiatives, including a global computer database to track vehicle repairs and cut reporting times about customer complaints from months to days. It also has extended deployment of rapid-response teams to determine the causes of accidents beyond the United States and Japan to other major markets, including China and Europe.

These initiatives include a multimillion-dollar, multilingual computer system manned by a dedicated unit of 20 employees who compile repair reports from Toyota dealerships worldwide, along with complaints on the Internet and safety concern information gathered by governments; then they mine those data to spot trends. Known internally as TAQIC, or Toyota Advanced Quality Information Center, this system will be made accessible to most employees on an as-needed basis.

The company also has named a managing director to oversee all safety-related issues. This official works on the research and engineering side of the business but collaborates with a separate quality-focused task force. Another initiative involves the so-called Swift Market Analysis Response Teams, known as Smart, set up to troubleshoot in the United States. These are now being rolled out globally in markets such as Europe, India, Southeast Asia, and China at a total annual cost to Toyota of some five billion yen ($60.4 million). The teams are responsible for tracking down what company insiders dub "S-ketten," a hybrid of an abbreviation for the English word *safety* and the Japanese term for defects. While these troubleshooting squads are new to the United States and other markets, Toyota revealed that it has maintained similar teams in Japan for years as a result of Japanese regulators' demands for quarterly reports following recalls. Since U.S. authorities didn't require Toyota to isolate the root cause of problems leading to recalls like their Japanese counterparts, the Smart groups weren't deployed outside Japan.

Toyota says the renewed focus on quality and safety will form an early-warning system of sorts to get a handle on potential problems before they can snowball. Toyota assigned 1,000 engineers to spot-check quality, setting up troubleshooting teams in the United States and adding at least four weeks to its new-car development schedules. It also has lowered its bar for requiring recalls.

At a new Toyota group factory opened in northern Japan to export its Yaris subcompacts to the United States and the Middle East, the company stressed its commitment to the highest levels of quality and safety. "We are at ground zero in the sense [that] the things we make here go directly to the customers, so we have a responsibility to get it right from the earliest stage of the manufacturing process," said Atsushi Niimi, executive vice president in charge of production engineering. However, Toyota has not instituted drastic changes to its assembly lines as a result of the recall, even at the new plant in Miyagi, which replaces an older factory in Sagamihara outside Tokyo. "We haven't done anything radically different in terms of quality checks," said Kenji Kinoshita, an assembly-line production engineer at Miyagi who was seconded from Kanto Auto Works Ltd. "We're just doing our normal everyday work to improve things little by little."

Discussion Questions

1. Develop a diagram that summarizes what Toyota has done in response to its recent quality recall problems. Focus on the changes by functional area (i.e., Management, Product Design, Quality, and Manufacturing).

2. Evaluate the statement in the case made by Toru Sakuragi that "Toyota has been caught between a need to cut costs to overcome the strong yen and the need to improve quality to prevent recalls," and that "[t]hey are now pursuing both strategies but they are essentially at odds with one another." Is this a realistic strategy? Do you have suggestions for how the strategy might be improved?

3. Suggest improvements that you feel could be made to Toyota's quality program. Also, what might Toyota do to improve its image to the consumer relative to quality?

Source: Adapted from Chester Dawson and Yoshio Takahashi, "Toyota Makes New Push to Avoid Recalls," *The Wall Street Journal*, February 24, 2011.

Case Part B: Quality Control Analytics at Toyota

As part of the process for improving the quality of their cars, Toyota engineers have identified a potential improvement to the process that makes a washer that is used in the accelerator assembly. The tolerances on the thickness of the washer are fairly large since the fit can be loose, but if it does happen to get too large, it can cause the accelerator to bind and create a potential problem for the driver. (*Note:* This part of the case has been fabricated for teaching purposes and none of these data were obtained from Toyota.)

Let's assume that as a first step to improving the process, a sample of 40 washers coming from the machine that produces the washers was taken and the thickness measured in millimeters. The following table has the measurements from the sample:

1.9	2.0	1.9	1.8	2.2	1.7	2.0	1.9	1.7	1.8
1.8	2.2	2.1	2.2	1.9	1.8	2.1	1.6	1.8	1.6
2.1	2.4	2.2	2.1	2.1	2.0	1.8	1.7	1.9	1.9
2.1	2.0	2.4	1.7	2.2	2.0	1.6	2.0	2.1	2.2

Discussion Questions

1. If the specification is such that no washer should be greater than 2.4 millimeters, assuming that the thicknesses are distributed normally, what fraction of the output is expected to be greater than this thickness?

2. If there are upper and lower specifications, where the upper thickness limit is 2.4 and the lower thickness limit is 1.4, what fraction of the output is expected to be out of tolerance?

3. What is the C_{pk} for the process?

4. What would be the C_{pk} for the process if it were centered between the specification limits (assume the process standard deviation is the same)?

5. What percentage of output would be expected to be out of tolerance if the process were centered?

6. Set up $\overline{X}$ and range control charts for the current process. Assume the operators will take samples of 10 washers at a time.

7. Plot the data on your control charts. Does the current process appear to be in control?

8. If the process could be improved so that the standard deviation were only about .10 millimeter, what would be the best that could be expected with the processes relative to the fraction defective?

PRACTICE EXAM

1. This refers to the inherent value of the product in the marketplace and is a strategic decision for the firm.
2. Relates to how well a product or service meets design specifications.
3. Relates to how the customer views quality dimensions of a product or service.
4. The series of international quality standards.
5. What is the enemy of good quality?
6. A Six Sigma process that is running at the center of its control limits would expect this defect rate.
7. The standard quality improvement methodology developed by General Electric.
8. Variation that can be clearly identified and possibly managed.
9. Variation inherent in the process itself.
10. If a process has a capability index of 1 and is running normally (centered on the mean), what percentage of the units would one expect to be defective?
11. An alternative to viewing an item as simply good or bad due to it falling in or out of the tolerance range.
12. Quality characteristics that are classified as either conforming or not conforming to specification.
13. A quality characteristic that is actually measured, such as the weight of an item.
14. A quality chart suitable for when an item is either good or bad.
15. A quality chart suitable for when a number of blemishes are expected on each unit, such as a spool of yarn.
16. Useful for checking quality when we periodically purchase large quantities of an item and it would be very costly to check each unit individually.
17. A chart that depicts the manufacturer's and consumer's risks associated with a sampling plan.

Answers to Practice Exam 1. Design quality 2. Conformance quality 3. Fitness for use 4. ISO 9000 5. Variation 6. 2 parts per billion units 7. DMAIC cycle 8. Assignable variation 9. Common variation 10. Design limits are at ±3σ or 2.7 defects per thousand 11. Taguchi loss function 12. Attributes 13. Variable 14. *p*-chart 15. *c*-chart 16. Acceptance sampling 17. Operating characteristic curve

INVENTORY MANAGEMENT

WILL WAREHOUSES BE NEEDED IN THE FUTURE?

Logistics visionaries have talked for years about eliminating—or at least drastically reducing—the role of inventory in modern supply chains. The most efficient, slack-free supply chains, after all, wouldn't require any inventory buffer because supply and demand would be in perfect sync. This vision certainly has its appeal: The death of inventory would mean dramatically reduced logistics costs and simplified fulfillment.

There's no need to write a eulogy for inventory just yet. Most companies haven't honed their networks and technologies well enough to eliminate the need for at least minimal inventory. Logistics managers have to perform a daily, delicate act balancing:

- Transportation costs against fulfillment speed,
- Inventory costs against the cost of stock outs,
- Customer satisfaction against the cost to serve,
- New capabilities against profitability.

What's more, two accelerating business trends are making it even harder to synchronize supply chains.

First, global sourcing is forcing supply chains to stretch farther across borders. The goods people consume are increasingly made in some other part of the world, particularly in Asia. This acceleration in global sourcing changes the logistics equation. When goods cross borders, considerations such as fulfillment speed (these are the activities performed once an order is received) and inventory costs get more complicated. Second, powerful retailers and other end customers with clout are starting to push value-added supply chain responsibilities further up the supply chain. More customers are asking manufacturers or third-party logistics providers to label and prepare individual items so the products are ready to go directly to store shelves. With added responsibilities, of course, come added costs. Upstream suppliers are always looking for ways to squeeze more costs out of other areas of the supply chain, such as transportation and distribution.

© Bloomberg/Getty Images

A growing number of companies are overcoming these barriers by taking a more direct approach to global fulfillment. This direct-to-store approach—also known as distribution center bypass or direct distribution—keeps inventory moving from manufacturer to end customer by eliminating stops at warehouses along the way. Because companies can shrink the fulfillment cycle and eliminate inventory costs, direct-to-store can offer a good balance between fulfillment speed and logistics costs.

Internet-enabled electronic links between supply chain partners have allowed better coordination and collaboration among the various supply chain segments. Meanwhile, at the front of the supply chain, increasingly sophisticated point-of-sale systems can capture product demand patterns. This information can then be fed up the supply chain to manufacturers and components suppliers. More accurate sales-forecasting tools take some of the guesswork out of production and reduce the need for large inventory safety stocks. Tracking and tracing tools are also available to follow orders across borders and through the hands of different supply partners.

In short, companies no longer need as much inventory gathering dust in warehouses because they can better synchronize production and distribution with demand. Direct-to-store lets them keep inventory in motion—across borders and around the world.

You should visualize inventory as stacks of money sitting on forklifts, on shelves, and in trucks and planes while in transit. That's what inventory is—money. For many businesses, inventory is the largest asset on the balance sheet at any given time, even though it is often not very liquid. It is a good idea to try to get their inventory down as far as possible.

UNDERSTANDING INVENTORY MANAGEMENT

LO11–1 Explain how inventory is used and understand what it costs.

The economic benefit from inventory reduction is evident from the following statistics: The average cost of inventory in the United States is 30 to 35 percent of its value. For example, if a firm carries an inventory of $20 million, it costs the firm more than $6 million per year to keep it in stock. These costs are due mainly to obsolescence, insurance, and opportunity costs. If the amount of inventory could be reduced to $10 million, for instance, the firm would save over $3 million, which goes directly to the bottom line; that is, the savings from reduced inventory results in increased profit.

This chapter and Chapter 9 present techniques designed to manage inventory in different supply chain settings. In this chapter, the focus is on settings where the desire is to maintain a stock of inventory that can be delivered to customers on demand. Recall in Chapter 6 the concept of *customer order decoupling point,* which is a point where inventory is positioned to allow processes or entities in the supply chain to operate independently. For example, if a product is stocked at a retailer, the customer pulls the item from the shelf and the manufacturer never sees a customer order. In this case, inventory acts as a buffer to separate the customer from the manufacturing process. Selection of decoupling points is a strategic decision that determines customer lead times and can greatly impact inventory investment. The closer this point is to the customer, the quicker the customer can be served.

The techniques described in this chapter are suited for managing the inventory at these decoupling points. Typically, there is a trade-off where quicker response to customer demand comes at the expense of greater inventory investment. This is because finished goods inventory is more expensive than raw material inventory. In practice, the idea of a single decoupling point in a supply chain is unrealistic. There may actually be multiple points where buffering takes place.

Good examples of where the models described in this chapter are used include retail stores, grocery stores, wholesale distributors, hospital suppliers, and suppliers of repair parts needed to fix or maintain equipment quickly. Situations in which it is necessary to have the item "in stock" are ideal candidates for the models described in this chapter. A distinction that needs to be made with the models included in this chapter is whether this is a one-time purchase, for example, for a seasonal item or for one used at a special event, or whether the item will be stocked on an ongoing basis.

Exhibit 11.1 depicts different types of supply chain inventories that would exist in a make-to-stock environment, typical of items directed at the consumer. In the upper echelons of the supply chain, which are supply points closer to the customer, stock usually is kept so that an item can be delivered quickly when a customer need occurs. Of course, there are many exceptions, but in general this is the case. The raw materials and manufacturing plant inventory held in the lower echelon potentially can be managed in a special way to take advantage of the planning and synchronization needed to efficiently operate this part of the supply chain. In this case, the models in this chapter are most appropriate for the upper echelon inventories (retail and warehouse), and the lower echelon should use the material requirements planning (MRP) technique described in Chapter 9. The

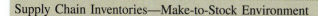

Supply Chain Inventories—Make-to-Stock Environment   **exhibit 11.1**

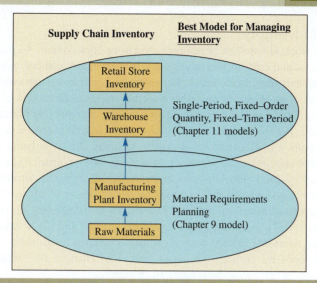

applicability of these models could be different for other environments such as when we produce directly to customer order as in the case of an aircraft manufacturer.

The techniques described here are most appropriate when demand is difficult to predict with great precision. In these models, we characterize demand by using a probability distribution and maintain stock so that the risk associated with stock out is managed. For these applications, the following three models are discussed:

1. **The single-period model.**   This is used when we are making a one-time purchase of an item. An example might be purchasing T-shirts to sell at a one-time sporting event.
2. **Fixed–order quantity model.**   This is used when we want to maintain an item "in stock," and when we resupply the item, a certain number of units must be ordered each time. Inventory for the item is monitored until it gets down to a level where the risk of stocking out is great enough that we are compelled to order.
3. **Fixed–time period model.**   This is similar to the fixed–order quantity model; it is used when the item should be in stock and ready to use. In this case, rather than monitoring the inventory level and ordering when the level gets down to a critical quantity, the item is ordered at certain intervals of time, for example, every Friday morning. This is often convenient when a group of items is ordered together. An example is the delivery of different types of bread to a grocery store. The bakery supplier may have 10 or more products stocked in a store, and rather than delivering each product individually at different times, it is much more efficient to deliver all 10 together at the same time and on the same schedule.

In this chapter, we want to show not only the mathematics associated with great inventory control but also the "art" of managing inventory. Ensuring accuracy in inventory records is essential to running an efficient inventory control process. Techniques such as ABC analysis and cycle counting are essential to the actual management of the system since they focus attention on the high-value items and ensure the quality of the transactions that affect the tracking of inventory levels.

Definition of Inventory

Inventory is the stock of any item or resource used in an organization. An *inventory system* is the set of policies and controls that monitor levels of inventory and determine what levels should be maintained, when stock should be replenished, and how large orders should be.

By convention, *manufacturing inventory* generally refers to items that contribute to or become part of a firm's product output. Manufacturing inventory is typically classified into *raw materials, finished products, component parts, supplies,* and *work-in-process.* In distribution, inventory is classified as *in-transit,* meaning that it is being moved in the system, and *warehouse,* which is inventory in a warehouse or distribution center. Retail sites carry inventory for immediate sale to customers. In services, *inventory* generally refers to the tangible goods to be sold and the supplies necessary to administer the service.

The basic purpose of inventory analysis, whether in manufacturing, distribution, retail, or services, is to specify (1) when items should be ordered and (2) how large the order should be. Many firms are tending to enter into longer-term relationships with vendors to supply their needs for perhaps the entire year. This changes the "when" and "how many to order" to "when" and "how many to deliver."

Purposes of Inventory

All firms (including JIT operations) keep a supply of inventory for the following reasons:

1. **To maintain independence of operations.** A supply of materials at a work center allows that center flexibility in operations. For example, because there are costs for making each new production setup, this inventory allows management to reduce the number of setups.

   Independence of workstations is desirable on assembly lines as well. The time it takes to do identical operations will naturally vary from one unit to the next. Therefore, it is desirable to have a cushion of several parts within the workstation so that shorter operation times can compensate for longer operation times. This way, the average output can be fairly stable.

2. **To meet variation in product demand.** If the demand for the product is known precisely, it may be possible (though not necessarily economical) to produce the product to exactly meet the demand. Usually, however, demand is not completely known, and a safety or buffer stock must be maintained to absorb variation.

3. **To allow flexibility in production scheduling.** A stock of inventory relieves the pressure on the production system to get the goods out at a precise time. The trade-off is that lead time may be increased, but smoother flow and lower-cost through larger lot-sizes may be possible. High setup costs, for example, favor producing a larger number of units once the setup has been made.

4. **To provide a safeguard for variation in raw material delivery time.** When material is ordered from a vendor, delays can occur for a variety of reasons: a normal variation in shipping time, a shortage of material at the vendor's plant causing backlogs, an unexpected strike at the vendor's plant or at one of the shipping companies, a lost order, or a shipment of incorrect or defective material.

5. **To take advantage of economic purchase order size.** There are costs to place an order: labor, phone calls, typing, postage, and so on. Therefore, the larger each order is, the fewer the orders that need be written. Also, shipping costs favor larger orders—the larger the shipment, the lower the per-unit cost.

Inventory
The stock of any item or resource used in an organization.

6. **Many other domain-specific reasons.** Depending on the situation, there are other reasons inventory may need to be carried. For example, in-transit inventory is material being moved from the suppliers to customers and depends on the order quantity and the transit lead time. Another example is inventory that is bought in anticipation of price changes such as fuel for jet planes or semiconductors for computers. There are many other examples.

For each of the preceding reasons (especially for items 3, 4, and 5), be aware that inventory is costly and large amounts are generally undesirable. Long cycle times are caused by large amounts of inventory and are undesirable as well.

© Brand X Pictures/PunchStock RF

Inventory Costs

In making any decision that affects inventory size, the following costs must be considered:

1. **Holding (or carrying) costs.** This broad category includes the costs for storage facilities, handling, insurance, pilferage, breakage, obsolescence, depreciation, taxes, and the opportunity cost of capital. Obviously, high holding costs tend to favor low inventory levels and frequent replenishment.

2. **Setup (or production change) costs.** Making each different product involves obtaining the necessary materials, arranging specific equipment setups, filling out the required papers, appropriately charging time and materials, and moving out the previous stock of material.

   If there were no costs or loss of time in changing from one product to another, many small lots would be produced. This would reduce inventory levels, with a resulting savings in cost. One challenge today is to try to reduce these setup costs to permit smaller lot sizes. (This is the goal of a JIT system.)

3. **Ordering costs.** These costs refer to the managerial and clerical costs to prepare the purchase or production order. Ordering costs include all the details, such as counting items and calculating order quantities. The costs associated with maintaining the system needed to track orders are also included in ordering costs.

4. **Shortage costs.** When the stock of an item is depleted, an order for that item must either wait until the stock is replenished or be canceled. When the demand is not met and the order is canceled, this is referred to as a stock out. A backorder is when the order is held and filled at a later date when the inventory for the item is replenished. There is a trade-off between carrying stock to satisfy demand and the costs resulting from stock outs and backorders. This balance is sometimes difficult to obtain because it may not be possible to estimate lost profits, the effects of lost customers, or lateness penalties. Frequently, the assumed shortage cost is little more than a guess, although it is usually possible to specify a range of such costs.

Establishing the correct quantity to order from vendors or the size of lots submitted to the firm's productive facilities involves a search for the minimum total cost resulting from the combined effects of four individual costs: holding costs, setup costs, ordering costs, and shortage costs. Of course, the timing of these orders is a critical factor that may impact inventory cost.

Independent versus Dependent Demand

In inventory management, it is important to understand the trade-offs involved in using different types of inventory control logic. Exhibit 11.2 is a framework that shows how characteristics of demand, transaction cost, and the risk of obsolete inventory map into different types of systems. The systems in the upper left of the exhibit are described in this chapter, and those in the lower right in Chapter 9.

Transaction cost is dependent on the level of integration and automation incorporated into the system. Manual systems such as simple *two-bin* logic depend on human posting of the transactions to replenish inventory, which is relatively expensive compared to using a computer to automatically detect when an item needs to be ordered. Integration relates to how connected systems are. For example, it is common for orders for material to be automatically transferred to suppliers electronically and for these orders to be automatically captured by the supplier inventory control system. This type of integration greatly reduces transaction cost.

The risk of obsolescence is also an important consideration. If an item is used infrequently or only for a very specific purpose, there is considerable risk in using inventory control logic that does not track the specific source of demand for the item. Further, items that are sensitive to technical obsolescence, such as computer memory chips and processors, need to be managed carefully based on actual need to reduce the risk of getting stuck with inventory that is outdated.

An important characteristic of demand relates to whether demand is derived from an end item or is related to the item itself. We use the terms **independent demand** and **dependent demand** to describe this characteristic. Briefly, the distinction between independent and dependent demand is this: In independent demand, the demands for various items are unrelated to each other. For example, a workstation may produce many parts

Independent demand The demands for various items are unrelated to each other.

Dependent demand The need for any one item is a direct result of the need for some other item, usually an item of which it is a part.

---

exhibit 11.2   Inventory-Control-System Design Matrix: Framework Describing Inventory Control Logic

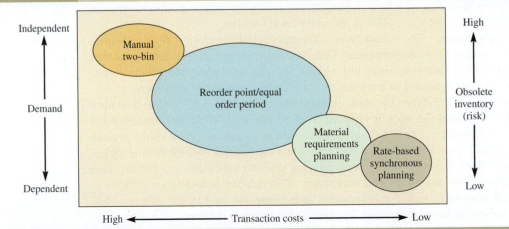

that are unrelated but that meet some external demand requirement. In dependent demand, the need for any one item is a direct result of the need for some other item, usually a higher-level item of which it is part.

In concept, dependent demand is a relatively straightforward computational problem. Required quantities of a dependent-demand item are simply computed, based on the number needed in each higher-level item in which it is used. For example, if an automobile company plans on producing 500 cars per day, then obviously it will need 2,000 wheels and tires (plus spares). The number of wheels and tires needed is *dependent* on the production levels and is not derived separately. The demand for cars, on the other hand, is *independent*—it comes from many sources external to the automobile firm and is not a part of other products; it is unrelated to the demand for other products.

To determine the quantities of independent items that must be produced, firms usually turn to their sales and market research departments. They use a variety of techniques, including customer surveys, forecasting techniques, and economic and sociological trends, as we discussed in Chapter 3 on forecasting. Because independent demand is uncertain, extra units must be carried in inventory. This chapter presents models to determine how many units need to be ordered, and how many extra units should be carried to reduce the risk of stocking out.

INVENTORY SYSTEMS

An inventory system provides the organizational structure and the operating policies for maintaining and controlling goods to be stocked. The system is responsible for ordering and receipt of goods: timing the order placement and keeping track of what has been ordered, how much, and from whom. The system also must follow up to answer such questions as: Has the supplier received the order? Has it been shipped? Are the dates correct? Are the procedures established for reordering or returning undesirable merchandise?

LO11–2 Analyze how different inventory control systems work.

This section divides systems into single-period systems and multiple-period systems. The classification is based on whether the decision is just a one-time purchasing decision where the purchase is designed to cover a fixed period of time and the item will not be reordered, or the decision involves an item that will be purchased periodically where inventory should be kept in stock to be used on demand. We begin with a look at the one-time purchasing decision and the single-period inventory model.

A Single-Period Inventory Model

Certainly, an easy example to think about is the classic **single-period** "newsperson" **problem**. For example, consider the problem a newsperson has in deciding how many newspapers to put in the sales stand outside a hotel lobby each morning. If the person does not put enough papers in the stand, some customers will not be able to purchase a paper and the newsperson will lose the profit associated with these sales. On the other hand, if too many papers are placed in the stand, the newsperson will have paid for papers that were not sold during the day, lowering profit for the day.

Single-period problem Answers the question of how much to order when an item is purchased only one time and it is expected that it will be used and then not reordered.

Actually, this is a very common type of problem. Consider the person selling T-shirts promoting a championship basketball or football game. This is especially difficult, since the person must wait to learn what teams will be playing. The shirts can then be printed with the proper team logos. Of course, the person must estimate how many people will actually want the shirts. The shirts sold prior to the game can probably be sold at a premium price, whereas those sold after the game will need to be steeply discounted.

© Paul Knivett/Alamy RF

A simple way to think about this is to consider how much risk we are willing to take for running out of inventory. Let's consider that the newsperson selling papers in the sales stand had collected data over a few months and had found that, on average, each Monday 90 papers were sold with a standard deviation of 10 papers (assume that during this time the papers were purposefully overstocked in order not to run out, so they would know what "real" demand was). With these data, our newsperson could simply state a service rate that is felt to be acceptable. For example, the newsperson might want to be 80 percent sure of not running out of papers each Monday.

Recall from your study of statistics, assuming that the probability distribution associated with the sales of the paper is normal, that if we stocked exactly 90 papers each Monday morning, the risk of stocking out would be 50 percent, since 50 percent of the time we expect demand to be less than 90 papers and 50 percent of the time we expect demand to be greater than 90. To be 80 percent sure of not stocking out, we need to carry a few more papers. From the "cumulative standard normal distribution" table given in Appendix E, we see that we need approximately 0.85 standard deviation of extra papers to be 80 percent sure of not stocking out. A quick way to find the exact number of standard deviations needed for a given probability of stocking out is with the NORM.S.INV(probability) function in Microsoft Excel: (NORM.S.INV(0.8) = 0.84162). Given our result from Excel, which is more accurate than what we can get from the tables, the number of extra papers would be $0.84162 \times 10 = 8.416$, or 9 papers. (There is no way to sell 0.4 paper!)

To make this more useful, it would be good to actually consider the potential profit and loss associated with stocking either too many or too few papers on the stand. Let's say that our newspaper person pays $0.20 for each paper and sells the papers for $0.50. In this case, the marginal cost associated with underestimating demand is $0.30, the lost profit. Similarly, the marginal cost of overestimating demand is $0.20, the cost of buying too many papers. The optimal stocking level, using marginal analysis, occurs at the point where the expected benefits derived from carrying the next unit are less than the expected costs for that unit. Keep in mind that the specific benefits and costs depend on the problem.

In symbolic terms, define

$$C_o = \text{Cost per unit of demand overestimated}$$
$$C_u = \text{Cost per unit of demand underestimated}$$

By introducing probabilities, the expected marginal cost equation becomes

$$P(C_o) \leq (1 - P)C_u$$

where P is the cumulative probability that the unit will not be sold and $1 - P$ is the probability of it being sold because one or the other must occur. (The unit is sold or is not sold.)

Then, solving for P, we obtain

$$P \leq \frac{C_u}{C_o + C_u} \qquad \text{[11.1]}$$

This equation states that we should continue to increase the size of the order, as long as the probability of selling what we order is equal to or less than the ratio $C_u/(C_o + C_u)$.

Returning to our newspaper problem, our cost of overestimating demand (C_o) is $0.20 per paper and the cost of underestimating demand (C_u) is $0.30. The probability therefore is $0.3/(0.2 + 0.3) = 0.6$. Now, we need to find the point on our demand distribution that corresponds to the cumulative probability of 0.6. Using the NORM.S.INV function to get the number of standard deviations (commonly referred to as the Z-score) of extra newspapers to carry, we get 0.253, which means we should stock $0.253(10) = 2.53$ or 3 extra papers. The total number of papers for the stand each Monday morning, therefore, should be 93 papers.

Single-period inventory models are useful for a wide variety of service and manufacturing applications. Consider the following:

1. **Overbooking of airline flights.** It is common for customers to cancel flight reservations for a variety of reasons. Here the cost of underestimating the number of cancellations is the revenue lost due to an empty seat on a flight. The cost of overestimating cancellations is the awards, such as free flights or cash payments, that are given to customers unable to board the flight.
2. **Ordering of fashion items.** A problem for a retailer selling fashion items is that often only a single order can be placed for the entire season. This is often caused by long lead times and limited life of the merchandise. The cost of underestimating demand is the lost profit due to sales not made. The cost of overestimating demand is the cost that results when it is discounted.
3. **Any type of one-time order.** For example, ordering T-shirts for a sporting event or printing maps that become obsolete after a certain period of time.

Example 11.1: Hotel Reservations

A hotel near the university always fills up on the evening before football games. History has shown that when the hotel is fully booked, the number of last-minute cancellations has a mean of 5 and a standard deviation of 3. The average room rate is $80. When the hotel is overbooked, the policy is to find a room in a nearby hotel and to pay for the room for the customer. This usually costs the hotel approximately $200 since rooms booked on such late notice are expensive. How many rooms should the hotel overbook?

SOLUTION

The cost of underestimating the number of cancellations is $80 and the cost of overestimating cancellations is $200.

$$P \le \frac{C_u}{C_o + C_u} = \frac{\$80}{\$200 + \$80} = 0.2857$$

Using NORM.S.INV(.2857) from Excel gives a Z-score of -0.56599. The negative value indicates that we should overbook by a value less than the average of 5. The actual value should be $-0.56599(3) = -1.69797$, or 2 reservations less than 5. The hotel should overbook 3 reservations on the evening prior to a football game.

Another common method for analyzing this type of problem is with a discrete probability distribution found using actual data and marginal analysis. For our hotel, consider that we have collected data and our distribution of no-shows is as follows:

NUMBER OF NO-SHOWS	PROBABILITY	CUMULATIVE PROBABILITY
0	0.05	0.05
1	0.08	0.13
2	0.10	0.23
3	0.15	0.38
4	0.20	0.58
5	0.15	0.73
6	0.11	0.84
7	0.06	0.90
8	0.05	0.95
9	0.04	0.99
10	0.01	1.00

Excel:
Inventory
Control

Using these data, we can create a table showing the impact of overbooking. The total expected cost of each overbooking option is then calculated by multiplying each possible outcome by its probability and summing the weighted costs. The best overbooking strategy is the one with minimum cost.

		NUMBER OF RESERVATIONS OVERBOOKED										
NO-SHOWS	PROBABILITY	0	1	2	3	4	5	6	7	8	9	10
0	0.05	0	200	400	600	800	1,000	1,200	1,400	1,600	1,800	2,000
1	0.08	80	0	200	400	600	800	1,000	1,200	1,400	1,600	1,800
2	0.1	160	80	0	200	400	600	800	1,000	1,200	1,400	1,600
3	0.15	240	160	80	0	200	400	600	800	1,000	1,200	1,400
4	0.2	320	240	160	80	0	200	400	600	800	1,000	1,200
5	0.15	400	320	240	160	80	0	200	400	600	800	1,000
6	0.11	480	400	320	240	160	80	0	200	400	600	800
7	0.06	560	480	400	320	240	160	80	0	200	400	600
8	0.05	640	560	480	400	320	240	160	80	0	200	400
9	0.04	720	640	560	480	400	320	240	160	80	0	200
10	0.01	800	720	640	560	480	400	320	240	160	80	0
Total cost		337.6	271.6	228	212.4	238.8	321.2	445.6	600.8	772.8	958.8	1,156

From the table, the minimum total cost is when three extra reservations are taken. This approach using discrete probability is useful when valid historic data are available. •

Multiperiod Inventory Systems

There are two general types of multiperiod inventory systems: **fixed–order quantity models** (also called the *economic order quantity*, EOQ, and **Q-model**) and **fixed–time period models** (also referred to variously as the *periodic* system, *periodic review* system, *fixed–order interval* system, and **P-model**). Multiperiod inventory systems are designed to ensure that an item will be available on an ongoing basis throughout the year. Usually the item will be ordered multiple times throughout the year where the logic in the system dictates the actual quantity ordered and the timing of the order.

The basic distinction is that fixed–order quantity models are "event triggered" and fixed–time period models are "time triggered." That is, a fixed–order quantity model initiates an order when the event of reaching a specified reorder level occurs. This event may take place at any time, depending on the demand for the items considered. In contrast, the fixed–time period model is limited to placing orders at the end of a predetermined time period; only the passage of time triggers the model.

To use the fixed–order quantity model (which places an order when the remaining inventory drops to a predetermined order point, R), the inventory remaining must be continually monitored. Thus, the fixed–order quantity model is a *perpetual* system, which requires that every time a withdrawal from inventory or an addition to inventory is made, records must be updated to reflect whether the reorder point has been reached. In a fixed–time period model, counting takes place only at the review period. (We will discuss some variations of systems that combine features of both.)

Some additional differences tend to influence the choice of systems (see Exhibit 11.3):

- The fixed–time period model has a larger average inventory because it must also protect against stock out during the review period, T; the fixed–order quantity model has no review period.
- The fixed–order quantity model is favored for more expensive items because average inventory is lower.
- The fixed–order quantity model is more appropriate for important items such as critical repair parts because there is closer monitoring and therefore quicker response to potential stock outs.
- The fixed–order quantity model requires more time to maintain because every addition or withdrawal is logged.

Fixed–order quantity model (Q-model)
An inventory control model where the amount requisitioned is fixed and the actual ordering is triggered by inventory dropping to a specified level of inventory.

Fixed–time period model (P-model)
An inventory control model that specifies inventory is ordered at the end of a predetermined time period. The interval of time between orders is fixed and the order quantity varies.

Fixed–Order Quantity and Fixed–Time Period Differences		**exhibit 11.3**
FEATURE	Q-MODEL FIXED–ORDER QUANTITY MODEL	P-MODEL FIXED–TIME PERIOD MODEL
Order quantity	Q—constant (the same amount ordered each time)	q—variable (varies each time order is placed)
When to place order	R—when inventory position drops to the reorder level	T—when the review period arrives
Recordkeeping	Each time a withdrawal or addition is made	Counted only at review period
Size of inventory	Less than fixed–time period model	Larger than fixed–order quantity model
Time to maintain	Higher due to perpetual recordkeeping	
Type of items	Higher-priced, critical, or important items	

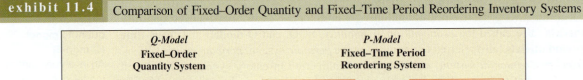

exhibit 11.4   Comparison of Fixed–Order Quantity and Fixed–Time Period Reordering Inventory Systems

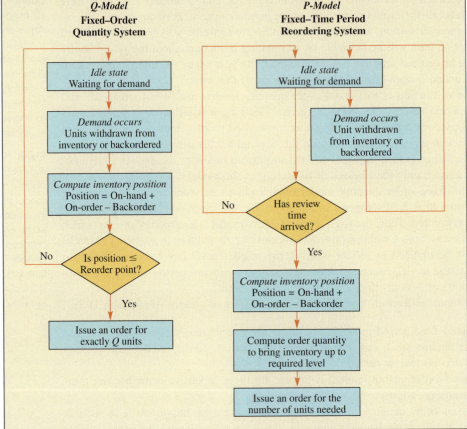

Exhibit 11.4 shows what occurs when each of the two models is put into use and becomes an operating system. As we can see, the fixed–order quantity system focuses on order quantities and reorder points. Procedurally, each time a unit is taken out of stock, the withdrawal is logged and the amount remaining in inventory is immediately compared to the reorder point. If it has dropped to this point, an order for Q items is placed. If it has not, the system remains in an idle state until the next withdrawal.

In the fixed–time period system, a decision to place an order is made after the stock has been counted or reviewed. Whether an order is actually placed depends on the inventory position at that time.

Fixed–Order Quantity Models

Fixed–order quantity models attempt to determine the specific point, R, at which an order will be placed and the size of that order, Q. The order point, R, is always a specified number of units. An order of size Q is placed when the inventory available (currently in stock and on-order) reaches the point R. **Inventory position** is defined as the on-hand plus on-order minus backordered quantities. The solution to a fixed–order quantity model

Inventory position
The amount on-hand plus on-order minus backordered quantities. In the case where inventory has been allocated for special purposes, the inventory position is reduced by these allocated amounts.

may stipulate something like this: When the inventory position drops to 36, place an order for 57 more units.

$$\text{Inventory position} = \text{On-hand} + \text{On-order} - \text{Backorder} \qquad [11.2]$$

The simplest models in this category occur when all aspects of the situation are known with certainty. If the annual demand for a product is 1,000 units, it is precisely 1,000— not 1,000 plus or minus 10 percent. The same is true for setup costs and holding costs. Although the assumption of complete certainty is rarely valid, it provides a good basis for our coverage of inventory models.

Exhibit 11.5 and the discussion about deriving the **optimal order quantity** are based on the following characteristics of the model. These assumptions are unrealistic, but they represent a starting point and allow us to use a simple example.

> **Optimal order quantity (Q_{opt})** This order size minimizes total annual inventory related costs.

- Demand for the product is constant and uniform throughout the period.
- Lead time (time from ordering to receipt) is constant.
- Price per unit of product is constant.
- Inventory holding cost is based on average inventory.
- Ordering or setup costs are constant.
- All demands for the product will be satisfied. (No backorders are allowed.)

The "sawtooth effect" relating Q and R in Exhibit 11.5 shows that when the inventory position drops to point R, a reorder is placed. This order is received at the end of time period L, which does not vary in this model.

In constructing any inventory model, the first step is to develop a functional relationship between the variables of interest and the measure of effectiveness. In this case, because we are concerned with cost, the following equation pertains:

$$\begin{array}{ccccc} \text{Total} \\ \text{annual cost} \end{array} = \begin{array}{c} \text{Annual} \\ \text{purchase cost} \end{array} + \begin{array}{c} \text{Annual} \\ \text{ordering cost} \end{array} + \begin{array}{c} \text{Annual} \\ \text{holding cost} \end{array}$$

or

$$TC = DC + \frac{D}{Q}S + \frac{Q}{2}H \qquad [11.3]$$

Basic Fixed–Order Quantity Model   exhibit 11.5

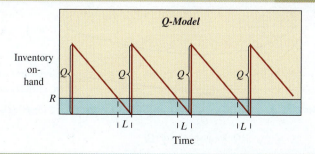

Excel:
Inventory
Control

OPERATIONS AND SUPPLY CHAIN MANAGEMENT

where

        TC = Total annual cost

        D = Demand (annual)

        C = Cost per unit

        Q = Quantity to be ordered (the optimal amount is termed the *economic order quantity*—EOQ—*or* Q_{opt})

        S = Setup cost or cost of placing an order

        R = Reorder point

        L = Lead time

        H = Annual holding and storage cost per unit of average inventory (often holding cost is taken as a percentage of the cost of the item, such as $H = iC$, where i is the percent carrying cost)

On the right side of the equation, DC is the annual purchase cost for the units, $(D/Q)S$ is the annual ordering cost (the actual number of orders placed, D/Q, times the cost of each order, S), and $(Q/2)H$ is the annual holding cost (the average inventory, $Q/2$, times the cost per unit for holding and storage, H). These cost relationships are graphed in Exhibit 11.6.

The second step in model development is to find that order quantity Q_{opt} at which the total cost is a minimum. In Exhibit 11.6, the total cost is minimal at the point where the slope of the curve is zero. Using calculus, we take the derivative of total cost with respect to Q and set this equal to zero. For the basic model considered here, the calculations are

$$TC = DC + \frac{D}{Q}S + \frac{Q}{2}H$$

$$\frac{dTC}{dQ} = 0 + \left(\frac{-DS}{Q^2}\right) + \frac{H}{2} = 0$$

$$Q_{opt} = \sqrt{\frac{2DS}{H}} \qquad \text{[11.4]}$$

Reorder point
An order is placed when the inventory position drops to this level.

Because this simple model assumes constant demand and lead time, neither safety stock nor stock-out cost is necessary, and the **reorder point**, R, is simply

$$R = \bar{d}L \qquad \text{[11.5]}$$

Excel:
Inventory
Control

exhibit 11.6   Annual Product Costs, Based on Size of the Order

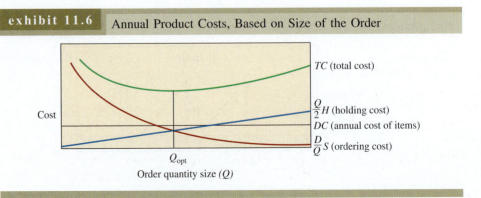

where

$\bar{d}$ = Average daily demand (constant)
L = Lead time in days (constant)

Example 11.2: Economic Order Quantity and Reorder Point

Find the economic order quantity and the reorder point, given

Annual demand (D) = 1,000 units

Average daily demand ($\bar{d}$) = 1,000/365

Ordering cost (S) = $5 per order

Holding cost (H) = $1.25 per unit per year

Lead time (L) = 5 days

Cost per unit (C) = $12.50

What quantity should be ordered?

Excel:
Inventory
Control

SOLUTION

The optimal order quantity is

$$Q_{opt} = \sqrt{\frac{2DS}{H}} = \sqrt{\frac{2(1,000)5}{1.25}} = \sqrt{8,000} = 89.4 \text{ units}$$

The reorder point is

$$R = \bar{d}L = \frac{1,000}{365}(5) = 13.7 \text{ units}$$

Rounding to the nearest unit, the inventory policy is as follows: When the inventory position drops to 14, place an order for 89 more.

The total annual cost will be

$$TC = DC + \frac{D}{Q}S + \frac{Q}{2}H$$

$$= 1,000(12.50) + \frac{1,000}{89}(5) + \frac{89}{2}(1.25)$$

$$= \$12,611.81$$

Note that the total ordering cost (1,000/89) × 5 = $56.18 and the total carrying cost (89/2) × 1.25 = $55.62 are very close but not exactly the same due to rounding Q to 89.

Note that in this example, the purchase cost of the units was not required to determine the order quantity and the reorder point because the cost was constant and unrelated to order size. •

Establishing Safety Stock Levels

The previous model assumed that demand was constant and known. In the majority of cases, though, demand is not constant but varies from day to day. Safety stock must therefore be maintained to provide some level of protection against stock outs. **Safety stock** can be defined as the amount of inventory carried in addition to the expected

Safety stock
The amount of inventory carried in addition to the expected demand.

demand. In a normal distribution, this would be the mean. For example, if our average monthly demand is 100 units and we expect next month to be the same, if we carry 120 units, then we have 20 units of safety stock.

Safety stock can be determined based on many different criteria. A common approach is for a company to simply state that a certain number of weeks of supply needs to be kept in safety stock. It is better, though, to use an approach that captures the variability in demand.

For example, an objective may be something like "set the safety stock level so that there will be only a 5 percent chance of stocking out if demand exceeds 300 units." We call this approach to setting safety stock the probability approach.

The Probability Approach Using the probability criterion to determine safety stock is pretty simple. With the models described in this chapter, we assume that the demand over a period of time is normally distributed with a mean and a standard deviation. *Again, remember that this approach considers only the probability of running out of stock, not how many units we are short.* To determine the probability of stocking out over the time period, we can simply plot a normal distribution for the expected demand and note where the amount we have on-hand lies on the curve.

Let's take a few simple examples to illustrate this. Say we expect demand to be 100 units over the next month, and we know that the standard deviation is 20 units. If we go into the month with just 100 units, we know that our probability of stocking out is 50 percent. Half of the months we would expect demand to be greater than 100 units; half of the months we would expect it to be less than 100 units. Taking this further, if we ordered a month's worth of inventory of 100 units at a time and received it at the beginning of the month, over the long run we would expect to run out of inventory in six months of the year.

If running out this often was not acceptable, we would want to carry extra inventory to reduce this risk of stocking out. One idea might be to carry an extra 20 units of inventory for the item. In this case, we would still order a month's worth of inventory at a time, but we would schedule delivery to arrive when we still have 20 units remaining in inventory. This would give us that little cushion of safety stock to reduce the probability of stocking out. If the standard deviation associated with our demand was 20 units, we would then be carrying one standard deviation worth of safety stock. Looking at the Cumulative Standard Normal Distribution (Appendix E), and moving one standard deviation to the right of the mean, gives a probability of 0.8413. So approximately 84 percent of the time we would not expect to stock out, and 16 percent of the time we would. Now if we order every month, we would expect to stock out approximately two months per year ($0.16 \times 12 = 1.92$). For those using Excel, given a z value, the probability can be obtained with the NORM.S.DIST function.

It is common for companies using this approach to set the probability of not stocking out at 95 percent. This means we would carry about 1.64 standard deviations of safety stock, or 33 units ($1.64 \times 20 = 32.8$) for our example. Once again, keep in mind that this does not mean we would order 33 units extra each month. Rather, it means we would still order a month's worth each time, but we would schedule the receipt so that we could expect to have 33 units in inventory when the order arrives. In this case, we would expect to stock out approximately 0.6 month per year, or that stock outs would occur in 1 of every 20 months.

Fixed–Order Quantity Model with Safety Stock

A fixed–order quantity system perpetually monitors the inventory level and places a new order when stock reaches some level, R. The danger of stock out in this model occurs only during the lead time, between the time an order is placed and the time it is received.

Fixed–Order Quantity Model

exhibit 11.7

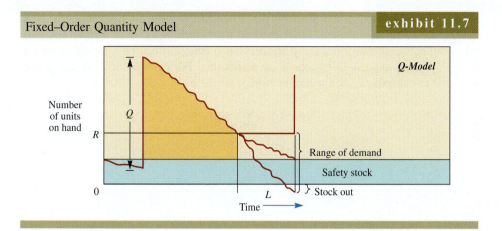

As shown in Exhibit 11.7, an order is placed when the inventory position drops to the reorder point, R. During this lead time L, a range of demands is possible. This range is determined either from an analysis of past demand data or from an estimate (if past data are not available).

The amount of safety stock depends on the service level desired, as previously discussed. The quantity to be ordered, Q, is calculated in the usual way considering the demand, shortage cost, ordering cost, holding cost, and so forth. A fixed–order quantity model can be used to compute Q, such as the simple Q_{opt} model previously discussed. The reorder point is then set to cover the expected demand during the lead time plus a safety stock determined by the desired service level. Thus, *the key difference between a fixed–order quantity model where demand is known and one where demand is uncertain is in computing the reorder point. The order quantity is the same in both cases.* The uncertainty element is taken into account in the safety stock.

The reorder point is

$$R = \bar{d}L + z\sigma_L \qquad [11.6]$$

where

R = Reorder point in units
$\bar{d}$ = Average daily demand
L = Lead time in days (time between placing an order and receiving the items)
z = Number of standard deviations for a specified service probability
σ_L = Standard deviation of usage during lead time

The term $z\sigma_L$ is the amount of safety stock. Note that if safety stock is positive, the effect is to place a reorder sooner. That is, R without safety stock is simply the average demand during the lead time. If lead time usage was expected to be 20, for example, and safety stock was computed to be 5 units, then the order would be placed sooner, when 25 units remained. The greater the safety stock, the sooner the order is placed.

Computing $\bar{d}$, σ_L, and z Demand during the replenishment lead time is really an estimate or forecast of expected use of inventory from the time an order is placed to when it is received. It may be a single number (e.g., if the lead time is a month, the demand may be taken as the previous year's demand divided by 12), or it may be a summation of expected demands over the lead time (such as the sum of daily demands over a 30-day lead time). For the daily demand situation, d can be a forecast demand using any of the models in Chapter 3 on forecasting. For example, if a 30-day period was used to calculate d, then a simple average would be

$$\bar{d} = \frac{\sum_{i=1}^{n} d_i}{n}$$

$$= \frac{\sum_{i=1}^{30} d_i}{30} \qquad [11.7]$$

where n is the number of days.

The standard deviation of the daily demand is

$$\sigma_d = \sqrt{\frac{\sum_{i=1}^{n}(d_i - \bar{d})^2}{n}}$$

$$= \sqrt{\frac{\sum_{i=1}^{30}(d_i - \bar{d})^2}{30}} \qquad [11.8]$$

Because σ_d refers to one day, if lead time extends over several days, we can use the statistical premise that the standard deviation of a series of independent occurrences is equal to the square root of the sum of the variances. That is, in general,

$$\sigma_L = \sqrt{\sigma_1^2 + \sigma_2^2 + \cdots + \sigma_L^2} \qquad [11.9]$$

For example, suppose we computed the standard deviation of demand to be 10 units per day. If our lead time to get an order is five days, the standard deviation for the five-day period, assuming each day can be considered independent, is

$$\sigma_5 = \sqrt{(10)^2 + (10)^2 + (10)^2 + (10)^2 + (10)^2} = 22.36$$

Next, we need to find z, the number of standard deviations of safety stock.

Suppose we wanted our probability of not stocking out during the lead time to be 0.95. The z value associated with a 95 percent probability of not stocking out is 1.64 (see Appendix E or use the Excel NORM.S.INV function). Given this, safety stock is calculated as follows:

$$SS = z\sigma_L$$
$$= 1.64 \times 22.36$$
$$= 36.67$$

We now compare two examples. The difference between them is that in the first, the variation in demand is stated in terms of standard deviation over the entire lead time, while in the second, it is stated in terms of standard deviation per day.

Example 11.3: Reorder Point

Consider an economic order quantity case where annual demand $D = 1,000$ units, economic order quantity $Q = 200$ units, the desired probability of not stocking out $P = .95$, the standard deviation of demand during lead time $\sigma_L = 25$ units, and lead time $L = 15$ days. Determine the reorder point. Assume that demand is over a 250-workday year.

SOLUTION

In our example, $\bar{d} = \frac{1000}{250} = 4$, and lead time is 15 days. We use the equation

$$R = \bar{d}L + z\sigma_L$$

$$= 4(15) + z(25)$$

In this case, z is 1.64.

Completing the solution for R, we have

$$R = 4(15) + 1.64(25) = 60 + 41 = 101 \text{ units}$$

This says that when the stock on-hand gets down to 101 units, order 200 more. •

Example 11.4: Order Quantity and Reorder Point

Daily demand for a certain product is normally distributed with a mean of 60 and standard deviation of 7. The source of supply is reliable and maintains a constant lead time of six days. The cost of placing the order is $10 and annual holding costs are $0.50 per unit. There are no stock-out costs, and unfilled orders are filled as soon as the order arrives. Assume sales occur over the entire 365 days of the year. Find the order quantity and reorder point to satisfy a 95 percent probability of not stocking out during the lead time.

Excel:
Inventory
Control

SOLUTION

In this problem, we need to calculate the order quantity Q as well as the reorder point R.

$$\bar{d} = 60 \qquad S = \$10$$
$$\sigma_d = 7 \qquad H = \$0.50$$
$$D = 60(365) \qquad L = 6$$

The optimal order quantity is

$$Q_{opt} = \sqrt{\frac{2DS}{H}} = \sqrt{\frac{2(60)365(10)}{0.50}} = \sqrt{876,000} = 936 \text{ units}$$

To compute the reorder point, we need to calculate the amount of product used during the lead time and add this to the safety stock.

The standard deviation of demand during the lead time of six days is calculated from the variance of the individual days. Because each day's demand is independent,

$$\sigma_L = \sqrt{\sum_{i=1}^{L} \sigma_d^2} = \sqrt{6(7)^2} = 17.15$$

Once again, z is 1.64.

$$R = \bar{d}L + z\sigma_L = 60(6) + 1.64(17.15) = 388 \text{ units}$$

To summarize the policy derived in this example, an order for 936 units is placed whenever the number of units remaining in inventory drops to 388. •

Fixed–Time Period Models

In a fixed–time period system, inventory is counted only at particular times, such as every week or every month. Counting inventory and placing orders periodically are desirable in situations such as when vendors make routine visits to customers and take orders for their complete line of products, or when buyers want to combine orders to save transportation costs. Other firms operate on a fixed time period to facilitate planning their inventory count; for example, distributor X calls every two weeks and employees know that all of distributor X's product must be counted.

Fixed–time period models generate order quantities that vary from period to period, depending on the usage rates. These generally require a higher level of safety stock than a fixed–order quantity system. The fixed–order quantity system assumes continual tracking of inventory on-hand, with an order immediately placed when the reorder point is reached. In contrast, the standard fixed–time period models assume that inventory is counted only at the time specified for review. It is possible that some large demand will draw the stock down to zero right after an order is placed. This condition could go unnoticed until the next review period. Then the new order, when placed, still takes time to arrive. Thus, it is possible to be out of stock throughout the entire review period, T, and order lead time, L. Safety stock, therefore, must protect against stock outs during the review period itself, as well as during the lead time from order placement to order receipt.

Fixed–Time Period Model with Safety Stock

In a fixed–time period system, reorders are placed at the time of review (T), and the safety stock that must be reordered is

$$\text{Safety stock} = z\sigma_{T+L} \qquad \text{[11.10]}$$

Exhibit 11.8 shows a fixed–time period system with a review cycle of T and a constant lead time of L. In this case, demand is randomly distributed about a mean d. The quantity to order, q, is

$$\begin{matrix} \text{Order} \\ \text{quantity} \end{matrix} = \begin{matrix} \text{Average demand} \\ \text{over the} \\ \text{vulnerable period} \end{matrix} + \begin{matrix} \text{Safety} \\ \text{stock} \end{matrix} - \begin{matrix} \text{Inventory currently} \\ \text{on-hand (plus on-} \\ \text{order, if any)} \end{matrix}$$

$$q \quad = \quad \bar{d}(T+L) \quad + \quad z\sigma \quad - \quad I \qquad \text{[11.11]}$$

exhibit 11.8　Fixed–Time Period Inventory Model

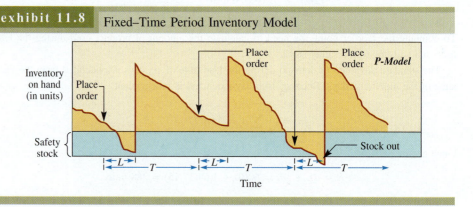

where

> q = Quantity to be ordered
> T = The number of days between reviews
> L = Lead time in days (time between placing an order and receiving it)
> $\bar{d}$ = Forecast average daily demand
> z = Number of standard deviations for a specified service probability
> σ_{T+L} = Standard deviation of demand over the review and lead time
> I = Current inventory level (includes items on-order)

Note: The demand, lead time, review period, and so forth can be any time units such as days, weeks, or years, as long as they are consistent throughout the equation.

In this model, demand ($\bar{d}$) can be forecast and revised each review period if desired, or the yearly average may be used if appropriate. We assume that demand is normally distributed.

The value of z is dependent on the probability of stocking out and can be found using Appendix E or by using the Excel NORM.S.INV function.

Example 11.5: Quantity to Order

Daily demand for a product is 10 units with a standard deviation of 3 units. The review period is 30 days, and lead time is 14 days. Management has set a policy of satisfying 98 percent of demand from items in stock. At the beginning of this review period, there are 150 units in inventory.

How many units should be ordered?

Excel:
Inventory
Control

SOLUTION

The quantity to order is

$$q = \bar{d}(T + L) + z\sigma_{T+L} - I$$
$$= 10(30 + 14) + z\sigma_{T+L} - 150$$

Before we can complete the solution, we need to find σ_{T+L} and z. To find σ_{T+L}, we use the notion, as before, that the standard deviation of a sequence of independent random variables equals the square root of the sum of the variances. Therefore, the standard deviation during the period $T + L$ is the square root of the sum of the variances for each day:

$$\sigma_{T+L} = \sqrt{\sum_{i=1}^{T+L} \sigma_d^2} \qquad [11.12]$$

Because each day is independent and σ_d is constant,

$$\sigma_{T+L} = \sqrt{(T + L)\sigma_d^2} = \sqrt{(30 + 14)(3)^2} = 19.90$$

the z value for $P = 0.98$ is 2.05.

The quantity to order, then, is

$$q = \bar{d}(T + L) + z\sigma_{T+L} - I = 10(30 + 14) + 2.05(19.90) - 150 = 331 \text{ units}$$

To ensure a 98 percent probability of not stocking out, order 331 units at this review period. •

Inventory Turn Calculations

Inventory turn
A measure of the
expected number of
times inventory is
replaced over a year.

It is important for managers to realize that how they run items using inventory control logic relates directly to the financial performance of the firm. A key measure that relates to company performance is **inventory turn**. Recall that inventory turn is calculated as follows:

$$\text{Inventory turn} = \frac{\text{Cost of goods sold}}{\text{Average inventory value}}$$

So what is the relationship between how we manage an item and the inventory turn for that item? Here, let us simplify things and consider just the inventory turn for an individual item or a group of items. First, if we look at the numerator, the cost of goods sold for an individual item relates directly to the expected yearly demand (D) for the item. Given a cost per unit (C) for the item, the cost of goods sold is just D times C. Recall that this is the same as what was used in calculating our total cost equation. Next, consider average inventory value. Recall from EOQ that the average inventory is $Q/2$, which is true if we assume that demand is constant. When we bring uncertainty into the equation, safety stock is needed to manage the risk created by demand variability. The fixed–order quantity model and fixed–time period model both have equations for calculating the safety stock required for a given probability of stocking out. In both models, we assume that when going through an order cycle, half the time we need to use the safety stock and half the time we do not. So, on average, we expect the safety stock (SS) to be on-hand. Given this, the average inventory is equal to the following:

$$\text{Average inventory value} = (Q/2 + SS)C \qquad [11.13]$$

The inventory turn for an individual item then is

$$\text{Inventory turn} = \frac{DC}{(Q/2 + SS)C} = \frac{D}{Q/2 + SS} \qquad [11.14]$$

Example 11.6: Average Inventory Calculation—Fixed–Order Quantity Model

Suppose the following item is being managed using a fixed–order quantity model with safety stock.

$$\text{Annual demand } (D) = 1{,}000 \text{ units}$$
$$\text{Order quantity } (Q) = 300 \text{ units}$$
$$\text{Safety stock } (SS) = 40 \text{ units}$$

What are the average inventory level and inventory turn for the item?

SOLUTION

$$\text{Average inventory} = Q/2 + SS = 300/2 + 40 = 190 \text{ units}$$
$$\text{Inventory turn} = \frac{D}{Q/2 + SS} = \frac{1{,}000}{190} = 5.236 \text{ turns per year} \bullet$$

Example 11.7: Average Inventory Calculation—Fixed–Time Period Model

Consider the following item that is being managed using a fixed–time period model with safety stock.

$$\text{Weekly demand } (d) = 50 \text{ units}$$
$$\text{Review cycle } (T) = 3 \text{ weeks}$$
$$\text{Safety stock } (SS) = 30 \text{ units}$$

What are the average inventory level and inventory turn for the item?

SOLUTION

Here, we need to determine how many units we expect to order each cycle. If we assume that demand is fairly steady, then we would expect to order the number of units we expect demand to be during the review cycle. This expected demand is equal to dT if we assume that there is no trend or seasonality in the demand pattern.

$$\text{Average inventory} = dT/2 + SS = 50(3)/2 + 30 = 105 \text{ units}$$

$$\text{Inventory turn} = \frac{52d}{dT/2 + SS} = \frac{52(50)}{105} = 24.8 \text{ turns per year}$$

Here, we assume the firm operates 52 weeks in the year. •

The Price-Break Model

The **price-break model** deals with the fact that, generally, the selling price of an item varies with the order size. This is a discrete or step change rather than a per-unit change. For example, wood screws may cost $0.02 each for 1 to 99 screws, $1.60 per 100, and $13.50 per 1,000. To determine the optimal quantity of any item to order, we simply solve for the economic order quantity for each price and at the point of price change. But not all of the economic order quantities determined by the formula are feasible. In the wood screw example, the Q_{opt} formula might tell us that the optimal decision at the price of 1.6 cents is to order 75 screws. This would be impossible, however, because 75 screws would cost 2 cents each.

> **Price-break model**
> This model is useful for finding the order quantity of an item when the price of the item varies with the order size.

In general, to find the lowest-cost order quantity we need to calculate the economic order quantity for each possible price and check to see whether the quantity is feasible. It is possible that the economic order quantity that is calculated is either higher or lower than the range to which the price corresponds. Any feasible quantity is a potential candidate for order quantity. We also need to calculate the cost at each of the price-break quantities, since we know that price is feasible at these points and the total cost may be lowest at one of these values.

The calculations can be simplified a little if holding cost is based on a percentage of unit price (they will be in all the examples and problems given in this book). In this case, we need to look only at a subset of the price-break quantities. The following two-step procedure can be used:

Step 1. Sort the prices from lowest to highest and then, beginning with the lowest price, calculate the economic order quantity for each price level until a feasible economic order quantity is found. By feasible, we mean that the quantity is in the correct corresponding range for that price.

| exhibit 11.9 | Curves for Three Separate Order Quantity Models in a Three-Price-Break Situation (red line depicts feasible range of purchases) |

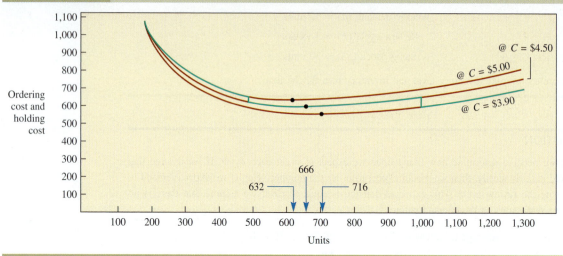

Step 2. If the first feasible economic order quantity is for the lowest price, this quantity is best and you are finished. Otherwise, calculate the total cost for the first feasible economic order quantity (you did these from lowest to highest price) and also calculate the total cost at each price break lower than the price associated with the first feasible economic order quantity. This is the lowest order quantity at which you can take advantage of the price break. The optimal Q is the one with the lowest cost.

Looking at Exhibit 11.9, we see that order quantities are solved from right to left, or from the lowest unit price to the highest, until a valid Q is obtained. Then, the order quantity at each *price break* above this Q is used to find which order quantity has the least cost—the computed Q or the Q at one of the price breaks.

Example 11.8: Price Break

Consider the following case, where

D = 10,000 units (annual demand)

S = $20 to place each order

i = 20 percent of cost (annual carrying cost, storage, interest, obsolescence, etc.)

C = Cost per unit (according to the order size; orders of 0 to 499 units, $5.00 per unit; 500 to 999, $4.50 per unit; 1,000 and up, $3.90 per unit)

What quantity should be ordered?

SOLUTION

The appropriate equations from the basic fixed–order quantity case are

$$TC = DC + \frac{D}{Q}S + \frac{Q}{2}iC$$

exhibit 11.10

Relevant Costs in a Three-Price-Break Model

	$Q = 632$ WHERE $C = \$5$	$Q = 667$ WHERE $C = \$4.50$	$Q = 716$ WHERE $C = \$3.90$	PRICE BREAK 1,000
Holding cost $\left(\dfrac{Q}{2}iC\right)$		$\dfrac{667}{2}(0.20)4.50 = \$300.15$		$\dfrac{1,000}{2}(0.20)3.90 = \$390$
Ordering cost $\left(\dfrac{D}{Q}S\right)$	Not feasible	$\dfrac{10,000(20)}{667} = \$299.85$	Not feasible	$\dfrac{10,000(20)}{1,000} = \$200$
Holding and ordering cost		$\$600.00$		$\$590$
Item cost (DC)		$10,000(4.50)$		$10,000(3.90)$
Total cost		$\$45,600$		$\$39,590$

and

$$Q = \sqrt{\frac{2DS}{iC}}$$

[11.15]

Solving for the economic order size, we obtain

@$C = \$3.90$,	$Q = 716$	Not feasible
@$C = \$4.50$,	$Q = 667$	Feasible, cost $= \$45,600$
Check $Q = 1,000$,	Cost $= \$39,590$	Optimal solution

In Exhibit 11.10, which displays the cost relationship and order quantity range, note that most of the order quantity–cost relationships lie outside the feasible range and that only a single, continuous range results. This should be readily apparent because, for example, the first order quantity specifies buying 632 units at $5.00 per unit. However, if 632 units are ordered, the price is $4.50, not $5.00. The same holds true for the third order quantity, which specifies an order of 716 units at $3.90 each. This $3.90 price is not available on orders of less than 1,000 units.

Exhibit 11.10 itemizes the total costs at the economic order quantities and at the price breaks. The optimal order quantity is shown to be 1,000 units. •

One practical consideration in price-break problems is that the price reduction from volume purchases frequently makes it seemingly economical to order amounts larger than the Q_{opt}. Thus, when applying the model, we must be particularly careful to obtain a valid estimate of product obsolescence and warehousing costs.

INVENTORY PLANNING AND ACCURACY

Maintaining inventory through counting, placing orders, receiving stock, and so on takes personnel time and costs money. When there are limits on these resources, the logical move is to try to use the available resources to control inventory in the best way. In other words, focus on the most important items in inventory.

In the nineteenth century, Villefredo Pareto, in a study of the distribution of wealth in Milan, found that 20 percent of the people controlled 80 percent of the wealth. This logic of the few having the greatest importance and the many having little importance has been broadened to include many situations and is termed the *Pareto principle*. This is true in our everyday lives

LO11–3 Analyze inventory using the *Pareto principle*.

(most of our decisions are relatively unimportant, but a few shape our future) and is certainly true in inventory systems (where a few items account for the bulk of our investment).

Any inventory system must specify when an order is to be placed for an item and how many units to order. Most inventory control situations involve so many items that it is not practical to model and give thorough treatment to each item. To get around this problem, the **ABC inventory classification** scheme divides inventory items into three groupings: high dollar volume (A), moderate dollar volume (B), and low dollar volume (C). Dollar volume is a measure of importance; an item low in cost but high in volume can be more important than a high-cost item with low volume.

ABC inventory classification
Divides inventory into dollar volume categories that map into strategies appropriate for the category.

ABC Classification

If the annual usage of items in inventory is listed according to dollar volume, generally, the list shows that a small number of items account for a large dollar volume and that a large number of items account for a small dollar volume. Exhibit 11.11A illustrates the relationship.

exhibit 11.11

A. Annual Usage of Inventory by Value

ITEM NUMBER	ANNUAL DOLLAR USAGE	PERCENTAGE OF TOTAL VALUE
22	$ 95,000	40.69%
68	75,000	32.13
27	25,000	10.71
03	15,000	6.43
82	13,000	5.57
54	7,500	3.21
36	1,500	0.64
19	800	0.34
23	425	0.18
41	225	0.10
	$233,450	100.00%

B. ABC Grouping of Inventory Items

CLASSIFICATION	ITEM NUMBER	ANNUAL DOLLAR USAGE	PERCENTAGE OF TOTAL
A	22, 68	$ 170,000	72.8%
B	27, 03, 82	53,000	22.7
C	54, 36, 19, 23, 41	10,450	4.5
		$233,450	100.0%

C. ABC Inventory Classification (inventory value for each group versus the group's portion of the total list)

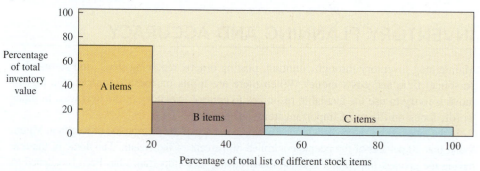

The ABC approach divides this list into three groupings by value: A items constitute roughly the top 15 percent of the items, B items the next 35 percent, and C items the last 50 percent. From observation, it appears that the list in Exhibit 11.11A can be meaningfully grouped, with A including 20 percent (2 of the 10), B including 30 percent, and C including 50 percent. These points show clear delineations between sections. The result of this segmentation is shown in Exhibit 11.11B and plotted in Exhibit 11.11C.

Segmentation may not always occur so neatly. The objective, though, is to try to separate the important from the unimportant. Where the lines actually break depends on the particular inventory under question and on how much personnel time is available. (With more time, a firm could define larger A or B categories.)

The purpose of classifying items into groups is to establish the appropriate degree of control over each item. On a periodic basis, for example, class A items may be more clearly controlled with weekly ordering, B items may be ordered biweekly, and C items may be ordered monthly or bimonthly. Note that the unit cost of items is not related to their classification. An A item may have a high dollar volume through a combination of either low cost and high usage or high cost and low usage. Similarly, C items may have a low dollar volume because of either low demand or low cost. In an automobile service station, gasoline would be an A item with daily or weekly replenishment; tires, batteries, oil, grease, and transmission fluid may be B items and ordered every two to four weeks; and C items would consist of valve stems, windshield wiper blades, radiator caps, hoses, fan belts, oil and gas additives, car wax, and so forth. C items may be ordered every two or three months or even be allowed to run out before reordering because the penalty for stock out is not serious.

Sometimes an item may be critical to a system if its absence creates a sizable loss. In this case, regardless of the item's classification, sufficiently large stocks should be kept on-hand to prevent runout. One way to ensure closer control is to designate this item an A or a B, forcing it into the category even if its dollar volume does not warrant such inclusion.

Inventory Accuracy and Cycle Counting

Inventory records usually differ from the actual physical count; inventory accuracy refers to how well the two agree. Companies such as Walmart understand the importance of inventory accuracy and expend considerable effort ensuring it. The question is, How much error is acceptable? If the record shows a balance of 683 of part X and an actual count shows 652, is this within reason? Suppose the actual count shows 750, an excess of 67 over the record. Is this any better?

Every production system must have agreement, within some specified range, between what the record says is in inventory and what actually is in inventory. There are many reasons why records and inventory may not agree. For example, an open stockroom area allows items to be removed for both legitimate and unauthorized purposes. The legitimate removal may have been done in a hurry and simply not recorded. Sometimes parts are misplaced, turning up months later. Parts are often stored in several locations, but records may be lost or the location recorded incorrectly. Sometimes stock replenishment orders are recorded as received, when in fact they never were. Occasionally, a group of parts is recorded as removed from inventory, but the customer order is canceled and the parts are replaced in inventory without canceling the record. To keep the production system flowing smoothly without parts shortages and efficiently without excess balances, records must be accurate.

A SALES CLERK AT TOKYO'S MITSUKOSHI DEPARTMENT STORE READS AN RFID TAG ON JEANS TO CHECK STOCK. MITSUKOSHI AND JAPAN'S ELECTRONIC GIANT FUJITSU PARTNERED TO USE RFID TO IMPROVE STOCK CONTROL AND CUSTOMER SERVICE.
© YOSHIKAZU TSUNO/Getty Images

How can a firm keep accurate, up-to-date records? Using bar codes and RFID tags is important to minimizing errors caused by inputting wrong numbers in the system. It is also important to keep the storeroom locked. If only storeroom personnel have access, and one of their measures of performance for personnel evaluation and merit increases is record accuracy, there is a strong motivation to comply. Every location of inventory storage, whether in a locked storeroom or on the production floor, should have a record keeping mechanism. A second way is to convey the importance of accurate records to all personnel and depend on them to assist in this effort. (It all boils down to this: Put a fence that goes all the way to the ceiling around the storage area so that workers cannot climb over to get parts; put a lock on the gate and give one person the key. Nobody can pull parts without having the transaction authorized and recorded.)

Another way to ensure accuracy is to count inventory frequently and match this against records. A widely used method is called *cycle counting*.

Cycle counting is a physical inventory-taking technique in which inventory is counted frequently rather than once or twice a year. The key to effective cycle counting and, therefore, to accurate records lies in deciding which items are to be counted, when, and by whom.

Virtually all inventory systems these days are computerized. The computer can be programmed to produce a cycle count notice in the following cases:

- When the record shows a low or zero balance on-hand. (It is easier to count fewer items.)
- When the record shows a positive balance but a backorder was written (indicating a discrepancy).

Cycle counting
A physical inventory-taking technique in which inventory is counted on a frequent basis rather than once or twice a year.

- After some specified level of activity.
- To signal a review based on the importance of the item (as in the ABC system) such as in the following table:

ANNUAL DOLLAR USAGE	REVIEW PERIOD
$10,000 or more	30 days or less
$3,000–$10,000	45 days or less
$250–$3,000	90 days or less
Less than $250	180 days or less

The easiest time for stock to be counted is when there is no activity in the stockroom or on the production floor. This means on the weekends or during the second or third shift, when the facility is less busy. If this is not possible, more careful logging and separation of items are required to count inventory while production is going on and transactions are occurring.

The counting cycle depends on the available personnel. Some firms schedule regular stockroom personnel to do the counting during lulls in the regular working day. Other companies hire private firms that come in and count inventory. Still other firms use full-time cycle counters who do nothing but count inventory and resolve differences with the records. Although this last method sounds expensive, many firms believe it is actually less costly than the usual hectic annual inventory count generally performed during the two- or three-week annual vacation shutdown.

The question of how much error is tolerable between physical inventory and records has been much debated. Some firms strive for 100 percent accuracy, whereas others accept a 1, 2, or 3 percent error. The accuracy level often recommended by experts is ± 0.2 percent for A items, ± 1 percent for B items, and ± 5 percent for C items. Regardless of the specific accuracy decided on, the important point is that the level be dependable so that safety stocks may be provided as a cushion. Accuracy is important for a smooth production process so that customer orders can be processed as scheduled and not held up because of unavailable parts.

CONCEPT CONNECTIONS

LO11–1 Explain how inventory is used and understand what it costs.

- Inventory is expensive mainly due to storage, obsolescence, insurance, and the value of the money invested.
- This chapter explains models for controlling inventory that are appropriate when it is difficult to predict exactly what demand will be for an item in the future and it is desired to have the item available from "stock."
- The basic decisions that need to be made are: (1) when should an item be ordered, and (2) how large should the order be.
- The main costs relevant to these models are: (1) the cost of the item itself, (2) the cost to hold an item in inventory, (3) setup costs, (4) ordering costs, and (5) costs incurred when an item runs short.

Inventory The stock of any item or resource used in an organization.

Independent demand The demand for various items are unrelated to each other.

Dependent demand The need for any one item is a direct result of the need for some other item, usually an item of which it is a part.

LO11–2 Analyze how different inventory control systems work.

- An inventory system provides a specific operating policy for managing items to be stock. Other than defining the timing and sizing of orders, the system needs to track the exact status of these orders (have the orders been received by the supplier, have they been shipped, what date is each expected, etc.).
- Single-period model—When an item is purchased only one time and it is expected that it will be used and then not reordered, the single-period model is appropriate.
- Multiple-period models—When the item will be reordered and the intent is to maintain the item in stock, multiple-period models are appropriate.
- There are two basic types of multiple-period models, with the key distinction being what triggers the timing of the order placement.
- With the fixed–order quantity model, an order is placed when inventory drops to a low level called the reorder point.
- With the fixed–time period model, orders are placed at fixed intervals of time, say every two weeks. The order quantity varies for each order.
- Safety stock is extra inventory that is carried for protection in case the demand for an item is greater than expected. Statistics are used to determine an appropriate amount of safety stock to carry based on the probability of stocking out.
- Inventory turn measures the expected number of times that average inventory is replaced over a year. It can be calculated in aggregate using average inventory levels or on an individual item basis.

Single-period problem Answers the question of how much to order when an item is purchased only one time and it is expected that it will be used and then not reordered.

Fixed–order quantity model (Q-model) An inventory control model where the amount requisitioned is fixed and the actual ordering is triggered by inventory dropping to a specified level of inventory.

Fixed–time period model (P-model) An inventory control model that specifies inventory is ordered at the end of a predetermined time period. The interval of time between orders is fixed and the order quantity varies.

Inventory position The amount on-hand plus on-order minus backordered quantities. In the case where inventory has been allocated for special purposes, the inventory position is reduced by these allocated amounts.

Optimal order quantity (Q_{opt})   This order size minimizes total annual inventory-related costs.

Reorder point   An order is placed when the inventory position drops to this level.

Safety stock   The amount of inventory carried in addition to the expected demand.

Inventory turn   A measure of the expected number of times that inventory is replaced over a year.

Price-break model   The model is useful for finding the order quantity of an item when the price of the item varies with the order size.

$$P \leq \frac{C_u}{C_o + C_u} \qquad [11.1]$$

$$\text{Inventory position} = \text{On-hand} + \text{On-order} - \text{Backorder} \qquad [11.2]$$

$$TC = DC + \frac{D}{Q}S + \frac{Q}{2}H \qquad [11.3]$$

$$Q_{opt} = \sqrt{\frac{2DS}{H}} \qquad [11.4]$$

$$R = \bar{d}L \qquad [11.5]$$

$$R = \bar{d}L + z\sigma_L \qquad [11.6]$$

$$\bar{d} = \frac{\sum_{i=1}^{n} d_i}{n} \qquad [11.7]$$

$$\sigma_d = \sqrt{\frac{\sum_{i=1}^{n}(d_i - \bar{d})^2}{n}} \qquad [11.8]$$

$$\sigma_L = \sqrt{\sigma_1^2 + \sigma_2^2 + \cdots + \sigma_L^2} \qquad [11.9]$$

$$\text{Safety stock} = z\sigma_{T+L} \qquad [11.10]$$

Order quantity	=	Average demand over the vulnerable period	+	Safety stock	−	Inventory currently on-hand (plus on-order, if any)	[11.11]
q	=	$\bar{d}(T + L)$	+	$z\sigma$	−	I	

$$\sigma_{T+L} = \sqrt{\sum_{i=1}^{T+L} \sigma_d^2} \qquad [11.12]$$

$$\text{Average inventory value} = (Q/2 + SS)C \qquad [11.13]$$

$$\text{Inventory turn} = \frac{DC}{(Q/2 + SS)C} = \frac{D}{Q/2 + SS} \qquad [11.14]$$

$$Q = \sqrt{\frac{2DS}{iC}} \qquad [11.15]$$

LO11–3 **Analyze inventory using the *Pareto principle*.**

- Most inventory control systems are so large that it is not practical to model and give a thorough treatment to each item. In these cases, it is useful to categorize items according to their yearly dollar value.
- A simple A, B, C categorization where A items are the high annual dollar value items, B items are the medium dollar value items, and C items are the low dollar value items is useful. This categorization can be used as a measure of the relative importance of an item.
- Typically, A items are roughly the top 15 percent of the items and represent 80 percent of the yearly dollar value. B items would be the next 35 percent and make up around 15 percent of the yearly dollar value. The C items would be the last 50 percent of the item, and have only 5 percent of the yearly dollar value.
- Cycle counting is a useful method for scheduling the audit of each item carried in inventory. Companies audit their inventory at least yearly to ensure accuracy of the records.

ABC inventory classification   Divides inventory into dollar volume categories that map into strategies appropriate for the category.

Cycle counting   A physical inventory-taking technique in which inventory is counted on a frequent basis rather than once or twice a year.

SOLVED PROBLEMS

LO11–2 **SOLVED PROBLEM 1**

A product is priced to sell at $100 per unit, and its cost is constant at $70 per unit. Each unsold unit has a salvage value of $20. Demand is expected to range between 35 and 40 units for the period; 35 definitely can be sold and no units over 40 will be sold. The demand probabilities and the associated cumulative probability distribution (*P*) for this situation are shown below.

NUMBER OF UNITS DEMANDED	PROBABILITY OF THIS DEMAND	CUMULATIVE PROBABILITY
35	0.10	0.10
36	0.15	0.25
37	0.25	0.50
38	0.25	0.75
39	0.15	0.90
40	0.10	1.00

How many units should be ordered?

Solution

The cost of underestimating demand is the loss of profit, or $C_u = \$100 - \$70 = \$30$ per unit. The cost of overestimating demand is the loss incurred when the unit must be sold at salvage value, $C_o = \$70 - \$20 = \$50$.

The optimal probability of not being sold is

$$P \leq \frac{C_u}{C_o + C_u} = \frac{30}{50 + 30} = .375$$

From the distribution data above, this corresponds to the 37th unit.

The following is a full marginal analysis for the problem. Note that the minimum cost occurs when 37 units are purchased.

		NUMBER OF UNITS PURCHASED					
UNITS DEMANDED	PROBABILITY	35	36	37	38	39	40
35	0.1	0	50	100	150	200	250
36	0.15	30	0	50	100	150	200
37	0.25	60	30	0	50	100	150
38	0.25	90	60	30	0	50	100
39	0.15	120	90	60	30	0	50
40	0.1	150	120	90	60	30	0
Total cost		75	53	43	53	83	125

SOLVED PROBLEM 2

Items purchased from a vendor cost $20 each, and the forecast for next year's demand is 1,000 units. If it costs $5 every time an order is placed for more units and the storage cost is $4 per unit per year, answer the following questions.

   a. What quantity should be ordered each time?
   b. What is the total ordering cost for a year?
   c. What is the total storage cost for a year?

Solution

   a. The quantity to be ordered each time is

$$Q = \sqrt{\frac{2DS}{H}} = \sqrt{\frac{2(1,000)5}{4}} = 50 \text{ units}$$

   b. The total ordering cost for a year is

$$\frac{D}{Q}S = \frac{1,000}{50}(\$5) = \$100$$

   c. The storage cost for a year is

$$\frac{Q}{2}H = \frac{50}{2}(\$4) = \$100$$

SOLVED PROBLEM 3

Daily demand for a product is 120 units, with a standard deviation of 30 units. The review period is 14 days and the lead time is 7 days. At the time of review, 130 units are in stock. If only a 1 percent risk of stocking out is acceptable, how many units should be ordered?

Solution

$$\sigma_{T+L} = \sqrt{(14 + 7)(30)^2} = \sqrt{18,900} = 137.5$$
$$z = 2.33$$
$$q = \bar{d}(T + L) + z\sigma_{T+L} - I$$
$$= 120(14 + 7) + 2.33(137.5) - 130$$
$$= 2,710 \text{ units}$$

SOLVED PROBLEM 4

A company currently has 200 units of a product on-hand that it orders every two weeks when the salesperson visits the premises. Demand for the product averages 20 units per day with a standard deviation of 5 units. Lead time for the product to arrive is seven days. Management has a goal of a 95 percent probability of not stocking out for this product.

The salesperson is due to come in late this afternoon when 180 units are left in stock (assuming that 20 are sold today). How many units should be ordered?

Solution

$$\text{Give } I = 180, T = 14, L = 7, d = 20$$
$$\sigma_{T+L} = \sqrt{21(5)^2} = 23$$
$$z = 1.64$$
$$q = \bar{d}(T + L) + z\sigma_{T+L} - I$$
$$= 20(14 + 7) + 1.64(23) - 180$$
$$q = 278 \text{ units}$$

SOLVED PROBLEM 5

Sheet Metal Industries Inc. (SMI) is a Tier 1 supplier to various industries that use components made from sheet metal in their final products. Manufacturers of desktop computers and electronic devices are its primary customers. SMI orders a relatively small number of different raw sheet metal products in very large quantities. The purchasing department is trying to establish an ordering policy that will minimize total costs while meeting the needs of the firm. One of the highest volume items it purchases comes in precut sheets direct from the steel processor. Forecasts based on historical data indicate that SMI will need to purchase 200,000 sheets of this product on an annual basis. The steel producer has a minimum order quantity of 1,000 sheets, and offers a sliding price scale based on the quantity in each order, as follows:

ORDER QUANTITY	UNIT PRICE
1,000–9,999	$2.35
10,000–29,999	$2.20
30,000 +	$2.15

The purchasing department estimates that it costs $300 to process each order, and SMI has an inventory carrying cost equal to 15 percent of the value of inventory.

Based on this information, use the price-break model to determine an optimal order quantity.

Solution

The first step is to take the information in the problem and assign it to the proper notation in the model.

$D = 200,000$ units (annual demand)

$S = \$300$ to place and process each order

$I = 15$ percent of the item cost

$C =$ cost per unit, based on the order quantity Q, as shown in the table above

Next, solve the economic order size at each price point starting with the lowest unit price. Stop when you reach a feasible Q.

$$Q_{\$2.15} = \sqrt{\frac{2 * 200,000 * 300}{.15 * 2.15}} = 19,290 \text{ (infeasible)}$$

The EOQ at $2.15 is not feasible for that price point. The best quantity to order at that price point is therefore the minimum feasible quantity of 30,000.

$$Q_{\$2.20} = \sqrt{\frac{2 * 200,000 * 300}{.15 * 2.20}} = 19,069 \text{ (feasible)}$$

The EOQ at $2.20 is feasible, therefore the best quantity to order at that price point is the EOQ of 19,069. Since we found a feasible EOQ at this price point, we do not need to consider any higher price points. The two ordering policies to consider are: Order 30,000 sheets each time at $2.15 apiece, or order 19,069 sheets each time at $2.20 each. The question is whether the purchase price savings at the $2.15 price point will offset the higher holding costs that would result from the higher ordering quantity. To answer this question, compute the total cost of each option.

$$TC_{Q=30,000} = 200,000 * \$2.15 + \frac{200,000}{30,000}(\$300) + \frac{30,000}{2}(.15)(\$2.15) \approx \$436,837$$

$$TC_{Q=19,069} = 200,000 * \$2.20 + \frac{200,000}{19,069}(\$300) + \frac{19,069}{2}(.15)(\$2.20) \approx \$446,293$$

The lowest total annual cost comes when ordering 30,000 units at $2.15, so that would be the best ordering policy. Are you surprised that the 5-cent difference in unit price would make such a difference in total cost? When dealing in large volumes, even tiny price changes can have a significant impact on the big picture.

DISCUSSION QUESTIONS

LO11–1
1. Distinguish between dependent and independent demand in a McDonald's restaurant, in an integrated manufacturer of personal copiers, and in a pharmaceutical supply house.
2. Distinguish between in-process inventory, safety stock inventory, and seasonal inventory.
3. Discuss the nature of the costs that affect inventory size. For example:
   a. How does shrinkage (stolen stock) contribute to the cost of carrying inventory? How can this cost be reduced?
   b. How does obsolescence contribute to the cost of carrying inventory? How can this cost be reduced?

LO11–2
4. Under which conditions would a plant manager elect to use a fixed–order quantity model as opposed to a fixed–time period model? What are the disadvantages of using a fixed–time period ordering system?
5. What two basic questions must be answered by an inventory control decision rule?
6. Discuss the assumptions that are inherent in production setup cost, ordering cost, and carrying costs. How valid are they?
7. "The nice thing about inventory models is that you can pull one off the shelf and apply it so long as your cost estimates are accurate." Comment.
8. Which type of inventory system would you use in the following situations?
   a. Supplying your kitchen with fresh food
   b. Obtaining a daily newspaper
   c. Buying gas for your car
   To which of these items do you impute the highest stock-out cost?

LO11–3
9. What is the purpose of classifying items into groups, as the ABC classification does?
10. When cycle counting inventory, why do experts recommend a lower acceptable error tolerance for A items than B or C items?

OBJECTIVE QUESTIONS

LO11–1

1. What is the term used to refer to inventory while in distribution—that is, being moved within the supply chain?

2. Almost certainly you have seen vending machines being serviced on your campus and elsewhere. On a predetermined schedule, the vending company checks each machine and fills it with various products. This is an example of which category of inventory model?

3. To support the manufacture of desktop computers for its customers, Dell needs to order all the parts that go into the computer, such as hard drives, motherboards, and memory modules. Obviously the demand for these items is driven by the production schedule for the computers. What is the term used to describe demand for these parts?

LO11–2

4. The local supermarket buys lettuce each day to ensure really fresh produce. Each morning, any lettuce that is left from the previous day is sold to a dealer that resells it to farmers who use it to feed their animals. This week, the supermarket can buy fresh lettuce for $4.00 a box. The lettuce is sold for $10.00 a box and the dealer that sells old lettuce is willing to pay $1.50 a box. Past history says that tomorrow's demand for lettuce averages 250 boxes with a standard deviation of 34 boxes. How many boxes of lettuce should the supermarket purchase tomorrow?

5. Next week, Super Discount Airlines has a flight from New York to Los Angeles that will be booked to capacity. The airline knows from past history that an average of 25 customers (with a standard deviation of 15) cancel their reservation or do not show for the flight. Revenue from a ticket on the flight is $125. If the flight is overbooked, the airline has a policy of getting the customer on the next available flight and giving the person a free round-trip ticket on a future flight. The cost of this free round-trip ticket averages $250. Super Discount considers the cost of flying the plane from New York to Los Angeles a sunk cost. By how many seats should Super Discount overbook the flight?

6. Solve the newsvendor problem. What is the optimal order quantity?

Probability	0.2	0.1	0.1	0.2	0.3	0.1
Value	1	2	3	4	5	6

Purchase cost $c = 15$
Selling price $p = 25$
Salvage value $v = 10$

7. Wholemark is an Internet order business that sells one popular New Year's greeting card once a year. The cost of the paper on which the card is printed is $0.05 per card, and the cost of printing is $0.15 per card. The company receives $2.15 per card sold. Since the cards have the current year printed on them, unsold cards have no salvage value. Its customers are from the four areas: Los Angeles, Santa Monica, Hollywood, and Pasadena. Based on past data, the number of customers from *each* of the four regions is normally distributed with a mean of 2,000 and a standard deviation 500. (Assume these four are independent.) What is the optimal production quantity for the card?

8. Lakeside Bakery bakes fresh pies every morning. The daily demand for its apple pies is a random variable with (discrete) distribution, based on past experience, given by

Demand	5	10	15	20	25	30
Probability	10%	20%	25%	25%	15%	5%

Each apple pie costs the bakery $6.75 to make and is sold for $17.99. Unsold apple pies at the end of the day are purchased by a nearby soup kitchen for 99 cents each. Assume no goodwill cost.

a. If the company decided to bake 15 apple pies each day, what would be its expected profit?

b. Based on the demand distribution above, how many apple pies should the company bake each day to maximize its expected profit?

9. Sally's Silk Screening produces specialty T-shirts that are primarily sold at special events. She is trying to decide how many to produce for an upcoming event. During the event, Sally can sell T-shirts for $20 apiece. However, when the event ends, any unsold T-shirts are sold for $4 apiece. It costs Sally $8 to make a specialty T-shirt. Sally's estimate of demand is the following:

DEMAND	PROBABILITY
300	.05
400	.10
500	.40
600	.30
700	.10
800	.05

a. What is the service rate (or optimal fractile)?

b. How many T-shirts should she produce for the upcoming event?

10. You are a newsvendor selling the *San Pedro Times* every morning. Before you get to work, you go to the printer and buy the day's paper for $0.25 a copy. You sell a copy of the *San Pedro Times* for $1.00. Daily demand is distributed normally with mean = 250 and standard deviation = 50. At the end of each morning, any leftover copies are worthless and they go to a recycle bin.

a. How many copies of the *San Pedro Times* should you buy each morning?

b. Based on part (*a*), what is the probability that you will run out of stock?

11. Famous Albert prides himself on being the Cookie King of the West. Small, freshly baked cookies are the specialty of his shop. Famous Albert has asked for help to determine the number of cookies he should make each day. From an analysis of past demand, he estimates demand for cookies as

DEMAND	PROBABILITY OF DEMAND
1,800 dozen	0.05
2,000	0.10
2,200	0.20
2,400	0.30
2,600	0.20
2,800	0.10
3,000	0.05

Each dozen sells for $0.69 and costs $0.49, which includes handling and transportation. Cookies that are not sold at the end of the day are reduced to $0.29 and sold the following day as day-old merchandise.

a. Construct a table showing the profits or losses for each possible quantity.

b. What is the optimal number of cookies to make?

c. Solve this problem by using marginal analysis.

12. Ray's Satellite Emporium wishes to determine the best order size for its best-selling satellite dish (Model TS111). Ray has estimated the annual demand for this model at 1,000 units. His cost to carry one unit is $100 per year per unit, and he has estimated that each order costs $25 to place. Using the EOQ model, how many should Ray order each time?

13. Dunstreet's Department Store would like to develop an inventory ordering policy with a 95 percent probability of not stocking out. To illustrate your recommended procedure, use as an example the ordering policy for white percale sheets.

Demand for white percale sheets is 5,000 per year. The store is open 365 days per year. Every two weeks (14 days) inventory is counted and a new order is placed. It takes 10 days for the sheets to be delivered. Standard deviation of demand for the sheets is 5 per day. There are currently 150 sheets on-hand.
How many sheets should you order?

14. Charlie's Pizza orders all of its pepperoni, olives, anchovies, and mozzarella cheese to be shipped directly from Italy. An American distributor stops by every four weeks to take orders. Because the orders are shipped directly from Italy, they take three weeks to arrive.

Charlie's Pizza uses an average of 150 pounds of pepperoni each week, with a standard deviation of 30 pounds. Charlie's prides itself on offering only the best-quality ingredients and a high level of service, so it wants to ensure a 98 percent probability of not stocking out on pepperoni.

Assume that the sales representative just walked in the door and there are currently 500 pounds of pepperoni in the walk-in cooler. How many pounds of pepperoni would you order?

15. Given the following information, formulate an inventory management system. The item is demanded 50 weeks a year.

PARAMETER	VALUE
Item cost	$10.00
Order cost	$250.00/order
Annual holding cost	33% of item cost
Annual demand	25,750 units
Average weekly demand	515/week
Standard deviation of weekly demand	25 units
Lead time	1 week
Service probability	95%

a. State the order quantity and reorder point.
b. Determine the annual holding and order costs.
c. If a price break of $50 per order was offered for purchase quantities of over 2,000, would you take advantage of it? How much would you save annually?

16. Lieutenant Commander Data is planning to make his monthly (every 30 days) trek to Gamma Hydra City to pick up a supply of isolinear chips. The trip will take Data about two days. Before he leaves, he calls in the order to the GHC Supply Store. He uses chips at an average rate of 5 per day (seven days per week) with a standard deviation of demand of 1 per day. He needs a 98 percent service probability. If he currently has 35 chips in inventory, how many should he order? What is the most he will ever have to order?

17. Jill's Job Shop buys two parts (Tegdiws and Widgets) for use in its production system from two different suppliers. The parts are needed throughout the entire 52-week year. Tegdiws are used at a relatively constant rate and are ordered whenever the remaining quantity drops to the reorder level. Widgets are ordered from a supplier who stops by every three weeks. Data for both products are as follows:

ITEM	TEGDIW	WIDGET
Annual demand	10,000	5,000
Holding cost (% of item cost)	20%	20%
Setup or order cost	$150.00	$25.00
Lead time	4 weeks	1 week
Safety stock	55 units	5 units
Item cost	$10.00	$2.00

a. What is the inventory control system for Tegdiws? That is, what is the reorder quantity and what is the reorder point?
b. What is the inventory control system for Widgets?

18. Demand for an item is 1,000 units per year. Each order placed costs $10; the annual cost to carry items in inventory is $2 each. In what quantities should the item be ordered?

19. The annual demand for a product is 15,600 units. The weekly demand is 300 units with a standard deviation of 90 units. The cost to place an order is $31.20, and the time from ordering to receipt is four weeks. The annual inventory carrying cost is $0.10 per unit. Find the reorder point necessary to provide a 98 percent service probability.

    Suppose the production manager is asked to reduce the safety stock of this item by 50 percent. If she does so, what will the new service probability be?

20. Daily demand for a product is 100 units, with a standard deviation of 25 units. The review period is 10 days and the lead time is 6 days. At the time of review, there are 50 units in stock. If 98 percent service probability is desired, how many units should be ordered?

21. Item X is a standard item stocked in a company's inventory of component parts. Each year the firm, on a random basis, uses about 2,000 of item X, which costs $25 each. Storage costs, which include insurance and cost of capital, amount to $5 per unit of average inventory. Every time an order is placed for more of item X, it costs $10.
    a. Whenever item X is ordered, what should the order size be?
    b. What is the annual cost for ordering item X?
    c. What is the annual cost for storing item X?

22. Annual demand for a product is 13,000 units; weekly demand is 250 units with a standard deviation of 40 units. The cost of placing an order is $100, and the time from ordering to receipt is four weeks. The annual inventory carrying cost is $0.65 per unit. To provide a 98 percent service probability, what must the reorder point be?

    Suppose the production manager is told to reduce the safety stock of this item by 100 units. If this is done, what will the new service probability be?

23. Gentle Ben's Bar and Restaurant uses 5,000 quart bottles of an imported wine each year. The effervescent wine costs $3 per bottle and is served only in whole bottles because it loses its bubbles quickly. Ben figures that it costs $10 each time an order is placed, and holding costs are 20 percent of the purchase price. It takes three weeks for an order to arrive. Weekly demand is 100 bottles (closed two weeks per year) with a standard deviation of 30 bottles.

    Ben would like to use an inventory system that minimizes inventory cost and will provide a 95 percent service probability.
    a. What is the economic quantity for Ben to order?
    b. At what inventory level should he place an order?

24. Retailers Warehouse (RW) is an independent supplier of household items to department stores. RW attempts to stock enough items for a 98 percent service probability.

    A stainless steel knife set is one item it stocks. Demand (2,400 sets per year) is relatively stable over the entire year. Whenever new stock is ordered, a buyer must ensure that numbers are correct for stock on-hand and then phone in a new order. The total cost involved to place an order is about $5. RW figures that holding inventory in stock and paying for interest on borrowed capital, insurance, and so on, add up to about $4 holding cost per unit per year.

    Analysis of the past data shows that the standard deviation of demand from retailers is about four units per day for a 365-day year. Lead time to get the order is seven days.
    a. What is the economic order quantity?
    b. What is the reorder point?

25. Daily demand for a product is 60 units with a standard deviation of 10 units. The review period is 10 days, and lead time is 2 days. At the time of review, there are 100 units in stock. If 98 percent service probability is desired, how many units should be ordered?

26. University Drug Pharmaceuticals orders its antibiotics every two weeks (14 days) when a salesperson visits from one of the pharmaceutical companies. Tetracycline is one of its most prescribed antibiotics, with an average daily demand of 2,000 capsules. The standard deviation of daily demand was derived from examining prescriptions filled over the past three months and was found to be 800 capsules. It takes five days for the order to arrive. University Drug would like to satisfy 99 percent of the prescriptions. The salesperson just arrived, and there are currently 25,000 capsules in stock.

    How many capsules should be ordered?

27. Sarah's Muffler Shop has one standard muffler that fits a large variety of cars. Sarah wishes to establish a reorder point system to manage inventory of this standard muffler. Use the following information to determine the best order size and the reorder point:

Annual demand	3,500 mufflers	Ordering cost	$50 per order
Standard deviation of daily demand	6 mufflers per working day	Service probability	90%
Item cost	$30 per muffler	Lead time	2 working days
Annual holding cost	25% of item value	Working days	300 per year

28. After graduation, you decide to go into a partnership in an office supply store that has existed for a number of years. Walking through the store and stockrooms, you find a great discrepancy in service levels. Some spaces and bins for items are completely empty; others have supplies that are covered with dust and have obviously been there a long time. You decide to take on the project of establishing consistent levels of inventory to meet customer demands. Most of your supplies are purchased from just a few distributors that call on your store once every two weeks.

    You choose, as your first item for study, computer printer paper. You examine the sales records and purchase orders and find that demand for the past 12 months was 5,000 boxes. Using your calculator, you sample some days' demands and estimate that the standard deviation of daily demand is 10 boxes. You also search out these figures:

> Cost per box of paper: $11
> Desired service probability: 98 percent
> Store is open every day.
> Salesperson visits every two weeks.
> Delivery time following visit is three days.

    Using your procedure, how many boxes of paper would be ordered if, on the day the salesperson calls, 60 boxes are on-hand?

29. A distributor of large appliances needs to determine the order quantities and reorder points for the various products it carries. The following data refer to a specific refrigerator in its product line:

Cost to place an order	$100/order
Holding cost	20 percent of product cost per year
Cost of refrigerator	$500/unit
Annual demand	500 units
Standard deviation of demand during lead time	10 units
Lead time	7 days

Consider an even daily demand and a 365-day year.

a. What is the economic order quantity?

b. If the distributor wants a 97 percent service probability, what reorder point, R, should be used?

30. It is your responsibility, as the new head of the automotive section of Nichols Department Store, to ensure that reorder quantities for the various items have been correctly established. You decide to test one item and choose Michelin tires, XW size 185 × 14 BSW. A perpetual inventory system has been used, so you examine this as well as other records and come up with the following data:

Cost per tire	$35 each
Holding cost	20 percent of tire cost per year
Demand	1,000 per year
Ordering cost	$20 per order
Standard deviation of daily demand	3 tires
Delivery lead time	4 days

Because customers generally do not wait for tires but go elsewhere, you decide on a service probability of 98 percent. Assume the demand occurs 365 days per year.

a. Determine the order quantity.

b. Determine the reorder point.

31. UA Hamburger Hamlet (UAHH) places a daily order for its high-volume items (hamburger patties, buns, milk, and so on). UAHH counts its current inventory on-hand once per day and phones in its order for delivery 24 hours later. Determine the number of hamburgers UAHH should order for the following conditions:

Average daily demand	600
Standard deviation of demand	100
Desired service probability	99%
Hamburger inventory	800

32. A local service station is open 7 days per week, 365 days per year. Sales of 10W40 grade premium oil average 20 cans per day. Inventory holding costs are $0.50 per can per year. Ordering costs are $10 per order. Lead time is two weeks. Backorders are not practical—the motorist drives away.

a. Based on these data, choose the appropriate inventory model and calculate the economic order quantity and reorder point. Describe in a sentence how the plan would work. *Hint:* Assume demand is deterministic.

b. The boss is concerned about this model because demand really varies. The standard deviation of demand was determined from a data sample to be 6.15 cans per day. The manager wants a 99.5 percent service probability. Determine a new inventory plan based on this information and the data in part (a). Use Q_{opt} from part (a).

33. Dave's Auto Supply custom mixes paint for its customers. The shop performs a weekly inventory count of the main colors used for mixing paint. Determine the amount of white paint that should be ordered using the following information:

Average weekly demand	20 gallons
Standard deviation of demand	5 gallons/week
Desired service probability	98%
Current inventory	25 gallons
Lead time	1 week

34. SY Manufacturers (SYM) is producing T-shirts in three colors: red, blue, and white. The monthly demand for each color is 3,000 units. Each shirt requires 0.5 pound of raw cotton that is imported from Luft-Geshfet-Textile (LGT)

Company in Brazil. The purchasing price per pound is $2.50 (paid only when the cotton arrives at SYM's facilities) and transportation cost by sea is $0.20 per pound. The traveling time from LGT's facility in Brazil to the SYM facility in the United States is two weeks. The cost of placing a cotton order, by SYM, is $100 and the annual interest rate that SYM is facing is 20 percent.

a. What is the optimal order quantity of cotton?
b. How frequently should the company order cotton?
c. Assuming that the first order is needed on April 1, when should SYM place the order?
d. How many orders will SYM place during the next year?
e. What is the resulting annual holding cost?
f. What is the resulting annual ordering cost?
g. If the annual interest cost is only 5 percent, how will it affect the annual number of orders, the optimal batch size, and the average inventory? (You are not expected to provide a numerical answer to this question. Just describe the direction of the change and explain your answer.)

35. Demand for a book at Amazon.com is 250 units per week. The product is supplied to the retailer from a factory. The factory pays $10 per unit, while the total cost of a shipment from the factory to the retailer when the shipment size is Q is given by

$$\text{Shipment cost} = \$50 + 2Q$$

Assume the annual inventory carrying cost is 20 percent.
a. What is the cost per shipment and annual holding cost per book?
b. What is the optimal shipment size?
c. What is the average throughput time?

36. Palin's Muffler Shop has one standard muffler that fits a large variety of cars. The shop wishes to establish a *periodic review* system to manage inventory of this standard muffler. Use the information in the following table to determine the optimal inventory target level (or order-up-to level).

Annual demand	3,000 mufflers	Ordering cost	$50 per order
Standard deviation of daily demand	6 mufflers per working day	Service probability	90%
Item cost	$30 per muffler	Lead time	2 working days
Annual holding cost	25% of item value	Working days	300 per year
Review period	15 working days		

a. What is the optimal target level (order-up-to level)?
b. If the service probability requirement is 95 percent, the optimal target level [your answer in part (a)] will (select one):
  I. Increase.
  II. Decrease.
  III. Stay the same.

37. Daily demand for a certain product is normally distributed with a mean of 100 and a standard deviation of 15. The supplier is reliable and maintains a constant lead time of 5 days. The cost of placing an order is $10 and the cost of holding inventory is $0.50 per unit per year. There are no stock-out costs, and unfilled orders are filled as soon as the order arrives. Assume sales occur over 360 days of the year.

Your goal here is to find the order quantity and reorder point to satisfy a 90 percent probability of not stocking out during the lead time.
a. What type of system is the company using?
b. Find the order quantity.
c. Find the reorder point.

38. A particular raw material is available to a company at three different prices, depending on the size of the order:

Less than 100 pounds	$20 per pound
100 pounds to 1,000 pounds	$19 per pound
More than 1,000 pounds	$18 per pound

The cost to place an order is $40. Annual demand is 3,000 units. The holding (or carrying) cost is 25 percent of the material price.

What is the economic order quantity to buy each time?

39. CU, Incorporated (CUI), produces copper contacts that it uses in switches and relays. CUI needs to determine the order quantity, Q, to meet the annual demand at the lowest cost. The price of copper depends on the quantity ordered. Here are price-break and other data for the problem:

Price of copper	$0.82 per pound up to 2,499 pounds
	$0.81 per pound for orders between 2,500 and 5,000 pounds
	$0.80 per pound for orders greater than 5,000 pounds
Annual demand	50,000 pounds per year
Holding cost	20 percent per unit per year of the price of the copper
Ordering cost	$30.00

Which quantity should be ordered?

LO11–3 40. In the past, Taylor Industries has used a fixed–time period inventory system that involved taking a complete inventory count of all items each month. However, increasing labor costs are forcing Taylor Industries to examine alternative ways to reduce the amount of labor involved in inventory stockrooms, yet without increasing other costs, such as shortage costs. Here is a random sample of 20 of Taylor's items.

ITEM NUMBER	ANNUAL USAGE	ITEM NUMBER	ANNUAL USAGE
1	$ 1,500	11	$ 13,000
2	12,000	12	600
3	2,200	13	42,000
4	50,000	14	9,900
5	9,600	15	1,200
6	750	16	10,200
7	2,000	17	4,000
8	11,000	18	61,000
9	800	19	3,500
10	15,000	20	2,900

a. What would you recommend Taylor do to cut back its labor cost? (Illustrate using an ABC plan.)

b. Item 15 is critical to continued operations. How would you recommend it be classified?

41. Alpha Products, Inc., is having a problem trying to control inventory. There is insufficient time to devote to all its items equally. Here is a sample of some items stocked, along with the annual usage of each item expressed in dollar volume.

ITEM	ANNUAL DOLLAR USAGE	ITEM	ANNUAL DOLLAR USAGE
a	$ 7,000	k	$80,000
b	1,000	l	400
c	14,000	m	1,100
d	2,000	n	30,000
e	24,000	o	1,900
f	68,000	p	800
g	17,000	q	90,000
h	900	r	12,000
i	1,700	s	3,000
j	2,300	t	32,000

    a. Can you suggest a system for allocating control time?

    b. Specify where each item from the list would be placed.

42. DAT, Inc., produces digital audiotapes to be used in the consumer audio division. DAT lacks sufficient personnel in its inventory supply section to closely control each item stocked, so it has asked you to determine an ABC classification. Here is a sample from the inventory records:

ITEM	AVERAGE MONTHLY DEMAND	PRICE PER UNIT	ITEM	AVERAGE MONTHLY DEMAND	PRICE PER UNIT
1	700	$ 6.00	6	100	$10.00
2	200	4.00	7	3,000	2.00
3	2,000	12.00	8	2,500	1.00
4	1,100	20.00	9	500	10.00
5	4,000	21.00	10	1,000	2.00

Develop an ABC classification for these 10 items.

ANALYTICS EXERCISE: INVENTORY MANAGEMENT AT BIG10SWEATERS.COM

Big10Sweaters.com is a new company started last year by two recent college graduates. The idea behind the company was simple. It will sell premium logo sweaters for Big Ten colleges with one major, unique feature. This unique feature is a special large monogram that has the customer's name, major, and year of graduation. The sweater is the perfect gift for graduating students and alumni, particularly avid football fans who want to show support during the football season. The company is off to a great start and had a successful first year while selling to only a few schools. This year it plans to expand to a few more schools and target the entire Big Ten Conference within three years.

You have been hired by Big10Sweaters.com and need to make a good impression by making good supply chain decisions. This is your big opportunity with a start-up. There are only two people in the firm and you were hired with the prospect of possibly becoming a principal in the future. You majored in supply chain (operations) management in school and had a great internship at a big retailer that was getting into Internet sales. The experience was great, but now you are on your own and have none of the great support that the big company had. You need to find and analyze your own data and make some big decisions. Of course, Rhonda and Steve, the partners who started the company, are knowledgeable about this venture and they are going to help along the way.

Rhonda had the idea to start the company two years ago and talked her friend from business school, Steve, into joining her. Rhonda is into Web marketing, has a degree in computer science, and has been working on completing an online MBA. She is as much an artist as a techie. She can really make the Website sing.

Steve majored in accounting and likes to pump the numbers. He has done a great job of keeping the books and selling the company to some small venture capital people in the area. Last year, he was successful in getting them to invest $2,000,000 in the company (a onetime investment). There were some significant strings attached to this investment in that it stipulated that only $100,000 per year could go toward paying the salary of the two principals. The rest had to be spent on the Website, advertising, and inventory. In addition, the venture capital company gets 25 percent of the company profits, before taxes, during the first four years of operation, assuming the company makes a profit.

Your first job is to focus on the firm's inventory. The company is centered on selling the premium sweaters to college football fans through a Website. Your analysis is important since a significant portion of the company's assets is the inventory that it carries.

The business is cyclic, and sales are concentrated during the period leading up to the college football season, which runs between late August and the end of each year. For the upcoming season, the firm wants to sell sweaters to only a few of the largest schools in the Midwest region of the United States. In particular, it is targeting the Ohio State University (OSU), University of Michigan (UM), Michigan State University (MSU), Purdue University (PU), and Indiana University (IU). These five schools have major football programs and a loyal fan base.

The firm has considered the idea of making the sweaters in its own factory, but for now it purchases them from a supplier in China. The prices are great, but service is a problem since the supplier has a 20-week lead time for each order and the minimum order size is 5,000 sweaters. The order can consist of a mix of the different logos, such as 2,000 for OSU, 1,500 for UM, 750 for MSU, 500 for PU, and 250 for IU. Within each logo sub lot, sizes are allocated based on percentages and the supplier suggests 20 percent X-large, 50 percent large, 20 percent medium, and 10 percent small based on its historical data.

Once an order is received, a local subcontractor applies the monograms and ships the sweaters to the customer. The subcontractor stores the inventory of sweaters for the company in a small warehouse area located at their site.

This is the company's second year of operation. Last year, it sold sweaters for only three of the schools, OSU, MU, and PU. It ordered the minimum 5,000 sweaters and sold all of them, but the experience was painful because the company had too many MU sweaters and not enough for OSU fans. Last year, it ordered 2,300 OSU, 1,800 MU, and 900 PU sweaters. Of the 5,000 sweaters, 342 had to be sold at a steep discount on eBay after the season. The company was hoping not to do this again.

For the next year, you have collected some data relevant to the decision. Exhibit 11.12 shows cost information for the product when purchased from the supplier in China. Here we see that the cost for each sweater, delivered to the warehouse of our monogramming subcontractor, is $60.88. This price is valid for any quantity we order above 5,000 sweaters. This order can be a mix of sweaters for each of the five schools we are targeting. The supplier needs 20 weeks to process the order, so the order needs to be placed around April 1 for the upcoming football season.

Our monogramming subcontractor gets $13 for each sweater. Shipping cost is paid by the customer when the order is placed.

In addition to the cost data, you also have some demand information, as shown in Exhibit 11.13. The exact sales numbers for last year are given. Sweaters sold at full retail price were sold for $120 each. Sweaters left over at the end of the season were sold through eBay for $50 each and these sweaters were not monogrammed by our subcontractor. Keep in mind that the retail sales numbers do not accurately reflect

Cost Information for the Big Ten Sweaters

exhibit 11.12

ITEM	COST	
Material	$32.00	
Labor	10.50	
Overhead	1.25	
Transportation within China	1.00	
Supplier profit	8.95	
Agent's fee	2.68	
Freight (ocean carrier)	1.50	
Duty, insurance, etc.	3.00	
Total China supplier cost		$60.88
Monogram material	5.00	
Labor	8.00	
Total subcontractor cost		$13.00
Total (per sweater)		$73.88

exhibit 11.13   Forecast Data for the Big Ten Sweaters

	AVERAGE FOOTBALL GAME ATTENDANCE	LAST YEAR'S ACTUAL SALES (FULL PRICE)	RHONDA'S FORECAST FOR NEXT YEAR	STEVE'S FORECAST FOR NEXT YEAR	MARKET RESEARCH FORECAST FOR NEXT YEAR	AVERAGE FORECAST	STANDARD DEVIATION
Ohio State	105,261	2,300	2,500	2,200	2,800	2,500	300
Michigan	108,933	1,468	1,800	1,500	2,000	1,767	252
Purdue	50,457	890	1,000	900	1,100	1,000	100
Michigan State	74,741	—	1,750	1,500	1,600	1,617	126
Indiana	41,833	—	600	500	450	517	76
Penn State	107,008						
Wisconsin	80,109						
Iowa	70,214						
Illinois	59,545						
Minnesota	50,805						
Northwestern	24,190						
Nebraska	85,071						
Total		4,658*	7,650	6,600	7,950	7,400	430**

*342 sweaters were sold through eBay for $50 each (the customer pays shipping on all orders).

**Calculated assuming the demand at each school is independent $\sqrt{\sum_{i=1}^{N} \sigma_i^2}$

Excel:
Ch10_Big10Sweaters

actual demand since they stocked out of the OSU sweaters toward the end of the season.

As for advertising the sweaters for next season, Rhonda is committed to using the same approach used last year. The firm placed ads in the football program sold at each game. These worked very well for reaching those attending the games, but she realized there may be ways to advertise that may open sales to more alumni. She has hired a market research firm to help identify other advertising outlets but has decided to wait at least another year to try something different.

Forecasting demand is a major problem for the company. You have asked Rhonda and Steve to predict what they think sales might be next year. You have also asked the market research firm to apply their forecasting tools. Data on these forecasts are given in Exhibit 11.13. To generate some statistics, you have averaged the forecasts and calculated the standard deviation for each school and in total.

Based on advice from the market research firm, you have decided to use the aggregate demand forecast and standard deviation for the aggregate demand. The aggregate demand was calculated by adding the average forecast for each item. The aggregate standard deviation was calculated by squaring the standard deviation for each item (this is the variance), summing the variance for each item, and then taking the square root of this sum. This assumes that the demand for

each school is independent, meaning that the demand for Ohio State is totally unrelated to the demand at Michigan and the other schools.

You will allocate your aggregate order to the individual schools based on their expected percentage of total demand. You discussed your analysis with Rhonda and Steve and they are OK with your analysis. They would like to see what the order quantities would be if each school was considered individually.

You have a spreadsheet set up with all the data from the exhibits called Big10Sweater.xls and you are ready to do some calculations.

Questions

1. You are curious as to how much Rhonda and Steve made in their business last year. You do not have all the data, but you know that most of their expenses relate to buying the sweaters and having them monogrammed. You know they paid themselves $50,000 each and you know the rent, utilities, insurance, and a benefit package for the business was about $20,000. About how much do you think they made "before taxes" last year? If they must make their payment to the venture capital firm, and then pay 50 percent in taxes, what was their increase in cash last year?

2. What was your reasoning behind using the aggregate demand forecast when determining the size of your

order rather than the individual school forecasts? Should you rethink this or is there a sound basis for doing it this way?
3. How many sweaters should you order this year? Break down your order by individual school. Document your calculations in your spreadsheet. Calculate this based on the aggregate forecast and also the forecast by individual school.

4. What do you think they could make this year? They are paying you $40,000 and you expect your benefit package addition would be about $1,000 per year. Assume that they order based on the aggregate forecast.
5. How should the business be developed in the future? Be specific and consider changes related to your supplier, the monogramming subcontractor, target customers, and products.

PRACTICE EXAM

1. The model most appropriate for making a one-time purchase of an item.
2. The model most appropriate when inventory is replenished only in fixed intervals of time, for example, on the first Monday of each month.
3. The model most appropriate when a fixed amount must be purchased each time an order is placed.
4. Based on an EOQ-type ordering criterion, what cost must be taken to zero if the desire is to have an order quantity of a single unit?
5. Term used to describe demand that can be accurately calculated to meet the need of a production schedule, for example.
6. Term used to describe demand that is uncertain and needs to be forecast.
7. We are ordering T-shirts for the spring party and are selling them for twice what we paid for them. We expect to sell 100 shirts and the standard deviation associated with our forecast is 10 shirts. How many shirts should we order?
8. We have an item that we stock in our store that has fairly steady demand. Our supplier insists that we buy 1,200 units at a time. The lead time is very short on the item, since the supplier is only a few blocks away and we can pick up another 1,200 units when we run out. How many units do you expect to have in inventory, on average?
9. For the item described in question 8, if we expect to sell approximately 15,600 units next year, how many

trips will we need to make to the supplier over the year?
10. If we decide to carry 10 units of safety stock for the item described in questions 8 and 9, and we implemented this by going to our supplier when we had 10 units left, how much inventory would you expect to have, on average, now?
11. We are being evaluated based on the percentage of total demand met in a year (not the probability of stocking out as used in the chapter). Consider an item that we are managing using a fixed–order quantity model with safety stock. We decide to double the order quantity but leave the reorder point the same. Would you expect the percent of total demand met next year to go up or down? Why?
12. Consider an item for which we have 120 units currently in inventory. The average demand for the item is 60 units per week. The lead time for the item is exactly 2 weeks and we carry 16 units for safety stock. What is the probability of running out of the item if we order right now?
13. If we take advantage of a quantity discount, would you expect your average inventory to go up or down? Assume that the probability of stocking out criterion stays the same.
14. This is an inventory auditing technique where inventory levels are checked more frequently than one time a year.

Answers to Practice Exam 1. Single-period model 2. Fixed–time period model 3. Fixed–order quantity model 4. Setup or ordering cost 5. Dependent demand 6. Independent demand 7. 100 shirts 8. 600 units 9. 13 trips 10. 610 units 11. Go up (we are taking fewer chances of running out) 12. 50 percent 13. Will probably go up if the probability of stocking out stays the same 14. Cycle counting

CHAPTER 12

LEAN SUPPLY CHAINS

Learning Objectives

LO12–1 Explain lean production.

LO12–2 Illustrate how lean concepts can be applied to supply chain processes.

LO12–3 Analyze supply chain processes using value stream mapping.

LO12–4 Apply lean concepts to service processes.

FROM LEAN SUPPLY CHAIN TO LEAN DESIGN

As seen in the diagram, the just-in-time approach to manufacturing has resulted in major reductions in inventory in U.S. companies over the past two decades. As we can see in the more recent data, some companies think it has gone too far and that having a little extra inventory might be a healthier option.

Although being lean helps companies hold down costs by keeping stockpiles of components and finished goods low, it can leave them high and dry if there is some disruption in the supply chain, such as an earthquake or some other natural disaster. Just-in-time makes sense, but it makes supply chains vulnerable to disruptions, so what we are seeing now is how these concepts are being adapted to meet the practical world.

Toyota Motors, the just-in-time pioneer, is adapting as well, and it has recently announced a new process call the Toyota New Global Architecture. In an effort to lower costs, Toyota is implementing a new global modular assembly program that extends back to the design of the vehicles. The new process takes advantage of greatly increased component sharing across the product line. Toyota will be able to order parts in bulk and save costs through greater economies of scale.

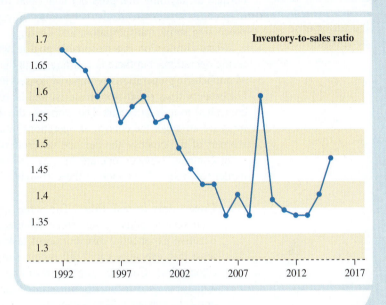

Inventory-to-sales ratio

LEAN PRODUCTION

The most significant operations and supply management approach of the past 50 years is **lean production**. In the context of supply chains, lean production refers to a focus on eliminating as much waste as possible. Moves that are not needed, unnecessary processing steps, and excess inventory in the supply chain are targets for improvement during the *leaning* process. Some consultants in industry have coined the phrase *value chain* to refer to the concept that each step in the supply chain processes that deliver products and services to customers should create value. If a step does not create value, it should be removed from the process. Lean production may be one of the best tools for implementing green strategies in manufacturing and service processes.

The basis of lean thinking came from the just-in-time (JIT) production concepts pioneered in Japan at Toyota. Even though JIT gained worldwide prominence in the 1970s, some of its philosophy can be traced to the early 1900s in the United States. Henry Ford used JIT concepts as he streamlined his moving assembly lines to make automobiles. For example, to eliminate waste, he used the bottom of the packing crates for car seats as the floor board of the car. Although elements of JIT were being used by Japanese industry as early as the 1930s, it was not fully refined until the 1970s when Tai-ichi Ohno of Toyota Motors used JIT to take Toyota's cars to the forefront of delivery time and quality.

Customer value, in the context of lean production, is defined as something for which the customer is willing to pay. Value-adding activities transform materials and information

LO12–1 Explain lean production.

Lean production
Integrated activities designed to achieve high-volume, high-quality production using minimal inventories of raw materials, work-in-process, and finished goods.

Customer value
In the context of lean production, something for which the customer is willing to pay.

Waste
Anything that does
not add value from
the customer's
perspective.

into something the customer wants. Non-value-adding activities consume resources and do not directly contribute to the end result desired by the customer. **Waste**, therefore, is defined as anything that does not add value from the customer's perspective. Examples of process wastes are defective products, overproduction, inventories, excess motion, processing steps, transportation, and waiting.

Waste elimination is a reasonable goal in service operations, just as it is in manufacturing operations, but there is a difference in the sources of variation that cause the waste. Manufacturing operations, compared to service operations, are far more controllable. Uncertainty does result from material and labor inputs, but those can be anticipated and controlled to a great extent. The workers, the design of the product, and the production tools are all under the control of operations to a very large extent. If sales and marketing are part of the process, the demand uncertainty also can be reduced.

In contrast, services operate in a sea of uncertainty and variability that are much harder to control. Let's look at these sources.

- **Uncertainty in task times.** The nature of service products is that the execution of each service delivery has some uniqueness. This variability typically leads to a negative exponential distribution of task times. Simply put, this means that while most task executions will fall within some tight range, some executions will take a long time. Consider airplane boarding. There's uncertainty here, yet Southwest found a way to reduce the uncertainty and achieve faster turnaround times at airports, increasing effective capacity.
- **Uncertainty in demand.** While service demand can be forecasted, no forecast is 100 percent perfect. Manufacturers can buffer this forecast uncertainty with some finished goods inventory. The simultaneous production and consumption in services precludes this tactic. The capacity must be available when the demand arises. Think about the number of available tables needed in a restaurant for peak dining hours.
- **Customers' production roles.** Both of the above uncertainties have much to do with customer involvement in service operations. Because customers typically have some role to play in the production of a service, variability is introduced based on how well the service provider performs his or her role. Customers usually have to provide information to service agents to initiate service, and they typically have tangible tasks to perform.

Lean production and Six Sigma work best in repeatable, standardized operations. While many services are repeatable, given the above, how well can they be truly standardized? Let's look at the recent experience of the airline industry.

Airline companies such as Southwest have very efficient operations, and they achieve high ratings in customer satisfaction—until a major storm causes a disruption. Consider the horrible storms that often strike the eastern third of the United States in the spring. Weather is one of those uncertainties that the airlines simply cannot control. Flights will be canceled, and passengers will need to be rebooked. This is an extreme example of demand uncertainty that leads to huge demand spikes.

At the same time, to eliminate waste and become more efficient, airlines have tended to cut capacity and fill flights. Today, you seldom fly on a plane that is not 90 to 100 percent booked. With few available seats, it can take days to rebook all passengers from flights canceled due to weather. Our point is that there is often a price to pay for being lean, and that price often is at the expense of customer service when unlikely events occur. Whether in a service or manufacturing business, potential trade-offs exist with lean production and must be dealt with.

Lean Production Pull System

exhibit 12.1

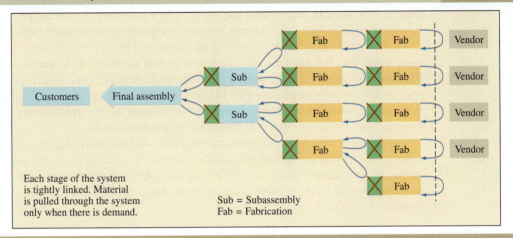

Each stage of the system is tightly linked. Material is pulled through the system only when there is demand.

Sub = Subassembly
Fab = Fabrication

This chapter starts by reviewing the evolution of lean concepts from Japan and Toyota. We then expand this view to encompass a complete supply chain. The remainder of the chapter is devoted to value stream mapping, a tool that can be used to drive out waste and improve the efficiency of the supply chain.

Lean production is an integrated set of activities designed to achieve production using minimal inventories of raw materials, work-in-process, and finished goods. Parts arrive at the next workstation "just-in-time" and are completed and move through the process quickly. Lean is also based on the logic that nothing will be produced until it is needed. Exhibit 12.1 illustrates the process. Production need is created by actual demand for the product. When an item is sold, in theory, the market pulls a replacement from the last position in the system—final assembly in this case. This triggers an order to the factory production line, where a worker then pulls another unit from an upstream station in the flow to replace the unit taken. This upstream station then pulls from the next station further upstream and so on back to the release of raw materials. To enable this pull process to work smoothly, lean production demands high levels of quality at each stage of the process, strong vendor relations, and a fairly predictable demand for the end product.

The Toyota Production System

In this section, we develop the philosophy and elements of lean production developed in Japan and embodied in the Toyota Production System—the benchmark for lean manufacturing. The Toyota Production System was developed to improve quality and productivity and is predicated upon two philosophies that are central to the Japanese culture: elimination of waste and respect for people.

Elimination of Waste Waste is anything that is not absolutely essential to production. An expanded lean definition identifies seven prominent types of waste to be eliminated from the supply chain: (1) waste from overproduction, (2) waste of waiting time, (3) transportation waste, (4) inventory waste, (5) processing waste, (6) waste of motion, and (7) waste from product defects.

Respect for People Respect for people is a key to the Toyota Production System. They have traditionally strived to ensure lifetime employment for permanent positions and to maintain level payrolls even when business conditions deteriorate. Permanent workers (about one-third of the total workforce of Japan) have job security and tend to be more flexible, remain with a company, and do all they can to help a firm achieve its goals. (Global recessions have caused many Japanese companies to move away from this ideal.)

Company unions at Toyota as well as elsewhere in Japan exist to foster a cooperative relationship with management. All employees receive two bonuses a year in good times. Employees know that if the company performs well, they will get a bonus. This encourages workers to improve productivity. Management views workers as assets, not as human machines. Automation and robotics are used extensively to perform dull or routine jobs so employees are free to focus on important improvement tasks.

Toyota relies heavily on subcontractor networks. Indeed, more than 90 percent of all Japanese companies are part of this supplier network of small firms. Some suppliers are specialists in a narrow field, usually serving multiple customers. Firms have long-term partnerships with their suppliers and customers. Suppliers consider themselves part of a customer's family.

LEAN SUPPLY CHAINS

LO12–2 Illustrate how lean concepts can be applied to supply chain processes.

Value stream
These are the value-adding and non-value-adding activities required to design, order, and provide a product from concept to launch, order to delivery, and raw materials to customers.

Waste reduction
The optimization of value-adding activities and elimination of non-value-adding activities that are part of the value stream.

The focus of the Toyota Production System is on elimination of waste and respect for people. As the concepts have evolved and become applied to the supply chain, the goal of maximizing customer value has been added. Customer value when considered from the entire supply chain should center on the perspective of the end customer with the goal being to maximize what the customer is willing to pay for a firm's goods or services. The **value stream** consists of the value-adding and non-value-adding activities required to design, order, and provide a product or service from concept to launch, order to delivery, and raw materials to customers. This all-inclusive view of the system is a significant expansion of the scope of application of the lean concepts pioneered by Toyota. When applied to supply chains, **waste reduction** relates to the optimization of the value-adding activities and the elimination of non-value-adding activities that are part of the value stream. In the next section, the value stream analysis tool is discussed.

In the following paragraphs, we discuss the different components of a supply chain and what would be expected using a lean focus:

Lean Suppliers Lean suppliers are able to respond to changes. Their prices are generally lower due to the efficiency of lean processes, and their quality has improved to the point that incoming inspection at the next link is not needed. Lean suppliers deliver on time and their culture is one of continuous improvement. To develop lean suppliers, organizations should include them in their value stream planning. This will help them fix problems and share savings.

Lean Procurement A key to lean procurement is automation. The term *e-procurement* relates to automatic transaction, sourcing, bidding and auctions using Web-based applications, and the use of software that removes human interaction and integrates with the financial reporting of the firm. The key to lean procurement is visibility. Suppliers must be able to "see" into the customers' operations and customers must be able to "see" into their suppliers' operations. The overlap of these processes needs to be optimized to maximize value from the end-customer perspective.

Lean Manufacturing Lean manufacturing systems produce what the customers want, in the quantity they want, when they want it, and with minimum resources. Applying lean concepts in manufacturing typically presents the greatest opportunities for cost reduction and quality improvement.

Lean Warehousing   This relates to eliminating non-value-added steps and waste in product storage processes. Typical functions include the following: receiving material; putting-away/storing; replenishing inventory; picking inventory; packing for shipment; and shipping. Waste can be found in many warehousing processes including shipping defects, which creates returns; overproduction or overshipment of products; excess inventory, which

© 4774344sean/Getty Images RF

requires extra space and reduces warehouse efficiency; excess motion and handling; waiting for parts; and inadequate information systems.

Lean Logistics   Lean concepts can be applied to the functions associated with the movement of material through the system. Some of the key areas include optimized mode selection and pooling orders; combined multistop truckloads; optimized routing; cross docking; import/export transportation processes; and backhaul minimization. Just as with the other areas, these logistics functions need to be optimized by eliminating non-value-adding activities while improving the value-adding activities.

Lean Customers   Lean customers have a great understanding of their business needs and specify meaningful requirements. They value speed and flexibility and expect high levels of delivery performance. Lean customers are interested in establishing effective partnerships with their suppliers. Lean customers expect value from the products they purchase and provide value to their customers.

The benefits of a lean supply chain primarily are in the improved responsiveness to the customer. As business conditions change, the supply chain adapts to dynamic needs. The ideal is a culture of rapid change with a bias for change when it is needed. The reduced inventory inherent in a lean supply chain reduces obsolescence and reduces flow time through the value-added processes. The reduced cost along with improved customer service allows the firms using a lean supply chain a significant competitive advantage when competing in the global marketplace.

HERE A WORKER VISUALLY CHECKS CARTONS OF KETCHUP AS THEY MOVE ON A SPIRAL CONVEYOR AND REPLACES BOTTLES THAT ARE NOT PERFECT. THIS PROCESS COULD PROBABLY BE MADE MORE EFFICIENT.

© AP Images/Ingo Wagner

VALUE STREAM MAPPING

Value stream mapping (VSM) is a special type of flowcharting tool that is valuable for the development of lean processes. The technique is used to visualize product flows through various processing steps. The tool also illustrates information flows that result from the process, as well as information used to control flow through the process. The aim of this section is to provide a brief introduction to VSM and to illustrate its use with an example.

To create a lean process, one needs to have a full understanding of the business, including production processes, material flows, and information flows. In this section, we discuss this in the context of a production process where a product is being made. VSM is not limited to this context and can be readily applied to service, logistics, distribution, or virtually any type of process.

In the context of a production process such as a manufacturing plant, the technique is used to identify all of the value-adding, as well as non-value-adding, processes that materials are subjected to within a plant, from raw material coming into the plant, through delivery to the customer. Exhibit 12.2 is a sample map that depicts a production process. With this map, identification of wasteful processes and flows can be made

---

exhibit 12.2   Manufacturing Process Map

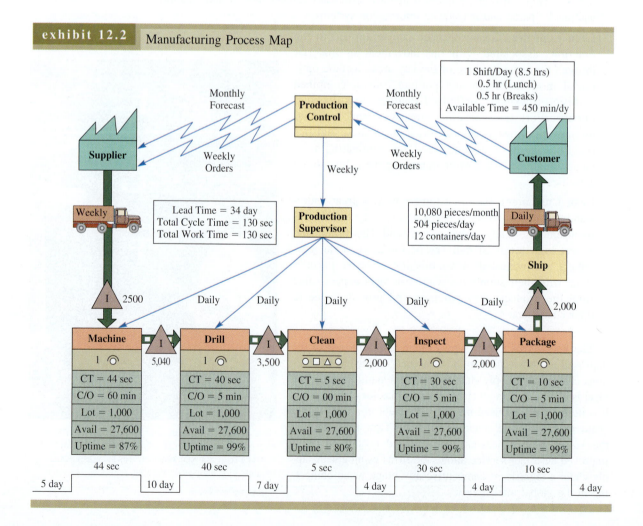

so that they can be modified or eliminated, and the manufacturing system made more productive.

Details explaining the symbols will be discussed later in the section, but here it is useful to discuss what the information in the map depicted in Exhibit 12.2 actually means. Starting from the left, we see that material is supplied on a weekly basis and deposited in a raw material inventory indicated by the triangle. The average level for this inventory is 2,500 units. This material is run through a five-step process consisting of machining, drilling, cleaning, inspection, and packaging. The machining, drilling, inspection, and packaging processes all use a single operator. Under each of these process symbols is the activity cycle time (CT), changeover time (C/O time to switch from one type of item to another), lot size, available number of seconds per day, and percent uptime. The cleaning activity is a multistep process where items are handled on a first come, first served basis. In between each process are inventory buffers with the average inventory in these buffers depicted in the exhibit. Material flows through the process at an average rate of 405 pieces/day over 20 days of operation each month.

Information flows are shown on the map. In Exhibit 12.2, we see that production control issues monthly demand forecasts, weekly orders to the supplier, and a weekly production schedule that is managed by the supervisor on a daily basis. Monthly forecasts are provided by the customer and they place their order on a weekly basis. The time line at the bottom shows the processing time for each production activity (in seconds) together with the average inventory wait time. Adding these times together gives an estimate of the lead time through the entire system.

VSM symbols are somewhat standardized, but there are many variations. Several common symbols are depicted in Exhibit 12.3. These are categorized as Process, Material, Information, and General symbols.

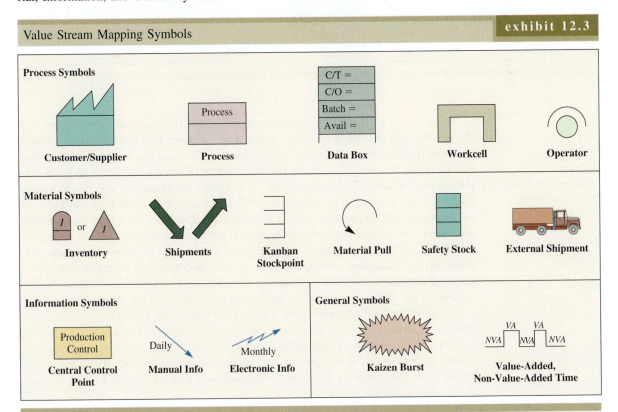

Value Stream Mapping Symbols   exhibit 12.3

Process Symbols

Customer/Supplier   Process   Data Box   Workcell   Operator

Data Box fields: C/T =, C/O =, Batch =, Avail =

Material Symbols

Inventory   Shipments   Kanban Stockpoint   Material Pull   Safety Stock   External Shipment

Information Symbols

Central Control Point (Production Control)   Manual Info (Daily)   Electronic Info (Monthly)

General Symbols

Kaizen Burst   Value-Added, Non-Value-Added Time (VA / NVA)

exhibit 12.4 Analysis Showing Potential Areas for Improving a Process

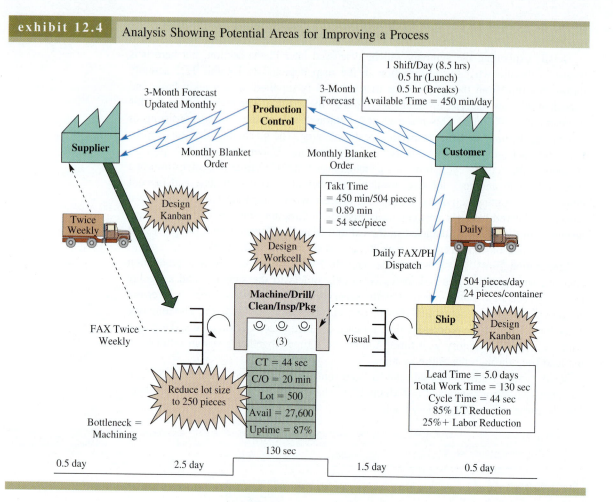

Value stream mapping is a two-part process—first, depicting the "current state" of the process, and second, a possible "future state." Exhibit 12.4 depicts another map of the same process with suggested improvements. The map has been annotated using Kaizen bursts that suggest the areas for improvement. **Kaizen** is the Japanese philosophy that focuses on continuous improvement. The Kaizen bursts identify specific short-term projects (often referred to as "Kaizen events") that teams work on to implement changes to the process. In this exhibit, we see a totally redesigned process where the individual production operations have been combined into a workcell operated by three employees. In addition, rather than "pushing" material through the system based on weekly schedules generated by production control, the entire process is converted to a pull system that is operated directly in response to customer demand. Note that the lead time in the new system is only 5 days, compared to the 34-day lead time with the old system.

To study another example using value stream mapping (VSM), consider Solved Problem 2 at the end of the chapter. VSM is a great visual way to analyze an existing system and to find areas where waste can be eliminated. Value stream maps are simple to draw and it is possible to construct the maps totally with paper and pencil. These maps can, however, be more easily constructed using standard office software or graphics packages.

Kaizen
Japanese philosophy that focuses on continuous improvement.

LEAN SUPPLY CHAIN DESIGN PRINCIPLES

Looking for ways to improve supply chain processes should be based on ideas that have been proven over time. In the following, we review a set of key principles that can guide the design of lean supply chains. We divide our design principles into three major categories. The first two sets of principles relate to internal production processes. These are the processes that actually create the goods and services within a firm. The third category applies lean concepts to the entire supply chain. These principles include

1. Lean Layouts
   a. Group technology
   b. Quality at the source
   c. JIT production
2. Lean Production Schedules
   a. Uniform plant loading
   b. Kanban production control system
   c. Determination of number of Kanbans needed
   d. Minimized setup times
3. Lean Supply Chains
   a. Specialized plants
   b. Collaboration with suppliers
   c. Building a lean supply chain

Lean Concepts

Lean requires the plant layout to be designed to ensure balanced workflow with a minimum of work-in-process inventory. Each workstation is part of a production line, whether or not a physical line actually exists. Capacity is balanced using the same logic for an assembly line, and operations are linked through a pull system. In addition, the system designer must visualize how all aspects of the internal and external logistics system tie to the layout.

Preventive maintenance is emphasized to ensure that flows are not interrupted by downtime or malfunctioning equipment. Preventive maintenance involves periodic inspection and repair designed to keep a machine reliable. Operators perform much of the maintenance because they are most familiar with their machines and because machines are easier to repair, since lean operations favor several simple machines rather than one large complex one.

Group Technology **Group technology** is a philosophy in which similar parts are grouped into families, and the processes required to make the parts are arranged in a manufacturing cell. Instead of transferring jobs from one specialized department to another, group technology considers all operations required to make a part and groups those machines together. Exhibit 12.5 illustrates the difference between the clusters of different machines grouped into cells versus departmental layouts. The group technology cells eliminate movement and queue (waiting) time between operations, reduce inventory, and reduce the number of employees required. Workers, however, must be flexible to run several machines and processes. Due to their advanced skill level, these workers have increased job security.

Quality at the Source **Quality at the source** means do it right the first time and, when something goes wrong, stop the process or assembly line immediately. Factory workers become their own inspectors, personally responsible for the quality of their output. Workers concentrate on one part of the job at a time so quality problems are uncovered. If the

Preventive maintenance
Periodic inspection and repair designed to keep equipment reliable.

Group technology
A philosophy in which similar parts are grouped into families, and the processes required to make the parts are arranged in a specialized workcell.

Quality at the source
Philosophy of making factory workers personally responsible for the quality of their output. Workers are expected to make the part correctly the first time and to stop the process immediately if there is a problem.

exhibit 12.5 **Group Technology versus Departmental Specialty**

Group Technology Manufacturing Cells . . .   **. . . Instead of Specialized Workcenters**

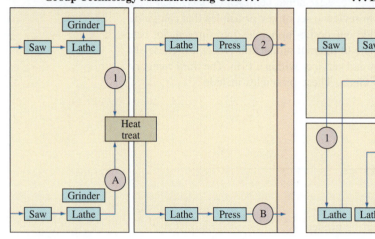
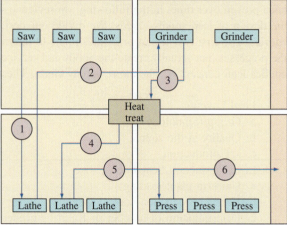

pace is too fast, if the worker finds a quality problem, or if a safety issue is discovered, the worker is obligated to push a button to stop the line and turn on a visual signal. People from other areas respond to the alarm and the problem. Workers are empowered to do their own maintenance and housekeeping until the problem is fixed.

JIT Production JIT (just-in-time) means producing what is needed when needed and no more. Anything over the minimum amount necessary is viewed as waste because effort and material expended for something not needed now cannot be utilized now. This is in contrast to relying on extra material just in case something goes wrong.

JIT is typically applied to repetitive manufacturing, which is when the same or similar items are made one after another. JIT does not require large volumes and can be applied to any repetitive segments of a business regardless of where they appear. Under JIT, the ideal lot size or production batch is one. Although workstations may be geographically dispersed, it is important to minimize transit time and keep transfer quantities small—typically one-tenth of a day's production. Vendors even ship several times a day to their customers to keep lot sizes small and inventory low. The goal is to drive all inventory queues to zero, thus minimizing inventory investment and shortening lead times.

When inventory levels are low, quality problems become very visible. Exhibit 12.6 illustrates this idea. If the water in a pond represents inventory, the rocks represent problems that could occur in a firm. A high level of water hides the problems (rocks). Management assumes everything is fine, but as the water level drops in an economic downturn, problems are presented. If you deliberately force the water level down (particularly in good economic times), you can expose and correct problems before they cause worse problems. JIT manufacturing exposes problems otherwise hidden by excess inventories and staff.

Level schedule
A schedule that pulls material into final assembly at a constant rate.

Lean Production Schedules

As noted earlier, lean production requires a stable schedule over a lengthy time horizon. This is accomplished by level scheduling, freeze windows, and underutilization of capacity. A **level schedule** is one that requires material to be pulled into final assembly in a

Inventory Hides Problems	exhibit 12.6

pattern uniform enough to allow the various elements of production to respond to pull signals. It does not necessarily mean that the usage of every part on an assembly line is identified hour by hour for days on end; it does mean that a given production system equipped with flexible setups and a fixed amount of material in the pipelines can respond to the dynamic needs of the assembly line.

The term **freeze window** refers to that period of time during which the schedule is fixed and no further changes are possible. An added benefit of the stable schedule is seen in how parts and components are accounted for in a pull system. Here, the concept of **backflush** is used where the parts that go into each unit of the product are periodically removed from inventory and accounted for based on the number of units produced. For example, if 1,000 road bicycles are made, 1,000 of the appropriate handlebars, 2,000 tires, one seat, and so on are automatically removed from on-hand inventory. This eliminates much of the shop-floor data collection activity, which is required if each part must be tracked and accounted for during production.

Underutilization and overutilization of capacity are controversial features of lean production. Conventional approaches use safety stocks and early deliveries as a hedge against production problems like poor quality, machine failures, and unanticipated bottlenecks in traditional manufacturing. Under lean production, excess labor, machines, and overtime provide the hedge. The excess capacity in labor and equipment that results is much cheaper than carrying excess inventory. When demand is greater than expected, overtime must be used. Often, part-time labor is used when additional capacity is needed. During idle periods, personnel can be put to work on other activities such as special projects, work group activities, and workstation housekeeping.

Uniform Plant Loading Smoothing the production flow to dampen the reaction waves that normally occur in response to schedule variations is called **uniform plant loading**. When a change is made in a final assembly, the changes are magnified throughout the line and the supply chain. The only way to eliminate the problem is to make adjustments as small as possible by setting a firm monthly production plan for which the output rate is frozen.

Freeze window
The period of time during which the schedule is fixed and no further changes are possible.

Backflush
Calculating how many of each part were used in production and using these calculations to adjust actual on-hand inventory balances. This eliminates the need to actually track each part used in production.

Uniform plant loading
Smoothing the production flow to dampen schedule variation.

	exhibit 12.7	Toyota Example of Mixed-Model Production Cycle in a Japanese Assembly Plant		
MODEL		MONTHLY QUANTITY	DAILY QUANTITY	MODEL CYCLE TIME (MINUTES)
Sedan		5,000	250	2
Hardtop		2,500	125	4
Wagon		2,500	125	4

Sequence: Sedan, hardtop, sedan, wagon, sedan, hardtop, sedan, wagon, and so on (one minute apart)

Toyota found it could do this by building the same mix of products every day in small quantities. Thus, it always has a total mix available to respond to variations in demand. A Toyota example is shown in Exhibit 12.7. Monthly car style quantities are reduced to daily quantities (assuming a 20-day month) in order to compute a model *cycle time* (defined here as the time between two identical units being completed on the line). The cycle time figure is used to adjust resources to produce the precise quantity needed. The speed of equipment or of the production line is adjusted so only the needed quantity is produced each day. JIT strives to produce on schedule, on cost, and on quality.

Kanban Production Control Systems A kanban control system uses a signaling device to regulate JIT flows. **Kanban** means "sign" or "instruction card" in Japanese. In a paperless control system, containers can be used instead of cards. The cards or containers make up the **kanban pull system**. The authority to produce or supply additional parts comes from downstream operations. Consider Exhibit 12.8, where we show an assembly line that is supplied with parts by a machine center. The machine center makes two parts, A and B. These two parts are stored in containers that are located next to the assembly line and next to the machine center. Each container next to the assembly line has a withdrawal kanban, and each container next to the machine center has a production kanban. This is often referred to as a two-card kanban system.

When the assembly line takes the first part A from a full container, a worker takes the withdrawal kanban from the container, and takes the card to the machine center storage area. In the machine center area, the worker finds a container of part A, removes the production kanban, and replaces it with the withdrawal kanban. Placement of this card on the container

Kanban
A signaling device used to control production.

Kanban pull system
An inventory or production control system that uses a signaling device to regulate flows.

exhibit 12.8	Flow of Two Kanbans

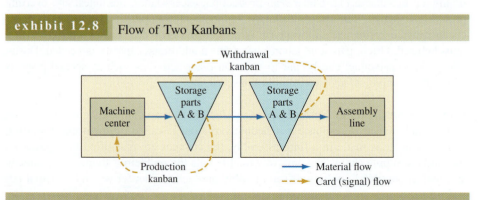

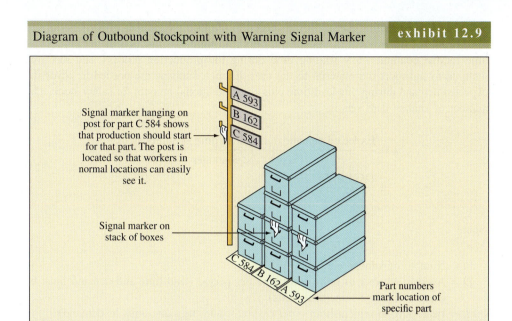

Signal marker hanging on post for part C 584 shows that production should start for that part. The post is located so that workers in normal locations can easily see it.

A 593
B 162
C 584

Signal marker on stack of boxes

C 584 / B 162 / A 593

Part numbers mark location of specific part

authorizes the movement of the container to the assembly line. The freed production kanban is placed on a rack by the machine center, which authorizes the production of another lot of material. A similar process is followed for part B. The cards on the rack visually show upcoming work for the machine center. Cards are not the only way to signal the need for production of a part; other visual methods are possible, as shown in Exhibit 12.9.

The following are some other possible approaches:

Kanban squares.   Some companies use marked spaces on the floor or on a table to identify where material should be stored. When the square is empty, the supplying operations are authorized to produce; when the square is full, no parts are needed.

Container system.   Sometimes the container itself can be used as a signal device. In this case, an empty container on the factory floor visually signals the need to fill it. The amount of inventory is adjusted by simply adding or removing containers.

Colored golf balls.   At a Kawasaki engine plant, when a part used in a subassembly is down to its queue limit, the assembler rolls a colored golf ball down a pipe to the replenishment machine center. This tells the operator which part to make next. Many variations have been developed on this approach.

The kanban pull approach can be used not only within a manufacturing facility but also between manufacturing facilities (pulling engines and transmissions into an automobile assembly operation, for example) and between manufacturers and external suppliers.

Determining the Number of Kanbans Needed Setting up a kanban control system requires determination of the number of kanban cards (or containers) needed. In a two-card system, we are finding the number of sets of withdrawal and production cards. The kanban cards represent the number of containers of material that flow back and forth between the supplier and the user areas. Each container represents the minimum production lot size to be supplied. The number of containers, therefore, directly controls the amount of work-in-process inventory in the system.

Accurately estimating the lead time needed to produce a container of parts is the key to determining the number of containers. This lead time is a function of the processing time for the container, any waiting time during the production process, and the time required to transport the material to the user. Enough kanbans are needed to cover the expected demand during this lead time plus some additional amount for safety stock. The number of kanban card sets is

$$k = \frac{\text{Expected demand during lead time} + \text{Safety stock}}{\text{Size of the container}}$$

$$= \frac{DL(1 + S)}{C}$$

[12.1]

where

k = Number of kanban card sets
D = Average number of units demanded per period (lead time and demand must be expressed in the same time units)
L = Lead time to replenish an order (expressed in the same units as demand)
S = Safety stock expressed as a percentage of demand during the lead time (this can be based on a service level and variance as shown in Chapter 11).
C = Container size

Observe that a kanban system does not produce zero inventory; rather, it controls the amount of material that can be in process at a time—the number of containers of each item. The kanban system can be easily adjusted to fit the current way the system is operating because card sets can be easily added or removed from the system. If the workers find that they are not able to consistently replenish the item on time, an additional container of material, with the accompanying kanban cards, can be added. If it is found that excess containers of material accumulate, card sets can be easily removed, thus reducing the amount of inventory.

Example 12.1: Determining the Number of Kanban Card Sets

Meritor, a company that makes muffler assemblies for the automotive industry, is committed to the use of kanban to pull material through its manufacturing cells. Meritor has designed each cell to fabricate a specific family of muffler products. Fabricating a muffler assembly involves cutting and bending pieces of pipe that are welded to a muffler and a catalytic converter. The mufflers and catalytic converters are pulled into the cell based on current demand. The catalytic converters are made in a specialized cell.

Catalytic converters are made in batches of 10 units and are moved in special hand carts to the fabrication cells. The catalytic converter cell is designed so that different types of catalytic converters can be made with virtually no setup loss. The cell can respond to an order for a batch of catalytic converters in approximately four hours. Because the catalytic converter cell is right next to the muffler assembly fabrication cell, transportation time is virtually zero.

The muffler assembly fabrication cell averages approximately eight assemblies per hour. Each assembly uses the same catalytic converter. Due to some variability in the process, management has decided to have safety stock equivalent to 10 percent of the needed inventory.

How many kanban sets are needed to manage the replenishment of the catalytic converters?

SOLUTION

In this case, the lead time for replenishment of the converters (*L*) is four hours. The demand (*D*) for the catalytic converters is eight per hour. Safety stock (*S*) is 10 percent of the expected demand, and the container size (*C*) is 10 units.

$$k = \frac{8 \times 4(1 + .1)}{10} = \frac{35.2}{10} = 3.52 \quad \text{or} \quad 4 \text{ sets}$$

In this case, we would need four kanban card sets, and we would have four containers of converters in the system. In all cases, when we calculate *k*, we will round the number up because we always need to work with full containers of parts. When the first unit of a batch of 10 catalytic converters is used in the muffler fabrication cell, a "signal" card is sent to the catalytic converter cell to trigger the production of another batch. •

Minimized Setup Times The reductions in setup and changeover times are necessary to achieve a smooth flow. Exhibit 12.10 shows the relationship between lot size and setup costs. Under a traditional approach, setup cost is treated as a constant, and the optimal order quantity is shown as six. Under the kanban approach, setup cost is significantly reduced and the corresponding optimal order quantity is reduced. In the exhibit, the order quantity has been reduced from six to two under lean methods by employing setup-time-saving procedures. This organization will ultimately strive for a lot size of one.

In a widely cited example from the late 1970s, Toyota teams of press operators producing car hoods and fenders were able to change an 800-ton press in 10 minutes, compared with the average of six hours for U.S. workers and four hours for German workers. (Now, however, such speed is common in most U.S. auto plants.) To achieve such setup time reduction, setups are divided into internal and external activities.

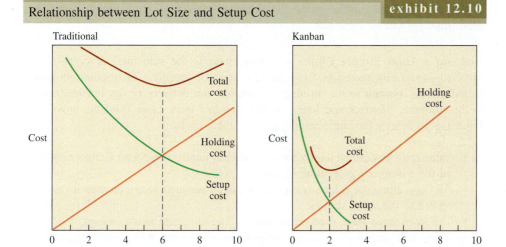

Relationship between Lot Size and Setup Cost — exhibit 12.10

Definitions: *Holding* cost includes the costs of storing inventory and the cost of money tied up in inventory. *Setup* cost includes the wage costs attributable to workers making the setup, and various administrative and supplies costs. (These are defined in total in Chapter 11, "Inventory Management.")

Internal setups must be done while a machine is stopped. External setups can be done while the machine is running. Other time-saving devices such as duplicate tool holders also are used to speed setups.

Lean Supply Chains

Building a lean supply chain involves taking a systems approach to integrating the partners. Supply must be coordinated with the need of the production facilities, and production must be tied directly to the demand of the customers for products. The importance of speed and steady consistent flow that is responsive to actual customer demand cannot be overemphasized. Concepts that relate to lean network design are discussed next.

Specialized Plants Small specialized plants rather than large vertically integrated manufacturing facilities are important. Large operations and their inherent bureaucracies are difficult to manage and not in line with the lean philosophy. Plants designed for one purpose can be constructed and operated more economically. These plants need to be linked together so they can be synchronized to one another and to the actual need of the market. Speed and quick response to changes are keys to the success of a lean supply chain.

Collaboration with Suppliers Just as customers and employees are key components of lean systems, suppliers are also important to the process. If a firm shares its projected usage requirements with its vendors, they have a long-run picture of the demands that will be placed on their production and distribution systems. Some vendors are linked online with a customer to share production scheduling and input needs data. This permits them to develop level production systems. Confidence in the supplier or vendor's delivery commitment allows reductions of buffer inventories. Maintaining stock at a lean level requires frequent deliveries during the day. Some suppliers even deliver directly to a location on the production line and not at a receiving dock. When vendors adopt quality practices, incoming receiving inspections of their products can be bypassed.

Building a Lean Supply Chain A supply chain is the sum total of organizations involved—from raw materials firms through tiers of suppliers to original equipment manufacturers, onward to the ultimate distribution and delivery of the finished product to the customer. Womack and Jones, in their seminal work *Lean Thinking,* provide the following guidelines for implementing a lean supply chain:

- Value must be defined jointly for each product family along with a target cost based on the customer's perception of value.
- All firms along the value stream must make an adequate return on their investments related to the value stream.
- The firms must work together to identify and eliminate *muda* (waste).
- When cost targets are met, the firms along the stream will immediately conduct new analyses to identify remaining *muda* and set new targets.
- Every participating firm has the right to examine every activity in every firm relevant to the value stream as part of the joint search for waste.

To summarize: To be lean, everyone's got to be on the same page!

LEAN SERVICES

Many lean techniques have been successfully applied by service firms. Just as in manufacturing, the suitability of each technique and the corresponding work steps depend on the characteristics of the firm's markets, production and equipment technology, skill sets, and corporate culture. Service firms are no different in this respect. Here are 10 of the more successful techniques applied to service companies:

LO12–4 Apply lean concepts to service processes.

1. **Organize Problem-Solving Groups**   Honeywell is extending its use of quality teams from manufacturing into its service operations. Other corporations as diverse as First Bank/Dallas, Standard Meat Company, and Miller Brewing Company are using similar approaches to improve service. British Airways used quality teams as a fundamental part of its strategy to implement new service practices.

2. **Upgrade Housekeeping**   Good housekeeping means more than winning the clean broom award. It means that only the necessary items are kept in a work area, that there is a place for everything, and that everything is clean and in a constant state of readiness. The employees clean their own areas.

   Service organizations such as McDonald's, Disneyland, and Speedi-Lube have recognized the critical nature of housekeeping. Their dedication to housekeeping has meant that service processes work better, the attitude of continuous improvement is easier to develop, and customers perceive that they are receiving better service.

3. **Upgrade Quality**   The only cost-effective way to improve quality is to develop reliable process capabilities. Process quality is quality at the source—it guarantees first-time production of consistent and uniform products and services.

   McDonald's is famous for building quality into its service delivery process. It literally "industrialized" the service delivery system so that part-time, casual workers could provide the same eating experience anywhere in the world. Quality doesn't mean producing the best; it means consistently producing products and services that give the customers their money's worth.

4. **Clarify Process Flows**   Clarification of flows, based on JIT themes, can dramatically improve the process performance. Here are three examples:

   First, Federal Express Corporation changed air flight patterns from origin-to-destination to origin-to-hub, where the freight is transferred to an outbound plane heading for the destination. This revolutionized the air transport industry. Second, the order-entry department of a manufacturing firm converted from functional subdepartments to customer-centered work groups and reduced the order processing lead time from eight to two days. Finally, Supermaids sends in a team of house cleaners, each with a specific responsibility, to clean a part of each house quickly with parallel processes. Changes in process flows can literally revolutionize service industries.

5. **Revise Equipment and Process Technologies**   Revising technologies involves evaluation of the equipment and processes for their ability to meet the process requirements, to process consistently within tolerance, and to fit the scale and capacity of the work group.

   Speedi-Lube converted the standard service station concept to a specialized lubrication and inspection center by changing the service bays from drive-in to drive-through and by eliminating the hoists and instead building pits under the cars where employees have full access to the lubrication areas on the vehicle.

   A hospital reduced operating room setup time so it had the flexibility to perform a wider range of operations without reducing the operating room availability.

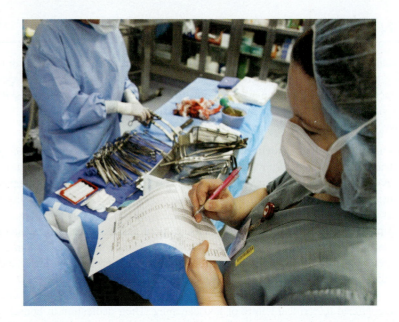

6. **Level the Facility Load**   Service firms synchronize production with demand. They have developed unique approaches to leveling demand so they can avoid making customers wait for service. McDonald's offers a special breakfast menu in the morning. Retail stores use take-a-number systems. The post office charges more for next-day delivery. These are all examples of the service approach for creating uniform facility loads.

7. **Eliminate Unnecessary Activities**   A step that does not add value is a candidate for elimination. A step that does add value may be a candidate for reengineering to improve the process consistency or to reduce the time to perform the tasks.

   A hospital discovered that significant time was spent during an operation waiting for an instrument that was not available when the operation began. It developed a checklist of instruments required for each category of operation. Speedi-Lube eliminated steps, but also added steps that did not improve the lubrication process but did make customers feel more assured about the work being performed.

8. **Reorganize Physical Configuration**   Work area configurations frequently require reorganization during a lean implementation. Often, manufacturers accomplish this by setting up manufacturing cells to produce items in small lots, synchronous to demand. These cells amount to microfactories inside the plant.

   Most service firms are far behind manufacturers in this area. However, a few interesting examples do come out of the service sector. Some hospitals—instead of routing patients all over the building for tests, exams, X-rays, and injections—are reorganizing their services into work groups based on the type of problem. Teams that treat only trauma are common, but other work groups have been formed to treat less immediate conditions like hernias. These amount to micro-clinics within the hospital facility.

9. **Introduce Demand-Pull Scheduling**   Due to the nature of service production and consumption, demand-pull (customer-driven) scheduling is necessary for operating a service business. Moreover, many service firms are separating their

operations into "back room" and "customer contact" facilities. This approach creates new problems in coordinating schedules between the facilities. The original Wendy's restaurants were set up so cooks could see cars enter the parking lot. They put a pre-established number of hamburger patties on the grill for each car. This pull system was designed to have a fresh patty on the grill before the customer even placed an order.

10. **Develop Supplier Networks**   The term *supplier networks* in the lean context refers to the cooperative association of suppliers and customers working over the long term for mutual benefit. Service firms have not emphasized supplier networks for materials because the service costs are often predominantly labor. Notable exceptions include service organizations like McDonald's, one of the biggest food products purchasers in the world, which has been developing lean practices. Manpower and other employment agencies have established lean-type relationships with a temporary employment service and a trade school to develop a reliable source of trained assemblers.

CONCEPT CONNECTIONS

LO12–1   Explain lean production.

- Lean production involves improving processes by eliminating waste and excess inventory.
- The just-in-time philosophy, pioneered by Toyota, is the basis for the concept.
- The concept includes the entire supply chain with the goal of creating value for the customer by eliminating all non-value-adding activities.

Lean production   Integrated activities designed to achieve high-volume, high-quality production using minimal inventories of raw materials, work-in-process, and finished goods.

Customer value   In the context of lean production, something for which the customer is willing to pay.

Waste   Anything that does not add value from the customer's perspective.

Value stream   These are the value-adding and non-value adding activities required to design, order, and provide a product from concept to launch, order to deliver, and from raw materials to customers.

Waste reduction   The optimization of value-adding activities and elimination of non-value-adding activities that are part of the value stream.

LO12–2   Illustrate how lean concepts can be applied to supply chain processes.

- Lean concepts can be applied to virtually all the processes in the supply chain.
- Key areas include production layout, the scheduling of production, and the design of the supply chain.
- Flow throughout the supply chain can be managed using just-in-time systems that pull material based on need.
- The kanban card is an example of this type of system.

Preventive maintenance   Periodic inspection and repair designed to keep equipment reliable.

Group technology   Philosophy in which similar parts are grouped into families, and the processes required to make the parts are arranged in a specialized workcell.

Quality at the source The philosophy of making workers personally responsible for the quality of their output. Workers are expected to make the part correctly the first time and to stop the process immediately if there is a problem.

Level schedule A schedule that pulls material into final assembly at a constant rate.

Freeze window The period of time during which the schedule is fixed and no further changes are possible.

Backflush Calculating how many of each part were used in production and using these calculations to adjust actual on-hand inventory balances. This eliminates the need to actually track each part used in production.

Uniform plant loading Smoothing the production flow to dampen schedule variation.

Kanban A signaling device used to control production.

Kanban pull system An inventory or production control system that uses a signaling device to regulate flow.

$$k = \frac{DL(1 + S)}{C}$$ [12.1]

LO12–3   **Analyze supply chain processes using value stream mapping.**

- Value stream mapping is a flowcharting tool used to visualize flows through a process.
- Features of the tool are the identification of value adding and non-value-adding activities together with a time line for each activity and the process as a whole.
- The tool can be applied to production, logistics, and distribution processes.
- The goal in using the tool is to identify ways to "lean" a process by eliminating waste and creating value for the customer.
- A Kaizen event is a short-term project designed to quickly improve a process.

Value stream mapping (VSM) A graphical way to analyze where value is or is not being added as material flows through a process.

Kaizen Japanese philosophy that focuses on continuous improvement.

LO12–4   **Apply lean concepts to service processes.**

- Lean concepts can be successfully applied by service firms.
- Just as with production processes, waste elimination and customer value creation are also goals of service processes.
- Often, services operate in an environment with more uncertainty, making them more difficult to control.

SOLVED PROBLEMS

LO12–2   SOLVED PROBLEM 1

A local hospital wants to set up a kanban system to manage its supply of blood with the regional blood bank. The regional blood bank delivers blood to the hospital each day with a one-day order lead time (an order placed by 6 P.M. today will be delivered tomorrow afternoon). Internally, the hospital purchasing group places orders for blood each day at 5 P.M. Blood is measured by the pint and is shipped in containers that contain six pints. For a particular blood type, the hospital uses an average of 12 pints per day. Due to the critical nature of a blood shortage, the hospital wants to carry a safety stock of two days' expected supply. How many kanban card sets should the hospital prepare?

Solution

This problem is typical of how a real application might look. Using the data given, the variables for this problem are as follows:

D = 12 pints per day (average demand)
L = 1 day (lead time)
S = 200 percent (safety stock; as a fraction, this is 2.0)
C = 6 pints (container size)

$$k = \frac{DL(1 + S)}{C} = \frac{12(1 + 2)}{6} = 6$$

This indicates that we need to prepare six kanban card sets. Each time a new container of blood (containing six pints) is opened, the card will be sent to purchasing and another six pints of blood will be ordered. When the blood is received, the card will be attached to the new container and moved to the blood storage area.

LO12–3   SOLVED PROBLEM 2

Value Stream Mapping Example: Bolt Manufacturing

A simple example will illustrate the use of value stream mapping. Exhibit 12.11 depicts a bolt manufacturing operation that ships 7,500 bolts per week. The current state map provides cycle time and setup time information for each of the 15 processes used, and it provides inventory levels at each location. The map also depicts information flow between the steel supplier, the bolt customer, and management via production scheduling. The total value-added time, denoted as processing time, is obtained by summing all of the individual value-added contributions at each processing step on the time line. For the example, it equals 28.88 seconds. At each inventory location, lead time is calculated by dividing inventory level by daily production demand, which is 1,500 bolts. Summing all of the lead time produces an overall production lead time of 66.1 days, which is the entire time it takes an individual bolt to make its way through the plant.

There are several possibilities to optimize the current production scenario. Exhibit 12.12 provides a few of these, shown as Kaizen bursts, including eliminating several processing steps, modifying some of the existing processes, and reducing travel distances between processes. Exhibit 12.13, the future state map, illustrates the incorporation of these modifications. As shown, the changes reduce production lead time to 50.89 days, which is a 23 percent reduction. The production scenario could be enhanced even more if pull systems were incorporated at various locations.

exhibit 12.11   Current State Map for Bolt Manufacturing Example

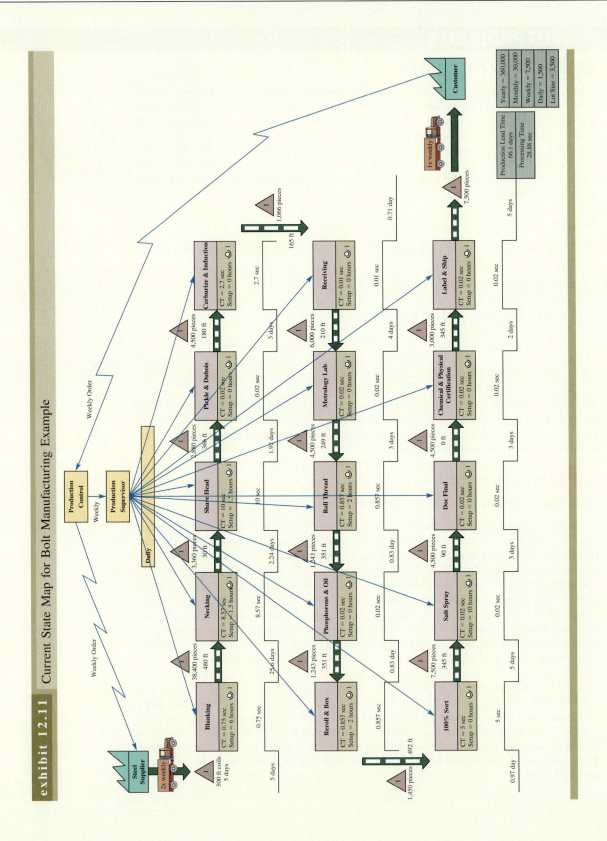

exhibit 12.12   Potential Process Changes for Bolt Manufacturing Example

Yearly = 360,000	
Monthly = 30,000	
Weekly = 7,500	
Daily = 1,500	
Lot Size = 3,500	

Production Lead Time	66.1 days
Processing Time	28.88 sec

Steel Supplier — 2x weekly — 500 ft coils, 5 days

Blanking — CT = 0.75 sec, Setup = 6 hours — 38,400 pieces, 480 ft

Combine Necking & Shaving w/ CNC — Setup — 8.57 sec — 60 pieces

Pickle & Dubois — CT = 0.02 sec, Setup = 0 hours — 2,880 pieces, 366 ft

Modify Hardening / Carburize & Induction — CT = 2.7 sec, Setup = 0 hours — 4,500 pieces, 180 ft

Eliminate Reroll — 1,243 pieces, 351 ft

Phosphorous & Oil — CT = 0.02 sec, Setup = 0 hours — 1,243 pieces, 351 ft

Roll Thread — CT = 0.857 sec, Setup = 2 hours — 4,500 pieces, 249 ft

Metrology Lab — CT = 0.02 sec, Setup = 0 hours — 6,000 pieces, 210 ft

Eliminate Receiving — Setup

Eliminate Sorting — 7,500 pieces, 345 ft

Eliminate Salt Spray — 4,500 pieces, 90 ft

Doc Final — CT = 0.02 sec, Setup = 0 hours — 4,500 pieces, 0 ft

Chemical & Physical Certification — CT = 0.02 sec, Setup = 0 hours — 3,000 pieces, 345 ft

Label & Ship — CT = 0.02 sec, Setup = 0 hours — 7,500 pieces

Customer — 1x weekly

Production Control — Weekly Order — Daily — Production Supervisor — Weekly

Timeline values: 0.97 day, 5 days, 0.75 sec, 25.6 days, 8.57 sec, 2.24 days, 0.857 sec, 0.83 day, 0.02 sec, 1.92 days, 0.02 sec, 3 days, 2.7 sec, 0.01 sec, 0.71 day, 0.02 sec, 0.02 sec, 10 sec, 0.857 sec, 3 days, 0.83 day, 4 days, 3 days, 5 days, 2 days, 5 days, 5 sec

exhibit 12.13 Future State Map for Bolt Manufacturing Example

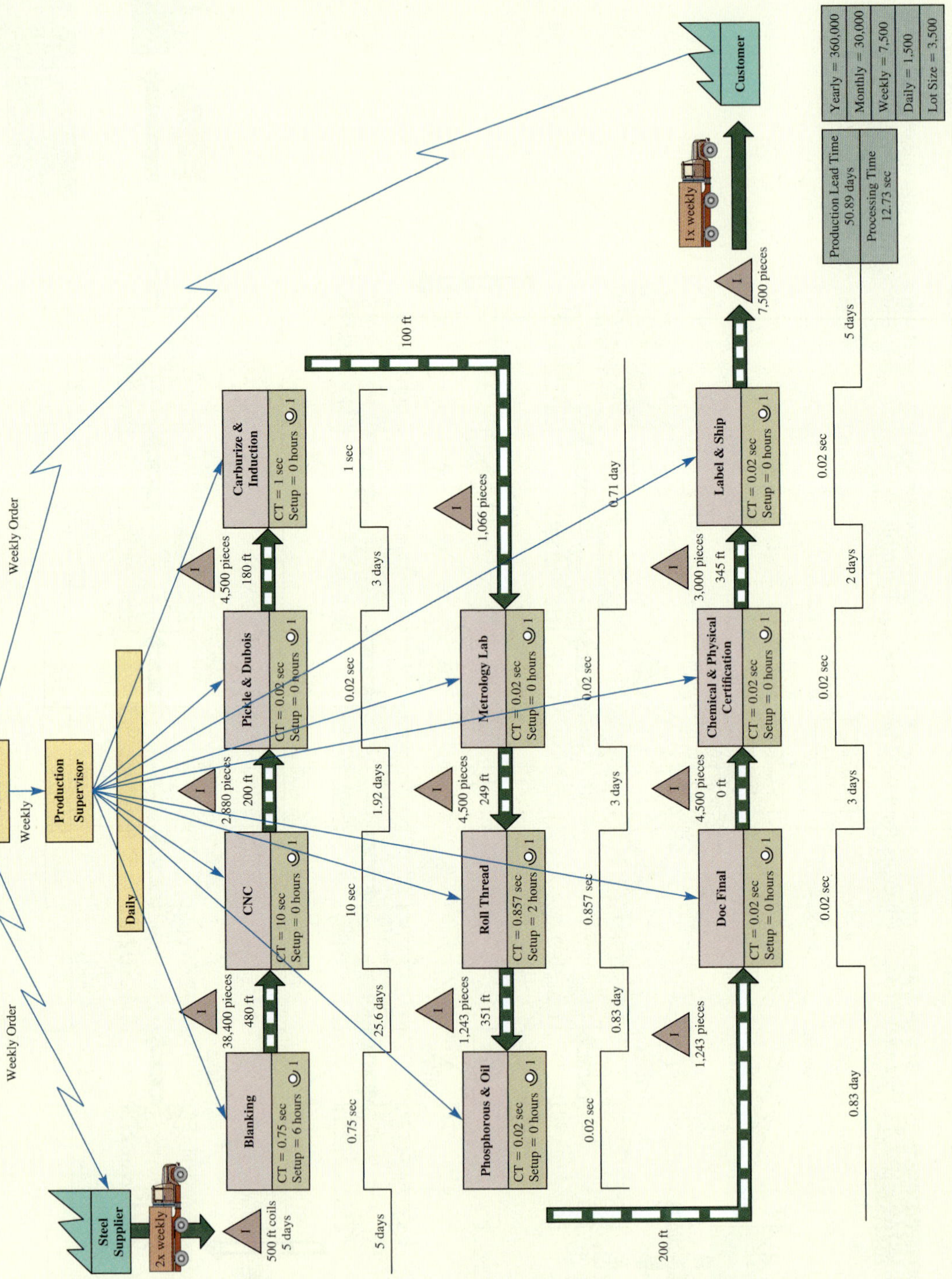

DISCUSSION QUESTIONS

LO12–1
1. Is it possible to achieve zero inventories? Why or why not?
2. One way to help achieve lean production systems is to employ flexible automated manufacturing equipment and automated material handling systems. A natural result of such a move is that fewer people are required in the process, an issue addressed regularly in negotiations with labor unions. Do you think there is a conflict between such a move and the principle of *Respect for People* in the Toyota Production System?
3. Can a supply chain become too lean? Explain your answer—using examples if possible.

LO12–2
4. Why must lean have a stable schedule?
5. What objections might a marketing manager have to uniform plant loading?
6. What are the implications for cost accounting of lean production?
7. What are the roles of suppliers and customers in a lean system?
8. Explain how cards are used in a kanban system.
9. In which ways, if any, are the following systems analogous to kanban: returning empty bottles to the supermarket and picking up filled ones; running a hot dog stand at lunchtime; withdrawing money from a checking account; raking leaves into bags?
10. Why is lean hard to implement in practice?
11. Explain the relationship between quality and productivity under the lean philosophy.

LO12–3
12. Stopping waste is a vital part of lean. Using value stream mapping, identify some sources of waste in your home or dorm and discuss how they may be eliminated.
13. How would you show a pull system in VSM symbols between the blanking and CNC stages of the bolt manufacturing Solved Problem 2?
14. What is value stream mapping?
15. What is the purpose of value stream mapping? How can it be achieved?

LO12–4
16. Will lean work in service environments? Why or why not?
17. Discuss ways to use lean to improve one of the following: a pizza restaurant, a hospital, or an auto dealership.

OBJECTIVE QUESTIONS

LO12–1
1. What phrase refers to the idea that all steps in supply chain processes that deliver goods and services to the customer should create value?
2. What term refers to the optimization of value-adding activities and the elimination of non-value-adding activities that are part of a value stream?
3. List at least four of the seven prominent types of waste that should be eliminated from the supply chain.
4. What lean concept relates to eliminating non-value-added steps and waste in product storage processes?

LO12–2
5. What term refers to a schedule that pulls material into final assembly at a constant rate?
6. The periodic inspection and repair of equipment designed to keep the equipment reliable, thus eliminating unplanned downtime due to malfunctions is called _____.
7. What term refers to the concept of doing things right the first time and, when problems occur, stopping the process to fix the source of the problem?

8. In some JIT systems, marked spaces on a table or the floor identify where material should be stored. Supplying operations are signaled to produce more when the space is empty. What are these spaces called?

9. Under a kanban approach to lean manufacturing, order quantities should be as small as possible. For a part that is manufactured in-house, what part of its manufacturing process needs to be reduced to reduce the optimal order quantity for an item?

10. A supplier of instrument gauge clusters uses a kanban system to control material flow. The gauge cluster housings are transported five at a time. A fabrication center produces approximately 10 gauges per hour. It takes approximately two hours for the housing to be replenished. Due to variations in processing times, management has decided to keep 20 percent of the needed inventory as safety stock. How many kanban card sets are needed?

11. Transmissions are delivered to the fabrication line four at a time. It takes one hour for transmissions to be delivered. Approximately four vehicles are produced each hour, and management has decided that 50 percent of expected demand should be maintained as safety stock. How many kanban card sets are needed?

12. A bottling plant fills 2,400 bottles every two hours. The lead time is 40 minutes and a container accommodates 120 bottles. The safety stock is 10 percent of expected demand. How many kanban cards are needed?

13. Refer to Example 12.1 as the basis for this problem. Meritor hires a team of consultants.

    The consultants suggest a partial robotic automation, as well as an increase in safety stock to 12.5 percent. Meritor implements these suggestions. The result is an increase in efficiency in both the fabrication of muffler assembly and the making of catalytic converters. The muffler assembly fabrication cell now averages 16 assemblies per hour and the lead time has been decreased to two hours' response time for a batch of 10 catalytic converters. How many kanban cards are now needed?

14. Meritor is so pleased with the outcome from previous suggestions that the consultants are invited back for more work. The consultants now suggest a more complete robotic automation of the making of muffler assemblies and also a reduction in container size to eight per container. Meritor implements these suggestions and the result is that the muffler assembly fabrication cell now averages approximately 32 assemblies per hour, and the catalytic converter assembly cell can now respond to an order for a batch of catalytic converters in one hour. The safety stock remains at 12.5 percent. How many kanban cards are needed?

LO12–3 15. In value stream mapping, what does an arrow in the shape of a lightning bolt mean?

16. What does a triangle represent in a value stream map?

17. In a data box on a value stream map, what do the abbreviations CT and C/O mean?

18. What is used to indicate suggested changes in a process that may lead to improvements in a value stream?

LO12–4 19. Compared to manufacturing systems, what is it about the environment of service operations that make them much harder to control?

20. The chapter presents multiple techniques that service firms can use to make their processes leaner. Which technique is demonstrated by a restaurant that offers special discounts midweek to attract more demand during a traditionally slow period?

CASE: QUALITY PARTS COMPANY

Quality Parts Company supplies gizmos for a computer manufacturer located a few miles away. The company produces two different models of gizmos in production runs ranging from 100 to 300 units.

The production flow of models X and Y is shown in Exhibit 12.14. Model Z requires milling as its first step, but otherwise follows the same flow pattern as X and Y. Skids can hold up to 20 gizmos at a time. Approximate times per unit by operation number and equipment setup times are shown in Exhibit 12.15.

Demand for gizmos from the computer company ranges between 125 and 175 per month, equally divided among X, Y, and Z. Subassembly builds up inventory early in the month to make certain that a buffer stock is always available. Raw

---

Gizmo Production Flow   **exhibit 12.14**

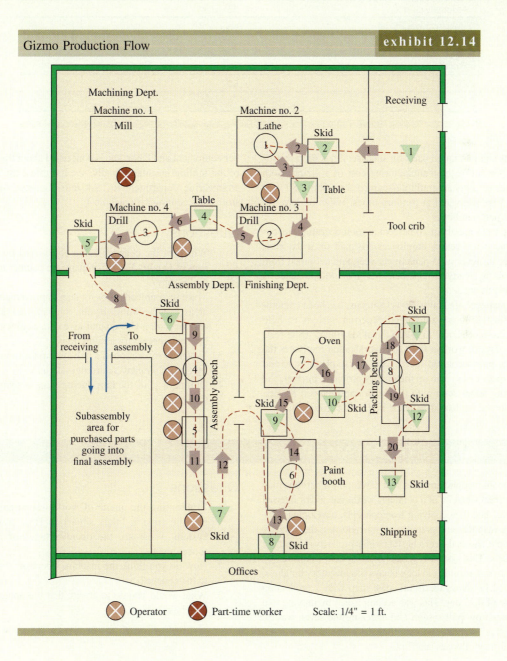

Scale: 1/4" = 1 ft.

exhibit 12.15	Operations and Setup Time	
OPERATION NUMBER AND NAME	OPERATION TIME (MINUTES)	SETUP TIME (MINUTES)
Milling for Model Z	20	60
1 Lathe	50	30
2 Mod. 14 drill	15	5
3 Mod. 14 drill	40	5
4 Assembly step 1	50	
Assembly step 2	45	
Assembly step 3	50	
5 Inspection	30	
6 Paint	30	
7 Oven	50	20
8 Packing	5	

materials and purchased parts for subassemblies each constitute 40 percent of the manufacturing cost of a gizmo. Both categories of parts are multiple-sourced from about 80 vendors and are delivered at random times. (Gizmos have 40 different part numbers.)

Scrap rates are about 10 percent at each operation, inventory turns twice yearly, employees are paid on a day rate, employee turnover is 25 percent per year, and net profit from operations is steady at 5 percent per year. Maintenance is performed as needed.

The manager of Quality Parts Company has been contemplating installing an automated ordering system to help control inventories and to "keep the skids filled." (She feels that two days of work in front of a workstation motivates the worker to produce at top speed.) She is also planning to add three inspectors to clean up the quality problem. Further, she is thinking about setting up a rework line to speed repairs. Although she is pleased with the high utilization of most of her equipment and labor, she is concerned about the idle time of the milling machine. Finally, she has asked the industrial engineering department to look into high-rise shelving to store parts coming off machine 4.

Questions

1. Which of the changes being considered by the manager of Quality Parts Company are counter to the lean philosophy?
2. Make recommendations for lean improvements in such areas as scheduling, layout, kanban, task groupings, and inventory. Use quantitative data as much as possible; state necessary assumptions.
3. Sketch the operation of a pull system for running Quality Parts Company's current system.
4. Outline a plan for introducing lean at Quality Parts Company.

CASE: VALUE STREAM MAPPING

Value stream mapping involves first developing a baseline map of the current situation of a company's external and/or internal operations, and then applying lean concepts, developing a future state map that shows improved operations. Exhibit 12.16, for example, shows the current state with a production lead time of 4.5 days. This system is a batch/push system (indicated by striped arrows) resulting in long delays and inventory buildups. Exhibit 12.17 shows the future state map with a production lead time of 0.25 day. This was accomplished by moving to a continuous-flow pull system and attacking the seven wastes. Value stream mapping uses a number of special icons and a display format of boxes and flows.

Questions

1. Eliminating the queue of work dramatically quickens the time it takes a part to flow through the system. What are the disadvantages of removing those queues?
2. How do you think the machine operators would react to the change?
3. What would you do to ensure that the operators were kept busy?

Map of the Current State

exhibit 12.16

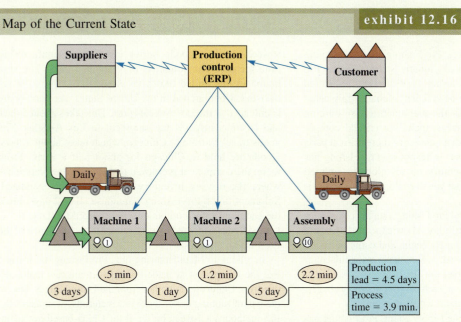

Source: Jared Lovelle, "Mapping the Value Stream," IIE Solutions 33, no. 2 (February 2001), p. 32.

Map of the Future State

exhibit 12.17

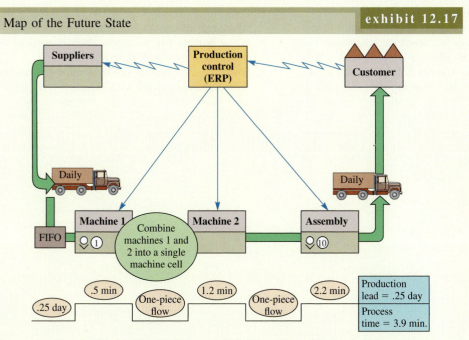

Source: Jared Lovelle, "Mapping the Value Stream," IIE Solutions 33, no. 2 (February 2001), p. 32.

CASE: PRO FISHING BOATS—A VALUE STREAM MAPPING EXERCISE

A fishing boat manufacturer, Pro Fishing Boats, is having many problems with critical globally sourced parts. Pro Fishing has two manufacturing facilities in the United States. The firm's reliance on efficient global supply chain operations is increasing as the manufacturer is sourcing more and more parts overseas, including critical components. Recent problems with a number of these critical parts have caused line shutdowns. In response, Pro Fishing has *mandated* a six-week inventory on all globally sourced parts. Management has asked you to evaluate whether this is the right decision.

First, you must understand Pro Fishing's supply chain. Currently, there is very little visibility (knowledge of the current status) of inventory in the supply chain, and communication with the supply base is minimal. In fact, the boat manufacturer does not have *any* visibility past the Tier I suppliers. Adding to the complexity of this problem, each part of the supply chain is handled by different departments within the company.

In order to understand the supply chain, Pro Fishing has asked you to map its supply chain. To do so, it has identified a critical component to follow in the supply chain. After having the opportunity to interview supply chain participants, including suppliers, you have collected the following information.

The component is manufactured overseas in China by the Tier I supplier, Manufacturing Inc. The Manufacturing Inc. production schedule is based on orders sent via fax from the Pro Fishing warehouse. It operates on a 90-60-30 day forecast along with a weekly order. Upon completion of the component, Manufacturing Inc. sends the component via truck to the Shanghai Port, where it is loaded onto a ship heading to the United States. Loading at the port takes 1 week, and truck transport takes 3 days. Manufacturing Inc. holds a 9-week finished goods buffer inventory. Manufacturing time for each component is only about 3 days. The ship bound to the United States takes about 14 days to travel overseas. Upon arrival in the United States, the component is unloaded at the Los Angeles port. This takes about 5 days and customs inspects the shipment in Los Angeles. The goods travel by train to Chicago, which takes about 7 days. Goods are held in Chicago for about half a week. From there, the component is trucked to a Pro Fishing warehouse where the 6-week inventory buffer has been mandated. Shipment to the Pro Fishing warehouse takes 2 days. From the warehouse, the components are trucked to plants in the United States triggered by electronic orders from each of the Pro Fishing plants.

In talking to Manufacturing Inc., Pro Fishing has learned that the component is made up of two main raw materials: one from China and the other from the United States. Due to the risk of running out of these raw materials, Manufacturing Inc. maintains a 4-week buffer of the China-based raw materials and a 12-week buffer of the U.S.-based raw materials. These Tier II supplier orders are by formal purchase order only. It is interesting to note that Manufacturing Inc. uses these suppliers due to Pro Fishing's strict supplier qualification requirements.

Questions

1. Create a value stream map (VSM) of this supply chain. What other information is needed?
2. Where is there risk for supply chain disruptions or stoppages to the flow of materials?
3. Where do opportunities reside in improving supply chain operations and how has VSM helped reveal these?

PRACTICE EXAM

1. Anything that does not add value from the customer's perspective.
2. An integrated set of activities designed to achieve production using minimal inventories of raw materials, work-in-process, and finished goods.
3. The Toyota Production System is founded on these two philosophies.
4. The set of value- and non-value-adding activities required to design, order, and provide a product from concept to launch, order to delivery, and raw materials to customers.
5. The Japanese philosophy that focuses on continuous improvement.
6. A philosophy in which similar parts are brought together in families for production purposes.
7. Means producing only what is needed when needed and no more.
8. A period of time during which the production schedule cannot be changed.
9. Producing a mix of products that matches demand as closely as possible.
10. A production control system that uses a signaling device to regulate the flow of material.
11. If the lead time for an item is exactly five days, the demand is a constant four units per day, and the shipment container contains two units, how many kanban card sets would be needed? (Assume 0 percent safety stock.)
12. A firm wants to justify smaller lot sizes economically. Management knows that it cannot change the cost to carry one unit in inventory since this is largely based on the value of the item. To justify a smaller lot size, what must it do?

CHAPTER 13

GLOBAL SOURCING AND PROCUREMENT

Learning Objectives

LO13–1 Explain what strategic sourcing is.

LO13–2 Explain why companies outsource processes.

LO13–3 Analyze the total cost of ownership.

LO13–4 Evaluate sourcing performance.

THE FACTORYLESS GOODS PRODUCERS

Consider a company like Apple Inc. and its iPhone and iPad. Apple handles every part of making its products except the actual fabrication. Currently, Apple outsources the production of many of its products to Taiwan's Hon Hai Precision Industry. Hon Hai, which is better known as Foxconn, draws 40–50 percent of its revenue from assembling Apple products.

As many industries have become global suppliers, this type of global outsourcing has become common for clothing, most retail household products, furniture, and computers. These factoryless goods producers do most of the functions of manufacturing, and in many cases, design the product and oversee distribution.

Much of the attraction for this arrangement is the traditionally low labor costs in Chinese factories. Because labor cost has recently surged in China, outsourcing specialists such as Foxconn have diversified their operations to other low-wage countries, including Vietnam, Indonesia, Turkey, Brazil, Mexico, and Hungary.

© Mick Ryan/Getty Images RF

STRATEGIC SOURCING

LO13–1 Explain what strategic sourcing is.

Strategic sourcing is the development and management of supplier relationships to acquire goods and services in a way that aids in achieving the immediate needs of the business. In the past, the term *sourcing* was just another term for purchasing, a corporate function that financially was important but strategically was not the center of attention. Today, as a result of globalization and inexpensive communications technology, the basis for competition is changing. A firm is no longer constrained by the capabilities it owns; what matters is its ability to make the most of available capabilities, whether they are owned by the firm or not. Outsourcing is so sophisticated that even core functions such as engineering, research and development, manufacturing, information technology, and marketing can be moved outside the firm.

Sourcing activities can vary greatly and depend on the item being purchased. Exhibit 13.1 maps different processes for sourcing or purchasing an item. The term **sourcing** implies a more complex process suitable for products that are strategically important. Purchasing processes that span from a simple "spot" or one-time purchase to a long-term strategic alliance are depicted on the diagram. The diagram positions a purchasing process according to the specificity of the item, contract duration, and intensity of transaction costs.

Strategic sourcing
The development and management of supplier relationships to acquire goods and services in a way that aids in achieving the needs of a business.

Sourcing
A process suitable for procuring products that are strategically important to the firm.

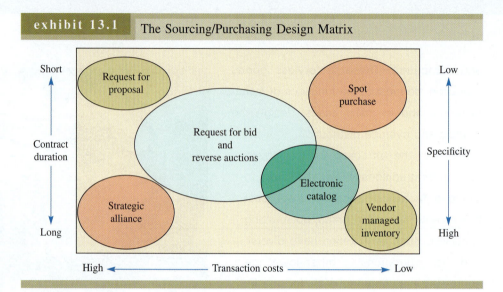

exhibit 13.1   The Sourcing/Purchasing Design Matrix

Short

Request for proposal

Spot purchase

Contract duration

Request for bid and reverse auctions

Specificity

Electronic catalog

Strategic alliance

Vendor managed inventory

Long

Low

High

High ◄—————— Transaction costs ——————► Low

Specificity
Refers to how commonly available the material is and whether substitutes can be used.

Request for proposal (RFP)
A solicitation that asks for a detailed proposal from a vendor interested in supplying an item.

Vendor managed inventory
When a customer allows the supplier to manage the inventory policy of an item or group of items.

Specificity refers to how common the item is and, in a relative sense, how many substitutes might be available. For example, blank DVD disks are commonly available from many different vendors and would have low specificity. A custom-made envelope that is padded and specially shaped to contain a specific item that is to be shipped would be an example of a high-specificity item.

Commonly available products can be purchased using a relatively simple process. For low-volume and inexpensive items purchased during the regular routine of work, a firm may order from an online catalog. Often, these online catalogs are customized for a customer. Special user identifications can be set up to authorize a customer's employees to purchase certain groups of items, with limits on how much they can spend. Other items require a more complex process.

A **request for proposal (RFP)** is commonly used for purchasing items that are more complex or expensive and where there may be a number of potential vendors. A detailed information packet describing what is to be purchased is prepared and distributed to potential vendors. The vendor then responds with a detailed proposal of how the company intends to meet the terms of the RFP. A request for bid or reverse auction is similar in terms of the information packet needed. A major difference is how the bid price is negotiated. In the RFP, the bid is included in the proposal, whereas in a request for bid or reverse auction, vendors actually bid on the item in real time and often using Internet software.

Vendor-managed inventory is when a customer actually allows the supplier to manage the inventory policy of an item or group of items for them. In this case, the supplier is given the freedom to replenish the item as they see fit. Typically, there are some

INSTEAD OF SENDING PURCHASE ORDERS, CUSTOMERS ELECTRONICALLY SEND DAILY DEMAND INFORMATION TO THE SUPPLIER. THE SUPPLIER GENERATES REPLENISHMENT ORDERS FOR THE CUSTOMER BASED ON THIS DEMAND INFORMATION.

© Charlie Westerman/The Image Bank/Getty Images

constraints related to the maximum that the customer is willing to carry, required service levels, and other billing transaction processes. Selecting the proper process depends on minimizing the balance between the supplier's delivered costs of the item over a period of time, say a year, and the customer's costs of managing the inventory. This is discussed later in the chapter in the context of the "total cost of ownership" for a purchased item.

The Bullwhip Effect

In many cases, there are adversarial relations between supply chain partners as well as dysfunctional industry practices such as a reliance on price promotions. Consider the common food industry practice of offering price promotions every January on a product. Retailers respond to the price cut by stocking up, in some cases buying a year's supply—a practice the industry calls **forward buying**. Nobody wins in the deal. Retailers have to pay to carry the year's supply, and the shipment bulge adds cost throughout the supplier's system. For example, the supplier plants must go on overtime starting in October to meet the bulge. Even the vendors that supply the manufacturing plants are affected because they must quickly react to the large surge in raw material requirements.

Forward buying
A term that refers to when a customer, responding to a promotion, buys far in advance of when an item will be used.

The impact of these types of practices has been studied at companies such as Procter & Gamble. Exhibit 13.2 shows typical order patterns faced by each node in a supply

Increasing Variability of Orders Up the Supply Chain

exhibit 13.2

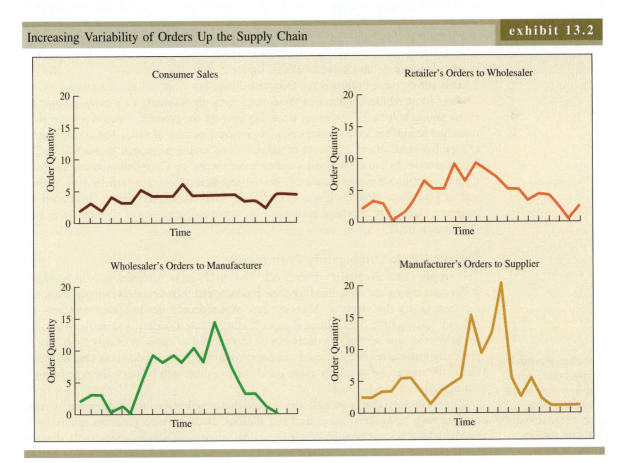

chain that consists of a manufacturer, a distributor, a wholesaler, and a retailer. In this case, the demand is for disposable baby diapers. The retailer's orders to the wholesaler display greater variability than the end-consumer sales; the wholesaler's orders to the manufacturer show even more oscillations; and, finally, the manufacturer's orders to its suppliers are the most volatile. This phenomenon of variability magnification as we move from the customer to the producer in the supply chain is often referred to as the **bullwhip effect**. The effect indicates a lack of synchronization among supply chain members. Even a slight change in consumer sales ripples backward in the form of magnified oscillations upstream, resembling the result of a flick of a bullwhip handle. Because the supply patterns do not match the demand patterns, inventory accumulates at various stages, and shortages and delays occur at others. This bullwhip effect has been observed by many firms in numerous industries, including Campbell Soup and Procter & Gamble in consumer products; Hewlett-Packard, IBM, and Motorola in electronics; General Motors in automobiles; and Eli Lilly in pharmaceuticals.

Campbell Soup pioneered a program called **continuous replenishment** that typifies what many manufacturers are doing to smooth the flow of materials through their supply chain. Here is how the program works. Campbell establishes electronic data interchange (EDI) links with retailers and offers an "everyday low price" that eliminates discounts. Every morning, retailers electronically inform the company of their demand for all Campbell products and of the level of inventories in their distribution centers. Campbell uses that information to forecast future demand and to determine which products require replenishment based on upper and lower inventory limits previously established with each supplier. Trucks leave the Campbell shipping plant that afternoon and arrive at the retailers' distribution centers with the required replenishments the same day. Using this system, Campbell can cut the retailers' inventories, which under the old system averaged four weeks of supply, to about two weeks of supply.

This solves some problems for Campbell Soup, but what are the advantages for the retailer? Most retailers figure that the cost to carry the inventory of a given product for a year equals at least 25 percent of what they paid for the product. A two-week inventory reduction represents a cost savings equal to nearly 1 percent of sales. The average retailer's profits equal about 2 percent of sales, so this saving is enough to increase profits by 50 percent. Because the retailer makes more money on Campbell products delivered through continuous replenishment, it has an incentive to carry a broader line of them and to give them more shelf space. Campbell Soup found that after it introduced the program, sales of its products grew twice as fast through participating retailers as they did through other retailers.

Supply Chain Uncertainty Framework

The supply chain uncertainty framework (Exhibit 13.3) is designed to help managers understand the nature of demand for their products and then devise the supply chain that can best satisfy that demand. Many aspects of a product's demand are important—for example, product life cycle, demand predictability, product variety, and market standards for lead times and service. Products can be categorized as either primarily functional or primarily innovative. Because each category requires a distinctly different kind of supply chain, the root cause of supply chain problems is a mismatch between the type of product and type of supply chain.

Functional products include the staples that people buy in a wide range of retail outlets, such as grocery stores and gas stations. Because such products satisfy basic needs, which do not change much over time, they have stable, predictable demand

Bullwhip effect
The variability in demand is magnified as we move from the customer to the producer in the supply chain.

Continuous replenishment
A program for automatically supplying groups of items to a customer on a regular basis.

Functional products
Staples that people buy in a wide range of retail outlets, such as grocery stores and gas stations.

and long life cycles. But their stability invites competition, which often leads to low profit margins. Specific criteria for identifying functional products include the following: product life cycle of more than two years, contribution margin of 5 to 20 percent, only 10 to 20 product variations, an average forecast error at time of production of only 10 percent, and a lead time for make-to-order products of from six months to one year.

To avoid low margins, many companies introduce innovations in fashion or technology to give customers an additional reason to buy their products. Fashionable clothes and personal computers are good examples. Although innovation can enable a company to achieve higher profit margins, the very newness of the innovative products makes demand for them unpredictable. These **innovative products** typically have a life cycle of just a few months. Imitators quickly erode the competitive advantage that innovative products enjoy, and companies are forced to introduce a steady stream of newer innovations. The short life cycles and the great variety typical of these products further increase unpredictability. Exhibit 13.3 summarizes the differences between functional and innovative products.

We expand on this idea by focusing on the "supply" side of the supply chain. While the Supply Chain uncertainty framework captures important demand characteristics, there are uncertainties revolving around the supply side that are equally important drivers for the right supply chain strategy.

A **stable supply process** is where the manufacturing process and the underlying technology are mature and the supply base is well established. In contrast, an **evolving supply process** is where the manufacturing process and the underlying technology are still under early development and are rapidly changing. As a result, the supply base may be limited in both size and experience. In a stable supply process, manufacturing complexity tends to be low or manageable. Stable manufacturing processes tend to be highly automated, and long-term supply contracts are prevalent. In an evolving supply process, the manufacturing process requires a lot of fine-tuning and is often subject to breakdowns and uncertain yields. The supply base may not be reliable, as the suppliers themselves are going through process innovations. Exhibit 13.3 summarizes some of the differences between stable and evolving supply processes.

While functional products tend to have a more mature and stable supply process, that is not always the case. For example, the annual demand for electricity and other

Innovative products Products such as fashionable clothes and high-end personal computers that typically have a life cycle of just a few months.

Stable supply process A process where the underlying technology is stable.

Evolving supply process A process where the underlying technology changes rapidly.

Product and Process Uncertainty Characteristics — exhibit 13.3

PRODUCT (DEMAND) CHARACTERISTICS	FUNCTIONAL	INNOVATIVE	MANUFACTURING (SUPPLY) PROCESS CHARACTERISTICS	STABLE	EVOLVING
Demand	Predictable	Unpredictable	Breakdowns	Few	Higher
Product Life	Long	Short	Process Yield	High	Lower
Inventory Value	Low	High	Quality Problems	Few	More
Product Variety	Low	High	Supply Sources	Many	Few
Volume	High	Low	Process Changes	Few	Many
Stock-out Cost	Low	High	Lead Time	Dependable	Difficult to predict

Based on research conducted by Marshall Fisher (Wharton School of Business, University of Pennsylvania).

exhibit 13.4	Supply Chain Uncertainty Framework

		PRODUCT (DEMAND) CHARACTERISTICS	
		FUNCTIONAL	INNOVATIVE
Manufacturing (Supply) Process Characteristics	Stable	**Efficient Supply Chain** Grocery, basic apparel, food, oil and gas	**Responsive Supply Chain** Fashion apparel, low-end computers, seasonal products
	Evolving	**Risk-Hedging Supply Chain** Hydroelectric power, food dependent on weather	**Agile Supply Chain** Cellphones, high-end computers, semiconductors

Based on research conducted by Hau Lee (Stanford University).

utility products in a locality tends to be stable and predictable, but the supply of hydroelectric power, which relies on rainfall in a region, can be erratic year by year. Some food products also have a very stable demand, but the supply (both quantity and quality) of the products depends on yearly weather conditions. Similarly, there are also innovative products with a stable supply process. Fashion apparel products have a short selling season and their demand is highly unpredictable. However, the supply process is very stable, with a reliable supply base and a mature manufacturing process technology. Exhibit 13.4 gives some examples of products that have different demand and supply uncertainties.

In most cases, it is more challenging to operate a supply chain that is in the right column of Exhibit 13.4 than in the left column, and similarly it is more challenging to operate a supply chain that is in the lower row of Exhibit 13.4 than in the upper row. Before setting up a supply chain strategy, it is necessary to understand the sources of the underlying uncertainties and explore ways to reduce these uncertainties. If it is possible to move the uncertainty characteristics of the product from the right column to the left or from the lower row to the upper, then the supply chain performance will improve.

Using the supply and demand characteristics discussed so far, four types of supply chain strategies, as shown in Exhibit 13.4, are possible. Information technologies play an important role in shaping such strategies.

- **Efficient supply chains.** These are supply chains that utilize strategies aimed at creating the highest levels of cost efficiency. For such efficiencies to be achieved, non-value-added activities should be eliminated, scale economies should be pursued, optimization techniques should be deployed to get the best capacity utilization in production and distribution, and information linkages should be established to ensure the most efficient, accurate, and cost-effective transmission of information across the supply chain.
- **Risk-hedging supply chains.** These are supply chains that utilize strategies aimed at pooling and sharing resources in a supply chain so that the risks in supply disruption can be shared. A single entity in a supply chain can be vulnerable to supply disruptions, but if there is more than one supply source or if alternative supply resources are available, then the risk of disruption is reduced. A company

may, for example, increase the safety stock of its key component to hedge against the risk of supply disruption, and by sharing the safety stock with other locations that also need this key component, the cost of maintaining this safety stock can be shared. This type of strategy is common in retailing, where different retail stores or dealerships share inventory. Information technology is important for the success of these strategies since real-time information on inventory and demand allows the most cost-effective management and transshipment of goods between partners sharing the inventory.

- **Responsive supply chains.**   These are supply chains that utilize strategies aimed at being responsive and flexible to the changing and diverse needs of the customers. To be responsive, companies use build-to-order and mass customization processes as a means to meet the specific requirements of customers.

- **Agile supply chains.**   These are supply chains that utilize strategies aimed at being responsive and flexible to customer needs, while the risks of supply shortages or disruptions are hedged by pooling inventory and other capacity resources. These supply chains essentially have strategies in place that combine the strengths of "hedged" and "responsive" supply chains. They are agile because they have the ability to be responsive to the changing, diverse, and unpredictable demands of customers on the front end, while minimizing the back-end risks of supply disruptions.

Demand and supply uncertainty is a good framework for understanding supply chain strategy. Innovative products with unpredictable demand and an evolving supply process face a major challenge. Because of shorter and shorter product life cycles, the pressure for dynamically adjusting and adopting a company's supply chain strategy is great. In the following section, we explore the concepts of outsourcing, green sourcing, and total cost of ownership. These are important tools for coping with demand and supply uncertainty.

OUTSOURCING

Outsourcing is the act of moving some of a firm's internal activities and decision responsibility to outside providers. The terms of the agreement are established in a contract. Outsourcing goes beyond the more common purchasing and consulting contracts because not only are the activities transferred, but also resources that make the activities occur, including people, facilities, equipment, technology, and other assets. The responsibilities for making decisions over certain elements of the activities are transferred as well. Taking complete responsibility for this is a specialty of contract manufacturers such as Flextronics.

The reasons why a company decides to outsource can vary greatly. Exhibit 13.5 lists examples of reasons to outsource and the accompanying benefits. Outsourcing allows a firm to focus on activities that represent its core competencies. Thus, the company can create a competitive advantage while reducing cost. An entire function may be outsourced, or some elements of an activity may be outsourced, with the rest kept in-house. For example, some of the elements of information technology may be strategic, some may be critical, and some may be performed less expensively by a third party. Identifying a function as a potential outsourcing target, and then breaking that function into its components, allows decision makers to determine which activities are strategic or critical

LO13–2 Explain why companies outsource processes.

Outsourcing
Moving some of a firm's internal activities and decision responsibility to outside providers.

exhibit 13.5	Reasons to Outsource and the Resulting Benefits

FINANCIALLY DRIVEN REASONS

Improve return on assets by reducing inventory and selling unnecessary assets.
Generate cash by selling low-return entities.
Gain access to new markets, particularly in developing countries.
Reduce costs through a lower cost structure.
Turn fixed costs into variable costs.

IMPROVEMENT-DRIVEN REASONS

Improve quality and productivity.
Shorten cycle time.
Obtain expertise, skills, and technologies that are not otherwise available.
Improve risk management.
Improve credibility and image by associating with superior providers.

ORGANIZATIONALLY DRIVEN REASONS

Improve effectiveness by focusing on what the firm does best.
Increase flexibility to meet changing demand for products and services.
Increase product and service value by improving response to customer needs.

and should remain in-house and which can be outsourced like commodities. As an example, outsourcing the logistics function will be discussed.

Logistics Outsourcing

Logistics

Management functions that support the complete cycle of material flow: from the purchase and internal control of production materials; to the planning and control of work-in-process; to the purchasing, shipping, and distribution of the finished product.

There has been dramatic growth in outsourcing in the logistics area. **Logistics** is a term that refers to the management functions that support the complete cycle of material flow: from the purchase and internal control of production materials; to the planning and control of work-in-process; to the purchasing, shipping, and distribution of the finished product. The emphasis on lean inventory means there is less room for error in deliveries. Trucking companies such as Ryder have started adding the logistics aspect to their businesses—changing from merely moving goods from point A to point B, to managing all or part of all shipments over a longer period, typically three years, and replacing the shipper's employees with their own. Logistics companies now have complex computer tracking technology that reduces the risk in transportation and allows the logistics company to add more value to the firm than it could if the function were performed in-house. Third-party logistics providers track freight using electronic data interchange technology and a satellite system to tell customers exactly where its drivers are and when deliveries will be made. Such technology is critical in some environments where the delivery window may be only 30 minutes long.

Federal Express has one of the most advanced systems available for tracking items being sent through its services. The system is available to all customers over the Internet. It tells the exact status of each item currently being carried by the company. Information on the exact time a package is picked up, when it is transferred between hubs in the company's network, and when it is delivered is available on the system. You can access this system at the FedEx Website (**www.fedex.com**). Select your country on the initial screen and then select "Track Shipments" in the Track box in the lower part of the page. Of course, you will need the actual tracking number for an item currently in the system to get information. Federal Express has integrated its tracking system with many of its customers' in-house information systems.

Another example of innovative outsourcing in logistics involves Hewlett-Packard. Hewlett-Packard turned over its inbound raw materials warehousing in Vancouver, British Columbia, to Roadway Logistics. Roadway's 140 employees operate the warehouse 24 hours a day, seven days a week, coordinating the delivery of parts to the warehouse and managing storage. Hewlett-Packard's 250 employees were transferred to other company activities. Hewlett-Packard reports savings of 10 percent in warehousing operating costs.

One of the drawbacks to outsourcing is the layoffs that often result. Even in cases where the outsourcing partner hires former employees, they are often hired back at lower wages with fewer benefits. Outsourcing is perceived by many unions as an effort to circumvent union contracts.

Framework for Supplier Relationships

In theory, outsourcing is a no-brainer. Companies can unload noncore activities, shed balance sheet assets, and boost their return on capital by using third-party service providers. But in reality, things are more complicated.

Exhibit 13.6 is a useful framework to help managers make appropriate choices for the structure of supplier relationships. The decision goes beyond the notion that "core competencies" should be maintained under the direct control of management of the firm and that other activities should be outsourced. In this framework, a continuum that ranges from vertical integration to arm's-length relationships forms the basis for the decision.

An activity can be evaluated using the following characteristics: required coordination, strategic control, and intellectual property. Required coordination refers to how difficult it is to ensure that the activity will integrate well with the overall process. Uncertain activities that require much back-and-forth exchange of information should not be

	OUTSOURCE	VERTICALLY INTEGRATE
		exhibit 13.6
A Framework for Structuring Supplier Relationships		
Required coordination	Standard interfaces: • Information is highly codified and standardized including: prices, quantities, delivery schedules, etc.	Nonstandard interfaces: • Manual adaption of data • Much exchange of implicit knowledge and learning-by-doing • Needed information is highly specific to the task
Strategic control	Very low requirement: • Large number of potential suppliers	Very high with investments in specialized assets that are needed to optimize processes: • Specialized facilities • Investment in branded assets • Proprietary activity with significant learning curve • Long-term investments in specialized R&D programs
Intellectual property protection	Strong protection: • Difficult-to-imitate technology • Distinct boundaries between different technological components	Unclear or weak intellectual property protection: • Easy-to-imitate technology • Complex and/or proprietary, interfaces between different technological components

outsourced, whereas activities that are well understood and highly standardized can easily move to business partners who specialize in the activity. Strategic control refers to the degree of loss that would be incurred if the relationship with the partner were severed. There could be many types of losses that would be important to consider, including specialized facilities, knowledge of major customer relationships, and investment in research and development. A final consideration is the potential loss of intellectual property through the partnership.

Intel is an excellent example of a company that recognized the importance of this type of decision framework in the mid-1980s. During the early 1980s, Intel found itself being squeezed out of the market for the memory chips it had invented by Japanese competitors such as Hitachi, Fujitsu, and NEC. These companies had developed stronger capabilities to develop and rapidly scale up complex semiconductor manufacturing processes. It was clear by 1985 that a major Intel competency was its ability to design complex integrated circuits, not in manufacturing or developing processes for more standardized chips. As a result, faced with growing financial losses, Intel was forced to exit the memory chip market.

Learning a lesson from the memory market, Intel shifted its focus to the market for microprocessors, which it had invented in the late 1960s. To keep from repeating the mistake with memory chips, Intel felt it was essential to develop strong capabilities in process development and manufacturing. A pure "core competency" strategy would have suggested that Intel focus on the design of microprocessors and use outside partners to manufacture them. Given the close connection between semiconductor product development and process development, however, relying on outside parties for manufacturing would likely have created costs in terms of longer development lead times. Throughout the late-1980s, Intel invested heavily in building world-class capabilities in process development and manufacturing. These capabilities are one of the chief reasons it has been able to maintain approximately 90 percent of the personal computer microprocessor market, despite the ability of competitors like AMD to "clone" Intel designs relatively quickly. Expanding its capabilities beyond its original core capability of product design has been a critical ingredient in Intel's sustained success.

Good advice is to keep control of—or acquire—activities that are true competitive differentiators or have the potential to yield a competitive advantage, and to outsource the rest. It is important to make a distinction between "core" and "strategic" activities. Core activities are key to the business, but do not confer a competitive advantage, such as a bank's information technology operations. Strategic activities are a key source of competitive advantage. Because the competitive environment can change rapidly, companies need to monitor the situation constantly, and adjust accordingly. As an example, Coca-Cola, which decided to stay out of the bottling business in the early 1900s, partnered instead with independent bottlers and quickly built market share. The company reversed itself in the 1980s when bottling became a key competitive element in the industry.

Green Sourcing

Being environmentally responsible has become a business imperative, and many firms are looking to their supply chains to deliver "green" results. A significant area of focus relates to how a firm works with suppliers where the opportunity to save money and benefit the environment might not be a strict trade-off proposition. Financial results can often be improved through cost reductions and by boosting revenues.

Deloitte (www.deloitte.com) has developed a green strategic sourcing process that can be used with conventional sourcing techniques to enhance sourcing savings by taking advantage of environmental factors. Before looking at its six-step process, it is worth considering the long-term benefits of this type of approach. Green sourcing is not just about finding new environmentally friendly technologies or increasing the use of recyclable materials. It can also help drive cost reductions in a variety of ways, including product content substitution, waste reduction, and lower usage.

A comprehensive green sourcing effort should assess how a company uses items that are purchased internally, in its own operations, or in its products and services. As costs of commodity items like steel, electricity, and fossil fuels continue to increase, properly designed green-sourcing efforts should find ways to significantly reduce and possibly eliminate the need for these types of commodities. As an example, consider retrofitting internal lighting in a large office building to a modern energy-efficient technology. Electricity cost savings of 10 to 12 percent per square foot can easily translate into millions of dollars in associated electricity cost savings.

Another important cost area in green sourcing is waste reduction opportunities. This includes everything from energy and water to packaging and transportation. A great example of this is the redesigned milk jug introduced recently by leading grocery retailers. Using the new jug, with more rectangular dimensions and a square base, cuts the associated water consumption of the jugs by 60 to 70 percent compared to earlier jug designs because the new design does not require the use of milk crates. Milk crates typically become filthy during use due to spillage and other natural factors; thus, they are usually hosed down before reuse, consuming thousands of gallons of water. The new design also reduces fuel costs. Since crates are no longer used, they also do not have to be transported back to the dairy plant or farm distribution point for future shipments. Furthermore, the new jugs have the unexpected benefit of fitting better in modern home refrigerator doors and allow retailers to fit more of them in their in-store coolers. Breakthrough results like the new milk jug can result from comprehensive partnerships between users and their suppliers working to find innovative solutions.

Working with suppliers can result in opportunities that improve revenue. They can be the opportunity to turn waste products into sources of revenue. For example, a leading beverage manufacturer operates a recycling subsidiary that sources used aluminum cans from a large number of suppliers. The subsidiary actually processes more aluminum cans than are used in the company's own products, consequently developing a strong secondary revenue stream for the company.

In other cases, green sourcing can help establish entirely new lines of business to serve environmentally conscious customers. In the cleaning products aisle of a supermarket, shoppers will find numerous "green" cleaning product options from a variety of consumer products companies. These products typically use natural ingredients in lieu of chemicals, and many are in concentrated amounts to reduce overall packaging costs.

Logistics suppliers could find business opportunities coming directly to them as a result of the green trend. A large automobile manufacturer completed a project to green its logistics/distribution network. The automaker analyzed the shipping carriers, locations, and overall efficiency of its distribution network for

© AP Images/Tony Dejak

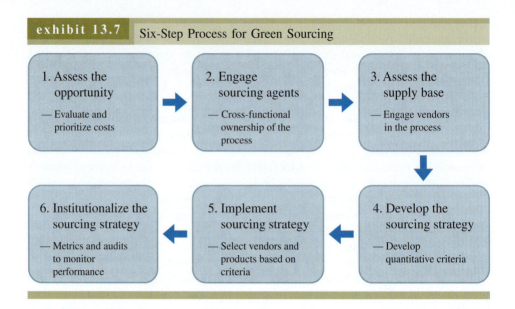

exhibit 13.7   Six-Step Process for Green Sourcing

1. Assess the opportunity
— Evaluate and prioritize costs

2. Engage sourcing agents
— Cross-functional ownership of the process

3. Assess the supply base
— Engage vendors in the process

4. Develop the sourcing strategy
— Develop quantitative criteria

5. Implement sourcing strategy
— Select vendors and products based on criteria

6. Institutionalize the sourcing strategy
— Metrics and audits to monitor performance

both parts and finished automobiles. By increasing the use of rail transportation for parts, consolidating shipments in fewer ports, and partnering with its logistics providers to increase fuel efficiency for both marine and road transportation, the company reduced its overall distribution-related carbon dioxide emissions by several thousand tons per year.

The following is an outline of a six-step process (see Exhibit 13.7) designed to transform a traditional process to a green-sourcing process:

1. **Assess the opportunity.**   For a given category of expense, all relevant costs need to be taken into account. The five most common areas include electricity and other energy costs; disposal and recycling; packaging; commodity substitution (alternative materials to replace materials such as steel or plastic); and water (or other related resources). These costs are identified and incorporated into an analysis of total cost (sometimes referred to as "spend" cost analysis) at this step. From this analysis, it is possible to prioritize the different costs based on the highest potential savings and criticality to the organization. This is important in directing effort to where it will likely have the most impact on the firm's financial position and cost-reduction goals.

2. **Engage internal supply chain sourcing agents.**   Internal sourcing agents are those within the firm that purchase items and have direct knowledge of business requirements, product specifications, and other internal perspectives inherent in the supply chain. These individuals and groups need to be "on-board" and be partners in the improvement process to help set realistic green goals. The goal of generating no waste, for example, becomes a cross-functional supply chain effort that relies heavily on finding and developing the right suppliers. These internal managers need to identify the most significant opportunities. They can develop a robust baseline model of what should be possible for reducing current and ongoing costs. In the case of procuring new equipment, for example, the baseline model would include not just the initial price of the equipment as in traditional sourcing, but also energy, disposal, recycling, and maintenance costs.

3. **Assess the supply base.** A sustainable sourcing process requires engaging new and existing vendors. As in traditional sourcing, the firm needs to understand vendor capabilities, constraints, and product offerings. The green process needs to be augmented with formal requirements that relate to green opportunities, including possible commodity substitutions and new manufacturing processes. These requirements need to be incorporated in vendor bid documents or the request for proposals (RFPs).

   A good example is concrete that uses fly ash, a by-product from coal-fired power plants. Fly ash can be substituted for Portland cement in ready-mix concrete or in concrete blocks to produce a stronger and lighter product with reduced water consumption. Fly ash substitution helps a company reduce its exposure to volatile and rapidly increasing prices for cement. At the same time, the reduced weight of the block lowers transportation costs to the company's new facilities. A company is also able to establish a specification incorporating fly ash for all new construction sites to follow. Finally, the substitution also helps power plants by providing a new market for fly ash, which previously had to be discarded.

FLY ASH IS GENERALLY STORED AT COAL POWER PLANTS OR PLACED IN LANDFILLS AS SHOWN HERE. ABOUT 43 PERCENT IS RECYCLED, REDUCING THE HARMFUL IMPACT ON THE ENVIRONMENT FROM LANDFILLS.

© AP Images/CAROLYN KASTER

4. **Develop the sourcing strategy.** The main goal with this step is to develop quantitative and qualitative criteria that will be used to evaluate the sourcing process. These are needed to properly analyze associated costs and benefits. These criteria need to be clearly articulated in bid documents and RFPs when working with potential suppliers so that their proposals will address relevant goals related to sustainability.

5. **Implement the sourcing strategy.** The evaluation criteria developed in step 4 should help in the selection of vendors and products for each business requirement. The evaluation process should consider initial cost and the total cost of ownership for the items in the bid. So, for example, energy-efficient equipment that is proposed with a higher initial cost may, over its productive life, actually result in a lower total cost due to energy savings and a related lower carbon footprint. Relevant green opportunities such as energy efficiency and waste reduction need to be modeled and then incorporated into the sourcing analysis to make it as comprehensive as possible and to facilitate an effective vendor selection process that supports the firm's needs.

6. **Institutionalize the sourcing strategy.** Once the vendor is selected and contracts finalized, the procurement process begins. Here, the sourcing and procurement department needs to define a set of metrics against which the supplier will be measured for the contract's duration. These metrics should be based on performance, delivery, compliance with pricing guidelines, and similar factors. It is vital that metrics that relate to the company's sustainability goals are considered as well. Periodic audits may also need to be incorporated in the process to directly observe practices that relate to these metrics to ensure honest reporting of data.

   A key aspect of green sourcing, compared to a traditional process, is the expanded view of the sourcing decision. This expanded view requires the incorporation of new criteria for evaluating alternatives. Further, it requires a wider range of internal integration such as designers, engineers, and marketers. Finally, visualizing and capturing the green-sourcing savings often involves greater complexity and longer payback periods compared to a traditional process.

TOTAL COST OF OWNERSHIP

LO13–3 Analyze the total cost of ownership.

Total cost of ownership (TCO)
Estimate of the cost of an item that includes all the costs related to the procurement and use of the item including disposing of the item after its useful life.

The **total cost of ownership (TCO)** is an estimate of the cost of an item that includes all the costs related to the procurement and use of an item, including any related costs in disposing of the item after it is no longer useful. The concept can be applied to a company's internal costs or it can be viewed more broadly to consider costs throughout the supply chain. To fully appreciate the cost of purchasing an item from a particular vendor, an approach that captures the costs of the activities associated with purchasing and actually using the item should be considered. Depending on the complexity of the purchasing process, activities such as pre-bid conferences, visits by potential suppliers, and even visits to potential suppliers can significantly impact the total cost of the item.

A TCO analysis is highly dependent on the actual situation; in general, though, the costs outlined in Exhibit 13.8 should be considered. The costs can be categorized into three broad areas: acquisition costs, ownership costs, and post-ownership costs. Acquisition costs are the initial costs associated with the purchase of materials, products, and services. They are not long-term costs of ownership but represent an immediate cash outflow. Acquisition costs include the prepurchase costs associated with preparing documents to distribute to potential suppliers, identifying suppliers and evaluating suppliers, and other costs associated with actually procuring the item. The actual purchase prices, including taxes, tariffs, and transportation costs, are also included.

Ownership costs are incurred after the initial purchase and are associated with the ongoing use of the product or material. Examples of costs that are quantifiable include energy usage, scheduled maintenance, repair, and financing (leasing situation). There can also be qualitative costs such as aesthetic factors (e.g., the item is pleasing to the eye), and ergonomic factors (e.g., productivity improvement or reducing fatigue). These ownership costs can often exceed the initial purchase price and have an impact on cash flow, profitability, and even employee morale and productivity.

Major costs associated with post-ownership include salvage value and disposal costs. For many purchases, there are established markets that provide data to help estimate reasonable future values, such as the *Kelley Blue Book* for used automobiles. Other areas that can be included are the long-term environmental impact (particularly when the firm has sustainability goals), warranty and product liabilities, and the negative marketing impact of low customer satisfaction with the item.

Overemphasis on acquisition cost or purchase price frequently results in failure to address other significant ownership and post-ownership costs. TCO is a philosophy for understanding all relevant costs of doing business with a particular supplier for a good or service. It is relevant not only for a business that wants to reduce its cost of doing business but also for a firm that aims to design products or services that provide the lowest total cost of ownership to customers. For example, some automobile manufacturers have extended the tune-up interval on many models to 100,000 miles, thereby reducing vehicle operating cost for car owners. Viewing TCO in this way can lead to an increased value of the product to existing and potential customers.

Total Cost of Ownership   exhibit 13.8

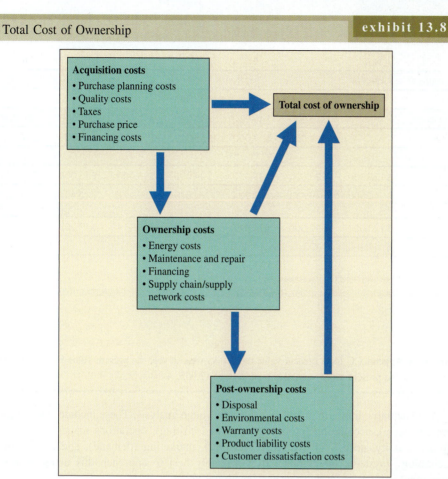

These costs can be estimated as cash inflows (the sale of used equipment, etc.) or outflows (such as purchase prices, demolition of an obsolete facility, etc.). The following example shows how this analysis can be organized using a spreadsheet. Keep in mind that the costs considered need to be adapted to the decision being made. Costs that do not vary based on the decision need not be considered, but relevant costs that vary depending on the decision should be included in the analysis.

Example 13.1: Total Cost of Ownership Analysis

Consider the analysis of the purchase of a copy machine as might be used in a copy center. The machine has an initial cost of $120,000 and is expected to generate income of $40,000 per year. Supplies are expected to be $7,000 per year and the machine needs to be overhauled during year 3 at a cost of $9,000. It has a salvage value of $7,500 when we plan to sell it at year 6.

SOLUTION

Laying out these costs over time can lead to the use of net present value analysis to evaluate the decision. Consider Exhibit 13.9, where the present values of each yearly stream are discounted to

exhibit 13.9   Analysis of the Purchase of an Office Copier

YEAR	NOW	1	2	3	4	5	6
Cost of copier including installation	−$120,000						
Manufacturer required overhaul				−$ 9,000			
Cash inflows from using the machine		$40,000	$40,000	$40,000	$40,000	$40,000	$40,000
Supplies needed to use the machine		−$ 7,000	−$ 7,000	−$ 7,000	−$ 7,000	−$ 7,000	−$ 7,000
Salvage value							$ 7,500
Total of annual streams	−$120,000	$33,000	$33,000	$24,000	$33,000	$33,000	$40,500
Discount factor from Appendix C (1 + .2)^−Year	1.000	0.833	0.694	0.579	0.482	0.402	0.335
Present value − yearly	−$120,000	$27,500	$22,917	$13,889	$15,914	$13,262	$13,563
Present value	−$ 12,955						

Discount factor = 20%.
Note: These calculations were done using the full precision of a spreadsheet.

now. (See Appendix C for a present value table.) As we can see, the present value in this analysis shows that the present value cost of the copier is $12,955. ·

TCO actually draws on many areas for a thorough analysis. These include finance (net present value), accounting (product pricing and costing), operations management (reliability, quality, need, and inventory planning), marketing (demand), and information technology (systems integration). It is probably best to approach this using a cross-functional team representing the key functional areas.

It is important that any analysis is adapted to the particular scenario. Such factors as exchange rates, the risk of doing business in a particular region of the world, transportation, and other items are often important. Depending on the alternatives, there are a host of factors, often going beyond cost, that need to be considered. Adapting this type of cost analysis and combining it with a more qualitative risk analysis are useful in actual company situations.

MEASURING SOURCING PERFORMANCE

LO13–4 Evaluate sourcing performance.

One view of sourcing is centered on the inventories that are positioned in the system. Exhibit 13.10 shows how hamburger meat and potatoes are stored in various locations in a typical fast-food restaurant chain. Here we see the steps that the beef and potatoes move through on their way to the local retail store and then to the customer. Inventory is carried at each step, and this inventory has a particular cost to the company. Inventory serves as a buffer, thus allowing each stage to operate independently of the others. For example, the distribution center inventory allows the system that supplies the retail stores to operate independently of the meat and potato packing operations. Because the inventory at each stage ties up money, it is important that the operations at each stage are synchronized to minimize the size of these buffer inventories. The efficiency of the supply chain can be measured based on the size of the inventory investment in the supply

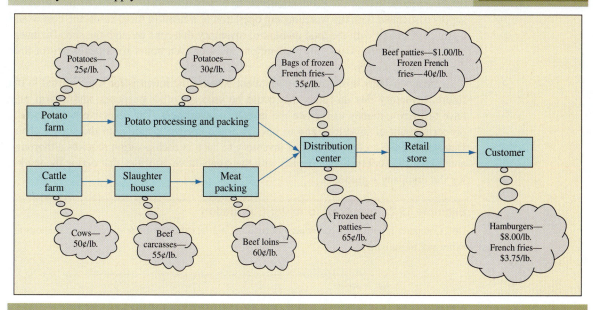

Inventory in the Supply Chain—Fast-Food Restaurant   exhibit 13.10

chain. The inventory investment is measured relative to the total cost of the goods provided through the supply chain.

Two common measures to evaluate supply chain efficiency are *inventory turnover* and *weeks-of-supply*. **Inventory turnover** is calculated as follows:

$$\text{Inventory turnover} = \frac{\text{Cost of goods sold}}{\text{Average aggregate inventory value}} \qquad [13.1]$$

The **cost of goods sold** is the annual cost for a company to produce the goods or services provided to customers; it is sometimes referred to as the *cost of revenue*. This does not include the selling and administrative expenses of the company. The **average aggregate inventory value** is the average total value of all items held in inventory for the firm valued at cost. It includes the raw material, work-in-process, finished goods, and distribution inventory considered owned by the company.

Good inventory turnover values vary by industry and the type of products being handled. At one extreme, a grocery store chain may turn inventory over 100 times per year. Values of six to seven are typical for manufacturing firms.

In many situations, particularly when distribution inventory is dominant, **weeks of supply** is the preferred measure. This is a measure of how many weeks' worth of inventory is in the system at a particular point in time. The calculation is as follows:

$$\text{Weeks of supply} = \left(\frac{\text{Average aggregate inventory value}}{\text{Cost of goods sold}} \right) \times 52 \text{ weeks} \qquad [13.2]$$

When company financial reports cite inventory turnover and weeks of supply, we can assume that the measures are being calculated firmwide. We show an example of this type of calculation in the example that follows using Dell Computer data. These calculations,

Inventory turnover
A measure of supply chain efficiency.

Cost of goods sold
The annual cost for a company to produce the goods or services provided to customers.

Average aggregate inventory value
The average total value of all items held in inventory for the firm, valued at cost.

Weeks of supply
Preferred measure of supply chain efficiency that is mathematically the inverse of inventory turn times 52.

though, can be done for individual entities within the organization. For example, we might be interested in the production raw materials inventory turnover or the weeks of supply associated with the warehousing operation of a firm. In these cases, the cost would be that associated with the total amount of inventory that runs through the specific inventory. In some very-low-inventory operations, days or even hours are a better unit of time for measuring supply.

A firm considers inventory an investment because the intent is for it to be used in the future. Inventory ties up funds that could be used for other purposes, and a firm may have to borrow money to finance the inventory investment. The objective is to have the proper amount of inventory and to have it in the correct locations in the supply chain. Determining the correct amount of inventory to have in each position requires a thorough analysis of the supply chain coupled with the competitive priorities that define the market for the company's products.

Example 13.2: Inventory Turnover Calculation

Dell Computer reported the following information in a recent annual report (all dollar amounts are expressed in millions):

Net revenue	$49,205
Cost of revenue	$40,190
Production materials on-hand	$ 228
Work-in-process and finished goods on-hand	$ 231
Days of supply in inventory	4 days

The cost of revenue corresponds to what we call cost of goods sold. One might think that U.S. companies, at least, would use a common accounting terminology, but this is not true. The inventory turnover calculation is

$$\text{Inventory turnover} = \frac{40,190}{228 + 231} = 87.56 \text{ turns per year}$$

This is amazing performance for a high-tech company, but it explains much of why the company is such a financial success.

The corresponding weeks of supply calculation is

$$\text{Weeks of supply} = \left(\frac{228 + 231}{40,190}\right) \times 52 = .59 \text{ week} \quad \bullet$$

CONCEPT CONNECTIONS

LO13–1 Explain what strategic sourcing is.

- Sourcing is a term that captures the strategic nature of purchasing in today's global and Internet connected marketplace.
- The sourcing/purchasing design matrix captures the scope of the topic that ranges from one-time spot purchases, to a complex strategic alliance arrangement with another firm.
- A phenomenon known as the bullwhip effect has been observed in many industries. This is when changes in demand are magnified as they move from the customer to the manufacturer. The phenomenon is caused by long lead times and the fact that there are often multiple stages in a supply chain.

- Supply chains can be categorized based on demand and supply uncertainty characteristics. Four types of supply chains are identified: (1) efficient, (2) risk-hedging, (3) responsive, and (4) agile.

Strategic sourcing   The development and management of supplier relationships to acquire goods and services in a way that aids in achieving the needs of a business.

Sourcing   A process suitable for procuring products that are strategically important to the firm.

Specificity   Refers to how commonly available the material is and whether substitutes can be used.

Request for proposal (RFP)   A solicitation that asks for a detailed proposal from a vendor interested in supplying an item.

Vendor managed inventory   When a customer allows the supplier to manage the inventory policy of an item or group of items.

Forward buying   A term that refers to when a customer, responding to a promotion, buys far in advance of when an item will be used.

Bullwhip effect   The variability in demand is magnified as we move from the customer to the producer in the supply chain.

Continuous replenishment   A program for automatically supplying groups of items to a customer on a regular basis.

Functional products   Staples that people buy in a wide range of retail outlets, such as grocery stores and gas stations.

Innovative products   Products such as fashionable clothes and high-end personal computers that typically have a life cycle of just a few months.

Stable supply process   A process where the underlying technology is stable.

Evolving supply process   A process where the underlying technology changes rapidly.

LO13–2 **Explain why companies outsource processes.**

- Outsourcing is when a firm contracts with an outside provider for activities essential to the firm's success.
- The transportation of a firm's products (referred to as logistics) is often outsourced.
- Whether an activity is outsourced or not often depends on criteria related to (1) coordination requirements, (2) strategic control, and (3) intellectual property issues.
- Green sourcing has become an imperative for many firms and it may create new markets for a firm's products.

Outsourcing   Moving some of a firm's internal activities and decision responsibility to an outside provider.

Logistics   Management functions that support the complete cycle of material flow: from the purchase and internal control of production materials; to the planning and control of work-in-process; to the purchasing, shipping, and distribution of the finished product.

LO13–3 **Analyze the total cost of ownership.**

- This is an approach to understanding the total cost of an item.
- Costs can generally be categorized into three areas: (1) acquisition costs, (2) ownership costs, and (3) post-ownership costs.

Total cost of ownership (TCO)   Estimate of the cost of an item that includes all the costs related to the procurement and use of the item including disposing of the item after its useful life.

LO13–4   **Evaluate sourcing performance.**

- Inventory turn and weeks of supply are the most common measures to evaluate supply chain efficiency. These measures can vary greatly depending on the industry.

Inventory turnover   A measure of supply chain efficiency.

Cost of goods sold   The annual cost for a company to produce the goods or services provided to customers.

Average aggregate inventory value   The average total value of all items held in inventory for the firm, valued at cost.

Weeks of supply   Preferred measure of supply chain efficiency that is mathematically the inverse of inventory turn times 52.

$$\text{Inventory turnover} = \frac{\text{Cost of goods sold}}{\text{Average aggregate inventory value}} \qquad [13.1]$$

$$\text{Weeks of supply} = \left(\frac{\text{Average aggregate inventory value}}{\text{Cost of goods sold}} \right) \times 52 \text{ weeks} \qquad [13.2]$$

DISCUSSION QUESTIONS

LO13–1
1. What recent changes have caused supply chain management to gain importance?
2. Describe the differences between functional and innovative products.
3. What are characteristics of efficient, responsive, risk-hedging, and agile supply chains? Can a supply chain be both efficient and responsive? Risk-hedging and agile? Why or why not?

LO13–2
4. With so much productive capacity and room for expansion in the United States, why would a company based in the United States choose to purchase items from a foreign firm? Discuss the pros and cons.
5. As a supplier, which factors about a buyer (your potential customer) would you consider to be important in setting up a long-term relationship?
6. Describe how outsourcing works. Why would a firm want to outsource?

LO13–3
7. Have you ever purchased a product based on purchase price alone and were surprised by the eventual TCO, either in money or in time? Describe the situation.
8. Why might managers resist buying a more expensive piece of equipment, known to have a lower TCO, than a less expensive item?

LO13–4
9. Why is it desirable to increase a company's inventory turnover ratio?
10. Research and compare the inventory turnover ratios of three large retailers: Walmart, Target, and Nordstrom. Use the same financial Website for all three, and compare numbers from the same time frame. What do these ratios tell you? Are you surprised by what you found?

OBJECTIVE QUESTIONS

LO13–1

1. What term refers to the development and management of supplier relationships in order to acquire goods and services in a way that helps achieve the immediate needs of a business?

2. Sometimes a company may need to purchase goods or services that are unique, very complex, and/or extremely expensive. These would not be routine purchases, but there may be a number of vendors that could supply what is needed. What process would be used to transmit the company's needs to the available vendors, asking for a detailed response to the needs?

3. Sony Electronics produces a wide variety of electronic products for the consumer marketplace, such as laptop computers, PlayStation game consoles, and tablet computers. What type of products would these be considered in the Supply Chain Uncertainty Framework?

4. One product that Staples sells a lot of is copy paper. According to the Supply Chain Uncertainty Framework, what supply chain strategy is appropriate for this product?

LO13–2

5. What is the term used for the act of moving some of a company's internal activities and decision-making processes to outside providers?

6. What is the term used for a company moving management of the complete cycle of material flow to an outside provider?

7. Many bottled water manufacturers have recently worked with their suppliers to switch over to bottles using much less plastic than before, reducing the amount of plastic that needs to be transported, recycled, and/or disposed of. What sourcing practice is this an example of?

8. What term is used to refer to those activities that are the key source of competitive advantage?

LO13–3

9. What three main categories of costs are considered in figuring the total cost of ownership?

10. Which category of lifetime product costs are sometimes overemphasized, leading to a failure to fully recognize the total cost of ownership?

11. One of your Taiwanese suppliers has bid on a new line of molded plastic parts that is currently being assembled at your plant. The supplier has bid $0.10 per part, given a forecast you provided of 200,000 parts in year 1; 300,000 in year 2; and 500,000 in year 3. Shipping and handling of parts from the supplier's factory is estimated at $0.01 per unit. Additional inventory handling charges should amount to $0.005 per unit. Finally, administrative costs are estimated at $20 per month.

    Although your plant is able to continue producing the part, the plant would need to invest in another molding machine, which would cost $10,000. Direct materials can be purchased for $0.05 per unit. Direct labor is estimated at $0.03 per unit plus a 50 percent surcharge for benefits; indirect labor is estimated at $0.011 per unit plus 50 percent benefits. Up-front engineering and design costs will amount to $30,000. Finally, management has insisted that overhead be allocated if the parts are made in-house at a rate of 100 percent of direct labor cost. The firm uses a cost of capital of 15 percent per year.

    What should you do, continue to produce in-house or accept the bid from your Taiwanese supplier?

12. Your company assembles five different models of a motor scooter that is sold in specialty stores in the United States. The company uses the same engine for all five models. You have been given the assignment of choosing a supplier for

these engines for the coming year. Due to the size of your warehouse and other administrative restrictions, you must order the engines in lot sizes of 1,000 each. Because of the unique characteristics of the engine, special tooling is needed during the manufacturing process for which you agree to reimburse the supplier. Your assistant has obtained quotes from two reliable engine suppliers and you need to decide which to use. The following data have been collected:

Requirements (annual forecast)	12,000 units
Weight per engine	22 pounds
Order processing cost	$125 per order
Inventory carry cost	20 percent of the average value of inventory per year

Note: Assume that half of the lot size is in inventory, on average (1,000/2 = 500 units).

Two qualified suppliers have submitted the following quotations:

ORDER QUANTITY	SUPPLIER 1 UNIT PRICE	SUPPLIER 2 UNIT PRICE
1 to 1,499 units/order	$510.00	$505.00
1,500 to 2,999 units/order	500.00	$505.00
3,000+ units/order	490.00	488.00
Tooling costs	$22,000	$20,000
Distance	125 miles	100 miles

Your assistant has obtained the following freight rates from your carrier:

Truckload (40,000 lb. each load):	$0.80 per ton-mile
Less-than-truckload:	$1.20 per ton-mile

Note: Per ton-mile = 2,000 lb. per mile

    a. Perform a total cost of ownership analysis and select a supplier.
    b. Would it make economic sense to order in truckload quantities? Would your supplier selection change if you ordered truckload quantities?

 13. Which supply chain efficiency measure is more appropriate when the majority of inventory is held in distribution channels?
  14. What do you call the average total value of all items held in inventory for a firm, at cost?
  15. The owner of a large machine shop has just finished its financial analysis from the prior fiscal year. Following is an excerpt from the final report:

Net revenue	$375,000
Cost of goods sold	322,000
Value of production materials on-hand	42,500
Value of work-in-process inventory	37,000
Value of finished goods on-hand	12,500

    a. Compute the inventory turnover ratio (ITR).
    b. Compute the weeks of supply (WS).
  16. The McDonald's fast-food restaurant on campus sells an average of 4,000 quarter-pound hamburgers each week. Hamburger patties are resupplied twice a week, and on average the store has 350 pounds of hamburger in stock. Assume that the hamburger patties cost $1.00 a pound. What is the inventory turnover for the hamburger patties? On average, how many days of supply are on-hand?
  17. U.S. Airfilter has hired you as a supply chain consultant. The company makes air filters for residential heating and air-conditioning systems. These filters are

made in a single plant located in Louisville, Kentucky, in the United States. They are distributed to retailers through wholesale centers in 100 locations in the United States, Canada, and Europe. You have collected the following data relating to the value of inventory in the U.S. Airfilter supply chain:

	QUARTER 1 (JANUARY THROUGH MARCH)	QUARTER 2 (APRIL THROUGH JUNE)	QUARTER 3 (JULY THROUGH SEPTEMBER)	QUARTER 4 (OCTOBER THROUGH DECEMBER)
Sales (total quarter):				
United States	300	350	405	375
Canada	75	60	75	70
Europe	30	33	20	15
Cost of goods sold (total quarter)	280	295	340	350
Raw materials at the Louisville plant (end-of-quarter)	50	40	55	60
Work-in-process and finished goods at the Louisville plant (end-of-quarter)	100	105	120	150
Distribution center inventory (end-of-quarter):				
United States	25	27	23	30
Canada	10	11	15	16
Europe	5	4	5	5

All amounts in millions of U.S. dollars.

a. What is the average inventory turnover for the firm?
b. If you were given the assignment to increase inventory turnover, what would you focus on? Why?
c. The company reported that it used $500M worth of raw material during the year. On average, how many weeks of supply of raw material are on-hand at the factory?

ANALYTICS EXERCISE: GLOBAL SOURCING DECISIONS— GRAINGER: REENGINEERING THE CHINA/ U.S. SUPPLY CHAIN

W. W. Grainger, Inc., is a leading supplier of maintenance, repair, and operating (MRO) products to businesses and institutions in the United States, Canada, and Mexico with an expanding presence in Japan, India, China, and Panama. The company works with more than 3,000 suppliers and runs an extensive Website (www.grainger.com), where it offers nearly 900,000 products. The products range from industrial adhesives used in manufacturing, to hand tools, janitorial supplies, lighting equipment, and power tools. When something is needed by one of its 1.8 million customers, it is often needed quickly, so quick service and product availability are key drivers to Grainger's success.

Your assignment involves studying a specific part of Grainger's supply chain. Grainger works with over 250 suppliers in the China and Taiwan region. These suppliers produce products to Grainger's specifications and ship to the United States using ocean freight carriers from four major ports in China and Taiwan. From these ports, product is shipped to U.S. entry ports in either Seattle, Washington, or Los Angeles, California. After passing through customs, the 20- and 40-foot containers are shipped by rail to Grainger's central distribution center in Kansas City, Kansas. The containers are unloaded and quality is checked in Kansas City. From there, individual items are sent to

regional warehouses in nine U.S. locations, a Canadian site, and Mexico.

The Current China/Taiwan Logistics Arrangement

The contracts that Grainger has with Chinese and Taiwanese suppliers currently specify that the supplier owns the product and is responsible for all costs incurred until the product is delivered to the shipping port. These are commonly referred to as free on board (FOB) shipping port contracts. Grainger works with a freight forwarding company that coordinates all shipments from the Asian suppliers.

Currently, suppliers have the option of either shipping product on pallets to consolidation centers at the port locations or packing the product in 20- and 40-foot containers that are loaded directly on the ships bound for the United States. In many cases, the volume from a supplier is relatively small and will not sufficiently fill a container. The consolidation centers are where individual pallets are loaded into the containers that protect the product while being shipped across the Pacific Ocean and then to Grainger's Kansas City distribution center. The freight forwarding company coordinates the efficient shipping of the 20- and 40-foot containers. These are the same containers that are loaded onto rail cars in the United States.

Currently, about 190,000 cubic meters of material are shipped annually from China and Taiwan. This is expected to grow about 15 percent per year over the next five years. About 89 percent of all the volume shipped from China and Taiwan are sent directly from the suppliers in 20- and 40-foot containers that are packed by the supplier at the supplier site.

Approximately 21 percent are packed in the 20-foot containers and 79 percent in 40-foot containers. The 20-foot containers can hold 34 cubic meters (CBM) of material and the 40-foot containers, 67 CBM. The cost to ship a 20-foot container is $480 and a 40-foot container, $600 from any port location in China or Taiwan and to either Los Angeles or Seattle. Grainger estimates that these supplier-filled containers average 85 percent full when they are shipped.

The remaining 11 percent shipped from China and Taiwan go through consolidation centers that are located at each port. These consolidation centers are run by the freight forwarding company and cost about $75,000 per year each to operate. At the volumes that are currently running through these centers, the variable cost is $4.90 per CBM. The variable cost of running a consolidation center could be reduced to about $1.40 per CBM using technology if the volume could be increased to at least 50,000 CBM per year. Now there is much variability in the volume run at each center and it only averages about 5,000 CBM per site.

Material at the consolidation centers is accumulated on an ongoing basis and as containers are filled they are sent to the port. Volume is sufficient that at least one 40-foot container is shipped from each consolidation center each week. Grainger has found that the consolidation centers can load all material into 40-foot containers and utilize 96 percent of the capacity of the container.

Grainger ships from four major port locations. Approximately 10 percent of the volume is shipped from the north China port of Qingdao and 42 percent is shipped from the central China port of Shanghai/Ningbo. Another 10 percent is shipped from Kaohsiung in Taiwan. The final 38 percent is shipped from the southern Yantian/Hong Kong port. Consolidation centers are currently run in each location.

Grainger management feels that it may be possible to make this part of its supply chain more efficient.

Specific Questions to Address in Your Analysis

1. Evaluate the current China/Taiwan logistics costs. Assume a current total volume of 190,000 CBM and that 89 percent is shipped direct from the supplier plants in containers. Use the data from the case and assume that the supplier-loaded containers are 85 percent full. Assume that consolidation centers are run at each of the four port locations. The consolidation centers use only 40-foot containers and fill them to 96 percent capacity. Assume that it costs $480 to ship a 20-foot container and $600 to ship a 40-foot container. What is the total cost to get the containers to the United States? Do not include U.S. port costs in this part of the analysis.

2. Evaluate an alternative that involves consolidating all 20-foot container volume and using only a single consolidation center in Shanghai/Ningbo. Assume that all the existing 20-foot container volume and the existing

consolidation center volume is sent to this single consolidation center by suppliers. This new consolidation center volume would be packed into 40-foot containers filled to 96 percent and shipped to the United States. The existing 40-foot volume would still be shipped direct from the suppliers at 85 percent capacity utilization.

3. What should be done based on your analytics analysis? What have you not considered that may make your analysis invalid or that may strategically limit success? What do you think Grainger management should do?

Many thanks to Gary Scalzitti of Grainger for help with developing this case.

PRACTICE EXAM

1. Refers to how common an item is or how many substitutes might be available.
2. When a customer allows the supplier to manage inventory policy for an item or group of items.
3. A phenomenon characterized by increased variation in ordering as we move from the customer to the manufacturer in the supply chain.
4. Products that satisfy basic needs and do not change much over time.
5. Products with short life cycles and typically high profit margins.
6. A supply chain that must deal with high levels of both supply and demand uncertainty.
7. In order to cope with high levels of supply uncertainty, a firm would use this strategy to reduce risk.
8. Used to describe functions related to the flow of material in a supply chain.
9. When a firm works with suppliers to look for opportunities to save money and benefit the environment.
10. Refers to an estimate of the cost of an item that includes all costs related to the procurement and use of an item, including the costs of disposing after its useful life.

Answers to Practice Exam 1. Specificity 2. Vendor managed inventory 3. Bullwhip effect 4. Functional products 5. Innovative products 6. Agile supply chain 7. Multiple sources of supply (pooling) 8. Logistics 9. Green sourcing 10. Total cost of ownership

CHAPTER 14

LOCATION, LOGISTICS, AND DISTRIBUTION

Learning Objectives

LO14–1 Explain what logistics is.

LO14–2 Contrast logistics and warehouse design alternatives.

LO14–3 Analyze logistics-driven location decisions.

PANAMA CANAL WIDENING MAY IMPACT FLOW OF GOODS TO UNITED STATES

Right now, about 70 percent of U.S. imports from Asia arrive by ship on the West Coast, and much of that gets transferred by rail to the rest of the country. It takes about 18 days to make the ship and train journey from Asia to the West Coast and then across the country to East Coast businesses. An alternative is the all-water route through the Panama Canal, which takes about 22 days. Taking the all-water route takes longer but can cost up to 25 percent less than the ship and train route.

The Panama Canal, completed in 1914, was one of the largest and most difficult engineering projects ever completed. The canal was built to accommodate the ships of that time. These vessels were much smaller than today's super container vessels, which are too large to pass through the canal's narrow locks.

This will all change when a much wider lane of locks opens. The new locks will allow today's largest container vessels to pass through. The economies of using these vessels will make the water route look even more attractive, at least from a cost view. Many logistics experts are calling the expansion a major game-changer and a threat to the Western ports and railroads.

© EvrenKalinbacak/Getty Images RF

LOGISTICS

A major issue in designing a great supply chain for manufactured goods is determining the way those items are moved from the manufacturing plant to the customer. For consumer products, this often involves moving product from the manufacturing plant to a warehouse and then to a retail store. You probably do not think about this often, but consider items such as a sweatshirt with "Made in China" on the label. That sweatshirt probably has made a trip longer than you may ever make. If you live in Chicago in the United States and the sweatshirt is made in the Fujian region of China, that sweatshirt traveled over 6,600 miles, or 10,600 kilometers, nearly halfway around the world, to get to the retail store where you bought it. To keep the price of the sweatshirt down, that trip must be made as efficiently as possible. There is no telling how that sweatshirt made the trip. It might have been flown in an airplane or might have traveled in a combination of vehicles, possibly going by truck part of the way and by boat or plane the rest. Logistics is about this movement of goods through the supply chain.

APICS, the supply chain and operations professional organization, defines **logistics** as "the art and science of obtaining, producing, and distributing material and product to the proper place and in proper quantities." This is a fairly broad definition, and this chapter will focus on how to analyze where we locate warehouses and plants and how

LO14–1 Explain what logistics is.

Logistics
The art and science of obtaining, producing, and distributing material and product to the proper place and in the proper quantities.

International logistics
All functions
concerned with
the movement of
materials and
finished goods on
a global scale.

to evaluate the movement of materials to and from those locations. The term **international logistics** refers to managing these functions when the movement is on a global scale. Clearly, if the China-made sweatshirt is sold in the United States or Europe, this involves international logistics.

There are companies that specialize in logistics, such as United Parcel Service (UPS), Federal Express (FedEx), and DHL. These global companies are in the business of moving everything from flowers to industrial equipment. Today, a manufacturing company most often will contract with one of those companies to handle many of its logistics functions. In this case, those transportation companies often are called a **third-party logistics company**. The most basic function would be simply moving the goods from one place to another. The logistics company also may provide additional services such as warehouse management, inventory control, and other customer service functions.

Third-party logistics company
A company that
manages all or part
of another
company's product
delivery operations.

Logistics is big business, accounting for 8 to 9 percent of the U.S. gross domestic product, and growing. Today's modern, efficient warehouse and distribution centers are the heart of logistics. These centers are carefully managed and efficiently operated to ensure the secure storage and quick flow of goods, services, and related information from the point of origin to the point of consumption.

DECISIONS RELATED TO LOGISTICS

LO14–2 Contrast
logistics and
warehouse design
alternatives.

The problem of deciding how best to transport goods from plants to customers is a complex one that affects the cost of a product. Major trade-offs related to the cost of transporting the product, speed of delivery, and flexibility in reacting to changes in demand are involved. Information systems play a major role in coordinating activities and include activities such as allocating resources, managing inventory levels, scheduling, and order tracking. A full discussion of these systems is beyond the scope of this book, but we cover basic inventory control in other chapters.

Transportation Modes

A key decision area is deciding how material will be transported. The Logistics-System Design Matrix shown in Exhibit 14.1 depicts the basic alternatives. There are six widely recognized modes of transportation: highway (trucks), water (ships), air (aircraft), rail (trains), pipelines, and hand delivery. Each mode is uniquely suited to handle certain types of products, as described next:

- **Highway (truck).** Actually, few products are moved without some highway transportation. The highway offers great flexibility for moving goods to virtually any location not separated by water. Size of the product, weight, and liquid or bulk can all be accommodated with this mode.
- **Water (ship).** Ships have very high capacity, and operating costs relative to this capacity are very low, but transit times are slow, and large areas of the world are not directly accessible to water carriers. This mode is especially useful for bulk items such as oil, coal, and chemical products.
- **Air.** Planes are fast but very expensive to operate. Small, light, expensive items are most appropriate for this mode of transportation.
- **Rail (trains).** This is a fairly low-cost alternative, but transit times can be long and may be subject to variability. The suitability of rail can vary depending on the rail infrastructure. The European infrastructure is highly developed, making this an attractive alternative compared to trucks, while in the United States, the infrastructure has declined over the last 50 years, making it less attractive.
- **Pipelines.** This is highly specialized and limited to liquids, gases, and solids in slurry forms. No packaging is needed and the costs per mile are low. The initial cost to build a pipeline is very high.
- **Hand Delivery.** This is the last step in many supply chains. Getting the product in the customer's hand is often a slow and costly activity due to the high labor content.

Logistics-System Design Matrix: Framework Describing Logistics Processes   **exhibit 14.1**

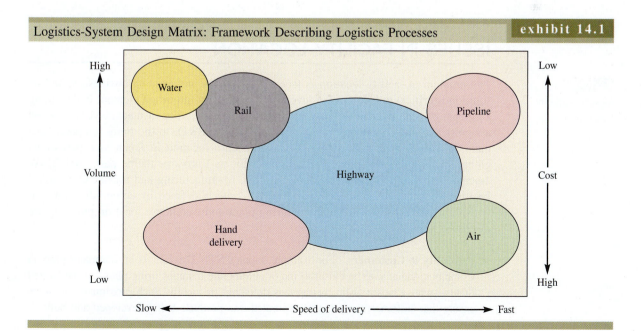

Few companies use a single mode of transportation. Multimodal solutions are the norm, and finding the correct multimode strategies can be a significant problem. The problem of coordination and scheduling the carriers requires comprehensive information systems capable of tracking goods through the system. Standardized containers often are used so that a product can be transferred efficiently from a truck to an airplane or ship.

Warehouse Design

Cross-docking
An approach used in consolidation warehouses where, rather than making larger shipments, incoming shipments are broken down into small shipments for local delivery in an area.

Special consolidation warehouses are used when shipments from various sources are pulled together and combined into larger shipments with a common destination. This improves the efficiency of the entire system. **Cross-docking** is an approach used in these consolidation warehouses, where, rather than making larger shipments, incoming shipments are broken down into small shipments for local delivery in an area. This often can be done in a coordinated manner so that the goods never are stored in inventory.

Retailers receive shipments from many suppliers in their regional warehouses and immediately sort those shipments for delivery to individual stores by using cross-docking systems coordinated by computerized control systems. This results in a minimal amount of inventory being carried in the warehouses.

Hub-and-spoke systems
Systems that combine the idea of consolidation and that of cross-docking.

Hub-and-spoke systems combine the idea of consolidation and that of cross-docking. Here, the warehouse is referred to as a "hub" and its sole purpose is sorting goods. Incoming goods are sorted immediately to consolidation areas, where each area is designated for shipment to a specific location. Hubs are located in strategic locations near the geographic center of the region they are to serve so as to minimize the distance a good must travel.

Designing a system is an interesting and complex task. The following section focuses on the plant and warehouse location problem as representative of the types of logistics decisions that need to be made. Logistics is a broad topic, and its elements evolve as the value-added services provided by major logistics vendors expand. Having the proper network design is fundamental to efficiency in the industry.

ISSUES IN FACILITY LOCATION

LO14–3 Analyze logistics-driven location decisions.

The problem of facility location is faced by both new and existing businesses, and its solution is critical to a company's eventual success. An important element in designing a company's supply chain is the location of its facilities. For instance, 3M has moved a significant part of its corporate activity, including R&D, to the more temperate climate of Austin, Texas. Toys "Я" Us has opened a location in Japan as a part of its global strategy. Disney chose Paris, France, for its European theme park, and BMW assembles the Z3 sports car in South Carolina. Manufacturing and service companies' location decisions are guided by a variety of criteria defined by competitive imperatives. Criteria that influence manufacturing plant and warehouse location planning are discussed next.

Proximity to Customers   For example, Japan's NTN Driveshafts built a major plant in Columbus, Indiana, to be closer to major automobile manufacturing plants in the United States—whose buyers want their goods delivered frequently. Such proximity also helps ensure that customer needs are incorporated into products being developed and built.

Business Climate   A favorable business climate can include the presence of similar-sized businesses, the presence of companies in the same industry, and, in the case of international locations, the presence of other foreign companies. Pro-business government legislation and local government intervention to facilitate businesses locating in an area via subsidies, tax abatements, and other support are also factors.

Total Costs   The objective is to select a site with the lowest total cost. This includes regional costs, inbound distribution costs, and outbound distribution costs. Land, construction, labor, taxes, and energy costs make up the regional costs. In addition, there are hidden costs that are difficult to measure. These involve (1) excessive moving of preproduction material between locations before final delivery to the customers and (2) loss of customer responsiveness arising from locating away from the main customer base.

Infrastructure   Adequate road, rail, air, and sea transportation is vital. Energy and telecommunications requirements also must be met. In addition, the local government's willingness to invest in upgrading infrastructure to the levels required may be an incentive to select a specific location.

Quality of Labor   The educational and skill levels of the labor pool must match the company's needs. Even more important are their willingness and ability to learn.

Suppliers   A high-quality and competitive supplier base makes a given location suitable. The proximity of important suppliers' plants also supports lean production methods.

Other Facilities   The location of other plants or distribution centers of the same company may influence a new facility's location in the network. Issues of product mix and capacity are strongly interconnected to the location decision in this context.

Free Trade Zones   A foreign trade zone or a **free trade zone** is typically a closed facility (under the supervision of the customs department) into which foreign goods can be brought without being subject to the normal customs requirements. There are about 260 such free trade zones in the United States today. Such specialized locations also exist in other countries. Manufacturers in free trade zones can employ imported components used in the production of the final product and delay the payment of customs duties until the product is shipped into the host country.

Political Risk   The fast-changing geopolitical scenes in numerous nations present exciting, challenging opportunities. But the extended phase of transformation that many countries are undergoing makes the decision to locate in those areas extremely difficult. Political risks in both the country of location and the host country influence location decisions.

Government Barriers   Barriers to enter and locate in many countries are being removed today through legislation. Yet many nonlegislative and cultural barriers should be considered in location planning.

Trading Blocs   The Central America Free Trade Agreement (CAFTA) is one of the new **trading blocs** in our hemisphere. Such agreements influence location decisions, both within and outside trading bloc countries. Firms typically locate, or relocate, within a bloc to take advantage of new market opportunities or the lower total costs afforded by the trading agreement. Other companies (those outside the trading bloc countries) decide on locations within the bloc so as not to be disqualified from

Free trade zone
A closed facility (under the supervision of government customs officials) into which foreign goods can be brought without being subject to the payment of normal import duties.

Trading blocs
A group of countries that agree on a set of special arrangements governing the trading of goods between member countries. Companies may locate in places affected by the agreement to take advantage of new market opportunities.

competing in the new market. Examples include the location of various Japanese auto manufacturing plants in Europe before 1992, as well as recent moves by many communications and financial services companies into Mexico in a post-NAFTA environment.

Environmental Regulation   The environmental regulations that impact a certain industry in a given location should be included in the location decision. Besides measurable cost implications, these regulations influence the relationship with the local community.

Host Community   The host community's interest in having the plant in its midst is a necessary part of the evaluation process. Local educational facilities and the broader issue of quality of life are also important.

Competitive Advantage   An important decision for multinational companies is the nation in which to locate the home base for each distinct business. Competitive advantage is created at a home base where strategy is set, the core product and process technology are created, and a critical mass of production takes place. Tax implications also play a role in the decision. So a company should move its home base to a country that stimulates innovation and provides the best environment for global competitiveness. This concept can also be applied to domestic companies seeking to gain sustainable competitive advantage. It partly explains the southeastern states' recent emergence as the preferred corporate destination within the United States (i.e., their business climate fosters innovation and low-cost production).

Plant Location Methods

As we will see, there are many techniques available for identifying potential sites for plants or other types of facilities. The process required to narrow the decision down to a particular area can vary significantly depending on the type of business we are in and the competitive pressures that must be considered. As we have discussed, there are often many different criteria that need to be considered when selecting from the set of feasible sites.

In this section, we sample three different types of techniques that have proven to be very useful to many companies. The first is the *factor-rating system* that allows us to consider many different types of criteria using simple point-rating scales. Next, we consider the *transportation method of linear programming*, a powerful technique for estimating the cost of using a network of plants and warehouses. Following this, we consider the *centroid method*, a technique often used by communications companies (cellphone providers) to locate their transmission towers. Finally, later in the chapter we consider how service firms such as McDonald's and State Farm Insurance use statistical techniques to find desirable locations for their facilities.

Keep in mind that each of the techniques described here would be used within the context of a more comprehensive strategy for locating a facility. Typically, the strategy would employ some type of search where major regions are first considered; it is narrowed down to areas, then to potential sites, and finally a choice is made between a few alternatives. Think of these techniques as simple tools used in different ways to zero in on a site. The factor-rating system is useful when nonquantitative factors are important. The linear programming and centroid methods are quantitative and may be tied to cost and service-related criteria. The statistical techniques are good when there is significant variability in criteria measures. The techniques are often used in combination to solve a real problem.

Factor-Rating Systems **Factor-rating systems** are perhaps the most widely used of the general location techniques because they provide a mechanism to combine diverse factors in an easy-to-understand format.

By way of example, a refinery assigned the following range of point values to major factors affecting a set of possible sites:

	RANGE
Fuels in region	0 to 330
Power availability and reliability	0 to 200
Labor climate	0 to 100
Living conditions	0 to 100
Transportation	0 to 50
Water supply	0 to 10
Climate	0 to 50
Supplies	0 to 60
Tax policies and laws	0 to 20

Factor-rating system
An approach for selecting a facility location by combining a diverse set of factors. Point scales are developed for each criterion. Each potential site is then evaluated on each criterion and the points are combined to calculate a rating for the site.

Each site was then rated against each factor, and a point value was selected from its assigned range. The sums of assigned points for each site were then compared. The site with the most points was selected.

A major problem with simple point-rating schemes is that they do not account for the wide range of costs that may occur within each factor. For example, there may be only a few hundred dollars' difference between the best and worst locations on one factor and several thousands of dollars' difference between the best and the worst on another. The first factor may have the most points available to it but provide little help in making the location decision; the second may have few points available but potentially show a real difference in the value of locations. To deal with this problem, it has been suggested that points possible for each factor be derived using a weighting scale based on standard deviations of costs rather than simply total cost amounts. In this way, relative costs can be considered.

Transportation Method of Linear Programming The **transportation method** is a special linear programming method. (Note that linear programming is developed in detail in Appendix A.) It gets its name from its application to problems involving transporting products from several sources to several destinations. The two common objectives of such problems are either (1) minimize the cost of shipping n units to m destinations or (2) maximize the profit of shipping n units to m destinations.

Transportation method
A special linear programming method that is useful for solving problems involving transporting products from several sources to several destinations.

Example 14.1: U.S. Pharmaceutical Company

Suppose the U.S. Pharmaceutical Company has four factories supplying the warehouses of four major customers and its management wants to determine the minimum-cost shipping schedule for its monthly output to these customers. Factory supply, warehouse demands, and shipping costs per case for these drugs are shown in Exhibit 14.2A.

exhibit 14.2

A. Data for U.S. Pharmaceutical Transportation Problem

| | | | | | SHIPPING COSTS PER CASE (IN DOLLARS) | | | |
FACTORY	SUPPLY	WAREHOUSE	DEMAND	FROM	To COLUMBUS	To ST. LOUIS	To DENVER	To LOS ANGELES
Indianapolis	15	Columbus	10	Indianapolis	$25	$35	$36	$60
Phoenix	6	St. Louis	12	Phoenix	55	30	25	25
New York	14	Denver	15	New York	40	50	80	90
Atlanta	11	Los Angeles	9	Atlanta	30	40	66	75

B. Transportation Matrix for U.S. Pharmaceutical Problem

From \ To	Columbus	St. Louis	Denver	Los Angeles	Factory supply
Indianapolis	25	35	36	60	15
Phoenix	55	30	25	25	6
New York	40	50	80	90	14
Atlanta	30	40	66	75	11
Destination requirements	10	12	15	9	46 / 46

The transportation matrix for this example appears in Exhibit 14.2B, where supply availability at each factory is shown in the far-right column and the warehouse demands are shown in the bottom row. The shipping costs are shown in the small boxes within the cells. For example, the cost to ship one unit from the Indianapolis factory to the customer warehouse in Columbus is $25. The actual flows would be shown in the cells intersecting the factory rows and warehouse columns.

SOLUTION

This problem can be solved by using Microsoft Excel's Solver function. If you are not familiar with the Solver, you should study Appendix A, "Linear Programming Using the Excel Solver." Exhibit 14.3 shows how the problem can be set up in the spreadsheet. Cells B6 through E6 contain the requirement for each customer warehouse. Cells F2 through F5 contain the amount that can be supplied from each plant. Cells B2 through E5 are the cost of shipping one unit for each potential plant and warehouse combination.

Cells for the solution of the problem are B9 through E12. These cells can initially be left blank when setting up the spreadsheet. Column cells F9 through F12 are the sum of each row, indicating how much is actually being shipped from each factory in the candidate solution. Similarly, row cells B13 through E13 are sums of the amount being shipped to each customer in the candidate solution. The Excel Sum function can be used to calculate these values.

The cost of the candidate solution is calculated in cells B16 through E19. Multiplying the amount shipped in the candidate solution by the cost per unit of shipping over that particular route

Excel Screen Showing the U.S. Pharmaceutical Problem   exhibit 14.3

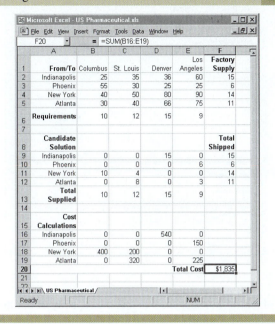

Excel:
US Pharmaceutical

makes this calculation. For example, multiplying B2 by B9 in cell B16 gives the cost of shipping between Indianapolis and Columbus for the candidate solution. The total cost shown in cell F20 is the sum of all these individual costs.

To solve the problem, the Excel Solver application needs to be accessed. The Solver is found by selecting Data and then Solver from the Excel menu. A screen similar to what is shown on the next page should appear. If you cannot find Solver at that location, the required add-in might not have been activated when Excel was initially installed on your computer. Solver can easily be added if you have your original Excel installation disk. •

Solver parameters now need to be set. First, set the target cell. This is the cell where the total cost associated with the solution is calculated. In our sample problem, this is cell F20, which sums the values in cells B16 through E19. Next, we need to indicate that we are minimizing this cell. Selecting the "Min" button does this. The location of our solution is indicated in the "By Changing Variable Cells." These cells are B9 through E12 in our example.

Next, we need to indicate the constraints for our problem. For our transportation problem, we need to be sure that customer demand is met and that we do not exceed the capacity of our manufacturing plants. To ensure that demand is met, click on "Add" and highlight the range of cells where we have calculated the total amount being shipped to each customer. This range is B13 to E13 in our example. Next select "=" indicating that we want the amount shipped to equal demand. Finally, on the right side, enter the range of cells where the actual customer demand is stated in our spreadsheet. This range is B6 to E6 in our example.

The second set of constraints that ensures that the capacity of our manufacturing plants is not exceeded is entered similarly. The range of cells that indicate how much is being shipped from each factory is F9 to F12. These values need to be less than or equal to ($<=$) the capacity of each factory, which is in cells F2 to F5.

Two options need to be set for solving transportation problems. First, set the solving method to "Simplex LP." This tells the Solver that there are no nonlinear calculations in our spreadsheet. This is important because the Solver can use a very efficient algorithm to calculate the optimal solution to this problem if this condition exists. Next, check the "Make Unconstrained Variables Non-Negative" box. This tells Solver that the values in our solution need to be greater than or equal to zero. In transportation problems, shipping negative quantities does not make any sense. Click "Solve" to actually solve the problem. Solver will notify you that it found a solution. Indicate that you want that solution saved. Finally, click OK to go back to the main spreadsheet. The solution should be in cells B9 to E12.

The transportation method can be used to solve many different types of problems if it is applied innovatively. For example, it can be used to test the cost impact of different candidate locations on the entire production–distribution network. To do this, we might add a new row that contains the unit shipping cost from a factory in a new location, say, Dallas, to the existing set of customer warehouses, along with the total amount it could supply. We could then solve this particular matrix for minimum total cost. Next, we would replace the factory located in Dallas in the same row of the matrix with a factory at a different location, Houston, and again solve for minimum total cost. Assuming the factories in Dallas and Houston would be identical in other important respects, the location resulting in the lower total cost for the network would be selected.

For additional information about using the Solver, see Appendix A, "Linear Programming Using the Excel Solver."

Centroid method
A technique for locating single facilities that considers the existing facilities, the distances between them, and the volumes of goods to be shipped.

Centroid Method The **centroid method** is a technique for locating single facilities that considers the existing facilities, the distances between them, and the volumes of goods

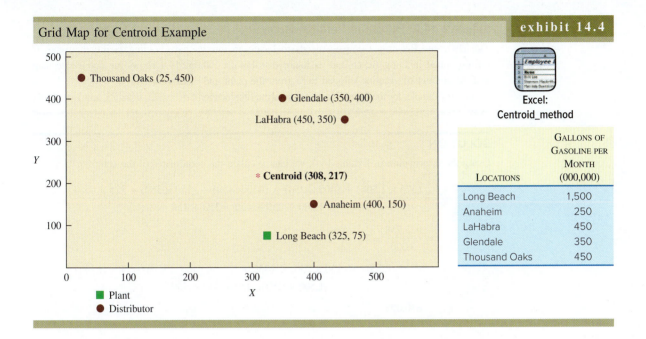

Grid Map for Centroid Example

exhibit 14.4

Excel:
Centroid_method

LOCATIONS	GALLONS OF GASOLINE PER MONTH (000,000)
Long Beach	1,500
Anaheim	250
LaHabra	450
Glendale	350
Thousand Oaks	450

■ Plant
● Distributor

to be shipped. The technique is often used to locate intermediate or distribution ware-houses. In its simplest form, this method assumes that inbound and outbound transporta-tion costs are equal, and it does not include special shipping costs for less than full loads.

Another major application of the centroid method today is the location of communi-cation towers in urban areas. Examples include radio, TV, and cellphone towers. In this application, the goal is to find sites that are near clusters of customers, thus ensuring clear radio signals. The centroid method finds a simple mathematical point. Once it is found, the problem should consider qualitative factors such as geography, roads, and utilities to find an exact location.

The centroid method begins by placing the existing locations on a coordinate grid system. Coordinates are usually based on longitude and latitude measures due to the rapid adoption of GPS systems for mapping locations. To keep it simple for our examples, we use arbitrary *X, Y* coordinates. Exhibit 14.4 shows an example of a grid layout.

The centroid is found by calculating the *X* and *Y* coordinates that result in the minimal transportation cost. We use the formulas

$$C_x = \frac{\Sigma d_{ix}V_i}{\Sigma V_i} \qquad C_y = \frac{\Sigma d_{iy}V_i}{\Sigma V_i}$$

[14.1]

where

C_x = X coordinate of the centroid
C_y = Y coordinate of the centroid
d_{ix} = X coordinate of the *i*th location
d_{iy} = Y coordinate of the *i*th location
V_i = Volume of goods moved to or from the *i*th location

Example 14.2: HiOctane Refining Company

The HiOctane Refining Company needs to locate an intermediate holding facility between its refining plant in Long Beach and its major distributors. Exhibit 14.4 shows the coordinate map and the amount of gasoline shipped to or from the plant and distributors.

In this example, for the Long Beach location (the first location), $d_{ix} = 325$, $d_{iy} = 75$, and $V_i = 1,500$.

SOLUTION

Using the information in Exhibit 14.4, we can calculate the coordinates of the centroid:

$$C_x = \frac{(325 \times 1,500) + (400 \times 250) + (450 \times 450) + (350 \times 350) + (25 \times 450)}{1,500 + 250 + 450 + 350 + 450}$$

$$= \frac{923,750}{3,000} = 307.9$$

$$C_y = \frac{(75 \times 1,500) + (150 \times 250) + (350 \times 450) + (400 \times 350) + (450 \times 450)}{1,500 + 250 + 450 + 350 + 450}$$

$$= \frac{650,000}{3,000} = 216.7$$

This gives management the X and Y coordinates of approximately 308 and 217, respectively, and provides an initial starting point to search for a new site. By examining the location of the calculated centroid on the grid map, we can see that it might be more cost-efficient to ship directly between the Long Beach plant and the Anaheim distributor than to ship via a warehouse near the centroid. Before a location decision is made, management would probably recalculate the centroid, changing the data to reflect this (i.e., decrease the gallons shipped from Long Beach by the amount Anaheim needs and remove Anaheim from the formula). •

Locating Service Facilities

Because of the variety of service firms and the relatively low cost of establishing a service facility compared to one for manufacturing, new service facilities are far more common than new factories and warehouses. Indeed, there are few communities in which rapid population growth has not been paralleled by concurrent rapid growth in retail outlets, restaurants, municipal services, and entertainment facilities.

Services typically have multiple sites to maintain close contact with customers. The location decision is closely tied to the market selection decision. If the target market is college-age groups, locations in retirement communities—despite desirability in terms of cost, resource availability, and so forth—are not viable alternatives. Market needs also affect the number of sites to be built and the size and characteristics of the sites. Whereas manufacturing location decisions are often made by minimizing costs, many service location decision techniques maximize the profit potential of various sites. Next, we present a multiple regression model that can be used to help select good sites.

Example 14.3: Screening Hotel Location Sites

Selecting good sites is crucial to a hotel chain's success. Of the four major marketing considerations (price, product, promotion, and location), location and product have been shown to be most important for multisite firms. As a result, hotel chain owners who can pick good sites quickly have a distinct competitive advantage.

	exhibit 14.5
Independent Variables Collected for the Initial Model-Building Stage	

CATEGORY	NAME	DESCRIPTION
Competitive	INNRATE	Inn price
	PRICE	Room rate for the inn
	RATE	Average competitive room rate
	RMS 1	Hotel rooms within 1 mile
	RMSTOTAL	Hotel rooms within 3 miles
	ROOMSINN	Inn rooms
Demand generators	CIVILIAN	Civilian personnel on base
	COLLEGE	College enrollment within 4 miles
	HOSP1	Hospital beds within 1 mile
	HOSPTOTL	Hospital beds within 4 miles
	HVYIND	Heavy industrial employment
	LGTIND	Light industrial acreage
	MALLS	Shopping mall square footage
	MILBLKD	Military base blocked
	MILITARY	Military personnel
	MILTOT	MILITARY+CIVILIAN
	OFC1	Office space within 1 mile
	OFCTOTAL	Office space within 4 miles
	OFCCBD	Office space in Central Business District
	PASSENGR	Airport passengers enplaned
	RETAIL	Scale ranking of retail activity
	TOURISTS	Annual tourists
	TRAFFIC	Traffic count
	VAN	Airport van
Demographic	EMPLYPCT	Unemployment percentage
	INCOME	Average family income
	POPULACE	Residential population
Market awareness	AGE	Years inn has been open
	NEAREST	Distance to nearest inn
	STATE	State population per inn
	URBAN	Urban population per inn
Physical	ACCESS	Accessibility
	ARTERY	Major traffic artery
	DISTCBD	Distance to downtown
	SIGNVIS	Sign visibility

Exhibit 14.5 shows the initial list of variables included in a study to help a hotel chain screen potential locations for its new hotels. Data were collected on 57 existing sites. Analysis of the data identified the variables that correlated with operating profit in two years. (See Exhibit 14.6.)

SOLUTION

An introduction into how *regression* models are constructed is included in Chapter 3. The details of how variables are selected for inclusion in the model are beyond the scope of this book. Basically, the variables that are the most strongly correlated (as shown in Exhibit 14.6) are used in a linear mathematical model to maximize the fit between profitability and characteristics of each potential site. The correlations are a relative measure of the amount of statistical variation explained by each variable. Variables with values closer to 1 or −1 explain more variation than those closer to zero.

exhibit 14.6 A Summary of the Variables That Correlated with Operating Margin

VARIABLE	YEAR 1	YEAR 2
ACCESS	.20	
AGE	.29	.49
COLLEGE		.25
DISTCBD		−.22
EMPLYPCT	−.22	−.22
INCOME		−.23
MILTOT		.22
NEAREST	−.51	
OFCCBD	.30	
POPULACE	.30	.35
PRICE	.38	.58
RATE		.27
STATE	−.32	−.33
SIGNVIS	.25	
TRAFFIC	.32	
URBAN	−.22	−.26

The analysis done by the hotel chain indicated that the best variables to include in the model were the following:

- State population per inn (STATE)
- Room rate for the inn (PRICE)
- Square root of the income of the area (INCOME)
- College enrollment within four miles (COLLEGE)

The final form for this model is as follows:

$$\text{Profitability} = 39.05 - 5.41 \times \text{State population per inn (1,000)}$$
$$+ 5.86 \times \text{Room rate for the inn}$$
$$- 3.91 \times \text{Square root of the income of the area (1,000)}$$
$$+ 1.75 \times \text{College enrollment within 4 miles}$$

The model shows that profitability is negatively affected by the state population per inn, positively affected by room rate, negatively affected by area income (the inns do better in lower-income areas), and positively affected by colleges nearby.

The hotel chain implemented the model on a spreadsheet and routinely uses the spreadsheet to screen potential real estate acquisitions. The founder and president of the hotel chain has accepted the model's validity and no longer feels obligated to personally select the sites.

This example shows that a specific model can be obtained from the requirements of service organizations and used to identify the most important features in site selection. •

CONCEPT CONNECTIONS

LO14–1 Explain what logistics is.

- Logistics covers the entire scope of obtaining, producing, and distributing material and product to the proper place and in the correct quantities.
- The focus here is on the movement of material and the location of warehouses and manufacturing plants with consideration of the cost of material movement.
- Third-party logistics companies, such as FedEx and DHL, provide services to many companies.

Logistics   The art and science of obtaining, producing, and distributing material and product to the proper place and in the proper quantities.

International logistics   All functions concerned with the movement of materials and finished goods on a global scale.

Third-party logistics company   A company that manages all or part of another company's product delivery operations.

LO14–2 Contrast logistics and warehouse design alternatives.

- Decision related to how material will be transported and where plants and warehouses are located have an impact on the cost of the product.
- Trade-offs relate to the cost of transporting the product, delivery speed, and the ability to efficiently react to changes in plans.
- Transportation alternatives, called "modes" of transportation, include water, rail, highways, air, pipelines, and hand delivery. Often, multiple modes are used as a product moves through the supply chain.
- Warehouses and distribution centers are used to consolidate shipments from various sources to improve the efficiency of the supply chain.
- Finding the optimal logistics-system design—consisting of manufacturing plants, distribution centers and warehouses, and ultimately, delivery to the final customer—is a complex task.

Cross-docking   An approach used in consolidation warehouses where, rather than making larger shipments, incoming shipments are broken down into small shipments for local delivery in an area.

Hub-and-spoke systems   Systems that combine the idea of consolidation and that of cross-docking.

LO14–3 Analyze logistics-driven location decisions.

- There are a variety of criteria that go beyond cost for determining the location of the facilities that form a company's supply chain.
- The factor-rating system is an analytical tool that allows consideration of many different types of criteria using point-rating scales for each criterion.
- Linear programming, in particular the transportation method, is useful when transportation cost is the major criterion in the decision.
- A third technique is the centroid method, which is useful for finding desirable geographic coordinates for a facility such as a cellphone tower.
- Locating service type businesses is often very dependent on how close the contact needs to be to customers. For example, an automatic teller machine for a bank needs to be in close proximity to existing and potential customers.

Free trade zone   A closed facility (under the supervision of government customs officials) into which foreign goods can be brought without being subject to the payment of normal import duties.

Trading blocs A group of countries that agree on a set of special arrangements governing the trading of goods between member countries. Companies may locate in places affected by the agreement to take advantage of new market opportunities.

Factor-rating system An approach for selecting a facility location by combining a diverse set of factors. Point scales are developed for each criterion. Each potential site is then evaluated on each criterion and the points are combined to calculate a rating for the site.

Transportation method A special linear programming method that is useful for solving problems involving transporting products from several sources to several destinations.

Centroid method A technique for locating single facilities that considers the existing facilities, the distances between them, and the volumes of goods to be shipped.

$$C_x = \frac{\Sigma d_{ix} V_i}{\Sigma V_i} \qquad C_y = \frac{\Sigma d_{iy} V_i}{\Sigma V_i} \qquad\qquad [14.1]$$

SOLVED PROBLEMS

LO14–3 SOLVED PROBLEM 1

Green Energy Technologies (GET) is planning to locate a new solar panel manufacturing plant in the southeastern United States to meet strongly growing demand in that market. It is considering three cities for this new plant: Montgomery, Alabama; Atlanta, Georgia; and Charleston, North Carolina. It has developed a list of important factors to consider in making its decision. After making site visits to each of the three cities, the facility location team has rated each of the cities as shown in the table below:

		CITY RATINGS		
FACTOR	MAX POINTS	MONTGOMERY	ATLANTA	CHARLESTON
Availability of labor	60	55	52	48
Availability of technical skills	50	37	46	41
Transportation infrastructure	40	34	37	32
Warehousing availability/costs	40	30	33	28
Proximity to customers	35	22	27	25
Proximity to suppliers	25	25	22	20
Taxation structure	15	12	10	14
Quality of life	10	7	8	9
Climate	5	3	3	4

Based on this factor-rating system and the points assigned by the facility location team, which location appears to be the best choice?

Solution

The difficulty in applying a factor-rating system lies in the design of the system and the evaluation of each potential site on every factor. Once this is accomplished, evaluating the results is a simple matter of adding up the total points for each candidate location. Based on the ratings shown above, the point totals are as follows.

Montgomery	225
Atlanta	238
Charleston	221

Based on the results of the rating system, Atlanta would appear to be the best choice.

LO14–3 **SOLVED PROBLEM 2**

Industrial Packaging Solutions (IPS) is a manufacturer of corrugated fiberboard shipping boxes used by companies across the United States. It sells to wholesalers, who in turn sell to resellers or end-user customers. Final products are consolidated on standard shipping pallets of uniform dimensions and weight. Because of this, the cost to ship a pallet to a single destination is the same regardless of the type of box loaded on the pallet. The standard unit for sales and operations planning at IPS is a pallet load.

After recently opening a new factory to satisfy growing demand for its products, IPS is concerned about allocating demand from its customers to the facilities in its production network. It wants to do so in a way that minimizes the total cost of shipping final products to the wholesalers.

It currently has three factories that service a network of eight major wholesalers. Relevant data for the next year are shown in the table below.

FACTORY LOCATION	PRODUCTION CAPACITY (PALLETS × 1,000)
Denver, CO	25
Chicago, IL	50
Baltimore, MD	35

WHOLESALER LOCATION	DEMAND (PALLETS × 1,000)
Spokane, WA	8.5
Los Angeles, CA	19.6
Kansas City, MO	9.3
Minneapolis, MN	8.8
Indianapolis, IN	11.8
Atlanta, GA	13.6
New York, NY	17.2
Orlando, FL	8.4

Based on contracts with its transportation suppliers, IPS is confident that the following transportation rates will be valid over the next year. Rates provided are to transport one pallet of product. There is no quantity discount given for volume shipments.

	DESTINATION CITY AND TRANSPORTATION RATES							
FACTORY LOCATION	SPOKANE	L.A.	K.C.	MINN.	INDY	ATLANTA	N.Y.	ORLANDO
Denver, CO	$42	$49	$45	$54	$56	$65	$70	$72
Chicago, IL	65	69	49	38	32	45	50	55
Baltimore, MD	75	77	68	62	43	44	35	38

Use the transportation method of linear programming to develop a low-cost transportation plan for IPS for the upcoming year.

Solution

The first step is to consolidate the capacity, demand, and cost data in a single table. This table is shown below. Note that the capacity and demand numbers have been converted to single pallets to match the transportation cost units. You could instead convert the transportation cost data into 1,000 pallet units. Either way is fine as long as you have consistent units for all data.

FACTORY LOCATION	DESTINATION CITY AND TRANSPORTATION RATES								CAPACITY
	SPOKANE	L.A.	K.C.	MINN.	INDY	ATLANTA	N.Y.	ORLANDO	
Denver, CO	$42	$49	$45	$54	$56	$465	$70	$72	25,000
Chicago, IL	$65	$69	$49	$38	$32	$45	$50	$55	50,000
Baltimore, MD	$75	$77	$68	$62	$43	$44	$35	$38	35,000
Demand:	8,500	19,600	9,300	8,800	11,800	13,600	17,200	8,400	

The next step is to insert this table in Excel along with a copy of the table to indicate the candidate solution and a smaller table to calculate the costs based on the candidate solution. The following screen capture from Excel shows how this would be set up.

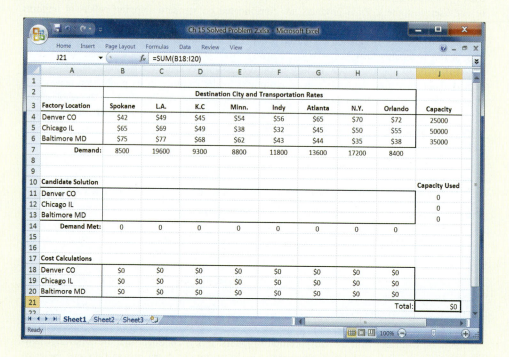

The blank cells in the candidate solution table represent the amount to ship from each factory to each destination—they will be set up as changing cells in Solver. The Demand Met row in that table sums up each column in the table, telling us how much demand is being met in each city by our solution. For example, the formula in cell B14 is 5SUM(B11:B13). Similarly, the Capacity Used column sums up each row in the table, telling us how much product is shipped from each plant in our solution. For example, the formula in cell J11 is 5SUM(Bl1:I11). The cells in the Cost Calculations table each multiply the relevant cells from the candidate solution and the cost data tables, telling us how much our candidate solution costs for each factory–customer combination. For example, the formula in B18 is 5B11*B4. The Total cell simply sums up all the costs in the table.

Next, we need to set up Solver to let it solve the problem for us. This is fairly easy given the structure of the tables above. We need to tell Solver the following things:

- We want to minimize the total cost.
- It can change the values of the empty cells in the Candidate Solution table.
- The amount shipped to each customer must match the amount demanded.
- The amount shipped from each factory must not exceed the capacity of that factory.

After starting Solver, we would set up the parameters as shown below. Be sure to set the options to "Assume Linear Model" and "Assume Non-Negative." (The latter could also be accomplished by adding a constraint that all changing cells be greater than or equal to zero.)

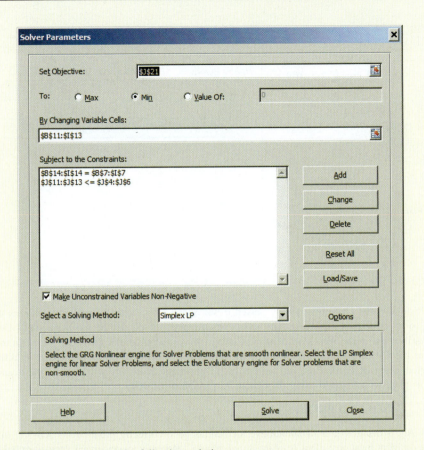

After running Solver, we get the following solution:

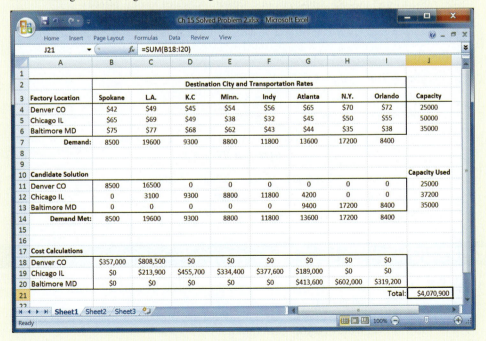

exhibit 14.7 Plant Location Matrix

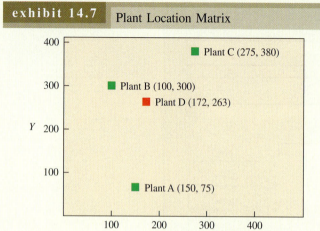

PLANT	COMPRESSORS REQUIRED PER YEAR
A	6,000
B	8,200
C	7,000

If IPS follows the plan presented by Solver, it will spend a little over $4 million to ship its products to its customers next year. The recommended plan should not be too surprising—Denver primarily satisfies the West Cost demand, Chicago serves the middle of the country, and Baltimore serves the East. This makes sense given the reality that transportation costs increase as distance traveled increases. Further, we can see that both Denver and Baltimore will max out their capacity in this plan, with Chicago using only about 75 percent of capacity.

LO14–3 **SOLVED PROBLEM 3**

Cool Air, a manufacturer of automotive air conditioners, currently produces its XB-300 line at three different locations: plant A, plant B, and plant C. Recently, management decided to build all compressors, a major product component, in a separate dedicated facility, plant D.

Using the centroid method and the information displayed in Exhibit 14.7, determine a location for plant D. Assume a linear relationship between volumes shipped and shipping costs (no premium charges).

Solution

$$d_{1x} = 150 \quad d_{1y} = 75 \quad V_1 = 6,000$$
$$d_{2x} = 100 \quad d_{2y} = 300 \quad V_2 = 8,200$$
$$d_{3x} = 275 \quad d_{3y} = 380 \quad V_3 = 7,000$$

$$C_x = \frac{\Sigma d_{ix} V_i}{\Sigma V_i} = \frac{(150 \times 6,000) + (100 \times 8,200) + (275 \times 7,000)}{6,000 + 8,200 + 7,000} = 171.9$$

$$C_y = \frac{\Sigma d_{iy} V_i}{\Sigma V_i} = \frac{(75 \times 6,000) + (300 \times 8,200) + (380 \times 7,000)}{21,200} = 262.7$$

Plant D[C_x, C_y] = D[172, 263]

DISCUSSION QUESTIONS

LO14–1
1. What motivations typically cause firms to initiate a facilities location or relocation project?
2. List five major reasons why a new electronic components manufacturing firm should move into your city or town.

LO14–2
3. Recent figures show that almost 60 percent of the volume of freight movements in the United States ship by truck. Railroads are far more fuel efficient on a

ton-mile basis—CSX advertises it can move a ton of freight 468 miles on a gallon of fuel. Why is it that rail does not have a greater share of the freight market in the United States?

4. What is required to make cross-docking a viable solution for a logistics provider?

LO14–3
5. What are the pros and cons of relocating a small or midsized manufacturing firm (that makes mature products) from the United States to China?
6. How do facility location decisions differ for service facilities and manufacturing plants?
7. If you could locate your new software development company anywhere in the world, which place would you choose, and why?

OBJECTIVE QUESTIONS

LO14–1
1. Some manufacturing firms contract with an outside company to manage the firm's logistics functions. What is the general term for a firm that provides such services?
2. Logistics accounts for about what percent of the U.S. gross domestic product?

LO14–2
3. What mode of transportation is involved in the movement of the greatest number of products?
4. What mode of transportation is limited to specialized products such as liquids and gases?

LO14–3
5. A manufacturer has decided to locate a new factory in the northwestern United States to serve the growing demand in that market. It has narrowed the potential sites down to two finalists: city A and city B. It has developed a list of important factors to consider in selecting a site, and rated each as shown in the following table:

FACTOR	CITY A	CITY B
Utility rates	100	115
Availability of skilled labor	78	75
Tax rates	40	35
Transportation	46	38
Proximity to suppliers	35	34
Quality of life	19	16

Based on these data, which city appears to be the better choice?

6. Logistics Consultants Inc. (LCI) provides various logistics analysis services to other firms, including facility location decisions. It has just completed a project for a major customer, but on the eve of its presentation it discovered a computer malfunction had partially deleted some of its data. One file that was impacted contains the final factor rating results. Following are the partial results it was able to recover. As you'll notice, some ratings are missing.

FACTOR	MAX POINTS	RATINGS CITY X	CITY Y
Availability of labor	150	130	123
Availability of utilities	130	122	110
Transportation infrastructure	80	73	
Warehousing availability/costs	75	70	63
Proximity to customers	65	59	
Business climate	40	30	24
Taxation structure	30	15	
Quality of life	25	22	17

If you were the project manager for LCI, what would you do given that you are missing some crucial data?

7. Bindley Corporation has a one-year contract to supply motors for all washing machines produced by Rinso Ltd. Rinso manufactures the washers at four locations around the country: New York, Fort Worth, San Diego, and Minneapolis. Plans call for the following numbers of washing machines to be produced at each location:

New York	50,000
Fort Worth	70,000
San Diego	60,000
Minneapolis	80,000

Bindley has three plants that can produce the motors. The plants and production capacities are

Boulder	100,000
Macon	100,000
Gary	150,000

Due to varying production and transportation costs, the profit Bindley earns on each 1,000 units depends on where they were produced and where they were shipped. The following table gives the accounting department estimates of the dollar profit per unit. (Shipment will be made in lots of 1,000.)

	SHIPPED TO			
PRODUCED AT	NEW YORK	FORT WORTH	SAN DIEGO	MINNEAPOLIS
Boulder	7	11	8	13
Macon	20	17	12	10
Gary	8	18	13	16

Given profit maximization as a criterion, Bindley would like to determine how many motors should be produced at each plant and how many motors should be shipped from each plant to each destination.

a. Develop a transportation grid for this problem.

b. Find the optimal solution using Microsoft Excel.

8. Rent'R Cars is a multisite car rental company in the city. It is trying out a new "return the car to the location most convenient for you" policy to improve customer service. But this means that the company has to constantly move cars around the city to maintain required levels of vehicle availability. The supply and demand for economy cars, and the total cost of moving these vehicles between sites, are shown below.

From \ To	D	E	F	G	Supply
A	$9	$8	$6	$5	50
B	9	8	8	0	40
C	5	3	3	10	75
Demand	50	60	25	30	165 / 165

a. Find the solution that minimizes moving costs using Microsoft Excel.

b. What would you have to do to the costs to assure that A always sends a car to D as part of the optimal solution?

9. Sycamore Plastics (SP) is a manufacturer of polyethylene plastic pellets used as a raw material by manufacturers of plastic goods around the U.S. SP currently operates four manufacturing centers in Philadelphia, PA; Atlanta, GA; St. Louis, MO; and Salt Lake City, UT. The plants have different capacities and production costs as indicated in the table below.

PLANT	MAXIMUM CAPACITY (× 100,000 LB.)	PROD. COSTS (PER 1,000 LB.)
Philadelphia	7.5	$325.00
Atlanta	9.0	$275.00
St. Louis	12.0	$305.00
Salt Lake City	10.3	$250.00

SP currently has six contract customers located in New York City; Birmingham, AL; Terre Haute, IN; Dallas, TX; Spokane, WA; and San Diego, CA. Transportation costs between the plants and various customers, as well as contracted demand from each customer, are shown in the table below.

	TRANSPORT COSTS PER 1,000 LB.					
FROM/TO	NYC	BIRMINGHAM	TERRE HAUTE	DALLAS	SPOKANE	SAN DIEGO
Philadelphia	$45	$52	$56	$62	$78	$85
Atlanta	$55	$42	$58	$59	$80	$82
St. Louis	$57	$60	$50	$54	$65	$70
Salt Lake City	$72	$71	$67	$57	$52	$60
Total Demand (× 1,000 lb.)	525	415	925	600	325	400

  a. Create a solver model and find the optimal solution to help SP develop a distribution plan that will minimize costs to supply the customers' demand.
  b. Comment briefly on your solution. Beyond the obvious, does your proposed solution have any other implications for SP?

10. A small manufacturing facility is being planned that will feed parts to three heavy manufacturing facilities. The locations of the current plants with their coordinates and volume requirements are given in the following table:

PLANT LOCATION	COORDINATES (x, y)	VOLUME (PARTS PER YEAR)
Peoria	300, 320	4,000
Decatur	375, 470	6,000
Joliet	470, 180	3,000

Use the centroid method to determine a location for this new facility.

11. DM Office Products (DMOP) is a wholesale supplier of office products with one facility in Pennsylvania. It has decided to build a new distribution warehouse in the state of New York to help serve the growing demand in that market. It has four major customers located in Buffalo, Syracuse, Albany, and New York City. Though New York City is the largest market, it also has the greatest competition, and DMOP is not a major player there. When DMOP ships an order to a customer, it uses its own small fleet of two trucks to deliver, so the cost of delivery is essentially the same for a full or partially full truck.

The expected number of annual shipments to each city and their coordinates on an x, y grid is shown in the following table.

CITY	x-COORDINATES	y-COORDINATES	NUMBER OF SHIPMENTS
Buffalo	325	850	78
Syracuse	1,420	900	82
Albany	2,300	630	122
New York	2,275	25	62

Use the centroid method to recommend a location for the new warehouse for DMOP. Round your coordinates to one decimal place.

12. Santa Cruz Bottling is a manufacturer of organic soft drinks on the coast of central California. Its products are enjoying a growing reputation and increased demand throughout the American Southwest. Because of the high cost of transporting soft drinks, it is considering a new plant to serve the states of New Mexico and Arizona. A key concern in its search for a new location is the resultant transportation costs to serve its key markets. Following is a list of cities where its main wholesale customers are located, along with estimated annual demand in cases of product for each.

CITY	x-COORDINATE	y-COORDINATE	NUMBER OF CASES
Phoenix	250	250	25,000
Tucson	350	125	20,000
Albuquerque	800	450	28,000
Santa Fe	850	520	17,000

a. Use the centroid method to recommend a location for the new bottling plant. Round your coordinates to one decimal place.
b. Do you have any concerns about the result? How would you deal with them?

ANALYTICS EXERCISE: DISTRIBUTION CENTER LOCATION

Grainger: Reengineering the China/U.S. Supply Chain

W. W. Grainger, Inc., is a leading supplier of maintenance, repair, and operating (MRO) products to businesses and institutions in the United States, Canada, and Mexico with an expanding presence in Japan, India, China, and Panama. The company works with more than 3,000 suppliers and runs an extensive Website (www.grainger.com) where Grainger offers nearly 900,000 products. The products range from industrial adhesives used in manufacturing, to hand tools, janitorial supplies, lighting equipment, and power tools. When something is needed by one of its 1.8 million customers, it is often needed quickly, so quick service and product availability are key drivers to Grainger's success.

Your assignment involves studying U.S. distribution in Grainger's supply chain. Grainger works with over 250 suppliers in the China and Taiwan region. These suppliers produce products to Grainger's specifications and ship to the United States using ocean freight carriers from four major ports in China and Taiwan. From these ports, product is shipped to U.S. entry ports in either Seattle, Washington, or Los Angeles, California. After passing through customs, the 20- and 40-foot containers are shipped by rail to Grainger's central distribution center in Kansas City, Kansas. The containers are unloaded and quality is checked in Kansas City. From there, individual items are sent to regional warehouses in nine U.S. locations, a Canadian site, and Mexico.

Grainger: U.S. Distribution

In the United States, approximately 40 percent of the containers enter in Seattle, Washington, and 60 percent at the

Los Angeles, California, port. Containers on arrival at the port cities are inspected by federal agents and then loaded onto rail cars for movement to the Kansas City distribution center. Variable costs for processing at the port are $5.00 per cubic meter (CBM) in both Los Angeles and Seattle. The rate for shipping the containers to Kansas City is $0.0018 per CBM per mile.

In Kansas City, the containers are unloaded and processed through a quality assurance check. This costs $3.00 per CMB processed. A very small percentage of the material is actually sent back to the supplier, but errors in quantity and package size are often found that require accounting adjustments.

Items are stored in the Kansas City distribution center, which serves nine warehouses in the United States. Items are also sent to warehouses in Canada and Mexico, but for the purposes of this study we focus on the United States. The nine warehouses each place orders at the distribution center that contains all the items to be replenished. Kansas City picks each item on the order, consolidates the items onto pallets, and ships the items on 53-foot trucks destined to each warehouse. Truck freight costs $0.0220 per CBM per mile. The demand forecasts for the items purchased from China/Taiwan for next year in cubic meters and shipping distances are given in the following table:

It is estimated that the Los Angeles facility could be upgraded at a one-time cost of $1,500,000 and then operated for $350,000 per year. In the new Los Angeles distribution center, containers would be unloaded and processed through a quality assurance check, just as is now done in Kansas City. The variable cost for doing this would be $5.00 per CBM processed, which includes the cost to move the containers from the Los Angeles port to the distribution center.

After the material is processed in Los Angeles, the amount needed to replenish the Los Angeles warehouse (approximately 18 percent) would be kept and the rest sent by rail to Kansas City. It would then be directly stocked in the Kansas City distribution center and used to replenish the warehouses. Grainger expects that very little would need to be shipped back to the Los Angeles warehouse after the new system was operating for about six months.

Grainger management feels that it may be possible to make this change, but it is not sure if it would actually save any money and whether it would be a good strategic change.

Specific Questions to Address in Your Analysis

1. Relative to the U.S. distribution network, calculate the cost associated with running the existing system.

	DEMAND (CBM)		DISTANCES		
WAREHOUSE	AVERAGE	% OF DEMAND	MILES FROM KANSAS CITY	MILES FROM LOS ANGELES	MILES FROM SEATTLE
Kansas City	20,900	11%	0	1,620	1,870
Cleveland	17,100	9%	800	2,350	2,410
Newark	24,700	13%	1,200	2,780	2,890
Jacksonville	15,200	8%	1,150	2,420	2,990
Chicago	22,800	12%	520	2,020	2,060
Greenville	15,200	8%	940	2,320	2,950
Memphis	17,100	9%	510	1,790	2,330
Dallas	22,800	12%	500	1,430	2,130
Los Angeles	34,200	18%	1,620	0	1,140
Total	190,000				

Although a high percentage of demand was from warehouses either south or east of Kansas City, the question has surfaced concerning the 18 percent that will be shipped to Kansas City and then shipped back to the Los Angeles warehouse. This double-transportation could potentially be eliminated if a new distribution center were built in Los Angeles. The idea might be to ship material arriving at the Seattle port by rail to a new Los Angeles distribution center, which would be located at the current location of the Los Angeles warehouse.

Assume that 40 percent of the volume arrives in Seattle and 60 percent in Los Angeles and the port processing fee for federal processing at both locations is $5.00 per CBM. Assume that everything is transferred to the Kansas City distribution center by rail, where it is unloaded and quality-checked. Assume that all volume is then transferred by truck to the nine existing warehouses in the United States.

2. Consider the idea of upgrading the Los Angeles warehouse to include a distribution center capable of

processing all the volume coming into the United States. Assume that containers coming into Seattle would be inspected by federal officials (this needs to be done at all port locations) and then immediately shipped by rail in their original containers to Los Angeles. All volume would be unloaded and quality-checked in Los Angeles (the quality check cost $5.00 per CBM when done in Los Angeles). Eighteen percent of the volume would then be kept in Los Angeles for distribution through that warehouse and the rest transshipped by rail to the Kansas City warehouse. Assume the cost to transship by rail is $0.0018 per CBM per mile. The material sent to Kansas City would not need to go through the "unload and quality check process," and would be stored directly in the Kansas City

distribution center. Assume that the remaining volume would be transferred by truck to the eight remaining warehouses in the United States at a cost of $0.0220 per CBM per mile.

3. What should be done based on your analytics analysis of the U.S. distribution system? Should the new Los Angeles distribution center be added? Is there any obvious change that Grainger might make to have this option be more attractive?

4. Is this strategically something that Grainger should do? What has the company not considered that may be important?

Many thanks to Gary Scalzitti of Grainger for help with developing this case.

PRACTICE EXAM

1. This is the art and science of obtaining, producing, and distributing material and product in the proper place and in the proper quantities.
2. A company that is hired to handle logistics functions.
3. A mode of transportation that is the most flexible relative to cost, volume, and speed of delivery.
4. When large shipments are broken down directly into smaller shipments for local delivery.
5. Sorting goods is the main purpose of this type of warehouse.
6. A place where foreign goods can be brought into the United States without being subject to normal customs requirements.
7. The main cost criterion employed when a transportation model is used for analyzing a logistics network.
8. The Microsoft Excel function used to solve the transportation model.
9. For the transportation model to be able to find a feasible solution, this must always be greater than or equal to total demand.
10. The "changing cells" in a transportation model represent this.
11. This is a method that locates facilities relative to an X, Y grid.
12. A technique that is useful for screening potential locations for services.

Answers to Practice Exam 1. Logistics 2. Third-party logistics company 3. Highway 4. Cross-docking 5. Hub 6. Free trade zone 7. Cost of shipping 8. Solver 9. Total capacity 10. Allocation of demand to a plant or warehouse 11. Centroid method 12. Regression analysis

APPENDIX A

LINEAR PROGRAMMING USING THE EXCEL SOLVER

The key to profitable operations is making the best use of available resources of people, material, plant and equipment, and money. Today's manager has a powerful mathematical modeling tool available for this purpose with linear programming. In this appendix, we will show how the use of the Microsoft Excel Solver to solve LP problems opens a whole new world to the innovative manager and provides an invaluable addition to the technical skill set for those who seek careers in consulting. In this appendix, we use a product-planning problem to introduce this tool. Here we find the optimal mix of products that have different costs and resource requirements. This problem is certainly relevant to today's competitive market. Extremely successful companies provide a mix of products, from standard to high-end luxury models. All these products compete for the use of limited production and other capacity. Maintaining the proper mix of these products over time can significantly bolster earnings and the return on a firm's assets.

We begin with a quick introduction to linear programming and conditions under which the technique is applicable. Then, we solve a simple product-mix problem. Other linear programming applications appear throughout the rest of the book.

Linear programming (or simply **LP**) refers to several related mathematical techniques used to allocate limited resources among competing demands in an optimal way. LP is the most widely used of the approaches falling under the general heading of mathematical optimization techniques and has been applied to many operations management problems. The following are typical applications:

Aggregate sales and operations planning: Finding the minimum-cost production schedule. The problem is to develop a three- to six-month plan for meeting expected demand given constraints on expected production capacity and workforce size. Relevant costs considered in the problem include regular and overtime labor rates, hiring and firing, subcontracting, and inventory carrying cost.

Service/manufacturing productivity analysis: Comparing how efficiently different service and manufacturing outlets are using their resources compared to the best-performing unit. This is done using an approach called data envelopment analysis.

Product planning: Finding the optimal product mix where several products have different costs and resource requirements. Examples include finding the optimal blend of chemicals for gasoline, paints, human diets, and animal feeds. Examples of this problem are covered in this chapter.

Product routing: Finding the optimal way to produce a product that must be processed sequentially through several machine centers, with each machine in the center having its own cost and output characteristics.

Vehicle/crew scheduling: Finding the optimal way to use resources such as aircraft, buses, or trucks and their operating crews to provide transportation services to customers and materials to be moved between different locations.

Process control: Minimizing the amount of scrap material generated by cutting steel, leather, or fabric from a roll or sheet of stock material.

LOA–1 Use Microsoft Excel Solver to solve a linear programming problem.

Linear programming (LP) Refers to several related mathematical techniques used to allocate limited resources among competing demands in an optimal way.

Inventory control: Finding the optimal combination of products to stock in a network of warehouses or storage locations.

Distribution scheduling: Finding the optimal shipping schedule for distributing products between factories and warehouses or between warehouses and retailers.

Plant location studies: Finding the optimal location of a new plant by evaluating shipping costs between alternative locations and supply and demand sources.

Material handling: Finding the minimum-cost routings of material-handling devices (such as forklift trucks) between departments in a plant, or, for example, hauling materials from a supply yard to work sites by trucks. Each truck might have different capacity and performance capabilities.

Linear programming is gaining wide acceptance in many industries due to the availability of detailed operating information and the interest in optimizing processes to reduce cost. Many software vendors offer optimization options to be used with enterprise resource planning systems. Some firms refer to these as *advanced planning option, synchronized planning,* and *process optimization.*

For linear programming to pertain in a problem situation, five essential conditions must be met. First, there must be *limited resources* (such as a limited number of workers, equipment, finances, and material); otherwise, there would be no problem. Second, there must be an *explicit objective* (such as maximize profit or minimize cost). Third, there must be *linearity* (two is twice as much as one; if three hours are needed to make a part, then two parts would take six hours and three parts would take nine hours). Fourth, there must be *homogeneity* (the products produced on a machine are identical, or all the hours available from a worker are equally productive). Fifth, there must be *divisibility:* Normal linear programming assumes products and resources can be subdivided into fractions. If this subdivision is not possible (such as flying half an airplane or hiring one-fourth of a person), a modification of linear programming, called *integer programming,* can be used.

When a single objective is to be maximized (like profit) or minimized (like costs), we can use linear programming. When multiple objectives exist, *goal programming* is used. If a problem is best solved in stages or time frames, *dynamic programming* is employed. Other restrictions on the nature of the problem may require that it be solved by other variations of the technique, such as *nonlinear programming* or *quadratic programming.*

The Linear Programming Model

Stated formally, the linear programming problem entails an optimizing process in which nonnegative values for a set of decision variables $X_1, X_2, \ldots, X_n$ are selected to maximize (or minimize) an objective function in the form

$$\text{Maximize(minimize)} \; Z = C_1 X_1 + C_2 X_2 + \cdots + C_n X_n$$

subject to resource constraints in the form

$$A_{11}X_1 + A_{12}X_2 + \cdots + A_{1n}X_n \leq B_1$$
$$A_{21}X_1 + A_{22}X_2 + \cdots + A_{2n}X_n \leq B_2$$
$$\cdot$$
$$\cdot$$
$$\cdot$$
$$A_{m1}X_1 + A_{m2}X_2 + \cdots + A_{mn}X_n \leq B_m$$

where C_n, A_{mn}, and B_m are given constants.

Depending on the problem, the constraints also may be stated with equal signs (=) or greater-than-or-equal-to signs (≥).

Example A.1: Puck and Pawn Company

We describe the steps involved in solving a simple linear programming model in the context of a sample problem, that of Puck and Pawn Company, which manufactures hockey sticks and chess sets. Each hockey stick yields an incremental profit of $2, and each chess set, $4. A hockey stick requires 4 hours of processing at machine center A and 2 hours at machine center B. A chess set requires 6 hours at machine center A, 6 hours at machine center B, and 1 hour at machine center C. Machine center A has a maximum of 120 hours of available capacity per day, machine center B has 72 hours, and machine center C has 10 hours.

If the company wishes to maximize profit, how many hockey sticks and chess sets should be produced per day?

SOLUTION

Formulate the problem in mathematical terms. If H is the number of hockey sticks and C is the number of chess sets, to maximize profit the objective function may be stated as

$$\text{Maximize } Z = \$2H + \$4C$$

The maximization will be subject to the following constraints:

$$4H + 6C \leq 120 \text{ (machine center A constraint)}$$
$$2H + 6C \leq 72 \text{ (machine center B constraint)}$$
$$1C \leq 10 \text{ (machine center C constraint)}$$
$$H, C \geq 0 \bullet$$

This formulation satisfies the five requirements for standard LP stated in the first section of this appendix:

1. There are limited resources (a finite number of hours available at each machine center).
2. There is an explicit objective function (we know what each variable is worth and what the goal is in solving the problem).
3. The equations are linear (no exponents or cross-products).
4. The resources are homogeneous (everything is in one unit of measure, machine hours).
5. The decision variables are divisible and nonnegative (we can make a fractional part of a hockey stick or chess set; however, if this were deemed undesirable, we would have to use integer programming).

Graphical Linear Programming

Though limited in application to problems involving two decision variables (or three variables for three-dimensional graphing), **graphical linear programming** provides a quick insight into the nature of linear programming. We describe the steps involved in

Graphical linear programming
Provides a quick insight into the nature of linear programming.

the graphical method in the context of Puck and Pawn Company. The following steps illustrate the graphical approach:

1. **Formulate the problem in mathematical terms.** The equations for the problem are given above.
2. **Plot constraint equations.** The constraint equations are easily plotted by letting one variable equal zero and solving for the axis intercept of the other. (The inequality portions of the restrictions are disregarded for this step.) For the machine center A constraint equation, when $H = 0$, $C = 20$, and when $C = 0$, $H = 30$. For the machine center B constraint equation, when $H = 0$, $C = 12$, and when $C = 0$, $H = 36$. For the machine center C constraint equation, $C = 10$ for all values of H. These lines are graphed in Exhibit A.1.
3. **Determine the area of feasibility.** The direction of inequality signs in each constraint determines the area where a feasible solution is found. In this case, all inequalities are of the less-than-or-equal-to variety, which means it would be impossible to produce any combination of products that would lie to the right of any constraint line on the graph. The region of feasible solutions is unshaded on the graph and forms a convex polygon. A convex polygon exists when a line drawn between any two points in the polygon stays within the boundaries of that polygon. If this condition of convexity does not exist, the problem is either incorrectly set up or is not amenable to linear programming.
4. **Plot the objective function.** The objective function may be plotted by assuming some arbitrary total profit figure and then solving for the axis coordinates, as was done for the constraint equations. Other terms for the objective function when used in this context are the *iso-profit* or *equal contribution line,* because it shows all possible production combinations for any given profit figure. For example, from the dotted line closest to the origin on the graph, we can determine all possible combinations of hockey

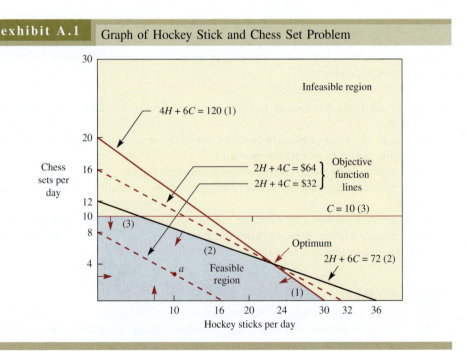

exhibit A.1   Graph of Hockey Stick and Chess Set Problem

sticks and chess sets that yield \$32 by picking a point on the line and reading the number of each product that can be made at that point. The combination yielding \$32 at point *a* would be 10 hockey sticks and three chess sets. This can be verified by substituting $H = 10$ and $C = 3$ in the objective function:

$$\$2(10) + \$4(3) = \$20 + \$12 = \$32$$

H	C	EXPLANATION
0	120/6 = 20	Intersection of Constraint (1) and C axis
120/4 = 30	0	Intersection of Constraint (1) and H axis
0	72/6 = 12	Intersection of Constraint (2) and C axis
72/2 = 36	0	Intersection of Constraint (2) and H axis
0	10	Intersection of Constraint (3) and C axis
0	32/4 = 8	Intersection of \$32 iso-point line (objective function) and C axis
32/2 = 16	0	Intersection of \$32 iso-profit line and H axis
0	64/4 = 16	Intersection of \$64 iso-profit line and C axis
64/2 = 32	0	Intersection of \$64 iso-profit line and H axis

5. **Find the optimum point.** It can be shown mathematically that the optimal combination of decision variables is always found at an extreme point (corner point) of the convex polygon. In Exhibit A.1, there are four corner points (excluding the origin), and we can determine which one is the optimum by either of two approaches. The first approach is to find the values of the various corner solutions algebraically. This entails simultaneously solving the equations of various pairs of intersecting lines and substituting the quantities of the resultant variables in the objective function. For example, the calculations for the intersection of $2H + 6C = 72$ and $C = 10$ are as follows:

Substituting $C = 10$ in $2H + 6C = 72$ gives $2H + 6(10) = 72$, $2H = 12$, or $H = 6$. Substituting $H = 6$ and $C = 10$ in the objective function, we get

$$\text{Profit} = \$2H + \$4C = \$2(6) + \$4(10)$$
$$= \$12 + \$40 = \$52$$

A variation of this approach is to read the H and C quantities directly from the graph and substitute these quantities into the objective function, as shown in the previous calculation. The drawback in this approach is that, in problems with a large number of constraint equations, there will be many possible points to evaluate, and the procedure of testing each one mathematically is inefficient.

The second and generally preferred approach entails using the objective function or iso-profit line directly to find the optimum point. The procedure involves simply drawing a straight line *parallel* to any arbitrarily selected initial iso-profit line so the iso-profit line is farthest from the origin of the graph. (In cost minimization problems, the objective would be to draw the line through the point closest to the origin.) In Exhibit A.1, the dashed line labeled $\$2H + \$4C = \$64$ intersects the most extreme point. Note that the initial arbitrarily selected iso-profit line is necessary to display the slope of the objective function for the particular problem. For this problem, the slope of the objective function is -2. This is important since a different objective function (try profit $= 3H + 3C$) might indicate that some other point is farthest from the origin. Given that $\$2H + \$4C = \$64$ is optimal, the amount of each variable to produce can be read from the graph: 24 hockey sticks and four chess sets. No other combination of the products yields a greater profit.

Linear Programming Using Microsoft Excel

Spreadsheets can be used to solve linear programming problems. In the desktop versions of Microsoft Excel an optimization tool called *Solver* is available. We will demonstrate the add-in tool by solving the hockey stick and chess problem. We invoke the Solver from the Data tab. A dialog box requests information required by the program. The following example describes how our sample problem can be solved using Excel.

If the Solver option does not appear in your Data tab, click on File → Options → Add-Ins → Go (Manage Excel Add-Ins) → Select the Solver Add-in. Solver should then be available directly from the Data tab for future use.

In the following example, we work in a step-by-step manner, setting up a spreadsheet and then solving our Puck and Pawn Company problem. Our basic strategy is to first define the problem within the spreadsheet. Following this, we invoke the Solver and feed it required information. Finally, we execute the Solver and interpret results from the reports provided by the program.

Step 1: Define Changing Cells A convenient starting point is to identify cells to be used for the decision variables in the problem. These are H and C, the number of hockey sticks and the number of chess sets to produce. Excel refers to these cells as changing cells in Solver. Referring to our Excel screen (Exhibit A.2), we have designated B4 as the location for the number of hockey sticks to produce and C4 for the number of chess sets. Note that we have set these cells equal to two initially. We could set these cells to anything, but a value other than zero will help verify that our calculations are correct.

Step 2: Calculate Total Profit (or Cost) This is our objective function and is calculated by multiplying profit associated with each product by the number of units produced.

exhibit A.2	Microsoft Excel Screen for Puck and Pawn Company

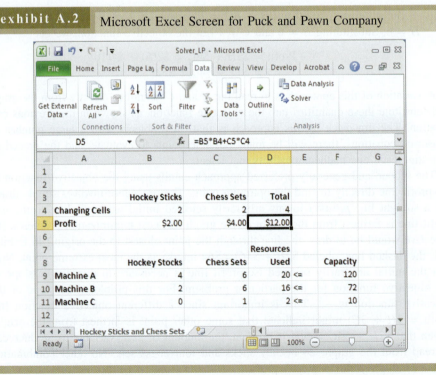

We have placed the profits in cells B5 and C5 ($2 and $4), so the profit is calculated by the following equation: B4*B5 + C4*C5, which is calculated in cell D5. Solver refers to this as the Target Cell, and it corresponds to the objective function for a problem.

Step 3: Set Up Resource Usage Our resources are machine centers A, B, and C as defined in the original problem. We have set up three rows (9, 10, and 11) in our spreadsheet, one for each resource constraint. For machine center A, 4 hours of processing time are used for each hockey stick produced (cell B9) and 6 hours for each chess set (cell C9). For a particular solution, the total amount of the machine center A resource used is calculated in D9 (B9*B4 + C9*C4). We have indicated in cell E9 that we want this value to be less than the 120-hour capacity of machine center A, which is entered in F9. Resource usage for machine centers B and C is set up in the exact same manner in rows 10 and 11.

Step 4: Set Up Solver Go to the Data tab and select the Solver option.

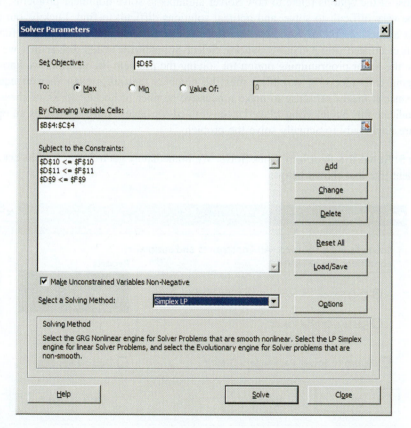

1. *Set Objective:* is set to the location where the value we want to optimize is calculated. This is the profit calculated in D5 in our spreadsheet.
2. *To:* is set to Max since the goal is to maximize profit.
3. *By Changing Variable Cells:* are the cells that Solver can change to maximize profit. Cells B4 through C4 are the changing cells in our problem.
4. *Subject to the Constraints:* corresponds to our machine center capacity. Here, we click on Add and indicate that the total used for a resource is less than or equal to the capacity available. A sample for machine center A follows. Click OK after each constraint is specified.

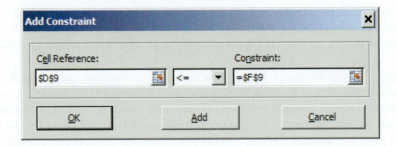

5. *Select a Solving Method* allows us to tell Solver what type of problem we want it to solve and how we want it solved. Solver has numerous options, but we will need to use only a few.

Most of the options relate to how Solver attempts to solve nonlinear problems. These can be very difficult to solve, and optimal solutions difficult to find. Luckily, our problem is a linear problem. We know this since our constraints and our objective function are all calculated using linear equations. Select Simplex LP to tell Solver that we want to use the linear programming option for solving the problem. In addition, we know our changing cells (decision variables) must be numbers that are greater than or equal to zero since it makes no sense to make a negative number of hockey sticks or chess sets. We indicate this by selecting Make Unconstrained Variables Non-Negative as an option. We are now ready to actually solve the problem.

Step 5: Solve the Problem Click Solve. We immediately get a Solver Results acknowledgment like that shown below.

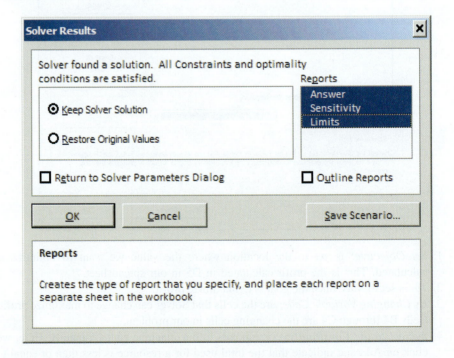

Solver acknowledges that a solution was found that appears to be optimal. On the right side of this box are options for three reports: an Answer Report, a Sensitivity Report, and a Limits Report. Click on each report to have Solver provide these. After highlighting the reports, click OK to exit back to the spreadsheet. Three new tabs have been created that correspond to these reports.

The most interesting reports for our problem are the Answer Report and the Sensitivity Report, both of which are shown in Exhibit A.3. The Answer Report shows the final answers for the total profit ($64) and the amounts produced (24 hockey sticks and 4 chess sets). In the constraints section of the Answer Report, the status of each resource is given. All of machine A and machine B are used, and there are six units of slack for machine C.

Excel Solver Answer and Sensitivity Reports — exhibit A.3

Answer Report

TARGET CELL (MAX)

CELL	NAME	ORIGINAL VALUE	FINAL VALUE
$D$5	Profit Total	$12	$64

ADJUSTABLE CELLS

CELL	NAME	ORIGINAL VALUE	FINAL VALUE
$B$4	Changing Cells Hockey Sticks	2	24
$C$4	Changing Cells Chess Sets	2	4

CONSTRAINTS

CELL	NAME	CELL VALUE	FORMULA	STATUS	SLACK
$D$11	Machine C Used	4	$D$11<=$F$11	Not Binding	6
$D$10	Machine B Used	72	$D$10<=$F$10	Binding	0
$D$9	Machine A Used	120	$D$9<=$F$9	Binding	0

Sensitivity Report

ADJUSTABLE CELLS

CELL	NAME	FINAL VALUE	REDUCED COST	OBJECTIVE COEFFICIENT	ALLOWABLE INCREASE	ALLOWABLE DECREASE
$B$4	Changing Cells Hockey Sticks	24	0	2	0.666666667	0.666666667
$C$4	Changing Cells Chess Sets	4	0	4	2	1

CONSTRAINT

CELL	NAME	FINAL VALUE	SHADOW PRICE	CONSTRAINT R.H. SIDE	ALLOWABLE INCREASE	ALLOWABLE DECREASE
$D$11	Machine C Used	4	0	10	1E+30	6
$D$10	Machine B Used	72	0.333333333	72	18	12
$D$9	Machine A Used	120	0.333333333	120	24	36

The Sensitivity Report is divided into two parts. The first part, titled "Adjustable Cells," corresponds to objective function coefficients. The profit per unit for the hockey sticks can be either up or down $0.67 (between $2.67 and $1.33) without having an impact on the solution. Similarly, the profit of the chess sets could be between $6 and $3 without changing the solution. In the case of machine A, the right-hand side could increase to 144 (120 + 24) or decrease to 84 with a resulting $0.33 increase or decrease per unit in the objective function. The right-hand side of machine B can increase to 90 units or decrease to 60 units with the same $0.33 change for each unit in the objective function. For machine C, the right-hand side could increase to infinity (1E+30 is scientific notation for a very large number) or decrease to 4 units with no change in the objective function.

CONCEPT CONNECTIONS

LOA–1 **Use Microsoft Excel Solver to solve a linear programming problem.**

- Linear programming is a powerful tool because it allows managers to make the best use of the available resources of material, plant, and equipment.
- Using Microsoft Excel Solver, we can solve problems dealing with aggregate sales and operations planning, service/manufacturing productivity analysis, product planning, product routing, and more.
- Using the Excel Solver involves the following steps: (1) define changing cells, (2) calculate total profit (or cost), (3) set up resource usage, (4) set up the Solver, and (5) solve the problem.

Linear programming (LP)   Refers to several related mathematical techniques used to allocate limited resources among competing demands in an optimal way.

Graphical linear programming   Provides a quick insight into the nature of linear programming.

SOLVED PROBLEMS

SOLVED PROBLEM 1

A furniture company produces three products: end tables, sofas, and chairs. These products are processed in five departments: the saw lumber, fabric cutting, sanding, staining, and assembly departments. End tables and chairs are produced from raw lumber only, and the sofas require lumber and fabric. Glue and thread are plentiful and represent a relatively insignificant cost that is included in operating expense. The specific requirements for each product are as follows:

RESOURCE OR ACTIVITY (QUANTITY AVAILABLE PER MONTH)	REQUIRED PER END TABLE	REQUIRED PER SOFA	REQUIRED PER CHAIR
Lumber (4,350 board feet)	10 board feet @ $10/foot = $100/table	7.5 board feet @ $10/foot = $75	4 board feet @ $10/foot = $40
Fabric (2,500 yards)	None	10 yards @ $17.50/yard = $175	None
Saw lumber (280 hours)	30 minutes	24 minutes	30 minutes
Cut fabric (140 hours)	None	24 minutes	None
Sand (280 hours)	30 minutes	6 minutes	30 minutes
Stain (140 hours)	24 minutes	12 minutes	24 minutes
Assemble (700 hours)	60 minutes	90 minutes	30 minutes

The company's direct labor expenses are $75,000 per month for the 1,540 hours of labor, at $48.70 per hour. Based on current demand, the firm can sell 300 end tables, 180 sofas, and 400 chairs per month. Sales prices are $400 for end tables, $750 for sofas, and $240 for chairs. Assume that labor cost is fixed and the firm does not plan to hire or fire any employees over the next month.

Required:

1. What is the most limiting resource to the furniture company?
2. Determine the product mix needed to maximize profit at the company. What is the optimal number of end tables, sofas, and chairs to produce each month?

Solution

Define X_1 as the number of end tables, X_2 as the number of sofas, and X_3 as the number of chairs to produce each month. Profit is calculated as the revenue for each item minus the cost of materials (lumber and fabric), minus the cost of labor. Since labor is fixed, we subtract this out as a total sum. Mathematically, we have $(400 - 100)X_1 + (750 - 75 - 175)X_2 + (240 - 40)X_3 - 75,000$. Profit is calculated as follows:

$$\text{Profit} = 300X_1 + 500X_2 + 200X_3 - 75,000$$

Constraints are the following:

Lumber:	$10X_1 + 7.5X_2 + 4X_3 \leq 4,350$
Fabric:	$10X_2 \leq 2,500$
Saw:	$.5X_1 + .4X_2 + .5X_3 \leq 280$
Cut:	$.4X_2 \leq 140$
Sand:	$.5X_1 + .1X_2 + .5X_3 \leq 280$
Stain:	$.4X_1 + .2X_2 + .4X_3 \leq 140$
Assemble:	$1X_1 + 1.5X_2 + .5X_3 \leq 700$
Demand:	
Table:	$X_1 \leq 300$
Sofa:	$X_2 \leq 180$
Chair:	$X_3 \leq 400$

Step 1: Define Changing Cells These are B3, C3, and D3. Note that these cells have been set equal to zero.

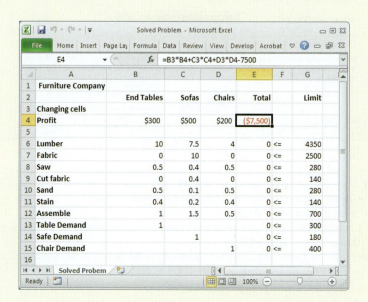

Step 2: Calculate Total Profit This is E4 (this is equal to B3 times the $300 revenue associated with each end table, plus C3 times the $500 revenue for each sofa, plus D3 times the $200 revenue associated with each chair). Note the $75,000 fixed expense that has been subtracted from revenue to calculate profit.

Step 3: Set Up Resource Usage In cells E6 through E15, the usage of each resource is calculated by multiplying B3, C3, and D3 by the amount needed for each item and summing the product (e.g., E6 = B3*B6 + C3*C6 + D3*D6). The limits on these constraints are entered in cells G6 to G15.

Step 4: Set Up Solver Go to Tools and select the Solver option.

a. *Set Objective:* is set to the location where the value we want to optimize is calculated. This is the profit calculated in E4 in this spreadsheet.
b. *To:* is set to Max since the goal is to maximize profit.
c. *By Changing Variable Cells:* are the cells that Solver can change to maximize profit (cells B3 through D3 in this problem).
d. *Subject to the Constraints:* is where a constraint set is added; we indicate that the range E6 to E15 must be less than or equal to G6 to G15.

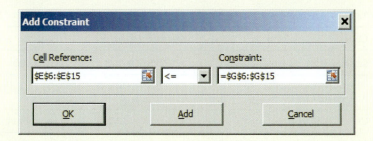

Step 5: Select a Solving Method There are a few options here, but for our purposes we just need to indicate Simplex LP and Make Unconstrained Variables Non-Negative. Simplex LP means all of our formulas are simple linear equations. Make Unconstrained Variables Non-Negative indicates that changing cells must be greater than or equal to zero.

Step 6: Solve the Problem Click Solve. We can see the solution and two special reports by highlighting items on the Solver Results acknowledgment that is displayed after a solution is found. Note that in the following report, Solver indicates that it has found a solution and all constraints and optimality conditions are satisfied. In the Reports box on the right, the Answer, Sensitivity, and Limits options have been highlighted, indicating that we would like to see these items. After highlighting the reports, click OK to exit back to the spreadsheet.

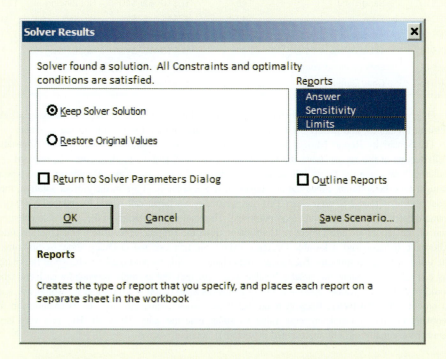

Note that three new tabs have been created: an Answer Report, a Sensitivity Report, and a Limits Report. The Answer Report indicates in the Target Cell section that the profit associated with this solution is $93,000 (we started at −$75,000). From the Target Cell section, we should make 260 end tables, 180 sofas, and no chairs. From the Constraints section, notice that the only constraints limiting profit are the staining capacity and the demand for sofas. We can see this from the column indicating whether a constraint is binding or nonbinding. Nonbinding constraints have slack, as indicated in the last column.

TARGET CELL (MAX)

CELL	NAME	ORIGINAL VALUE	FINAL VALUE
$E$4	Profit Total	−$75,000	$93,000

ADJUSTABLE CELLS

CELL	NAME	ORIGINAL VALUE	FINAL VALUE
$B$3	Changing Cells End Tables	0	260
$C$3	Changing Cells Sofas	0	180
$D$3	Changing Cells Chairs	0	0

CONSTRAINTS

CELL	NAME	CELL VALUE	FORMULA	STATUS	SLACK
$E$6	Lumber Total	3,950	$E$6<=$F$6	Not Binding	400
$E$7	Fabric Total	1,800	$E$7<=$F$7	Not Binding	700
$E$8	Saw Total	202	$E$8<=$F$8	Not Binding	78
$E$9	Cut Fabric Total	72	$E$9<=$F$9	Not Binding	68
$E$10	Sand Total	148	$E$10<=$F$10	Not Binding	132
$E$11	Stain Total	140	$E$11<=$F$11	Binding	0
$E$12	Assemble Total	530	$E$12<=$F$12	Not Binding	170
$E$13	Table Demand Total	260	$E$13<=$F$13	Not Binding	40
$E$14	Sofa Demand Total	180	$E$14<=$F$14	Binding	0
$E$15	Chair Demand Total	0	$E$15<=$F$15	Not Binding	400

Of course, we may not be too happy with this solution because we are not meeting all the demand for tables, and it may not be wise to totally discontinue the manufacturing of chairs.

The Sensitivity Report (shown below) gives additional insight into the solution. The Adjustable Cells section of this report shows the final value for each cell and the reduced cost. The reduced cost indicates how much the target cell value would change if a cell that was currently set to zero were brought into the solution. Since the end tables (B3) and sofas (C3) are in the current solution, their reduced cost is zero. For each chair (D3) that we make, our target cell would be reduced $100 (just round these numbers for interpretation purposes). The final three columns in the adjustable cells section of the report are the Objective Coefficient from the original spreadsheet and columns titled Allowable Increase and Allowable Decrease. Allowable Increase and Decrease show by how much the value of the corresponding coefficient could change so there would not be a change in the changing cell values (of course, the target cell value would change). For example, revenue for each end table could be as high as $1,000 ($300 + $700) or as low as $200 ($300 − $100), and we would still want to produce 260 end tables. Keep in mind that these values assume nothing else is changing in the problem. For the allowable increase value for sofas, note the value 1E + 30. This is a very large number, essentially infinity, represented in scientific notation.

ADJUSTABLE CELLS

CELL	NAME	FINAL VALUE	REDUCED COST	OBJECTIVE COEFFICIENT	ALLOWABLE INCREASE	ALLOWABLE DECREASE
$B$3	Changing Cells End Tables	260	0	299.9999997	700.0000012	100.0000004
$C$3	Changing Cells Sofas	180	0	500.0000005	1E+30	350.0000006
$D$3	Changing Cells Chairs	0	−100.0000004	199.9999993	100.0000004	1E+30

CONSTRAINTS

CELL	NAME	FINAL VALUE	SHADOW PRICE	CONSTRAINT R.H. SIDE	ALLOWABLE INCREASE	ALLOWABLE DECREASE
$E$6	Lumber Total	3,950	0	4,350	1E+30	400
$E$7	Fabric Total	1,800	0	2,500	1E+30	700
$E$8	Saw Total	202	0	280	1E+30	78
$E$9	Cut Fabric Total	72	0	140	1E+30	68
$E$10	Sand Total	148	0	280	1E+30	132
$E$11	Stain Total	140	749.9999992	140	16	104
$E$12	Assemble Total	530	0	700	1E+30	170
$E$13	Table Demand Total	260	0	300	1E+30	40
$E$14	Sofa Demand Total	180	350.0000006	180	70	80
$E$15	Chair Demand Total	0	0	400	1E+30	400

For the Constraints section of the report, the actual final usage of each resource is given in Final Value. The Shadow Price is the value to our target cell for each unit increase in the resource. If we could increase staining capacity, it would be worth $750 per hour. The Constraint Right-Hand Side is the current limit on the resource. Allowable Increase is the amount the resource could be increased while the shadow price is still valid. Another 16 hours' work of staining capacity could be added with a value of $750 per hour. Similarly, the Allowable Decrease column shows the amount the resource could be reduced without changing the shadow price. There is some valuable information available in this report.

The Limits Report provides additional information about our solution.

CELL	TARGET NAME	VALUE
$E$4	Profit Total	$93,000

CELL	ADJUSTABLE NAME	VALUE	LOWER LIMIT	TARGET RESULT	UPPER LIMIT	TARGET RESULT
$B$3	Changing Cells End Tables	260	0	15,000	260.0000002	93,000
$C$3	Changing Cells Sofas	180	0	3,000	180	93,000
$D$3	Changing Cells Chairs	0	0	93,000	0	93,000

Total profit for the current solution is $93,000. The current value for B3 (end tables) is 260 units. If this were reduced to 0 units, profit would be reduced to $15,000. At an upper limit of 260, profit is $93,000 (the current solution). Similarly, for C3 (sofas), if this were reduced to 0, profit would be reduced to $3,000. At an upper limit of 180, profit is $93,000. For D3 (chairs), if this were reduced to 0, profit is $93,000 (current solution), and in this case the upper limit on chairs is also 0 units.

Acceptable answers to the questions are as follows:

1. *What is the most limiting resource to the furniture company?*
   In terms of our production resources, staining capacity is really hurting profit at this time. We could use another 16 hours of capacity.
2. *Determine the product mix needed to maximize profit at the furniture company.*
   The product mix would be to make 260 end tables, 180 sofas, and no chairs.

Of course, we have only scratched the surface with this solution. We could actually experiment with increasing staining capacity. This would give insight into the next most limiting resource. We also could run scenarios where we are required to produce a minimum number of each product, which is probably a more realistic scenario. This could help us determine how we could possibly reallocate the use of labor in our shop.

SOLVED PROBLEM 2

It is 2:00 on Friday afternoon and Joe Bob, the head chef (grill cook) at Bruce's Diner, is trying to decide the best way to allocate the available raw material to the four Friday night specials. The decision has to be made in the early afternoon because three of the items must be started now (Sloppy Joes, Tacos, and Chili). The table below contains the information on the food in inventory and the amounts required for each item.

FOOD	CHEESE BURGER	SLOPPY JOES	TACO	CHILI	AVAILABLE
Ground Beef (lb.)	0.3	0.25	0.25	0.4	100 lb.
Cheese (lb.)	0.1	0	0.3	0.2	50 lb.
Beans (lb.)	0	0	0.2	0.3	50 lb.
Lettuce (lb.)	0.1	0	0.2	0	15 lb.
Tomato (lb.)	0.1	0.3	0.2	0.2	50 lb.
Buns	1	1	0	0	80 buns
Taco Shells	0	0	1	0	80 shells

One other fact relevant to Joe Bob's decision is the estimated market demand and selling price.

	CHEESE BURGER	SLOPPY JOES	TACO	CHILI
Demand	75	60	100	55
Selling Price	$2.25	$2.00	$1.75	$2.50

Joe Bob wants to maximize revenue since he has already purchased all the materials that are sitting in the cooler.

Required:

1. What is the best mix of the Friday night specials to maximize Joe Bob's revenue?
2. If a supplier offered to provide a rush order of buns at $1.00 a bun, is it worth the money?

Solution

Define X_1 as the number of Cheese Burgers, X_2 as the number of Sloppy Joes, X_3 as the number of Tacos, and X_4 as the number of bowls of Chili made for the Friday night specials.

$$\text{Revenue} = \$2.25\ X_1 + \$2.00\ X_2 + \$1.75\ X_3 + \$2.50\ X_4$$

Constraints are the following:

Ground Beef:	$0.30\ X_1 + 0.25\ X_2 + 0.25\ X_3 + 0.40\ X_4 \leq 100$
Cheese:	$0.10\ X_1 + 0.30\ X_3 + 0.20\ X_4 \leq 50$
Beans:	$0.20\ X_3 + 0.30\ X_4 \leq 50$
Lettuce:	$0.10\ X_1 + 0.20\ X_3 \leq 15$
Tomato:	$0.10\ X_1 + 0.30\ X_2 + 0.20\ X_3 + 0.20\ X_4 \leq 50$
Buns:	$X_1 + X_2 \leq 80$
Taco Shells:	$X_3 \leq 80$

Demand:

Cheese Burger	$X_1 \leq 75$
Sloppy Joes	$X_2 \leq 603$
Taco	$X_3 \leq 100$
Chili	$X_4 \leq 55$

Step 1: Define the Changing Cells These are B3, C3, D3, and E3. Note the values in the changing cell are set to 10 each so the formulas can be checked.

Formula bar: F7 = SUMPRODUCT(B3:E3,B7:E7)

	A	B	C	D	E	F	G	H
1								
2		Cheese Burger	Sloppy Joes	Taco	Chili			
3	Changing Cells	10	10	10	10			
4		<=	<=	<=	<=			
5	Demand	70	60	100	55			
6						Total		
7	Revenue	$2.25	$2.00	$1.75	$2.50	$85.00		
8								
9								
10	Ingredients:	Cheese Burger	Sloppy Joes	Taco	Chili	Total		Available
11	Ground beef (lbs.)	0.3	0.25	0.25	0.4	12	<=	100
12	Cheese (obs.)	0.1	0	0.3	0.2	6	<=	50
13	Beans (lbs.)	0	0	0.2	0.3	5	<=	50
14	Lettuce (lbs.)	0.1	0	0.2	0	3	<=	15
15	Tomato (lbs.)	0.1	0.3	0.2	0.2	8	<=	50
16	Buns	1	1	0	0	20	<=	80
17	Taco Shells	0	0	1	0	10	<=	80

Step 2: Calculate Total Revenue This is in cell F7 (it is equal to B3 times the $2.25 for each Cheese Burger, plus C3 times the $2.00 for a Sloppy Joe, plus D3 times the $1.75 for each Taco, plus E3 times the $2.50 for each bowl of Chili; the SUMPRODUCT function in Excel was used to make this calculation faster). Note that the current value is $85, which is a result of selling 10 of each item.

Step 3: Set Up the Usage of the Food In cells F11 to F17, the usage of each food is calculated by multiplying the changing cells row times the per item use in the table and then summing the result. The limits on each of these food types are given in H11 through H17.

Step 4: Set Up Solver and Select the Solver Option

a. *Set Objective:* is set to the location where the value we want to optimize is calculated. The revenue is calculated in F7 in this spreadsheet.
b. *To:* is set to Max since the goal is to maximize revenue.
c. *By Changing Variable Cells:* are the cells that tell how many of each special to produce.
d. *Subject to the Constraints:* is where we add two separate constraints, one for demand and one for the usage of food.

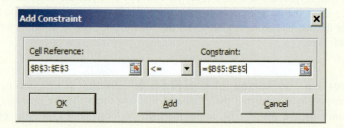

Step 5: Select a Solving Method We will leave all the settings as the default values and only need to make sure of two changes: (1) Simplex LP option and (2) check the Make Unconstrained Variables Non-Negative. These two options make sure that Solver knows that this is a linear programming problem and that all changing cells should be nonnegative.

Step 6: Solve the Problem Click Solve. We will get a Solver Results box. Make sure it says that it has the following statement: "Solver found a solution. All constraints and optimality conditions are satisfied."

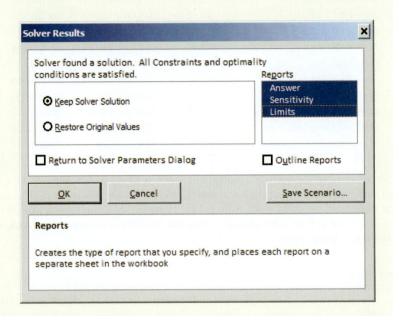

On the right-hand side of the box, there is an option for three reports: Answer, Sensitivity, and Limit. Click on all three reports and then click OK; this will exit you back to the spreadsheet, but you will have three new worksheets in your workbook.

The answer report indicates that the target cell has a final solution of $416.25 and started at $85. From the adjustable cells area, we can see that we should make 20 Cheese Burgers, 60 Sloppy Joes, 65 Tacos, and 55 bowls of Chili. This answers the first requirement from the problem of what the mix of Friday night specials should be.

TARGET CELL (MAX.)

CELL	NAME	ORIGINAL VALUE	FINAL VALUE
$F$7	Revenue Total	$85.00	$416.25

ADJUSTABLE CELLS

CELL	NAME	ORIGINAL VALUE	FINAL VALUE
$B$3	Changing Cells Cheeseburger	10	20
$C$3	Changing Cells Sloppy Joes	10	60
$D$3	Changing Cells Taco	10	65
$E$3	Changing Cells Chili	10	55

CONSTRAINTS

CELL	NAME	CELL VALUE	FORMULA	STATUS	SLACK
$F$11	Ground Beef (lb.) Total	59.25	$F$11<=$H$11	Not Binding	40.75
$F$12	Cheese (lb.) Total	32.50	$F$12<=$H$12	Not Binding	17.5
$F$13	Beans (lb.) Total	29.50	$F$13<=$H$13	Not Binding	20.5
$F$14	Lettuce (lb.) Total	15.00	$F$14<=$H$14	Binding	0
$F$15	Tomato (lb.) Total	44.00	$F$15<=$H$15	Not Binding	6
$F$16	Buns Total	80.00	$F$16<=$H$16	Binding	0
$F$17	Taco Shells Total	65.00	$F$17<=$H$17	Not Binding	15
$B$3	Changing Cells Cheeseburger	20	$B$3<=$B$5	Not Binding	55
$C$3	Changing Cells Sloppy Joes	60	$C$3<=$C$5	Binding	0
$D$3	Changing Cells Taco	65	$D$3<=$D$5	Not Binding	35
$E$3	Changing Cells Chili	55	$E$3<=$E$5	Binding	0

The second required answer was whether it is worth it to pay a rush supplier $1 a bun for additional buns. The answer report shows us that the buns constraint was binding. This means that if we had more buns, we could make more money. However, the answer report does not tell us whether a rush order of buns at $1 a bun is worthwhile. In order to answer that question, we have to look at the sensitivity report.

ADJUSTABLE CELLS

CELL	NAME	FINAL VALUE	REDUCED COST	OBJECTIVE COEFFICIENT	ALLOWABLE INCREASE	ALLOWABLE DECREASE
$B$3	Changing Cells Cheeseburger	20	0	2.25	0.625	1.375
$C$3	Changing Cells Sloppy Joes	60	0.625	2	1E+30	0.625
$D$3	Changing Cells Taco	65	0	1.75	2.75	1.25
$E$3	Changing Cells Chili	55	2.5	2.5	1E+30	2.5

CONSTRAINTS

CELL	NAME	FINAL VALUE	SHADOW PRICE	CONSTRAINT R.H. SIDE	ALLOWABLE INCREASE	ALLOWABLE DECREASE
$F$11	Ground Beef (lb.) Total	59.25	0.00	100	1E+30	40.75
$F$12	Cheese (lb.) Total	32.50	0.00	50	1E+30	17.5
$F$13	Beans (lb.) Total	29.50	0.00	50	1E+30	20.5
$F$14	Lettuce (lb.) Total	15.00	8.75	15	3	13
$F$15	Tomato (lb.) Total	44.00	0.00	50	1E+30	6
$F$16	Buns Total	80.00	1.38	80	55	20
$F$17	Taco Shells Total	65.00	0.00	80	1E+30	15

We have highlighted the buns row to answer the question. We can see that buns have a shadow price of $1.38. This shadow price means that each additional bun will generate $1.38 of profit. We also can see that other foods such as ground beef have a shadow price of $0. The items with a shadow price of $0 add nothing to profit since we are currently not using all that we have now. The other important piece of information we have on the buns is that they are only worth $1.38 up until the next 55 buns, and that is why the allowable increase is 55. We also can see that a pound of lettuce is worth $8.75. It might be wise to also look for a rush supplier of lettuce so we can increase our profit on Friday nights.

Acceptable answers to the questions are as follows:

1. *What is the best mix of the Friday night specials to maximize Joe Bob's revenue?*
   20 Cheese Burgers, 60 Sloppy Joes, 65 Tacos, and 55 bowls of Chili.
2. *If a supplier offered to provide a rush order of buns at $1.00 a bun, is it worth the money?*
   Yes, each additional bun brings in $1.38, so if they cost us $1, then we will net $0.38 per bun. However, this is true only up to 55 additional buns.

OBJECTIVE QUESTIONS

1. Solve the following problem with Excel Solver:

$$\text{Maximize } Z = 3X + Y$$
$$12X + 14Y \leq 85$$
$$3X + 2Y \leq 18$$
$$Y \leq 4$$

2. Solve the following problem with Excel Solver:

$$\text{Minimize } Z = 2A + 4B$$
$$4A + 6B \geq 120$$
$$2A + 6B \geq 72$$
$$B \geq 10$$

3. A manufacturing firm has discontinued production of a certain unprofitable product line. Considerable excess production capacity was created as a result. Management is considering devoting this excess capacity to one or more of three products: X_1, X_2, and X_3.

   Machine hours required per unit are

	PRODUCT		
MACHINE TYPE	X_1	X_2	X_3
Milling machine	8	2	3
Lathe	4	3	0
Grinder	2	0	1

The available time in machine hours per week is

	MACHINE HOURS PER WEEK
Milling machines	800
Lathes	480
Grinders	320

The salespeople estimate they can sell all the units of X_1 and X_2 that can be made. But the sales potential of X_3 is 80 units per week maximum.

Unit profits for the three products are

	UNIT PROFITS
X_1	$20
X_2	6
X_3	8

a. Set up the equations that can be solved to maximize the profit per week.

b. Solve these equations using the Excel Solver.

c. What is the optimal solution? How many of each product should be made, and what should the resultant profit be?

d. What is this situation with respect to the machine groups? Would they work at capacity, or would there be unused available time? Will X_3 be at maximum sales capacity?

e. Suppose an additional 200 hours per week can be obtained from the milling machines by working overtime. The incremental cost would be $1.50 per hour. Would you recommend doing this? Explain how you arrived at your answer.

4. A diet is being prepared for the University of Arizona dorms. The objective is to feed the students at the least cost, but the diet must have between 1,800 and 3,600 calories. No more than 1,400 calories can be starch, and no fewer than 400 can be protein. The varied diet is to be made of two foods: *A* and *B*. Food *A* costs $0.75 per pound and contains 600 calories, 400 of which are protein and 200 starch. No more than 2 pounds of food *A* can be used per resident. Food *B* costs $0.15 per pound and contains 900 calories, of which 700 are starch, 100 are protein, and 100 are fat.

a. Write the equations representing this information.

b. Solve the problem graphically for the amounts of each food that should be used.

5. Do problem 4 with the added constraint that not more than 150 calories shall be fat and that the price of food has escalated to $1.75 per pound for food *A* and $2.50 per pound for food *B*.

6. Logan Manufacturing wants to mix two fuels, *A* and *B*, for its trucks to minimize cost. It needs no fewer than 3,000 gallons to run its trucks during the next month. It has a maximum fuel storage capacity of 4,000 gallons. There are 2,000 gallons of fuel *A* and 4,000 gallons of fuel *B* available. The mixed fuel must have an octane rating of no less than 80.

When fuels are mixed, the amount of fuel obtained is just equal to the sum of the amounts put in. The octane rating is the weighted average of the individual octanes, weighted in proportion to the respective volumes.

The following is known: Fuel *A* has an octane of 90 and costs $1.20 per gallon. Fuel *B* has an octane of 75 and costs $0.90 per gallon.

a. Write the equations expressing this information.

b. Solve the problem using the Excel Solver, giving the amount of each fuel to be used. State any assumptions necessary to solve the problem.

7. You are trying to create a budget to optimize the use of a portion of your disposable income. You have a maximum of $1,500 per month to be allocated to food, shelter, and entertainment. The amount spent on food and shelter combined must not exceed $1,000. The amount spent on shelter alone must not exceed $700. Entertainment cannot exceed $300 per month. Each dollar spent on food has a satisfaction value of 2, each dollar spent on shelter has a satisfaction value of 3, and each dollar spent on entertainment has a satisfaction value of 5.

Assuming a linear relationship, use the Excel Solver to determine the optimal allocation of your funds.

8. C-town brewery brews two beers: Expansion Draft and Burning River. Expansion Draft sells for $20 per barrel, while Burning River sells for $8 per barrel. Producing a barrel of Expansion Draft takes 8 pounds of corn and 4 pounds of hops. Producing a barrel of Burning River requires 2 pounds of corn, 6 pounds of rice, and 3 pounds of hops. The brewery has 500 pounds of corn, 300 pounds of rice, and 400 pounds of hops. Assuming a linear relationship, use the Excel Solver to determine the optimal mix of Expansion Draft and Burning River that maximizes C-town's revenue.

9. BC Petrol manufactures three chemicals at their chemical plant in Kentucky: BCP1, BCP2, and BCP3. These chemicals are produced in two production processes known as zone and man. Running the zone process for an hour costs $48 and yields three units of BCP1, one unit of BCP2, and one unit of BCP3. Running the man process for one hour costs $24 and yields one unit of BCP1 and one unit of BCP2. To meet customer demands, at least

20 units of BCP1, 10 units of BCP2, and six units of BCP3 must be produced daily. Assuming a linear relationship, use the Excel Solver to determine the optimal mix of processes zone and man to minimize costs and meet BC Petrol daily demands.

10. A farmer in Wood County has 900 acres of land. She is going to plant each acre with corn, soybeans, or wheat. Each acre planted with corn yields a $2,000 profit; each with soybeans yields $2,500 profit; and each with wheat yields $3,000 profit. She has 100 workers and 150 tons of fertilizer. The table below shows the requirement per acre of each of the crops. Assuming a linear relationship, use the Excel Solver to determine the optimal planting mix of corn, soybeans, and wheat to maximize her profits.

	CORN	SOYBEANS	WHEAT
Labor (workers)	0.1	0.3	0.2
Fertilizer (tons)	0.2	0.1	0.4

APPENDIX B

ANSWERS TO SELECTED OBJECTIVE QUESTIONS

Chapter 1
1. Strategy, processes, and analytics
3. *a.* Receivables turnover ratio = 5.453,
   b. inventory turnover ratio = 4.383,
   c. asset turnover ratio = 2.306

Chapter 2
1. Triple bottom line
17. Productivity (hours), Deluxe = 0.20,
    Limited = 0.20; Productivity (dollars),
    Deluxe = 133.33, Limited = 135.71

Chapter 3
4. 3rd most recent = 1,000, 2nd most
   recent = 1,175, most recent = 975
   weighted moving average = 1,031.25
6. *a.* February 84, March 86, April 90, May 88,
   June 84; *b.* MAD = 15
21. *a.* MAD = 90, TS = −1.67; *b.* TS acceptable
    for now, but is trending downward.

Chapter 4
1. Capacity utilization rate = 89.1%
8. NPV − Small factory = $4.8 million,
   NPV − Do nothing = $0.0
   NPV − Large factory = $2.6 million,
   therefore build small factory.
10. Capacity utilization rate = 75%; they are
    in the critical zone on these nights.

Chapter 4A
5. 4,710 hours
7. Learning rate − Labor = 80%, Learning
   rate − Parts = 90%; Labor = 11,556 hours,
   Parts = $330,876

Chapter 5
9. *b.* A-C-F-G-I and A-D-F-G-I, 18 weeks;
   c. C: one week, D: one week, G: one week;
   d. Two paths: A-C-F-G-I and A-D-F-G-I,
   16 weeks.
14. *a.* A-E-G-C-D; *b.* 26 weeks; *c.* No difference
    in completion date.

Chapter 6
15. *b.* 120 seconds/unit; *c.* station 1 (AD), station 2
    (BC), station 3 (EF), station 4 (GH); *d.* 87.5%
19. *a.* 33.6 seconds/unit; *b.* 3.51 → 4 workstations;
    d. station 1 (AB), station 2 (DF), station 3 (C),
    station 4 (EG), station 5 (H); *e.* 70.2%;
    f. Reduce cycle time to 32 seconds and work
    6.67 minutes overtime; *g.* 1.89 hours overtime,
    may be better to re-balance.

Chapter 6A
2. Break even = 7,500 units
6. Break even (dollars) = $27,778
   Break even (units) = 2,222 units

Chapter 7
1. Service package
4. Face-to-face tight specs
15. *a.* 33.33%, *b.* 1/3 hour or 20 minutes,
    c. 1.33 students, *d.* 44.44%
28. *a.* .2333 minutes or 14 seconds; *b.* 2.083 cars in
    queue, 2.92 cars in the system

Chapter 8
7. Total cost = $416,600
10. Total cost = $413,750

Chapter 9
11. *a.*

	Level
Z	0
A(2) B(4)	1
C(3) D(4)	2
E(2)	3

b. Z Planned order release (POR) period 8 for
50 units 8(50),
A POR 7(100),
B POR 7(200),
C POR 6(300),
D POR 6(400),
E POR 3(800).

21. Least total cost order 180 to cover periods 4 through 8. Least unit cost is tied for ordering 180 for periods 4 through 8, or order 220 units to cover 4 through 9, therefore either 180 or 220 units in period 2.

Chapter 10

9. DPMO = 15,333; this is not very good.
14. Opportunity flow diagram.
17. *a.* Cost when not inspecting = $20/hr, cost to inspect = $9/hr, therefore inspect; *b.* $0.18 each; *c.* $0.22 per unit.
22. *a.* .333, *b.* No, the machine is not capable of a high enough quality.
25. UCL = 1014.965, LCL = 983.235 for X-bar chart; UCL = 49.552, LCL = 0.00 for the R-chart.

Chapter 11

4. Purchase 268 boxes of lettuce.
14. $q = 713$
17. *a.* $Q = 1,225, R = 824$; *b.* $q = 390 - I$

Chapter 12

10. 5 kanban card sets
14. 5 kanban card sets

Chapter 13

11. Buy NPV = $143,226.27, make NPV = $84,442.11, we should accept the bid.
16. Inventory turn = 148.6, weeks of supply = .350 (1/3 of a week's supply on-hand)

Chapter 14

9. Total cost $1,056.770; *b.* Should consider closing the Philadelphia plant since we are using very little of the capacity from that plant.
10. $C_x = 373.8$, $C_y = 356.9$

Appendix A

2. Optimal combination is $B = 10, A = 15$, and $Z = 70$
4. *a.* $600A + 900B <= 3,600$
       $600A + 900B >= 1,800$
       $200A + 700B <= 1,400$
       $400A + 100B >= 400$
       $A <= 2$
       Minimize $.75A + .15B$
   b. $A = 0.54$
       $B = 1.85$
       Obj = 0.68

APPENDIX C

PRESENT VALUE TABLE

| table C.1 | | Present Value of $1 |

YEAR	1%	2%	3%	4%	5%	6%	7%	8%	9%	10%	12%	14%	15%
1	.990	.980	.971	.962	.952	.943	.935	.926	.917	.909	.893	.877	.870
2	.980	.961	.943	.925	.907	.890	.873	.857	.842	.826	.797	.769	.756
3	.971	.942	.915	.889	.864	.840	.816	.794	.772	.751	.712	.675	.658
4	.961	.924	.889	.855	.823	.792	.763	.735	.708	.683	.636	.592	.572
5	.951	.906	.863	.822	.784	.747	.713	.681	.650	.621	.567	.519	.497
6	.942	.888	.838	.790	.746	.705	.666	.630	.596	.564	.507	.456	.432
7	.933	.871	.813	.760	.711	.665	.623	.583	.547	.513	.452	.400	.376
8	.923	.853	.789	.731	.677	.627	.582	.540	.502	.467	.404	.351	.327
9	.914	.837	.766	.703	.645	.592	.544	.500	.460	.424	.361	.308	.284
10	.905	.820	.744	.676	.614	.558	.508	.463	.422	.386	.322	.270	.247
11	.896	.804	.722	.650	.585	.527	.475	.429	.388	.350	.287	.237	.215
12	.887	.788	.701	.625	.557	.497	.444	.397	.356	.319	.257	.208	.187
13	.879	.773	.681	.601	.530	.469	.415	.368	.326	.290	.229	.182	.163
14	.870	.758	.661	.577	.505	.442	.388	.340	.299	.263	.205	.160	.141
15	.861	.743	.642	.555	.481	.417	.362	.315	.275	.239	.183	.140	.123
16	.853	.728	.623	.534	.458	.394	.339	.292	.252	.218	.163	.123	.107
17	.844	.714	.605	.513	.436	.371	.317	.270	.231	.198	.146	.108	.093
18	.836	.700	.587	.494	.416	.350	.296	.250	.212	.180	.130	.095	.081
19	.828	.686	.570	.475	.396	.331	.276	.232	.194	.164	.116	.083	.070
20	.820	.673	.554	.456	.377	.312	.258	.215	.178	.149	.104	.073	.061
25	.780	.610	.478	.375	.295	.233	.184	.146	.116	.092	.059	.038	.030
30	.742	.552	.412	.308	.231	.174	.131	.099	.075	.057	.033	.020	.015

YEAR	16%	18%	20%	24%	28%	32%	36%	40%	50%	60%	70%	80%	90%
1	.862	.847	.833	.806	.781	.758	.735	.714	.667	.625	.588	.556	.526
2	.743	.718	.694	.650	.610	.574	.541	.510	.444	.391	.346	.309	.277
3	.641	.609	.579	.524	.477	.435	.398	.364	.296	.244	.204	.171	.146
4	.552	.516	.482	.423	.373	.329	.292	.260	.198	.153	.120	.095	.077
5	.476	.437	.402	.341	.291	.250	.215	.186	.132	.095	.070	.053	.040
6	.410	.370	.335	.275	.227	.189	.158	.133	.088	.060	.041	.029	.021
7	.354	.314	.279	.222	.178	.143	.116	.095	.059	.037	.024	.016	.011
8	.305	.266	.233	.179	.139	.108	.085	.068	.039	.023	.014	.009	.006
9	.263	.226	.194	.144	.108	.082	.063	.048	.026	.015	.008	.005	.003
10	.227	.191	.162	.116	.085	.062	.046	.035	.017	.009	.005	.003	.002
11	.195	.162	.135	.094	.066	.047	.034	.025	.012	.006	.003	.002	.001
12	.168	.137	.112	.076	.052	.036	.025	.018	.008	.004	.002	.001	.001
13	.145	.116	.093	.061	.040	.027	.018	.013	.005	.002	.001	.001	.000
14	.125	.099	.078	.049	.032	.021	.014	.009	.003	.001	.001	.000	.000
15	.108	.084	.065	.040	.025	.016	.010	.006	.002	.001	.000	.000	.000
16	.093	.071	.054	.032	.019	.012	.007	.005	.002	.001	.000	.000	
17	.080	.060	.045	.026	.015	.009	.005	.003	.001	.000	.000		
18	.069	.051	.038	.021	.012	.007	.004	.002	.001	.000	.000		
19	.060	.043	.031	.017	.009	.005	.003	.002	.000	.000			
20	.051	.037	.026	.014	.007	.004	.002	.001	.000	.000			
25	.024	.016	.010	.005	.002	.001	.000	.000					
30	.012	.007	.004	.002	.001	.000	.000						

Using Microsoft Excel®, these are calculated with the equation: $(1 + \text{interest})^{-\text{years}}$.

APPENDIX D

NEGATIVE EXPONENTIAL DISTRIBUTION: VALUES OF e^{-x}

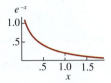

X	e^{-x} (VALUE)	X	e^{-x} (VALUE)	X	e^{-x} (VALUE)	X	e^{-x} (VALUE)
0.00	1.00000	0.50	0.60653	1.00	0.36788	1.50	0.22313
0.01	0.99005	0.51	.60050	1.01	.36422	1.51	.22091
0.02	.98020	0.52	.59452	1.02	.36060	1.52	.21871
0.03	.97045	0.53	.58860	1.03	.35701	1.53	.21654
0.04	.96079	0.54	.58275	1.04	.35345	1.54	.21438
0.05	.95123	0.55	.57695	1.05	.34994	1.55	.21225
0.06	.94176	0.56	.57121	1.06	.34646	1.56	.21014
0.07	.93239	0.57	.56553	1.07	.34301	1.57	.20805
0.08	.92312	0.58	.55990	1.08	.33960	1.58	.20598
0.09	.91393	0.59	.55433	1.09	.33622	1.59	.20393
0.10	.90484	0.60	.54881	1.10	.33287	1.60	.20190
0.11	.89583	0.61	.54335	1.11	.32956	1.61	.19989
0.12	.88692	0.62	.53794	1.12	.32628	1.62	.19790
0.13	.87809	0.63	.53259	1.13	.32303	1.63	.19593
0.14	.86936	0.64	.52729	1.14	.31982	1.64	.19398
0.15	.86071	0.65	.52205	1.15	.31664	1.65	.19205
0.16	.87514	0.66	.51685	1.16	.31349	1.66	.19014
0.17	.84366	0.67	.51171	1.17	.31037	1.67	.18825
0.18	.83527	0.68	.50662	1.18	.30728	1.68	.18637
0.19	.82696	0.69	.50158	1.19	.30422	1.69	.18452
0.20	.81873	0.70	.49659	1.20	.30119	1.70	.18268
0.21	.81058	0.71	.49164	1.21	.29820	1.71	.18087
0.22	.80252	0.72	.48675	1.22	.29523	1.72	.17907
0.23	.79453	0.73	.48191	1.23	.29229	1.73	.17728
0.24	.78663	0.74	.47711	1.24	.28938	1.74	.17552
0.25	.77880	0.75	.47237	1.25	.28650	1.75	.17377
0.26	.77105	0.76	.46767	1.26	.28365	1.76	.17204
0.27	.76338	0.77	.46301	1.27	.28083	1.77	.17033
0.28	.75578	0.78	.45841	1.28	.27804	1.78	.16864
0.29	.74826	0.79	.45384	1.29	.27527	1.79	.16696
0.30	.74082	0.80	.44933	1.30	.27253	1.80	.16530
0.31	.73345	0.81	.44486	1.31	.26982	1.81	.16365
0.32	.72615	0.82	.44043	1.32	.26714	1.82	.16203
0.33	.71892	0.83	.43605	1.33	.26448	1.83	.16041
0.34	.71177	0.84	.43171	1.34	.26185	1.84	.15882
0.35	.70469	0.85	.42741	1.35	.25924	1.85	.15724
0.36	.69768	0.86	.42316	1.36	.25666	1.86	.15567
0.37	.69073	0.87	.41895	1.37	.25411	1.87	.15412
0.38	.68386	0.88	.41478	1.38	.25158	1.88	.15259
0.39	.67706	0.89	.41066	1.39	.24908	1.89	.15107
0.40	.67032	0.90	.40657	1.40	.24660	1.90	.14957
0.41	.66365	0.91	.40252	1.41	.24414	1.91	.14808
0.42	.65705	0.92	.39852	1.42	.24171	1.92	.14661
0.43	.65051	0.93	.39455	1.43	.23931	1.93	.14515
0.44	.64404	0.94	.39063	1.44	.23693	1.94	.14370
0.45	.63763	0.95	.38674	1.45	.23457	1.95	.14227
0.46	.63128	0.96	.38289	1.46	.23224	1.96	.14086
0.47	.62500	0.97	.37908	1.47	.22993	1.97	.13946
0.48	.61878	0.98	.37531	1.48	.22764	1.98	.13807
0.49	.61263	0.99	.37158	1.49	.22537	1.99	.13670
0.50	.60653	1.00	.36788	1.50	.22313	2.00	.13534

Using Microsoft Excel, these values are calculated with the equation: 1 − EXPONDIST(x, 1, TRUE).

APPENDIX E

AREAS OF THE CUMULATIVE STANDARD NORMAL DISTRIBUTION

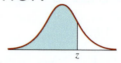

An entry in the table is the proportion under the curve cumulated from the negative tail.

z	G(z)	z	G(z)	z	G(z)
−4.00	0.00003	−1.30	0.09680	1.40	0.91924
−3.95	0.00004	−1.25	0.10565	1.45	0.92647
−3.90	0.00005	−1.20	0.11507	1.50	0.93319
−3.85	0.00006	−1.15	0.12507	1.55	0.93943
−3.80	0.00007	−1.10	0.13567	1.60	0.94520
−3.75	0.00009	−1.05	0.14686	1.65	0.95053
−3.70	0.00011	−1.00	0.15866	1.70	0.95543
−3.65	0.00013	−0.95	0.17106	1.75	0.95994
−3.60	0.00016	−0.90	0.18406	1.80	0.96407
−3.55	0.00019	−0.85	0.19766	1.85	0.96784
−3.50	0.00023	−0.80	0.21186	1.90	0.97128
−3.45	0.00028	−0.75	0.22663	1.95	0.97441
−3.40	0.00034	−0.70	0.24196	2.00	0.97725
−3.35	0.00040	−0.65	0.25785	2.05	0.97982
−3.30	0.00048	−0.60	0.27425	2.10	0.98214
−3.25	0.00058	−0.55	0.29116	2.15	0.98422
−3.20	0.00069	−0.50	0.30854	2.20	0.98610
−3.15	0.00082	−0.45	0.32636	2.25	0.98778
−3.10	0.00097	−0.40	0.34458	2.30	0.98928
−3.05	0.00114	−0.35	0.36317	2.35	0.99061
−3.00	0.00135	−0.30	0.38209	2.40	0.99180
−2.95	0.00159	−0.25	0.40129	2.45	0.99286
−2.90	0.00187	−0.20	0.42074	2.50	0.99379
−2.85	0.00219	−0.15	0.44038	2.55	0.99461
−2.80	0.00256	−0.10	0.46017	2.60	0.99534
−2.75	0.00298	−0.05	0.48006	2.65	0.99598
−2.70	0.00347	0.00	0.50000	2.70	0.99653
−2.65	0.00402	0.05	0.51994	2.75	0.99702
−2.60	0.00466	0.10	0.53983	2.80	0.99744
−2.55	0.00539	0.15	0.55962	2.85	0.99781
−2.50	0.00621	0.20	0.57926	2.90	0.99813
−2.45	0.00714	0.25	0.59871	2.95	0.99841
−2.40	0.00820	0.30	0.61791	3.00	0.99865
−2.35	0.00939	0.35	0.63683	3.05	0.99886
−2.30	0.01072	0.40	0.65542	3.10	0.99903
−2.25	0.01222	0.45	0.67364	3.15	0.99918
−2.20	0.01390	0.50	0.69146	3.20	0.99931
−2.15	0.01578	0.55	0.70884	3.25	0.99942
−2.10	0.01786	0.60	0.72575	3.30	0.99952
−2.05	0.02018	0.65	0.74215	3.35	0.99960
−2.00	0.02275	0.70	0.75804	3.40	0.99966
−1.95	0.02559	0.75	0.77337	3.45	0.99972
−1.90	0.02872	0.80	0.78814	3.50	0.99977
−1.85	0.03216	0.85	0.80234	3.55	0.99981
−1.80	0.03593	0.90	0.81594	3.60	0.99984
−1.75	0.04006	0.95	0.82894	3.65	0.99987
−1.70	0.04457	1.00	0.84134	3.70	0.99989
−1.65	0.04947	1.05	0.85314	3.75	0.99991
−1.60	0.05480	1.10	0.86433	3.80	0.99993
−1.55	0.06057	1.15	0.87493	3.85	0.99994
−1.50	0.06681	1.20	0.88493	3.90	0.99995
−1.45	0.07353	1.25	0.89435	3.95	0.99996
−1.40	0.08076	1.30	0.90320	4.00	0.99997
−1.35	0.08851	1.35	0.91149		

Using Microsoft Excel, these probabilities are generated with the NORM.S.DIST(z) function.

NAME INDEX

A page number followed by an *n* indicates a note on that page.

SUBJECT INDEX

A page number followed by an *e* indicates an exhibit on that page.